Sustainable and Responsible Entrepreneurship and Key Drivers of Performance

Cristina Raluca Gh. Popescu
University of Bucharest, Romania & The Bucharest University of Economic Studies, Romania & University of Craiova, Romania & The National Institute for Research and Development in Environmental Protection (INCDPM), Romania & National Research and Development Institute for Gas Turbines (COMOTI), Romania

Rahul Verma
Delhi University, India

IGI Global
PUBLISHER of TIMELY KNOWLEDGE

A volume in the Advances in Business Strategy and Competitive Advantage (ABSCA) Book Series

Published in the United States of America by
IGI Global
Business Science Reference (an imprint of IGI Global)
701 E. Chocolate Avenue
Hershey PA, USA 17033
Tel: 717-533-8845
Fax: 717-533-8661
E-mail: cust@igi-global.com
Web site: http://www.igi-global.com

Library of Congress Cataloging-in-Publication Data

Names: Popescu, Cristina Raluca Gh., 1983- editor. | Verma, Rahul, 1989- editor.
Title: Sustainable and responsible entrepreneurship and key drivers of performance / Cristina Raluca Gh. Popescu and Rahul R. Verma, editor.
Description: Hershey, PA : Business Science Reference, [2021] | Includes bibliographical references and index. | Summary: "This book provides an updated view of the newest trends, novel practices and latest tendencies concerning the sustainable and responsible entrepreneurship, in a world permanently dominated by insecurity and dramatic economic, political, and managerial changes"-- Provided by publisher.
Identifiers: LCCN 2021005791 (print) | LCCN 2021005792 (ebook) | ISBN 9781799879510 (hardcover) | ISBN 9781799879527 (paperback) | ISBN 9781799879534 (ebook)
Subjects: LCSH: Social entrepreneurship. | Social responsibility of business. | Sustainable development.
Classification: LCC HD60 .S884667 2021 (print) | LCC HD60 (ebook) | DDC 658.4/08--dc23
LC record available at https://lccn.loc.gov/2021005791
LC ebook record available at https://lccn.loc.gov/2021005792

This book is published in the IGI Global book series Advances in Business Strategy and Competitive Advantage (ABSCA) (ISSN: 2327-3429; eISSN: 2327-3437)

British Cataloguing in Publication Data
A Cataloguing in Publication record for this book is available from the British Library.

Advances in Business Strategy and Competitive Advantage (ABSCA) Book Series

Patricia Ordóñez de Pablos
Universidad de Oviedo, Spain

ISSN:2327-3429
EISSN:2327-3437

Mission

Business entities are constantly seeking new ways through which to gain advantage over their competitors and strengthen their position within the business environment. With competition at an all-time high due to technological advancements allowing for competition on a global scale, firms continue to seek new ways through which to improve and strengthen their business processes, procedures, and profitability.

The **Advances in Business Strategy and Competitive Advantage (ABSCA) Book Series** is a timely series responding to the high demand for state-of-the-art research on how business strategies are created, implemented and re-designed to meet the demands of globalized competitive markets. With a focus on local and global challenges, business opportunities and the needs of society, the **ABSCA** encourages scientific discourse on doing business and managing information technologies for the creation of sustainable competitive advantage.

Coverage

- International Business Strategy
- Cost Leadership Strategy
- Strategic Management
- Ethics and Business Strategy
- Customer-Orientation Strategy
- Globalization
- Entrepreneurship & Innovation
- Outsourcing
- Core Competencies
- Value Creation

IGI Global is currently accepting manuscripts for publication within this series. To submit a proposal for a volume in this series, please contact our Acquisition Editors at Acquisitions@igi-global.com or visit: http://www.igi-global.com/publish/.

The Advances in Business Strategy and Competitive Advantage (ABSCA) Book Series (ISSN 2327-3429) is published by IGI Global, 701 E. Chocolate Avenue, Hershey, PA 17033-1240, USA, www.igi-global.com. This series is composed of titles available for purchase individually; each title is edited to be contextually exclusive from any other title within the series. For pricing and ordering information please visit http://www.igi-global.com/book-series/advances-business-strategy-competitive-advantage/73672. Postmaster: Send all address changes to above address.

Titles in this Series

For a list of additional titles in this series, please visit:
http://www.igi-global.com/book-series/advances-business-strategy-competitive-advantage/73672

Emerging Challenges, Solutions, and Best Practices for Digital Enterprise Transformation
Kamaljeet Sandhu (University of New England, Australia)
Business Science Reference • © 2021 • 387pp • H/C (ISBN: 9781799885870) • US $215.00

Emerging Ecosystem-Centric Business Models for Sustainable Value Creation
Xenia Ziouvelou (University of Southampton, UK) and Frank McGroarty (University of Southampton, UK)
Business Science Reference • © 2021 • 335pp • H/C (ISBN: 9781799848431) • US $225.00

Handbook of Research on Reinventing Economies and Organizations Following a Global Health Crisis
Teresa Gomes da Costa (Polytechnic Institute of Setúbal, Portugal) Inês Lisboa (CARME, School of Management and Technology, Polytechnic of Leiria, Portugal) and Nuno Miguel Teixeira (Center for Research in Business and Administration, School of Business Sciences, Polytechnic Institute of Setúbal, Portugal)
Business Science Reference • © 2021 • 400pp • H/C (ISBN: 9781799869269) • US $345.00

Handbook of Research on Disruptive Innovation and Digital Transformation in Asia
Patricia Ordóñez de Pablos (The University of Oviedo, Spain) Xi Zhang (Tianjin University, China) and Mohammad Nabil Almunawar (School of Business and Economics, University of Brunei Darussalam, Brunei)
Business Science Reference • © 2021 • 661pp • H/C (ISBN: 9781799864776) • US $295.00

Disruptive Technology and Digital Transformation for Business and Government
Kamaljeet Sandhu (University of New England, Australia)
Business Science Reference • © 2021 • 410pp • H/C (ISBN: 9781799885832) • US $225.00

Handbook of Research on Entrepreneurship, Innovation, Sustainability, and ICTs in the Post-COVID-19 Era
Luisa Cagica Carvalho (Polytechnic Institute of Setubal, Portugal & CEFAGE, University of Évora, Portugal) Leonilde Reis (Polytechnic Institute of Setubal, Portugal) and Clara Silveira (Polytechnic Institute of Guarda, Portugal)
Business Science Reference • © 2021 • 451pp • H/C (ISBN: 9781799867760) • US $295.00

Disruptive Technologies and Innovative Strategies for Organizational Success
Nilsa I. Elias (Western Governors University, USA) Terry M. Walker (University of Louisiana, USA) and Robin Walker (Metropolitan State University, USA)
Business Science Reference • © 2021 • 315pp • H/C (ISBN: 9781799837909) • US $225.00

IGI Global
PUBLISHER of TIMELY KNOWLEDGE

701 East Chocolate Avenue, Hershey, PA 17033, USA
Tel: 717-533-8845 x100 • Fax: 717-533-8661
E-Mail: cust@igi-global.com • www.igi-global.com

Editorial Advisory Board

Table of Contents

Detailed Table of Contents

Literature on university quality systems and teaching performance measurement addresses only tangentially the neutrality of measurement instruments in relation to the different teaching methodologies. This chapter explores this issue posing the following question: Should we use identical assessment instruments on teachers who apply different teaching methodologies? The authors attempt to answer this question by focusing the debate on the two most widespread methodological approaches in the university: the behaviourist and the constructivist. The study addresses this task from the perspective of measurement instruments with behavioural episodes. The authors present two instruments to assess teaching performance: one aimed at evaluating teachers who use behaviourist approaches and the other aimed at assessing teachers who apply constructivist approaches. The work reveals divergences between the two questionnaires addressing the importance of using different teaching appraisal instruments to measure, responsibly, the performance of teachers who apply different teaching methodologies.

Entrepreneurship is a key element for developing of economies in recent years. Turkey is a country that is experiencing entrepreneurship both in national and international area. The Turkish economy, especially after 1980, opened its doors to the world global economy, and entrepreneurship became more important in this new order. Before 1980, the big companies were established only in the big cities of Turkey. But after that time, they started to be founded in small cities, too. There are governmental support organizations in Turkey, which fund the entrepreneurship intentions. And there are also new regulations in recent years in Turkey, which enable entrepreneurship activities to establish online on internet processes. By comparison with other countries, it could easily be said that Turkey is also in the arena with facilitation and developing of entrepreneurship in the world scene. Turkish people know more about the increasing importance of entrepreneurship now.

Employee engagement refers to an employee's highest degree of loyalty, commitment, and participation towards organizational goals, objectives, vision, and mission. It is a technique for instilling an intrinsic desire and passion for excellence in employees by winning their head, heart, and soul. In other words, it can be said it is an art and science of engaging people in authentic and recognized connections to strategy, roles, performance, organization, community, relationship, customers, development, energy, and well-being as we leverage, sustain, and transform our work linkages into results. An engaged employee understands the market context and collaborates with co-workers to enhance job performance for the

The chapter established the effects of Nigerian market environment on SMEs performance. An empirical study was conducted with survey research design of 21,444 firms and a sample size of 1,102 was arrived at scientifically. Probability sampling methods were employed. An adapted validated questionnaire, and a 0.82-0.96 reliability coefficients range was used. Inferential statistics were used to analyse the data using SPSS software version 22.0. The findings reveal that Nigerian market environment had significant negative effects on the SME performance. The different components of the Nigerian market environment have different effects on the SME performance. The results imply that the environmental turbulence could be responsible for the high failure rate of SMEs in Nigeria. The study contributes to the body of knowledge on environmental and performance management by noting the criticality of the industry market environment in facilitating organizational performance.

In order to build a successful strategy for any type of business, a strategic analysis needs to be performed. A strategic analysis consists of multiple elements, but it always starts with environmental scanning. This research focuses on that very first step by conducting an environmental analysis. It is a strategic tool that identifies all the external and internal elements, which could possibly affect the organization's performance. The aim of this research was not to provide all the final and conclusive answers. It was merely to explore the research topic with varying levels of depth. Additionally, this research tended to tackle new problems on which little or no previous research has been done by combining and elaborating well-known models, such as PESTEL, Porter´s 5 forces, and SWOT. The research problem of this chapter can be described as to determine the possibilities of starting a successful commercial business within the social welfare sector of Portugal.

Foreword

The book *Sustainable and Responsible Entrepreneurship and Key Drivers of Performance* tackles today's entrepreneurial practices operate in a continuously challenging, highly dynamic, and ever-changing environment. In these times of change, it is important to examine up-to-date theoretical infrastructure on the most powerful and representative approaches to sustainable and responsible entrepreneurship.

What is more, the book *Sustainable and Responsible Entrepreneurship and Key Drivers of Performance* covers an updated view of the newest trends, novel practices, and latest tendencies concerning sustainable and responsible entrepreneurship in a world dominated by insecurity and dramatic economic, political, and managerial changes. The book presents theoretical infrastructure on approaches to sustainable and responsible entrepreneurship as well as empirical results that make a tremendous contribution to the analysis of organizations' performance key drivers. Elaborating on topics such as greening economy, intellectual capital, knowledge management, sustainable entrepreneurial ecosystems, and social responsibility, this text is essential for entrepreneurs, managers, executives, academicians, scientists, researchers, students, practitioners, and policymakers worldwide.

The theme of Corporate Social Responsibility (CSR) is widely diffused in the literature. Simply put, sustainability is a business approach to creating long-term value by organization operates in the ecological, social and economic environment. Management should address these topics separately-not mesh them together. Significantly in both business and academic areas, further research from different supply chain viewpoints, such as collaboration, economies have become key players in supply chains, mainly due to market globalization to define sustainable performance as a term related to results that measure. It is perceived as a key activity for large Multi-National Corporations (MNCs). This is referred to as Sustainable Business Model Innovation (SBMI) of value: from mainly economic to also include social and environmental value. In the short term, social economy actors have assisted the recovery by promoting inclusive and sustainable economic models. Create and share tools to provide data on social impact that are not onerous but can document whose business models are built around such principles can help. But Small and Medium-sized Enterprises (SME) are lagging behind in the digital transition and disruptive. For many start-ups and Small and Medium-sized Enterprises (SME), access to finance in the appropriate forms is difficult. Small and Medium-sized Enterprises (SME) are the main source of jobs in the business sector and those who don't have strong growth aspirations, often remain small throughout their life cycle. Its capability should not be considered in isolation but rather should be integrated and the key factors that facilitate the transformation is the KM cycle, it contributes to meeting their business objectives. We then examine several bases for organizational design and redesign: Perhaps the most noteworthy change in the environment for business, for example, globalization, which may be the most important economic force changes in the organization itself, and hence alter its performance.

But technological change and innovation need to be directed towards business and academia. However, basic financial and entrepreneurial skills requires agility in education.

In terms of topics covered, it should be acknowledged that the book *Sustainable and Responsible Entrepreneurship and Key Drivers of Performance* refers to many academic areas which include, but are not limited to key concepts, such as: agility, entrepreneurship, entrepreneurship finance, greening economy, innovation, intellectual capital, international entrepreneurship, knowledge management, organizational performance, responsible entrepreneurship, social responsibility, sustainable development, sustainable entrepreneurial ecosystems, and women entrepreneurship.

Anand Shukla
Mewar University, India

Sarvottam Dixit
Mewar University, India

Preface

Today's entrepreneurial practices operate in a continuously challenging, highly dynamic, and ever-changing environment. The term 'business environment' means the sum total of all individuals, and the economic, social, political, technological and other forces, which operate. All types of enterprises facing increasingly dynamic environment. They continuously monitor their environment and adopt suitable business practices. Any organisation operating in today's uncertain, complex, and competitive global business environment, managers and organisations are faced with highly dynamic and complex operating environmental conditions by continually introducing changes. Entrepreneurial development today has become very significant; in view of this value creation activity is performed continuously in the midst of uncertain business environment, therefore, entrepreneurship is regarded as a dynamic to continuously evaluate the existing modes of business operations. The problem this presents is that the environment constantly changes and the firm has little control. Today's business environment is generally very dynamic. We live in a dynamic environment that changes all the time. It is complicated and continuously changing. Moreover, the organization does not operate in a vacuum but must interact with its environment in actual practice, since both external and internal forces interact and impact. Identify the most important changes in your business environment and see tips to adapt successfully to a rapidly changing business environment combining to force top management to re-evaluate company operations on changed circumstances and the challenges they present. Today's turbulent business environment, characterised by rapid technological changes that are necessary for coping with the ever changing business environment. It's been greatly challenged in the past few years as the business environment earlier work on turbulence can be traced back to the work on capitalism. In a world of constant change, the spoils go to the nimble. Globalization, new technologies, and greater transparency have combined to upend the business environment as has the size of the gap between winners. All this uncertainty poses a tremendous challenge for strategy making. What are the sectors of the business environment, and how do changes in a dynamic environment that has a direct influence on how they operate and are generally beyond the control of management and change constantly. They are difficult to predict, define, and measure because they can be very subjective. Organizational change is pervasive today, as organizations struggle to adapt or perhaps the most noteworthy change in the environment for business in the societal structure of work-some in traditional solo practice. This is the challenge to be met by those who would posit or create the high-reliability.

In these times of change, it is important to examine up-to-date theoretical infrastructure on the most powerful and representative approaches to sustainable and responsible entrepreneurship. But if we are to achieve all of the Sustainable Development Goals, more needs to be done. It is essential to consider ways and means by which the international community can deal more. Human resource development is a crucial requirement not only to build up technical path that is sustainable in a physical sense could theoretically be pursued. It provides a clear sense of the principles that make sustainability more important.

Sustainable and Responsible Entrepreneurship and Key Drivers of Performance covers an updated view of the newest trends, novel practices, and latest tendencies concerning sustainable and responsible entrepreneurship in a world dominated by insecurity and dramatic economic, political, and managerial changes. In a time when the global economy continues to stutter, climate change and development ranks high on the political agenda, but the barriers appear still too intricate. Some organizations are accepting deteriorating environmental and economic environment. This is one of the core philosophies of sustainable business practices. Successful sustainable businesses are focused on the creation of new, recognizing change, pursuing opportunity, and taking on risk and responsibility. The theme of Corporate Social Responsibility (CSR) is widely diffused in the literature and the debate among scholars of different disciplines. New ways of finding answers for future, unforeseeable threats, to be ready to identify the key drivers of change that will shape and reshape our world. Defence policy, strategy and capability development, making it more relevant and developments that may have a dramatic impact on water sustainability are already.

The book presents theoretical infrastructure on approaches to sustainable and responsible entrepreneurship as well as empirical results that make a tremendous contribution to the analysis of organizations' performance key drivers. This research will help in studying the role of social entrepreneurs in creating new social institutions and structures. In the last century, the economic performance and innovation is a great success. Digital technologies may not only result in business opportunities; they determine future avenues for contributing sustainability implications of entrepreneurship. In the review approach with the analysis of bibliographic networks, the results showed that apart from a huge contribution, sustainability or making opportunities for realizing Industry 4.0, is one of the main technologies of Industry 4.0 (next to CPS and big data) performance of smart manufacturing. The main contribution of this book is to revisit the governance performance of networks and entrepreneurship in family firm internationalisation. The comparison is based on key factors namely: manpower and technology.

Elaborating on topics such as greening economy, intellectual capital, knowledge management, sustainable entrepreneurial ecosystems, and social responsibility, this text is essential for entrepreneurs, managers, executives, academicians, scientists, researchers, students, practitioners, and policymakers worldwide. Evolution and sustainability of entrepreneurial ecosystems nurtures entrepreneurs. The main purpose of this book is to help to develop sustainable information and ideas. An entrepreneurial ecosystems or entrepreneurship ecosystems are peculiar systems of interdependent actors and relations directly or indirectly supporting the creation and growth of new ventures. Ecosystems including the social and the economic environment affect local and economies of scale can be explored in business functions. Social entrepreneurship typically attempts to further broad social, cultural, and environmental goals often associated with the voluntary sector in numerous areas. Entrepreneurial Ecosystems and Growth Oriented Entrepreneurship successful cashed out entrepreneurs reinvest their time, money and expertise in supporting new. Finally, it is important that policy-makers develop and research also shows that these firms invest heavily in human capital and are more. Women and girls' human rights is fundamental to achieving sustainable green economy and gender equality for gender-responsive sustainable development. Emerging Economic Models considers the issues of social and sustainable entrepreneurship to business growth and market leadership and concentrates on the economic and managerial contributions for the collection of information.

ORGANIZATION OF THE BOOK

The chapters that are part of this book are extremely complex and address numerous up-to-date problems:

In this matter, Chapter 1, entitled "Sustainable and Responsible Entrepreneurship for Sustainable Energy Development", Dalia Streimikiene, Asta Mikalauskiene, emphasizes the linkages between sustainable energy development and entrepreneurship are focused and studies in this field are critically discussed in this article, while pointing out that the new sustainable energy technologies and other innovations are presented, such as solar powered trains, electric tires, liquid sunlight, etc. The role of entrepreneurs' in developing of new sustainable energy technologies and other innovations in sustainable energy is emphasized, focusing on the idea that the policies and measures targeting these barriers are analysed and discussed.

Chapter 2, entitled "Sustainable and Responsible Entrepreneurship for Value-Based Cultures, Economies, and Societies: Increasing Performance Through Intellectual Capital in Challenging Times", Cristina Raluca Gh. Popescu, emphasizes the importance of entrepreneurship, stressing the fact that nowadays, entrepreneurship represents the very basis of powerful societies and the essence of robust economies, bringing unique contributions to both sustainable development and economic growth processes. Thus, on one hand, this chapter reviews the theory on sustainable and responsible entrepreneurship as the core of environmental and societal success, and on the other hand, it focuses on the manner in which intangible business assets and intellectual capital yield creativity, innovation, motivation, productivity, and value, in challenging times (COVID-19 pandemic). This multidisciplinary study, based on quantitative and qualitative indicators, reports that intellectual capital factor plays a dominant role in constructing new products, rules and services for the marketplace, and highlights main economic, social, and environmental effects of current business practices.

In continuation, Chapter 3, entitled "Crisis Situation and Financial Planning for Sustainability: A Case of the Czech SMEs", Jarmila Duháček Šebestová, points out the fact that, in any crisis or uncertain situation, it is necessary to carefully decide about three main points when, what to invest and which financial sources will be used, which leads to the idea that a profit reinvestment would be an effective and safe way of circulating money flows in a company. Under these given circumstances, according to the author, the main goal of this chapter is to compare the reinvestment behaviour in the company before the crisis based on primary research data (at least 425 respondents), the chapter including results of different preferences influenced by COVID-19 uncertainty and factor analysis had shown that availability of internal resources were important so survive restrictions and to be able to continue in financial planning to sustainable develop the business.

In continuation, Chapter 4, "Sustain or Perish: A Simple Choice – Collective Action for Sustainability, Not Wishful Thinking", Vishwas Gupta, Amit Bhattacharya, point out that till date, homo-sapiens is a natural creature and hence, Man-Nature relationship is inseparable. Thus, the authors believe that if, in the next few decades designer babies are produced enemas in laboratories like currency notes and their life and living gets programmed by Artificial Intelligence; the issue of 'Reimagining Man-Nature relationship will become more complex provided, the mankind may reach up to that future with its present self-destructive activities. In this matter, according to the authors, without being negative or cursing the flight of Capitalism and Technology, this paper endeavours to record and analyse few recent issues and its impact on human existence and suggests some simple measures that might re-structure value-based consumption-production pattern to ensure liveable conditions and sustainability for the 7 billion people and the next generations on this beautiful planet Earth until next ice-age hits, which means that Mankind is left with no alternative but rectifying partially 'corrupted' portion of 'mind-ware' and re-shaping the man-nature relationship for real survival and growth.

The next work, represented by Chapter 5, "Sustainopreneurship", Rahul Verma introduces the concept of "Sustainopreneurship" (innovation and entrepreneurship for sustainability) which may be a concept that has risen from the prior concepts ecopreneurship and social entrepreneurship, through sustainability entrepreneurship and which implies to utilize creative business organizing to unravel issues related to sustainability to make environmental and social sustainability as a vital purpose and objective, at the same time respecting the boundaries set in order to preserve the life support frameworks within the process. According to the author, it could be a "business with a cause"-where the world issues are turned into business openings by arrangement of sustainability innovations.

Furthermore, Chapter 6, entitled "Quality Systems for a Responsible Management in the University: Measuring the Performance of Teaching Staff", Luis Matosas-López, Roberto Soto-Varela, Melchor Gómez-García, Moussa Boumadan, explores the idea of Quality Systems for a Responsible Management in the University: Measuring the Performance of Teaching Staff posing the following question: Should we use identical assessment instruments on teachers who apply different teaching methodologies? The authors attempt to answer this question by focusing the debate on the two most widespread methodological approaches in the university: the behaviourist and the constructivist.

In Chapter 7, "Turkey's Entrepreneurship Development", Yunus Emre Genç, the author considers entrepreneurship as a key element for developing of economies in recent years, stating that Turkey is a country that experiencing entrepreneurship within years both in national and international area and also that Turkish economy, especially after year 1980, opened its doors to the world global economy and entrepreneurship became more important in this new order.

Also, in Chapter 8, "Employee Engagement, 'Myth or Reality': A Critical Analysis of Entrepreneur and Employee Relationship in Recession Phase of Business Cycle", Bhagawan Chandra Sinha, employee engagement refers to an employee's highest degree of loyalty, commitment and participation towards organization's goals, objectives, vision and mission, which is a technique for instilling an intrinsic desire and passion for excellence in employees by winning their head, heart, and soul. In other words, according to the author, it can be said it is an art and science of engaging people in authentic and recognized connections to strategy, roles, performance, organization, community, relationship, customers, development, energy, and well-being as we leverage, sustain, and transform our work connections into results.

What is more, Chapter 9, "Policy Approaches to Promote Women Entrepreneurship in India", discusses the status and problems along with the solutions of women entrepreneurs in India. It also includes significance of women's entrepreneurship and to analyse the policies of the Indian government for women in urban and rural areas. The authors will initiate a dialogue with policymakers on how to foster enhanced innovation in women-owned enterprises in India.

What is more, Chapter 10, "The Role of University, Structural, and Social Support Means on the Intention of Entrepreneurship: An Empirical Study on the Sample of University Youth", targets at studying the effect of the implicit factors on the intention of establishing an institution for the students of the Algerian university. The authors showed that educational and social support factors affect the entrepreneurial spirit of students more than structural support.

While analysing Chapter 11, "Managerial Pamperdom and Prestige Entrepreneurship", Fahri Özsungur, it should be taken into consideration that entrepreneurship has started to be used as a tool for individual interests as well as the implementation of innovative ideas and sustainability in entrepreneurship requires corporate social responsibility and ethical principles in leadership. Thus, according to the author, especially managerial pamperdom and prestige entrepreneurship that emerged in professional organizations are introduced to the literature for the first time. It is thought that this chapter will make significant contributions to the fields of entrepreneurship, business, management, and strategy.

In like manner, Chapter 12, "Moderated Mediation Effect of Institutional Environment and Entrepreneurship Orientation: The Enterprising Self-Efficacy and Small and Medium-Sized Enterprises (SME) Advancement", Anthony Eniola, presents business enterprise as a significant driver of feasible financial development, autonomous of social, economic, and international condition while the creation and support of effective Small and Medium-sized Enterprises (SME) zeroed in on business is a significant test.

When addressing Chapter 13, "Enhanced Innovation Process as a Key Driver of Bakery Performance", Kafigi Jeje, Vannie Naidoo, Rahul Verma, it should be stressed that Small and Medium-sized Enterprises (SME) in the food sector play a pivotal role in contributing to the developing county's economy, and in order to improve a Small and Medium-sized Enterprises (SME), one key driver is innovation and for innovation initiatives to grow and succeed it depends largely on the leadership and the innovation capabilities of the firm. In this matter, this work sheds more light on the impact of the enhanced innovation process on the performance of Small and Medium-sized Enterprises (SME) bakeries.

While referring to Chapter 14, "Business Environment as Key Driver of SME Performance", Olalekan Asikhia, Vannie Naidoo, it should be stated that the chapter established the effects of Nigerian market environment on Small and Medium-sized Enterprises (SME) Performance and the study contributes to the body of knowledge on environmental and performance management by noting the criticality of the industry market environment in facilitating organizational performance.

In the end, Chapter 15, "Key Drivers of Performance and Profitability in a Social Business", Daisy van Steenbergen, Paulo Ramos, Bruno Sousa, argues that, in order to build a successful strategy for any type of business, a strategic analysis needs to be performed, while a strategic analysis exists of multiple elements, but it always starts with environmental scanning, which implicates that this research focuses on that very first step by conducting an environmental analysis. The authors' aim of this research was not to provide all the final and conclusive answers, it was merely to explore the research topic with varying levels of depth, and additionally, this research tended to tackle new problems on which little or no previous research has been done by combining and elaborating well known models, such as PESTEL, Porter´s 5 forces, and SWOT. The research problem of this chapter can be described as followed: to determine the possibilities of starting a successful commercial business within the social welfare sector of Portugal.

Acknowledgment

The editors would like to acknowledge the help of all the people involved in this project and, more specifically, to the authors and reviewers that took part in the review process. Without their support, this book would not have become a reality.

First, the editors would like to thank each one of the authors for their contributions. Our sincere gratitude goes to the chapter's authors who contributed their time and expertise to this book.

Second, the editors wish to acknowledge the valuable contributions of the reviewers regarding the improvement of quality, coherence, and content presentation of chapters. Most of the authors also served as referees; we highly appreciate their double task.

Cristina Raluca Gh. Popescu
University of Bucharest, Romania & The Bucharest University of Economic Studies, Romania & University of Craiova, Romania & The National Institute for Research and Development in Environmental Protection (INCDPM), Romania & National Research and Development Institute for Gas Turbines (COMOTI), Romania

Rahul Verma
Delhi University, India

Chapter 1
Sustainable and Responsible Entrepreneurship for Sustainable Energy Development

Dalia Streimikiene
https://orcid.org/0000-0002-3247-9912
Vilnius University, Lithuania

Asta Mikalauskiene
Vilnius University, Lithuania

ABSTRACT

The linkages between sustainable energy development and entrepreneurship are focussed, and studies in this field are critically discussed in this chapter. The new sustainable energy technologies and other innovations are presented, such as solar powered trains, electric tires, liquid sunlight, etc. The role of entrepreneurs in developing new sustainable energy technologies and other innovations in sustainable energy is emphasized. The main barriers and drivers of entrepreneurship and innovations in sustainable energy are scrutinized and grouped in regulatory, economic, informational, technological, etc. barriers based on comprehensive literature review. The policies and measures targeting these barriers are analysed and discussed.

INTRODUCTION

Energy is an essential driving force and basis of human life. The different eras of human civilization have been shaped by innovation and the ways in which various energy sources are consumed. Energy can be defined as a cornerstone of social life and a decisive factor in industrial and economic development. Today, the global energy system is highly dependent on fossil fuels, with fossil fuels currently producing about 78.4% of the world's electricity. Combustion of fossil fuels releases various types of

DOI: 10.4018/978-1-7998-7951-0.ch001

toxic and dangerous pollutants that have negative impact on environment and human health through the food chain in a variety of ways. Although this way of energy generation has a negative impact on the environment: on groundwater, soil, air, vegetation, biodiversity etc., the most important problems are linked to air pollution, the greenhouse effect and climate change. Burning fossil fuels releases huge amounts of greenhouse gases into the atmosphere, also classical pollutants such as sulphur and nitrogen dioxides, slid particulates, carbon monoxide etc. In addition, burning of fossil fuels have an increasing negative impact on public health and on people's financial condition and quality of life. For this reason, the implementation of the sustainable energy concept, in particular increase of use of renewable energy sources, is currently receiving a great deal of attention among scholars, decision makers and general public.

The future of global energy must first and foremost be about implementing the concept of sustainable energy development. The main goal of sustainable energy development policy is the development of energy services by reducing the impact of energy production and consumption on the environment and ensuring the implementation of long - term development goals of humanity. In order to respond to high and fluctuating energy prices, growing energy import dependence, rapidly growing global energy demand and global warming, it is necessary to clearly define and pursue energy policies at both national and global levels. In general, energy policy seeks to ensure security of energy supply, affordability, competitiveness and reduction of environmental impacts. Energy security and the completion of the internal market is one of the main priority areas for energy policy. Security of energy supply, energy scarcity and climate change are global challenges. Global energy policy and a balanced response of countries to the current situation in energy markets, diversification of energy supply and promotion of Energy Efficiency (EE) and use of Renewable Energy Sources (RES) are particularly important in addressing energy security issues. Energy and climate change policies already transcend national or regional borders. An effective fight against climate change is only possible with the involvement of all regions of the world. The innovations are playing the key role in providing sustainable energy development and implementing the main Sustainable Development Goals (SDG). However, there are many challenges facing innovation process in delivering sustainable energy targets.

This chapter of the book deals with the main barriers and drivers of entrepreneurship and innovations in sustainable energy and develops recommendations for policies and measures necessary to overcome these barriers and promote entrepreneurship and innovations in sustainable energy. Renewable energy are the main sustainable energy issues discussed in the article. Therefore, innovations in energy sector are linked to new technologies based on renewables and providing energy efficiency improvements also allows to implement Green House Gas (GHG) emission reduction targets. As, there are still a lot of barriers and market failures preventing fast penetration of advanced sustainable energy technologies, public policies are necessary to address these barriers and to promote entrepreneurship and innovations in sustainable energy area.

The chapter deals with the following issues addressed in three sections: the linkages between sustainable energy development and entrepreneurship are analysed; the new sustainable energy technologies are discussed; the main barriers and drivers of entrepreneurship and innovations in sustainable energy are scrutinized and grouped in regulatory, economic, informational, technological etc. barriers based on comprehensive literature review. The policies and measures targeting these barriers are analysed and analytically assessed in terms of their weaknesses and strengths to overcome regulatory, economic, informational and technological barriers and recommendations for enhancement of policies and measures targeting promotion of entrepreneurship and innovations in sustainable energy are given.

BACKGROUND

Sustainable Development and Entrepreneurship

Energy plays a key role in achieving the interlinked economic, social and environmental goals of sustainable development. Sustainable energy is described as energy production and consumption, ensuring the long - term goals of human development, taking into account all three aspects of sustainable development: economic, social and environmental. Liberalization of energy markets increases the security of energy supply by offering more options, more suppliers and thus ensuring competition in the energy market, but it also poses new challenges. Liberalization of international markets, including energy markets, has been a key element of successful growth strategies. The security of energy supply means accesses to energy in all its forms at any time, in sufficient quantities and at affordable prices. Ensuring security of energy supply would successfully implement important issue of the sustainable energy concept. However, along with the liberalized energy market and its benefits, new challenges are emerging due to deprived energy consumers who are withdrawing from the market and facing the constant threat of an insecure energy supply and experiencing fuel and energy poverty. For moving towards low carbon future In Europe Union it is necessary to ensure just transition to carbon free economy by 2050 as the most vulnerable groups of population should protected and problems of distributional, procedural and recognition justices are properly addressed by policies.

Equally important for the sustainability of energy development is the reduction of the negative environmental impact of energy production and consumption. All forms of electricity generation have an impact on the environment. Energy consumption and production activities account for two thirds of total Green House Gas (GHG) emissions. In general, energy also has the greatest potential to help slow down climate change caused by greenhouse gases by accelerating the pace of innovation and supporting the deployment of large - scale renewable energy technologies.

However, this innovation keeps pace with the growing challenges of climate change and the growing demand for energy. Despite the recent rapid increase in investment in clean energy and the empowerment of policies, investment in clean energy research and development is too low and significant barriers to innovation still remain in energy sector.

The White Paper identifies the need for a systematic approach to innovation, as well as global catalysts and actions that can enhance innovation at different stages and technologies. This White Paper also sets out a number of ideas to inspire decision - makers and stimulate debate on the next steps needed for sustainable energy innovation. The main ones are:

- The approach to energy innovation needs to be systematic in order to better connect isolated teams of experts and fill gaps that hinder the faster transformation of basic research into commercially viable projects.
- There is a need to provide better support for capital - intensive innovation areas and to foster cooperation in the pre - competitive stages of innovation by mobilizing R&D investment from countries, companies and philanthropists.
- Measures need to be put in place to invest with public venture capital investors in public R&D grants in order to better target grant recipients, reduce the administrative requirements for grant applications, develop cooperation between public and private capital sources and facilitate fair and transparent grant award.

- Technological plans for the public and private sectors and for cross - border design must be aimed at improving security of energy supply by accelerating commercialization and pooling technical and financial forces that are able to innovate.
- Redesigned and integrated procurement strategies need to be viable, results - oriented rather than technology - specific, offering early - stage "demand - side support" for innovation in areas where there are no technological solutions.
- Transparency of public R&D spending on sustainable energy innovation is important, using existing multilateral frameworks to facilitate data sharing between countries and addressing areas of under - innovation.

The development of renewable energy sources is seen as an important national challenge, ensuring the sustainable development of the energy sector and the country's energy independence. Using more energy from Renewable Energy Sources (RES) reduces the need to import fossil fuels, ensures more efficient use of the country's local energy resources, reduces greenhouse gas emissions and reduces the energy sector's negative impact on climate change.

It is increasingly understood that change is needed to reduce the negative impacts of unsustainable business development on society and the environment (Hall et al., 2010; Stiglitz, 2016). Entrepreneurship is proposed as a particularly effective practice for sustainable and inclusive economic growth. Despite the promises of entrepreneurship to promote sustainable development goals and address the challenges of climate change, the role and nature of entrepreneurship remain unclear. In addition, scientific literature on sustainability and sustainable business is still relatively rare in the general entrepreneurial literature (Hall et al., 2010). Thus, despite the fact that entrepreneurship has been recognized as one of the drivers of potential change for a more sustainable economy, there are still significant gaps in research and knowledge of how and whether this transition is actually taking place. At the same time, the literature on entrepreneurship does not take into account other key aspects of the problem, such as the quality of the institution, the level of innovation or the openness of the economy to trade.

Many authors, such as Schumpeter (1934, 1942), Drucker (1985), and Matos and Hall (2007), have examined, among others, the links between entrepreneurship and global problems - solving. Researchers Cohen and Winn (2007) show that there are several types of market failures like externalities having negative impact on environment. They can also be seen as sources of significant entrepreneurial opportunities to lay the foundations for an emerging model of sustainable entrepreneurship that slows down degradation and gradually improves ecosystems.

Similarly, York & Venkataraman (2010) suggest entrepreneurship as a solution for environmental degradation. The authors have developed a model that encompasses entrepreneurial potential, complementing regulation, corporate social responsibility, and activism in addressing environmental issues. Entrepreneurial actions can reduce environmental pollution and deforestation, preserve the ecosystem and improve the supply of fresh water and the quality of agricultural products. Thus, entrepreneurship could be a solution to many environmental and social problems (Wheeler et al., 2005; Senge et al., 2007; Hall et al., 2010). It follows that entrepreneurship can be seen as a tool for achieving the Sustainable Development Goals (SDGs) in all sectors, including energy, which is particularly relevant in addressing the economic, environmental and social challenges facing this sector.

Innovative entrepreneurs have the potential to create new jobs, restructure the economy and increase sustainability (Silvestre, 2015). Innovation is a catalyst for change through which institutions, organizations and countries can increase the quantity and quality of more sustainable products and services

(Silvestre, 2015). Research shows that society is demanding more initiatives and investment from businesses, educational institutions and governments to make innovative solutions to current sustainability challenges (Almeida et al., 2013). Thus, entrepreneurship and innovation can be recognized as solutions for such global challenges as security of energy supply and scarcity, energy vulnerability and poverty, atmospheric pollution and climate change (York & Venkataraman, 2010). Therefore, a reconsideration of innovations important role in building a sustainable, carbon free economy is necessary.

Any business model clearly reflects the way a company makes a profit. At the same time, business must meet the expectations of stakeholders. However, achieving the SDGs requires the development of new business models that link economic goals to the SDGs. If an element of sustainability is included in the business model, the business can create higher value through customer trust, which is reflected in the important aspect of sustainability inclusion. The added value created in this way also creates a competitive advantage for companies in the market. Therefore, the crucial question of how to create a sustainable business model with the help of innovative entrepreneurs and successfully exploiting the opportunities of entrepreneurship is currently emerging.

The sustainable business model is like an example of a company's business logic that reflects sustainability. If a simple business model includes four key elements: product (service) value, customer, infrastructure, and finance, then in a sustainable business model, sustainability aspects should be included in all four elements. It is recommended to add another element to these four elements, which may be referred to as the "non - market element". The fifth aspect refers to "the configuration of resources and activities that links the value proposition of a business model to technical, legal, regulatory, and policy issues that are (currently) not subject to market mechanisms and market relationships" (Lüdeke - Freund, 2020).

Sustainable Energy Development and Responsible Entrepreneurship

Currently, the focus is on sustainable business models in energy, as energy is important for both economic and social development of societies. A reliable, secure and clean energy sources are essential for achieving all the goals of sustainable development. This is evident in a global context, as one sees the very painful problems of the developing world, where energy is relatively expensive because access to it is still limited. As a result, many projects are being implemented at both the public and private levels, based on innovative business models that tend to focus on the wider use of renewable energy. (Kolk & van - de - Buuse, 2012).

However, renewable energy is not only suitable in niche markets such as rural areas in developing countries. Companies in developed countries are exploring new and innovative business models to develop renewable energy and to ensure successful penetration of these technologies in the mass market. In this case, it is very important which business model the company chooses, because its competitive advantage depends on it. In general, the two most important factors that determine the choice of business model are strategic management of internal resources and management of external factors. To this end, it is necessary to identify the following internal factors that promote entrepreneurship: the opportunities and importance of technological progress and competitive price. However, there are external factors that are also very important to assess, namely social, political and institutional factors (Chalikas et al., 2014; Aravossis et al., 2019).

The innovation process can be seen as a process with three stages: research, demonstration and commercialization. In the research phase, feasibility studies are carried out, in the demonstration phase, prototype planning and implementation are carried out, and in the last commercialization phase, commercial activities are carried out in order to achieve large - scale production, independence and business maturity. The renewable energy industry is a policy - based or policy - sensitive industry. Policies in this area act as a strong institutional factor and play a key role in the development of renewable energy.

The capacity to innovate in renewable energy technologies is the result of many factors that vary greatly depending on the national and sub - national context (Kyriakopoulos et al., 2010). Whatever the technology at stake, economic and educational and energy support and policy coordination are crucial for an effective renewable energy technology innovation policy (Kyriakopoulos et al., 2019). Economic support, public education and successful project coordination and implementation are general conditions for a successful innovation policy. In addition, specific policies often need to be tailored to the specificities of each country and the choice of technologies available. These sectoral innovation policy conditions are an important focus of the renewable energy technology innovation policy process (Kapsalis et al., 2019).

The process of innovation policy for renewable energy technologies describes a three - step process. Each step is designed to shape the approach to developing innovative energy policies (Miller et al., 2015):

- Evaluation phase. This phase focuses on a structured assessment of existing resources and capacities, identifying appropriate ways to innovate in renewable energy technologies and clarifying key policy objectives that are the long - term drivers of innovation policy.
- Strategy phase. This phase focuses on identifying specific circumstances for the successful deployment of renewable energy technologies and the development of a comprehensive policy strategy to support innovation in these areas.
- Implementation phase. This phase focuses on the selection and application of specific policies, together with the establishment of appropriate governance structures to support the implementation of renewable energy technologies.

These three stages are used as an analytical or deductive 'funnel' to move from general to specific aspects of renewable energy technology innovation policy. The innovation policy process for renewable energy technologies aims to cover the whole innovation policy - making cycle. In this way, efforts are made to assess the specific existing opportunities for innovation and the appropriate policies for innovation. It is equally important to identify and explain roles and responsibilities in supporting the effective implementation of renewable energy technologies (Bell & Pavitt, 1993).

Renewable energy technology innovation policy is based on two assumptions:

1. There are many opportunities for innovation in the value chains of various renewable energy technologies.
2. These opportunities for innovation are strongly influenced by contextual factors.

Using the traditional model of innovation, technological inventions are called "linear" because the movement of such inventions from idea to market is linear, i.e., from high - tech research laboratories at an early commercial stage and eventually to markets. Renewable energy technologies are special in that they are not purely physical, as they are designed and developed in a specific policy context and a set of systems consisting of skills and knowledge on how to adopt, implement and use new technologies. Moreover, in the process of implementation of this type of innovation, another component emerges, which the further, the more and more weight is gained - the social acceptance of new renewable energy technologies (Miller et. al., 2015).

However, the introduction of renewable energy technology innovation has some limitations. In particular, it is the economic constraints that limit investment in RES innovation. More specifically, RES innovators cannot always expect to benefit from the positive effects of their investments, thus reducing the incentive to invest. This is a crucial factor both in the innovation phase (e.g., it is difficult to prevent other market players from copying and benefiting from "leading" R&D projects) and in the dissemination phase (where reducing negative externalities does not necessarily mean profit). These two barriers to investing in innovation are well known as the problem of "double externality" (Rennings, 2000). In addition to these external aspects, RES innovations take place in deeply embedded infrastructure systems, which can severely limit the pace and scope of innovation implementation (Musiolik & Markard, 2011).

In Figure 1 the linkages between sustainable development, responsible entrepreneurship and innovations in energy field are addressed.

Figure 1. The Linkages between Sustainable Development, Business - Entrepreneurship and Innovations in Energy Sector
Source: Own

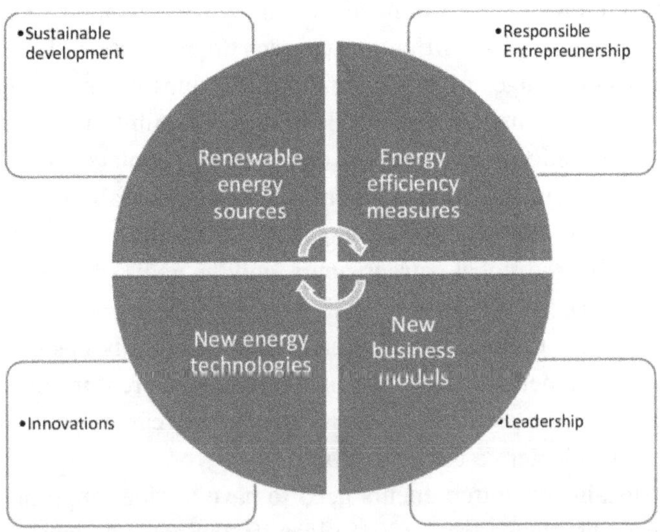

As one can see from Figure 1, the main linkages between sustainable development and business - entrepreneurship and innovations in energy sector are transferred to use of new business models and penetration of new clean energy technologies based on renewable energy sources and providing for energy efficiency improvements. Responsible entrepreneurship allows to implement sustainable development targets in energy sector by innovations linked to sustainable energy development. However, state support and policies and measures are necessary to easier the main barriers of innovations and creation of favourable business environment for innovating companies. The leadership is also playing an important role in fostering responsible entrepreneurship.

Specific contextual factors are very important in the development of innovation policy. Existing resources, human and institutional capacity, energy needs, stakeholder networks, etc. - all brings important input to innovation policy success. Decision - makers who understand these various aspects can make better decisions by rigorously assessing technical, institutional, human, and financial capital in the country. All these issues will be further addressed in other sections of this chapter in more details.

MAIN FOCUS OF THE CHAPTER

Sustainable Entrepreneurship

Traditional and sustainable entrepreneurship is currently widely discussed. While traditional entrepreneurship is still vital to the economies of many countries, it is increasingly acknowledged the need for responsible, sustainable entrepreneurship and business that are not only able to adapt to changing market conditions, but also envisage the sustainable development of society as a whole, ensuring long - term and high - quality of well - being in safe and clean environment. Such business is socially and economically responsible and addresses issues of society very seriously (Lüdeke - Freund, 2020). Successful sustainable business can be achieved through innovations that allow to improve operational efficiency of enterprises. The success of sustainable business can be described in terms of financial and non - financial benefits (profits from an improved innovation environment, solving environmental and social problems, etc.).

Sustainable entrepreneurship has a different approach to business risk compared to traditional entrepreneurship and faces challenges of private and social values when setting up a business entity. Representatives of sustainable business are more likely to face institutional barriers due to the lack of financial, administrative, and information support observed by scholars (Hoogendoorn et al., 2019). However, sustainable entrepreneurs are much more afraid of personal failures and this leads to complex relationships with stakeholders (Hoogendoorn et al., 2019). Nevertheless, environmental and social issues are tackled sluggishly by traditional entrepreneurs, and the goals of sustainable entrepreneurs are much more complex and broader than those of traditional entrepreneurs, who are mainly focusing on profit and pay very little or no attention to social and environmental issues of business development. In addition, sustainable entrepreneurship faces the uncertainties inherent in such entrepreneurship - the causality and consequences of the problem, as decision - making can often be unpopular and provide for a little economic benefit (Fichter & Tiemann, 2020).

Scholars argue that sustainable entrepreneurs need to have a wide range of specific competencies in order to achieve their goals. Ploum et al. (2018) identify the competencies that are necessary for a sustainable entrepreneur:

- Strategic management and actions that include business diversification opportunities and interdisciplinary;
- Systemic thinking;
- Normative competencies;
- Insightful thinking;
- Interpersonal competencies.

Sustainable entrepreneurs also include traits that well facilitate business creation and management: knowledge management, motivation, a focus on sustainable consumption, and continuous improvement (Fichter & Tiemann, 2020). By introducing their products to the market, sustainable entrepreneurs not only meet and adapt to the needs of consumers, but also promote their attitudes towards the environment and society. These entrepreneurs publicize the features and benefits of their products as sustainable business practices and use this as additional tools for market differentiation.

Examining the concept of sustainable entrepreneurship, it is observed that sustainable entrepreneurship is an integral part of sustainable development (Popescu & Popescu, 2019). There is currently a wide - ranging debate on how sustainable development strategies can be developed, in which the promotion of entrepreneurship, in particular sustainable entrepreneurship, and the possibilities for achieving sustainable development goals through sustainable entrepreneurship promotion models can play an important role. At the same time, it is necessary to define exactly the main features of sustainable entrepreneur and establish main criteria the entrepreneur must meet in order to be named as sustainable entrepreneur. This sustainable entrepreneurship approach can be applied to the successful development of sustainable business strategy (Popescu, 2019, 2020).

Sustainable entrepreneurship is defined as a vision that can be successfully implemented by a business leader with a set strategy (Tassigny, 2013). If we support such an approach, we must assume that an organization with such a leader becomes completely dependent on his actions, attitudes, and understanding of business and business models. In this case, when developing a business strategy, it is likely to be adapted to the experience of the leader, and his desire to adapt to the changing internal and external conditions of the organization he is leading.

Sustainable Leadership

Sustainable leadership brings together all types of leadership through three dimensions of sustainable development (economic, social, and environmental). The core values of sustainable leadership are clearly visible in the articulated vision and mission. Sustainable leadership includes the principles of sustainable leadership, which are declared and expressed in values that help preserve the world around us. Sustainable leadership is characterized by a focus on the team and followers, as it aims not only for short - term goals, but also for the continuity of leadership and the development of new leaders. Sustainable leadership not only accepts and implements the goals of the organization, but is committed to the community and society as a whole. Sustainable leadership is an ongoing, stable process that uses reasonable means of influence over team members.

In the course of its activities, the organization is constantly facing changes in the business environment and fierce competition. Creating a sustainable organization requires management practices that allow you to successfully respond to changes in the business environment and maintain a competitive advantage. Therefore, a sustainable organization also develops an appropriate organizational culture, the principle of which is also considered to be sustainable leadership.

Researchers Hargreaves & Fink (2004) provided a definition of sustainable leadership and singled out the principles of sustainable leadership:

- Sustainable leadership matters. The first and key principle of sustainable leadership is to be a leader while learning and taking care of others.
- Sustainable leadership lasts. It preserves and continually enhances the most valuable aspects of life year after year, moving from one leader to another. The challenges of succession and continuity of leadership are the basis for sustainable leadership.

- Sustainable leadership spreads. It supports the leadership of others and depends on it. In a complex world, no leader, institution or nation can control everything without the help of others. Sustainable leadership, first of all, is distributed and shared leadership.
- Sustainable leadership does no harm to and actively improves the surrounding environment. It does not 'steal' from others. It does not try to thrive at the expense of others. It does not damage other organisations but actively seeks for ways how to share with them its knowledge and resources. Sustainable leadership is not egocentric; it is socially just.
- Sustainable leadership promotes cohesive diversity. Strong organisations promote diversity and avoid standards that weaken learning, adaptability and resilience not only to those changes and threats. Sustainable leadership promotes teaching and learning diversity and learns from it. It encourages to move forward by combining completely different components.
- Sustainable leadership develops and does not deplete material and human resources. It takes care of its leaders by encouraging them to take care of themselves. It renews people's energy resources. Sustainable leadership is wise and smart leadership, which does not waste either its financial or human resources.
- Sustainable leadership honours and learns from the best of the past to create an even better future. In the chaos of changes, sustainable leadership firmly protects and retains its long term goals. Many theories of change refer to changes, despite or without remembering the past. Sustainable leadership 'refreshes' the memory of organisations and respects the wisdom behind it as a way of learning, preserving and improving.

These 7 universal principles of sustainable leadership can be distinguished, which apply to both public and private sector organizations (Hargreaves & Fink, 2004):

- Sustainable leadership creates and maintains long - term sustainable activities of the organization.
- Sustainable leadership promotes long - term progress.
- Sustainable leadership strengthens the leadership of others and develops new leaders.
- Sustainable leadership is socially just.
- Sustainable leadership encourages to develop human and material resources and not just waste them.
- Sustainable leadership encourages to create a diverse environment and develop skills of community members.
- Sustainable leadership actively impacts the environment where the organisation is located.

Sustainable leadership must undoubtedly become a commitment to all leaders. If the changes in sustainable development that are spreading and last for a long time are important for the society, sustainable leadership must become a guiding principle in the systems where leaders have to do their job.

Sustainable Energy Sector Development

Sustainable economic growth requires a responsible approach to energy resources. Sustainable energy will ensure national and global security, strengthen the use of renewable energy sources, thus reducing greenhouse gas emissions. Sustainable energy allows to improve the quality of life of society by ensuring the achievement of the general goals of sustainable development. There is no doubt that the deterioration of air quality and climate change are directly linked to the energy sector, which is responsible for most of the greenhouse gas emissions. The situation is changing by the fast penetration of renewable energy sources in the energy markets and moving towards a low - carbon economic development model.

Renewable energy in 2016 accounted for 17.5 percent total energy consumption (IEA, IRENA, UNSD, WB, WHO, 2019). 2019 The Energy Progress Report presented in 2006 indicates that the use of renewable energy sources for electricity generation is increasing, but that the heat and transport sectors are lagging far behind. Increasing the availability, reliability and sustainable production and consumption of energy is essential for the wider use of renewable energy (IEA, IRENA, UNSD, WB, WHO, 2019).

The energy sector has important input for the sustainable development of the world. Energy is necessary for all other sectors of the economy and for the development of sustainable entrepreneurship as well. Therefore, sustainable entrepreneurship in energy sector is mainly linked with increased use of renewable energy sources and development of new advanced energy efficient low carbon technologies.

Therefore, it is very important that, the chief executives (leaders) of an energy companies must have a vision of sustainable business development that can be implemented through novel and flexible decisions. However, the organization in energy sector may face difficulties in implementing the business leader's strategy because this type of strategy is often accepted by the employees of an organization as autocratic, reflecting the attitudes and expectations of only one person - leader. To avoid this, a lot of time is necessary for the discussing of strategy in a team and aligning it with common documents and activities. The mission of the organization is also very important for this purpose, which must clearly reflect the directions that the organization should follow (Tassigny, 2013). All doubts are mitigated by the clear direction of business development set by the business leader. It is also very important to anticipate opportunities to change the business development course in order to adapt to new short and long challenges which are difficult to predict.

For sustainable entrepreneurship in energy sector, where companies are mostly medium and large, especially in the energy production sector, the idea of sustainable entrepreneurship and leadership is of core importance as allows to solve many emerging problems in this sector linked to pollution, corruption risks etc. This is especially true because by envisioning sustainable business strategies, the business leader has a great opportunity to innovate and maintain an organic and flexible organizational structure at the company.

New structures are being set up to clarify the links between sustainable business and sustainable energy and to achieve the common goals of sustainable development. These goals be achieved by sustainable entrepreneurs and leaders by combining different approaches through training, the acquisition of new knowledge, improvement and refinement. Such features are met by an innovative organization, where decision - making does not depend on the decision of one person, but takes into account the competencies of all team members, the latest knowledge, expert recommendations, and allows urgent and necessary decisions and actions at different levels. This type of organization requires open and flexible operations, rapid identification and resolution of problems, stable technological change, and a responsible approach to the surrounding environment.

The interaction of individual elements of an organization's operations is essential for a business strategy to become holistic and take into account both the internal and external operating environment of the organization. Therefore, innovation must be constantly introduced and maintained at all levels of the organization's activities, thus creating a holistic vision of business development through innovation process (Kobayashi, 2000).

Often, the strategies of energy companies are implemented through strategic directions, which are envisaged taking into account the country's level of economic development, political situation, attitudes of energy consumers and other aspects. However, most of sustainable leaders uses strategic directions: competitiveness, reliability, reducing the impact of climate change and ambient air pollution (energy saving and use of green energy), and the involvement of other business entities and developing clusters in achieving innovations and progress in sustainable energy development. Thus, the need for sustainable entrepreneur and leader for the sustainable development of the energy sector is necessary.

Renewable energy sources and energy efficiency are currently widely discussed as the main ways to achieve sustainable energy development and climate change mitigation. Consumer needs must be met in an environmentally friendly way, contributing to climate change mitigation by reducing greenhouse gas emissions, providing access to energy for all, improving energy security and encouraging consumers to use energy efficiently.

Changes in the share of renewable energy in world's primary energy production since 1965 are shown in Figure 2.

Figure 2. Share of Renewable Energy in Primary Energy Production
Source: Our World in Data https://ourworldindata.org/renewable-energy#how - much - of - our - primary - energy - comes - from - renewables

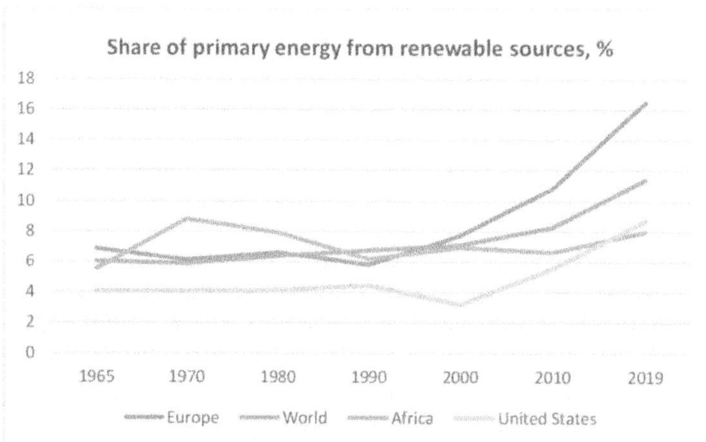

Also, one can notice from Figure 1 above, the share of energy from renewable sources in primary energy supply is growing steadily, and Europe is an example of energy sector with the 2.5 times increase of the share of renewable energy sources (RES) from 1965 to 2019. Globally the share of RES has almost doubled (1.9 times) during the same period. The share of RES has also doubled in US during the mentioned period. The dynamics of renewable energy production in the world is provided in Fig. 3.

As can be seen from Figure 3, the world's renewable energy production is growing, with hydropower accounting for the largest share, followed by wind and solar energy.

Improving energy efficiency is another important sustainable energy development direction providing for the reduction of energy import dependency, climate change mitigation, increase of competitiveness of country, as well as energy security. In most cases, energy efficiency is being assessed by estimating the GDP energy intensity of primary and final energy. The latter indicator shows how much energy

Figure 3. Global Renewable Energy Production
Source: Our World in Data https://ourworldindata.org/renewable-energy#how - much - of - our - primary - energy - comes - from - renewables

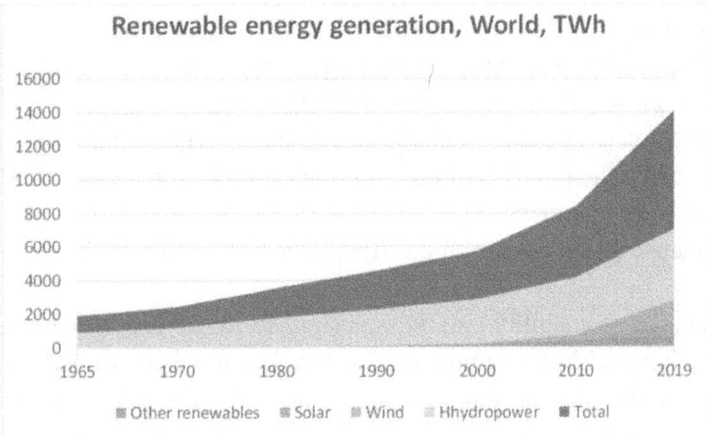

consumption was spent on creating a specific amount of goods and services in the country (ratio of energy consumption of the national economy to GDP). Generally, energy efficiency is understood as the reduction of energy consumption to perform the same task, in other words, the main goal is not to waste energy. The greatest energy saving potential is in the industrial, residential, building and transport sectors.

New renewable energy technologies can also provide for similar benefits, however new advanced energy technologies are expensive and often become an important burden on the economies of economically weaker countries, while increasing of energy efficiency is the cheapest way to reduce the use of fossil fuels and GHG emissions.

Corporate Social Responsibility

When it comes to responsible business, it is worth to emphasize the idea of Corporate Social Responsibility (CSR) and the main periods of CSR development. Corporate social responsibility itself is not a new phenomenon in the business world. A concept has been defined firstly defined in 1953. The first concept of CSR states that social responsibility is the duty of entrepreneurs to make decisions based not only on the profits of the company, but also on the goals and values of society (Bowen, 1953). The concept was later supplemented by other definitions, like statements that a firm must not only fulfil certain economic and financial obligations, but it must also have a binding responsibility to society (McGuire, 1963). The evolution of corporate social responsibility can be seen in three stages: the first is related to maximizing corporate profits, the second is related to trust when stakeholder involvement is initiated and the third is related to the integration of corporations into society. During the last period of CSR development, with the help of responsible corporations, attempts were made to address the major social problems of society. It is worth noting that in the seventies such problems like unemployment, environmental pollution, quality of products, health of workers, etc. emerged (Choi & Gray, 2008). Even later, then the idea was conceptualized in 1975, it became clear it is not possible to consider about environmental and social problems in isolation, because they are very closely interrelated and should be solved together.

Social responsibility can be classified into five main dimensions (Dahlsrud, 2006):

- Environmental dimension (focuses on the company's environmental policy, ensuring a cleaner environment, sustainable use of resources, raw materials and solving other environmental problems),
- Social dimension (seeks cooperation and integration of business as an organizational unit with the business environment),
- Economic dimension (aimed at ensuring the long - term economic viability of operations, while contributing to global sustainable economic development),
- Stakeholder dimension (emphasizes that the company, in carrying out socially responsible activities, takes into account the interests of all stakeholders and the interests of all employees, suppliers, customers and other partners),
- Volunteering dimension (a philanthropic activity where the company is volunteering for charity.

This division of social responsibility into 5 dimensions shows a very strong link of all of them with sustainable development, which is being understood through three main dimensions: economic, social and environmental in addition taking into account institutional dimension helping to implement all three dimensions. Consequently, the model of social responsibility can be called an extended model of sustainable development.

The three traditional sectors - public (government), private (business) and social (non - profit) - have blurred in the new millennium as social and environmental objectives increasingly blend together with development of new business approaches. This can be seen everywhere, from civil and municipal enterprises, financial institutions, public organisations, sustainable businesses or social enterprises. Whatever they are called, they all are dedicating more resources to delivering social and environmental benefits. In addition, public and social sector organisations are attempting to operate in a more business - like manner in targeting sustainable development goals.

Figure 4 shows how social businesses and enterprises fit within two criteria: where they receive their revenue from and how they distribute their profits.

In one direction we categorise organisations by their "bottom line ". It is necessary to define do these enterprises seek to maximise the financial benefits or do they seek to maximise the social benefit to the community as a whole. In the other direction, it is necessary to categorise them by their source of income by answering an important question: does their income come primarily from earned sources (sales) or does it originate from some contributed source such as charity, grants, taxes or subsidies.

Using these criteria, we can distinguish between traditional business for - profits, business for - profits with corporate social responsibility goals, and social businesses models. At the other end of the spectrum is the traditional non - profit business, following by a social enterprise that seeks direct earned income on behalf of the non - profit. Finally, there is the true social business pursuing social and environmental aims through the use of business methods.

Therefore, corporate social responsibility is a kind of business development system that integrates the observance of ethical norms in profit - making activities, using modern and up - to - date sustainable management systems. This presupposes that socially responsible business organizations not only base their activities on the pursuit of profit, but also use certain innovative management systems that control whether the business process meets the set environmental and social standards.

It is very important for socially responsible companies to create a strong organizational culture that reflects the values cherished by the responsible entrepreneurs themselves. Creating a harmonious organizational culture makes it much easier for a company to develop sustainable business practices, attract new employees, raise their attitudes towards society and environment, increase their qualifications and

Figure 4. Defining Social Businesses and Enterprises
Source: Adapted From Fourth Sector Network, 2009

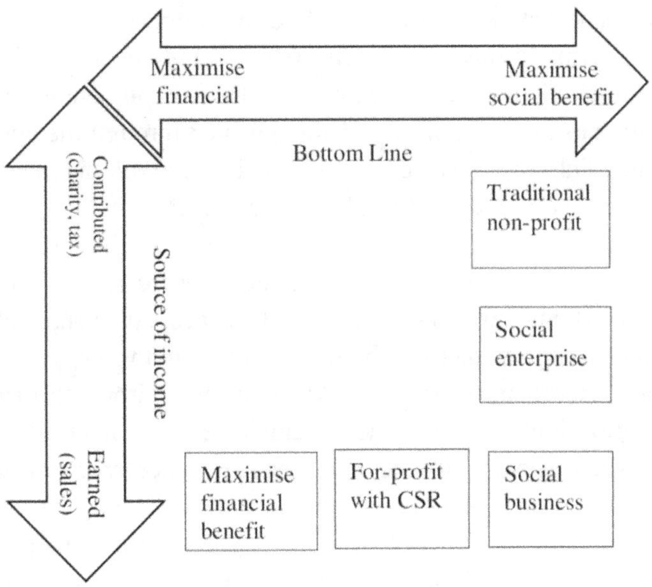

develop mutual understanding and responsibility. However, for this, the personal values of most employees must coincide with the values of the company, and the overall goal of the company's activities must be part of the personal goals of employees.

The importance and benefits of organizational culture can be defined in many different ways, but in all cases organizational culture creates coherence between the organization and employees, strengthens the stability of the social system, and distinguishes one organization from another by revealing the uniqueness of the latter. The organizational culture creates business continuity and the ability to respond quickly and effectively to the changing environment by implementing the principles of social responsibility through innovation.

Although there is a general interest in the links between organizational culture and organizational efficiency in the search for opportunities to increase operational efficiency, much attention has recently been paid to organizational culture as a basis for sustainable business development. Through organizational culture, it is possible to successfully combine the personal attitudes of each employee (sustainable consumption, and environmental protection) with the general attitudes and culture of the entire organization. Strong and cohesive organizational culture allows for the creation of a community that is believed to be effective and works like a family (Choi & Gray, 2008).

Thus, a socially responsible business does not necessarily offer goods and services that are suitable for all consumers, these products do not necessarily have to be available to everyone. The strategy of a socially responsible business reflects the economic reality: strong competition in the market, and the advantage of competitors using economies of scale. Therefore, using higher costs for responsible business products requires a differentiated business strategy. This strategy would highlight the essential advantages of responsible business, which are linked with sustainable development in general and the dimensions of social responsibility in a broader sense. Unlike traditional businesses, socially responsible businesses can often envision a strategy that would reduce a company's profits in the short term but will provide increase of profits in long - term.

It is important to understand that the idea of sustainable development of an organization can be realized in both the short and long term. To this end, organizations should develop their operational strategies, involving stakeholders, improving not only economic but also environmental performance. Thus, at the organizational level, sustainable development is communicated through the concept of organizational social responsibility, which links the activities of the organization with the main aspects of sustainable development (Tauraitė - Janušauskienė, 2019; Rahdari et al., 2016).

The terms sustainable organization and social responsibility are similar, but cannot be used interchangeably. In both cases, the aim is to maximize the total value created for society and both integrate elements of the three - dimensional bottom - up line, but the concept of sustainable development, unlike in the case of social responsibility, emphasizes both levels of shared value - society and stakeholders in the organization and its long - term impact on stakeholders and the environment (Tauraitė - Janušauskienė, 2019). Therefore, all organizations that apply the sustainable development model to their activities are socially responsible, but social responsibility does not mean acceptance by organization of all sustainability practices. Consequently, if an organization focuses its social responsibility on a short - term perspective and applies only to some individual activities (usually they are not integrated into the organization's business strategy), then social responsibility of such company will be one of the stages in achieving long - term sustainable development goals.

The change in values currently observed in societies is directly related to the long - term economic development of the states. In countries that have crossed a certain line of development, entering the so - called era of post - materialist values, there are higher consumer needs for self - expression, self - realization, security and social justice. Social justice is becoming a societal priority and socially responsible business is serving to realize this societal need (Tauraitė - Janušauskienė, 2019; Rahdari et al., 2016).

Energy companies are considered to be the most important, because the activity of other economic sectors depends on their efficiency. The activities of companies in the energy sector have long relied on the use of fossil fuels, which has made it necessary to address environmental problems in this sector. Recently, the activities of energy service companies have been reorganized throughout the chain, from energy production to trade, including energy distribution. Given that the energy sector has long been considered the most polluting sector, there is a need to improve environmental efficiency, reduce energy supply costs and increase the reliability of energy systems. As a result, energy companies around the world are reviewing their business models to adapt them to changing environmental conditions.

As energy companies and the energy sector as a whole are forced to take responsibility for the environment and society, the idea of corporate social responsibility has proved to be appropriate in the choice of energy companies' strategies to meet consumer expectations and remain competitive. CSR practices have shown that the implementation of social responsibility principles helps to address key challenges related to the environment, competition, customer loyalty and others. Most energy companies focus on social responsibility when developing sustainable business ideas. The implementation of these practices takes place at the institutional level.

The energy production sector must take responsibility for preserving the surrounding environment and are therefore encouraged to phase out the use of fossil fuels in the gradual transition to renewable energy sources. Energy companies are also forced to pursue business strategies that focus on reducing greenhouse gas emissions and improving the quality of life in society and conserving biodiversity.

The implementation of the principles of social responsibility in energy companies is based on three dimensions of sustainable development: economic, social and environmental. At first sight, the solution to economic issues does not seem to raise any debate. However, economic responsibility is misunderstood as a solution to financial issues and is often considered to be an expression of the implementation of social responsibility. The economic aspect of sustainability must take into account the direct and indirect economic impact that the organisation's activities have on the community and the company's stakeholders (Stjepcevic & Siksnelyte, 2017).

From the point of view of corporate social responsibility, companies in the energy sector must not only generate profits, but must also contribute to the sustainable economic development of the country. Such a contribution to the implementation of sustainable development goals can be made through investments in infrastructure through the creation of new infrastructure objects and the reconstruction and modernization of old ones. The economic dimension of social responsibility also includes the introduction and development of new energy technologies, the adoption of innovative solutions to improve the security and reliability of energy supply. It is essential that energy companies far from consumers are responsible for the entire energy supply chain. In contributing to the development of the local economy, these companies need to assess the needs of consumers in the short and long term. Based on this, plan new energy capacity without exceeding the planned energy demand. Energy efficiency and reliability are also very important. Increasing efficiency requires economic capacity that would allow the introduction of new energy - saving technologies not only in large companies, but also to offer them to the population at the lowest cost. Security of energy supply allows consumers to be assured that they will be supplied with the right amount of energy at any time of the day. It also requires economic capacity. Thus, the economic dimension of sustainable development, and thus of social responsibility, is very important and must be appreciated.

The social aspects of sustainable development have been increasingly discussed during the implementation of corporate social responsibility. Most energy companies actively address social issues by assessing the impact of their activities (both direct and indirect) not only on the company's own employees, but also on the wider society. In this way, organizations build their image and, by solving social problems correctly, build a long - term and stable positive reputation. Building such a reputation comes at a cost, but it is a very important factor in increasing competitiveness. The social aspects of corporate social responsibility also include public information, recommendations on energy efficiency, the development of new technologies, the reduction of emissions, and so on.

The importance of the social responsibility aspects of environmental energy companies is not in doubt, as this topic has been widely discussed for a long time. Energy production and transmission clearly have a significant impact on the environment, and addressing these issues today is a concern not only for environmentalists but also for energy strategists, politicians and the general public. As environmental problems are clearly visible around the world, the environmental burden created by the energy sector extends beyond the national state. There are many ways to determine the environmental impact of energy companies, so energy development strategies include environmental or energy capacity reduction measures in addition to infrastructure or energy capacity development.

Many environmental problems are solved by the use of renewable energy sources. Electricity generated from RES can be successfully supplied to large electricity networks, although in many cases the decentralization of this type of source is considered a disadvantage of RES use. The use of RES can help solve many problems in remote rural areas, where it is expensive and uneconomical to build electricity transmission networks. Economically difficult developing countries can use RES to supply electricity to the population without connecting remote consumers to the centralized electricity supply network. However, innovative energy technologies face barriers.

SOLUTIONS AND RECOMMENDATIONS

Innovative Energy Technologies

Existing energy technologies are already well known and used in everyday life. Meanwhile, renewable electricity sources are natural resources, the emergence of which and the extent to which they are renewed are caused by natural processes.

There are following already developed and constantly improved, electricity generation technologies based on renewable energy sources:

- Bioenergy - biomass;
- Direct solar energy - solar panels;
- Geothermal energy - production of geothermal power.
- Hydropower - hydroelectric power plants.
- Wind energy - wind power plants.

These are existing and at the same time constantly technically updated and improved renewable electricity generation sources, thanks to the new technologies of which renewable electricity is obtained. This electricity from renewable energy sources is used to avoid dependence on fossil fuels, to mitigate the effects of climate change, and so on (IPCC, 2012).

In addition to conventional renewable electricity sources, new innovative renewable electricity technologies are being developed. The aim of these innovations is to create advanced and socially adaptable devices that will benefit people. These technologies are divided into 5 groups: solar, wind, water, bio and others.

The following are 5 examples from each group of new renewable electrical technologies are provided.

The new solar energy technologies:

- Saltwater solar thermal ponds. Solar ponds are thermal solar collectors that have their own separate power storage system. They accumulate electricity from direct and diffuse sunlight (Qiblawey & Banat, 2007).
- Multi - node solar cells or tandem cells. These solar cells are composed of a combination of two different cells, which allows for much more efficient conversion of electricity without loss of electricity (Kim et al., 2007).
- Photo electrochemical solar cells. Transfers solar energy directly to electricity using an electrolyte - coated material. The electrical network is created when the conductor anode is in contact with the metal cathode and they are both in contact with the electrolyte.
- Paint - sensitive solar cells. It is a cheap and easy alternative to solar cells. It is transparent, flexible and long - lasting (Zhu et al., 2006).
- Thin film organic photovoltaic cells or polymeric solar cells. The organic and plastic composition of this technology can be easily manufactured and adapted to different forms (Yoo et al., 2004).

Therefore, the innovative solar technologies are characterized by the development of new elements that use micro - technologies to extract electricity from direct or indirect sunlight and have the potential to store such energy within themselves that can then be transmitted and distributed to the electricity grid.

The innovative wind - based energy generation technologies are:

- Vertical axis wind turbines. They can be of the Darrieus or Savonius type and are characterized by a low wind speed (4 m / s) to operate.
- Concentrated wind accelerators or a diffuser augmented wind turbine or a ducted turbine. These are efficient wind farms that collect about 1.5 to 2 times more electricity than conventional wind mills farms.
- Knife tip power system. This technology allows to start collecting electricity at very weak winds, which reaches only 2 m / s, while the average wind speed required for the operation of traditional wind systems is 6 - 8 m / s.
- High altitude wind turbines and air wind turbines. A high - pitched wind farm is much more efficient because it is not dependent on fluctuations in wind speed close to the ground and can produce large amounts of electricity.
- Wind belt. This technology is driven by static gas motion, which is created by repeating a naturally moving object through which energy moves aerodynamically (Balaguru, 2013).

One can notice, that innovative wind technologies are characterized by the development of new wind turbines - an architecture that improves the existing structure of wind farms. Taking advantage of the new architectural type and new possibilities of wind turbines, the most optimal option for obtaining electricity from wind power is being sought.

There are following new hydro technologies:

- Micro and peak hydroelectric power plants. These are very small - sized, natural water - changing micro - tubes that spin a small turbine generator that produces electricity, and the water is then returned back to its source (Razak et al., 2009).
- Eddy power hydrokinetic hydroelectric power plant. When one object is placed in a fluid flow path the other will create or turbulence in that fluid. By applying certain fins in the flowing liquid, electricity can be extracted from such low speeds as 2 knots (Tytell, 2006).
- Ocean current hydrokinetic power plant. It provides possibility to extract electricity from strong underwater currents. It is an indirect source of solar energy because ocean currents are caused by the energy emitted by solar heat (Myers & Bahaj, 2007).
- Osmotic power or salinity gradient power plant. In places where clean water mixes with salt water, a voltage is created on the salt water side, which allows this water to run through a turbine and generate electricity (She et al., 2012).
- Ocean thermal energy change. The water that is at the bottom of the oceans is much cooler than at the surface. This principle makes it possible to create a heat engine with a low - pressure system that would allow the extraction of electricity by means of heat exchange.

So, innovative water technologies focus on new types of hydropower plants that are able to generate electricity from new, hydrokinetic, renewable electricity sources - offshore currents, wave battles, space power and thermal energy change.

Innovative bio - electricity technologies are:

- Synthesis gas, biomass biofuel. Specially emitted gases can be used in new hybrid electric and gas cars that would be powered by these gases (Pino et al., 2003).
- Fuels derived from pyrolysis, biomass biofuels. During pyrolysis, by burning organic matter, energy can be extracted from the heat released, which would later be converted into electricity.
- Biomass microbial fuel cells. Oxidation of glucose can directly generate electricity using special microbial fuel cells (Chaudhuri & Lovley, 2003).

Therefore, the innovative bio - electricity technologies focus on the development of biomass biofuels from alternative, renewable electricity sources - diesel, gas fusion, etc. These bio - sources can be used to generate electricity instead of not being used at all.

Other innovative energy technologies are:

- Yield of kinetic energy. Possibility to use mechanical force stress and convert it into electricity. This technology can be used to install special devices in shoes or on the curbs where electricity can be extracted from the energy that is generated by the flow of people.
- Micro natural energy yield. It is the conversion of small amounts of natural energy into electricity. Natural energy can come from various forms - solar, wind, mechanical vibration, thermal energy, etc. This energy can be extracted and stored or used in small, wireless, autonomous devices, i.e., electronic devices, wireless networks or biomedical devices.
- Mechanical electricity tanks. Mechanical electrical reservoirs allow electricity to be stored from mechanical energy. The energy is transferred to a mechanical device, which starts operating from the acquired energy. In the event of a power demand, this device is mechanically braked and the previously used energy is recovered (Chen et al., 2018).
- Thermal electricity tanks. The most widely used thermal power tanks are designed to store solar energy. The main function of such tanks is to store as much electricity as possible during the day, which would then be used for as long as possible during the night and thus exploit the full potential of solar collectors (Kuravi et al., 2013).
- Updated electricity network to help store electricity. This technology makes it possible to exploit the potential of both the electricity supplier - user and consumer - to store electricity and use it at the right time, using renewable electricity sources (Wade et al., 2010).

Other innovative energy technologies described above summarize the potential for energy from natural sources where energy is unused. Much attention is paid to electricity savings in electricity storages. This can be done using both batteries and mechanical storage or thermal storage tanks.

Barriers of Innovations in Energy Sector and Policies and Measures to Overcome Them

The implementation of innovation can be limited by various barriers, both external and internal. Internal barriers to innovation include a lack of internal funding, a lack of technical expertise, a lack of management time and lack of innovative culture. External barriers to innovation include difficulties in accessing technical information, external finance, lack of customer demand, risk perception, and government regulation and policy (Hadjimanolis, 1999). These barriers hamper the implementation of innovation or slow down the pace of innovation.

Such barriers to innovation have a negative impact on the performance of organizations, reducing their competitiveness in the market, as the lack or absence of innovation prevents the improvement of products and services to adapt to market needs. From the government's point of view, this is also undesirable because innovation is important to the economy to sustain and improve economic growth processes.

Barriers of innovations faced by companies can be divided into four categories:

- Administrative,
- Financial,
- Political, and
- Legal.

Administrative barriers are related to the time that can be devoted to the implementation of innovation in the organization, as administrative procedures require a lot of time and this hinders the efficiency of innovation process. Financial barriers include a lack of internal resources and problems linked with external funding. Innovation usually requires both internal and external funding. Political obstacles create uncertainty and question the feasibility of innovation after a certain period of time (e.g., elections, attitudes of individual parties in power, etc.). Legal barriers are related to existing weak innovation regulations. Excessively stringent innovation requirements can hamper innovation and lead to additional legislation requirements and in this way slows and hampers innovation process.

The government uses subsidies to achieve certain policy goals. This is done "by supporting producers through direct or indirect measures to reduce costs, increase income, employment, or stimulate the country's economy" (Guiyang, 2007). The indirect effect of a subsidy is to reduce the cost and price of a good or service, which can increase the demand for that good. In other words, the government wants to encourage the use of a particular good, service, product, or achieve a particular policy goal. The aid scheme reduces costs for the company, which in turn reduces costs for producers, making production, investment or innovation cheaper. In the case of innovation, the support scheme reduces required investments or innovation costs by increasing in this way the number of innovations. Innovation support schemes are based on two market failures. Technological spills can occur through research and development and / or innovation.

Companies do not include certain additional aspects in the cost - benefit analysis because it is difficult to predict what the market demand for a good or service will be. Due to the lack of cost - benefit analysis, the level of private investment will be not optimal from a public perspective. Support schemes are used to increase R&D activities to social optimality (Bronzini & Piselli, 2016). The second reason concerns the asymmetry of information. Innovation can be vague and risky, making private investors reluctant to invest. This is important reason for limited access to private market financing for innovations (Bronzine & Piselli, 2016). Subsidies and fiscal incentives are the most common support schemes. The purpose of support schemes is to encourage innovation. In this way public funding compensates for the lack of private funding (Bronzine & Piselli, 2016).

Small and medium - sized enterprises make up 99% of companies in the European Union. Kaufmann & Tödtling (2002) described the barriers faced by small and medium - sized enterprises as "specific size barriers". Small and medium - sized enterprises are also hampered by the same obstacles to innovation: financial, administrative and legal. Research shows that access to external funding depends on the size of the organization, the duration of the activity, and the form of ownership (Beck et al., 2006). In the case of small and medium - sized enterprises, own financial resources are severely limited, so it is very important to have sufficient external funding. Limited external funding reduces the innovativeness of these companies, as innovation requires a large share of external funding. Therefore, the situation of small and medium - sized enterprises in the field of innovation implementation compared to large business is quite complicated. In addition, small and medium - sized enterprises have small not only financial but also human resources, which also negatively affects the innovative environment of the organization.

Government policies affect the innovative capacity of companies. The nature of regulations and support schemes can have a positive or negative impact on innovation. Pelkmans & Renda (2014) recommend an innovation policy that "combines compliance, timing, flexibility, and legal certainty".

The ideal innovation policy consists of:

- not too strict technological requirements,
- sufficient time to comply with regulatory requirements,
- where regulation is more performance - based than stringent technological requirements; and
- when regulatory requirements do not change so often (Pelkmans & Renda, 2014).

Frenken & Hekkert (2017) see fixed government policy as an important factor for innovation as well. Innovation is more effective if policies have clear expectations about the role of different technologies. Clear expectations contribute to the creation of new markets and consumer requirements that deliver products to businesses. Expectations must be reflected in the available innovation funds. Policies need to identify which technologies will be important in the future and align innovation funds with them. There is general agreement that public funding is needed for innovation in the energy sector. Clausen (2009) argues that the return on private investment does not outweigh the benefits to society, making public funding desirable. Therefore, due to low private returns, investors are reluctant to invest in innovation.

The market penetration of new energy production technologies, such as those using renewable energy sources is driven by a number of factors, including policies and measures promoting renewable and energy efficiency improvements. These policies and measures were developed to address the main barriers of renewables.

Though due to economies of scale new renewable energy technologies can compete with fossil fuel - based technologies in energy markets, the social, economic, technological, regulatory and behavioural barriers to the further development of these new technologies still exist. (Zyadin et al., 2014; Nasirov, 2015).

There are social barriers of RES development like public resistance for RES projects. This is linked with the lack of information and public awareness of RES (Raza et al., 2015; Paravantis et al., 2014; Zhao et al., 2016). Other social barriers of RES project are linked to the land and natural resource competition with other sectors of economy like fishery, tourism and recreation (Boie et al., 2014; Edomah et al., 2017).

There is also "Not in My Yard" or "NIMBY" syndrome which cause many conflicts with local communities due to implementation of big RES projects on local level like wind farms, big solar panels areas (Nasirov et al. 2015).

There is lack of capacities due to the weakness of education systems in developing experts in renewable energy field. The lack of skilled labour for the development of RES projects is also important barrier for RES projects (Karakaya & Sriwannawit, 2015).

The main policies and measures to deal with identified social barriers of RES are various information dissemination campaigns, large demonstration projects, establishment of various curricula in higher and professional education institutions (Sovacool, 2009; Paravantis et al., 2014; Kilinc - Ata, 2016; Seetharaman et al., 2019).

There are serious economic and financial barriers to the development of RES projects such as high start - up capital needs to implement such projects, the lack of financial institutions and investors (Byrnes et al. 2013; Raza et al., 2015; Sun & Nie, 2015). RES projects usually have a long payback period (Lyu & Shi, 2018; Painuly, 2001) and RES project developers are usually facing many problems linked with financing of these projects (Ohunakin et al., 2014) therefore RES projects are treated as risky projects.

External costs of environmental damage are not fully integrated in the price of energy and due to shrinking prices of fossil fuels and low environmental taxes not reflecting full external costs of fossil fuel cycles, these traditional fuels are successfully competing with clean renewable energy sources (Jovovic et al., 2017).

The main economic and financial policies necessary to deal with economic barriers to the development of RES technologies: preferential loans, subsidies and grants for RES projects, green certificates and greenhouse gas emissions trading; GHG taxes or tax incentives for RES; fixed feed - in electricity prices or feed - in price auctions, development of new financial institutions to subsidize RES projects, (Harrison, 2015; Sun & Nie, 2015; Zeng et al., 2018).

The main technological barriers to the market penetration of RES technologies are the following: inadequate infrastructure, lack of storages, scares financing of research and development. Infrastructure barriers (Gullberg et al., 2014; Zhao et al., 2016; Boie et al., 2014; Raza et al., 2015) are very important for RES projects. Infrastructure necessary for RES projects is very costly as includes financing of additional transmission lines to connect RES to the grid and storage technologies are necessary to deal with intermittency of RES.

Inadequate financing of research and development prevents RES technologies from competing effectively with conventional energy technologies (Cho et al., 2013). The low culture of operation and maintenance of RES technologies also prevents penetration of these technologies in energy markets.

The main policies and measures to overcome technological barriers of RES technologies are: public support for RES infrastructure, reduction of import taxes, VAT and other tax breaks to ensure reduction of high infrastructure costs of RES technologies (Boie et al., 2014; Edomah et al., 2017; Lyu & Shi, 2010).

There are following regulatory barriers of RES projects development: the lack of political support and pour regulatory framework supporting RES, bureaucratic burdens and over - regulation; insufficient incentives, institutional corruption and lobbying for fossil fuels or nuclear energy (Malik et al., 2019).

The main regulatory policies and measures to overcome regulatory barriers: development of predictable energy policy and high political confidence in RES projects (Zhang et al., 2014).

Policies and measures should be developed to remove regulatory barriers: establishment of the share of renewables in final energy, in electricity and heat, in transport and other obligations and mandates; public procurement of RES electricity and heat; renewable energy quotas and other obligations (Boie et al., 2014; Cadoret & Padovano, 2016; Kilinc - Ata, 2016; Malik et al., 2019).

In Table 1 barriers and policies to overcome these barriers are evaluated based on the ability to deal with main barriers of innovations in sustainable energy development.

As on can see from Table 1, for successful implementation of policies and measures to promote sustainable energy and innovations in energy sector, the several important issues should be taken into account then implementing these policies and measures. Most of the instruments in order to be successful

Table 1. Assessment of Policies and Measures Targeting Innovations in Energy Sector and Sustainable Energy Development

Policy instruments	Assessment of success in dealing with barriers	Factors of success in overcoming barriers
Regulatory and control instruments		
Appliance standards	High	Only effective if periodical updated, if independent control is being ensured, Provision of information, communication, education is crucial for success
Building codes	High	Only effective if enforced and periodically updated, monitoring and control is also important. Provision of information, communication, and education is crucial for success.
Energy efficiency or renewable energy obligations and quotas	Medium	Only effective if continuous improvements are ensured such as new energy efficiency measures and technologies
Mandatory audit requirement	Medium	Mostly they are effective if combined with other measures
Mandatory and voluntary labelling and certification programs	Medium	Mandatory programs are more effective than voluntary ones. Mostly they are effective if combined with other measures
Demand - side management programs	High	These instruments are more cost - effective for the commercial buildings and do not fit very well for residential buildings
Economic and market - based instruments		
Energy savings performance contracting (ESCO)	Medium	Provision of information, communication, education is crucial for success
Cooperative procurement	Medium	Only effective in combination with standards and labelling etc.
White certificates and green certificates	Mcdium	Requires high monitoring and enforcement costs and institutional support, not clear interaction with other measures
Fiscal instruments and incentives		
Taxation	Low	Effectiveness is linked to price elasticity. Most effective when combined with other tools
Tax exemptions / reductions	Medium	Effective just if they are properly structured to stimulate large scale energy renovation
Public benefit charges	Medium	Successful if independent administration of funds is ensured, regular monitoring &feedback and simple &clear design are necessary
Capital subsidies, grants, soft loans	Low	They can provide access to capital of low - income population
Support, information and voluntary action		
Voluntary and negotiated agreements	Medium	Only effective when regulations are difficult to enforce. Combined with financial incentives can provide for better results
Public leadership programs	Medium	Mandatory leadership programs have higher potential than voluntary programmes. Combined with financial incentives can provide for better results
Education and information programs	Low	Most effective then they are implemented with other measures
Detailed billing and disclosure programs	Medium	Successful in combination with other measures. It is necessary to ensure periodic evaluation for success

Sources: Stokes, 2013; Sun & Nie, 2015; Zhang et al., 2014; Gullberg et al., 2014; Zhao et al., 2016; Boie et al., 2014; Raza et al., 2015

in promoting innovations in energy sector should be implemented in combination with other instruments. Especially it is important for measures aiming to support, information and voluntary actions. Regulatory and informative policies would also provide for more effective results if are well structured and enforced in combination with other measures like economic and market based.

However, there are also other barriers like information asymmetries and lack of information, fragmented initiatives, lack of transparency and other behavioural barriers (Browne et al., 2015; Huang et al., 2013). The most important are behavioural barriers having negative impact on penetration of innovative sustainable energy technologies.

FUTURE RESEARCH DIRECTIONS

Most modern climate change mitigation strategies and measures have been developed on the basis of a rational decision - making model; however, household's decision - making systematically deviates from rational choice economic theory. Therefore, the important recommendation is to shape policies seeking to remove behavioural barriers.

There are "nudges" and "boosts" can be applied in energy policies. Nudging mechanism is designed in a way to provide humans with the choices that direct them to make decisions through the automatic or intuitive process. This mechanism does not obscure the freedom of choice instead facilitates people for making wise decisions conveniently and predictably. Nudging can deploy one or a range of intervention techniques based on the context and requirements.

The "boost" measures can deal with such behavioural barriers like scarcity of information, barriers to cognition, social comparison and behavioural limitation, and include important policies and measures such as education, information dissemination, capacity building, and community empowerment.

All policies and measures aiming to support penetration of RES technologies need to be harmonized and the best way is to develop policy packages aiming to address all complex barriers together like supplementing fiscal instruments with information dissemination and behavioural measures like nudges and boosts.

Additional research is necessary to addresses policies and measures design by incorporating relevant non - economic issues in the decision making especially those linked to behavioural change which are not being adequately addressed by current policies and measures targeting new innovative energy generation technologies.

Therefore, considerable analysis is necessary to reconcile many issues about behavioural failures and their influence on deployment of RES technologies. It is very important to define how behavioural and other market failures and barriers are related and how these all - overlapping failures may be corrected through well shaped and innovative policies and measures.

CONCLUSION

- Entrepreneurship is particularly effective practice for ensuring sustainable economic growth. Despite the promises of entrepreneurship to promote sustainable development goals and address the challenges of climate change, there are still significant gaps in research and knowledge of how and whether this transition is actually taking place.

- The Entrepreneurship is necessary to ensure innovation process which can be seen as a process with three stages: research, demonstration and commercialization. In the research phase, feasibility studies are carried out, in the demonstration phase, prototype planning and implementation are carried out, and in the last commercialization phase, commercial activities are carried out in order to achieve large - scale production, independence and business maturity.
- All these stages are specific for specific goods and sector. Innovations in energy sector are mainly linked to renewable energy generation technologies. As renewable energy industry is a policy - based or policy - sensitive industry. Policies in this area act as a strong institutional factor and play a key role in the development of renewable energy technologies and their uptake in the market.
- Use of renewable energy based new energy technologies and their rapid uptake by the market can provide for many social benefits like reduction of negative environmental and public health effects linked to fossil fuel generation, greenhouse gas emission reduction, increase in security of energy supply and reduction of energy import dependency as well as creation of new jobs and positive impact of economic growth and business development including growth of income and reduction of energy poverty and vulnerability. However, socially optimal level of these technologies' deployment can't be reached due to various market failures and barriers which need to be properly appraised and addressed.
- Though there are many innovative RES based energy technologies successfully competing with conventional energy sources on the market in many parts of the world, there are still many barriers to the further development and market uptake of these new technologies. Thus, the rapid market penetration of new energy generation technologies is hampered by a number of social, economic, technological and regulatory and behavioural barriers. Researchers have identified these barriers as the main reasons preventing the widespread use of new innovative energy generation technologies based on renewable energy sources.
- For overcoming social, economic, technological and regulatory barriers to the development of new energy generation technologies the well - targeted policies that effectively address these barriers are necessary. However, the success and impact of this policy in overcoming barriers to new energy production technologies need to be assessed on the basis of concrete examples also taking into account behavioural and psychological barriers which are site specific and culturally based.
- Most of the policy instruments in order to be successful should be implemented in combination of other instruments. Especially it is important for support, information and voluntary actions. Regulatory and informative policies would also provide for more effective results if are well structured and enforced in combination with other measures. The policy packages being introduced together became more popular in recent years however they do not provide evidence so far on their effectiveness in dealing with climate change mitigation paradox at households.
- The main reason of weak performance of implemented policies and measures to overcome the identified barriers of penetration of new innovative energy generation technologies in the market is the overlooked behavioural and psychological barriers in shaping these policy instruments.

REFERENCES

Almeida, C. M. V. B., Bonilla, S. H., Giannetti, B. F., & Huisingh, D. (2013). Cleaner Production initiatives and challenges for a sustainable world: An introduction to this special volume. *Journal of Cleaner Production*, *47*, 1–10.

Aravossis, K. G., Kapsalis, V. C., Kyriakopoulos, G. L., & Xouleis, T. G. (2019). Development of a holistic assessment framework for industrial organizations. *Sustainability*, *11*(14), 3946.

Balaguru, P., Raj, B. V., & Vignesh, B. E. (2013). Low Cost Energy Production Using Wind Belt Technology. *International Journal of Engineering and Innovative Technology*, *2*(9).

Beck, T., & Demirguc-Kunt, A. (2006). Small and medium - size enterprises: Access to finance as a growth constraint. *Journal of Banking & Finance*, *30*(11), 2931–2943.

Bell, M., & Pavitt, K. (1993). Technological Accumulation and Industrial Growth: Contrasts between Developed and Developing Countries. *Industrial and Corporate Change*, *2*, 157–210.

Boie, I., Fernandes, C., Frías, P., & Klobasa, M. (2014). Efficient strategies for the integration of renewable energy into future energy infrastructures in Europe - An analysis based on transnational modelling and case studies for none European regions. *Energy Policy*, *67*, 170–185.

Bowen, H. R. (1953). *Social responsibilities of the businessman*. Harper and Row.

Bronzini, R., & Piselli, P. (2016). The impact of R&D subsidies on firm innovation. *Research Policy*, *45*(2), 442–457.

Browne, O., Poletti, S., & Young, D. (2015). How does market power affect the impact of large scale wind investment in 'energy only' wholesale electricity markets? *Energy Policy*, *87*, 17–27. doi:10.1016/j.enpol.2015.08.030

Byrnes, L., Brown, C., Foster, J., & Wagner, L. D. (2013). Australian renewable energy policy: Barriers and challenges. *Renewable Energy*, *60*(1), 711–721. doi:10.1016/j.renene.2013.06.024

Cadoret, I., & Padovano, F. (2016). The political drivers of renewable energies policies. *Energy Economics*, *56*, 261–269. doi:10.1016/j.eneco.2016.03.003

Chalikias, M., Kyriakopoulos, G., Skordoulis, M., & Koniordos, M. (2014). Knowledge Management for Business Processes: Employees' Recruitment and Human Resources' Selection: A Combined Literature Review and a Case Study. *Communications in Computer and Information Science*, *466*, 505 - 520.

Chaudhuri, S. K., & Lovley, D. R. (2003). Electricity generation by direct oxidation of glucose in mediator less microbial fuel cells. *Nature Biotechnology*, *21*(10), 1229–1232. PMID:12960964

Chen, J., Cheng, S., Vinko, N., & Song, M. (2018). Quo Vadis? Major players in global coal consumption and emissions reduction. *Transformations in Business & Economics*, *17*(1), 112–132.

Cho, C., Yang, L., Chu, Y., & Yang, H. (2013). Renewable energy and renewable R&D in EU countries: A cointegration analysis. *Asian Journal of Natural and Applied Sciences*, *2*(1), 10–16.

Choi, D. Y., & Gray, E. R. (2008). Socially responsible entrepreneurs: What do they do to create and build their companies? *Business Horizons, 51*, 341–352.

Clausen, T. H. (2009). Do subsidies have positive impacts on R&D and innovation activities at the firm level? *Structural Change and Economic Dynamics, 20*(4), 239–253.

Cohen, B., & Winn, M. I. (2007). Market imperfections, opportunity and sustainable entrepreneurship. *Journal of Business Venturing, 22*, 29–49.

Dahlsrud, A. (2006). How Corporate Social Responsibility is defined: An Analysis of 37 Definitions. *Corporate Social Responsibility and Environmental Management, 15*, 1–13.

Drucker, P. F. (1985). *Innovation and Entrepreneurship: Practice and Principles*. Harper Business.

Edomah, N., Foulds, C., & Jones, A. (2017). Influences on energy supply infrastructure: A comparison of different theoretical perspectives. *Renewable & Sustainable Energy Reviews, 79*, 765–778. doi:10.1016/j.rser.2017.05.072

Fichter, K., & Tiemann, I. (2020). Impacts of promoting sustainable entrepreneurship in generic business plan competitions. *Journal of Cleaner Production, 267*, 122076. Advance online publication. doi:10.1016/j.jclepro.2020.122076

Fourth Sector Network. (2009). *The Emerging Fourth Sector About Fourth Sector Network*. Fourth Sector Network.

Frenken, K., & Hekkert, M. P. (2017). *Innovatiebeleid in tijden van maatschappelijke uitdagingen*. Retrieved on https://www.mejudice.nl/artikelen/detail/innovatiebeleid-in-tijden-van-maatschappelijke-uitdagingen

Guiyang, Z. (2007). Energy subsidy policies and their reform: Providing economic incentives for climate change mitigation. *Advances in Climate Change Research, 3*, 92–96.

Gullberg, A. T., Ohlhorst, D., & Schreurs, M. (2014). Towards a low carbon energy Future - Renewable energy cooperation between Germany and Norway. *Renewable Energy, 68*, 216–222. doi:10.1016/j.renene.2014.02.001

Hadjimanolis, A. (1999). Barriers to innovation for SMEs in a small less developed country (Cyprus). *Technovation, 19*(9), 561–570.

Hall, J. K., Daneke, G. A., & Lenox, M. J. (2010). Sustainable Development and Entrepreneurship: Past Contributions and Future Directions. *Journal of Business Venturing, 25*, 439–448.

Hargreaves, A., & Fink, D. (2004). The seven principles of sustainable leadership. Educational Leadership. *Journal of the Department of Supervision and Curriculum Development, NEA, 61*(7), 8–13.

Harrison, B. (2015). Expanding the renewable energy industry through tax subsidies using the structure and rationale of traditional energy tax subsidies. *University of Michigan Journal of Law Reform. University of Michigan. Law School, 48*(3), 845–877.

Hoogendoorn, B., Van der Zwan, P., & Thurik, R. (2019). Sustainable Entrepreneurship: The Role of Perceived Barriers and Risk. *Journal of Business Ethics, 157*(3). Advance online publication. doi:10.100710551 - 017 - 3646 - 8

Huang, S., Lo, S., & Lin, Y. (2013). To re - explore the causality between barriers to renewable energy development: A case study of wind energy. *Energies, 6*(9), 4465–4488. doi:10.3390/en6094465

IEA, IRENA, UNSD, WB, & WHO. (2019). Tracking SDG 7: The Energy Progress Report 2019. Washington, DC: Author.

IPCC. (2012). *Intergovernmental panel on climate change. Renewable energy sources and climate change mitigation. Summary for policymakers and technical summary.* https://archive.ipcc.ch/

Jovovic, R., Simanaviciene, Z., & Dirma, V. (2017). Assessment of Heat Production Savings Resulting from Replacement of Gas with Biofuels. *Transformations in Business & Economics, 16*(1), 34–51.

Kapsalis, V. C., Kyriakopoulos, G. L., & Aravossis, K. G. I. (2019). Investigation of ecosystem services and circular economy interactions under an inter - organizational framework. *Energies, 12*(9), 1734.

Karakaya, E., & Sriwannawit, P. (2015). Barriers to the adoption of photovoltaic systems: The state of the art. *Renewable & Sustainable Energy Reviews, 49*, 60–66. doi:10.1016/j.rser.2015.04.058

Kaufmann, A., & Tödtling, F. (2002). How effective is innovation support for SMEs? An analysis of the region of Upper Austria. *Technovation, 22*(3), 147–159.

Kilinc - Ata, N. (2016). The evaluation of renewable energy policies across EU countries and US states: An econometric approach. *Energy for Sustainable Development, 31*, 83–90. doi:10.1016/j.esd.2015.12.006

Kim, J. Y., Lee, K., Coates, N. E., Moses, D., Nguyen, T. Q., Dante, M., & Heeger, A. J. (2007). Efficient tandem polymer solar cells fabricated by all - solution processing. *Science, 317*(5835), 222–225. PMID:17626879

Kobayashi, S. (2000). *Renewal of logistics: how to define global physical distribution strategies. Traduzido por Valéria Custódio dos Santos*. Atlas.

Kolk, A., & van de Buuse, D. (2012). In search of viable business models for development: Sustainable energy in developing countries. *Corporate Governance, 12*(4), 551–567. doi:10.1108/14720701211267865

Kuravi, S., Trahan, J., Goswami, D. Y., Rahman, M. M., & Stefanakos, E. K. (2013). Thermal energy storage technologies and systems for concentrating solar power plants. *Progress in Energy and Combustion Science, 39*(4), 285–319.

Kyriakopoulos, G. L., Kapsalis, V. C., Aravossis, K. G., Zamparas, M., & Mitsikas, A. (2019). Evaluating circular economy under a multi - parametric approach: A technological review. *Sustainability, 11*(21), 6139.

Kyriakopoulos, G. L., Kolovos, K. G., & Chalikias, M. S. (2010). Woodfuels prosperity towards a more sustainable energy production. *Communications in Computer and Information Science, 112*, 19–25.

Lüdeke-Freund, F. (2020). Sustainable Entrepreneurship, Innovation, and Business Models: Integrative Framework and Propositions for Future Research. *Business Strategy and the Environment, 29*(2), 665–681.

Lyu, X., & Shi, A. (2018). Research on the Renewable Energy Industry Financing Efficiency Assessment and Mode Selection. *Sustainability, 10*(1), 222. doi:10.3390u10010222

Malik, K., Rahman, S. M., Khondaker, A. N., Abubakar, I. R., Aina, Y. A., & Hasan, M. A. (2019). Renewable energy utilization to promote sustainability in GCC countries: Policies, drivers, and barriers. *Environmental Science and Pollution Research International*, *26*(20), 20798–20814. doi:10.100711356 - 019 - 06138 - 2 PMID:31104248

Matos, S., & Hall, J. (2007). Integrating sustainable development in the extended value chain: The case of life cycle assessment in the oil and gas and agricultural biotechnology industries. *Journal of Operations Management*, *25*, 1083–1102.

McGuire, J. W. (1963). *Business and society*. McGrawHill.

Miller, M., Bustamante, C., Roesch, R., Boshell, F., & Ayuso, M. (2015). *Renewable Energy Technology Innovation Policy. A Process Development Guide*. IRENA Innovation and Technology Centre.

Musiolik, J., & Markard, J. (2011). Creating and Shaping Innovation Systems: Formal Networks in the Innovation System for Stationary Fuel Cells in Germany. *Energy Policy*, *39*(4), 1909–1922.

Myers, L., & Bahaj, A. S. (2007). Wake studies of a 1/30th scale horizontal axis marine current turbine. *Ocean Engineering*, *34*(5), 758–762.

Nasirov, S., Silva, C., & Agostini, C. A. (2015). Investors' perspectives on barriers to the deployment of renewable energy sources in Chile. *Energies*, *8*(5), 3794–3814. doi:10.3390/en8053794

Ohunakin, O. S., Adaramola, M. S., Oyewola, O. M., & Fagbenle, R. O. (2014). Solar energy applications and development in Nigeria: Drivers and barriers. *Renewable & Sustainable Energy Reviews*, *32*, 294–301. doi:10.1016/j.rser.2014.01.014

Painuly, J. P. (2001). Barriers to renewable energy penetration; a framework for analysis. *Renewable Energy*, *24*(1), 73 - 89. https://doi: (00)00186-5 doi:10.1016/S0960 - 1481

Paravantis, J. A., Stigka, E. K., & Mihalakakou, G. K. (2014). An analysis of public attitudes towards renewable energy in Western Greece. *Renewable & Sustainable Energy Reviews*, *32*, 100–106. doi:10.1109/IISA.2014.6878776

Pelkmans, J., & Renda, A. (2014). *Does EU regulation hinder or stimulate innovation?* https://www.ceps.eu/ceps-publications/does-eu-regulation-hinder-or-stimulate-innovation/

Pino, L., Vita, A., Cordaro, M., Recupero, V., & Hegde, M. S. (2003). A comparative study of Pt/CeO 2 catalysts for catalytic partial oxidation of methane to syngas for application in fuel cell electric vehicles. *Applied Catalysis A, General*, *243*(1), 135–146.

Ploum, L., Blok, V., Lans, T., & Omta, O. (2018). Toward a validated competence framework for sustainable entrepreneurship. *Organization & Environment*, *31*, 113–132. PMID:30886514

Popescu, C. R., & Popescu, G. N. (2019). The Social, Economic, and Environmental Impact of Ecological Beekeeping in Romania. In G. Popescu (Ed.), *Agrifood Economics and Sustainable Development in Contemporary Society* (pp. 75–96). IGI Global. doi:10.4018/978 - 1 - 5225 - 5739 - 5.ch004

Popescu, C. R. G. (2019). Addressing Intellectual Capital in the Context of Integrated Strategy and Performance: Emphasizing the Role of Companies' Unique Value Creation Mechanism, While Targeting Better Organizational Reporting In Romania: The Case of Green Marketing and Green Marketing Strategies. *Journal of Marketing Research & Case Studies, 672821*. Advance online publication. doi:10.5171/2019.672821

Popescu, C. R. G. (2020). Sustainability Assessment: Does the OECD/G20 Inclusive Framework for BEPS (Base Erosion and Profit Shifting Project) Put an End to Disputes Over The Recognition and Measurement of Intellectual Capital? *Sustainability, 12*(23), 10004. doi:10.3390u122310004

Qiblawey, H. M., & Banat, F. (2008). Solar thermal desalination technologies. *Desalination, 220*(1), 633–644.

Rahdari, A., Sepasi, S., & Moradi, M. (2016). Achieving sustainability through Schumpeterian social entrepreneurship: The role of social enterprises. *Journal of Cleaner Production, 137*, 347–360.

Raza, W., Saula, H., Islam, S. U., Ayub, M., Saleem, M., & Raza, N. (2015). Renewable energy resources: Current status and barriers in their adaptation for Pakistan. *Journal of Bioprocessing and Chemical Engineerin, 3*(3), 1–9.

Razak, J. A., Sopian, K., Ali, Y., Alghoul, M. A., Zaharim, A., & Ahmad, I. (2009). Optimization of PV - wind - hydro - diesel hybrid system by minimizing excess capacity. *European Journal of Scientific Research, 25*(4), 663–671.

Rennings, K. (2000). Redefining Innovation— Ecoinnovation Research and the Contribution from Ecological Economics. *Ecological Economics, 32*(2), 319–332.

Schumpeter, J. (1934). *The Theory of Economic Development*. Harvard University Press.

Schumpeter, J. (1942). *Capitalism, Socialism, and Democracy*. Harper.

Seetharaman, M. K., Patwa, N., Saravan, & Gupta, Y. (2019). Breaking barriers in deployment of renewable energy. *Heliyon, 5*(1), 1–23. doi:10.1016/j.heliyon.2019.e01166 PMID:30723834

Senge, P., Lichtenstein, B., Kaeufer, K., Bradbury, H., & Carroll, J. (2007). Collaborating for systemic change. *MIT Sloan Management Review, 48*, 44–53.

She, Q., Jin, X., & Tang, C. Y. (2012). Osmotic power production from salinity gradient resource by pressure retarded osmosis: Effects of operating conditions and reverse solute diffusion. *Journal of Membrane Science, 401*, 262–273.

Silvestre, B. S. (2015). A hard nut to crack! Implementing supply chain sustainability in an emerging economy. *Journal of Cleaner Production, 96*, 171–181.

Sovacool, B. K. (2009). Rejecting renewables: The socio - technical impediments to renewable electricity in the United States. *Energy Policy, 37*(11), 4500–4513. doi:10.1016/j.enpol.2009.05.073

Stiglitz, J. (2016). An agenda for sustainable and Inclusive growth for emerging Markets. *Journal of Policy Modeling, 38*(4), 693–710.

Stjepcevic, J., Siksnelyte, I. (2017). Corporate Social Responsibility in Energy Sector. *Transformations in Business & Economics, 16*(1), 21 - 33.

Sun, P., & Nie, P. (2015). A comparative study of feed - in tariff and renewable portfolio standard policy in renewable energy industry. *Renewable Energy, 74*, 255–262. doi:10.1016/j.renene.2014.08.027

Tassigny, M. (2013). *Sustainable Entrepreneurship in the Energy Sector*. https://www.researchgate.net/publication/292604425_Sustainable_Entrepreneurship_in_the_Energy_Sector

Tauraitė-Janušauskienė, G. (2019). The role of organizational social entrepreneurship in the context of sustainable development. *Regional Formation and Development Studies, 3*(29).

Tytell, E. D. (2006). Median fin function in bluegill sunfish Lepomis macrochirus: Stream wise vortex structure during steady swimming. *The Journal of Experimental Biology, 209*(8), 1516–1534. PMID:16574809

Wade, N. S., Taylor, P. C., Lang, P. D., & Jones, P. R. (2010). Evaluating the benefits of an electrical energy storage system in a future smart grid. *Energy Policy, 38*(11), 7180–7188.

Wheeler, D., McKague, K., Thomson, J., Davies, R., Medalye, M., & Prada, M. (2005). Creating sustainable local enterprise networks. *MIT Sloan Management Review, 47*, 33–40.

Yoo, S., Domercq, B., & Kippelen, B. (2004). Efficient thin - film organic solar cells based on pentacene/C - 60 heterojunctions. *Applied Physics Letters, 85*(22), 5427–5429.

York, J. G., & Venkataraman, S. (2010). The entrepreneur - environment nexus: Uncertainty, innovation, and allocation. *Journal of Business Venturing, 25*, 449–463.

Zeng, S., Jiang, C., Ma, C., & Su, B. (2018). Investment efficiency of the new energy industry in China. *Energy Economics, 70*, 536–544. doi:10.1016/j.eneco.2017.12.023

Zhang, H., Li, L., Zhou, D., & Zhou, P. (2014). Political connections, government subsidies and firm financial performance: Evidence from renewable energy manufacturing in China. *Renewable Energy, 63*, 330–336. doi:10.1016/j.renene.2013.09.029

Zhao, Z., Chang, R., & Chen, Y. (2016). What hinder the further development of wind power in China? A socio - technical barrier study. *Energy Policy, 88*, 465–476. doi:0.1016/j.enpol.2015.11.004

Zhu, K., Neale, N. R., Miedaner, A., & Frank, A. J. (2006). Enhanced charge - collection efficiencies and light scattering in dye - sensitized solar cells using oriented TiO2 nanotubes arrays. *Nano Letters, 7*(1), 69–74. PMID:17212442

Zyadin, A., Halder, P., Kähkönen, T., & Puhakka, A. (2014). Challenges to renewable energy: A bulletin of perceptions from international academic arena. *Renewable Energy, 69*, 82–88. doi:10.1016/j.renene.2014.03.029

Chapter 2
Sustainable and Responsible Entrepreneurship for Value-Based Cultures, Economies, and Societies:
Increasing Performance Through Intellectual Capital in Challenging Times

Cristina Raluca Gh. Popescu
https://orcid.org/0000-0002-5876-0550
University of Bucharest, Romania & The Bucharest University of Economic Studies, Romania & University of Craiova, Romania & The National Institute for Research and Development in Environmental Protection (INCDPM), Romania & National Research and Development Institute for Gas Turbines (COMOTI), Romania

ABSTRACT

Entrepreneurship represents the very basis of powerful societies and the essence of robust economies, bringing unique contributions to both sustainable development and economic growth processes. In addition, corporate social responsibility constitutes the key ingredient for all businesses, encouraging competitiveness, ensuring performance, and enabling excellence, while promising a safe and sustainable environment. On one hand, this chapter reviews the theory on sustainable and responsible entrepreneurship as the core of environmental and societal success, and on the other hand, it focuses on the manner in which intangible business assets and intellectual capital yield creativity, innovation, motivation, productivity, and value in challenging times (COVID-19 pandemic). This multidisciplinary study, based on quantitative and qualitative indicators, reports that intellectual capital factor plays a dominant role in constructing new products, rules, and services for the marketplace and highlights the main economic, social, and environmental effects of current business practices.

DOI: 10.4018/978-1-7998-7951-0.ch002

INTRODUCTION

Nowadays, sustainable and responsible entrepreneurship has managed to become a major challenge and a paramount concern for both developed and developing countries, while seeking for the key drivers of performance has managed to occupy a top priority and a leading target for all emerging and emergent markets.

Under these given circumstances, entrepreneurship represents the very basis of all dominant and powerful societies and the very essence of robust and resilient economies, bringing unique contributions to both sustainable development and economic growth processes.

In addition, corporate social responsibility constitutes the key ingredient for all businesses worldwide, brining competitive advantages and encouraging competitiveness, ensuring performance and enabling excellence, while promising a safe and sustainable environment.

On one hand, this chapter reviews the theory on sustainable and responsible entrepreneurship seen as the core of environmental and societal success, and on the other hand, this work focuses on the manner in which intangible business assets and intellectual capital yield creativity, initiate innovation, arouse motivation, generate productivity, and increase value, in challenging times (with a particular emphasis on these current times, namely COVID - 19 pandemic).

Nevertheless, this multidisciplinary study, which contains research based on quantitative and qualitative indicators, reports that intellectual capital factor plays a dominant role in constructing new products, rules and services for the marketplace, and highlights the main economic, social, and environmental effects of current business practices not only at a national, but also at an international level.

The central question (the main Research Question - RQ) in this book chapter asks how sustainable and responsible entrepreneurship will be able to influence in a positive and constructive manner the 21st - century organizational landscape, while emphasizing human and intellectual capital importance and roles as drivers for performance management at a global level.

In particular, this scientific research paper, will also examine six secondary research questions derived from the main aforementioned question:

- (RQ1) what does sustainable and responsible entrepreneurship stand for?
- (RQ2) what influences does sustainable and responsible entrepreneurship have on today's organizational landscape?
- (RQ3) which are the opportunities, challenges and uncertainties brought by sustainable and responsible entrepreneurship during the current COVID - 19 pandemic?
- (RQ4) what influence do tangible and intangible assets have and in which way are these assets able to influence the role, importance and implications for sustainable and responsible entrepreneurship?
- (RQ5) does entrepreneurship represent a key solution in increasing sustainable development worldwide and which are the ways of increasing performance through intellectual capital in challenging times?
- (RQ6) which are the main solutions and recommendations due to be considered while addressing the need for sustainable and responsible entrepreneurship, when focusing on the influence of intellectual capital?

This paper has been divided into five parts. The first part deals with the general background, focusing on key concepts, such as, sustainability, responsibility, environmental performance and environmental management system, social integration and constant engagement with today's society, corporate responsibility and secure awareness and working environment, entrepreneurs and entrepreneurship, value - based cultures, economies and societies, performance, tangible and intangible assets, human resources and human resources management, intellectual capital and intellectual property, challenging times (current COVID - 19 pandemic). The second part targets the presentation of the opportunities, challenges and uncertainties specific to the sustainable and responsible entrepreneurship, during the current COVID - 19 pandemic. In continuation, the third part is meant to bring into attention the implications of sustainable and responsible entrepreneurship on the priorities and core of business strategy, human resource management, with a particular emphasis on tangible and intangible assets, while addressing the role, importance and implications for sustainable and responsible entrepreneurship, supportive and healthy working conditions, employment of competent and engaged workforce, and effective and gender - balanced management. The last part of this work, namely the fourth section, is represented by a case study concerned with developing a model for inclusive and sustainable entrepreneurship, and the ways of increasing performance through intellectual capital in challenging times, with reference to the implications and importance of a sustainable organizational financial management, keen on issues such as, internal control and risk management.

Besides all the elements presented above, this chapter offers several solutions and recommendations, as well as consistent conclusion in terms of creating and promoting sustainable and responsible entrepreneurship for value - based cultures, economies and societies, with the defining purpose of increasing performance through intellectual capital in challenging times, since it tackles aspects concerning the need for reasonable assurance that Earth's resources are properly managed, the organizations' financial management respect the inclusive sustainable growth and development principles, and that the control, the organizations' development and growth procedures offer all the necessary guarantees concerning the legality and regularity of undertaken transactions in order to ensure that no fraud and irregularities might arise, the implementation of the human resources modernization focuses on fully exploiting the potential of intellectual capital, while managing usefully intellectual property.

It should also be brought to the attention the fact that this book chapter also possesses a section addressing solutions and recommendations for the subjects chosen for the analyses, conclusions and limitations of the study and the references part which highlights a few representative studies already published on the generous and vast domains of business administration, economics and management.

BACKGROUND

The first section of this paper entitled suggestively "Background" will examine the literature review on the key concepts specific to the chosen theme, namely: business model, entrepreneurship, intangible assets, intellectual capital, COVID - 19 pandemic, corporate social responsibility, sustainability, responsibility, transparency, accountability, integrity, and value - based cultures, economies and societies.

Also, the first section of this paper entitled suggestively "Background" will seek to present the following determining elements, namely: firstly, addressing the meaning of the notions sustainable and responsible entrepreneurship for value - based cultures, economies and societies in the attempt of understanding the concepts and emphasizing the differences; secondly, presenting the role of intellectual capital in challenging times in enhancing organizations' performance in the 21st - century organizational landscape and stressing the differences between tangible and intangible assets; and thirdly, aiming at painting the importance of intellectual capital for organizational success and addressing key questions in order to find optimum answers to the current evolving business paradigms as well as today's COVID - 19 pandemic.

Because of the continuous challenges that humanity are facing these days, social conduct has become crucial when addressing sensible and valuable concepts such as social responsibility, corporate social responsibility, communities well - being and happiness, especially in those delicate situations in which the appropriate level of government intervention and government regulations in the marketplace cannot really be determined in a manner capable to not cause a general unbalance, and consumers and producers distress (Dai, 2019; Pokrovskaia et al., 2019; Rao et al., 2014; Sakaki, 2019; Tan et al., 2008; Velenturf et al., 2019).

At the same time, due to the steady increase in the preoccupations concerning social conduct, producers' and consumers' ethical behaviour and equality, reputed organisms worldwide are demanding, on a regular basis, greater transparency on both environmental and social matters (Gallagher et al., 2019; Gómez - Bezares et al., 2019; Kucharcikova et al., 2019; Paprocka, 2019; Popescu & Popescu, 2018a; Popescu, 2019c; Popescu, 2019f; Stankevičiūtė & Savanevičienė, 2018) (see Table 1).

Given the fact that sustainable and responsible entrepreneurship is becoming more and more important for these days society - since it is able to reflect how committed are, in fact, businesses to ethical, sustainable, responsible and transparent practices, determining which are today's key drivers of performance, as well as understanding these drivers and emphasizing the differences between them, are considered crucial elements in the creation process of successful future business models (European Commission, 2018c; Hamadamin & Atan, 2019; Popescu & Popescu, 2019b).

Several studies investigating the role of sustainable and responsible entrepreneurship, have managed to position ethical behaviour among the key concepts for performance, since it seriously contributes to economic development, thus enhancing job creation, investment in projects capable to support sustainable development and environmental well - being, quality of life and workforce, local and global communities growth (García - Alcaraz et al., 2018; Joshi & Islam, 2018; Sinclair & Phillips, 2018; Sokas et al., 2019) (see Figure 1).

The impact of intellectual capital on organizational performance needs constant investigation, especially since managers ought to be aware of the implications of accounting in business administration, economy and management, in order to take the right decisions with regard to the future of the organizations (Popescu, 2019a).

Under these circumstances, financial reports are considered an important index for decision - making for managers and investors (European Commission, 2019).

It should be noted, however, that intellectual capital has a special role in the knowledge era, in general, and in the knowledge economy, in particular, given the fact that intellectual capital may be found in a large part in the value of the products, although the traditional annual financial statements report only in part the value of intangible assets - with direct reference, for example, to concessions, intellectual property, licenses, patents, trademarks, and so on (Darooneh, 2005; Dobrin et al., 2012; Liu et al., 2019; Popescu, 2019b; Venkatasubramanian, 2009).

Throughout this paper, the term intellectual capital will reflect an important activity performed by an organization, which will aim to be efficient and effective on marketplace, thus focusing on a constant basis to obtain sustainable competitive advantages and ensure inclusive well - adapted and well - performing models for growth and development (Ruan et al., 2019; Zagonari, 2016; Nguyen et al., 2019) (see Table 2):

Table 1. Sustainable and Responsible Entrepreneurship (SRE) and Key Drivers of Performance: Understanding the Concepts and Emphasizing the Differences

	Sustainable and Responsible Entrepreneurship (SRE)	Key Drivers of Performance
Definitions:	• SRE tackles elements specific to sustainable and inclusive entrepreneurship, starting from the idea that human lives and environmental protection are the central concern when it comes to obtaining Sustainable Development Goals (Lombardi *et al.*, 2019; Rodríguez - Sánchez *et al.*, 2019; Tociu *et al.*, 2017).	• Entrepreneurship represents, according to specialists, one of the main key drivers of performance in today's society, especially in the context in which the economic agents focus on inclusive and sustainable development, as the Sustainable Development Goals require (European Commission, 2017; Ijadi Maghsoodi *et al.*, 2019; Ulrich *et al.*, 2019).
	• SRE addresses individuals' wellbeing when it comes to obtaining Sustainable Development Goals, focusing on sustainable growth, development and progress for all nations and all people, as well as for all the segments existing in the society (Pirmana *et al.*, 2019; Popescu, 2020).	• Microenterprises and small and medium - sized enterprises represent, according to specialists, another of the main key drivers of performance in today's society, especially in the context in which they position themselves as main drivers for employment and facilitators of income, by respecting, in the same time, the concept and the practices specific to responsible and dedicated to human beings and environment businesses (Holban *et al.*, 2017; Witek - Crabb, 2019).
	• SRE drives economic growth, by positioning entrepreneurship as the main performance and production key driver in a society, and facilitates the creation of jobs, by promoting social cohesion, reducing inequalities among people and expending opportunities for all human beings (Popescu & Popescu, 2015).	• Human Resources Management (HRM) represents, according to specialists, one of the main key drivers of performance in today's society, especially in the context in which the focus of responsible and sustainable business practices and inclusive business models is represented by the wellbeing and safety of individuals worldwide (Aykan *et al.*, 2019; European Commission, 2018a).
	• SRE encourages innovation and promotes the implementation of new inventions, knowledge, and information, thus successfully improving quality of life for all people (Midttun *et al.*, 2019; Popescu, 1997; Popescu & Popescu, 2000).	• Intellectual Capital (IC) represents, according to specialists, one of the main key drivers of performance in today's society, especially in the context in which, due to limited access to resources, products and facilities, organizations are dedicating their time and efforts to innovation, inclusive business models, commercially sustainable and viable models (European Commission, 2018b).
Examples:	• SRE (with the aid of Sustainable Development Goals) helps the reiteration of "the pledge that no one will be left behind, reaffirming the recognition that the dignity of the human person is fundamental and the wish to see the Sustainable Development Goals and targets met for all nations and peoples and for all segments of society" (United Nations, 2019).	• Inclusive businesses, mainly focused on the implementation of the benefits derived from the use of intangible assets, such as HRM and IC, have the power of providing goods, livelihoods, products, and services to all individuals, offering equal access to all, including to the categories of people belonging to disadvantages groups (Popescu & Dumitrescu, 2016a).
	• SRE (with the aid of Sustainable Development Goals) helps the expansion of opportunities for all individuals, mainly addressing the specific issues of women (Popescu *et al.*, 2015), people with disabilities, and most vulnerable categories in the society (United Nations, 2019; Zhang *et al.*, 2019).	• Responsible business practices and inclusive businesses are encouraged to constantly take proactive measures in achieving the Sustainable Development Goals in the benefit of individuals worldwide (Popescu & Dumitrescu, 2016b).

Source: Own

The importance of intellectual capital for organizational success implicates finding an answer to the following decisive questions, namely:

- "How can intellectual capital help the organizations meet their aims, goals and objectives?"

Figure 1. Presenting The Role Of Sustainable And Responsible Entrepreneurship In Enhancing Organizations' Performance In The 21st - Century Organizational Landscape And Stressing The Key Arguments That Position Entrepreneurship As The Core Of Environmental And Societal Success
Source: Own

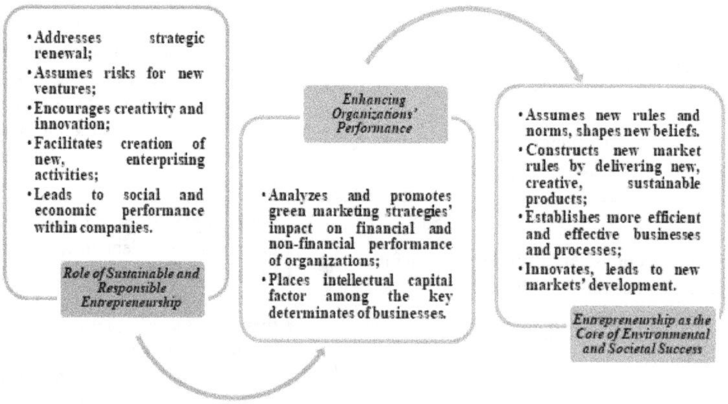

- "Which are the main reasons for organizations to have coherent and powerful intangible assets strategies, and mainly focus on the benefits of the implementation of intellectual capital strategies?"
- "Which are the organizations' main (business) drivers that are imperative for organizational success, especially when bringing light the particularities of today's challenges derived from COVID - 19 pandemic?", and
- "Does intellectual capital become these days a valuable tool for management to ensure development, efficiency, efficacy, growth, performance, and success?" (See Figure 2).

Table 2. Intellectual Capital (IC) Factor's Great Influences On To The Modern Knowledge - Based Organizations And On The Development Of All The Economic Activity That Take Place In Today's Market Economy

	Intellectual Capital (IC) factor's great influences on to the modern knowledge - based organizations and on the development of all the economic activity that take place in today's market economy
Influences and general context:	• Today's market economy is based on the benefits brought by different forms of intangible assets, such as, mainly IC and derived components, among which should be mentioned intellectual property (IP) (Van - Dierendonck *et al.*, 2016).
	• Inclusive and sustainable business models are commercially viable models that bring benefits to low - income individuals, businesses and communities, and that may be successfully included in the organizations' value chain in order to create innovative projects, especially when focusing on the benefits and use of intangible assets (Popescu, 2019e).
	• IC enables businesses to create and use a wide range of innovative and sustainable projects, mainly focused on sustainable earnings, costs, and productivity (Zappalà *et al.*, 2019).
	• IC provides a great empowerment to inclusive and sustainable business models, by bringing benefits to producers and consumers, as well as bottom - line and top growth (Popescu & Banța, 2019).
	• IC helps organizations to create well - structured and well - developed frameworks capable to monitor the success of planned outcomes, while focusing on improving people's health and well - being and reducing environmental impacts, thus preserving the future of next generations to come (Yi *et al.*, 2019).

Source: Own

Figure 2. Importance of Sustainable and Responsible Entrepreneurship for Organizational Success: Addressing Key Questions In Order To Find Optimum Answers To the Current Evolving Business Paradigms
Source: The Authors

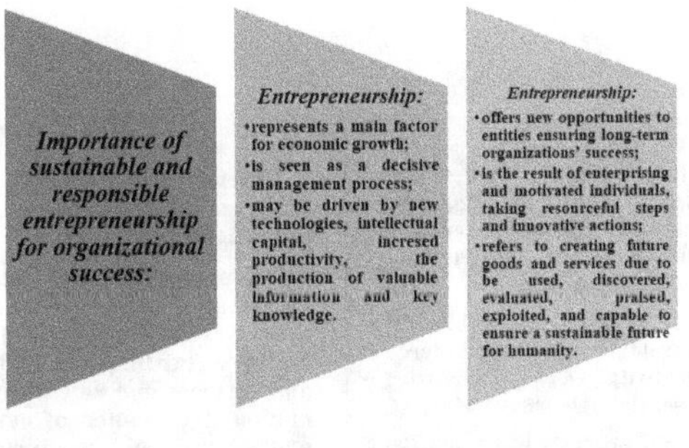

SUSTAINABLE AND RESPONSIBLE ENTREPRENEURSHIP: OPPORTUNITIES, CHALLENGES, AND UNCERTAINTIES DURING THE CURRENT COVID - 19 PANDEMIC

The second section of this paper entitled suggestively "Sustainable and responsible entrepreneurship: opportunities, challenges and uncertainties during the current COVID - 19 pandemic" will successfully examine the implications and the involvement of today's sustainable and responsible entrepreneurship, addressing the opportunities, presenting the challenges and discovering the uncertainties that managed to arouse during the current COVID - 19 pandemic (see Figure 3).

The United Nations Conference on Trade and Development (UNCTAD) (2020) has showed a deep interest in intellectual capital, when aiming to bring a substantial contribution to the implementation of the Sustainable Development Goals (SDGs) by:

- "building capacity in developing countries on the use of appropriate investment and intellectual property (IP) frameworks to promote partnerships and the transfer of emerging technologies", such as, for example, pharmaceuticals, biotechnology, clean energy, information and communication technologies;
- "advising developing countries on the role of investment and IP policies on emerging technologies, IP implications of big data solutions and artificial intelligence and the application to public health"; and
- "promoting cooperation on investment to tackle Anti - Microbial Resistance (AMR), considering the specific situation in developing countries and the need to prevent stock outs of essential generic antimicrobial treatments" (United Nations Conference on Trade and Development (UNCTAD), 2020).

The analysis of the need for a sustainable and responsible entrepreneurship, based on the opportunities, challenges and uncertainties that during a sustainable and responsible entrepreneurship may ensure during the current COVID - 19 pandemic, stressed the fact that between the intellectual capital and the organizations' performance is a significant relationship, as follows:

Figure 3. Sustainable and Responsible Entrepreneurship: Opportunities, Challenges, and Uncertainties during the Current COVID - 19 Pandemic
Source: Own

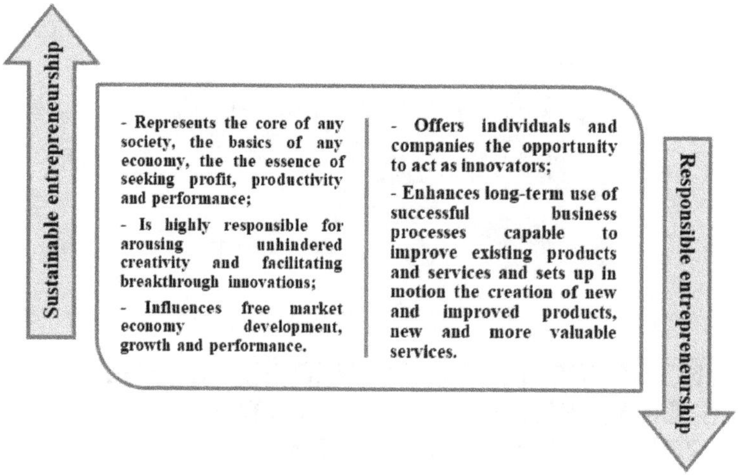

- creativity, innovation, and technical progress are meant to increase organizational performance far more than macroeconomic policies results or financial balance and tangible assets influence (Argyris, 1960; Armstrong, 2006; Cole, 2011; Popescu & Popescu, 2002; Popescu, 2019d; Urquijo et al., 2019);
- the quality of human, structural, and relational factors are believed to have a heavy influence organizational performance, especially in the cases of learning organizations, where managers are investing in knowledge, under different forms, such as, education, research and development, and innovation (Guglielmo - D'Amico et al., 2019; Lo, 2019; Maree & Di Fabio, 2018; Ying Lee et al., 2019; Tang et al., 2019).

The elements specific to this section of this paper entitled suggestively "Sustainable and responsible entrepreneurship: opportunities, challenges and uncertainties during the current COVID - 19 pandemic" that needs to be addressed focus on several key concepts, such as:

- **Performance Management:** which is seen as crucial for organizations' worldwide, since it helps entities to embrace all opportunities and all possibilities, and it empowers companies to value intangible assets - more specifically, intellectual capital, focusing on creativity, education, information, innovation, knowledge, new technologies and ground - braking techniques, in order to encompass present and future challenges.
- **Human Capital:** which is regarded as a multilevel and multidimensional concept, tackling people's specific characteristics and intellectual qualities that are able to empower organizations prevail in challenging times, aiding entities to react to different market challenges and changes, adapt to all forms of environment and strive to successfully meet consumers' expectations and needs.
- **Intellectual Capital:** which is acknowledged as a dominant and powerful intangible asset of organizations, strongly connected to performance management and human capital, having a posi-

tive influence on development, growth and inclusive sustainable and responsible entrepreneurship methods, models, and strategies.

- **Sustainability:** which is a dominant concept in today's society, as it addresses the needs belonging to human beings and future generations to come, eco - systems and bio - systems, and environment, while being influenced by numerous components and factors, such as, intellectual capital - as a key trigger for inclusive and resilient business models, human, social and organizational capital - as main sources for competitive advantages, and organizational performance - as major accomplishment when referring to corporate social responsibility, good governance, good business practices, ethics, transparency, diligent and correct business behaviour.
- **Sustainable and Responsible Entrepreneurship:** which represents a major asset to all entities these days, especially when analysed together with intangible assets, intellectual capital, human capital, innovation, and creativity, positive impact of intangible assets and entities higher performance.

TANGIBLE AND INTANGIBLE ASSETS: ROLE, IMPORTANCE, AND IMPLICATIONS FOR SUSTAINABLE AND RESPONSIBLE ENTREPRENEURSHIP

The third section of this paper entitled suggestively "Tangible and intangible assets: role, importance and implications for sustainable and responsible entrepreneurship" addresses both human capital and intellectual capital as drivers for performance management, in the attempt to describe and analyse the constructive ways capable to ensure both employees' fulfilment and the realization of the management's objectives, focusing on the fact that the innovative performance of organizations requires constant care and constant investment in knowledge and intellectual capital management - which could be seen as key areas for all successful entities worldwide (see Figure 4).

The United Nations Conference on Trade and Development (UNCTAD) (2020) has proved to be extremely interested in aspects related to intellectual property and emerging technologies, thus stressing the fact that "intellectual property architecture needs to respond to the dynamics and economic realities of big data/artificial intelligence, climate change technologies, genetic engineering and other emerging technologies" (United Nations Conference on Trade and Development (UNCTAD), 2020).

What is more, the United Nations Conference on Trade and Development (UNCTAD) (2020) has been promoting the idea that "beyond technology, intellectual property is an important element in the realization of other domestic public policy objectives". Thus, in order "to avoid conflict, governments need to design coherent domestic policies and pursue international cooperation", while "countries are engaged at regional and multilateral levels on various issues of technology, intellectual property, and investment as part of negotiations on global challenges including climate change or initiatives to tackle Anti - Microbial Resistance (AMR)" (United Nations Conference on Trade and Development (UNCTAD), 2020).

Furthermore, the United Nations Conference on Trade and Development (UNCTAD) (2020) has concentrated lately on the following key areas of interest, which also address aspects related to knowledge and intellectual capital:

- (a). "new models of investment"; "consensus building at the international level on key questions, such as unilateral trade policy review mechanisms and multilateralism, and other issues suggested by member states";

- (c) "research, analysis and policy advice on the implications of regional trade agreements on public policy topics such as public health, the environment, cultural protection and industrial development and on how to implement international intellectual property obligations in harmony with domestic public policy objectives"; and
- (d) "consensus building on the role of South - South cooperation for supply of technology goods, specifically uninterrupted supply of pharmaceuticals and their intermediaries and for the transfer of related know - how" (United Nations Conference on Trade and Development (UNCTAD), 2020).

Figure 4. Sustainability - Driven Entrepreneurship: Human and Intellectual Capital as Drivers for Planning A Sustainability Management System Program
Source: Own

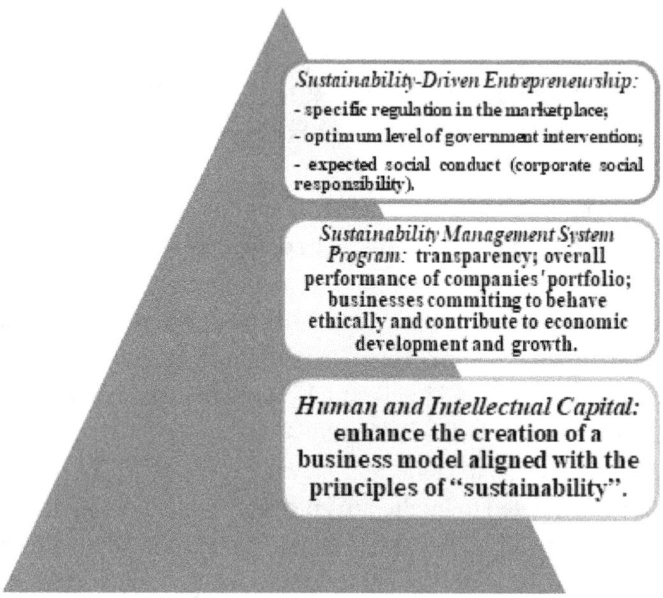

When analysing the connections existing between an inclusive, sustainable and responsible entrepreneurship, value - based cultures, economies and societies, long - term organizational performance, and human and intellectual capital - as key drivers for performance management especially during current challenging times, the following elements need to be addressed in order to have a broad picture of the constructive ways meant to ensure the successful process of reaching organizations' goals, ensuring employees' fulfilment and realizing the management's objectives:

- First of all, it should be acknowledged that knowledge and intellectual capital management represent key areas for most organizations worldwide (Becker, 1964; Keenan, 2015; Popescu et al., 2008).
- Second of all, it should be stressed that knowledge and intellectual capital management are the dominant key areas for knowledge - intensive and learning organizations (Becker, 1993; Popescu et al., 2016).

- Third of all, it should be emphasized that intellectual capital represents a key factor for creative and innovative performance, thus being regarded as one of the most critical, crucial and strategic value entities may have (Cole, 2011; Popescu & Popescu, 2018b; Popescu & Popescu, 2019a).
- Forth of all, it should be highlighted that knowledge - intensive and learning organizations use intellectual capital with maximum efficiency and efficacy, since intellectual capital represents their main resource, thus being able to reduce the consumption of other resources and focus on creative and innovative solutions in order to ensure a successful intellectual capital management (Andersen et al., 2019; García - Mestanza et al., 2019; Kuitto et al., 2019; Taylor & van - der - Velden, 2019).

In the process of determining the way in which intellectual capital and can ensure a balance between individual goals and organizational goals, specialists have suggested that, due to the strong influence of intellectual capital on organizational performance, the focus should be on the organizations' ability to create value by using intangible assets rather than tangible assets, since this represents a multilevel analysis of entities critical assets, where managers' investments need to address aspects, such as: improving and increasing employees' knowledge and skills, adapting to current economic challenges and realities, facing and coping with the organizational and inter - organizational processes, addressing the opportunities and challenges derived from applying different forms specific to business process management (Beier et al., 2019; Gallagher et al., 2019; Popescu et al., 2015; Popescu et al., 2017a,b,c,d; Popescu, 2017; Popescu, 2018; Zhao et al., 2019).

Moreover, intellectual capital consists of numerous activities including the ones presented and described in the lines below:

Figure 5. Intellectual Capital (IC) and Ways of Ensuring A Balance between Individual Goals and Organizational Goals
Source: Own

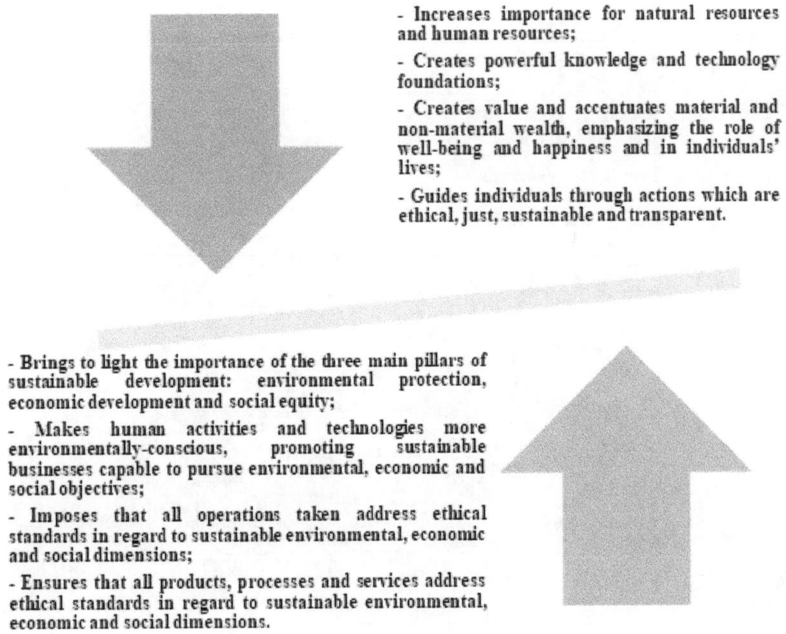

Figure 6. Intellectual Capital (IC): Definitions, Functions, and General Objectives
Source: The Authors

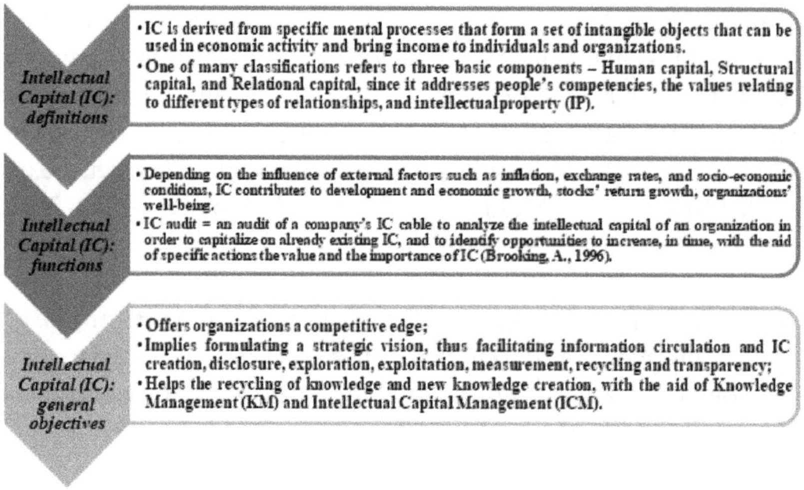

- Assembling a set of knowledge and information resources and analysing this set of knowledge and information resources, since intellectual capital has become the new core of economic progress (Fournier et al., 2018; Ying Lee et al., 2019);

Figure 7. Developing a Model for Long - Term Sustainable and Responsible Entrepreneurship for Value - Based Cultures, Economies and Societies and Creating an Inclusive Framework Capable To Enhance Organizations' Performance through Intellectual Capital in Challenging Times
Source: Own

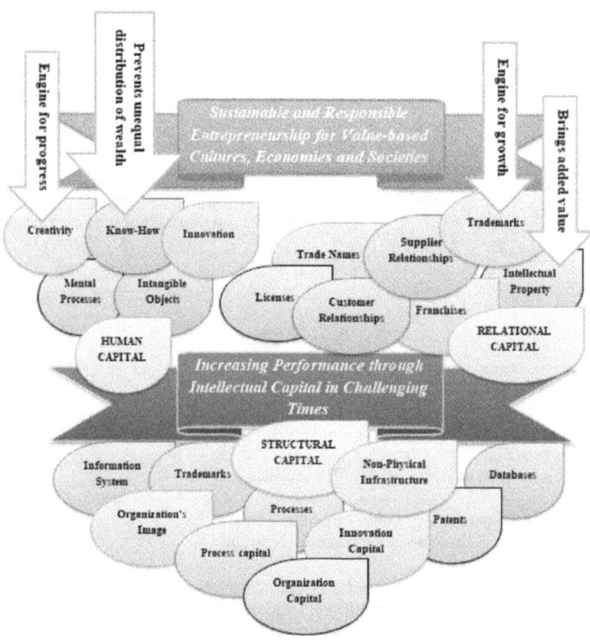

- Supports the actions that contribute and lead to achieving organizational performance, starting from the idea that human resources and intellectual capital are the most essential resources an organization might have access to (Ulrich et al., 2019; Urquijo et al., 2019);
- Intangible assets, such as, for example, employees' abilities and skills to use different information, organizational culture, and intellectual property, are regarded as significant in helping organizations achieve the long - desired and expected performance (Lombardi et al., 2019; Popescu, 2019d) (see Figure 5).

Since human and intellectual capital represents key drivers for performance management, organizations these days have placed among their priorities the following key steps: firstly, the shift from traditional assets and traditional accounting, to the accounting mainly focused on the benefits derived from intangible assets; secondly, placing access to information, intelligence and knowledge - which are valuable parts of human and intellectual capital, on top positions in ensuring organizational performance, thus focusing on creativity, innovation, and intellectual freedom, in order to confer organizations a better advantage on the market; and, thirdly, understanding and valuing intellectual assets and intellectual capital, starting from the ideas that these assets are invisible, reflect employees' knowledge and experience in relation to the organizations' technologies, customers, clients and partners, and have the power to offer unlimited future opportunities to entities when used in an appropriate manner (García - Alcaraz et al., 2019; Hamadamin & Atan, 2019; Kell & Lang, 2017; Van - Dierendonck et al., 2016) (see Figure 6).

Figure 8. Main Characteristics Of A Model For Long - Term Sustainable And Responsible Entrepreneurship For Value - Based Cultures, Economies And Societies And Creating An Inclusive Framework Capable To Enhance Organizations' Performance Through Intellectual Capital In Challenging Times
Source: The Authors

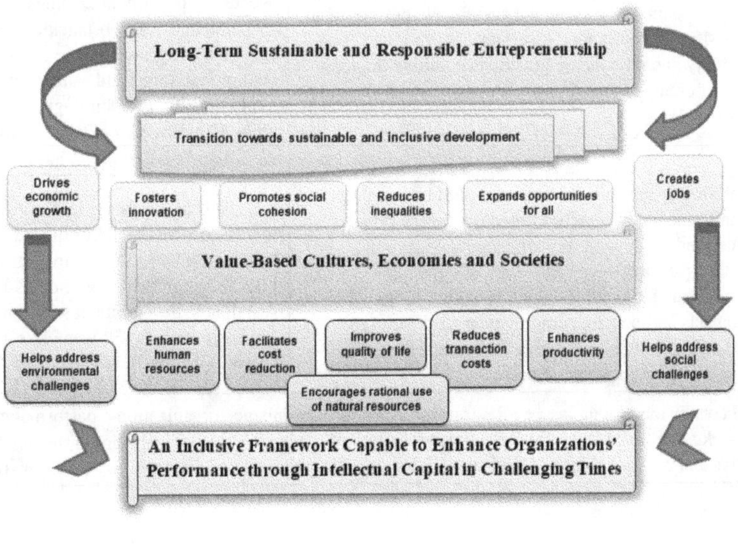

CASE STUDY: ENTREPRENEURSHIP AND WAYS OF INCREASING PERFORMANCE THROUGH INTELLECTUAL CAPITAL IN CHALLENGING TIMES

The fourth section of this paper entitled suggestively "Case study: Entrepreneurship and ways of increasing performance through intellectual capital in challenging times" seeks to present a model for entrepreneurship and the ways of increasing performance through intellectual capital in challenging times (see Figure 7).

Developing a model for long - term sustainable and responsible entrepreneurship for value - based cultures, economies and societies and creating an inclusive framework capable to enhance organizations' performance through intellectual capital in challenging times is related to addressing and presenting the main characteristics of a model for long - term sustainable and responsible entrepreneurship for value - based cultures, economies and societies and creating an inclusive framework capable to enhance organizations' performance through intellectual capital in challenging times (see Figure 8).

In the same way, creating an inclusive sustainable and responsible entrepreneurship model for value - based cultures, economies and societies framework capable to enhance organizations' performance on the long - term, proves to be crucial in finding solutions for increasing performance through intellectual capital in challenging times (see Table 3).

Table 3. An Inclusive Sustainable and Responsible Entrepreneurship for Value - Based Cultures, Economies and Societies Framework Capable To Enhance Organizations' Performance on the Long - Term: Solutions for Increasing Performance through Intellectual Capital in Challenging Times

	Sustainable and Responsible Entrepreneurship (SRE) Framework:	**Ways to enhance Organizations' Performance on the long - term, with the aid of Intellectual Capital (IC):**
Solutions:	• SRE and inclusive and sustainable business frameworks models should seek both economic and social viability by prioritizing social and environmental objectives, by encouraging economic growth and sustainable development, and by positioning corporate governance, corporate social responsibility and democratic governance among the top priorities of organizations (Palová & Šebestová, 2020; Tak *et al.*, 2019).	• All types of organizations (large companies, microenterprises and small and medium - sized enterprises) should: (a.) centre themselves on innovative inclusive businesses in order to ensure long - term success, especially in challenging times (COVID - 19 pandemic); and (b.) tackle all sectors, such as, agriculture, agribusiness, education, energy, housing, health care, water and sanitation, information and communications technology, and transport. (Brooking, 1996; Gismera *et al.*, 2019; Latifi & Lim, 2019; Zuo *et al.*, 2019; Wu *et al.*, 2019).
	• One of SRE framework main aims should be to enlarge the global value chain usually formed by multinational companies and large domestic companies, with microenterprises, start - ups and small and medium - sized enterprises, thus facilitating social cohesion, increase in social impacts and benefits, employment, and inclusive and sustainable growth (Aghayeva & Ślusarczyk, 2019; Pokorná, 2019; Štreimikienė, 2019).	• Organizations' performance can be successfully increased with the aid of inclusive and sustainable businesses, by providing infrastructure, market access, knowledge, information, innovative, original, and sustainable development solutions (Lai *et al.*, 2019; Leksono *et al.*, 2019; Kiseľáková *et al.*, 2019; Pérez - Ordás *et al.*, 2019; Ullrich *et al.*, 2019).
	General conclusion: An inclusive SRE framework capable to enhance organizations' performance on the long - term should seek at all times to ensure the full transparency of the business process, business sustainability, creative, innovative and original solutions, and sustainable - development related solutions to continuously pressing challenges.	

Source: Own

SOLUTIONS AND RECOMMENDATIONS

A number of researchers claim that intangible assets (especially human resources and intellectual capital) represent the future of successful companies, focused on integrated forms of sustainable entrepreneurship and development, long - term performance of their portfolios and business models aligned with the principles and values of sustainability (García - Alcaraz et al., 2018; Joshi & Islam, 2018; Sinclair & Phillips, 2018; United Nations & United Nations Economic Commission for Europe, 2013), which has led to a clear focus on determining a consistent set of solutions and recommendations concerning sustainable and responsible entrepreneurship for value - based cultures, economies and societies, in the attempt to increase performance through intellectual capital in challenging times (see Table 4):

Table 4. Solutions and Recommendations Concerning Sustainable and Responsible Entrepreneurship for Value - Based Cultures, Economies, and Societies: Increasing Performance through Intellectual Capital in Challenging Times

	Solutions and recommendations:	**Targeting the creation of an inclusive sustainable and responsible entrepreneurship framework capable to enhance organizations' performance on the long - term, with main focus on intellectual capital:**
Solutions and recommendations:	• Concern for quality education:	• Inclusive business models should promote access to quality education for future and current employees, thus meeting society's development needs (Cho & Ahn, 2018; García - Sánchez *et al.*, 2018; Harwood, 2016).
	• Concern for financial inclusion and opportunities:	• Inclusive business models should promote access to infrastructure, knowledge, market access, reduced transaction costs, high quality products and services (Watkin *et al.*, 2019; Popescu, 2019g).
	• Concern for ensuring equal opportunities for all:	• Inclusive business models should promote access to equal opportunities for all, by helping women and individuals from disadvantaged categories to have access to education and, later on, by encouraging them to obtain jobs (Hosseininia & Ramezani, 2016; Huang *et al.*, 2016; Preuss, 2016; Yin *et al.*, 2019).
	• Concern for inclusive solutions in organizations' reporting:	• Inclusive business models should promote inclusive solutions in organizations' reporting and should constantly raise awareness when it comes to accounting and audit activities, and increasing the role and the importance of intangible assets in organizations (Popescu, 2019a, b, c; Šebestová, 2020; Šebestová & Sroka, 2020).
	• Concern for having a holistic approach to business:	• Inclusive business models should promote holistic approaches, which should be able to address environmental and social needs, corporate social responsibility, good governance, substantial investments in innovation, knowledge and intellectual capital, sustainable consumption and production patterns, models and frameworks (Ernst, 2019; Hoang, 2019; Malara *et al.*, 2019; Naveed *et al.*, 2019; Parastuty & Bögenhold, 2019; Streimikiene & Balezentis, 2019).

Source: Own

CONCLUSION

This research extends our knowledge of sustainable and responsible entrepreneurship for value - based cultures, economies, and societies in the 21st - century organizational landscape, strives to discuss the main implications of human and intellectual capital as drivers for performance management, and addresses the main concern of organizations' management regarding the ways of increasing performance through intellectual capital in challenging times.

As a consequence, given the current situation, it has become clear that sustainable entrepreneurship represents a challenging but correct route to accomplish sustainable development and growth, which should take into account the following main objectives:

- First of all, it should be acknowledged that enterprises seeking success must be financially sustainable, in order to respect current norms, face today's regulatory systems, and be part of sustainable and inclusive successful economic models. In this matter, truly implicated organizations could receive help from governments in the form of different subsidies, which could ensure that some money is going to environmental work.
- Second of all, it should be stressed that enterprises wishing to help the environment and enable human beings well - being must get involved in steady philanthropic activities, concentrating on medium - term and long - term environmental values. For instance, a good example in this case could be represented by fair trade organizations willing to sell fair trade products, which will lead to helping, in time, disadvantaged communities and regions, thus taking them out of poverty.
- Third of all, it should be stressed that enterprises wishing to help the environment and enable human beings well - being must get involved diminishing, as much as possible, the level of pollution that is generated by the production process and also the level of pollution that is generated by the use of certain goods and services by the consumers. In this case, organizations should focus their actions on determining in what manner does the production process affect the environment, in what proportion is the environment damaged in the process of transporting the goods across the world to the consumers - thus, causing climate change, and in what manner does the use of the goods and services affect the environment while being used by consumers - thus, causing the depletion of natural resources, pesticides, and hazardous waste, while increasing the level of pollution and damaging the ecosystems.

REFERENCES

Aghayeva, K., & Ślusarczyk, B. (2019). Analytic Hierarchy of Motivating and Demotivating Factors Affecting Labour Productivity in the Construction Industry: The Case of Azerbaijan. *Sustainability*, *11*(21), 5975. doi:10.3390u11215975

Andersen, L. L., Jensen, P. H., Meng, A., & Sundstrup, E. (2019). Strong Labour Market Inequality of Opportunities at the Workplace for Supporting a Long and Healthy Work - Life: The Senior Working Life Study. *International Journal of Environmental Research and Public Health*, *16*(18), 3264. doi:10.3390/ijerph16183264

Argyris, C. (1960). *Understanding Organizational Behaviour*. Dorsey Press.

Armstrong, M. (2006). *A Handbook of Human Resource Management Practice* (8th ed.). Kogan Page.

Aykan, E., Karakuş, G., & Karakoç, H. (2019). The Effect of University Students' Individual Innovation and Lifelong Learning Trends on Entrepreneurship Orientation. *Sustainability, 11*(22), 6201. doi:10.3390u11226201

Becker, G. S. (1964). *Human Capital: A Theoretical and Empirical Analysis, with Special Reference to Education*. National Bureau of Economic Research.

Becker, G. S. (1993). *Human Capital: A Theoretical and Empirical Analysis, with Special Reference to Education* (3rd ed.). University of Chicago. doi:10.7208/chicago/9780226041223.001.0001

Beier, M. E., Kell, H. J., & Lang, J. W. B. (2019). Commenting on the "Great Debate": General Abilities, Specific Abilities, and the Tools of the Trade. *Journal of Intelligence*, *7*(1), 5. doi:10.3390/jintelligence7010005 PMID:31162384

Brooking, A. (1996). *Intellectual Capital, Core Assets for the Third Millennium Enterprise*. International Thomson Business Press.

Cho, H. J., & Ahn, J. Y. (2018). The Dark Side of Wars for Talent and Layoffs: Evidence from Korean Firms. *Sustainability, 10*(5), 1365. doi:10.3390u10051365

Cole, G. A. (2011). *Management Theory and Practice* (8th ed.). South - Western Cengage Learning.

D'Amico, G., Lika, A., & Petroni, F. (2019). Risk Management of Pension Fund: A Model for Salary Evolution. *Int. J. Financial Stud.*, *7*(3), 44. doi:10.3390/ijfs7030044

Dai, W. (2019). V - Shaped Responsibility of China's Social Welfare for the Elderly: Based on Analysing Historical Evolution and Future Sustainability. *Sustainability, 11*(8), 2385. doi:10.3390u11082385

Darooneh, A. H. (2005). Physical Premium Principle: A New Way for Insurance Pricing. *Entropy (Basel, Switzerland)*, *7*(1), 97–107. doi:10.3390/e7010097

Dobrin, C. O., Popescu, G. N., Popescu, V. A., & Popescu, C. R. G. (2012). The concept of performance in business organizations - Case study on the employee performance in Romanian business organizations, In *Proceedings of the 6th International Management Conference: Approaches in Organisational Management* (pp. 310 - 316). Editura ASE.

Ernst, E. (2019). Finance and Jobs: How Financial Markets and Prudential Regulation Shape Unemployment Dynamics. *J. Risk Financial Manag.*, *12*(1), 20. doi:10.3390/jrfm12010020

European Commission. (2017). *Directorate General Human Resources and Security: Performance through People, Management Plan 2017*. Retrieved from https://ec.europa.eu/info/sites/info/files/management-plan-hr-2017_en_0.pdf

European Commission. (2018a). *Directorate General Human Resources and Security: Performance through People, Management Plan 2018*. Retrieved from https://ec.europa.eu/info/sites/info/files/management-plan-hr-2018_en.pdf

European Commission. (2018b). Thematic Paper: Human Resource Management: How to Attract, Retain and Develop Talent. doi:10.2767/89866

European Commission. (2018c). Human Resources: Performance through People, Human Resources in 2018. Luxembourg: Publications Office of the European Union. doi:10.2774/259615

European Commission. (2019). *Directorate General Human Resources and Security: Performance through People, Management Plan 2018*. Retrieved from https://ec.europa.eu/info/sites/info/files/management-plan-hr-2019_en.pdf

Fournier, G., Zimmermann, H., Masdonati, J., & Gauthier, C. (2018). Job Loss in a Group of Older Canadian Workers: Challenges in the Sustainable Labour Market Reintegration Process. *Sustainability, 10*(7), 2245. doi:10.3390u10072245

Gallagher, H., Yang, L., & Liang, J. (2019). 'I Respect You but I Am Not Willing to Be You': Critical Reflections of Western Teaching of Social Work to Students in China - What Can be Learned Both Ways? *Soc. Sci., 8*(10), 272. doi:10.3390ocsci8100272

García-Alcaraz, J. L., Alor-Hernández, G., Sánchez-Ramírez, C., Jiménez-Macías, E., Blanco-Fernández, J., & Latorre-Biel, J. I. (2018). Mediating Role of the Six Sigma Implementation Strategy and Investment in Human Resources in Economic Success and Sustainability. *Sustainability,* 10.

García-Alcaraz, J. L., Flor-Montalvo, F. J., Avelar-Sosa, L., Sánchez-Ramírez, C., & Jiménez-Macías, E. (2019). Human Resource Abilities and Skills in TQM for Sustainable Enterprises. *Sustainability, 11*(22), 6488. doi:10.3390u11226488

García Mestanza, J., Cerezo Medina, A., & Cruz Morato, M. A. (2019). A Model for Measuring Fair Labour Justice in Hotels: Design for the Spanish Case. *Sustainability, 11*(17), 4639. doi:10.3390u11174639

García-Sánchez, E., García-Morales, V., & Martín-Rojas, R. (2018). Influence of Technological Assets on Organizational Performance through Absorptive Capacity, Organizational Innovation and Internal Labour Flexibility. *Sustainability, 10*(3), 770. doi:10.3390u10030770

Gismera, E., Fernández, J. L., Labrador, J., & Gismera, L. (2019). Suffering at Work: A Challenge for Corporate Sustainability in the Spanish Context. *Sustainability, 11*(15), 4152. doi:10.3390u11154152

Gómez-Bezares, F., Przychodzen, W., & Przychodzen, J. (2019). Corporate Sustainability and CEO - Employee Pay Gap—Buster or Booster? *Sustainability, 11*(21), 6023. doi:10.3390u11216023

Hamadamin, H. H., & Atan, T. (2019). The Impact of Strategic Human Resource Management Practices on Competitive Advantage Sustainability: The Mediation of Human Capital Development and Employee Commitment. *Sustainability, 11*(20), 5782. doi:10.3390u11205782

Harwood, R. (2016). What Has Limited the Impact of UK Disability Equality Law on Social Justice? *Laws, 5*(4), 42. doi:10.3390/laws5040042

Hoang, D. (2019). Labour Standards in the Global Supply Chain: Workers' Agency and Reciprocal Exchange Perspective. *Societies (Basel, Switzerland), 9*(2), 38. doi:10.3390oc9020038

Holban, E., Diacu, E., Matei, M., Ghita, G., Raischi, M., Fronescu, S., Daescu, A., Gheorghe, I. P., Ilie, M., Szep, R., Daescu, V., Dumitru, D., Marinescu, F., Tociu, C., Popescu, I., & Gh. Popescu, C. R. (2017). Assessment of atmospheric pollution in a cement factory area situated in the eastern part of Romania. *Journal of Environmental Protection and Ecology, 18*(3), 819–830.

Hosseininia, G., & Ramezani, A. (2016). Factors Influencing Sustainable Entrepreneurship in Small and Medium - Sized Enterprises in Iran: A Case Study of Food Industry. *Sustainability*, *8*(10), 1010. doi:10.3390u8101010

Huang, K.-W., Huang, J.-H., & Tzeng, G.-H. (2016). New Hybrid Multiple Attribute Decision - Making Model for Improving Competence Sets: Enhancing a Company's Core Competitiveness. *Sustainability*, *8*(2), 175. doi:10.3390u8020175

Ijadi Maghsoodi, A., Azizi-ari, I., Barzegar-Kasani, Z., Azad, M., Zavadskas, E., & Antucheviciene, J. (2019). Evaluation of the Influencing Factors on Job Satisfaction Based on Combination of PLS - SEM and F - MULTIMOORA Approach. *Symmetry*, *11*(1), 24. doi:10.3390ym11010024

Joshi, P. R., & Islam, S. (2018). E - Government Maturity Model for Sustainable E - Government Services from the Perspective of Developing Countries. *Sustainability*, *10*(6), 1882. doi:10.3390u10061882

Keenan, T. (2015). *Human Resource Management*. Edinburgh Business School Heriot - Watt University. Retrieved from https://www.ebsglobal.net/EBS/media/EBS/PDFs/Human-Resource-Management-Course-Taster.pdf

Kell, H. J., & Lang, J. W. (2017). Specific Abilities in the Workplace: More Important Than g? *Journal of Intelligence*, *5*(2), 13. doi:10.3390/jintelligence5020013 PMID:31162404

Kiseľáková, D., Šofranková, B., Gombár, M., Čabinová, V., & Onuferová, E. (2019). Competitiveness and Its Impact on Sustainability, Business Environment, and Human Development of EU (28) Countries in terms of Global Multi - Criteria Indices. *Sustainability*, *11*(12), 3365. doi:10.3390u11123365

Kucharcikova, A., Miciak, M., Malichova, E., Durisova, M., & Tokarcikova, E. (2019). The Motivation of Students at Universities as a Prerequisite of the Education's Sustainability within the Business Value Generation Context. *Sustainability*, *11*(20), 5577. doi:10.3390u11205577

Kuitto, K., Salonen, J., & Helmdag, J. (2019). Gender Inequalities in Early Career Trajectories and Parental Leaves: Evidence from a Nordic Welfare State. *Soc. Sci.*, *8*(9), 253. doi:10.3390ocsci8090253

Lai, S. L., Pham, H.-H., Nguyen, H.-K. T., Nguyen, T.-C., & Le, A.-V. (2019). Toward Sustainable Overseas Mobility of Vietnamese Students: Understanding Determinants of Attitudinal and Behavioural Loyalty in Students of Higher Education. *Sustainability*, *11*(2), 383. doi:10.3390u11020383

Latifi, K. A. N., & Lim, S. (2019). Strategic Human Resource Management in the Afghanistan Ministry of Mines and Petroleum: A Network Perspective. *Sustainability*, *11*(14), 3830. doi:10.3390u11143830

Leksono, E. B., Suparno, S., & Vanany, I. (2019). Integration of a Balanced Scorecard, DEMATEL, and ANP for Measuring the Performance of a Sustainable Healthcare Supply Chain. *Sustainability*, *11*(13), 3626. doi:10.3390u11133626

Liu, Y., Wang, G. G., & Chen, Y. (2019). Why Are Corporations Willing to Take on Public CSR? An Organizational Traits Approach. *Sustainability*, *11*(2), 524. doi:10.3390u11020524

Lo, C.-H. (2019). A Study of the Influence of Career Counselling Perception on the Employment Competencies of Design Students in Central Taiwan. *Applied Sciences (Basel, Switzerland)*, *9*(23), 5072. doi:10.3390/app9235072

Malara, J., Plebankiewicz, E., & Juszczyk, M. (2019). Formula for Determining the Construction Workers Productivity Including Environmental Factors. *Buildings, 9*(12), 240. doi:10.3390/buildings9120240

Maree, J. G., & Di Fabio, A. (2018). Integrating Personal and Career Counselling to Promote Sustainable Development and Change. *Sustainability, 10*(11), 4176. doi:10.3390u10114176

Midttun, A., Næss, K. M., & Piccini, P. B. (2019). Biofuel Policy and Industrial Transition - A Nordic Perspective. *Energies, 12*(14), 2740. doi:10.3390/en12142740

Naveed, A., Ahmad, N., Esmaeilzadeh, R., & Naz, A. (2019). Self - Employment Dynamics of Immigrants and Natives: Individual - level Analysis for the Canadian Labour Market. *Sustainability, 11*(23), 6671. doi:10.3390u11236671

Nguyen, H. V., Nguyen, N., Nguyen, B. K., Lobo, A., & Vu, P. A. (2019). Organic Food Purchases in an Emerging Market: The Influence of Consumers'. *Personal Factors and Green Marketing Practices of Food Stores. Int. J. Environ. Res. Public Health, 16*, 1037. PMID:30909390

Palová, Z., & Šebestová, J. (2020). Competencies, Skills, and Goals Needed for Social Enterprises: Case of the Czech Republic. In Developing Entrepreneurial Competencies for Start - Ups and Small Business (pp. 109 - 128). IGI Global. .ch008 doi:10.4018/978-1-7998-2714-6

Paprocka, I. (2019). Evaluation of the Effects of a Machine Failure on the Robustness of a Job Shop System - Proactive Approaches. *Sustainability, 11*(1), 65. doi:10.3390u11010065

Parastuty, Z., & Bögenhold, D. (2019). Paving the Way for Self - Employment: Does Society Matter? *Sustainability, 11*(3), 747. doi:10.3390u11030747

Pérez-Ordás, R., Aznar Cebamanos, M., Nuviala, R., & Nuviala, A. (2019). Evaluation of Extracurricular Sports Activities as an Educational Element for Sustainable Development in Educational Institutions. *Sustainability, 11*(12), 3474. doi:10.3390u11123474

Pirmana, V., Alisjahbana, A. S., Hoekstra, R., & Tukker, A. (2019). Implementation Barriers for a System of Environmental - Economic Accounting in Developing Countries and Its Implications for Monitoring Sustainable Development Goals. *Sustainability, 11*(22), 6417. doi:10.3390u11226417

Pokorná, P., Šebestová, J., & Čemerková, Š. (2019). Dilemma of Directions for Reinvestment. *Forum Scientiae Oeconomia, 7*(4), 83–99. doi:10.23762/FSO_VOL7_NO4_6

Pokrovskaia, N. N., Ababkova, M. Y., & Fedorov, D. A. (2019). Educational Services for Intellectual Capital Growth or Transmission of Culture for Transfer of Knowledge - Consumer Satisfaction at St. Petersburg Universities. *Education in Science, 9*(3), 183. doi:10.3390/educsci9030183

Popescu, C. R. G. (2017). The Role of Total Quality Management in Developing the Concept of Social Responsibility to Protect Public Interest in Associations of Liberal Professions. *Amfiteatru Economic, 19*(11), 1091 – 1106. Retrieved from https://www.amfiteatrueconomic.ro/temp/Article_2685.pdf

Popescu, C. R. G. (2018). "Intellectual Capital" - Role, Importance, Components and Influences on the Performance of Organizations - A Theoretical Approach. *Proceedings of the 32nd International Business Information Management Association Conference.*

Popescu, C. R. G. (2019a). Evaluating intellectual capital and its influence on companies' performance - a Case Study on Romania's Experience. *INTED2019 Proceedings*. doi: 10.21125/inted.2019

Popescu, C. R. G. (2019b). Intellectual capital evaluation and measuring effectiveness - A Case Study on Romania's Experience in terms of performance and excellence. *INTED2019 Proceedings*. doi: 10.21125/inted.2019

Popescu, C. R. G. (2019c). "Intellectual Capital": Major Role, Key Importance and Decisive Influences on Organizations' Performance. *Journal of Human Resources Management Research*. doi:10. 5171/2019

Popescu, C. R. G. (2019d). Addressing Intellectual Capital in the Context of Integrated Strategy and Performance: Emphasizing the Role of Companies' Unique Value Creation Mechanism, While Targeting Better Organizational Reporting In Romania: The Case of Green Marketing and Green Marketing Strategies. *Journal of Marketing Research & Case Studies, 2019*, 672821. doi:10. 5171/2019

Popescu, C. R. G. (2019e). Business development opportunities: Demonstrating present and future performance, auditing intellectual capital - a case study on Romanian organizations. *Proceedings of the 33nd International Business Information Management Association Conference*.

Popescu, C. R. G. (2019f). Intellectual capital, integrated strategy and performance: focusing on companies' unique value creation mechanism and promoting better organizational reporting in Romania - a framework dominated by the impact of green marketing and green marketing strategies. *Proceedings of the 33nd International Business Information Management Association Conference*.

Popescu, C. R. G. (2019g). Corporate Social Responsibility, Corporate Governance and Business Performance: Limits and Challenges Imposed by the Implementation of Directive 2013/34/EU in Romania. *Sustainability, 11*(19), 5146. doi:10.3390u11195146

Popescu, C. R. G. (2020). Sustainability Assessment: Does the OECD/G20 Inclusive Framework for BEPS (Base Erosion and Profit Shifting Project) Put an End to Disputes Over The Recognition and Measurement of Intellectual Capital? *Sustainability, 12*(23), 10004. doi:10.3390u122310004

Popescu, C. R. G., & Banța, V. C. (2019). Performance Evaluation of the Implementation of the 2013/34/EU Directive in Romania on the Basis of Corporate Social Responsibility Reports. *Sustainability, 11*(9), 2531. doi:10.3390u11092531

Popescu, C. R. G., & Dumitrescu, M. (2016a). The Importance of Change Typology - a Key Element in the Enterprise's Organizational Dynamics. *Manager Journal, Issue*, (23), 116–123.

Popescu, C. R. G., & Dumitrescu, M. (2016b). A New Configuration: Management's Paradigms - Acting in the Context of Social Economy. *Manager Journal, Issue*, (23), 124–137.

Popescu, C. R. G. & Popescu, G. N. (2018a). Risks of cyber - attacks on financial audit activity. *Audit Financiar, 16*(1), 140 – 147. Doi:10.20869/AUDITF/2018/149/006

Popescu, C. R. G., & Popescu, G. N. (2018b). Methods of Evaluating "Intellectual capital" of an Organization and Ways of Enhancing Performance in the Knowledge - based Economy - A Synthetically Approach. *Proceedings of the 32nd International Business Information Management Association Conference*.

Popescu, C. R. G., & Popescu, G. N. (2019a). The Social, Economic, and Environmental Impact of Ecological Beekeeping in Romania. In G. Popescu (Ed.), *Agrifood Economics and Sustainable Development in Contemporary Society* (pp. 75–96). IGI Global. doi:10.4018/978-1-5225-5739-5.ch004

Popescu, C. R. G., & Popescu, G. N. (2019b). An Exploratory Study Based on a Questionnaire Concerning Green and Sustainable Finance, Corporate Social Responsibility, and Performance: Evidence from the Romanian Business Environment. *J. Risk Financial Manag.*, *2019*(12), 162. doi:10.3390/jrfm12040162

Popescu, C. R. G., Popescu, G. N., & Popescu, V. A. (2017a). Assessment of the State of Implementation of Excellence Model Common Assessment Framework (CAF) 2013 by the National Institutes of Research - Development - Innovation in Romania. *Amfiteatru Economic*, *19*(44), 41–60. https://www.amfiteatrueconomic.ro/temp/Articol_2593.pdf

Popescu, C. R. G., Popescu, G. N., & Popescu, V. A. (2017b). Sustainability Leadership, the Key to a Better World - A Case Study on Romania's Situation. *Proceedings of the 29th International Business Information Management Association Conference.*

Popescu, C. R. G., Popescu, G. N., & Popescu, V. A. (2017c). Creating Comprehensive Human Resources Management Policies and Instruments by Using Strategic Personnel Planning - A Case Study on Romania's Situation: A Quantitative and Qualitative Analysis. *Manager Journal, Issue*, (25), 133–146.

Popescu, C. R. G., & Popescu, V. A. (2015). The Assessment Methodology PDCA/PDSA - A Methodology for Coordinating the Efforts to Improve the Organizational Processes to Achieve Excellence. In Proceedings "CKS - Challenges of the Knowledge Society" (pp. 693 - 696). "Nicolae Titulescu" University Publishing House.

Popescu, C. R. G., Popescu, V. A., & Popescu, G. N. (2015). The Entrepreneur's Role in the Performance Growth of the Financial Audit Activity in Romania. *Amfiteatru Economic*, *17*(38), 228–246.

Popescu, C. R. G., Popescu, V. A., & Popescu, G. N. (2017d). Forecasting of Financial Markets and Monetary, Fiscal, Financial, Economic and Political Freedom Features in Nowadays Society - A Case Study on Romania's Situation. *Manager Journal, Issue*, (25), 116–132.

Popescu, G. N. (1997). *Procedurile controlului intern şi auditul financiar*. Editura Gestiunea.

Popescu, G. N., Popescu, C. R. G., & Popescu, V. A. (2016). The Macro Environment and the Companies' Economic, Social and Research - Development - Innovation Potential - Nowadays Key Elements. *Perspectives and Challenges, Manager Journal, Issue*, (24), 214–230.

Popescu, G. N., & Popescu, V. A. (2000). *Impozitul pe venit şi contabilitatea în partidă simplă*. Editura Gestiunea.

Popescu, G. N., Popescu, V. A., & Popescu, C. R. G. (2008) Interdisciplinary Research regarding the Role of Virtual Components in Knowing and Modelling Complex Economical - Social Phenomena and Processes. In *Proceedings of The International Scientific Session "Challenges of the Knowledge Society"*. University of Bucharest Publishing House.

Popescu, V. A., & Popescu, G. N. (2002). Manualul inspectorului de salarii. Bucharest: Editura Gestiunea.

Popescu, V. A., Popescu, G. N., & Popescu, C. R. G. (2015). Competitiveness and sustainability - a modern economic approach to the industrial policy. *Metalurgija, 54*(2), 426 - 428.

Preuss, U. (2016). Sustainable Digitalization of Cultural Heritage - Report on Initiatives and Projects in Brandenburg, Germany. *Sustainability, 8*(9), 891. doi:10.3390u8090891

Rao, R., Zhang, X., Shi, Z., Luo, K., Tan, Z., & Feng, Y. (2014). A Systematical Framework of Schedule Risk Management for Power Grid Engineering Projects' Sustainable Development. *Sustainability, 6*(10), 6872–6901. doi:10.3390u6106872

Rodríguez-Sánchez, J.-L., Montero-Navarro, A., & Gallego-Losada, R. (2019). The Opportunity Presented by Technological Innovation to Attract Valuable Human Resources. *Sustainability, 11*(20), 5785. doi:10.3390u11205785

Ruan, Z., Liu, W., Na, S., Tan, X., & Xue, T. (2019). Regional Marketization, OFDI, and Sustainable Employment: Empirical Analysis in China. *Sustainability, 11*(15), 4101. doi:10.3390u11154101

Sakaki, S. (2019). Equality in Income and Sustainability in Economic Growth: Agent - Based Simulations on OECD Data. *Sustainability, 11*(20), 5803. doi:10.3390u11205803

Šebestová, J. (2020). *Developing Entrepreneurial Competencies for Start - Ups and Small Business.* IGI Global., doi:10.4018/978-1-7998-2714-6

Šebestová, J., & Sroka, W. (2020). Sustainable development goals and SMEs decisions: Czech Republic vs. Poland. *Journal of Eastern European and Central Asian Research, 7*(1), 39–50. doi:10.15549/jeecar.v7i1.418

Sinclair, M., & Phillips, C. J. C. (2018). International Animal Protection Society Leadership: The Right People for the Right Issues. *Animals (Basel), 8*(6), 89. doi:10.3390/ani8060089 PMID:29880748

Sokas, R. K., Dong, X. S., & Cain, C. T. (2019). Building a Sustainable Construction Workforce. *International Journal of Environmental Research and Public Health, 16*(21), 4202. doi:10.3390/ijerph16214202 PMID:31671567

Stankevičiūtė, Ž., & Savanevičienė, A. (2018). Raising the Curtain in People Management by Exploring How Sustainable HRM Translates to Practice: The Case of Lithuanian Organizations. *Sustainability, 10*(12), 4356. doi:10.3390u10124356

Streimikiene, D., & Balezentis, T. (2019). Innovative Policy Schemes to Promote Renovation of Multi - Flat Residential Buildings and Address the Problems of Energy Poverty of Aging Societies in Former Socialist Countries. *Sustainability, 11*(7). . doi:10.3390u11072015

Štreimikienė, D., Mikalauskienė, A., Atkočiūnienė, Z., & Mikalauskas, I. (2019). Renewable energy strategies of the Baltic States. *Energy & Environment, 30*(2), 363–381. doi:10.1177/0958305X18790961

Tak, J., Seo, J., & Roh, T. (2019). The Influence of Authentic Leadership on Authentic Followership, Positive Psychological Capital, and Project Performance: Testing for the Mediation Effects. *Sustainability, 11*(21), 6028. doi:10.3390u11216028

Tan, H. P., Plowman, D., & Hancock, P. (2008). The evolving research on intellectual capital. *Journal of Intellectual Capital, 9*(4), 585–608. doi:10.1108/14691930810913177

Tang, C., Liu, C., Fang, P., Xiang, Y., & Min, R. (2019). Work - Related Accumulated Fatigue among Doctors in Tertiary Hospitals: A Cross - Sectional Survey in Six Provinces of China. *International Journal of Environmental Research and Public Health, 16*(17), 3049. doi:10.3390/ijerph16173049 PMID:31443480

Taylor, M. B., & van der Velden. (2019). Resistance to Regulation: Failing Sustainability in Product Lifecycles. *Sustainability, 11*(22), 6526. doi:10.3390u11226526

Tociu, C., Szep, R., Anghel, A. M., Marinescu, F., Ilie, M., Holban, E., Ghita, G., Matei, M., Dumitru, F. D., Popescu, I., Moncea, A., Laslo, L., Daescu, A. I., & Gh. Popescu, C. R. (2017). Possibilities For Efficient Use Of Valuable Materials From Aluminium Slag To Remove Specific Pollutants In Wastewater. *Journal of Environmental Protection and Ecology, 18*(3), 842–852.

Ullrich, D., Koleňák, J., Ambrozová, E., Pokorný, V., & Milichovský, F. (2019). Global X - tream Index and its Partial Parameters for Identifying the Level of Potential Individual Characteristics in the Challenging Conditions of a Modern Corporate and Security Environment. *Sustainability, 11*(12), 3325. doi:10.3390u11123325

Ulrich, E., Hurdelbrink, J., Perepelkin, J., & Welter, K. (2019). Financial Incentive Required for Pharmacy Students to Accept a Post - Graduation Position in Rural and Undesirable Pharmacy Settings. *Pharmacy (Basel, Switzerland), 7*(3), 109. doi:10.3390/pharmacy7030109 PMID:31390805

United Nations. (2019). *Responsible and Sustainable Business Practices and Corporate Social Responsibility and Enterprise Development*. United Nations Conference on Trade and Development, Trade and Development Board Investment, Enterprise and Development Commission Multi - year Expert Meeting on Investment, Innovation and Entrepreneurship for Productive Capacity - building and Sustainable Development, Seventh session Geneva, 17 - 19 June 2019, Item 3 of the provisional agenda. Retrieved from https://unctad.org/system/files/official-document/ciimem4d20_en.pdf

United Nations & United Nations Economic Commission for Europe. (2013). *Human Resources Management and Training: Compilation of good practices in statistical offices.* Retrieved from https://www.unece.org/fileadmin/DAM/stats/publications/HRMT_w_cover_resized.pdf

United Nations Conference on Trade and Development (UNCTAD). (2020). *Intellectual Property*. https://unctad.org/Topic/Science-Technology-and-Innovation/Intellectual-Property

Urquijo, I., Extremera, N., & Azanza, G. (2019). The Contribution of Emotional Intelligence to Career Success: Beyond Personality Traits. *International Journal of Environmental Research and Public Health, 16*(23), 4809. doi:10.3390/ijerph16234809 PMID:31795505

Van Dierendonck, D., Lankester, A., Zmyslona, M., & Rothweiler, H. (2016). Linking HRM Practices and Institutional Setting to Collective Turnover: An Empirical Exploration. *Administrative Sciences, 6*(4), 18. doi:10.3390/admsci6040018

Velenturf, A. P., Jensen, P. D., Purnell, P., Jopson, J., & Ebner, N. (2019). A Call to Integrate Economic, Social and Environmental Motives into Guidance for Business Support for the Transition to a Circular Economy. *Administrative Sciences*, *9*(4), 92. doi:10.3390/admsci9040092

Venkatasubramanian, V. (2009). What is Fair Pay for Executives? An Information Theoretic Analysis of Wage Distributions. *Entropy (Basel, Switzerland)*, *11*(4), 766–781. doi:10.3390/e11040766

Watkin, L. J., Ruangpan, L., Vojinovic, Z., Weesakul, S., & Torres, A. S. (2019). A Framework for Assessing Benefits of Implemented Nature - Based Solutions. *Sustainability*, *11*(23), 6788. doi:10.3390u11236788

Witek-Crabb, A. (2019). CSR Maturity in Polish Listed Companies: A Qualitative Diagnosis Based on a Progression Model. *Sustainability*, 11.

Wu, K. J., Chen, Q., Qi, Y., Jiang, X., Gao, S., & Tseng, M. L. (2019). Sustainable Development Performance for Small and Medium Enterprises Using a Fuzzy Synthetic Method - DEMATEL. *Sustainability*, *11*(15), 4119. doi:10.3390u11154119

Yi, L., Uddin, M. A., Das, A. K., Mahmood, M., & Sohel, S. M. (2019). Do Transformational Leaders Engage Employees in Sustainable Innovative Work Behaviour? Perspective from a Developing Country. *Sustainability*, *11*(9), 2485. doi:10.3390u11092485

Yin, J., Yan, Q., Lei, K., Baležentis, T., & Streimikiene, D. (2019). Economic and Efficiency Analysis of China Electricity Market Reform Using Computable General Equilibrium Model. *Sustainability*, *11*(2), 350. . doi:10.3390u11020350

Ying Lee, C., Lotsu, S., Islam, M., Yoshida, Y., & Kaneko, S. (2019). The Impact of an Energy Efficiency Improvement Policy on the Economic Performance of Electricity - Intensive Firms in Ghana. *Energies*, *12*(19), 3684. doi:10.3390/en12193684

Zagonari, F. (2016). Four Sustainability Paradigms for Environmental Management: A Methodological Analysis and an Empirical Study Based on 30 Italian Industries. *Sustainability*, *8*(6), 504. doi:10.3390u8060504

Zappalà, S., Toscano, F., & Licciardello, S. A. (2019). Towards Sustainable Organizations: Supervisor Support, Commitment to Change and the Mediating Role of Organizational Identification. *Sustainability*, *11*(3), 805. doi:10.3390u11030805

Zhang, L., Guo, X., Lei, Z., & Lim, M. K. (2019). Social Network Analysis of Sustainable Human Resource Management from the Employee Training's Perspective. *Sustainability*, *11*(2), 380. doi:10.3390u11020380

Zhao, H., Zhao, Q. H., & Ślusarczyk, B. (2019). Sustainability and Digitalization of Corporate Management Based on Augmented / Virtual Reality Tools Usage: China and Other World IT Companies' Experience. *Sustainability*, *11*(17), 4717. doi:10.3390u11174717

Zuo, Z., Li, Y., Fu, J., & Wu, J. (2019). Human Resource Scheduling Model and Algorithm with Time Windows and Multi - Skill Constraints. *Mathematics*, *7*(7), 598. doi:10.3390/math7070598

KEY TERMS AND DEFINITIONS

Human Capital: Is regarded as a multilevel and multidimensional concept, tackling people's specific characteristics and intellectual qualities that are able to empower organizations prevail in challenging times, aiding entities to react to different market challenges and changes, adapt to all forms of environment and strive to successfully meet consumers' expectations and needs.

Intellectual Capital: Is acknowledged as a dominant and powerful intangible asset of organizations, strongly connected to performance management and human capital, having a positive influence on development, growth and inclusive sustainable and responsible entrepreneurship methods, models, and strategies.

Performance Management: Is seen as crucial for organizations' worldwide, since it helps entities to embrace all opportunities and all possibilities, and it empowers companies to value intangible assets - more specifically, intellectual capital, focusing on creativity, education, information, innovation, knowledge, new technologies and ground - braking techniques, in order to encompass present and future challenges.

Sustainability: Is a dominant concept in today's society, as it addresses the needs belonging to human beings and future generations to come, eco-systems and bio-systems, and environment, while being influenced by numerous components and factors, such as intellectual capital—as a key trigger for inclusive and resilient business models—, human, social, and organizational capital—as main sources for competitive advantages—, and organizational performance—as major accomplishment when referring to corporate social responsibility, good governance, good business practices, ethics, transparency, diligent, and correct business behaviour.

Sustainable and Responsible Entrepreneurship: Represents a major asset to all entities these days, especially when analysed together with intangible assets, intellectual capital, human capital, innovation, and creativity, positive impact of intangible assets and entities higher performance.

Chapter 3
Crisis Situation and Financial Planning for Sustainability:
A Case of the Czech SMEs

Jarmila Duháček Šebestová
https://orcid.org/0000-0002-7493-0759
School of Business Administration in Karvina, Silesian University in Opava, Czech Republic

ABSTRACT

In any crisis or uncertain situation, it is necessary to carefully decide about three main points: when, what to invest, and which financial sources will be used. A profit reinvestment would be an effective and safe way of circulating money flows in a company. The first wave of COVID-19 has changed business conditions not only in the Czech Republic, but also it has an influence on financial decisions of entrepreneurs on how to use financial resources in individual segments of the company. The main goal of this chapter is to compare the reinvestment behavior in the company before the crisis based on primary research data (at least 425 respondents). The chapter includes results of different preferences influenced by COVID-19 uncertainty, and factor analysis has shown that availability of internal resources was important to survive restrictions and to be able to continue in financial planning to sustainably develop the business. Unfortunately, the relationship between business experience and main motives to invest wasn't confirmed.

INTRODUCTION

Businesses are diverse and each is specific, but decision - making processes must be planned, applied and analysed in everyone, whether in a large multinational enterprise or a micro enterprise. A planning helps businesses to achieve predefined goals, make decisions quickly and efficiently on the basis of elaborated documents, and achieve operational goals faster than without them. It also helps to focus on a clearly defined goal and not to deviate from, for example, business goals (Delmar & Shane, 2003). There are researches where companies grew faster and, according to a specific research by Brinckmann et al. (2010), companies that use planning at their inception grew faster than those who did not. An entrepre-

DOI: 10.4018/978-1-7998-7951-0.ch003

neur always carries a degree of uncertainty and risk, which is related to the fact that he coordinates the plans, introduces new goods and production processes supported by reinvestment, especially in crisis situation as represented by COVID - 19.

Human behaviour, even rational human and business behaviour is not to be accounted for optimal variants. In real life we could assume perfect adaptation to the business environment, but it depends on economic literacy of business owner, its experience and problems of company. There are so many different techniques for observing decision - making behaviour, which combine financial statements, business perceptions and business environment factors (Simon, 1979, Walker et al., 2011, Illés, 2016). All models want to answer the question of profit maximization, especially in profit reinvestment in explicit or implicit way, when the main problem is not actually the reinvestment rate, but the critical reinvestment rate (Meyer, 1979). Financial planning is closely connected with many areas such as: planning, calculating and reporting to prepare entrepreneurs for a more prospective future, especially in area of financial management and resource management within appropriate business education (Pittaway & Cope, 2016; Fiet, 2001). In a line with that, a company development, when reinvestment process plays an important part of the decision - making process in financial management not only small businesses (Zhou, 2017). According that small businesses prefer own capital and their behaviour depends on previous experience (Wellalage & Reddy, 2020).

The aim of the chapter is to analyse and describe main factors based on primary research who made decision about allocation of their resources within COVID - 19 situation. The research sample consists more than 400 SMEs form whole Czech Republic. The survey was conducted during summer 2020. The main results are presented in the form of a case study.

BACKGROUND

The business level is intersected by strategic dilemmas that affect the understanding of organizations not only services that have their goals, strategy and want to achieve success. Companies that positively influence the market can divide the business strategy into 3 fundamental categories. The first are companies that support a precisely planned and written strategic plan. The second group of them does not incorporate a written strategy, but it provides a strategic focus. Most of them are small to medium - sized enterprises, where the dominant position is occupied by the owner of the company, who typically has key goals in his head. Such enterprises rely purely on the invention and potential of the owner on whom the most considerable burden of responsibility. The business's strategy is practically replaced by corporate culture. The culture is characterized by a friendly, participatory and team thinking, supported by employee loyalty. The third specific group of companies does not include an effective strategy. At this place, the corporate culture fulfils a significant role, which in a way influences the strategic document and the essential management is a reflection of the corporate culture (i.e. attitudes, standards, which management or owner holds). Naturally, corporate culture cannot function optimally as an effective strategy in the long run, and therefore other companies are characterized primarily by inconsistent management and untargeted steps in decision - making. (Havlíček, 2011). From previous analyses of various types of entities on the market, several groups of internal strategic dilemmas can be deduced (Šebestová & Antonová, 2011, Šebestová & Nowáková, 2013), which can also be applied in small companies in general:

- The dilemma of ethics and business. Is it necessary to do good things or things right as an entrepreneur? Is it really possible to combine mastering both roles, i.e. professionalism and entrepreneurial role?
- The dilemma of strategic selection of business partners. Intuitive or analytical business decisions predominate - but when will the business be more successful? Will business be its own life philosophy? Will the owner want to be more involved in decision - making in one company or does he want to have more shares in the chain of companies?
- The dilemma of survival and growth. What managerial skills and business strategies are needed in a competitive environment? Is the growth and development of the company good or will it endanger the quality of products or services? How can we differentiate a service so that it is perceived as a "niche"? How do you know that business is getting out of hand and you need to seek professional help? How to withstand external threats and, conversely, take advantage of the challenges arising from market opportunities?
- The financial management dilemma for innovation and control. Can we still do business without external financial resources? What kind of innovation will benefit the business? Will they bring a sustainable competitive advantage to the business? Is activity control really necessary? Does the control not jeopardize trust in employees?

Other dilemmas include the way to strategy development in companies, where it is a concise breakdown according to Swayne et al. (2006), and dividing approaches into 2 groups:

- Strategies founded on an analytical approach. Leads to the process management of the organization and the established system, but the delay changes and dynamics, because everything is acquired "rationally";
- Strategies based on an intuitive approach, sometimes called "emergency", which are based on experience and learning. The strategy maker is typically part of the management.
- In practice, both approaches are combined, because from the nature of business. We can conclude, that an analytical style to strategy is valid when it comes to a long - term matter within a stable business environment. The second approach in the event of sudden changes, crisis situations and we will utilize it in operational planning.

The idea consists of a combination of previous approaches is also supported by Hurst (2002), who added:

"The question is not which approach is better, but whether the one who manages completely comprehends what he is preparing. Modern management is described by periods of calm and reversals, when nothing works in the company. Sometimes deeper analyses are needed, other times we can do it with previous experience".

A comparison of development approaches from intuitive strategy to process management is shown in the following table 1.

In the relevant literature we should find significant models, based on empirical studies, which describe dynamic factors to protect business from uncertainty and a crisis environment. The most used business models for the performance of firms are the - SSP model (Strategy - Structure - Performance model);

Table 1. Analytical and Intuitive Strategy Comparison

	Intuitive Approach			Analytical Approach	
	Elements	*Definition*		*Elements*	*Definition*
Strategy	People	Basic resources, especially in services, influenced by the environment, demography (customers)	Strategy	Change	Assignment of persons responsible for tasks.
	Roles	Have the right person in the right place at the right time. Be able to evaluate the situation according analysis or previous experience.		Task	Tasks given according to specializations.
	Teams	Hectic group formation.		Structure	It is created according to groups that have already been created
	Network	Open communication channels, high level of variability.		System	Stabilization of external and internal relations, formalization
	Recognition	A sense of belonging, unsustainable in the long run, cash rewards frequently used.		Rewards	Work evaluation system and creating a motivational and reward system.

Source: Hurst, 2002; Swayne et al., 2006

SCP model (Strategy - Conduct - Performance model) and RBV model (Resource - Based View model) as a response for interaction between company, environment, and performance (Lo, 2013).

The SSP model suggest that strategy, followed by organizational change would bring about a dynamic response to a changing environment, other factors such as resource allocations and leadership style are determined by long term goals and the proper type of strategy (Chandler, 1962; Ansoff, 1965). Other scholars add the influence of the external environment to balance resources for strategy success (Pfeffer & Salanick, 1978).

The SCP model was developed by Porter and is based on industrial structure, the behaviour of a firm in the market and its bargaining power (the model is academically known as "Porter's five forces"; Porter, 1996).

The RBV model, presented by Barney (1991) proposes a combination of internal resources as a competitive advantage of the company. The difference in responding to the business environment and the self - interests of companies brings about constraints on being dynamic. Many companies have as the main goal for their future not innovation, but merely survival.

MAIN FOCUS OF THE CHAPTER

Role of Strategy in Financial Planning

Strategic methods and tools are closely connected with strategic management use in general. A strategic management can be defined as a set of theories and frameworks, supported by special methods, tools and techniques, which are primarily designed to assist managers of organizations in thinking, planning and acting strategically (Stonehouse & Pemberton, 2002; Berisha et al., 2017). On the other hand, strategy tool is could be a generic name for any method, model, technique, tool, technology, framework, methodology or approach used to support strategic management work in the non - stable business environment (Stenfors et al., 2007; Golsorkhi et al., 2010; Vaara & Whittington, 2012). Since most of strategic tools were developed for the sector of large companies, the raising question is how successful would be the transformation process of original method to the SME company use (Abosede et al., 2016; Krasniqi & Kume, 2013). Those differences can be distinguished within literature comparison (Holmes & Ferrill, 2005; Jun et al., 2013; Popper, 2008; Phillips, 2013) in the table 2.

Table 2. A Comparison in Strategy Thinking

Criteria	SME Company (< 250 Employees)	Large Company (>250 Employees)
Main motivation to use / prepare strategy	Finding a new investor Adaptation to changes in the business environment	Innovative strategy Risk analysis for decision - making Entry to the new market
Attributes of strategy	Description of current stage Transfer knowledge from other	Systematic, long term work New knowledge creation
Resources for strategy implementation	Limited by the company stage and the company size	A budget is closely connected with planned company changes
Tools, techniques	Tools for the environment observation Creative tools - Brainstorming, Brain - writing	Approx. combination of five to six tools, together with a trend analysis, own research, an expert estimation.
Main barriers	Most of time is spent by operative management Lack of the future anticipation	Company size and organizational structure, stability in managerial positions.

Source: Šebestová, 2018

The practice in the business area allows becoming familiar with problems and avoiding a turbulent and non - dynamic decisional spiral. Traditional models of skills cover only a few variables such as the structure of an organization, climate, processes and leadership without dynamic points such as the behaviour of other elements (Burke & Litwin, 1992; Damanpour, 1991; Kimberly & Cook, 2008). The successfulness of each strategy depends on behavioural models, but all models need the below stated four significant steps (Tidd et al., 2007; Rylková & Chobotová, 2011): (1) Copy main goals from strategy, (2) Effective internal and external linkage with other subjects in the market, (3) Support for conducting changes in an organization, (4) Supportive environment.

Strategy tools. The use of strategic management tools depends on expected results in comparison to costs. Despite this, little progress has been made in the work of Vishnevskiy & Egorova (2015) who divided strategic tools, used in SMEs according previously presented criteria. These authors presented four groups of tools, used by SMEs such as:

- **Low – Cost:** These tools are easy to transfer to SME Company to use, but result could be limited due to experience of the final user or data inputs, which were used for the analysis (e.g. SWOT, Interviews, and reviews).
- **Highly Informative:** In comparison to previous group, these tools bring deeper range of information at lower costs (e.g. Expert panels, Benchmarking, Scenarios).
- **Highly Specialized:** These tools achieve mostly positive effect on using. Opposite to that, they are time and finance consuming. Specialized personnel are needed for data collection and final report preparation (e.g. Modelling, Extrapolation, and Indicator setting).
- **Resource Consuming:** These methods were originally designed for large companies, so implementation at SME level could be quite difficult (e.g. Surveys, Delphi)

Global level of strategy tools use. Rigby & Bilodeau (2018, 13,000 respondents) stated, that large companies use in average 8.1 tools, medium - sized 7.6 and small companies 5.3 tools, when table 3 provides an overview of significant strategy tools used in SMEs between years 2000 - 2017.

One interesting finding is, that Strategic planning as "whole package" of tools and procedures placed in the TOP 5 during whole observed period. Second popular method globally used was benchmarking. However, these results were not very encouraging in area of SMEs strategic tools use, when most of

Table 3. Significant Strategy Tools Used In Years 2000 To 2017

	2000	2006	2008	2010	2012	2014	2017
1	Strategic Planning	Strategic Planning	Benchmarking	Benchmarking	Strategic Planning	CRM	Strategic Planning
2	Mission and Vision Statement	CRM	Strategic Planning	Strategic Planning	Supply Chain Management	Benchmarking	CRM
3	Benchmarking	Customer Segmentation	Mission and Vision Statement	Mission and Vision Statement	Employee Engagement Surveys	Employee Engagement Surveys	Benchmarking
4	Outsourcing	Benchmarking	CRM	CRM	Benchmarking	Strategic Planning	Advanced Analytics
5	Customer Satisfaction	Mission and Vision Statement	Outsourcing	Outsourcing	BSC	Outsourcing	Supply Chain Management
6	Growth Strategies	Core Competencies	BSC	BSC	Core Competencies	BSC	Customer Satisfaction
7	Strategic Alliances	Outsourcing	Customer Segmentation	Change Management Programs	Outsourcing	Mission and Vision Statement	Change management
8	Pay - for - Performance	Business Process Reengineering	Business Process Reengineering	Core Competencies	Change Management	Supply Chain Management	TQM
9	Customer Segmentation	Scenario and Contingency Planning	Scenario and Contingency Planning	Strategic Alliances	Supply Chain Management	Change Management	Digital transformation
10	Core Competencies	Knowledge Management	Mergers and Acquisitions	Customer Segmentation	Mission and Vision Statement	Customer Segmentation	Mission and Vision Statement

Source: Rigby & Bilodeau 2018

them depend on group of time and resource consuming tools (Vishnevskiy & Egorova, 2015). On the other hand, in spite of these recent findings about the role of strategic tools in SMEs, national studies showed country differences. Alkan & Bozkurt (2013) argued that small business owners in Turkey prefer traditional and well explained tools like SWOT analysis, strategic scenarios and financial planning. In the same way, Afonina & Chalupský (2013) and supported those findings by their results in the Czechia, where SWOT, PEST, and model of Five Porter forces are dominating in respondent's answers. Finally, Ogbadu et al. (2017) mentioned financially oriented tools and pro - innovative approach to strategy in Nigeria. Those findings confirmed use of low - cost tools in the sectors of SMEs and it could have an influence on financial planning skills.

Strategy Evaluation. Equations are often used to evaluate strategy structure models and to describe dependent values in strategy behaviour or to describe successful business theories. We should mention the research of managerial choices and strategy components in reaction to the external environment as equations (Bourgeois, 1984). Others connect strategy positions and business performance in one equation. In theory, we should imagine their dynamics as the relationship between one resource and another which produces the same effect as an equal relationship between other combinations, because we use them equally. We should imagine the combination of the relationships between factors as in the Bernoulli mathematical spiral of development. This imaginative picture explains the relationship between triangle tops, represented by strategic pillars and these tops are connected by one spiral. The optimal ratio between vertices, represented by the distance from A to B and B to C is named φ, with the value of 0.618 (Häuser, 2007), for strategy optimization, the value means the dynamics of resources used for sustainable development in each group. His evaluation and models are especially developed for industrial organizations, (Keeley& Roure, 1990). This evaluation opens up areas for financial planning (desired effect for company) in strategic behaviour.

Sustainability in Financial Planning

Financial planning, especially reinvestments are mostly realized in the area of science and research and human resources that means to attract new employees hired to develop innovation, which companies make more profit (Hasuch & Pyka, 2007; Chakravarty & Xiang, 2011). Business profit is usually limited in 2 ways. Once, entrepreneur's don´t have so many stable customers which will generate sustainable profit, secondly, limitation of enterprise capacity, which limits amount of orders that they cannot accept more ones.

Reinvestments are, as the name suggests, profit already generated from a successful investment, and this financial amount will be reused for business development as investment money. Lazonick (2014) has been involved in the decision - making process of redistributing the resources of large US companies for several years and mentioned a trend where companies have tended to withhold profit and are just doing the reinvestment process, especially in the areas of increasing human resources skills to increase competitiveness.

Sustainability in financial area means finding a new combination of resources and opportunities to adapt to new conditions as quickly as possible. However, the question arises as to how to measure sustainability, predict or successfully cope with change through the individual skills of the entrepreneur, and how each of the presented approaches affects the creation of strategy. The practical application of the results of empirical analyses is the creation of a business model, according to which entrepreneurs try to implement their strategy. From the point of view of sustainability, the business model is understood as a long - term concept of a company, which includes "the structure of products, services, information flows that create and bring the value" (Osterwalder et al., 2010). It means that the model should cover not only how the company should work, but what factors cause problems or success, but how value is created at each stage or process of the company. One of the milestones of any business model that shifts the dimension of profit gain to sustainability is the connection with the current socio - economic environment, and therefore the basic six elements include (Osterwalder et al., 2010; Zott et al., 2011):

- Definition of values
- Product or service innovation
- Infrastructure management
- Customer relationship management

- Financial sustainability
- Value for the owner
- Regular sources of revenue.

The internal dynamics as the effect of egocentric uncertainty, where owners have difficulty understanding or predicting how changes in the business environment will affect them, shows the opposite side of external strategy dynamics, and what it can happen and when a small business does not properly understand outside impulses. This behaviour can easily lead to a business downfall because it rely solely on marketing tools (Aragon - Corea & Sharma, 2003). Business profit is usually limited in 2 ways. Once, entrepreneurs' don´t have so many stable customers which will generate sustainable profit, secondly, limitation of enterprise capacity, which limits amount of orders that they cannot accept more ones. There could be one solution to both problems in form of reinvestment to employees, machines, other products and appropriate promotion. The fact that businesses could allow reinvestment to accept reinforcement to help us handle orders can be a key element that moves business into a different dimension. When the company reinvests profits to themselves, the money is used for research and development, debt repayment, or possibly has a net cash flow from investment activities. On the contrary to that a joint stock company which pays out to shareholders, usually increases dividends and buys back its shares. Main motivation to plan this process would be (1) profit maximization; (2) maximizing the current value of future net cash inflows with cost minimization or (3) maximization of profits in the long run and the prestige of the enterprise according to the owner or owners (Kędzierski, 2017; Kaczmarek, 2014).

Factors like adaptability, innovation and strategy are very important. Without these components, the firm cannot adapt to changes in the regional environment. From knowledge of current modern methods of management and business management services in general it can be inferred that the enterprise can develop an open system that is capable of rapidly adapting to positive and negative external influences such as special tax treatment at the employee level with non - deductible impact at corporate level (Blechová, 2011). The basis of maintaining adaptability to environmental changes, growth, business competitiveness and long - term business growth is the ability of firms to innovate. Each sector has different characteristics and priorities - some are sensitive to the scale of production, others to scientific research or the range of or sensitivity to demographic changes. Therefore, an analysis of the strategic elasticity of small and medium - sized businesses could help to find an answer to the question of how this business segment could deal with challenges from the external environment and what type of strategies they might use to achieve their goals. It is anticipated that the research findings will illuminate the definition by Krupski (2005), who described elasticity of strategy within unstable environment in four dimensions as: (i) reactive, (ii) adaptive, (iii) defensive, (iv) creative as attributes of the strategy of an observed firm.

Sustainability seems to be acceptable in the form of repetition of the business habits (supporting the idea of Schumpeter) that entrepreneurs have formed during their customer relationships, competition, employee relations, and this behaviour forms the basis of an unwritten, strong business strategy (Cohen, 2006). These routine activities and decisions are stable and not susceptible to change because they are related to the person using them and are closely influenced by corporate culture (Winter, 2000; Cohen & Bacdayan, 1994). However, if changes occur, we can call the process improvisation, which is directly dependent on the previous experience and skills of the strategy creator, because the strategy usually does not have a written form. It follows that in enterprises, especially small ones, where an informal form of strategy - making predominates, it will also have an informal form of monitoring progress and control (March, 1991; Nelson 1991). Brown & Eisenhardt (1998) support the possibility of predicting the response of change by arguing that the complexity of strategy is linked to the speed of change in the organization. There is a reason why external support is needed to eliminate external risk. A need of cooperation corresponds with other, quite similar research data in area of sustainable business. The authors confirm, the best way for sustainability is cooperation, not only between business units, but via spin - offs (Androniceanu & Drăgulănescu, 2012). Investments into research and development as well as innovation are positive factors for the future (Tidd, 2007), but they bring a higher level of risk. However, it can be argued and agreed that by examining small businesses, the degree of adaptability can be identified and the factors that lead to adaptability and their strength in the concept of strategic management can be described.

In a line of studies, mentioned in the table 4, most of them use financial indicators as main factors of sustainability evaluation. To broader this, we have to mention that financial evaluation tools often play a secondary role in corporate investment choices (Cooremans, 2011). It means that sustainable investments not only in time of crisis have a strategic character (Sorrell et al., 2000; Sandberg & Söderström, 2003). In times of crisis, the main goal is to get out of it and to find out alternative ways, how to reinvest the profit. This situation, especially in sustainable point of view, we could imagine as crisis situation and we are able to apply methods closely connected with that area, namely balanced scorecard as an example (Kolumber et al., 2020). Crisis management involves active change. The principle of change management is, among other things, the identification of resistance to change and the conversion of this

Table 4. Previous Studies Comparison

Author	Study Focus	Sources Of Financial Sustainability
Jensen, 1986	A study on “free cash flow” relationship to investment	Availability of internal funds
Fazzari et al., 1988	Empirical study of firm investment decisions, impact on cash flow	Liquidity, cash flow fluctuations
Kaplan & Zingales, 1997	Investment - liquidity sensitivities across different groups of firms	Sensitiveness on the internal resources
Perera et al., 1997	A study on non - financial indicators	Adoption of non - financial indicators
Xu et al., 2006	Variation between strategy standardization and company performance (marketing oriented)	Strategy and firm performance relationship
McKenzie, 2006	Study confirmed relationship a positive relationship between financial behaviour and (re)investment skills	Experience and age of investor
Alkaraan & Northcott, 2006	Study of 83 UK companies about factors influencing investments	Financial evaluation tools
Gupta et al., 2015	A study of prosperous and non - prosperous companies with variables size, capital structure, management structure	Company size, access to external sources
Bartosova & Kral, 2017	Study on financial analysis of Slovak companies	Financial indicators
Valaskova et al., 2018	Risk modelling and prediction	Risk assessment
Astanaqulov & Asatullayev, 2020	A study of investments in Uzbekistan, describing factors influencing investment behaviour	Activity of an individual or in the acquisition, planning and production of property

Source: Own

energy into positive energy, which not only accelerates the process of change and its course, but also ensures the successful effect of change. Thus, change leads to a new level that is qualitatively higher than the previous state (Boyatzis & McKee, 2011). We must realize that every change evokes in natural systems (which are also a person, i.e. subordinate, colleague and superior) a certain form of resistance, which he transforms into an undesirable form of energy or work. In proportion to the resistance, it is then necessary to expend a reasonable dose of energy only to eliminate this resistance, which is all the more difficult from the point of view of the idea of introducing a change. Adequate amount of investment activity and in a crisis situation financing to ensure timely delivery of change and sustainability. It is a long - term orientation of the company and several factors come into play, namely the level of indebtedness, attitude to risk and the emphasis placed on reinvesting profit. This trend, especially in the area of reinvestment activities related to sustainability is supported by other authors: Pakšiová (2017), MacGregor - Pelikánová (2019) or Popescu & Banta (2019).

It is important to optimize the structure of resources and develop a sustainable competitive advantage. Seisebaeva (2015) suggested financial anti - crisis management to support sustainability in simple steps:

Step 1: Financial Anti - Crisis Management: A system that uses financial mechanisms to prevent or overcome financial problems.

Step 2: Anti - Crisis Management: Restoration of financial stability of the enterprise. This is one of the main task that ensure implementation of the main goal of anti - crisis management of the enterprise, which requires little effort and cost of financial resource.

Step 3: Financial Management: Minimizing the negative consequences of the financial crisis of the enterprise. This task is realized by consolidating the positive results of removing the company from the state of the financial crisis.

To be able to evaluate financial planning for investments is necessary to set investment categories. The investment category influences the financial criteria used (duration, capital budgeting tool, and discount rate) and the procedure as type of analysis carried out, sources of information and development of the project (Chen, 1995; De - Bodt & Bouquin, 2001). These previous studies have generally not shown that financial factors are more important with regard to the investment process for smaller companies (Carr et al., 2010; Fazzari, et al., 1998; Liu and Pang, 2009). Because they have limited access to capital markets, they are forced to rely more on internal funds such as, for example, personal savings or funds borrowed from relatives or friends (Gill et al., 2012). The research gap was found that in earlier studies was found that terms such as planning, calculations, changes in reinvestments are closely connected but there are not studies, which are connecting all those variables together. Entrepreneurs mirror modern present - day developments, which might be extra dynamic, mainly within the SME sector. To be able to survive those changes, they need to use actively their competences. The level of these competencies can influence a business surroundings evaluation by using the personal level of satisfaction. All characteristics have long - term consequences and that they have closer links to organizational performance inside current enterprise surroundings. Following that, we have developed 2 hypotheses, focused on relationship on financial planning and relationship to business experience:

Hypothesis 1: Business experience has an influence on a financial management decision - a decision of structure of external and internal resources.

Hypothesis 2: Business experience has an influence on a change in priorities within investment categories after crisis.

Financial Planning Within Crisis Situation: A Case Study

Previously presented studies analysing financial behaviour was valid within "normal" situation without any problems, which comes to whole economies due to COVID - 19 pandemic from March 2020. Many enterprises in the Czech Republic had to be closed or limited due to anti - epidemic restriction provided by national government. FAPI research (2020), conducted on 90 sole proprietors and companies has shown that due to COVID - 19 situation were "closed" their business de jure 28%, de facto others had possibility to use alternative ways, how to deliver their services and products to customers (via social media, e - shops, etc.). Their profits decreased to 60%. In a line with that, those people tried to find some ways, how to survive in that situation as others. They used a costs reduction (38%), a close of establishments / offices (32%) and a reduction of business activities (29%). The main costs which they have to cover are rent, energies and lease payments. In words of financial planning those entrepreneurs stated, that they would have a reserve fund to cover 3 month cost (46%). In terms of future plans, 39% of respondents plan to invest in gaining new customers, expanding activities or expanding into new markets. This results and existing list of support were a starting point for finding a current research gap - to observe a change in behaviour in area of a financial planning and internal funds use in context of existing public support, which isn't covered in previous studies (Pokorná, 2020).

The main focus of this interviews was to describe a change in planning behaviour during first wave of COVID - 19 situation and main motives to invest within changed conditions, which was in a line of study of Kaplan & Zingales (1997), Gupta et al. (2015) and Astanaqulov & Asatullayev (2020) in combination with age and experience of business owner McKenzie (2006). To acquire relevant information in the field of companies and their activity in a financial decision making within crisis situation, a combination of primary and secondary research was needed (Zott et. al, 2011).

Methodology and Data Collection

The case study precedes complete field research conducted in the form of a questionnaire. Data was collected from the second half of 2020 to December 2020 by a combination of an online form and a personal interview of the team members. A total of 425 respondents had replied to the questionnaire as of December 28, 2020. Data was collected using a semi - structured interview and online form. The interviews were conducted by telephone when 66% of semi - structured interviews were conducted interviews were conducted by telephone. A total of 1,206 entrepreneurs were addressed and 425 entrepreneurs attended the research, when 78.5% of answers to questions about numbers (qualitative evaluation, descriptive variables) were obtained directly from entrepreneurs and 21.5% of responses were taken directly from the enterprise records. Of all the companies in the Czech Republic we were only interested in companies meeting the following conditions (quota selection by region in value of one per mile of companies per one region):

- Only Sole proprietor and Limited Liability Companies (Joint Stock Companies have a large turnover and a large share of GDP, but we are interested in the number of opinions).

- Turnover min. CZK 1 (to eliminate inactive enterprises according Czech statistical office evaluation).
- The maximum number of employees being 249. This is due to the fact that managers are employed in large enterprises and therefore have no experience in setting up an enterprise.

A SPSS statistical package was used for data evaluation. A Cramer´s V coefficient was used to confirm significance between variables at $\alpha = 0.05$. A bootstrapping was used to robust dataset. To obtain a main set of factors for financial planning within crisis situation, a factor analysis with VARIMAX rotation was applied, when Kaiser - Meyer - Olkin Measure of Sampling Adequacy was above 0.6.

Data Sample Description

The findings presented here are founded on the authors' interpretation of in - depth interviews with enterprises managers. In this study, the sample consists from 425 respondents, who dedicated their time for the interview, based on phone call. One call lasts 20 to 30 minutes in average. The main group of respondents were men (74.2%). When we focused on their experience, the majority of them have an experience more than 20 years (30.9%), 11 to 20 years (19.5%), 4 to 10 years (21.4%) and the shortest experience - till 3 years (7.8%). This sample represents people with long business experience, so they have competencies to evaluate precisely the current situation. Those descriptive variables were found as statistically significant for evaluation of overall situation, when Cramer V coefficient = 0.745 and Sig. = 0.001

Main Results

Decision making and financial planning in financial management are closely related to the company's survival in a globalized market and with competitiveness, which is specifically reflected in the continuous process of the improvement of goods and services as well as financial processes and the economic potential evaluation of enterprises within crucial situation, especially crisis situation. At first, we obtained main motives to invest profit into company. According previous literature review, the main motive as availability of internal resources is the driver to reinvestment (Jensen, 1986; Table 5).

As significant were found 2 factors (1) payback period and (2) extra benefits. This approach with absolute first motive "extra benefits" extents a study of Alkaraan & Northcott (2006), who examined mostly the motive of payback period and financial ratios.

In the next step respondents answer the question about the amount of profit they reinvested back in examined period. To get easier information, they use a percentage share from their profit. As illustrated in the Table 6, the main group reinvests 60% and more, so we could confirm, that those companies prefer internal financial resources for their activities.

As confirmed by statistical tests, the change before 2 period and 2 nominal values aren't significant in that moment. It is not surprise that the group of companies who reinvest more that 80% of its profit increased due to uncertain situation.

To extend a study of McKenzie (2006) we evaluated factors in relationship with business experience not related to current age of the business owner and factors were divided according steps, mentioned by Seisebaeva (2015; Table 7). Author added one group more, named "main motives" lead to investment before financial management within crisis situation was applied.

Table 5. Main Motives for Profit Re - Investments

Factor	No	Yes
Interest rate in bank	54.4%	45.6%
Payback period	17.5%	82.5%
Tax deductions	41.1%	58.9%
Extra benefits to yields	12.3%	87.7%
Competitive advantage	33.9%	66.1%
Financial ratios	29.8%	70.2%

Source: Own

This evaluation has shown that business experience isn't playing a significant role within crisis situation as presented by COVID - 19 situation. The most significant factor, related to business experience was age (0.496, sig. 0.000) and other factors, supporting a growth of investments or anti - crisis activity

Table 6. Change in the Investment Share

	How much profit do you reinvest back to your enterprise? (in percentage share)						Evaluation	
Period	0%	20%	40%	60%	80%	100%	Cramer V	Sig.
B: During COVID - 19	9.4%	1.6%	7.8%	18.8%	34.4%	28.1%	0.096	0.480
A:Before COVID - 19	0.0%	10.5%	10.5%	26.3%	31.6%	21.1%	0.130	0.205
Difference B - A	+9.4%	- 8.6%	- 2.7%	- 7.5%	+2.8%	+7%	0.132	0.832

Source: Own

had statistically significant tie, but the value of the coefficient was rather small (below 0.3). Finally, we provided a confirmatory factor analysis to evaluate a data sample to explain main factor groups, which have an influence on financial planning within crisis environment (Table 8). The data factor loading was 59.969% and we obtained 9 factor groups (Bartlett's Test of Sphericity - Approx. Chi - Square 1052.286, Sig. 0.000)

As presented in the table above, we have extracted nine factors. First factor group (F1) describes a company owner related to experience and age. This affects the second factor group (F2) when business owners have to decide about the changes in financial planning due to crisis situation and they are not able to invest according previous plans and they have to update the financial plan. Third factor group reveals their main motives such as extra benefits and payback period, because financial sources are limited within this period. Main focus in that period is to invest resources into company development to be sustainable (F4). Then education is often used (F5). Company development is supported by appropriate mixture of internal and external resources (F6). To continue in sustainable development a company needs to invest to the equipment and technologies (F7) but those projects seem to be financed from external resources, when F8 factors had shown dependence on interest rates and tax deductions. Finally, all the cycle will

Table 7. Bootstrapped Evaluation of Factors Influencing Financial Planning Related To Business Experience

Factor	Cramer V	Bias	Std. Error	Approx. Sig
Main motive: Interest rate in bank	0.092	0.025	0.041	0.311
Main motive: Payback period	0.072	0.030	0.042	0.536
Main motive: Tax deductions	0.111	0.020	0.040	0.157
Main motive: Extra benefits to yields	0.100	0.020	0.041	0.233
Main motive: Competitive advantage	0.152*	0.013	0.040	0.020
Main motive: Financial ratios	0.030	0.049	0.033	0.943
An amount of reinvestment in percentage share (Financial anti - crisis management)	0.141	0.000	0.000	0.046
Investment category: Marketing (Financial anti - crisis management)	0.146*	0.027	0.026	0.027
Investment category: Company development (Financial anti - crisis management)	0.093	0.040	0.025	0.759
Investment category: Human Resources (Financial anti - crisis management)	0.086	0.041	0.023	0.849
Investment category: Equipment and Technologies (Financial anti - crisis management)	0.122	0.035	0.023	0.209
Anti - crisis management: reserve fund	0.121*	0.024	0.025	0.029
Anti - crisis management: use of internal resources during crisis	0.119	0.037	0.022	0.253
Anti - crisis management: A ratio between external and internal financial resources	0.150	0.042	0.024	0.121
Financial planning: A change in priorities within investment categories after crisis	0.153*	0.025	0.023	0.003
Financial planning: A growth of support in selected investment	0.260*	0.016	0.025	0.004
Financial planning: A concrete percentage of growth of financial investment	0.120	0.044	0.022	0.428
Financial planning: Reduction of support in selected investment	0.144	0.028	0.029	0.340
Financial planning: A concrete percentage of reduction of financial investment	0.145	0.041	0.027	0.085
Descriptive variable: Gender	0.168*	0.015	0.045	0.008
Descriptive variable: Age	0.496*	0.003	0.022	0.000
Descriptive variable: Education	0.072	0.033	0.022	0.673

NOTE: Unless otherwise noted, bootstrap results are based on 488 stratified bootstrap samples.* significant at $\alpha = 0.05$.
Source: Own

differ when the decision will be made by man or woman business owner (F9) due to different risk perception. This evaluation gave us a suggestion of decision - making process according following steps:

Step 1: The business owner evaluate the situation according its previous business experience, which is closely connected with life experience (age of respondent, F1)

Step 2: In this step the owner has to make a crucial decision, which segment in company have to be supported and which have to be reduced due to unstable situation. (Financial planning for sustainability, F2).

Table 8. Rotated Component Matrix

Factor / Loading	F1 8.280%	F2 7.503%	F3 7.221%	F4 6.880%	F5 6.327%	F6 6.300%	F7 6.034%	F8 6.009%	F9 5.414%
Descriptive variable: Experience	0.908								
Descriptive variable: Age	0.894								
Financial planning: A concrete percentage of growth of financial investment		0.813							
Financial planning: A concrete percentage of reduction of financial investment		0.779							
Main motive: Extra benefits to yields			0.743						
Main motive: Payback period			0.626						
Investment category: Company development (Financial anti - crisis management)				0.708					
Descriptive variable: Education					0.715				
Anti - crisis management: use of internal resources during crisis						0.745			
Anti - crisis management: A ratio between external and internal financial resources						0.683			
Investment category: Equipment and Technologies (Financial anti - crisis management)							0.816		
Main motive: Interest rate in bank								0.724	
Main motive: Tax deductions								0.717	
Descriptive variable: Gender									0.783

Source: Own

Step 3: When decided, which segments are prioritized, the main indicators have to be set to create optimal financial scenarios, because of financial limits (Limited budget, indicators, F3).

Step 4: Within unstable business environment, such as crisis situation, COVID - 19 is necessary to survive the restrictions, so the owner focuses on company development to survive (F4).

Step 5: To be able to decide for sustainability, the education and knowledge is needed to make right decisions (F5).

Step 6: Each investments, planned in the step 4 need an appropriate mixture of company capital (F6).

Step 7: When first wave of crisis situation is overcoming, company could focus on technology and innovations (F7).

Step 8: Innovative projects are costly, so external resources are needed and owner have to think about advantage of the cheapest resources. (F8)

Step 9: The final project and the decision will differ according the gender of the owner (F9).

Hypotheses Evaluation

To evaluate all the hypotheses a statistical tests and models has been used. Firstly, we computed data distribution, according to each hypothesis criteria. Secondly, Cramer V tests were made, to establish which factors affect the final relationship between variables.

Hypothesis 1: Business experience has an influence on a financial management decision - a decision of structure of external and internal resources.

The relationship was examined in the table 7. Hypothesis one have to be rejected because the relationship between business experience and indicator "a ratio between external and internal financial resources between external and internal financial resources" wasn't confirmed, when the Cramer V test wasn't found as significant (Cramer V = 0.150, sig. = 0.121). It means that this type of decision is connected with other factors, predominantly the age of respondents (Cramer V = 0.496, sig. = 0.000).

Hypothesis 2: Business experience has an influence on a change in priorities within investment categories after crisis.

The evaluation is based in analysis in the table 7. Hypothesis 2 have to be confirmed. (Cramer V = 0.156, sig. = 0.005). There is a statistically significant tie between experience and prioritization in investment activities, but the value of coefficient is rather low. Nowadays, most of respondents is solving a company development within unstable business conditions. Unfortunately, the lack of internal resources stopped other investment projects to different segments.

SOLUTIONS AND RECOMMENDATIONS

This case study confirmed a knowledge from the study of McKenzie (2006), when factor analysis extracted as first factor a combination of an age and business experience. The factor analysis also suggested a crisis behaviour of business owners, so we are able to precise steps of financial management within crisis situation as suggested by Seisebaeva (2015). We summarized those actions to lead to sustainable financial planning according following 3 steps (Table 9).

Table 9. Updated Steps in Crisis Financial Management

Step	Actions Named By Seisebaeva (2015)	Actions Added (Based On The Case Study)
Financial anti - crisis management	Prevention action	Main motives for investment wasn't included (Table 5) Investment limits wasn't set (Table 6)
Anti - crisis management	Activities for stability	Concrete actions - a ratio between external and internal resources
Financial planning	Actions for future development	Investment segments, priorities were added (Table 7), change management

Source: Own

This could help in decision making in financial management. We recommend to evaluate main motives for investments at first. Following that, each business owner is able to make decision how much amount of profit will invest for the future (set the limit of internal resources). In the next step a mixture of available resources is set and a business owner is able to react to current unstable situation to change priorities to support sustainability of financial resources within crisis and change management principles and in some cases they behave as zombies (Blažková & Dvouletý, 2020).

FUTURE RESEARCH DIRECTIONS

The limitations of the study can be seen in the validation of results, where they describe the subjective opinion of each respondent. This choice was appropriate for the chosen research problem which was to identify different behavioural models for social groups support based on their socio - economic and sociocultural backgrounds (Alaslani & Collins, 2017). The future research will be expanding the existing knowledge about crisis financial management in combination with factor of public support, offered by national government during COVID - 19 restrictions.

CONCLUSION

Financial behaviour within uncertain situation as COVID - 19 pandemic had shown the significant change in financial behaviour in companies, when they prefer to trust internal resources and they reinvest to segments, which could help them to survive in that very hard situation. Some decisions could be affected by public support (especially in area of compensation bonuses for employees), but further research could confirm if those respondents combined just internal resources to survive uncertainty or they use public support. Unfortunately, the lack of internal resources stopped other investment activities.

REFERENCES

Abosede, A. J., Obasan, K. A., & Alese, O. J. (2016). Strategic Management and Small and Medium Enterprises (SMEs) Development: A Review of Literature. *International Review of Management and Business Research*, *5*(1), 315–335.

Afonina, A., & Chalupský, V. (2013). Investigation of strategic management tools and techniques. *Acta Universitatis Agriculturae et Silviculturae Mendelianae Brunensis*, *61*(4), 833–840. doi:10.11118/actaun201361040833

Alaslani, M., & Collins, J. (2017). The Blocked Mobility Hypothesis and Muslim Immigrant Entrepreneurship in Sydney, Australia. *Review of Integrative Business and Economics Research*, *6*(3), 333–357.

Alkan, A., & Bozkurt, Ö. Ç. (2013). The Choice and Use of Strategic Planning Tools and Techniques in Turkish SMEs According to Attitudes of Executives. *Procedia: Social and Behavioral Sciences*, *99*, 1016–1025. doi:10.1016/j.sbspro.2013.10.575

Alkaraan, F., & Northcott, D. (2006). Capital investment decision - making: A role for strategic management accounting. *The British Accounting Review, 38*(2), 49–73. doi:10.1016/j.bar.2005.10.003

Androniceanu, A., & Drăgulănescu, I. V. (2012). Sustainability of the Organizational Changes in the Context of Global Economic Crisis. *Amfiteatru Economic, 14*(32), 366–379.

Ansoff, H. I. (1965). *Corporate strategy*. Prentice Hall.

Aragón-Correa, J. A., & Sharma, S. (2003). A Contingent Resource - Based View of Proactive Corporate Environmental Strategy. The Academy of Management Review, 28(1), 71 - 88.

Astanaqulov, O., & Asatullayev, K. (2020). Improving Investment Decisions in the Context of the Coronavirus Pandemy. *International Finance and Accounting, 3*(28), 1–12.

Barney, J. B. (1991). Firm Resources and Sustained Competitive Advantage. *Journal of Management, 17*(1), 99–120. doi:10.1177/014920639101700108

Bartosova, V., & Kral, P. (2017). Methodological framework of financial analysis results objectification in Slovak Republic. *J. Mod. Account. Audit., 13*, 394–400.

Berisha, Q. A., Kutllovci, E., & Shiroka, P. J. (2017). Strategic Management Tools and Techniques: A Comparative Analysis of Empirical Studies. *Croatian Economic Survey, 19*(1), 67–99. doi:10.15179/ces.19.1.3

Blažková, I., & Dvouletý, O. (2020). Zombies: Who are they and how do firms become zombies? *Journal of Small Business Management*, 1–27. Advance online publication. doi:10.1080/00472778.2019.1696100

Blechová, B. (2011). The influence of tax policy on the emergence of financial crisis. In *13th International Conference on Finance and Banking*. Karvina: SU OPF.

Boyatzis, R., & McKee, A. (2011). Neuroscience and leadership: The promise of insights. *Ivey Business Journal, 75*(1), 1–3.

Brinckmann, J., Grichnik, D., & Kapsa, D. (2010). Should entrepreneurs plan or just storm the castle? A Meta - analysis on contextual factors impacting the business planning - performance relationship in small firms. *Journal of Business Venturing, 25*(1), 24–40. doi:10.1016/j.jbusvent.2008.10.007

Brown, S. L., & Eisenhardt, K. M. (1998). *Competing on the edge: strategy as structured chaos*. Harvard Business School Press.

Burke, W. W., & Litwin, G. H. (1992). A causal model of organizational performance and change. *Journal of Management, 18*(3), 523–545. doi:10.1177/014920639201800306

Carr, C., Kolehmainen, K., & Mitchell, F. (2010). Strategic investment decision making practices: A contextual approach. *Management Accounting Research, 21*(3), 167–184. doi:10.1016/j.mar.2010.03.004

Chakravarty, S., & Meifang, X. (2011). Determinants of Profit Reinvestment by Small Businesses in Emerging Economies. *Financial Management, 40*(3), 553–590. doi:10.1111/j.1755-053X.2011.01153.x

Chandler, A. D. (1962). *Strategy and structure: Chapters in the history of American enterprise*. M.I.T. Press.

Chen, S. (1995). An empirical examination of capital budgeting techniques: Impact of investment types and firm characteristics. *The Engineering Economist, 40*(2), 145–170. doi:10.1080/00137919508903142

Cohen, M. D. (2006). What's Different is Routine. *Industrial and Corporate Change, 15*(2), 387–390. doi:10.1093/icc/dtl001

Cohen, M. D., & Bacdayan, P. (1994). Organizational Routines Are Stored As Procedural Memory: Evidence from a Laboratory Study. *Organization Science, 5*(4), 554–568. doi:10.1287/orsc.5.4.554

Cooremans, C. (2011). Make it strategic! Financial investment logic is not enough. *Energy Efficiency, 4*(4), 473–492. doi:10.100712053-011-9125-7

Damanpour, F. (1991). Organizational innovation: A Meta - analysis of effects of determinants and moderators. *Academy of Management Journal, 34*(3), 555–590.

De Bodt, E., & Bouquin, H. (2001). Le contrôle de l'investissement. In *Images de l'investissement, Ouvrage collectif coordonné par G. Charreaux* (pp. 115–166). Vuibert.

Delmar, F., & Shane, S. (2003). Does Business Planning Facilitate the Development of New Ventures? *Strategic Management Journal, 24*(12), 1165–1185. doi:10.1002mj.349

FAPI. (2020). *Průzkum COVID - 19: Víme, jak koronavirus zasáhl podnikatele a firmy*. Retrieved from https://fapi.cz/pruzkum-covid-19-vime-jak-koronavirus-zasahl-podnikatele-a-firmy/

Fazzari, S. M., Hubbard, R. G., & Peterson, B. C. (1998). Financing Constraints and Corporate Investment. *Brookings Papers on Economic Activity, 1*, 141–195.

Fiet, J. O. (2001). The pedagogical side of entrepreneurship theory. *Journal of Business Venturing, 16*(2), 101–117. doi:10.1016/S0883-9026(99)00042-7

Gill, A. S., Sharma, S. P., & Mathur, N. (2012). The Impact of Debt Policy on the Investment Decision of Small Business Owners in India. *International Research Journal of Finance and Economics*, (97), 6–13.

Golsorkhi, D., Rouleau, L., Seidl, D., & Vaara, E. (2010). *Cambridge handbook of strategy as practice*. Cambridge University Press. doi:10.1017/CBO9780511777882

Gupta, J., Gregoriou, A., & Healey, J. (2015). Forecasting bankruptcy for SMEs using hazard function: To what extent does size matter? *Review of Quantitative Finance and Accounting, 45*(4), 845–869. doi:10.100711156-014-0458-0

Hasuch, H., & Pyka, A. (2007). *Elgar companion to Neo - Schumpeterian Economics*. Edward Elgar Publishing.

Häuser, S. (2007). *Krizové řízení v turbulentním prostředí.Studijní opora*. Slezská univerzita v Opavě. Matematický ústav v Opavě.

Havlíček, K. (2011). Strategické řízení podniku. *Moderní řízení*, 32 - 34.

Holmes, H., & Ferriill, M. (2005). The application of operation and technology road - mapping to aid Singaporean SMEs identify and select emerging technologies. *Technological Forecasting and Social Change, 72*(3), 349–357. doi:10.1016/j.techfore.2004.08.010

Hurst, D. K. (2002). *Crisis: meeting the challenge of organizational change*. Harvard Business School Press.

Illés, M. (2016). The Real Reinvestment Rate Assumption as a Hidden Pitfall. Theory, Methodology. *Practice*, *12*(1), 47–60.

Jensen, M. C. (1986). Agency costs of free cash flow, corporate finance, and takeovers. *The American Economic Review*, *76*, 323–329.

Jun, S. P., Seo, J. H., & Son, J. K. (2013). A study of the SME technology road - mapping program to strengthen R&D planning capability of Korean SMEs. *Technological Forecasting and Social Change*, *80*(5), 1002–1014. doi:10.1016/j.techfore.2012.10.022

Kaczmarek, J. (2014). Czynnik czasu a modyfikacja dynamicznych miar oceny efektywności inwestycji. Zeszyty Naukowe Uniwersytetu Szczecińskiego. Finanse, Rynki Finansowe. *Ubezpieczenia*, *66*, 111–121.

Kaplan, S. N., & Zingales, L. (1997). Do financing constraints explain why investment is correlated with cash flow? *The Quarterly Journal of Economics*, *112*, 169–215. doi:10.1162/003355397555163

Kędzierski, L. (2017). Determinanty oddziaływania inwestycji finansowych na maksymalizację wartości rynkowej przedsiębiorstwa. *Studia Gdańskie. Wizje i rzeczywistość*, *14*, 179 - 196.

Keeley, R. H., & Roure, J. B. (1990). Management, Strategy, and Industry Structure As Influences on the Success of New Firms: A Structural Model. *Management Science*, *36*(10), 1256–1267. doi:10.1287/mnsc.36.10.1256

Kimberly, J., & Cook, J. M. (2008). Organizational Measurement and the Implementation of Innovations in Mental Health Services. *Administration and Policy in Mental Health*, *35*(1-2), 11–20. doi:10.100710488-007-0143-x PMID:17990096

Kolumber, Š., Tkačíková, L., & Menšík, M. (2020). Increasing the Competitiveness of Businesses By Using The Balance Scorecard Methodology. *Economics Management Innovation*, *12*(3), 49–68.

Krasniqi, E., & Kume, A. (2013). Entrepreneurship and Strategic Management In Emerging Economies: Kosovo's Perspective. *Annales Universitatis Apulensis Series Oeconomica*, *15*(1), 267–279. doi:10.29302/oeconomica.2013.15.1.22

Krupski, R. (2005). *Zarządzanie przedsiębiorstwem w turbulentnym otoczeniu. Ku superelastycznej organizacji*. PWE.

Lazonick, W. (2014). Profits without prosperity. *Harvard Business Review*, *92*(9), 46–55.

Liu, J., & Pang, D. (2009). Financial Factors and Company Investment Decisions in Transitional China. *Managerial and Decision Economics*, *30*(2), 91–108. doi:10.1002/mde.1440

Lo, F. Y. (2013). The dynamic adjustment of environment, strategy, structure, and resources on firm performance. *The International Entrepreneurship and Management Journal*, *9*(2), 217–227. doi:10.100711365-012-0222-7

MacGregor Pelikánová, R. (2019). Corporate Social Responsibility Information in Annual Reports in the EU - A Czech Case Study. *Sustainability*, *11*(1), 237. doi:10.3390u11010237

March, J. G. (1991). Exploration and Exploitation in Organizational Learning. *Organization Science, 2*(1), 71–87. doi:10.1287/orsc.2.1.71

McKenzie, D. J. (2006). Disentangling age, cohort, and time effects in the additive model. *Oxford Bulletin of Economics and Statistics, 68*(4), 473–495. doi:10.1111/j.1468-0084.2006.00173.x

Meyer, R. L. (1979). A Note on Capital Budgeting Techniques and the Reinvestment Rate. *The Journal of Finance, 34*(5), 1251–1254. doi:10.1111/j.1540-6261.1979.tb00070.x

Nelson, R. R. (1991). Why do firms differ, and how does it matter? *Strategic Management Journal, 12*(2), 61–74. doi:10.1002mj.4250121006

Ogbadu, E., Aduku, D., & Nafiu, A. (2017). Small Firms' Strategy Adoption and Business Outcomes in Business Games: An Empirical Investigation from Nigeria. Asian Journal of Economics. *Business and Accounting, 4*(1), 1–13.

Osterwalder, A., Pigneur, Y., & Clark, T. (2010). *Business model generation: a handbook for visionaries, game changers, and challengers*. Wiley.

Pakšiová, R. (2017). The Critical Analysis of Profit for its Allocation Decision - Making. *Scientific Annals of Economics and Business, 64*(s1), 41–56. doi:10.1515aeb-2017-0039

Perera, S., Harrison, G., & Poole, M. (1997). Customer - focused manufacturing strategy and the use of operations - based non - financial performance measures: A research note. *Accounting, Organizations and Society, 22*(6), 557–572. doi:10.1016/S0361-3682(96)00048-7

Pfeffer, J., & Salanick, G. R. (1978). *The External Control of Organization*. Harper and Row.

Phillips, J. (2013). *Technology foresight for small - to medium - sized enterprises*. LAP Lambert Academic Publishing.

Pittaway, L., & Cope, J. (2016). Entrepreneurship Education. *International Small Business Journal: Researching Entrepreneurship, 25*(5), 479–510. doi:10.1177/0266242607080656

Pokorná, P. (2020). Financial Sources for Company Scale - Up. In J. Šebestová (Ed.), *Developing Entrepreneurial Competencies for Start - Ups and Small Business* (pp. 97–108). Advances in Business Strategy and Competitive Advantage. IGI Global. doi:10.4018/978-1-7998-2714-6.ch007

Popescu, C. R. G., & Banța, V. C. (2019). Performance Evaluation of the Implementation of the 2013/34/ EU Directive in Romania on the Basis of Corporate Social Responsibility Reports. *Sustainability, 11*, 2531. doi:10.3390u11092531

Popper, R. (2008). *Foresight methodology. The Handbook of Technology Foresight. Northhampton.* Edward Elgar.

Porter, M. E. (1996). Competitive Advantage, Agglomeration Economies, and Regional Policy. *International Regional Science Review, 19*(1 - 2), 85 - 90.

Rigby, D., & Bilodeau, B. (2018). *Management tools and trends 2017*. Bain & Company. Retrieved from http://www.bain.com/publications/articles/management-tools-and-trends-2017.aspx

Rylková, Ž. & Chobotová, M. (2011). Přizpůsobování organizací na změny v konkurenčním prostředí. *Periodica Academica, 6*, 65 - 82.

Sandberg, P., & Söderström, M. (2003). Industrial energy efficiency: The need for investment decision support from a manager perspective. *Energy Policy, 31*(15), 1623–1634. doi:10.1016/S0301-4215(02)00228-8

Šebestová, J. (2018). Strategic Management Tools in the Small and Medium Sized Enterprises: A Long - Term View. In International Day of Science 2018 - Economics, Management, Innovation. In *Proceedings of the International Scientific Conference*. Olomouc: Moravian University College Olomouc.

Šebestová, J., & Antonová, B. (2011). Adaptabilita podnikání v reakci na turbulentní politicko - ekonomické prostředí v kontextu strategického řízení. *Periodica Academica, 6*(1), 218–230.

Šebestová, J., & Nowáková, K. (2013). Dynamic strategy and sustainable business development: Lessons learned from the crisis. *Acta Universitatis Agriculturae et Silviculturae Mendelianae Brunensis, 61*(7), 2827–2833. doi:10.11118/actaun201361072827

Seisebaeva, N. G. (2015). Analysis of theoretical approaches to the definition of the essence of the concept of crisis financial management in the enterprise. *Bulletin of the Zaporizhzhya National University, 4*, 116–123.

Simon, H. (1979). Rational Decision Making in Business Organizations. *The American Economic Review, 69*(4), 493–513.

Sorrell, S. (2000). *Reducing barriers to energy efficiency in public and private organisations*. Final Report, SPRU, JOS3CT970022, Research funded in part by the European Commission in the framework of the Non-Nuclear Energy Programme JOULE III.

Stenfors, S., Tanner, L., Syrjänen, M., Seppälä, T., & Haapalinna, I. (2007). Executive views concerning decision support tools. *European Journal of Operational Research, 181*(2), 929–938. doi:10.1016/j.ejor.2006.06.024

Stonehouse, G., & Pemberton, J. (2002). Strategic planning in SMEs - some empirical findings. *Management Decision, 40*(9), 853–861. doi:10.1108/00251740210441072

Swayne, L. E., Duncan, W., & Ginter, P. M. (2006). *Strategic management of health care organizations* (5th ed.). Blackwell Pub.

Tidd, J., Bessant, J., & Pavitt, K. (2007). *Řízení inovací*. Computer Press.

Vaara, E., & Whittington, R. (2012). Strategy as practice: Taking social practices seriously. *The Academy of Management Annals, 6*(1), 285–336. doi:10.5465/19416520.2012.672039

Valaskova, K., Kliestik, T., Svabova, L., & Adamko, P. (2018). Financial Risk Measurement and Prediction Modelling for Sustainable Development of Business Entities Using Regression Analysis. *Sustainability, 10*(7), 2144. doi:10.3390u10072144

Vishnevskiy, K., & Egorova, O. (2015). *Strategic Foresight for SMEs: Choice of the Most Relevant Methods*. XXVI ISPIM Conference - Shaping the Frontiers of Innovation Management, Budapest, Hungary.

Walker, J. S., Check, H. F. Jr, & Randall, K. L. (2011). Does the Internal Rate of Return Calculation Require a Reinvestment Rate Assumption? There Is Still No Consensus. *West Chester University: Pennsylvania Economic Association Proceedings Annual Conference*, 118 - 130.

Wellalage, N. H., & Reddy, K. (2020). Determinants of profit reinvestment undertaken by SMEs in the small island countries. *Global Finance Journal*, *43*, 1–13. doi:10.1016/j.gfj.2017.11.001

Winter, S. G. (2000). The Satisficing Principle in Capability Learning. *Strategic Management Journal*, *21*(10-11), 981–996. doi:10.1002/1097-0266(200010/11)21:10/11<981::AID-SMJ125>3.0.CO;2-4

Xu, S., Cavusgil, S. T., & White, J. C. (2006). The impact of strategic fit among strategy, structure, and processes on multinational corporation performance: A multi - method assessment. *Journal of International Marketing*, *14*(2), 1–31. doi:10.1509/jimk.14.2.1

Zhou, W. (2017). Institutional environment, public - private hybrid forms, and entrepreneurial reinvestment in a transition economy. *Journal of Business Venturing*, *32*(2), 197–214. doi:10.1016/j.jbusvent.2016.11.002

Zott, C., Amit, R., & Massa, L. (2011). The Business Model: Recent Developments and Future Research. *Journal of Management*, *37*(4), 1019–1042. doi:10.1177/0149206311406265

KEY TERMS AND DEFINITIONS

Business Survival: It is one of business objective. Business survival refers to keeping the business operating for a certain amount of time, especially when some crisis situation comes.

External Financial Resources: A source of financing of business activity, which comes outside of business unit such as bank (loans, guaranties), friends, family, business angels, and public support (grants and subsidies).

Financial Planning: It is a process to achieve financial goals and planned amount of profit or financial ratios. This planning covers all activities and resources needed to manage all the financial process.

Financial Sustainability: It means selling a product or service at a price that not only cover expenses but also creates a profit. In the crisis situation it means to meet financial obligation within have other alterative possibilities to fund your activities (be able to be self-financed).

Internal Financial Resources: A source of financing of business activity, which comes from own profit, own capital or from selling own assets.

Investment: The role of investment is to generate the profit in the future. An investment is planned action for the long period. The investment could have different form (financial or nonfinancial assets).

Investment Segments: There are main investment types, or asset classes, that you can choose from, each with distinct characteristics, risks, and benefits. In this chapter they are closely connected with strategy goals as well as marketing, company development, human resources, and equipment and technologies.

Reinvestment: The act or practice of taking profits or other proceeds from investments and making other investments with them.

Chapter 4
Sustain or Perish:
A Simple Choice – Collective Action for Sustainability, Not Wishful Thinking

Vishwas Gupta
Lovely Professional University, India

Amit M. Bhattacharya
RIDA, India

ABSTRACT

Without being negative or cursing the flight of capitalism and technology, this chapter endeavors to record and analyze a few recent issues and their impact on human existence and suggests some simple measures that might restructure value-based consumption-production patterns to ensure livable conditions and sustainability for the seven billion people and the next generations on this beautiful planet Earth until the next ice age hits. Mankind is left with no alternative but rectifying the partially 'corrupted' portion of 'mind-ware' and reshaping the man nature relationship for real survival and growth.

INTRODUCTION

Till date, homo - sapiens is a natural creature and hence, Man - Nature relationship is inseparable. If, in the next few decades designer babies are produced enemas in laboratories like currency notes and their life and living gets programmed by Artificial Intelligence; the issue of 'Reimagining Man - Nature relationship will become more complex provided, the mankind may reach up to that future with its present self - destructive activities. The human civilization is in deep trouble since the invention of steam - power as civilization is continuously threatened by three of its in - built frenemies i.e., 'greed', 'intelligence', and 'curiosity' which is capable of transforming known and unknown natural resources into various tangible and intangible things. While, on the one hand, this intelligence and curiosity has minimized physical toil and drudgery; the greed has rapidly pushed the flora - fauna system to the verge of extinction on the other hand. The interplay of skewed perception of 'growth and 'development' is continuously repositioning the mankind against the Laws of Nature because ever - inflating human Ego

DOI: 10.4018/978-1-7998-7951-0.ch004

has waged a war to exploit Nature's last unit of resources and for taming its infinite forces to its 'Greed'. The issue of "re - imagining man - nature relationship" has arisen as global concern because mankind is experiencing unbearable pressure and discomfort in its efforts for peaceful sustenance. In the frantic pursuit of wealth creation; not only the man - nature relationship is becoming extremely vitiated but also its social and emotional relationship is in regular jeopardy.

Mathematics, though basically based on postulates, establish that 'minus into minus results into plus.' A philosophical interpretation might be when someone achieves a 'positive' thing; one has to accept two in - built 'negatives' and that too, in a multiplied form. Strangely, Mathematics to manoeuvrability, physics to philosophy, physicality to spirituality all function with the objective of providing 'betterment of life and living for mankind.'

Some leading scientists have perceived the human mind like 'software' embedded in 'hardware' of physique existing within a given Natural ecosystem. The 'software' is getting progressively 'corrupted' due to greed - based acts and risking its own hardware resulting from 'Egocentricism.' Without being negative or cursing the flight of Capitalism and Technology, this paper endeavours to record and analyse few recent issues and its impact on human existence and suggests some simple measures that might re - structure value - based consumption - production pattern to ensure liveable conditions and sustainability for the 7 billion people and the next generations on this beautiful planet Earth until next ice - age hits. Mankind is left with no alternative but rectifying partially 'corrupted' portion of 'mind - ware' and re - shaping the man - nature relationship for real survival and growth.

BACKGROUND

Geoffrey Garver and Peter G. Brown point out "The global economy today is overwhelming the ability of the earth to maintain life's abundance (Brown & Garver, 2009). We are getting something terribly wrong (Donnelley, 2009)." The teachings of Mahatma Gandhi are becoming repeatedly highlighted in the context of latest report of international NGO Oxfam that raised accusing fingers to the developed countries in the perspective of imminent environmental catastrophe. The report came out almost on the same day when the United Nations initiated international conference to rectify the 'wrongs' caused to the global environment on 2nd December, 2019 in Madrid, Spain for initiating immediate and collective steps. Oxfam reveals that around 20 million people are displaced in the last decade following sudden and violent change in the environment. Such displacement is seven times higher than the people displaced due to volcanic eruption, earthquakes or frequent ethnic frictions in various parts of the world. One person is being displaced in every two seconds either due to Hurricane - cyclone or wild - fire conditions anywhere in the world. Bitterly criticizing the role played by the First World, the report says that they have not extended any helping hands to rescue the poor nations neither have they made any fund provisions to meet their exigencies. It further said that the rich nations rather added fuel to the fire and the poor nations paid heavy price for the same. The Secretary General of the UN, Mr. Antonio Gutteres, in his inaugural speech of the Conference said, "When the human civilization is facing extinction due to climate change, there is no option left to the mankind to choose between 'hope' and 'surrender'." He expressed his deep anguish as the people are continuously surrendering to the 'bad habits' at large being oblivious to the catastrophic climatic change. While, Ms. Nancy Pellosi, the Speaker of the US House of Representative, said that the world should not lose confidence on US though, Mr. Donald Trump had decided to walk out of Paris Accord recently. The glaring contradiction is while Ms. Pellosi is expressing hope; the State Secretary of the US recently declared that incremental global pollution would fetch 'huge financial gains' to their country and that withdrawal of the US from the Accord was a well - thought - out strategy in the interest of the nation.

The human history of development has been driven by 'endless desires and 'consumption' that led to complex economic relationships and interactions. The present precarious condition is direct by - product of reckless desires for convenience in material living over the centuries. Ruined Roman, Mayan, and Easter Island civilizations are glaring historical examples (Brown & Garver, 2009).

Right Relationship with the Ecosystem: The fundamental values of any relationship are perceived as (1) Respect (2) Trust (3) Care and (4) Dedication, which are repeatedly, advocated by the world's major religious and spiritual traditions for maintaining "right relationship" with anything existing on the Earth pointing out to the universally respected moral principles of the Golden Rule. The questions as to what the relationship be maintained and why it is so important to maintain such relationship; the graffiti becomes loud and clear - with Nature and for Living and Growing peacefully. The glorification of 'consumerism' by the capitalistic system undermines the primary values like 'respect' and 'care' and continuously fan the 'Ego'(show off) and 'Greed'(demanding more of everything without knowing the purpose of desire) among the people to break the phenomenon of 'Common - Wealth.' Over concentration of capacity of utilizing the natural resources for reaping huge wealth has poisoned the global environment to that extent that even the richest people now cannot escape its disastrous effects.

Australia: Growth for Whom and at Whose Cost

The 24 - hour rolling PM 2.5 averages at Bradfield Highway. Liverpool and Katoomba in Sydney were 582, 453, and 263 microgram/cubic meter, respectively, on 10th December; according to New South Wales government website. Authorities warned people with respiratory conditions, or heart problems, to stay indoors.

[Reported by TNN to AGENCIES, Times of India, 11th December, 2019]

Though 65 countries, including many of the European Union (EU) nations - France, Germany, Italy and UK - figured in the list of the nations which will work together on 'net zero emissions' by 2050, they hardly account for 37% of the global emissions. Pursuing all the countries to keep aside their current political differences and to find common consensus on the climatic issue, Guterres warned that the failure to operationalize Article 6 would undermine overall climate efforts and hence; the rule is compulsory for all. It is good to listen but what if, some powerful countries simply ignore the rules? The US has already opted out of the Paris Agreement without an iota of regret for flouting the rules framed by the international community for protecting the climate. 'Greta Thunberg is absolutely right in pointing out that the young people are bearing the brunt of leaders' failures. The adults have signed them onto suicide pact by proxy" (Bisht, 2009).

MAIN FOCUS OF THE CHAPTER

Part I: Building Highways of Mass Destruction

Scene I

However, the legitimacy of the Swedish teenager Greta Thunberg's movement gets critically underpinned by the mining extractions of coal from the last and biggest coal mine of the world situated at Botswana in Africa continent. Coincidentally, the extraction of this national wealth will start from the same day when Greta would raise her voice through BBC 'Today' program. The geophysics scientists had located the largest stock of coal in 1960s but it remained untouched till now because, the population of Botswana is only 2.3 million in 2019 and the export infrastructure of the country is underdeveloped. However, the situation will change very soon. Botswana administration is at seventh heaven perceiving the enormous stock of 'black diamond' and its imminent astronomical dividends. Augmenting GDP to the extent by selling and exporting coal will be the easiest way for the country. The Government knows well that the business of exporting coal to the South Africa would expand to a number of countries shortly. An assessment of the stock of coal was made in 2012 reveals that the stock is around 2850 crores of tons and it stands to be the highest among five large coal mines in other countries of the world. Surprisingly, only one small coal mine was being used to meet the demand of electricity of the country by the government till last year. Now a good number of multinational companies have assembled there to extract coal in a huge way side - lining the national government altogether. Consequently, the annually extracted stock of five lakh tons of coal will now exceed 12 lakh tons per annum. Further that few big players are waiting in disguise to enter into the mining business in Botswana. Under the condition it may easily be understood as to what would be the disastrous scenario when all the miners would exploit the coal stock jointly.

The global environmentalists stand horrified thinking of the future of African environment as well as the imminent calamity for the world at large. They understand well that if they fail to hold the global warming at the 1.50 Celsius, it may go more than 3.50 Celsius by the end of the 21 century which will result in widespread catastrophe. Burning of the quantum of coal from Botswana mines will upload extra 8400 tons of carbon - di - oxide in the environment and cause perennial physical and mental sufferings for the people globally. The coal procuring country is, of course, South Africa because of its fast - depleting oil stock. Botswana needs foreign currency and South Africa is compelled to keep its industries running through adequate electricity supply. The 'comparative advantage' theory is serving the economic interest of the duo without having iota of respect for the environment issues. A leading policymaker of Botswana, protecting the emerging reckless mining activities commented that the rich nations had continuously exploited the natural resources for achieving magnificent economic well - being without caring for the environmental issues, and when a poor nation like Botswana was working hard for betterment, the rich nations and the environmentalists' criticism held no legitimacy. Greta Thunberg's war against polluters seems to be extremely difficult and it looks like David is throwing small pebbles to stop the atrocities of roaring Goliaths.

Scene II

In its April 2019 issue, the world - renowned magazine National Geography published a spine - chilling research paper titled 'This is the world's most destructive oil operation - and it's growing'. The paper detailed the quantum of sinful activities committed to the Mother Earth and the mankind as such in the name of Economic Development (Taft, 2017). Alberta Tar Sands, the largest industrial project located in western Canada. This oil extracting industry has consciously attempted to reversing the man - nature relationship to that extent that the surrounding forests, rivers, wetlands, and lakes have become polluted and contaminated and permeating its heating effects globally through 'ripple effect'. In this case, 'the chain of refineries and waste materials spread out from it, affect 'as far west as China and as far south as Texas.' The environmental experts observed that the surface of the earth is stripped of all animal or plant habitats around life - giving 168 km long Athabaska river (Brown & Garver, 2009).

The disturbed ecological hazard has also affected the social relationships among the people of the area. Huge migration of workers in the sites has resulted in steep crime rates. The big cities like Calgary, Fort McMurray, Edmonton and Fort Chipewyan are witnessing abnormally rising cost of living, prostitution and homelessness. Further that human trafficking, drug peddling and addiction, reckless alcohol consumption and highway accidents along with widespread depression, frustration, xenophobia and rigors of shift work are also increasing which is permeating a deep sense of insecurity and uncertainty within the community.

India: Ostrich - Head in Sand

Deadly nitrous oxide has attained 123% and carbon dioxide levels are higher than that was before four lakh years and situation is getting worse; a responsible minister's declaration in the Lower House leave the whole world clueless. The statement came at the time when Conference for climate control is undergoing in Madrid. Any sensible man knows that Aerosol is polluting the air, water, vegetation and anything and everything and causing irreversible mutation in organic ecosystem, such comments really stunned every Indian being vulnerable to range of sickness and untimely and painful death following Greenhouse gases. In the year 2018, the government of India transferred the 64% of accumulated fund of National Green Tribunal, which was kept exclusively to augment atmospheric quality and which was non - transferable by force of law, to make up the deficit of GST for the year. This single act of the GOI shows the seriousness of the system in attaining the quality of life of its citizens.

Lost Fundamental Right to Breathe - in Fresh Air

Only on 25th of November, 2019, the two judges bench (comprising of Justice Arun Mishra and Justice Deepak Gupta) of the Supreme Court had harshly told the government to 'opt for killing the citizens of Delhi - NCR region by bombing than to kill them in the gas chamber.' and 'if the government was incapable of fixing the 'wrongs' within ten days they would hold no right to be on their designated posts.' All the capital cities and even C class cities in India are facing Air Quality Index ranging from 256 to 494, which is well past disastrous AQI level of 200 on most of the days in winter. It is well known fact that a physician can treat a disease when the patient accepts the truth and undergoes proper diagnostic process. First and foremost, thing is to 'accepting' the ailing atmospheric conditions and initiating serious operation against it. For the last forty years innumerable rounds of national and international talks and agreements have taken place internationally but the non - acceptance of seriousness of the pollution and its impact on health and life has kept on distorting the way of living. Rampant consumerism and the emission of CO_2 are increasing regularly. The adverse man - nature relationship can be easily reversed provided the mankind resorts to 'common - sense' and 'austerity' immediately. 'But in the world where the rich countries are busy in negotiating to buy and sell Greenland, wildfire of Amazon forest is viewed as commercially beneficial issue, respiratory troubles take a backseat behind glittering firecracker shows; talking about saving the climate and thus planet Earth religiously is a ridiculous issue.' Hence, the desperate Meenakshi Reddy Mahadevan who lives in Delhi writes 'Get out of Mumbai, see that you do, the sea is coming for me and you. Get out of Bengaluru I'd recommend, before the water comes to an end. Move to Goa? It's pretty dire, you might end up dead in garbage fire; so, get out? Why bother? Just choose your tomb" (Madhavan, 2007).

However, Prakash Javadekar's statement is in total contrast with Global Burden of Disease Study 2017, titled "Impact of air pollution on deaths, disease burden and life expectancy across the states of India". These studies clearly found that incremental polluting elements is linked to deaths and its shorter life spans too. The study was funded by Bill & Melinda Gates Foundation and Indian Council of Medical Research - that exclusively comes under the Union Ministry of Health and Family Welfare.

Children in Delhi Smoke 10 Cigarettes A Day Just by Breathing

The study said: 1•24 million deaths in India in 2017, which were 12•5% of the total deaths, were attributable to air pollution, including 0•67 million from ambient particulate matter pollution and 0•48 million from household air pollution (Rampal, 2019).

However, writing the eulogy for PM on 4th December, 2019, the same Prakash Javadekar writes, "The central government has launched National Clean Air Programme (NCAP) as a long term, time - bound, national level strategy with targets to achieve 20%, to 30% reduction in PM 10 and PM 2.5 concentration by 2024."

The minister accepted that the Centre had allocated Rs. 3,175 crores for 2019 - 20 to fund pollution control activities Rs. 10 crores each to 210 assorted cities in India. When the very minister in charge is in dilemma about his statements and commitments, it is quite understandable to what extent the action would be and how much amount would be utilized to control pollution and human activities in the coming five years. When such a massive budget is allocated for the very purpose, does 'All is well' approach of the minister hold any merit?

As of now, the man - nature relationship at its worse and heading to worst, faster than estimation, exposing 7 billion people on Earth to passive euthanasia primarily due to man - made conditions itself.

Part II: Disconnect Dysfunction, Failure, and Hope

After Great Recession, political economy has been showing particular inclination towards 'growth economy.' The political leaders and the policy makers are in fierce competition in exploiting natural resources to attaining growth parameters like GDP, GNP, FDI investment etc. to accumulate more and more wealth than their competitors. The most logical questions as to what mankind needs and how will it be achieved and to what extent have lost in thin air in the rat - race of monetary value - addition. This has led to pervasive disconnect with the nature, communities, societies and individuals and dysfunction of the well - defined and well - designed natural and man - made systems. Amassing 'peso' (wealth) at the cost of 'peace' (social stability) has failed a large number of economies worldwide although, such happens in disguise.

Even few decades back, atmospheric calamity was perceived the dynamism of nature however, gradually the international community realized that flood, famine, wild - fire, hunger, rising oceanic levels, a range of devastating diseases are mostly man - made fallouts. In this blitzkrieg of global growth economy, poverty and death from hunger have grown manifolds. Recently, the Secretary General of the UN, Antonio Guteres has alerted that not less than thirty million people are facing acute starvation in the wake of 2021 AD. Around 2.6 million people have lost their lives due to Covid19 but the death by starvation may surpass the number beyond imagination. In spite of that, the 21st century has witnessed overproduction of food grains, 69 crore people are facing food shortages and 8 crore people are suffering from acute hunger. In both the cases, food - shortage was not the cause of such starvation rather, the decision about the procurement and proper distribution of food articles by the policy makers were major reasons. Guteres alerted critically that the famine and starvation was created artificially thereby pushing a large section of people to starvation.

When can death by starvation be a negligible issue? History speaks when Winston Churchill retrieved million tons of food grains from India to feed the World War II soldiers or Mao Je Dong deployed red army to annihilate the rightists in China. The incidents proved that when the conflict takes at a larger scale in the society, the food security gets neglected. The UN report reveals that all the 36 countries which are facing acute starvation, involved in long drawn wars and civil wars. The countries like Sudan, Yemen, Congo, and Afghanistan are the foremost ones that are passing through worst wars, internal conflicts and destabilization. Hunger has posed a greatest menace in the region. A vicious cycle of conflict for food - shortage and food - shortage leading to conflict is going on endlessly over there whereas world is witnessing glut in food grains and allied products.

India is no exception. The country, already being ethnically and religiously fragmented for ages, went on blindly copying the western way of life and economic model thereby endangering its social texture as well as its economic harmony. Although; India's most of the major religious texts emphasize upon 'austerity' as a normal way of life and respect the 'Mother Nature' in their every activity thereby connecting their sacred relationship with nature, the teachings and traditions gradually drifted away from practice and mostly turned to 'ritualistic' following tremendous bombardment of western thoughts and capitalistic persuasion for materialistic way of life. Resultant permeation of tacit competition, egocentricism and belittling age - old socio - religious values not only disconnected individuals within their respective societies but also skewed their mass behaviour to ignore and disrespect the Nature. Right from their dressing, eating, living and behaving sense got altogether changed and to manifest their 'progressiveness' and 'modernity' most of the Indians opted to ignore, ridicule and look down those age - old teachings and practices that defined the 'spirit of India'.

Politicians and the policy makers of India, being grossly influenced by the western models of 'growth' often hold short - term view, limited to their working tenure mostly of five - year terms. Although they know that the industries and companies to work for longer periods and most of the times their technology and huge capital investment result in long - term harm to the climate and make the societies more and more vulnerable and dysfunctional; they fear to bring fundamental changes in the policies, technological innovations and in the production system because that may adversely affect their political career forever. They are, in unison with the mega industries and mammoth corporate houses, promote consumerism in view of their 'personal gains' as well as to manifest the country's phenomenal economic growth to impress the western world for attracting more and more international debts, assistance and investments without an iota of care for its adverse impact on the consumption - production pattern of this poor country.

Consumer - culture tremendously abhors philosophies where continuous fulfilment of desires is considered to be the central constituent of a sinful life. Hence, people, to their detriment, develop a culture in which consumption is regarded as the end in itself and ethics that present other worthwhile ends are out rightly discarded. Here lies the crux of partially 'corrupt' mind - wire.

Where People Fail

Peter Kahn, psychology professor, University of Washington undertook landmark research on man - nature relationships observes "I first began to recognize the problem of environmental generational amnesia. How could these kids not know it?" (Matei, 2017)

Similarly, it was largely hailed by the press and the academics, but its specific proposals to change consumption patterns received 'only scant attention.' The proposal on mainly focused on the 'measures such as eco - labelling, assessing the full life - cycle of products, reducing wasteful packaging of materials, and encouraging recycling at the consumer level. In spite of that the intension of the proposal was noble, it failed to make any visible impact because environmental policy seriously accepted that the consumers' desires were immutable even when the destructive consequences of fulfilling them were undeniable.

"Or perhaps the problem of over - consumption is considered simply intractable." Elaborating the dreadful account of reckless consumption pattern, the author writes "The strain placed upon energy resources as a result of this increased activity is unsustainable at this rate. Every day the worldwide economy burns an amount of energy the planet required 10,000 days to create, while twenty - seven years' worth of stored solar energy is burned (Hawken, 1992). When the environmental effects of the industrial economy are measured on a per capita basis, the picture appears even bleaker. The average American consumer "produces twice his weight per day in household, hazardous, and industrial waste, and an additional half - ton per week when gaseous wastes such as carbon dioxide are included. Every American consumes about 36 pounds of resources a week, while 2,000 pounds of resources are discarded to support that consumption' (Bourdeau, 2004).

Decidedly, the perceptions of capitalistic consumerism, political economy and technological blitzkrieg has distorted the man - nature relationship to that extent that it may take five decades of strong collective commitment and conscious efforts to re - establish the natural relationship with the nature henceforth. The individual commitment of cutting down carbon footprint will reshape their behaviour and restore the requisite respect for the nature. Criticizing the capitalistic system or restraining technology will not work anymore because both the elements are hard facts and have added wings to the productive efforts of mankind for a long time and working for regularly opening up new opportunities to earn livelihood. However, frenetic use of technology, which is perceived to be the greatest reason for re - shaping human behaviour and drifting away man from nature to make their lives complicated and mechanical, the same technological wave in its finest form, would relieve the mankind from thousands of miseries enabling them to enjoy the elixir of natural life with everlasting possibilities of sustainability. The world, at the threshold of 2020 - 2030 decade, is bound to fall in love with such disruptive and innovative technology that would facilitate the mankind to embrace Nature again passionately for pleasure and peace.

HOPE: Full Circle

Mixed Reality or MR, propagated by the Tesseract and Imaginate companies, highlighting the fusion of AR and VR technologies announces its imminent appearance which will nullify the idea of AI based hologram companion Joi that would establish relationship with Ryan Gosling in 2049. The MR enabled cross - device communication over wearable VR and AR would work for better collaboration in the industrial sector. Similarly, the innovators in Southampton have developed a device that can display 3D animated objects which can talk and interact with the curious audience. World's first AI - powered news anchor is successfully working as human anchor in Xinhua News Agency in China. DataGrid Incorporation of Japan is using generative adversarial networks (GANs) that generate full - size images of non - existent persons with high resolutions through AI technology.

Bill Gates' promoted Heliogen Company has invented a technology by using solar power that would replace fossil fuels with carbon - free, ultra - high temperature. The company uses large field of mirrors that works as a multi - acre magnifying glass for concentrating sunlight. The technology will be commercially available in 2020 and would dramatically reduce the carbon emission to negligible level.

A French firm called Ciel et Terre, has set up solar roadways in Netherlands which remains laminated throughout the nights without any help of electricity. To reduce land use 'Floating Solar' projects have been set up in France, England, Japan, India and California as pilot projects and finding it remarkably successful, the company is going to place it in various parts of the world on commercial basis (D'Monte, 2019).

Mutual trust, which is becoming progressively rare element in the society, can not only be restored but also augmented through IOT and humanoid robots to the extent. A survey undertaken by Oracle in September 2017 showed that people at workplace trusts the robots more than their human managers. The study, indicates that the workers in India (78%) and China (77%) and have trusted AI based managers much more than their counterpart in France (32%) and Japan (29%). The perception about robot managers is that they provide un - biased information, maintains flawless work schedules and perform much better tasks than the human managers. Surprisingly, in India and China such believers figure almost 90% that indicates there is serious lack of trust in the society.

The days are closer than expected when the solar power - driven satellites would process the sunlight and directly supply power to the all the industries, corporate houses and devices at a dirt - cheap price and with zero - emission. Entrepreneurs like Elon Musk are putting their wealth and intelligence to make the world a better place where people are closer to nature being assisted by greener technology.

Gaining popularity of moneyless economy is going to facilitate Bit - coin and various forms of Crypto - currencies would eliminate huge note printing machineries and raw - materials of paper currencies thereby eliminating huge carbon footprint from the global economic system (Gupta, 2020).

Quick Response codes will incrementally be used for payments, and IOT will set to dominate payment channels, though the pace of adoption of 5G by the emerging economies like India which will mitigate carbon emission to the extent.

Further, at home, the scientists at the Indian Institute of Chemical Biology (CSIR - IICB) and the Institute of Genomics and Integrative Biology (IGIB) and are closer to find the technique that would rectify genetic mutations in their laboratories using CRISPR Cas9 with remarkable preliminary results. Once the CRISPR Cas9 is commercially launched, it would not only snip out more than 90% of all genetic diseases but also eliminate the mammoth carbon emitting medicine manufacturing industries thereby leading to eliminating production of medicine packaging accessories.

Big Data and Data mining are most modern factors of production that are carrying out the uncontrollable carbon emitting tangible goods to virtual goods and services enabling the climate on Earth more and more clean and sustainable.

The glimpses of emerging technologies raise high hopes that the technology, which caused disintegration and dysfunction of socio - economic life, will restore and redefine the man - nature relationship with new paradigms.

SOLUTIONS AND RECOMMENDATIONS

From 80:20 to 20:80

When Petteri Taalas, Secretary - General of the World Meteorological Organization; in his opening speech on 2nd December, 2019, reveals at COP25 that "Global warming continues… has risen by about 1.1°C… the ocean has warmed by half a degree." Consequently, "220 million people suffered from heat - waves last year. Now we have more than 800 million people suffering from lack of food," a spine - chilling sense of imminent destruction is perceived in 80% of Growth and 20% of Development of ongoing formula of the world economic system.

Similarly, the COP25 President and Chile's Environment Minister Carolina Schmidt warned that "This conference must change the course of action. National commitments are necessary but not sufficient." Without any lapse of time and shunning the political blame - game because the bush burning in Australia will ultimately cause mutation in global flora fauna system and the whole mankind will suffer its consequences.

Gandhian Approach - The Ultimate Panacea for Mankind

It is a pleasing coincidence that the world is celebrating 150th anniversary of Mahatma Gandhi, and world renowned 'Nature' magazine as well as apolitical COP25 in Madrid, Spain at the threshold of 2020. Mahatma Gandhi had never visited USA in his lifetime but highest number of his statues is there across US than anywhere else in the world. This shows his greatness impact of his teachings that an ultra - materialistic country like US tacitly agrees with. The Hippie culture and movement propagated by John Lennon in 1960s was a warning against 'madding consumerism' and 'crony capitalism' which polluted the idealism of 'simple living and harmony' thereby causing immense harm to natural man - nature relationship.

Mahatma was not an environmentalist and throughout his writings and speeches he never uttered the word 'environment protection' or 'ecological imbalance' rather he always advocated for "Tena Tyaktena Bhunjeeta", (The literal meaning appears to be enjoying with a sense of renunciation to blissfully support oneself from His permeated bounties) Gandhiji had so much respect and dedication for nature that he established huge Sabarmati Ashram in such eco - friendly manner that British architect Laurie Baker had incessantly cried by observing the simplicity and utility of the design and sensing the mental make - up of Bapu and had commented that he was not capable of adapting such elegant way of natural living. Gandhi therefore, always called for limiting wants and desires so that the consumers' stress on nature could be mitigated. Super ordinariness of the London returns barrister and his most natural lifestyle made Mahatma an extra - ordinary man for all times to come.

In an interview with IDR, Vance G Martin, the president of the WILD Foundation, revealed the importance of people - and culture - based models of development and emphasized the need to mobilize people to reverse climate breakdown. Replying to a question as to what mistakes India made in adopting 'development model'; Van said that "there's a Western paradigm of development that I believe 'modern' India has accepted. What happens then?"

Dams silt up quickly because they are not accompanied by a biodiversity conservation program. Biodiversity supports life. Corruption for money (and / or power), and influence. Corruption exists everywhere and it is the number one issue with bad development." Cautioning that, standing against the system status - quo sometimes bring the fate of Martin Luther King Jr, John Lennon, or Mahatma Gandhi, he asked to connect people to create an effective shield against the powerful rulers with vested interests.

FUTURE RESEARCH DIRECTIONS

- AR, VR and MR technology can reduce the use of polythene/polypropylene to the extent of ninety per cent.
- Community housing and group living may drastically cut the building of sky - scrappers and rampant use of use of cement, concrete and vinyl paints etc.
- Combination of Nanotechnology and natural sources of energy can mitigate the use of hydrocarbon to the extent.
- Extensive and planned community forestry may bring down the environmental temperature in the surrounding areas by 5%.

CONCLUSION

We need relationships. Things live, die, evolve, and everything is connected. Economic development requires systemic or holistic thinking. And where do we get this thinking? We get it from looking at nature. Things live, die, evolve, and everything is connected. I observe wilderness because it helps me understand how to priorities relationships. We know where that ends up! Suggestion of simple solution to save mankind from catastrophe is:

1. Reduce personal consumption by half to reduce personal carbon footprint
2. Learn and promote use of finer technologies relating to natural sources of energy
3. Connect people and promote non - violent ways of politics, social interaction and co - operation
4. Teach the generations to be naturally innovative and respect and care for Nature on each count
5. Teach the generations to live dignified life of simplicity

The desperate voice and concern reflected during COP25 in Madrid generates much hope and confidence that the world leaders and communities understand that science and technology is just a tool for making life peaceful and sustainable and not an end in itself. Concerted global efforts sans politics would minimize consumerism and thus mad exploitation of natural resources resulting into global warming and related catastrophe. Whether by compulsion or by self - propelled movements; general conscience and austerity will surely re - establish man - nature relationship with new understanding of 'Common - wealth of Life' and passive euthanasia of 7 billion people will prove to be just a myth by 2030.

REFERENCES

Bisht, R. (2019). The children are cursing us: Can we rescue humanity from the Suicide Pact of the 7 Billion? *Times of India*.

Bourdeau, P. (2004). The man - nature relationship and environmental ethics. *Journal of Environmental Radioactivity, 72*(1 - 2), 9 - 15.

Brown, P. G., & Garver, G. (2009). *Right relationship: Building a whole earth economy*. Berrett - Koehler Publishers.

D'Monte, L. (2019). *Five technologies that may alter India in 2020.* Retrieved from mint: https://www.livemint.com/technology/tech-news/five-technologies-that-may-alter-india-in-2020-11575819146057.html

Donnelley, S. (2009). *Minding Nature, Minding Ourselves.* Centre for Humans & Nature.

Gupta, V. (2020). A Case Study on Economic Development of Tanzania. *Journal of the International Academy for Case Studies, 26*(1), 1–16.

Hawken, P. (1992). The ecology of commerce. *Inc., 14*(4), 93–97.

Madhavan, M. R. (2007). *You are here.* Penguin Books India.

Matei, A. (2017). *Technology is changing our relationship with nature as we know it.* Retrieved from Quartz: https://qz.com/1048433/technology-is-changing-our-relationship-with-nature-as-we-know-it/

Rampal, N. (2019). *India Today.* Retrieved from https://www.indiatoday.in/diu/story/delhi-air-quality-toxic-smoke-smog-cigarettes-1621410-2019-11-21

Taft, K. (2017). *Oil's Deep State: How the petroleum industry undermines democracy and stops action on global warming - in Alberta, and in Ottawa.* James Lorimer & Company.

KEY TERMS AND DEFINITIONS

Carbon Footprint: It is the sum amount of all the greenhouse gases including carbon - di - oxide and methane emitted by a person or a company or any action in a year.

Ego-Centricity: When people are unable to understand the other's perspective. This may happen due to innate nature of due to recklessness. Sometimes people can't differentiate self and other problems.

Frenemies: A wolf in sheep's clothing. A person pretends to be as your friend but actually he may harm you in future.

Greed: Mankind is becoming more and more materialistic. There is no limit of wants and desires of people. They are ready to harness the nature to any limit to fulfil their desires.

Laws of Nature: Nature supports human being only if humans support the nature. If human beings do not follow the rules of nature, we have to see so many unorthodox changes in nature which may not be favourable to human beings.

Mass Extinction: If any living organism or species do not follow the laws of nature may lead to the mass extinction of that organism.

Restructure: The healing of nature is need of hour. The mankind has to think to restructure those all alterations done to nature.

Chapter 5
Sustainopreneurship

Rahul Verma
Delhi University, India

ABSTRACT

Sustainopreneurship (innovation and entrepreneurship for sustainability) may be a concept that has risen from the prior concepts ecopreneurship and social entrepreneurship through sustainability entrepreneurship. The concept implies to utilize creative business organizing to unravel issues related to sustainability to make environmental and social sustainability a vital purpose and objective while at the same time respecting the boundaries set in order to preserve the life support frameworks within the process. In other words, it could be a "business with a cause" where the world issues are turned into business openings by arrangement of sustainability innovations.

INTRODUCTION

Sustainopreneurship (innovation and entrepreneurship for sustainability) may be a concept that has risen from the prior concepts ecopreneurship and social entrepreneurship, through sustainability entrepreneurship. The concept implies to utilize creative business organizing to unravel issues related to sustainability to make environmental and social sustainability as a vital purpose and objective, at the same time respecting the boundaries set in order to preserve the life support frameworks within the process. In other words, it could be a "business with a cause" - where the world issues are turned into business openings by arrangement of sustainability innovations.

Social entrepreneurship is an approach by entrepreneurs or start - up companies, groups, or individuals, in which they implement, fund and develop solutions to environmental, cultural, or social issues (PBS Foundation, 2021). This concept may be connected to a wide range of organizations, which vary in beliefs, aims, and size (Dees, 2001). For - profit entrepreneurs ordinarily measure performance using business measurements like increases in stock prices, revenues and profit. Social entrepreneurs, in any case, are either non - profits, or they mix for - profit objectives with creating a positive "return to society". In this manner, they use diverse measurements. Social entrepreneurship regularly endeavours to advance wide environmental, cultural, and social objectives frequently related with the voluntary sector (Thompson, 2002) in zones such as community development, health care, and poverty alleviation.

DOI: 10.4018/978-1-7998-7951-0.ch005

At times, profit - making social ventures may be set up to back the cultural or social objectives of the organization but not as a conclusion in themselves. For case, an organization that points to supply employment and housing to the homeless may operate an eatery, both to provide employment and to raise money for the homeless. In the 2010 social entrepreneurship was encouraged by the use of the web, especially social media websites and social networking. These websites empower social entrepreneurs to reach various individuals who aren't topographically near however who share the same objectives and energize them to collaborate online, learn about the issues, spread data about the group's activities and events, and raise funds through crowd funding. In recent years, analysts are calling for a better understanding of the environment in which social ventures operate, and social entrepreneurship exists (De - Bruin & Teasdale, 2019). This will assist them define better strategy and assist accomplish their twofold bottom line goal (Purkayastha et al., 2020; Bloom & Dees, 2008).

Ecopreneurship could a term coined to represent the method of standards of entrepreneurship being connected to form businesses that operate sustainably or solve environmental problems. The term started to be broadly utilized within the 1990's, and it is otherwise alluded to as "environmental entrepreneurship." Within the book Merging Economic and Environmental Concerns Through Ecopreneurship, composed by Gwyn Schuyler in 1998, ecopreneurs are characterized as follows: In spite of the fact that ecopreneurship activities can span a wide range of issues from food waste to recycling to ocean pollution, they tend to take after reoccurring environmental principles such as triple bottom line accounting, cradle to cradle product design, systems thinking, etc.

BACKGROUND

The definition first presented in a conference article in 2006 (Abrahamsson, 2006):

- Deployment of sustainability innovations: Innovation and Entrepreneurship for sustainability.
- Short for sustainability intra / entre - preneurship.
- To centre on one or more (sustainability / social / world - related) problem (s), identify / find and / or design a solution to the problem (s) and bring the innovation to the market by making a productive organization. With the (modern alt. profound change of an ancient) mission / cause - oriented sustainability business adding social / economical / ecological gains and values, with a predisposition towards the intangible - through re - socialization / dematerialization. The value included at the same time enhancing, restoring and / or ultimately preserving the basic utilized capital stock, in order to preserve the capacity to satisfy the wants of present and coming eras of stakeholders.

The business world has been assigned as a head force for making a sustainable world (Hart, 2005; Prahalad, 2004), particularly when acting as a source of creativity and innovation - e. g. as Robinson puts it (Robinson, 2004): In expansion to joining over areas, sustainability must also be co - ordinated over interests or sectors. It is evident that governments alone have neither the capability nor the will to achieve sustainability on their own. The private division, as the chief engine of economic activity on the planet, and a major source for entrepreneurship, innovation and creativity, must be included in attempting to accomplish sustainability.

Sustainopreneurship could be a candidate to be the complementing figure to allow indeed more use to powers rising from world of business activities to contribute to sustainability. The concept of

Sustainopreneurship was to begin with presented as a term in 2000 (Schaltegger, 2000) where it was overwhelmingly related to the proactive change management approaches related with process adjustment with expanded regard to the environment. The phenomenon created with publications in 2003 (Hockerts, 2003; Gerlach, 2003a; Gerlach, 2003b), and further advanced and was probably characterized in 2006 by Anders Abrahamsson (Abrahamsson, 2006). This conditional definition was observationally tested in his Master thesis (Abrahamsson, 2007a), where the enactive research process (Johannisson, 2002; Johannisson, 2005) affirmed that the definition stood the test differentiating it towards the auto - ethnographical empirical material. A paper to ascertain future research challenges was made past this in 2007 (Abrahamsson, 2007b), and created further with a book chapter published in September 2008 (Abrahamsson, 2008).

In common, the entrepreneurial talk has opened up to move past an entirely economic phenomenon, instead of being seen fundamentally as a social process at large (Steyaert & Katz, 2004). Going before the conceptual arrangement were two traces of eco - preneurship and social entrepreneurship, managing basically with the ecological and social dimensions of sustainability. Essential affiliations with social entrepreneurship have too been setting up charities and not - for - profit venturing to innovatively solve and address social issues, though ecopreneurship has been fundamentally centered on understanding environmental issues (Gerlach, 2003b).

Both these traces of conceptual improvement are taken past, integrate and merge into the proposed conceptual build at hand, where distinctions are made from both of these concepts - sustainopreneurial forms taking place organizationally through for - profit organizing, but not with profit as its fundamental driving force. Sustainopreneurial venturing is done in an encompassing way that meets both social and ecological challenges at the same time with respect to both process and purpose.

MAIN FOCUS OF THE CHAPTER

Three Main Dimensions

The definition of Sustainopreneurship has to be highlighted by three recognizing dimensions with all three being at the same time present within the applied (inter) action it reflects. The first is situated towards "why" - its motive and purpose. The second and third are replicating two "how" - allied dimensions - its procedure.

1. Sustainopreneurship Consciously Sets Out To Create And / Or Find Innovations to Solve Sustainability - Related Problems

The cognizant mission that guides the activity, particularly within the beginning 'preneurial' stage before venturing forms and formalizes into an institutionalized business entity, is to intentionally discover innovative and practical solutions to problems related to the sustainability plan. This is the main key to recognize this category of entrepreneurial behaviour and activity named Sustainopreneurship from non - specific entrepreneurial action: the cause - oriented intention that places the driving - force, purpose and core motive of the business exercises. To further grasp and identify what is implied by sustainability issues, central sources within the worldwide sustainable development talk are recognized, which direct us to what is implied operationally and practically by sustainability in activity. The result of assorted sources are summarized in this list of "sustainability - related issues", decided by the political action plan reported in Agenda 21 (UN, 1992a), the Millennium Declaration characterizing the Millennium Development Goals (UN, 2000), both concurred at the Millennium Summit in New York 2000, and the WSSD Plan of Implementation chosen upon at the World Summit on Sustainable Development in Johannesburg 2002 (UN, 2002b). This list, synthesized and derived from these sources, lines up areas with related values to create, goals to reach, and problems to solve:

- Poverty
- Sanitation and Water
- Health
- Illiteracy / Education
- Sustainable consumption and production patterns
- Energy systems and climate change
- Chemicals
- Urbanization
- Land use, biological diversity, and ecosystems
- Utilization of sea resources
- Agriculture and food
- Trade justice
- Good governance, democracy, and social stability
- Security and peace

2. Sustainopreneurship Means to Get Solutions to the Market through Creative Organizing

The line - up over could make one effortlessly discouraged. But then again, a vital approach to maintain and acquire when this list of sustainability - related difficulties is collected and then well - thought - out to escape dropping into despair and disempowerment. It is of core significance to take the plan as entrepreneurial challenges - to see resistance as a resource, obstacles as opportunities, and problems as possibilities, whatever the nature of the resistance. If the solution is created by creativity, it is similarly critical to take it to the market in an innovative and creative way. The market is utilized as well, not society basically, since it implies business foundation - a sustainability business that still knows its role and place in the holarchy specified earlier. Getting something to the market at the same time gets it to society and our shared physical environment. There's nothing that actually varies from the general entrepreneurial depiction contributed to, in this dimension, but this comes normal since Sustainopreneurship may be a conceptual development and extension on or after the social sensation so - called entrepreneurship, and as a result accede to one of its professed important dimensions, "entrepreneurship as creative organizing" (Johannisson, 2005).

3. Sustainopreneurship in Process Adds Sustainability Value with Respect for Life Support Systems

The mindfulness that the (economic) market is an implanted sub - framework in the "socio - sphere" that's in turn a portion of the 'bio - sphere' is made unequivocal. This mindfulness self - evidently and naturally makes the sustainopreneurial team maximize harmony with life support systems within the process. With pride and joy the epitome of the nonexclusive definition of "sustainable development" lives in business venturing. In brief - living the nonexclusive definition of sustainable development as characterized by WCED (UN, 1987), with regard to the requirements of future and present stakeholders, keeping the holistic world - view and making it direct everyday (inter) action.

SOLUTIONS AND RECOMMENDATIONS

It has been recommended, in spite of the fact that, to keep the research connected, to recognize institutional barriers and obstacles, and how to overcome them; i.e. encouraging components for Sustainopreneurship, researching imminent approaches, enablers and tools. Suitable domains and areas for Sustainopreneurship connected are recommended to be processed. Research strategies recommended are Enactive Research (Johannisson, 2002; Johannisson, 2005) and Open Space Technology, since they include instant value among stakeholders, and in themselves actually builds fields where Sustainopreneurship proliferates and evolves. For progress, past these "how" - related pointers, the key is to single out "the huge questions", getting answers through collaborative, collective conversation and dialogue, with an unequivocal interaction and results orientation. Topics and Issues have been outlined and formulated, where it is of striking significance with an deliberation to pull authentic forces possibly hearing this call of investigating the phenomenon further, with the reason to breakdown the degrees of partition in between the stakeholders of the sustainopreneurial concept - in applied interaction, reflective practice and idea to create collaborative and collective intelligence for a more profound understanding of the concept. An affiliation with this purpose is in its interim stages, Association of Enactive Research, Education, and Application for Sustainopreneurship (Interim) or AEREAS (I).

FUTURE RESEARCH DIRECTIONS

Given its recent date, there's a need for future research, as said over (Abrahamsson, 2007b; Abrahamsson, 2008). Fundamental discoveries here are that conceptually, a more profound examination is required to be conducted with a detailed and nuanced framework and taxonomy made of sustainability innovations, the centre of Sustainopreneurship, essentially by categorizing and cataloguing case stories. It is furthermore desirable to create a further comprehensive depiction to re - count sustainopreneurship to further perceptions in the broader, general awareness - sphere of the "business case of sustainability", within the modern - day superfluity of "buzz - words", acronyms, methods, and approaches that by this time subsists - and in this circumstance too to encourage why this conception improves value.

CONCLUSION

Sustainability vs. Sustainable Entrepreneurship

With these dimensions clarified and distinctions made a common conceptual lack of clarity or vagueness ought to be addressed, where a solid need to recognize clearly between Sustainability vs. Sustainable entrepreneurship is distinguished. From this point of view, a really vital refinement with the concept shaped is claimed - sustainability entrepreneurship as within the concept Sustainopreneurship; the use of entrepreneurial action in a decided activity introduction towards tackling a sustainability - related issue with (creative) business organizing as a means to solve the issue (s) - business with a cause: to turn business movement from a portion of the issue to a portion of the solution. Sustainable entrepreneurship is just a nonexclusive entrepreneurial process that takes into thought the boundaries set by sustainability, and doesn't address where to and why, the aim, the purpose or the destination of the venture. The key aim and the business idea in itself aren't related to sustainability per se, sustainability just being a "connection" to the entrepreneurial process. The second and third dimensions are spoken to, but not the first. Sustainability entrepreneurship, in contrast, takes as its root of presence and key point to unravel a sustainability - related issue. This implies that all three dimensions are at the same time present: to require a sustainability innovation to the market through inventive organizing with regard for life - supporting frameworks within the process.

REFERENCES

Abrahamsson, A. (2006). Sustainopreneurship - Business with a Cause. in Science Sustainable Development - Starting Points and Critical Reflections. Uppsala: VHU - Föreningen Vetenskap för Hållbar Utveckling.

Abrahamsson, A. (2007a). *Sustainopreneurship - Business with a Cause: Conceptualizing Entrepreneurship for Sustainability* [Master Thesis in Business Administration]. Växjö: Reports from Växjö University: Business Administration and Economics. http://www.diva-portal.org/vxu/abstract.xsql?dbid=1254

Abrahamsson, A. (2007b). *Researching Sustainopreneurship - conditions, concepts, approaches, arenas and questions. An invitation to authentic sustainability business forces.* Paper presented at the 13th International Sustainable Development Research Conference, Mälardalens Högskola, Västerås.

Abrahamsson, A. (2008). Sustainopreneurship - Business with a Cause. The Promise of Creative Organizing for Sustainability. In Bridging the Functional and Territorial Views on Regional Entrepreneurship and Development. Örebro: FSF (Swedish Foundation for Small Business Research).

Bloom, P. N., & Dees, J. G. (2008). Cultivate Your Ecosystem. *Stanford Social Innovation Review*, *6*(1), 47–53.

De-Bruin, A., & Teasdale, S. (2019). A Research Agenda for Social Entrepreneurship. Edward Elgar Publishing.

Dees, J. G. (2001). *The Meaning of Social Entrepreneurship.* Caseatduke.org.

PBS Foundation. (2021). *What is a Social Entrepreneur. Enterprising Ideas. A social entrepreneur, in our view, is a person or entity that takes a business approach to effectively solving a social problem.* Author.

Gerlach, A. (2003a). *Sustainable entrepreneurship and innovation.* Centre for Sustainability Management. University of Lueneburg.

Gerlach, A. (2003b). *Innovativität und Sustainability Intrapreneurship.* Paper presented at Sustainable Management in Action '03, University of St. Gallen, Schweiz.

Hart, S. L. (2005). *Capitalism at the Crossroads: the Unlimited Business Opportunities in Solving the World's Most Difficult Problems*. Wharton School Publishing.

Hockerts, K. (2003). *Sustainability Innovation: Ecological and Social Entrepreneurship and the Managing of Antagonistic Assets* (PhD Dissertation). University of St. Gallen, Schweiz.

Johannisson, B. (2002). *Enacting Entrepreneurship - Using Auto - Ethnography to Study Organization Creation*. Paper presented the conference Ethnographic Organizational Studies, University of St. Gallen, Switzerland.

Johannisson, B. (2005). *Entreprenörskapets väsen*. Studentlitteratur.

Prahalad, C. K. (2004). *The Fortune at the Bottom of the Pyramid - Eradicating Poverty Through Profits*. Wharton School Publishing.

Purkayastha, D., Tripathy, T., & Das, B. (2020). Understanding the ecosystem of microfinance institutions in India. *Social Enterprise Journal,* 243 - 261.

Robinson, J. (2004). Squaring the Circle? Some thoughts on the idea of Sustainable Development. *Ecological Economics, 48*(4), 369–384. doi:10.1016/j.ecolecon.2003.10.017

Schaltegger, S. (2000). *Vom Bionier zum Sustainopreneur*. Presentation at Rio Impuls Management Forum 2000.

Steyaert, C., & Katz, J. (2004). Reclaiming the space of entrepreneurship in society: Geographical, discursive and social dimensions. *Entrepreneurship and Business Development, 2004*(3), 179–196.

Thompson, J. L. (2002). The World of the Social Entrepreneur. *The International Journal of Public Sector Management, 15*(4/5), 413. Doi: 10.1108 / 09513550210435746

UN. (1987). *World Commission on Environment and Development. Our Common Future*. Oxford University Press.

UN. (1992a). *Conference on Environment and Development Main Documents*. https://www.un.org/esa/sustdev/documents/docs_unced.htm

UN. (2000). *Millennium Development Goals*. https://www.un.org/millenniumgoals

UN. (2002b). *World Summit on Sustainable Development*. http://www.johannesburgsummit.org

KEY TERMS AND DEFINITIONS

Entrepreneurship: The extraction or creation of value.
Sustainability: Capacity for human civilization and Earth's biosphere to co - exist.
Sustainopreneurship: Entrepreneurship and innovation for sustainability.

Chapter 6
Quality Systems for a Responsible Management in the University:
Measuring the Performance of Teaching Staff

Luis Matosas-López
https://orcid.org/0000-0001-7313-0146
Rey Juan Carlos University, Spain

Roberto Soto-Varela
Antonio de Nebrija University, Spain

Melchor Gómez-García
Autonomous University of Madrid, Spain

Moussa Boumadan
Autonomous University of Madrid, Spain

ABSTRACT

Literature on university quality systems and teaching performance measurement addresses only tangentially the neutrality of measurement instruments in relation to the different teaching methodologies. This chapter explores this issue posing the following question: Should we use identical assessment instruments on teachers who apply different teaching methodologies? The authors attempt to answer this question by focusing the debate on the two most widespread methodological approaches in the university: the behaviourist and the constructivist. The study addresses this task from the perspective of measurement instruments with behavioural episodes. The authors present two instruments to assess teaching performance: one aimed at evaluating teachers who use behaviourist approaches and the other aimed at assessing teachers who apply constructivist approaches. The work reveals divergences between the two questionnaires addressing the importance of using different teaching appraisal instruments to measure, responsibly, the performance of teachers who apply different teaching methodologies.

DOI: 10.4018/978-1-7998-7951-0.ch006

INTRODUCTION

Quality Systems in University Management

Quality has become a key concept in modern societies. Any organized activity can be optimized, and this optimization occurs thanks to the implementation of control systems. These systems audit the effectiveness, functionality, and reliability of the activity being evaluated and this, by definition, is the basis for preserving and improving quality in any context.

Today, quality systems are implemented in all relevant areas of society: production processes, agriculture, food industry, government programs, health systems, urban development, logistics, etc. (De - La - Orden, 2009). No space of action remains outside these processes of control and, of course, the field of university management is not an exception.

Management of university organizations has experienced significant changes in the last few years, and this has also had implications for the administration of their quality systems (Restrepo - Abondano, 2008). Ruiz - Carrascosa (2000) points out that the importance of the university as a key service in society beside the substantial investment of funds that it requires - whether this funding is public or private - intensifies concerns about the monitoring of its quality. In the same line, Sierra - Sánchez (2012) suggests that quality control has become one of the greatest challenges for a responsible management in the university of the 21st century.

However, measuring quality of the intangible, as in the case of higher education institutions, is not an easy task. The concept of quality in the university context is a complex issue that is undoubtedly determined by the confluence of different factors. These elements, which configure the concept of quality, extend from the attention of the service staff to the soundness of the curricula; including the facilities, or the offer of social activities in the institution (Resino - Blázquez et al., 2013; Veciana - Vergés & Capelleras - I - Segura, 2004). The following studies show the variety of variables that can be considered when measuring this manifold concept.

Gil - Edo et al. (1999), in their study on quality models in public universities, highlight seven components: Technical Dimension of Teaching Staff, Functional Dimension of Teaching Staff, Accessibility and Academic Structure, Attention of Service Staff, Tangible Aspect of the Facilities, Visible Aspect or Appearance of the Staff, and Complementary Services (catering, reprography, etc.).

Along the same lines, Veciana - Vergés et al. (2004) highlight the importance of four relevant aspects when defining quality in the university environment: Attitude and Competence of the Teaching Staff, Curricular Contents, Technical Equipment and Facilities, and Organizational Efficiency in the Institution.

Resino - Blázquez et al. (2013), in their research on quality indicators that condition student satisfaction, highlight three dimensions: Facilities and Resources (library services, transport, etc.), Academic Aspects (teaching staff, reputation, etc.), and Social Aspects (sports activities, exchange programs, etc.).

Similarly, the study by Alvarado - Lagunas et al. (2016) on quality in universities from the student's point of view, addresses the existence of four critical aspects: Physical Infrastructure, Teaching Staff, Teaching Resources, and Student's Development.

Finally, Álvarez - Rojo et al. (1999), based on discussion groups with professors, indicate that university quality is defined by the interaction of four variables: Teaching Skills, Teaching Attitude, Structural and Social Conditions (administrative processes, job opportunities, group size, etc.), and the Management of the Typical Dilemmas in the University Context (research vs. teaching, innovation vs. inertia).

Sustainable Development, Responsible Social Entrepreneurship, and University

The comprehension of the universities' impact to sustainable development requires consideration of the different aspects that affect universities' behavior, such as organizational management, non - financial regulation, the external environment, or the entrepreneurship responsibilities in its social setting (Pizzi et al., 2020). The contribution of these issues to the discussion surrounding the Sustainable Development Goals (SDGs) (United Nations, 2015) and their impact for quality systems in university management has grown exponentially giving rise also to the concept of social entrepreneurship (Kivarina et al., 2020).

In this sense, in the last years, these 2 issues have been analyzed in works such as those of Abdelnaeim & El - Bassiouny (2020), Cervello - Royo et al. (2020), Nor - Aishah et al. (2020), Aquino et al. (2018), Cave et al. (1997), or Guthrie & Neumann (2007).

Abdelnaeim & El - Bassiouny (2020) analyze the relationship between entrepreneurial cognitive scripts and sustainability orientation, to understand whether entrepreneurial cognitive scripts act as a driver toward sustainability developments. The study by Cervello - Royo et al. (2020) aims to identify the combinations of the economic and sustainable development factors that may be related to opportunity - driven entrepreneurship. Nor - Aishah et al. (2020) delve into the effect of entrepreneurship on the economic, environmental, and social aspects of organizational sustainable performance; increasing concern in the field of social entrepreneurship. The work by Aquino et al. (2018) explores responsible and sustainable management practices considering management alternative approaches and innovative holistic strategies for a sustainable development in the community. Finally, there are also studies on the impact and consequences of applying financial, or non - financial, performance indicators for the sustainable measurement of university quality, especially when it comes to public universities (Cave et al., 1997; Guthrie & Neumann, 2007).

BACKGROUND

Focusing on the higher education context, when it comes to measuring the concept of quality in the university, there is an element that is ubiquitous and on which all the authors agree. That is the performance of the teaching staff. The performance of teaching staff is not only recurring element and cornerstone in any research in this area, but it is also an aspect that sometimes overlaps with the concept of quality itself in its broadest sense.

The Performance of Teaching Staff

Many authors agree in placing the start of teaching effectiveness measurement systems in the studies carried out by Remmers (Adams & Umbach, 2012), at Purdue University in Indiana (USA), during the 1920s (Remmers, 1928).

Since then, literature on teaching performance in university organizations has addressed a wide variety of topics. These include instruments' validity and reliability (Marsh, 1982), questionnaires' dimensionality (Lemos et al., 2011), surveys' careless responding (Meade & Craig, 2012), low rates of student participation (Stanny & Arruda, 2017), or the development of specific appraisal instruments for distance learning modalities (Bangert, 2006).

However, while the academic community has dealt with topics such as those mentioned above, it seems to ignore the issue of the indifference of teaching assessment instruments to different teaching methodologies.

Moore (2006) emphasizes the importance of teaching methodologies in measuring teaching performance and even Kember & Wong (2000) highlight the need to consider the form of instruction, applied by the teacher, when designing questionnaires. However, authors' literature review reveals the absence of works presenting differentiated instruments to evaluate teaching performance according to the method of instruction.

The Different Teaching Methodologies

Whilst we can identify multiple methodological approaches in the teaching - learning processes, Sobrino - Morrás (2011) points out the existence of three main streams: The Cognitive, The Behaviorist and the Constructivist. The first is an approach in which the focus is on understanding learning processes, in general, and on cognitive processes in particular (assimilation of information, problem solving, thinking, language or concept generation) (Piaget, 1981). Nevertheless, the other 2 streams are the ones that stand out from the rest of methodologies.

The behaviorist approach, originally promoted by Watson (1970), focuses on knowledge, content, skills, and measurable learning. In this, the student has a secondary role, being the teacher the main source of knowledge and the one responsible for taking decisions in the learning process.

Meanwhile, the constructivist movement, which has Vygotskiĭ (1978) as its main forerunner, focuses on the active role of the student during learning; learning which is generated from experiences, interpretation of reality and integration of multiple perspectives in collaboration with others.

For behaviorism, knowledge is an external element that must be transferred to the student. Therefore, the act of teaching focuses on the manipulation of handbooks or exercises, with the purpose of transmitting knowledge to the student in a cumulative way. On the contrary, constructivism postulates that the student can construct knowledge. Consequently, the act of teaching must focus on helping the student to generate personal meanings from his or her own experiences.

These 2 approaches, depending on the author, received different denominations. Although one of the most repeated categorizations is that which speaks of teaching - centered approaches and learning - centered approaches (Kember, 1997; Pegalajar - Palomino, 2016; Samuelowicz & Bain, 2001), there are also others. Regardless of the name, its essence is the same and its nature is antagonistic. The first one, mainly passive, focused on the teacher and the teaching process. The second, definitely active, focused on the student and the learning flows.

MAIN FOCUS OF THE CHAPTER

Despite the antagonistic nature of the behaviorist and constructivist approaches, the systems used to measure teaching performance ignore these differences, using identical instruments for both teaching methodologies.

The present work delves into the issue of the non - differentiation of measurement instruments for different methodologies. The authors explore this issue posing the following question: Should we use identical assessment instruments on teachers who apply different teaching methodologies? Alternatively,

Table 1. Main Features of Behaviorist and Constructivist Approaches

	Behaviourist Approach	Constructivist Approach
Samuelowicz & Bain (1992)	It focuses on teaching and providing information to the student.	It focuses on helping students to develop their own experiences.
	It focuses on transmitting knowledge and content to the student.	It focuses on supporting and motivating students to create their own knowledge.
Kember (1997)	It focuses on providing information to the student.	It focuses on facilitating students' understanding.
	It focuses on transmitting knowledge to the student in a structured way.	It focuses on achieving an intellectual development in the student.
Samuelowicz & Bain (2001)	Teacher - student relationship based on unidirectional interactions.	Teacher - student relationship based on 2 - way dialogue.
	Content built externally and contextualized within the framework of the course.	Content built in a personalized and contextualized in professional scenarios.
Martinez - Geijo (2008)	Teacher: exposes, explains, maintains order, asks questions, corrects, examines, and evaluates.	Teacher: facilitates the expression of ideas for confrontation with other points of view.
	Content is taught using a variety of handbooks and exercises.	Content is learned based on problems detected, considering the student's background.
Hernandez - Pina & Maquilón - Sanchez (2010)	Student has a passive role, being the focus of interest in the content.	Student has an active role, being the focus of interest on learning achievements.
	Teacher transfers knowledge to the student in an organized and structured way.	Teacher generates spaces of professionalization with the purpose of making the student think like a professional.
Pegalajar - Palomino (2016)	Student perceives that teacher controls the course content and facilitates its organisation and understanding.	Student perceives that teacher understands the knowledge as something agreed between teacher and student.
	Teacher is positioned as a competent manager within the learning process.	Student is positioned as an autonomous, responsible, and active learner within the learning process.
Homero - Orozco et al. (2018)	It focuses on the contents of handbooks presented by the teacher.	It focuses on problem solving and development of problem - solving activities.
	Knowledge is built from a selection of what has been produced by scientific research.	Knowledge is built from the management of the problems posed.

Source: Own elaboration

expressed in another way: Does it make sense to use identical appraisal questionnaires for teachers who use different teaching approaches?

The authors attempt to answer these questions by focusing the debate on the 2 most widespread methodological approaches in the university context. On the one hand, the behaviorist methodology and, on the other, the constructivist approach.

The study addresses this task from the perspective of teaching assessment instruments with Behavioral Anchored Rating Scales (BARS). The work developed by the authors describes the construction of 2 questionnaires to measure the performance of teaching staff. One aimed at evaluating the performance of teachers who use behaviorist approaches. The other aimed to assess the performance of teachers who apply constructivist methodologies. The comparison of both instruments provides a good approximation to answer the questions raised by the authors.

Methodology

The 2 measurement instruments, following the recommendations for the construction of Behavioral Anchored Rating Scales (BARS) (Dickinson & Zellinger, 1980), are designed with the participation of teachers and students. 15 teachers and 974 students from Rey Juan Carlos University (from now on URJC) - a medium - sized Spanish university located in Madrid - took part in the study.

The Behavioral Anchored Rating Scales (BARS) method takes the different teaching categories, gathering, for each one of them, behavioral episodes. Behavioral episodes that, after being screening and categorized through different stages, serve to form the anchor points in the final measurement instrument. Based on this method, the authors, following the proposal of Matosas-Lopez et al. (2019), use a construction process with seven different stages:

Step 1. Description of Teaching Categories: In the first stage, a panel of faculty members (n = 5) make a brief description of the 10 categories of teaching being considered. These categories are those measured by URJC in its faculty appraisal processes. The categories are: Course Introduction, Evaluation System Description, Time Management, General Availability, Organizational Coherence, Assessment Implementation, Dealing with Doubts, Explicative Capacity, Follow - Up Easiness, and Overall Satisfaction.

Step 2. Compilation of Behavioral Episodes: During the second stage, a group of post - graduate students (n = 25) provide behavioral episodes (efficient and inefficient) in teaching. This task is developed through a series of semi - structured group interviews coordinated by the researchers.

Step 3. Screening Of Behavioral Examples: In the third stage, a second panel of faculty members (n = 5) review all behavioral episodes collected during the previous stage. Here faculty members proceed to discard those episodes that are ambiguous or redundant before moving on to the next stage.

Step 4. Relocation of Behavioral Episodes: During the fourth stage, a second group of students (n = 70) relocate the remaining behavioral episodes into the 10 teaching categories above indicated. Those episodes that are not correctly relocated by at least 80% of the participants in the teaching category, for which they were formulated, are discarded (Bernardin, 1977).

Step 5. Clustering Of Behavioral Episodes Into Subcategories: In the fifth stage, a third panel of faculty members (n = 5) take the behavioral episodes that have fallen into each category and proceed to regroup them into subcategories with common aspects. These subcategories are called Core Behavioral Aspects (CBAs) (Matosas, 2018). At this stage, the behavioral episodes are synthesized in 40 Core Behavioral Aspects (CBAs) subcategories (4 Core Behavioral Aspects (CBAs) per category).

Step 6. Dual Evaluation of Behavioral Episodes: During the sixth stage, a third group of students (n = 879) tackle a dual evaluation process. To undertake this evaluation, students take as reference the performance of one of their professors during the previous term.

The tasks to be undertaken by the student are 2: (a) dichotomous evaluation of the Core Behavioral Aspects (CBAs) of each category in terms of “Fulfilled” or “Not fulfilled”, and (b) rating of a statement of each category on a scale from “1 - Strongly disagree” to “5 - Strongly agree”.

The first task in this dual evaluation generates different combinations of Core Behavioral Aspects (CBAs), some of them fulfilled and some of them not. The second task reflects the numerical score that would be attached to each combination of Core Behavioral Aspects (CBAs), according to the student’s perspective. This dual evaluation makes it possible to determine the combination of Core Behavioral Aspects (CBAs) that the student links to each level of performance on a scale from 1 to 5.

Before undertaking the 2 tasks previously described, the participants answer a first question to indicate the teaching methodology used by the professor whose work they are going to evaluate. In this question, the participants find 2 alternatives designed according to the features identified in the literature (Homero - Orozco et al., 2018; Martínez - Geijo, 2008; Samuelowicz & Bain, 2001) for the approaches under examination. In this question, participants must indicate which sequence of statements best describes the way in which the teacher, taken as reference, address the course. Option A represents the use of a behaviorist approach, while option B indicates the application of a constructivist approach.

Option A: Classes are usually a monologue by the teacher / Classes focus on the contents of handbooks / Contents are not contextualized in professional scenarios / Teacher exposes, maintains order, asks questions, corrects, and evaluates.

Option B: Classes allow for a dialogue between teacher and group / Classes focus on problem - solving and developing activities to solve them / Contents are contextualized in professional scenarios / Teacher facilitates the expression of different ideas and points of view.

Once the dual evaluation described above is completed, researchers proceed to calculate the mean and Standard Deviation (SD) of the Core Behavioral Aspects (CBAs) combinations in each category. The mean value identifies the point on the scale that the combination could occupy in the final instrument, while Standard Deviation (SD) describes the degree of agreement among raters in placing the combination of Core Behavioral Aspects (CBAs) at the point indicated by the mean.

Step 7. Generation of the Final Scale: The information gathered in the previous stage on the type of approach used by the teacher (Option A for behaviorist approach / Option B for constructivist approach) allows the data obtained to be used independently. This makes it possible to generate 2 separate scales, one for evaluating the performance of teachers who apply behaviorist methodologies and the other for those who maintain a constructivist approach.

The researchers generate the final scales using the combinations of surviving Core Behavioral Aspects (CBAs) as anchor points. The combinations of Core Behavioral Aspects (CBAs) are assigned to each interval according to the mean value obtained in the previous step. Consequently, each combination of Core Behavioral Aspects (CBAs) falls into a particular class interval. Likewise, when more than one combination of Core Behavioral Aspects (CBAs) falls in a given interval, the choice is made by taking the combination with the lowest Standard Deviation (SD).

Each of the 2 instruments generated consist of 10 questions - or items - to evaluate the 10 teaching categories covered. In addition, each question presents 5 anchor points represented by a single or combination of Core Behavioral Aspects (CBAs). Each anchor point therefore refers to an action or set of actions that unequivocally describe teacher's performance in the context of its category.

Both instruments are included in Appendices 1 (Assessment instrument for teachers who apply behaviorist methodologies) and 2 (Assessment instrument for teachers who apply constructivist methodologies).

SOLUTIONS AND RECOMMENDATIONS

Even though the scales of both instruments start from the same set of behavioral episodes (sharing stages 1 to 5 during the instrument construction), the "teaching approach question" (Option A / Option B), introduced in stage 6, splits the data to generate 2 independent instruments. The first questionnaire, designed to measure the performance of teachers who apply behavioral approaches, is constructed from the responses of the 470 students who indicate option A in the "teaching approach question". The second questionnaire, created to assess the performance of teachers who use constructivist approaches, is designed based on the answers of the 409 students who selected option B in the "teaching approach question".

The observation and comparison of both questionnaires reveal the existence of substantial differences between them. Of the 50 anchor points (5 per question or item) used to create the scales of each instrument, 28 differ depending on whether it is a questionnaire or another. Likewise, none of the 10 questions has the same grouping of Core Behavioral Aspects (CBAs) in the 5 anchor points of its scale in both instruments.

The scales of the items Evaluation System Description, Organizational Coherence, Explicative Capacity, and Overall Satisfaction are the ones that show more coincidences in both questionnaires. On the contrary, the questions on General Availability and Dealing with Doubts, in which 4 of the 5 anchor points are different, are the ones that show the greatest divergence between the 2 instruments.

Table 2. Coincidences / Divergences in the Anchor Points between the 2 Instruments

Questions Or Teaching Categories	No. Of Coincident Anchor Points On The Scale	No. Of Divergent Anchor Points On The Scale
Course Introduction	2	3
Evaluation System Description	3	2
Time Management	2	3
General Availability	1	4
Organisational Coherence	3	2
Assessment Implementation	2	3
Dealing With Doubts	1	4
Explicative Capacity	3	2
Follow - Up Easiness	2	3
Overall Satisfaction	3	2
Total	**22**	**28**

Source: Own Elaboration

Table 3 shows the detail of the coincidences and divergences detected between the 2 questionnaires in each of the 5 anchor points of the scale for each question. It shows us that only in the fifth anchor point exists a total coincidence between the 2 instruments. In this last point of the scale, which denotes the maximum level of teaching performance, all the students, in both teaching approaches, agreed in determining that the maximum level of effectiveness is reached when the teacher satisfactorily fulfils all the Core Behavioral Aspects (CBAs) stated in the question.

Table 3. Matrix of Coincidences / Divergences per Question and Anchor Point between the 2 Instruments

Questions Or Teaching Categories	Coincidences Between The 2 Instruments				
	Anchor Point 1	Anchor Point 2	Anchor Point 3	Anchor Point 4	Anchor Point 5
Course Introduction	No	No	Yes	No	Yes
Evaluation System Description	Yes	Yes	No	No	Yes
Time Management	Yes	No	No	No	Yes
General Availability	No	No	No	No	Yes
Organisational Coherence	Yes	No	No	Yes	Yes
Assessment Implementation	Yes	No	No	No	Yes
Dealing With Doubts	No	No	No	No	Yes
Explicative Capacity	Yes	Yes	No	No	Yes
Follow - Up Easiness	Yes	No	No	No	Yes
Overall Satisfaction	Yes	Yes	No	No	Yes

Source: Own Elaboration

In contrast, the midpoints of the scale - the third and fourth anchor points - are the ones that show the greatest divergence. In the third point, only the item Course Introduction presents the same grouping of Core Behavioral Aspects (CBAs) in both instruments. In the fourth point, a single coincidence is observed for the Organizational Coherence item.

The content's examination of the Core Behavioral Aspects (CBAs) that constitute the different anchor points in the 10 items of both questionnaires also yields interesting results. Some of them are presented below:

- **Assessment Instrument for Teachers who Apply Behaviorist Methodologies:** In the instrument for behaviorist approaches, the scale generated for the question Course Introduction shows in its first anchor point, that the basic level of performance expected by the students is linked to the provision of an adequate bibliography to follow the course (Appendix 1). This finding, in line with previous research (Martínez - Geijo, 2008; Samuelowicz & Bain, 2001), corroborates the importance given in behaviorist methodologies to the external construction of knowledge through the use of handbooks and exercises.

In addition, other points of interest are also observed in this instrument. The Organizational Coherence item is an example of this. In this item, the first anchor point is represented by a situation of non - fulfillment of all the Core Behavioral Aspects (CBAs) contemplated in the question. Consequently, the minimum level of performance appears in the second point and is represented by the Core Behavioral Aspect (CBA): "Teacher respects the chronological plan of contents designed for every week" (Appendix 1). This fact, in accordance with various authors (Hernandez - Pina & Maquilón - Sánchez, 2010; Kember, 1997), reiterates the importance of an adequate structure of the course and its contents.

- **Assessment Instrument for Teachers who Apply Constructivist Methodologies:** Unlike what happens in the Course Introduction item in the behaviorist instrument, in the constructivist questionnaire the minimum level of performance is not linked to the presentation of the bibliographic materials, but to a relevant exposition of the course in academic and professional terms (Appendix 2). This finding is consistent with previous studies, which highlight the importance of framing the learning in the professional context in which the competencies acquired will be applied in the future (Hernandez - Pina & Maquilón - Sánchez, 2010; Samuelowicz & Bain, 2001).

The constructivist instrument also reflects other significant details. The anchor points that define the minimum efficiency in the items Dealing with Doubts and Follow - Up Easiness are a good example of this (Appendix 2). In the question Dealing with Doubts the first anchor point is represented by the Core Behavioral Aspect (CBA): "Teacher generates a suitable atmosphere that encourages students to formulate doubts or share opinions". Similarly, the item Follow - Up Easiness, in which the first anchor point is represented by a situation of non - fulfillment of all the Core Behavioral Aspects (CBAs), the minimum level of performance appears in the anchor point. This anchor is represented by the Core Behavioral Aspect (CBA): "Teacher encourages student to participate in the course in different ways (class work, class queries, online discussion forums…)". Both examples emphasize the concepts of support, motivation, participation, and dialogue, which have been repeatedly highlighted in the literature on constructivist approaches by different authors (Martínez - Geijo, 2008; Pegalajar - Palomino, 2016; Samuelowicz & Bain, 1992, 2001).

CONCLUSION

The instruments designed for the 2 teaching methodologies differ substantially from each other. The differences between the 2 questionnaires are evident, in the order and grouping of the behavioral episodes in every anchor point. The results show the alignment between the content of the Core Behavioral Aspects (CBAs) used in the different anchor points and several of the typical features of behaviorist and constructivist approaches presented in the previous literature (Martínez - Geijo, 2008; Samuelowicz & Bain, 2001).

Thus, for example, in the questionnaire designed to evaluate the performance of teachers who use behaviorist methodologies, it is observed that students think it is essential that the teacher provide a bibliography with the handbooks necessary to follow the course. In this instrument it is also reflected how the student taught under these methodologies considers of critical importance the planning and chronological organization of the course contents.

Similarly, in the questionnaire constructed for teachers aligned with constructivist approaches, it is evident the relevance given to the subject contextualization within the professional field for which the student is being prepared. Likewise, in this second instrument, the importance of aspects such as dialogue, motivation, or student participation in debates is also highlighted.

Divergences between the 2 questionnaires are evident, not only in terms of the behavioral episodes to be evaluated but also in terms of the importance given to them in each approach. However, the quality systems, used so far, irresponsibly ignore the fact that teachers' performance in different teaching approaches should be assessing by applying different measurement instruments.

This situation is especially important if we consider that the instruments used to measure the performance of teaching staff, besides being an essential part of the quality systems applied in the management of university organizations (Ruiz - Carrascosa, 2005), are also one of the indicators on which depends the promotion of teaching staff. In light of the above, it does not seem responsible to assess the effectiveness of teachers who apply antagonistic methodologies using identical instruments.

If we take into consideration, the aforementioned example of the item Course Introduction is not reasonable to give the same value to the provision of bibliographical references in teachers who use a behaviorist methodology as for teachers who use a constructivist approach. In the first one, the bibliographic contents are indispensable in the construction of knowledge. In the second, as knowledge is built through the development of experiences and the confrontation of different points of view, these materials are merely accessory. Consequently, it would be irresponsible and unfair to evaluate the performance of a constructivist teacher based on the exploitation of bibliographical materials, as it would be negligent to assess the performance of a behaviorist teacher by focusing on whether he or she employs debates to develop the students' knowledge.

Managerial and Practical Implications

Therefore, in order to move towards quality systems that allow a responsible and sustainable management in the university; each teacher, must be evaluated with the appropriate instrument, depending on whether he or she applies one approach or another.

This change would have associated important changes in terms of management. These changes would have implications in 2 ways. Firstly, pre - assessment implications, those that concern the management changes required before introducing the measurement system proposed by the authors. Secondly, post - assessment implications, those that affect the management adjustments that would be necessary after the implementation of the 2 - instruments evaluation postulated in the study. Several examples of these pre - assessment and post - assessment implications are shown in Table 4.

Table 4. Pre - assessment and Post - assessment Managerial Implications

Pre - Assessment Managerial Implications	Post - Assessment Managerial Implications
The university must categorize its teaching staff based on the teaching methodology applied.	The university must monitor the professional evolution of its teaching staff based on the methodology applied, offering differentiated career plans.
The university must design a double administration, management, and distribution system of surveys for the 2 instruments considered.	The university must design double processes of data cleaning, data analysis and results reporting for the 2 instruments considered.
The university must design incentive systems to apply rewards associated with the performance indicators for both instruments (professional promotion, reduction of class hours, etc.).	The university should make effective the rewards associated with the performance indicators of both instruments (professional promotion, reduction of class hours, etc.).
The quality assessment agencies must design incentive systems to apply rewards associated with the performance indicators of both instruments (funding incentives, salary improvements, curricular recognitions, etc.).	The quality assessment agencies should make effective the rewards associated with the performance indicators of both instruments (funding incentives, salary improvements, curricular recognitions, etc.).

Source: Own Elaboration

As can be seen in Table 4, these managerial implications, in line with previous research (Cave et al., 1997; Guthrie & Neumann, 2007), would impact both the university management itself, and the management responsibilities of the quality assessment agencies at the national level. Affecting aspects such as administrative and reporting processes, teacher's contractual conditions, salary situation, or the distribution of class hours, among others.

FUTURE RESEARCH DIRECTIONS

The present work can be improved in several ways. First, the sample could be augmented in order to explore more deeply the observed phenomena. Our study comprises only participants from social sciences; further research should involve teachers and students from other disciplines, covering health sciences, experimental sciences, or engineering, amongst others. The inclusion of participants from a wider variety of fields could provide distinct findings from those presented in this investigation.

Second, this study is carried out exclusively in a Spanish university. Consequently, future research could also consider undertaking comparative studies among different countries. This approach will help the academic community to reveal in which extend the conclusions offered here can be generalized or not.

Third, even though the questionnaires for both teaching methodologies were successfully designed, these instruments have not yet been effectively implemented. This work, consequently, shows the initial stage of a project that is currently being evaluated by the management teams of different universities in Spain.

Finally, the work focuses exclusively on the performance of teaching staff in the university context. Consequently, even though the proposed investigation could be replicated, in future studies, to improve quality management in schools, the instruments designed by the authors focus on the performance assessment of university teachers.

The issues aforementioned address new avenues of study, confirming that further research is still needed to expand our understanding on university management and the measurement of teaching staff performance.

REFERENCES

Abdelnaeim, S. M., & El-Bassiouny, N. (2020). The relationship between entrepreneurial cognitions and sustainability orientation: The case of an emerging market. *Journal of Entrepreneurship in Emerging Economies*, *20*(12), 12–29.

Adams, M. J. D., & Umbach, P. D. (2012). Nonresponse and Online Student Evaluations of Teaching: Understanding the Influence of Salience, Fatigue, and Academic Environments. *Research in Higher Education*, *53*(5), 576–591. doi:10.100711162-011-9240-5

Alvarado-Lagunas, E., Ramirez, D. M., & Tellez, E. A. (2016). Perception of educational quality: Case applied to students of the Autonomous University of Nuevo León and the Technological Institute of Higher Studies of Monterrey. *Revista de la Educación Superior*, *45*(180), 55–74.

Álvarez-Rojo, V., Garcia-Jimenez, E., & Gil Flores, J. (1999). The quality of university education from the perspective of the professors who are best valued by students. *Review of Education*, *319*, 273–290.

Aquino, R. S., Luck, M., & Schanzel, H. A. (2018). A conceptual framework of tourism social entrepreneurship for sustainable community development. *Journal of Hospitality and Tourism Management, 37*, 23–32. doi:10.1016/j.jhtm.2018.09.001

Bangert, A. W. (2006). The development of an instrument for assessing online teaching effectiveness. *Journal of Educational Computing Research, 35*(3), 227–244. doi:10.2190/B3XP-5K61-7Q07-U443

Bernardin, H. J. (1977). Behavioral expectation scales versus summated scales. *The Journal of Applied Psychology, 62*(4), 422–427. doi:10.1037/0021-9010.62.4.422

Cave, M., Hanney, S., Henkel, M., & Kogan, M. (1997). The use of performance indicators in higher education. In *Higher Education Policy Series*. Jessica Kingsley Publishers.

Cervelló-Royo, R., Moya-Clemente, I., Perelló-Marín, M. R., & Ribes-Giner, G. (2020). Sustainable development, economic and financial factors that influence the opportunity-driven entrepreneurship. An fsQCA approach. *Journal of Business Research, 115*, 393–402. doi:10.1016/j.jbusres.2019.10.031

De-La-Orden, A. (2009). Quality and evaluation: Analysis of a model. *Estudios Sobre Educación, 16*, 17–36.

Dickinson, T. L., & Zellinger, P. M. (1980). A comparison of the behaviorally anchored rating and mixed standard scale formats. *The Journal of Applied Psychology, 65*(2), 147–154. doi:10.1037/0021-9010.65.2.147

Gil-Edo, M. T., Roca Puig, V., & Camisón Zornoza, C. (1999). Towards customer - oriented service quality models in public universities: The case of Universitat Jaume I. *Investigaciones Europeas de Dirección y Economía de la Empresa, 5*(2), 69–92.

Guthrie, J., & Neumann, R. (2007). Economic and non - financial performance indicators in universities. *Public Management Review, 9*(2), 231–252. doi:10.1080/14719030701340390

Hernandez-Pina, F., & Maquilón-Sánchez, J. J. (2010). Conceptions of teaching. Contributions to teacher training. *Revista Electrónica Interuniversitaria de Formación Del Profesorado, 13*(3), 17–25.

Homero-Orozco, G., Sola-Olalla, M. R., & Martinez-Abad, F. (2018). Didactic Models at the High Education: A reality that can change. Profesorado. *Revista de Curriculum y Formación Del Profesorado, 22*(2), 447–469.

Kember, D. (1997). A reconceptualization of the research into university academics' conceptions of teaching. *Learning and Instruction, 7*(3), 255–275. doi:10.1016/S0959-4752(96)00028-X

Kember, D., & Wong, A. (2000). Implications for evaluation from a study of students' perceptions. *Higher Education, 40*(1), 69–97. doi:10.1023/A:1004068500314

Kivarina, M., Kulikov, S., Zagorodnikov, K., Zhiltsov, V., & Khan, N. (2020). Economic Growth Humanization: Responsibility of Business and Social Entrepreneurship. *Quality - Access to Success, 21*(176), 16–21.

Lemos, M. S., Queirós, C., Teixeira, P. M., & Menezes, I. (2011). Development and validation of a theoretically based, multidimensional questionnaire of student evaluation of university teaching. *Assessment & Evaluation in Higher Education*, *36*(7), 843–864. doi:10.1080/02602938.2010.493969

Marsh, H. W. (1982). SEEQ: A reliable, valid, and useful instrument for collecting students' evaluations of university teaching. *The British Journal of Educational Psychology*, *52*(2), 77–95. doi:10.1111/j.2044-8279.1982.tb02505.x

Martínez-Geijo, P. (2008). Learning styles: Methodological guidelines for working in the classroom. *Revista Complutense de Educación*, *19*(1), 77–94.

Matosas, L. (2018). Core behavioral aspects of university professors in Student Evaluation of Teaching (SET) for blended learning models. *Espacios*, *39*(10), 10–24.

Matosas-Lopez, L., Leguey-Galan, S., & Doncel-Pedrera, L. M. (2019). Converting Likert scales into Behavioral Anchored Rating Scales (Bars) for the evaluation of teaching effectiveness for formative purposes. *Journal of University Teaching & Learning Practice*, *16*(3), 1–24.

Meade, A. W., & Craig, S. B. (2012). Identifying careless responses in survey data. *Psychological Methods*, *17*(3), 437–455. doi:10.1037/a0028085 PMID:22506584

Moore, T. (2006). Teacher Evaluations and Grades: Additional Evidence. *The Journal of American Academy of Business, Cambridge*, *9*(2).

Nor-Aishah, H., Ahmad, N. H., & Thurasamy, R. (2020). Entrepreneurial Leadership and Sustainable Performance of Manufacturing SMEs in Malaysia: The Contingent Role of Entrepreneurial Bricolage. *Sustainability*, *12*(8), 3100. doi:10.3390u12083100

Pegalajar-Palomino, M. D. C. (2016). Percepciones del alumnado de posgrado acerca de la metodología docente y evaluativa. Profesorado. *Revista de Curriculum y Formación Del Profesorado*, *20*(2), 98–119.

Piaget, J. (1981). Piaget's theory. *Journal for the Study of Education and Development*, *4*(sup 2), 13 - 54.

Pizzi, S., Caputo, A., Corvino, A., & Venturelli, A. (2020). Management research and the UN sustainable development goals (SDGs): A bibliometric investigation and systematic review. *Journal of Cleaner Production*, *276*, 1–15. doi:10.1016/j.jclepro.2020.124033

Remmers, H. H. (1928). The relationship between students' marks and student attitude toward instructors. *School & Society*, *28*, 759–760.

Resino-Blázquez, J. J., Chamizo Gonzalez, J., Cano Montero, E. I., & Gutierrez Broncano, S. (2013). Quality of college life: Identifying the key indicators of student satisfaction. *Review of Education*, *362*, 458–484.

Restrepo-Abondano, J. M. (2008). Managerial consequences of credit system introduction: A Colombian case. *Cuadernos Americanos*, *21*(37), 11–36.

Ruiz-Carrascosa, J. (2000). The evaluation of teaching by students in the national plan for evaluating the quality of universities. Construction of an assessment instrument. *Revista de Investigación Educacional*, *18*(2), 433–445.

Ruiz-Carrascosa, J. (2005). The evaluation of the teaching process in universities quality improvement plans. *Educación XX1, 8*(5), 87 - 102.

Samuelowicz, K., & Bain, J. D. (1992). Conceptions of teaching held by academic teachers. *Higher Education, 24*(1), 93–111. doi:10.1007/BF00138620

Samuelowicz, K., & Bain, J. D. (2001). Revisiting academics' beliefs about teaching and learning. *Higher Education, 41*(3), 299–325. doi:10.1023/A:1004130031247

Sierra-Sánchez, J. (2012). Factors influencing a student's decision to pursue a communications degree in Spain. *Intangible Capital, 8*(1), 43–60.

Sobrino-Morrás, Á. (2011). Teaching-learning process and web 2.0: Valuation of connectivism as a post - constructivist learning theory. *Estudios Sobre Educación, 20*, 117–140.

Stanny, C. J., & Arruda, J. E. (2017). A comparison of student evaluations of teaching with online and paper - based administration. *Scholarship of Teaching and Learning in Psychology, 3*(3), 198–207. doi:10.1037tl0000087

United Nations. (2015). Post - 2015 Development Agenda. In Integrated and coordinated implementation and monitoring of the results of major United Nations conferences and summits in the economic and social and related fields: Vol. A 69/L.85. Author.

Veciana-Vergés, J. M., & Capelleras-I-Segura, J. L. (2004). Quality of service in university teaching development and validation of a measurement scale. *Revista Europea de Dirección y Economía de La Empresa, 13*(4), 55–72.

Vygotskiĭ, L. S. (1978). *Mind in society: The development of higher psychological processes*. Harvard University Press.

Watson, J. B. (1970). *Behaviorism*. The Norton Library.

KEY TERMS AND DEFINITIONS

Anchor Point: Each of the levels that are part of a measurement scale.

Behavioral Anchored Rating Scales (BARS): Type of questionnaire employed to measure effectiveness in different labor contexts, using behavioral episodes.

Behaviorist Methodology: Approach that states that knowledge is an external element that must be transferred to the student.

Core Behavioral Aspects (CBA): Clustering of behavioral episodes that are reorganized into subcategories with common traits.

Clustering: Process of segregating a big group of elements into subgroups of elements with similar traits and characteristics.

Cognitive Methodology: Approach in which the focus is on understanding learning processes, in general, and on cognitive processes in particular.

Constructivist Methodology: Approach that states that knowledge can be constructed or generated by the student.

Dual Evaluation: Assessment procedure that consists of 2 different steps that take place sequentially.

Screening: Process in which several elements are examined with the purpose of identifying and removing those elements that present inconsistencies.

APPENDIX 1

Assessment Instrument for Teachers who Apply Behaviorist Methodologies

Question 1: Course introduction (Mark only one of the next 5 statements)

1. Teacher provides a detailed description of the bibliography / supporting materials, besides the form of using them
2. Teacher describes the chronological plan of contents on the course and the time effort required in each part (classes, exams, homework...) and teacher provides a detailed description of the bibliography / supporting materials, besides the form of using them
3. Teacher presents all the key points on the teaching guide at the beginning of the course (syllabus, competencies, objectives, working methodology, ECTS, location of the materials in the eLearning platform ...) and teacher provides a detailed description of the bibliography / supporting materials, besides the form of using them
4. Teacher presents all the key points on the teaching guide at the beginning of the course (syllabus, competencies, objectives, working methodology, ECTS, location of the materials in thc cLcarning platform ...); teacher describes the chronological plan of contents on the course and the time effort required in each part (classes, exams, homework...); and teacher provides a detailed description of the bibliography / supporting materials, besides the form of using them
5. Teacher presents all the key points on the teaching guide at the beginning of the course (syllabus, competencies, objectives, working methodology, ECTS, location of the materials in the eLearning platform ...); teacher addresses the course importance in academic / professional terms; teacher describes the chronological plan of contents on the course and the time effort required in each part (classes, exams, homework...); and teacher provides a detailed description of the bibliography / supporting materials, besides the form of using them

Question 2: Evaluation system description (Mark only one of the next 5 statements)

1. Teacher does NOT explain all the key points on the evaluation system (nº of exams, exam dates, % of theoretical / practical evaluation, assignments, quizzes, retake exams…); teacher does NOT describe specific aspects relative to the exam (supporting material, correction criteria, exam length…); teacher does NOT outline the main key contents subject to evaluation; and teacher does NOT explain the way class participation, attendance or supplementary activities are considered in course evaluation
2. Teacher explains the way class participation, attendance or supplementary activities are considered in course evaluation
3. Teacher explains all the key points on the evaluation system (nº of exams, exam dates, % of theoretical / practical evaluation, assignments, quizzes, retake exams…); and teacher explains the way class participation, attendance or supplementary activities are considered in course evaluation

4. Teacher explains all the key points on the evaluation system (nº of exams, exam dates, % of theoretical / practical evaluation, assignments, quizzes, retake exams…) and teacher describes specific aspects relative to the exam (supporting material, correction criteria, exam length…)
5. Teacher explains all the key points on the evaluation system (nº of exams, exam dates, % of theoretical / practical evaluation, assignments, quizzes, retake exams…); teacher describes specific aspects relative to the exam (supporting material, correction criteria, exam length…); teacher outlines the main key contents subject to evaluation; and teacher explains the way class participation, attendance or supplementary activities are considered in course evaluation

Question 3: Time management (Mark only one of the next 5 statements)

1. Teacher is NOT punctual in class arrival to prepare the required teaching materials (notes, projections, multimedia resources...); teacher does NOT manage class time effectively, retrieving delays or potential absences if necessary; teacher does NOT notify possible changes in class times in advance or absences if necessary; and teacher does NOT maintain a homogeneous time of instruction on daily / weekly basis
2. Teacher outlines the main key contents subject to evaluation and teacher explains the way class participation, attendance or supplementary activities are considered in course evaluation
3. Teacher manages class time effectively, retrieving delays or potential absences if necessary and teacher maintains a homogeneous time of instruction on daily / weekly basis
4. Teacher is punctual in class arrival to prepare the required teaching materials (notes, projections, multimedia resources...); teacher maintains a homogeneous time of instruction on daily / weekly basis; and teacher notifies possible changes in class times in advance or absences if necessary
5. Teacher is punctual in class arrival to prepare the required teaching materials (notes, projections, multimedia resources...); teacher manages class time effectively, retrieving delays or potential absences if necessary; teacher notifies possible changes in class times in advance or absences if necessary; and teacher maintains a homogeneous time of instruction on daily / weekly basis

Question 5: Organizational coherence (Mark only one of the next 5 statements)

1. Teacher does NOT maintain the working methodology initially presented at the beginning of the course; teacher does NOT respect the chronological plan of contents designed for every week; teacher does NOT develop exactly the content in the course syllabus (No more no less content); and teacher does NOT prioritize key contents to achieve course objectives / competencies and indicates the specific competencies developed in each training activity
2. Teacher respects the chronological plan of contents designed for every week
3. Teacher maintains the working methodology initially presented at the beginning of the course
4. Teacher maintains the working methodology initially presented at the beginning of the course; teacher develops exactly the content in the course syllabus (No more no less content) and teacher prioritizes key contents to achieve course objectives / competencies and indicates the specific competencies developed in each training activity
5. Teacher maintains the working methodology initially presented at the beginning of the course; teacher respects the chronological plan of contents designed for every week; teacher develops exactly

the content in the course syllabus (No more no less content); and teacher prioritizes key contents to achieve course objectives / competencies and indicates the specific competencies developed in each training activity

Question 7: Dealing with doubts (Mark only one of the next 5 statements)

1. Teacher does NOT generate a suitable atmosphere that encourage students to formulate doubts or share opinions; teacher does NOT establish specific breaks during classes to formulate doubts; teacher is NOT able to face student´s doubts presenting one single concept in several ways and; teacher does NOT resolve students' doubts using practical examples / supporting materials to fix the idea
2. Teacher establishes specific breaks during classes to formulate doubts
3. Teacher generates a suitable atmosphere that encourage students to formulate doubts or share opinions; teacher establishes specific breaks during classes to formulate doubts; and teacher resolves students' doubts using practical examples / supporting materials to fix the idea
4. Teacher generates a suitable atmosphere that encourage students to formulate doubts or share opinions; teacher is able to face student´s doubts presenting one single concept in several ways; and teacher resolves students' doubts using practical examples / supporting materials to fix the idea
5. Teacher generates a suitable atmosphere that encourage students to formulate doubts or share opinions; teacher establishes specific breaks during classes to formulate doubts; teacher is able to face student´s doubts presenting one single concept in several ways; and teacher resolves students' doubts using practical examples / supporting materials to fix the idea

Question 9: Follow - up easiness (Mark only one of the next 5 statements)

1. Teacher does NOT connect contents across course stages to create a general perspective of the subject; teacher does NOT assign an achievable weekly / monthly workload to the student; teacher does NOT encourage student to participate in the course in different ways (class work, class queries, online discussion forums…); and teacher does NOT summarize daily / weekly the main ideas previously explained in class
2. Teacher assigns an achievable weekly / monthly workload to the student and teacher summarizes daily / weekly the main ideas previously explained in class
3. Teacher assigns an achievable weekly / monthly workload to the student and teacher encourages student to participate in the course in different ways (class work, class queries, online discussion forums…)
4. Teacher assigns an achievable weekly / monthly workload to the student; teacher encourages student to participate in the course in different ways (class work, class queries, online discussion forums…) and teacher summarizes daily / weekly the main ideas previously explained in class
5. Teacher connects contents across course stages to create a general perspective of the subject; teacher assigns an achievable weekly / monthly workload to the student; teacher encourages student to participate in the course in different ways (class work, class queries, online discussion forums…); and teacher summarizes daily / weekly the main ideas previously explained in class

Question 10: Overall satisfaction (Mark only one of the next 5 statements)

1. Teacher does NOT contribute decisively on the achievement of the expected objectives / competencies on the course; teacher does NOT influence the academic / professional development of the student; teacher does NOT exhibit a recognize knowledge on the field besides the ability to convey that knowledge; and teacher is NOT able to raise student interest in the field of instruction
2. Teacher exhibits a recognize knowledge on the field besides the ability to convey that knowledge
3. Teacher contributes decisively on the achievement of the expected objectives / competencies on the course and teacher exhibits a recognize knowledge on the field besides the ability to convey that knowledge
4. Teacher contributes decisively on the achievement of the expected objectives / competencies on the course; teacher influences the academic / professional development of the student; and teacher exhibits a recognize knowledge on the field besides the ability to convey that knowledge
5. Teacher contributes decisively on the achievement of the expected objectives / competencies on the course; teacher influences the academic / professional development of the student; teacher exhibits a recognize knowledge on the field besides the ability to convey that knowledge; and teacher is able to raise student interest in the field of instruction

APPENDIX 2

Assessment Instrument for Teachers who Apply Constructivist Methodologies

Question 1: Course introduction (Mark only one of the next 5 statements)

1. Teacher addresses the course importance in academic / professional terms
2. Teacher addresses the course importance in academic / professional terms and teacher provides a detailed description of the bibliography / supporting materials, besides the form of using them
3. Teacher presents all the key points on the teaching guide at the beginning of the course (syllabus, competencies, objectives, working methodology, ECTS, location of the materials in the eLearning platform ...) and teacher provides a detailed description of the bibliography / supporting materials, besides the form of using them
4. Teacher presents all the key points on the teaching guide at the beginning of the course (syllabus, competencies, objectives, working methodology, ECTS, location of the materials in the eLearning platform ...); teacher addresses the course importance in academic / professional terms; and teacher describes the chronological plan of contents on the course and the time effort required in each part (classes, exams, homework...)
5. Teacher presents all the key points on the teaching guide at the beginning of the course (syllabus, competencies, objectives, working methodology, ECTS, location of the materials in the eLearning

platform ...); teacher addresses the course importance in academic / professional terms; teacher describes the chronological plan of contents on the course and the time effort required in each part (classes, exams, homework...); and teacher provides a detailed description of the bibliography / supporting materials, besides the form of using them

Question 2: Evaluation system description (Mark only one of the next 5 statements)

1. Teacher does NOT explain all the key points on the evaluation system (nº of exams, exam dates, % of theoretical / practical evaluation, assignments, quizzes, retake exams…); teacher does NOT describe specific aspects relative to the exam (supporting material, correction criteria, exam length…); teacher does NOT outline the main key contents subject to evaluation; and teacher does NOT explain the way class participation, attendance or supplementary activities are considered in course evaluation
2. Teacher explains the way class participation, attendance or supplementary activities are considered in course evaluation
3. Teacher explains all the key points on the evaluation system (nº of exams, exam dates, % of theoretical / practical evaluation, assignments, quizzes, retake exams…) and teacher outlines the main key contents subject to evaluation
4. Teacher explains all the key points on the evaluation system (nº of exams, exam dates, % of theoretical / practical evaluation, assignments, quizzes, retake exams…); teacher describes specific aspects relative to the exam (supporting material, correction criteria, exam length…); and teacher outlines the main key contents subject to evaluation
5. Teacher explains all the key points on the evaluation system (nº of exams, exam dates, % of theoretical / practical evaluation, assignments, quizzes, retake exams…); teacher describes specific aspects relative to the exam (supporting material, correction criteria, exam length…); teacher outlines the main key contents subject to evaluation; and teacher explains the way class participation, attendance or supplementary activities are considered in course evaluation

Question 3: Time management (Mark only one of the next 5 statements)

1. Teacher is NOT punctual in class arrival to prepare the required teaching materials (notes, projections, multimedia resources...); teacher does NOT manage class time effectively, retrieving delays or potential absences if necessary; teacher does NOT notify possible changes in class times in advance or absences if necessary; and teacher does NOT maintain an homogeneous time of instruction on daily / weekly basis
2. Teacher maintains a homogeneous time of instruction on daily / weekly basis and teacher manages class time effectively, retrieving delays or potential absences if necessary
3. Teacher maintains a homogeneous time of instruction on daily / weekly basis and teacher notifies possible changes in class times in advance or absences if necessary
4. Teacher is punctual in class arrival to prepare the required teaching materials (notes, projections, multimedia resources...) and teacher notifies possible changes in class times in advance or absences if necessary

5. Teacher is punctual in class arrival to prepare the required teaching materials (notes, projections, multimedia resources...); teacher manages class time effectively, retrieving delays or potential absences if necessary; teacher notifies possible changes in class times in advance or absences if necessary; and teacher maintains an homogeneous time of instruction on daily / weekly basis

Question 5: Organizational coherence (Mark only one of the next 5 statements)

1. Teacher does NOT maintain the working methodology initially presented at the beginning of the course; teacher does NOT respect the chronological plan of contents designed for every week; teacher does NOT develop exactly the content in the course syllabus (No more no less content); and teacher does NOT prioritize key contents to achieve course objectives / competencies and indicates the specific competencies developed in each training activity
2. Teacher maintains the working methodology initially presented at the beginning of the course
3. Teacher maintains the working methodology initially presented at the beginning of the course; and teacher respects the chronological plan of contents designed for every week
4. Teacher maintains the working methodology initially presented at the beginning of the course; teacher develops exactly the content in the course syllabus (No more no less content); and teacher prioritizes key contents to achieve course objectives / competencies and indicates the specific competencies developed in each training activity
5. Teacher maintains the working methodology initially presented at the beginning of the course; teacher respects the chronological plan of contents designed for every week; teacher develops exactly the content in the course syllabus (No more no less content); and teacher prioritizes key contents to achieve course objectives / competencies and indicates the specific competencies developed in each training activity

Question 7: Dealing with doubts (Mark only one of the next 5 statements)

1. Teacher generates a suitable atmosphere that encourage students to formulate doubts or share opinions
2. Teacher is able to face student´s doubts presenting one single concept in several ways; and teacher resolves students' doubts using practical examples / supporting materials to fix the idea
3. Teacher generates a suitable atmosphere that encourage students to formulate doubts or share opinions; and teacher establishes specific breaks during classes to formulate doubts
4. Teacher establishes specific breaks during classes to formulate doubts; teacher is able to face student´s doubts presenting one single concept in several ways; and teacher resolves students' doubts using practical examples / supporting materials to fix the idea
5. Teacher generates a suitable atmosphere that encourage students to formulate doubts or share opinions; teacher establishes specific breaks during classes to formulate doubts; teacher is able to face student´s doubts presenting one single concept in several ways; and teacher resolves students' doubts using practical examples / supporting materials to fix the idea

Question 9: Follow - up easiness (Mark only one of the next 5 statements)

1. Teacher does NOT connect contents across course stages to create a general perspective of the subject; teacher does NOT summarize daily / weekly the main ideas previously explained in class; teacher does NOT encourage student to participate in the course in different ways (class work, class queries, online discussion forums…); and teacher does NOT assign an achievable weekly / monthly workload to the student
2. Teacher encourages student to participate in the course in different ways (class work, class queries, online discussion forums…)
3. Teacher encourages student to participate in the course in different ways (class work, class queries, online discussion forums…); and teacher assigns an achievable weekly / monthly workload to the student
4. Teacher connects contents across course stages to create a general perspective of the subject; teacher summarizes daily / weekly the main ideas previously explained in class; and teacher assigns an achievable weekly / monthly workload to the student
5. Teacher connects contents across course stages to create a general perspective of the subject; teacher summarizes daily / weekly the main ideas previously explained in class; teacher encourages student to participate in the course in different ways (class work, class queries, online discussion forums…); and teacher assigns an achievable weekly / monthly workload to the student

Question 10: Overall satisfaction (Mark only one of the next 5 statements)

1. Teacher does NOT contribute decisively on the achievement of the expected objectives / competencies on the course; teacher does NOT influence the academic / professional development of the student; teacher does NOT exhibit a recognize knowledge on the field besides the ability to convey that knowledge; and teacher is NOT able to raise student interest in the field of instruction
2. Teacher exhibits a recognize knowledge on the field besides the ability to convey that knowledge
3. Teacher contributes decisively on the achievement of the expected objectives / competencies on the course; teacher influences the academic / professional development of the student; and teacher exhibits a recognize knowledge on the field besides the ability to convey that knowledge
4. Teacher contributes decisively on the achievement of the expected objectives / competencies on the course; teacher exhibits a recognize knowledge on the field besides the ability to convey that knowledge; and teacher is able to raise student interest in the field of instruction
5. Teacher contributes decisively on the achievement of the expected objectives / competencies on the course; teacher influences the academic / professional development of the student; teacher exhibits a recognize knowledge on the field besides the ability to convey that knowledge; and teacher is able to raise student interest in the field of instruction

Chapter 7
Turkey's Entrepreneurship Development

Yunus Emre Genç
https://orcid.org/0000-0003-3924-6094
Giresun University, Turkey

ABSTRACT

Entrepreneurship is a key element for developing of economies in recent years. Turkey is a country that is experiencing entrepreneurship both in national and international area. The Turkish economy, especially after 1980, opened its doors to the world global economy, and entrepreneurship became more important in this new order. Before 1980, the big companies were established only in the big cities of Turkey. But after that time, they started to be founded in small cities, too. There are governmental support organizations in Turkey, which fund the entrepreneurship intentions. And there are also new regulations in recent years in Turkey, which enable entrepreneurship activities to establish online on internet processes. By comparison with other countries, it could easily be said that Turkey is also in the arena with facilitation and developing of entrepreneurship in the world scene. Turkish people know more about the increasing importance of entrepreneurship now.

INTRODUCTION

Entrepreneurship is not new, however its popularity is still growing rapidly as a result of a wide range of factors. Removal of the trade barriers, global economic recessions, improvement in information and telecommunication technologies, corporate restructurings, downsizing, mergers and acquisitions are among the major factors that lead the topic to sustain its critical importance. As a result of the above mentioned states, entrepreneurship is increasingly catching the attention of the academia as well as the governments, policy makers, NGOs and other profit or non-profit institutions. While many governments are working on new policies to support entrepreneurship, higher education institutions (HEI) are continuously launching new and innovative programs, courses and seminars on entrepreneurship. All these efforts have one common final target which is fostering and encouraging entrepreneurial activities and innovation (Demirci, 2013, p.21).

DOI: 10.4018/978-1-7998-7951-0.ch007

Entrepreneurship and entrepreneurs are described as an exit from economic turmoil for the economies in whole world in the sense of development of economies and decreasing unemployment problems. Increase in production and employment thanks to new entrepreneurs has great importance in the sense of Turkish economy as well. Therefore in order to develop entrepreneurship culture and activities and creating new entrepreneurs for different sectors, both state and private institutions in Turkey have been begun to increase their operations rapidly in recent years. Works on entrepreneurship which also contribute inter-sectoral relations becomes popular country-wide in Turkey (Sönmez and Toksoy, 2014, p. 41).

Entrepreneurship is an key element for developing of economies in recent years. Turkey is a country that experiencing entrepreneurship within years both in national and international area. Turkish economy, especially after year 1980, opened its doors to the world global economy and entrepreneurship became more important in this new order. Before 1980 the big companies were established only in the big cities of Turkey. But after that time they were started to be founded in small cities, too. There is govermental support organizations in Turkey, which funds the entrepreneurship intentions. And there is also new regulations in recent years in Turkey, which enables entrepreneurship activities, in starting to establishment process even online on internet (via e-state gateway) so. By comparison with other countries it could easily said that Turkey is also on the arena with facilitation and developing of entrepreneurship in the world scene. Turkish people knows more about the increasing importance of the entrepreneurship day by day now.

DEFİNİTİON OF ENTREPRENEURSHİP

In literature, it is possible to find various definitions to the required qualifications of an entrepreneur emphasized on different specifications. In this context leads to many different definitions with examination of qualifications posessed by an entrepreneur, examination of entrepreneur's functions and examination of entrepreneur's behavious and activities. It is communicable that within a definition which emphasizes on behaviours and activities of an entrepreneur the following specifications shall become pronounced (GISEP 2015-2018, p. 3):

- Combining the required resources with already available ones and organizing their conversion to products or present resources to get use of the opportunities that are present or the entrepreneur has formed,
- Performing spontaneous initiatives at any stage of starting a business and show leadership qualities,
- Calculating risks at during these processes and despite these risks taking relevant measures and carry on the path,
- Continiously seeking innovation and beyond being sensitive towards customer expectations, creating his/her own expectations.

ENTREPRENEURSHIP IN TURKEY

According to TOBB President, M. Rifat HİSARCIKLIOĞLU:

Turkey has come a long way in terms of economic and private sector development since 1980s, and now classified as one of the efficiencydriven economies in the world, in a group that includes high-growth economies such as Brazil and China. Firms in an efficiency-driven economy compete and grow by cutting down costs, while firms in an innovation-driven economy compete and grow by creating unique value at the global level. In order to upgrade to an innovation-driven stage, Turkish economy needs high-impact enterprises that are able to scale-up to the global level by creating unique value. Entrepreneurship is a key factor in creating high-impact enterprises. (GEM Report Turkey, 2010, p. 7)

Entrepreneurship is an key element for developing of economies recently. Turkey is a country that experiencing entrepreneurship within years both in national and international area. Turkish economy, especially after year 1980, opened its door to the world global economy and entrepreneurship became more important in this new order. Before 1980 the big companies were established only in big cities in Turkey. But after that time they were started to be founded in small cities, too. There is governmental support organizations in Turkey, which funds the entrepreneurship intentions. And there is also new regulations in recent years in Turkey, which enables entrepreneurship activities, in starting to establishment process even online on internet (via e-state gateway) so. By comparison with other countries it could easily said that Turkey is also on the arena with facilitation and developing of entrepreneurship in the world scene. Turkish people knows more about the increasing importance of the entrepreneurship day by day now.

From the historical perspective, evolution of entrepreneurial thought in Turkey can be studied in three periods (Demirci, 2013, p. 27):

Prior to Turkish Republic. In the Ottoman Empire, non-muslim population was taking the major role in commercial activities. Nevertheless, Muslim population's ignorance for commerce could never be explained by Islamic rules, that do not forbid the commercial activities. Furthermore there is no evidence that the governmental regulations were restraining the muslim population from doing business with non-muslims. Lately, the Empire in decline missed the commercial opportunities sourced by the industrial revolution. On the other hand, artisans -under umbrella of their organisations- were efficient in production, whilst manufacturing locally they were fulfiling in-state needs until the imperial edict of gülhane in 1839, which enables to found establish without any roof (cited from Müftüoğlu, 2013, p. 27, Bülbül, 2010, p. 40).

1923-1980 Period. After the Turkish Republic was formed in 1923, republicans constantly emphasized the importance of entrepreneurial activities. Despite the regulations towards supporting entrepreneurial initiatives, protectionist and state-led economic policies were in use. In late 1930s, companies owned by the state were the major players in Turkish economy. Dominance of the state-owned companies continued until the beginning of the 1980s.

After the 1980s in summary. After beginning of 1980s, as a result of a shift from protectionist economic policies to free market economy, private sector started to get stronger whilst the stateowned companies losing ground especially in industrial sector. Another shift was in the perceptions of Turkish people that people started to get familiar with the concepts like the markets, competition and quality. In this term, many structural reforms had been introduced in the general structure of Turkish economy. Some of these reforms are the liberalization of foreign trade, currency and investments, freely floating exchange rates, elimination of price controls, new interest rate policy to enhance savings, strictly controlled public expenditures and last an open and flexible foreign investment policy.

The entrepreneurship ecosystem is evolving day by day with Turkish and foreign partners in Turkey and makes the atmosphere more available for new start-ups. The ministry of education has put entrepreneurship courses into the curriculum of middle and high schools since 2009. Turkish government agencies are taking active and integral roles now in this ecosystem through monetary and non-monetary support programs provided by TUBİTAK and KOSGEB. Financial supports available in the Turkish entrepreneurship ecosystem, especially through the KOSGEB new entrepreneur support programs, are the first examples of its kind and can therefore be set as good practice for other countries want to support their entrepreneurs. Notable increase in businesses founded and numbers of businesses supported by government agencies during the last decade is such a result. In Turkey, the regulations for angel investors were introduced and have enabled interested individuals to become a part of this ecosystem in 2013. The entrepreneurial spirit is accelerated rapidly in Turkey with evolvement of contextual factors for supporting entrepreneurship (Öner and Kunday, 2016, p. 68).

Although the effects of entrepreneurship on the economy have been an important debate issue in the literature for a long time, entrepreneurship's effects on business cycles and economic growth, with the impact of globalization, has emerged as a subject of intensive research on how it affects employment and unemployment. According to the findings released by the study of Apaydın, the increases in entrepreneurship in Turkey reduce unemployment. In this regard, the application and development of policies that encourage entrepreneurship is important to reduce unemployment. Because the fact that; attempt with unemployment is based solely on these policies should not be appeared as the only solution, determining the structural reasons of unemployment and producing policies accordingly will be the healthiest way in order to find a consistent solution to the problem. (Apaydın, 2018, pp. 11-12).

According to Demirci (2013, p. 28) GEM Global Report 2010 sorts Turkey among efficiency-driven economies. Table 1 shows the entrepreneurship activities in selected efficiency-driven economies.

Table 1. Global Entrepreneurship Monitor's (GEM) Total Entrepreneurial Activity (TEA) Figures in Selected Countries

Country	Total Early-Stage Entrepreneurship Activity	Established Business Ownership Rate	Discontinuation of Businesses
Peru	27.2	7.2	9.2
Brazil	17.5	15.3	5.3
China	14.4	13.8	5.6
Argentina	14.2	12.4	3.8
Latvia	9.7	7.6	4.2
Turkey	8.6	10.7	4.6
Hungary	7.1	5.4	2.9
Romania	4.3	2.1	2.6
Russia	3.9	2.8	0.8
Average (unweighted)	**11.7**	**7.6**	**4.4**

Turkey has a lower entrepreneurship rate compared to the average TEA rates for efficiency-driven economies. In terms of the start-up survival rates, Turkish new ventures perform close to average among efficiency-driven economies (Demirci, 2013, p. 28).

Entrepreneurship is a crucial part of national economic growth and development. Turkey is currently at the efficiency-driven stage of economic development group with the other countries included as follows: Argentina, Bosnia and Herzegovina, Brazil, Chile, China, Colombia, Costa Rica, Croatia, Ecuador, Hungary, Latvia, Macedonia, Malaysia, Mexico, Montenegro, Peru, Romania, Russia, South Africa, Taiwan, Trinidad and Tobago, Tunisia, and Uruguay (GEM Report Turkey, 2010, p. 11).

In general terms, and to summarize, results of Report "GEM Turkey 2010" indicate that while people of low-to-middle income embark on or have embarked on a business tend to be necessity-driven entrepreneurs, conversely, at the highest income level, persons tend to be opportunity-driven entrepreneurs (GEM Report Turkey, 2010, p. 12).

A few most important factors in terms of entrepreneurship could be pointed out for Turkey according to Zbierowski (2015, p. 84)'s research:

- the level of intent is the highest in Europe (over 30% of people consider the possibility of starting up a business within next three years),
- high level of opportunity recognition, lower than in just a few European countries,
- lowest level of fear of failure in Europe,
- high level of early-stage entrepreneurial activity,
- lower level of established businesses ownership,
- high growth expectations,
- considerable gender gap.

Ali Sabancı, Chairman of TOBB Young Entrepreneurs Board, Turkey, states that:

The development of our country depends on the achievements of young entrepreneurs. We should encourage our young people to choose entrepreneurship as a career path. Therefore, we need to create awareness about entrepreneurship and increase the number of role models in Turkey. (GEM Global Report, 2010, p. 32)

About KOSGEB (https://en.kosgeb.gov.tr/site/tr/genel/detay/347/about-kosgeb, 13 July 2018 **date** last **accessed**)

KÜSGEM (Small Industry Development Center), which was established in the Ministry of Industry and Trade, in the form of a pilot project in Gaziantep in 1973 within the frame of the International Treaty between the Government of Republic of Turkey and United Nations Industrial Development Organization, was started to provide service with community facility workshops for the small –scale industrial enterprises.

Those efforts were subjected to a further improvment in the following years and KÜSGET (Small Industry Development Organization General Directorate) started its activities under the International Treaty on the "Development of Publication Services of Small Industry", which was published in the Official Gazette dated September 6th 1984 and numbered 18157 basing on the Cabinet Decree dated June 17th 1983 and numbered 83/6744. KÜSGET, which has provided technical consultancy services with Centers of Development of Small Scaled Enterprises, put modern administration principles into application in enterprises, showed efforts for the establishment and spread of quality awareness at world standards, rising technologic production level and increasing employment capacity and tried to perform the services for strengthening the technical infrastructure in order to provide contemporary management skills.

Under the International Treaty on the "Provision of Industrial Training Services", which entered into force after being acceded with the Cabinet Decree dated November 10th 1978 and numbered 7/16728, SEGEM (Industrial Training and Development Center General Directorate) put forward its activities. SEGEM was organised to include both in-class seminar type education and in-factory, at-work implementation; to prepare training programs for the new university and higher education school graduates in order to provide them with the fundamental experiences for ensuring them make a good start for their professional carriers and to respond to the specific, special needs of industrial organizations; and has been an organization providing service with the purpose of increasing the working skills of university or higher education school graduate personnel in the industry through in-factory, on-the-job training programs and preparing them for higher positions in the organizations, where they work.

Due to reasons such as the limited period of those services, which KÜSGET and SEGEM tried to perform within the frame of project agreements and their inability to sufficiently meet the needs in the entire country, the "Law on the Establishment of Small and Medium Scaled Industry Development and Support Directorate" numbered 3624 was prepared with the purpose of joining those two organizations under KOSGEB's roof to provide more comprehensive, continuous and widespread services in the entire country and entered into force being published in the Official Gazette dated April 20th 1990 and numbered 20498.

KOSGEB provided services and supports only for the production industry SMEs until 2009. However, due to the increase in the added value production and employment creation potentials of the sectors other than the production sector in our country and due to the requests got from SMEs in the sectors other than the production sector, the necessity to arise to enlarge the target population of KOSGEB in a way to cover all SMEs.

In line with this objective, the "Law numbered 5891 on Amending the KOSGEB Establishment Law numbered 3624" was published in the Official Gazette dated May 5th 2009 and numbered 27219. The law amendment enabled the necessary legal grounds for KOSGEB to support SMEs other than the ones in the production industry sectors. The Cabinet Decree numbered 15431 on the "Determination of Sector and Regional Priorities of Small and Medium Enterprises that will Benefit from the Services and Supports to be Provided by KOSGEB" was published in the Official Journal dated September 18th 2009 and numbered 27353, and with this decree, the sectoral and regional priorities related with the enterprises that will benefit from the services and supports to be provided by KOSGEB were designed.

ENTREPRENEURSHİP EDUCATİON AND TRAİNİNG İN TURKEY

Gürol and Atsan (2006, p. 36) suggest that in Turkey a national perspective on entrepreneurship education should be developed to encourage more universities to provide courses on entrepreneurship and offer a major on entrepreneurship, and, furthermore, to consider founding new institutions to teach only entrepreneurship. Course content on entrepreneurship in Turkey generally entails information on the founding and managing of new businesses. However, Gürol and Atsan question if enterprise education should be tied to the specifics of starting a business. There is a strong event to be made that higher education should be seeking to nurture and develop the entrepreneurial characteristics discussed in their study in all students. As a country seeking EU membership, Turkey is in need of being more innovative, more "entrepreneurial" so to speak, if she wishes to raise income per capita and to decrease the rate of unemployment in the line with needed economic performance criteria. Enterprising graduates can nominate a driving force in this process.

Yavuzaslan and Barıscıl (2017, p. 129) states that entrepreneurship is vital to all societies of the world to sustain economic and social development. Generally speaking, promoting entrepreneurship among university students before they begin their career is unavoidable. It is very challenging to study the future entrepreneurial intentions of university students preparing themselves for their respective professional career. Young people attending higher education institutions are theoretically better equipped; at first glance, it is thought that they should be more entrepreneurial than their counterparts who have lower degrees of education.

Yavuzaslan and Barıscıl's paper (2017, p. 136) argues that there are many factors influencing career choices for university students. One of them is entrepreneurship and it has become an unavoidable factor in the modern world. Unemployment has become a serious subject in many parts of the world. Therefore, entrepreneurship is a quite important factor in economy for the creation of employment opportunities. The general problem of false self-employment is also becoming an subject, and, with the increasing number of graduate unemployment, cannot be disregarded.

1980S AND ENTREPRENEURSHIP DEVELOPMENT

Kurtuluş (1987, pp. 67-69) states on "Entrepreneurship in Turkey" that:

Turkey's export markets diversified after 1980. Regional distribution of foreign trade for the last two years indicates that more than one-half of Turkish export and import trade is done with OECD countries, in which EEC countries have a major share. Islamic countries have a 43 percent share in Turkish exports and a 33 percent share in Turkish imports (mostly crude oil). As a result of the success of export policies, the balance of payments has improved. In 1985, the deficit amounted to $1,013 trillion, a decrease of $394 million over 1984.

All of these developments constitute a very positive and challenging atmosphere for entrepreneurs. During recent years, two major developments have affected both the quantity and the quality of Turkish firms. The first relates to changes in the size and legal structure of Turkish firms. On the one hand, the largest Turkish corporations have become even larger, and many have become holding companies. On the other hand, increasing numbers of new firms have been entering the market each year. The failure rate, too, has been increasing, for both large and small firms as a result of increased competition, high inflation, and other factors.

Because of the high inflation rate, replacement costs have become prohibitive. Without sufficient working capital, firms have faced serious borrowing problems. High interest rates have also made the cost of borrowing prohibitive for many firms. Moreover, the government's anti-inflationary monetary policy also increased the demand for money.

Large firms have adapted to these changes in different ways, one of which has been a general trend toward the use of professional managers. Of course, large firms have several distinct advantages over smaller ones. Apart from economies of scale and more professional management, large firms are able to minimize market risks by diversifying operations. In addition, large firms can influence public opinion more easily than medium- or small-sized firms. Their lobbying efforts are also more efficient. As a result, they have been more successful in obtaining government support.

During recent years, even the largest holding companies have asked for government help in rescheduling their debts to banks, in delaying their tax payments, and so forth. In many cases, the demands of these firms have been met by the Turkish government, while medium- or small-sized firms having the same problems went on into bankruptcy because of lack of official support. Very high bankruptcy rates have resulted among these smaller firms.

Yet despite the many failures, a number of small- or medium-sized firms in Turkey have been quite successful. These firms are generally more creative than larger firms in Turkey, and in Turkey as elsewhere, smaller firms are clearly more innovative. In order to promote entrepreneurship, the gap between large and small firms in terms of government attention and support must be narrowed. There is a real need for a formal, government-sponsored small business administration council to provide financial, technological, research and development, and managerial support. One way to do this may be to work through existing management education programs.

Turkey, as a rapidly industrializing nation, has been faced with major economic shifts. The dynamics of a free market economy and foreign competition, coupled with the lack of a comprehensive government policy regarding enterpreneurship/small business, have made conditions very difficult for new and existing small firms. At the same time, however, the shift toward a free market economy and less reliance on imports has also created new and challenging opportunities. Many new firms have entered the market, but many have failed. Large firms have a distinct advantage in terms of government attention and support. To encourage economic growth, the government must devote more attention to incentives and management support and training for smaller firms.

Management education, in general, and business education, in particular, should place more emphasis on integrating entrepreneurship and small business courses into the curriculum. Business history courses are a good starting point, hut they do not go nearly far enough. Models for entrepreneurship education can be found in British and American programs, which could be adapted to meet the needs of entrepreneurs and small business owners in Turkey. Projects dealing with these problems should he developed with the assistance of related national (for example, USAID) and/or international (for example, UNDP) organizations.

EU ENTREPRENEURSHİP PROGRAMS THAT TURKEY PARTİCİPATES

GISEP 2015-2018 (p. 32-34) states:

According to the studies regarding the SBA in Turkey, it is needed that every policy, strategy, action plan, application etc regarding SME's shall be realized appropriate to the principles of Europe Small

Businesses Law. Because of that, the 2011/6 numbered "Europe Small Businesses Law Principles" is published in the gazette numbered 27955 dated 05th June 2011.

In the extent of "Europe Small Businesses Law Application Project in Balkan Countries and Turkey" All the participated countries and European Commission contained by OECD, Europe Education Foundation, Europe Development and Zoning Bank are participated in the preparing the project and countries' SME policies, indicators that is devlared in the range of the project are evaluated. Small businesses Law evaluation frame comprises 12 policy fields that contains 10 principles of the law, 21 sub fields and 108 indicators. Each indicator is evaluated according to the five levels policy reforms. (1 is the weakest while 5 is the strongest). In the "Entrepreneurship education and women entrepreneurship" SBA principles Turkey's score is 2,52 while mean of the 8 countries are 2,41.

Since Turkey is participated in the SBA evaluation for the first time, a comparisation to the last year is not accessible. While being higher than the 8 countries' average in the 2012 evaluation, she has a performance distribution unlike the principles. It can be said that SME services and institutional framework in Turkey is strong of technical standards, inventiveness and encouragement of the export. In the fields of accessing the finance, Innovativeness and encouraging the green economy, Turkey is a little higher than the average. Entrepreneurship education and women entrepreneurship is the lowest evaluation points in the study. Applying the regulating reforms, regulating effect analysis, founding the company and e-government services are weak in Turkey.

Turkey, since 2011, besides the EU countries and Zealand, Norway and Serbia, participated in the European Entrepreneurship Incentive Awards that has been arranged by the sponsorship of the European Commission since 2006. KOSGEB is employed for the announcing the Award Program in Turkey and designating 2 nominees from Turkey and notified to the commission. Project of the Düzce University's Beekeeping Research and Development Departments named "We Can Do More Together" that is selected as nominee by the KOSGEB in 2011 in the "Developing the Entrepreneurship Spirit", in 2012 project of Denizli Municipality's "Handicapped People Are Working" in the "Responsible Entrepreneurship" category, in 2013 "Developed Gürsu with Unlimited Clean Energy" of Bursa Gürsu Municipality in the "Developing the Resource Activities and Environment Friendly (Green) Markets" category has won the grand prize. The project of "Creation of the Example Models in the Textile Finishing Sector For Clean Producting" went on the finals in 2014 in the category of "Developing the Resource Activities and Environment Friendly (Green) Markets".

The COSME pact was signed in16th October 2014 in Brussels. Therefore, Turkey, as in the Horizon 2020 and other EU programs, took its place in the harmony and integration period with EU which provide very crucial opportunities and possibilities to the country's SME's and entrepreneurs. Turkey is the fourth country that is signed this pact from out of the EU after the Montenegro, Macedonia and Moldova.

Consistency of the common studies of Turkey with the EU concerning to the SMEs is ensured by the participation of Turkey to the COSME program. Turkey has important experience in participating to the community programs of EU concerning to the SMEs. Between 2002-2006 Turkey participated to MAP, between 2007-2013 to CIP and EIP programs. Turkey provides access to the variable innovative SME supportive tools and stands in the platforms formed by the EU SME policies by the help of the participating mentioned programs.

KOSGEB is authorized as national coordinator institution about COSME program. COSME is especially targeting the SMEs. It attaches importance to the potential, new, young and women entrepreneurs in micro businesses, businesses regarding the craftings, businesses with single employees, liberal professions and social businesses.

Main aim of the instrument for Pre-accession Assistance- IPA of the EU to the applicants and potential countries, BROP which was applied by the Ministry of Science, Industry and Technology is increasing the regional competitiveness by supporting the businesses and developing the working environment. In the range of this aim, 3 prior aspects are included by BROP (Developing the Working Environment, Increasing the Business Capacities and Inventiveness of the Entrepreneurship and Technical Support) and 8 measurements under the mentioned priorities. 565 millions of Euros are resourced by Europan Comission and Ministry of Science, Indistury and Technology for the measurements mentioned.

CONCLUSION

Turkey is experiencing its entrepreneurial spirit development since prior the Turkish Republic.

After the beginning of 1980s, as a result of a shift from protectionist economic policies to free market economy, private sector started to get stronger while the stateowned companies losing ground especially in industrial sector. Another shift was in the perceptions of Turkish people that people started to get in touch with the concepts like the markets, competition and quality. In this term, much many structural reforms had been introduced in the general structure of Turkish economy (Demirci, 2013, p. 27).

KOSGEB (Small and Medium Scaled Industry Development and Support Directorate) is authorized as national coordinator institution about COSME program in Turkey. COSME is especially targeting the SMEs and attaches importance to the potential, new, young and women entrepreneurs in micro businesses, businesses regarding the craftings, businesses with single employees, liberal professions and social businesses.

According to Gürol and Atsan (2006, p. 36), in Turkey a national perspective on entrepreneurship education should be developed to encourage more universities to provide courses on entrepreneurship and offer a major on entrepreneurship, and, furthermore, to consider founding new institutions to teach only entrepreneurship. Course content on entrepreneurship generally includes information on the founding and managing of new businesses in Turkey.

In conclusion we could say that Turkish economy should rely much more on entrepreneurship for its growth. University-Industry Collaboration gains importance with its outputs: spin-offs and student-run startups. Turkish education system should be reshaped on this concept. Free market economy needs private sector. Other parts of Turkey except Istanbul, Ankara and Izmir should have big companies, as well.

REFERENCES

AboutKOSGEB. (n.d.). Retrieved from https://en.kosgeb.gov.tr/site/tr/genel/detay/347/about-kosgeb

Apaydın, Ş. (2018). The Relations Between Unemployment and Entrepreneurship in Turkey: Schumpeter or Refugee Effect? *Fiscaoeconomia*, *2*(2).

Bülbül, Y. (2010). *Osmanlı'dan Cumhuriyet'e Özel Girişimciliğe Yönelik Devlet Politikaları*. İTO Yayınları.

Demirci, A. E. (2013). Cross-Cultural Differencies in Entrepreneurial Tendencies: An Exploratory View in Turkey and Canada. *International Journal of Entrepreneurship*, 17.

GEM. (2010). *Report, Entrepreneurship in Turkey*. Author.

Gürol, Y., & Atsan, N. (2006). Entrepreneurial characteristics amongst university students. *Education + Training*, *48*(1), 25–38. doi:10.1108/00400910610645716

KOSGEB. (n.d.). *Türkiye Girişimcilik Stratejisi ve Eylem Planı (GISEP) (2015-2018)*. https://www.kosgeb.gov.tr/Content/Upload/Dosya/Mali%20Tablolar/Gisep_2015-2018_TR.pdf

Kurtuluş, K. (1987). Entrepreneurship in Turkey. *Journal of Small Business Management.*

Öner, M. A., & Kunday, Ö. (2016). A study on Schumpeterian and Kirznerian entrepreneurship in Turkey: 2006–2013. *Technological Forecasting and Social Change*, 102.

Sönmez, A., & Toksoy, A. (2014). Türkiye'de Girişimcilik ve Türk Girişimci Profili Üzerine Bir Analiz. *Yönetim ve Ekonomi*, *21*(2).

Yavuzaslan, A., & Barıscıl, A. (2017). Career in Entrepreneurship: Perceptions of Hungarian and Turkish Students. *Revista Romaneasca pentru Educatie Multidimensionala*, *9*(3).

Zbierowski, P. (2015). New impulse for European economy? Comparison of entrepreneurship in Turkey and Poland. *Journal of Economics and Management*, *20*(A).

Chapter 8
Employee Engagement, "Myth or Reality"?
A Critical Analysis of the Entrepreneur and Employee Relationship in the Recession Phase of the Business Cycle

Bhagawan Chandra Sinha
Sarala Birla University, India

ABSTRACT

Employee engagement refers to an employee's highest degree of loyalty, commitment, and participation towards organizational goals, objectives, vision, and mission. It is a technique for instilling an intrinsic desire and passion for excellence in employees by winning their head, heart, and soul. In other words, it can be said it is an art and science of engaging people in authentic and recognized connections to strategy, roles, performance, organization, community, relationship, customers, development, energy, and well-being as we leverage, sustain, and transform our work linkages into results. An engaged employee understands the market context and collaborates with co-workers to enhance job performance for the betterment of the company. Engaged employees want their organization to be successful and excel because they are physically, professionally, emotionally, and even spiritually associated with its goals, objectives, purpose, vision, and mission. Employee engagement has grown into a vital component of business performance today.

INTRODUCTION

According to Gallup's recent 142 - country report on the State of the Global Workplace, only 13% of workers worldwide are engaged at work. To put it another way, approximately one out of every eight workers is physically, mentally, even emotionally dedicated to their employment and is likely to be contributing positively to their organisations. As per engagement report 2011 - 12, 24% of employees

DOI: 10.4018/978-1-7998-7951-0.ch008

were found actively disengaged, 63% were found neutral or not engaged employee and only 13% of employees are engaged.

Gallup's findings that the vast majority of workers worldwide have had a negative work experience and that only one in every eight are completely engaged in and excited about their careers .It is important to understand why the global recovery has been so slow and social and workforce instability is rampant in many countries.

Employee involvement must be raised to new heights by business leaders around the world. Growing workplace participation is critical for businesses, societies, and countries to achieve long - term growth, and for the global economy to return to a more stable and peaceful future especially in present Covid - 19 pandemic where lot of business houses has to close their operations due to lack cash flow.

Employees can be divided into three groups depending on their degree of engagement: actively disengaged, neutral, or not engaged (neither engaged nor disengaged), and engaged. Employees that are disengaged have a pessimistic attitude about the company and are involved with it with a negative outlook. These workers generally exhibit rebellious and aggressive characteristics, and they are more likely to engage in predatory labour union practises.

Employees who are neutral or not engaged are neither engaged nor disengaged. These workers are more concerned about retaining their membership in the association, as well as their salary, benefits, and earned time off. These workers are only concerned with performing their duties in compliance with their employment contracts and are unconcerned about the organization's goals, intent, vision, task, or strategic objectives. Employees those are solely focused on themselves are unlikely to cause problems in the workplace.

The engaged employee is the organization's third form of employee. These committed employees not only give their hand, head, heart, and soul to the firm, but they also put the business's interests ahead of their own. These workers are constantly looking for organisational competence and a competitive advantage. Employees who are engaged are usually linked to the organization not only physically, psychologically, and emotionally, but also spiritually. Spiritual association with any entity tends to be more metaphysical and scholarly in nature. In other terms, employee commitment is nothing more than meeting all of the psychological contract's obligations.

Nowadays, committed and productive employees are the only resource that matters. Access to other resources is no longer a constraint; capital flows freely across borders, companies have access to technology, raw materials can be exported globally thanks to globalisation, and knowledge is available to everyone who wants to flag it down on the high digital super road., There is a scarcity of committed employees who are spiritually connected to the enterprise and willing to go above and beyond to accomplish the organisation's vision, mission, objectives, goals and strategies. Owing to the global depression, the global economy is constantly under serious strain, resulting in downsizing and other cost - cutting steps. Also engaged employees are suffering from a psychological crisis, and whether employee's commitment is a blessing or a bane is a point of contention.

BACKGROUND

As per Macey & Schneider (2008), employee engagement is an attachment, dedication, motivation, loyalty, zeal, keenness, focused endeavour, vigour, and liveliness towards achievement of organizational goals and obligations. Maslach et al. (2001) visualized employee engagement as contrary to the three burnout attributes: fatigue, scepticism, and feeling of inefficacy. Schaufeli et al., (2003) defined engagement as an optimistic, gratifying work environment that is endowed by dynamism, perseverance, and assimilation. As per Kahn (1990), employee engagement is harnessing of workforce to their work roles, workforce expresses themselves physically, cognitively, and emotionally during role performance and psychological differences of individual impact their ability to engage or disengage in their role performance. As per Seijts & Crim (2006) there are ten 'C', connect, carrier, clarity, convey, congratulate, contribute, collaborate, control, credibility and confidence provide a blueprint to employee engagement to leaders.

Bakker et al. (2004) stressed that employees who are engaged earn higher scores in their role performance from their co - workers, suggesting that employees who are engaged perform well and are able to perform more. In his article, Bakker et al. (2008) cited four reasons why engaged employees perform better than non - engaged workers. Engaged staff: first, optimistic feelings are always encountered with zeal, commitment, optimism, happiness, and enthusiasm; second, improved psychological and physical wellbeing is experienced; third, build their own assignment and personal resources (e.g., encouragement from others); and finally pass their dedication to others

Wellins & Concelman (2005) suggested that employee engagement is concerned with an amalgamation of commitment, loyalty, productivity and ownership and at the same time is an imaginary power which pulls the workforce to give some extra effort for higher level of performance. As per Crabtree (2013) (Gallup report) on America's workforce showed that employees either not engaged or disengaged causing a total loss of 500 billion USD. As per Shaw (2005) employee engagement basically deals with poignant, rational and mental loyalty to the work and workplace and self - propelled power required to perform it. Robinson et al. (2004) states engagement is one level higher of commitment.

Several literatures lead to the conclusion that personal resources often have a significant role to play in deciding the level of work commitment in addition to job efficacy. Studies performed by Xanthopoulou et al. (2007), found that workers engaged are highly self - effective, confident and feel they can perform. In their analysis of female school principals, Bakker et al. (2006) found that those with the most personal resources scored highest on job commitment. A broad cross - sectional study of 1,910 South African police officers was conducted by Rothmann & Storm (2003) and found that dedicated police officers are problem - focused, taking aggressive action to try and eliminate or rearrange hooligans.

MAIN FOCUS OF THE CHAPTER

This is an exploratory research focuses mainly on understanding the concept of employee engagement. In economic slowdown as top line and bottom line don't allow the company to continue even the services of engaged employee and at the same time it is only engaged employee who can facilitate combat the recession. This chapter tries to map the psychology of both the parties i.e. employer and employee and a sincere effort has been made provide a solution to dilemma.

Research Objective

- To explore employee engagement concept and its interaction with slowdown / recession phase of business cycle.
- To study critically employee engagement is a myth or reality especially in recession phase of business cycle.

- To assess the impact of economic meltdown on terms, conditions and morale of engaged employee.
- To conclude by giving recommendations how to cope up the downturn using employee engagement as a major instrument.

Research Methodology

This is an exploratory and qualitative study relying on secondary data and real - world knowledge of professionals, academicians, researchers, HR consultants, and research institutions. Several individuals and organisations have performed comprehensive research and have shared their data and information, which are either in the public domain or have been published in journals, newsletters, research studies, books or digital source.

The researcher compiled a list of available sources and attempted to rationalise them in context of the current socioeconomic, technological, and political climate. While there is a plethora of literature on this topic, there is a scarcity of written material on the effect of economic downturn on employee engagement mechanisms. This research paper is an attempt to critically examine and broaden one's knowledge base.

Dynamics of Employee Engagement

Dynamics of employee engagement can be expressed by The Zinger Model on Employee Engagement and Maslow's Hierarchy of Needs Framework for Improving Employee Engagement.

The Zinger Model on Employee Engagement

David Zinger has introduced a workable model that sheds light on various aspects of employee participation, commitment, and engagement based on his comprehensive and detailed work on the topic. The model outlines 14 keys that a manager must obey in order to produce meaningful performance.

The 14 Employee Engagement Elements

- **Achieve Results:** The aim of employee engagement is to produce results. The model's first key, on the far right, starts with the outcomes that the company, department, team, or person wants to achieve. The most critical question for this model is what do you want to achieve, and how will you know when you've achieved it?
- **Craft Strategy:** One need to develop a plan to get there in order to achieve their goals. For achieving their goals one has to craft a strategy. Is there awareness and the plan to make it success?
- **Connect:** Connection is a crucial aspect of employee engagement. In certain cases, connection and engagement are synonymous. How connected are workers to other aspects of commitment, such as their company and the genuine happiness? The core keys of CARE embedded in the employee engagement model begin with Connect.
- **Authentic:** Authenticity is the second letter of the acronym CARE. Employee participation must be real. Employees and consumers can tell whether anything is fake from a mile away or even in a split second. We must move beyond shallow relationships, culture, or pleasure to heartfelt commitment. True and robust engagement is the hallmark of successful engagement.

- **Recognition:** The 'R' in CARE stands for recognition or acknowledgment. Good employee involvement necessitates strong recognition. One should not just provide long service certificates or memento. Are workers completely recognized and compensated? Do workers understand the significance of their job and how it relates to outcomes?
- **Engage:** CARE comes to a close with the letter 'E', which stands for engage. We always use the verb "engage" instead of a static noun when we speak about "engagement". Engage focuses on the engagement actions. Engagement isn't a one - time metric or a constant condition. To fully observe and contribute to the diverse elements of workforce, one must engage.
- **Enliven Work Roles:** To fully participate, one must perform a variety of roles. A role is a set of behaviors, rights and obligations at work. While staying completely involved in the roles one must avoid taking on too many roles or role overload. Leaders and managers should not ignore their own positions as employees.
- **Excel At Performance:** Successful performance can be achieved by engagement with outcomes. It is a common perception engaged employee should be star performers. Engaged employee who are star performers assist each employee in achieving at least their performance standard for the benefit of their customers, the company, and themselves.
- **Esteem Organization:** How well does the employee fit into the company? Is there a link between the corporate and individual brands? Do workers feel as though they are an integral part of the company? Are they proud of working in company and equally proud to recommend it to others and serve as brand ambassador?
- **Foster Community:** Strong bond with community or society is a key factor in employee engagement. These connections and communities may be personal or via social media. Do we build lasting relationships and outcomes? Relationships and culture are at the heart of work. Organizations that do not turn into societies run the risk of being outdated or forgotten.
- **Serve Customers:** Employees are expected to represent the organization, and there are clear links between employee and customer interaction. Is the employee so pleased with the company and management that he or she is willing and able to give the same quality of service to external and internal customers?
- **Develop Career:** Employees should be able to enjoy the rewards of their jobs. Employees should have opportunities for both personal and professional growth through work that involves everything from learning and development to improving their own value, exposure, and engagement. One spends too much time at work, and it should help one achieve his full potential.
- **Leverage Energies:** Energy is the raw material of engagement. Does one have the stamina to completely participate? Does one provide the energy to boost the company or sucks energy of their coworkers? Mastery of physical, mental, emotional, moral, and organisational resources is required for effective engagement. The most important resource for engaged working is energy, not time.
- **Experience Well - Being:** Job should be, at the end, contributing to the happiness of its employees. Employees must be able to participate in healthy activities as well as enjoyment. The wellbeing and efficiency of individual workers are critical to the success of an organisation.

David Zinger Model on Employee Engagement considers all important aspects that could impact the involvement, engagement and dedication of employees.

Maslow's Hierarchy of Needs Framework for Improving Employee Engagement

Maslow's Hierarchy of Needs is a strong and comprehensive structure for comprehending the needs of today's workforce. Talent engagement has become a business priority as a result of the post - COVID economic slowdown. Maslow's theory provides companies in honing talent and growing employee engagement by delivering the right kind of gratification.

Levels 1 and 2 of Maslow's theory are what we call the bare minimum or basic needs of a human being, such as water, food, shelter, financial protection, and stability, and they are represented by a pyramid with five levels. Levels 3 and 4 are higher - order needs, such as the need for attachment, social standing, respect, and acceptance that are more psychological in nature. Maslow's hierarchy can be rearranged and used in a number of cases.

It promotes a bi - directional model at work, which is a two - way interaction between employee and employer. It offers a scale for assessing job satisfaction and heading toward improved fulfilment and effect at work from the employee's perspective. From the standpoint of an organisation, it aid in the development of a positive work culture, which increases morale, commitment, and, eventually, success.

In the context of employment engagement, office space, financial incentives, and benefits, most companies may fulfil the first two levels of needs. The discrepancy is found at levels 3 and 4. Equal pay and decent working conditions, as later researchers such as American psychologist Frederick Herzberg demonstrated are simply "hygiene factors" that prevent disengagement. To put it another way, their absence can lead to disengagement, but their presence does not lead to constructive engagement. As a result, companies must concentrate on levels 3 and 4 in order to increase employee engagement.

Although Maslow's hierarchy of needs has been shown to be valid for people and societies all over the world, Maslow himself has stated that the theory only defines a general order of needs and that individual needs will differ. Some individuals, for example, may place a higher value on emotional connection than financial protection, while others may place a higher value on status and recognition than group affiliations. As a result, it's critical for companies to figure out which category of Maslow's needs pyramid best corresponds to individual workers and then map similar recognition categories. HR leaders can use technical tool to get the data they need to personalize and iterate their employee engagement programme for the best performance.

Engagement A Pious Bond Between Entrepreneur and Employees

Professors Gerard Seijts and Dan Crim, have provided highly relevant blueprint to leaders for employee engagement:

- **Career:** Employees must be challenged and motivated in the workplace in order to advance their careers and stay active. Simultaneously, they must be equipped with the resources and skills necessary to meet these new challenges.
- **Clarity:** Employees thrive when they recognize how their position contributes to the broader organization's mission, vision, and goals. Can they express their own priorities, how they plan to accomplish them, and how they contribute to the company's overall goals?
- **Connect:** Often engagement begins with an employee's relationship with their supervisor. Is the employee convinced that their boss is concerned about them? If not, money spent on other projects is a waste of money.

- **Collaborate:** Research study good, trustworthy team relationships have been shown to result in improved productivity. Employees are more likely to be involved if they feel valued by their co-workers and have the opportunity to contribute to their teams.
- **Contribute:** Do employees realize how their contributions have an impact on company's success? Individuals who feel like cogs in a wheel whose operations are hidden from view can feel disengaged from the larger task.
- **Convey:** Leaders must provide continuous input to their subordinates, so that they are aware of how their success is being addressed and how they can improve. Managers are well placed to share their insights with their teams on a weekly or regular basis, as performance evaluation shifts away from annual reviews and toward ongoing input.
- **Congratulate:** We have a tendency to provide feedback only when an employee has failed to meet standards, and we neglect to compliment them on their accomplishments. Praise and recognition are effective communication tools.
- **Control:** Include the employees in the decision - making process, particularly if the result would have an impact on them personally. Allow them to choose how to get things done, coordinate their workflow, and solve problems as much as possible (this will vary based on skill level). This increases a person's sense of worth, their confidence in management, and their sense of control over their work.
- **Credibility:** Is your team proud of your company's name and reputation? You develop the brand externally and give your team another reason to believe in what they do by ensuring that your business maintains high ethical standards.
- **Confidence:** Individuals must have confidence in their organisation and its leaders' decisions in order to become committed workers. Keep in mind that you set the bar high in terms of both ethics and success.

With a sample size of 1500 million, Gallup's study reveal majority of workers worldwide, 63%, are "not engaged or neutral" which means they are unmotivated and less likely to devote discretionary attention to organisational goals or outcomes. And 24% are "highly disengaged," meaning they are depressed and unproductive at work, as well as likely to spread negativity to their colleagues. In rough numbers, this amounts to 900 million employees who are not engaged or neutral and 340 million who are actively disengaged all over the world.

In the 2011 - 2012 report, 13% of workers were engaged, up from 11% in Gallup's previous global workplace survey, conducted in 2009 - 2010. Furthermore, the percentage of people who are "actively disengaged" has decreased from 27% to 24%. Low levels of global worker participation, on the other hand, continue to impasse increases in economic productivity and quality of life in many parts of the world.

Employee engagement levels vary across global regions and countries within those regions, as they did in Gallup's employee report. North America (that is, the United States and Canada) has the largest proportion of engaged employees (29%) led by Australia and New Zealand (24%) at the regional level at the same time least engaged employee were found from East Asian region which is only 6%.

Employees have varying levels of dedication and participation, and its understanding varies from company to company.

- **Satisfied Employees:** are those workers who want to be a part of the company and are satisfied with the status quo. Satisfied workers aren't necessarily efficient workers.

- **Motivated Employees:** is more concerned with individual objectives and makes additional efforts to reward organizational activities that meet his or her ultimate requirements.
- **Committed Employees:** committed to the company's priorities, goals, objectives combined with personal goals.
- **Engaged Employees:** are emotionally attached with the organization and are institution builders. They know the desired expectations for their role so they can meet and exceed them. They're naturally curious about their company and their place in it. They perform at consistently high levels. They want to use their talents and strengths at work every day. They work with passion and they drive innovation and move their organization forward.

Employee engagement relates to workers' ability to dedicate their physical, mental, and emotional energy to their job and organisation. Employee involvement, in simple words, enables employees to work not only with their heads and bodies, but also with their souls. When someone puts their heart and soul into their work, it creates a cordial atmosphere in which organisational and individual goals can be met more effectively. Employee engagement is a multifaceted framework made up of cognitive, emotional, behavioural, and individual role performance components.

Any business would like to have engaged staff because they are more likely to be innovative and imaginative, it is more significant when In a period of growth in which the organization tries to hit new heights in the corporate world in order to achieve a competitive advantage. Staffs who are engaged have a high level of confidence in the organisation, a voluntary willingness and passion for loving and enjoying their jobs, and a wider view of the company's vision and mission. Employee involvement, without a doubt, is a partnership between an organisation and its workers in which everyone works together to achieve organisational goals and individual objectives.

Only a devoted employee is mentally and emotionally linked to the company, deeply cares for its goals, and is dedicated to its objectives. He goes above and beyond by linking himself to the company's guiding principles. Employees who are committed are more likely to stick with the company and support its products or services. Employee engagement is described as employees' positive attitude toward the organization and its values. It is rightly said that committed workers are a company's only long - term competitive advantage. Employees who are engaged care for the company's success and are willing to put in extra effort to help it achieve its goals. Employee engagement, not employee satisfaction, is used to determine an organization's productivity.

When the economy is in a slump, employers are under pressure to implement cost - cutting measures. Almost all companies are experiencing financial difficulties as a result of the economic crisis, as demand for goods and services have plummeted. With a drop in demand, it's critical to cut costs, resulting in a surplus of jobs. Wages and wages account for the greatest portion of all variable costs. Most businesses have no choice but to accept lower salaries, no raises, and decreased fringe benefits, as well as lower social and welfare costs, increased working hours, turnover, layoffs, and retrenchment. Workers' morale is at an all - time low, and they are frequently negative, as a result of the above - mentioned working conditions. And the employees who are involved are looking for a way out. They have no idea whether his position will be safe the next morning. Following the layoffs of their co - workers, these employees are afraid of being obsolete, expecting the worst and conceiving no need to offer everything. Fear of losing their jobs has sparked a "psychological crisis" among hardworking people. This is a vital and pathetic situation for both parties.

According to study, engaged employees are more vulnerable than disengaged employees. Committed employees are more identified with the organisation and feel more stress and mental pain when they consider leaving the present company. Engaged employees align their interests and priorities with the company's vision, purpose, and intent, and it's difficult to break the emotional and spiritual bond. Companies, on the other hand, do not want to risk their stars that are instrumental in achieving the organization's aspirations, dreams, missions, and objectives. Companies understand that only these diligent employees are capable of assisting in times of turmoil and combating the recession demon. As a result of the economic downturn wreaking havoc on industries, these companies are in serious financial trouble, and lowering their financial burden has become inevitable for them. Organisations are reluctantly forced to discharge their engaged employees in this economic environment, and retrenchment has become a necessity. When businesses downsize engaged employees due to a decrease in net profit, this is a major concern for both staff and employers, since these organisations also know that only the engaged employee can help them get out of financial trouble.

SOLUTIONS AND RECOMMENDATIONS

Employee Engagement as a Beacon of Pride in the Wake of Recession

In a bad economy, a motivated employee is a competitive advantage because it makes the company more resilient and helps it get through challenging times. The engagement of committed employees makes it easier to bounce back from bad news and focus on opportunities to grow the company right away. Employee loyalty should be maintained because it provides competitive advantages during a downturn. In times of adversity and extreme economic conditions, employee involvement becomes much more important and significant. Staffs are able to give their best when they are treated well and valued, and the ability to channel their ability is a strategic distinction. It is their choice, decision, attitude, and behaviour that decide the outcome. In a recession - prone economy, it is critical for companies to maintain a focus on employee engagement and to develop emotional and spiritual bonds with workers, resulting in highly satisfying and productive relationships with employees that can contribute to an organization's long - term success.

Managers should actively encourage their staff to provide input on key business issues, think innovatively, and leverage their talents to help build an organisation where employees want to work and achieve business goals, and managers should actively empower their workers to provide feedback on key business challenges, think innovatively, and exploit their talents to help create an organisation of agility and strategic strength to fight the inevitable problem of economic recession.

FUTURE RESEARCH DIRECTIONS

Present research paves the way of further research which can be based on identifying the measuring instruments which can measure level of engagement in the time of economic recession or slowdown. Research can be based on if there is any compulsion to the organisation to retrench or layoff the workforce, how it can be it implemented with human face so it hurts least to both the parties and steps to be taken to continue the pre - retrenchment bond. Research can be based on if there is any compulsion to the organisation to retrench or layoff the workforce, then to what extent retrenched or laid of employee will be still remain engaged to the organisation and show willingness to re - join when called to do so. Research can be based on if there is any compulsion to the organisation to retrench or layoff the workforce, then if retrenched or laid of employee remains engaged to the organisation then to what extent commitment and engagement will fade away lapse of time. Upcoming research can be based on change in perception of engaged employee towards the organisation when they are retrenched. Upcoming research can be based on how employee engagement can be made a pull factor rather than a push factor to combat recession.

CONCLUSION

The study concludes that employers should be patient with changes in terms and conditions of employment, and any layoff or retrenchments should be done with the human face in mind. It is critical to avoid layoffs or retrenchments of engaged workers. Reduced salaries, no raises, work sharing, sabbaticals, wage - free leave, redeployment, outplacement, and all other solutions should be tried first, and dedicated workers should be laid off only when all other options have been exhausted, since these employees are the organization's most valuable assets.

The most crucial aspect is communication. Whether or not they ask for it, keep the workers updated. In these tough economic times, it is much more important to disseminate information and ensure that everybody in the company receives the messages. It's important to keep lines of communication open, but don't wait for questions or issues to be raised; predict what workers want to know and give them the information they need. Individuals and small groups should be able to share their fears and concerns. Inform them of your knowledge of the situation, accept their strong feelings, and value their opinions. It could be a rough bumpy road and a long way toward growing employee involvement and building confidence. Employee engagement dealt with creating a conducive atmosphere, successful leadership, as well as ownership of the workplace and position, product and service advocacy, and brand ambassadorship, but ultimately it is concerned with creating an organisation that provides real business performance especially in economic crisis.

REFERENCES

Bakker, A. B., Demerouti, E., & Verbeke, W. (2004). Using the job demands: Resources model to predict burnout and performance. *Human Resource Management*, *43*(1), 83–104. doi:10.1002/hrm.20004

Bakker, A. B., Gierveld, J. H., & Van Rijswijk, K. (2006). *Success factors among female school principals in primary teaching: A Study on Burnout, Work Engagement, and Performance, Right Management Consultants*. Diemen.

Bakker, A. B., & Schaufeli, W. B. (2008). Positive organizational behavior: Engaged employees in flourishing organizations. *Journal of Organizational Behavior*, *29*(2), 147–154. doi:10.1002/job.515

Crabtree. (2013). *Worldwide, 13% of employees are engaged at work*. Available at https://www.gallup.com/poll/165269/worldwide-employees-engaged-work.aspx

Kahn, W. A. (1990). Psychological conditions of personal engagement and disengagement at work. *Academy of Management Journal, 33*, 692–724.

Macey, W. H., & Schneider, B. (2008). The meaning of employee engagement. *Industrial and Organizational Psychology: Perspectives on Science and Practice, 1*(1), 3–30. doi:10.1111/j.1754-9434.2007.0002.x

Maslach, C., Schaufeli, W. B., & Leiter, M. P. (2001). Job burnout. *Annual Review of Psychology, 52*(1), 397–422. doi:10.1146/annurev.psych.52.1.397 PMID:11148311

Robinson, D., Perryman, S., & Hayday, S. (2004). *The Drivers of Employee Engagement, Institute for Employment Studies*. IES Report 408.

Rothmann, S., & Storm, K. (2003). *Work engagement in the South African Police Service*. Paper presented at the 11th European Congress of Work and Organizational Psychology, Lisbon.

Schaufeli, W. B., & Bakker, A. B. (2003). *UWES – utrecht work engagement scale: test manual*. Department of Psychology, Utrecht University. Available at www.schaufeli.com

Seijts, G. H., & Crim, D. (2006). What engages employees the most or The Ten C's of employee engagement. Ivey Business Journal, 70(4), 1-5.

Shaw, K. (2005). An engagement strategy process for communicators. *Strategic Communication Management, 9*(3), 26–29.

Wellins, R., & Concelman, J. (2005). *Creating a culture for engagement*. Workforce Performance Solutions. Retrieved from www.WPSmag.com

Xanthopoulou, D., Bakker, A. B., Demerouti, E., & Schaufeli, W. B. (2007). *How job and personal resources influence work engagement and financial turnover: A diary study in a Greek fast - Food Company*. Academic Press.

KEY TERMS AND DEFINITIONS

Downsizing: Reducing number of workforce.

Economic Meltdown: Is an economic collapse which may be due to bad financial conditions, like recession, bankruptcy, and high joblessness.

Employee Engagement: Is a term that defines level of commitment of an employee i.e to what extent an employee is emotionally attached to organisation.

Global Recession: Economic slowdown across the world.

Layoff: Temporary expulsion/discharge of a worker.

Morale: Sense of belongingness to a team or group.

Psychological Crisis: Facing mental or emotional trauma.

Resource: Productive power of natural things.

Retrenchment: Permanent expulsion/discharge of a worker.

Chapter 9
Policy Approaches to Promote Women Entrepreneurship in India

Nishi Tyagi
https://orcid.org/0000-0002-9698-0503
Sharda University, Greater Noida, India

Rinkal Sharma
Sharda University, Greater Noida, India

Pallavi Jain
SRM Institute of Science and Technology, Ghaziabad, India

ABSTRACT

Women are traditionally regarded as homemakers and are restricted to household affairs and family customs. At the same time, the Indian society is a male-dominated one in the sociological setup, and the women are considered weak and dependent. The major problems of women's entrepreneurship development in India are poor degree of financial freedom for rural women, lack of direct ownership of the property, low risk bearing ability, and lack of contact with successful women entrepreneurs. Through their diligent work, determination, integrity, and dedication, these ambitious women are making a reputation for themselves and gained wealth. The primary objective of this chapter is to discuss the status and problems along with the solutions of women entrepreneurs in India. It also includes the significance of women's entrepreneurship and analyzes the policies of the Indian government for women in urban and rural areas. It will initiate a dialogue with policymakers on how to foster enhanced innovation in women-owned enterprises in India.

DOI: 10.4018/978-1-7998-7951-0.ch009

INTRODUCTION

Today, there is a need to know about Women Entrepreneurs. It is a fact that we have very little knowledge or information about women entrepreneurs. One main reason can be that women entrepreneurs are involved in so called petty business - like running shops from home or involved in small cottage industries that too not in main cities or town. Women entrepreneurs are a category that has been understudied. We know very little about women entrepreneurs, and our lack of understanding of this important demographic is a major concern in any effort to increase the total number of entrepreneurs in our economy. They have entrusted themselves to petty business and small cottage industries by and wide. Business established or owned by women is about the place of Women in Society as well as acceptance in entrepreneurs' group. As per latest reports out of total recorded entrepreneur's 10% share goes to women and it is increasing at a steady pace. This signifies the role of females to transform and lead the business. Women's entrepreneurship is concerned with both the status of women in society and the role of entrepreneurs. Women increasingly strengthen, lead, and transform the face of how business is done today. It is reported that about 10% of the total entrepreneurs in India are currently female entrepreneurs. It is also clear that this percentage is increasing year after year. However, since traditions are deeply entrenched in Indian culture, Indian women will have to put in a lot of effort to achieve parity in terms of rights and roles. Although present day women have much more support from family as well as society but still financial liberty and dependence on family plays a major part to come forward to start a business. Women's entrepreneurship growth in India is hampered by a lack of financial independence for rural women, a lack of direct property ownership, a lack of risk - taking capacity, and a lack of communication with established women entrepreneurs. Many women have been influential in their work, despite all the social barriers. Through their diligent work, determination, integrity, and dedication, these ambitious women are making a reputation for themselves and gained wealth (Dhameja et al., 2000).

The growing status of women as entrepreneurs has resulted in a shift in the country's market demographics and economic development. Women - owned businesses resulted in societal empowering and job creation in the country. To promote successful growth in the country, women entrepreneurs must develop sustainably, and Start - up India is entrusted to ushering the environment for women entrepreneurship. Because of the push and pull factors, female entrepreneurs participate in the business, allowing women to have an autonomous profession and stand on their feet. In this complex environment, women entrepreneurs have become a component of the global expedition for long - term monetary and social growth change. The wave of women - owned businesses is gaining momentum in almost all places of world because of rapid urbanisation, industrialization, and the expansion of reach to quality education and personal rights. Women's entrepreneurship is a rising industry worldwide. It is on the agenda of several National and international development organisations. Agencies and multilateral organizations and are a priority of several civil society organizations and foundations. Women, however, remain significantly under - represented as entrepreneurs, even in countries where women are not represented. Participation in the labour market has risen gradually. In addition, some gaps in information remain on the obstacles that impede the role of women in promoting sustainability (Coughlin & Thomas, 2002).

Many other recent policy initiatives to assist women entrepreneurs are emerging. Several countries are looking into the possibility of using procurement processes to help women gain access to new markets. They are attempting to increase funding for progressive female entrepreneurs. With dedicated support incubator and acceleration initiatives, the need to offer better opportunities for innovative women entrepreneurs is required. Lower levels of entrepreneurial expertise, intimidating social and cultural attitudes, challenges in receiving start - up funding, less successful entrepreneurial channels, and policy environments that discourage women from participating in entrepreneurship are among the obstacles that women encounter when starting a business. Traditional methods including training and funding do not cover the entire population, so these strategies must be extended (Chandra, 1991).

In a modern organization, it is not possible to identify an entrepreneur because he (she) is not a single person. The entrepreneur is no doubt the creator and manager of a business. He is not to be treated as a specific type of individual. Rather, as Donnelly has rightly suggested, "entrepreneurship can be considered a behaviour, encompassing an individual's pursuit of opportunity without regard to the resources the entrepreneur currently controls". Any single female or a group who innovate imitates for the purpose of implementing an economic operation is referred to as a woman entrepreneur. To put it another way, any woman or group of women who operates a business enterprise. As per Indian government women entrepreneur means, any enterprise which is controlled and owned by a woman who is having at least 51% OF FINIANCIAL interest in it, a woman entrepreneur is defined as, an enterprise possessed and owned by women, with a minimum financial interest in 51% of the employment generated in the enterprise.

BACKGROUND

Women are better entrepreneurs than men because of their nurturing skills such as developing others, building relationships, since they are emotionally intelligent about the human side of business, are fairer negotiators and are considered more open - minded. In fact, female leaders were better rated on many levels of business such as innovativeness, problem solving, taking initiatives, etc.

The country has 13.5 - 15.7 million women possessed enterprises, which is 20% of all the enterprises. They lead to a direct employment of 22 to 27 million people. India has seen a spurt in the number of entrepreneurs coming up, but it has left behind an important demographic, its women. Women's involvement in the labour force has reduced further.

In the coming decade, India will have the largest working age population of more than one billion people. The private sector and the government alone cannot provide jobs for everyone. It is exactly why we need entrepreneurs springing up everywhere. Entrepreneurship among women is even more important because it not only helps with creation of jobs, but also transforms the lives of children and the entire family.

India should compare its numbers with other countries and treat it as a benchmark to increase female entrepreneurship in the country (Brush & Cooper, 2012). Adhering to such benchmarks will create 30 million women - owned businesses, which can employ more than 150 - 170 million people. It also represents more than a quarter of the new jobs needed for the entire working - age population from this year to 2030.

- **More Jobs:** We should observe that most India's women have not participated in the labour force. When the government gives them sops or provides benefits to start their own venture, there will be a spurt in jobs suddenly. It will turn the economy around because there will be more people (especially women) who will be able to afford more things. The entire demographic has been largely non - existent in the female entrepreneurship space. The opportunities are wide open, although one must admit that India is not the easiest country to start a business in. India is ranked 63rd out of 190 countries in the World Bank's Ease of Doing Business report.

- **More Women in The Ecosystem:** When there are women in power, you will find them adding more women to the workforce. Women will be more open to working in establishments that are run by women. Encouraging women entrepreneurship also results in better social outcomes for education, childcare, and health.
- **Narrows Gender Gap:** Needless to say, that India's Record put us on shame when we talk about Gender Gap, we are ranked 123rd in the world. The gender gap will reduce when there are more women entrepreneurs in the fray. The next generation of women will have role models to look up to, which will increase participation of women in the labour force and the number of women entrepreneurs.
- **Safe Workplace:** Women tend to be a lot more empathetic and are driven towards creating workplaces that are safe and inclusive. Since women struggle with work - life balance, they are more inclined to create a work culture that encourages people to have the best of both worlds. Because of the flexibility and safety that women - led businesses offer, more women will feel comfortable to join these enterprises.

Women who are unable to demonstrate their full potential in society miss out on tremendous opportunities for job creation, economic growth, and other benefits. A recent study revealed that if India were to close the gender gap, it could increase its GDP by 6.8% . India needs to do more to encourage its women to take up entrepreneurship. The Indian government has created many schemes to encourage female entrepreneurship like Mudra Yojana Scheme, Annapurna Scheme, Dena Shakti Scheme, etc. All of these are government - enabled schemes that offer financial assistance and mentorship for women to start their enterprises.

MAIN FOCUS OF THE CHAPTER

Problems of Women Entrepreneurs

In India, women entrepreneurs still face several structural challenges. Records shows that companies started or raised by only women had a really a hard time raising enough money. As per August 2020 report released by the Global Alliance for Mass Entrepreneurship (GAME), an organisation of medium, minor and micro enterprises, 80% plus of women entrepreneurs in India are involved in solo businesses, out of which 86% being self - funded. In addition, just 0.6% of the total $ 13 billion, raised by Indian start - ups in 2018 went to all feminine founding teams, and women entrepreneurs account for just % of India's total production in the industry, according to the GAME survey women entrepreneur face several problems like male entrepreneurs (Pramanik, 2020). They have more issues than male entrepreneurs.

These problems can be classified into sets:

- General problems challenged by all the entrepreneurs
- Specific problems challenged by women entrepreneurs

Figure 1. General Problems Faced By Entrepreneurs

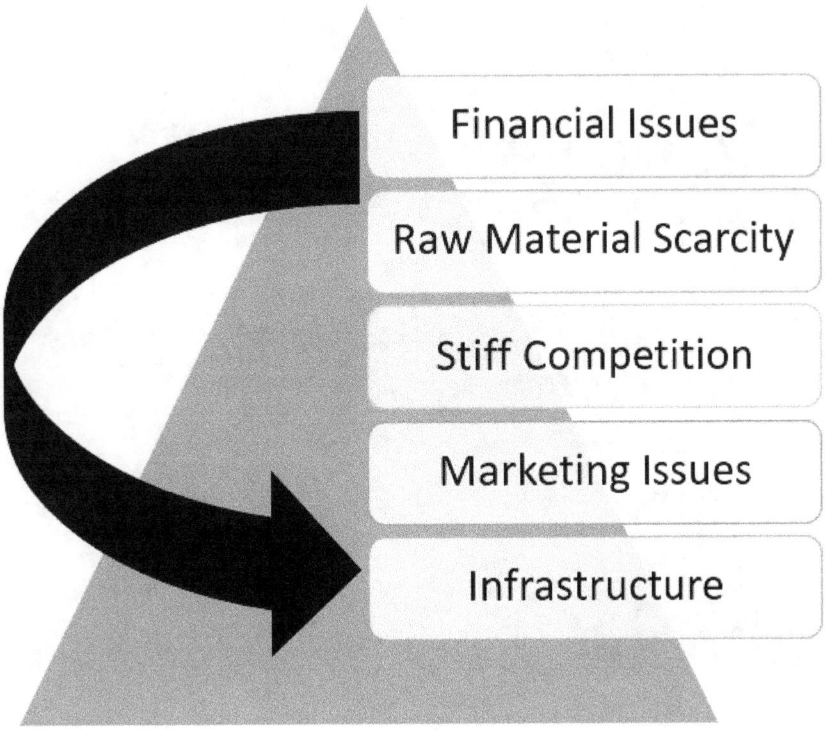

General Problems

- **Financial Problems:** Finance is considered to be the backbone of every company, whether large or small. Women entrepreneurs face a lack of funds for two main reasons. First, women in general do not own property in their own names that can be used as collateral security to obtain loans from outside sources. Hence, their access to external sources of funds is limited. Second, unfortunately, banks continue to view women as less creditworthy and discourage female borrowers, based on the belief that they could leave their business at any time for any reason.

Under such circumstances, Women are forced to rely on their own savings as well as loans from family and friends. And most of times it's not possible to get a healthy finance to start a business. This is a major hindrance to start a business for women entrepreneur.

- **Raw Material Scarcity:** Mostly women find it very hard to obtain the raw materials and other necessary inputs from far flung areas. In addition, during initial years due to their new entry, they may be compelled to pay high prices for the raw materials, and they may not be able to get any trade discount or timely supply of such raw materials etc. The scarcity of essential raw materials or their non - availability in time put the enterprises, run by women, in danger of shutting down.
- **High Competition:** Being new to business women do not have an adequate organisational set up to infuse in a lot of money for advertising to popularise their products. Thus, they face a tough competition from existing products to get market for their products. Also, many of times they do

Figure 2. Prominent Obstacles Faced By Women Entrepreneurs

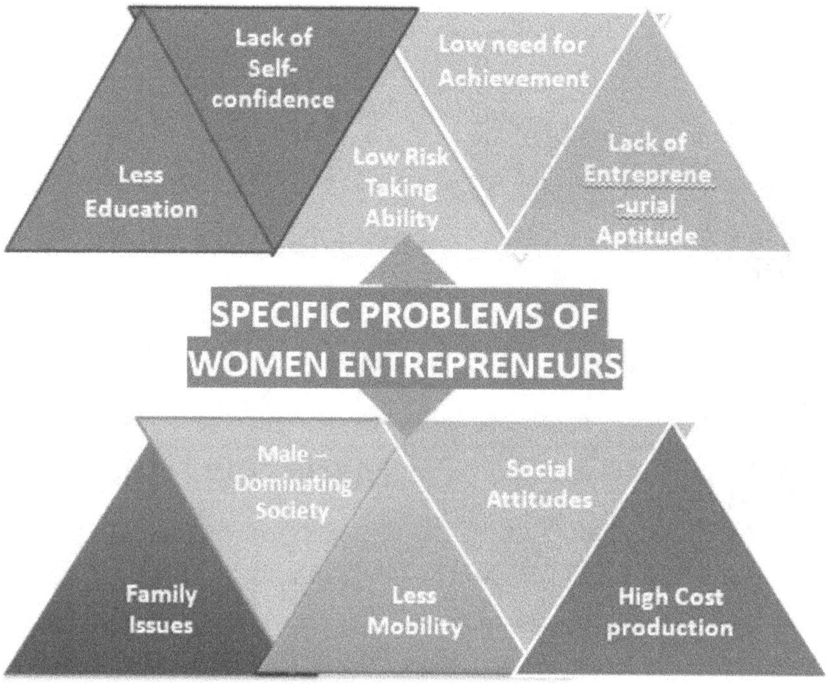

not get proper support from their male counterparts. This could be a reason for early closure of pack - up of an enterprise started by a woman.

- **Marketing Problems:** Women normally find it very difficult to enter in a new market and to promote the sale of their products. The middlemen are most likely to exploit the women entrepreneurs in various ways.
- **Infrastructure Problems:** Women entrepreneurs do not have adequate infrastructural facilities either for setting up their manufacturing activity or for making activity as such infrastructural activities require heavy investment which is beyond the capacity of women entrepreneurs.

Specific Problems to Women Entrepreneurs (Mauchi et al., 2014)

- **Playing Safe Strategy:** In India generally, women are brought up in a different manner. Normally they are less exposed to world. They are less educated and economically more dependent on others. In other words, they are economically not independent. Therefore, these factors reduce their ability to take risks involved in business and they try to play safe by not taking risk. Risk - taking is an essential requisite of a successful entrepreneurship. But women entrepreneurs have a low capacity to bear financial and other risks. Inferiority complex, low education, unplanned but protected growth, lack of infrastructure, etc., are the main factors for their low ability to take or bear risks.
- **Dearth of Self - Confidence:** A female entrepreneur is normally not very much confident in doing anything independently, particularly in India. They hesitate to take risks. They are conservative in

their outlook. The public in general look at women entrepreneurs with suspicion and they do not support nor encourage them.

- **Lack of Entrepreneurial Aptitude:** Women generally lack entrepreneurial aptitude. They lack any entrepreneurial bent of mind as well as entrepreneurial creativity, motivation, behaviour, etc.
- **Lack of Mobility:** Women, particularly in India, lack mobility. In other words, their mobility is highly limited due to various reasons. Women cannot travel alone freely and safely nor can they deal courageously with men or male officers who always try to humiliate women, when approached for any official or business work. Travelling is also not possible and feasible for women entrepreneurs. Thus, the mobility of women entrepreneurs is very limited, particularly in India.
- **Family Problems:** In our country it is supposed that woman will take care her children and other family members. Lot of time and energy will have to be used by the woman in looking after her family affairs. As a result, her involvement in family matters leaves her with little time and energy for work. Therefore, married women entrepreneurs must make a satisfactory balance between family burden and business burden.

Their success in this connection depends upon the willing support of their husband and other family members. Because without the consent and full support of her husband and without the cooperation and encouragement from the other members of her family, no woman entrepreneur can hope to succeed in her business. Otherwise, there arises a role of conflict for women entrepreneurs in their business life. Such conflicts prevent them from taking prompt and sound decisions in their business. The movement of women has been slowed down because of the traditions and family responsibilities, despite modernisation. Further, the work - related background of the families, and educational level of the husbands will have a great impact on the development of women entrepreneurship. The development of kindergartens, day - time nurseries, creches, and family planning and most important one, desire for a larger income and higher standard of living, have to some extent helped the women entrepreneurs to carry on their business without affecting the social prestige of their husbands.

- **Male - Dominated Society:** We live in a society which is dominated by males. Although our constitution speaks of equality between men and women, but women are not treated equal to men. Women are looked down upon as weak and incapable in all respects. Women suffer from male reservations about their role, ability, and capacity. Such an attitude of men towards women creates an obstacle to women's entry into business.
- **Social Attitudes:** The biggest problem faced by the women entrepreneurs is the problem of social attitudes towards women and the constraints in which women entrepreneurs work and life. Despite constitutional equality, there is a great discrimination against women. In our society, which is bound by customs and traditions, women suffer from many reservations imposed by men on their role and capacity. This is particularly true in rural India. In rural areas, women face struggle not only from the male members but also from the elderly female members who do not accept the principle of equality. The overbearing presence of the elders in the family restrains the young girls from venturing out.

Though the rural women have the potential to become entrepreneurs, they are not properly trained and given scope. It is believed that the skill imparted to a girl is lost when she is married. Hence, girls, though having entrepreneurial talent, continue to be helpless in rural handicrafts and small scale and tiny industries and hence they do not become entrepreneurs.

- **Lack of Education:** Not only in India but also in the world women get less opportunity for education to enhance their skills especially in marketing, business development, technology, etc. Nearly 48% of women in India are still illiterate as per 2001 census. Low level of knowledge or education among women is a major reason for the lower level of achievement motivation. Therefore, a low level of education is a hindrance for setting up and enterprise by a woman. Lack of education leads to a lack of knowledge and experience among women creates still more problems for them in their business i.e., because of their inability to deal with outsiders.
- **High Cost of Production:** Another issue that women entrepreneurs face is high investment in some areas of production, which reduces efficiency and limits the growth of entrepreneurship among women. The assistance given by the government and other agencies in the form of grants and subsidies may enable them to tide over this difficulty but to ensure their ultimate success and survival, it becomes necessary for them to improve their efficiency, expand their productive capacity, and lower their production costs. Even so, women entrepreneurs face a number of challenges, including labour, human resource, infrastructure, legal formalities, a lack of family support, and so on.
- **Low Need for Achievement:** Need for high achievement, independence, autonomy and freedom are the prerequisites for success in entrepreneurship. But women, by nature, prefer to grow under some assured shelter and glory of their parents, husbands, brothers, sons, etc. They have got some preconceived notions about their role in life and this attitude of women inhibits their achievements. There should be a keen usage for achievement in women, but it is true that all women cannot be expected to have such an urge. Only these women who have got such an exceptional urge for achievement and independence are most likely to succeed in their business.

SOLUTIONS AND RECOMMENDATIONS

Solutions of the Problems of Women Entrepreneurs

- **Finance Cells:** In various financial institutions and banks, special finance cells should be opened for providing easy finance to women entrepreneurs. Such finance cells should be managed by women officers and clerks. The finance cells should provide to women entrepreneurs at nominal interest rate with a long duration of repayment.
- **Marketing Co - Operatives:** Women entrepreneurs should be encouraged and given all assistance for setting up marketing cooperatives. The Government and semi - government bodies should give highest preference to such women's marketing cooperatives while making their purchases. Such cooperatives will be able to eliminate the middlemen while making their purchases of inputs and selling their products at remunerative prices.
- **Supply of Raw Materials and Other Inputs:** The government should make necessary arrangements for the supply of scarce and imported raw materials and other inputs required by the women

Figure 3. Solutions for Women Entrepreneurs

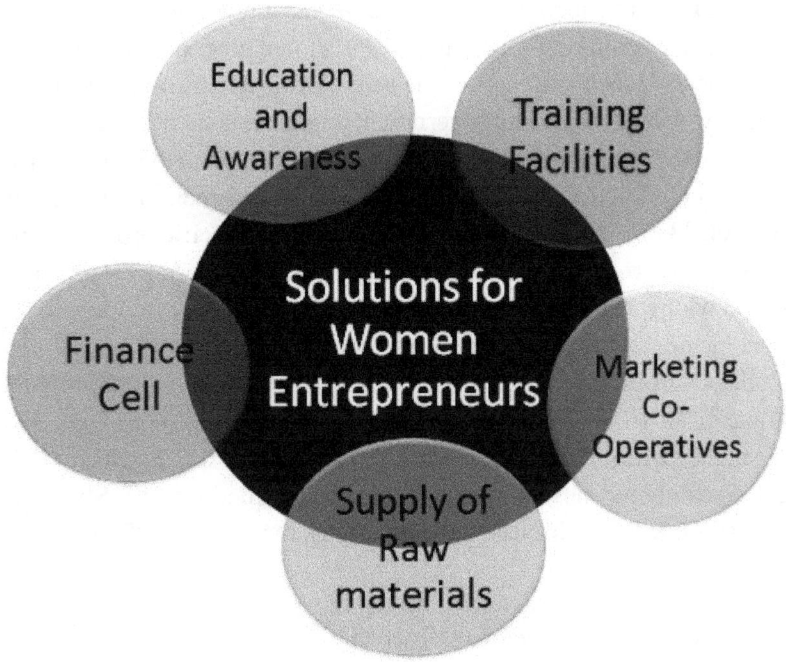

entrepreneurs. The government should also give subsidies to the women entrepreneurs to make their products cost - competitive and sell them at competitive prices.

- **Education and Awareness:** Intensive educational and awareness programmes should be arranged so as to change the negative or unfavourable attitudes towards women. The attitude of the elders, particularly, the elderly women whether mothers or mothers - in - law, should be made aware of the potential of the girls and their due role in the society. The social attitudes of these people should be made positive to enable the women entrepreneurs to achieve progress in their venture.
- **Training Facilities:** Training and skill development are quite essential for growth of entrepreneurs. Special training schemes should be designed to suit the women entrepreneurs so as to create self - confidence in their mind about the success of their entrepreneurship. Since family members will not be permitted to go too far distant places for training, mobile training centres should be arranged.
- Similarly, part - time training facilities should also be provided during weekends and holidays. In addition, stipend, good hygienic creches, transport facilities, and such other facilities should also be provided to appeal more and more women - entrepreneurs to the training centres.

Government Schemes of Women Entrepreneurs Need to Know About

According to the studies, financially independent women raise their households out of poverty, their children are happier, and the country's economy benefits. Women in the workforce would be able to contribute to community growth, creativity, and job creation, among other things. Society should be willing to recognize more entrepreneurs because of the direct and direct and indirect benefits that more women entrepreneurs bring to the economy. The government should play a significant role for promoting entrepreneurship among Indian women, because it has the resources and reach and because it is its job.

Millions of Indians' lives would be affected if government schemes are properly enforced. More than 30% of the 138 lakh projects launched as part of the Prime Minister's Employment Generation Program (PMEGP) were started by women. When the government implements such programmes, women are motivated to take advantage of them because they have a financial cushion in the form of a loan or mentoring.

The Indian government has taken several initiatives to enable women to start ventures. Last year, the government set aside Rs. 28,600 crore ($3.9 billion) for women - specific programmes, which included, among other things, schemes to address the root cause of problems faced by women in need like safety, security, education and widow care along with women in distress. However, people feel that the budget has nothing to encourage new women entrepreneurs.

During April, India's Citizen Engagement Platform MyGov, in collaboration with United Nations Women, provided financial assistance and mentorship to six women - led start - ups fighting COVID - 19 with innovative ideas. The government - run Women's Entrepreneurship Platform (WEP), which assists women in starting and scaling businesses, received a much - needed facelift. Some of the schemes that have been introduced (Figure 4) are discussed below (Jayashree & Priya, 2016).

Figure 4. Government Schemes for Women Entrepreneurs

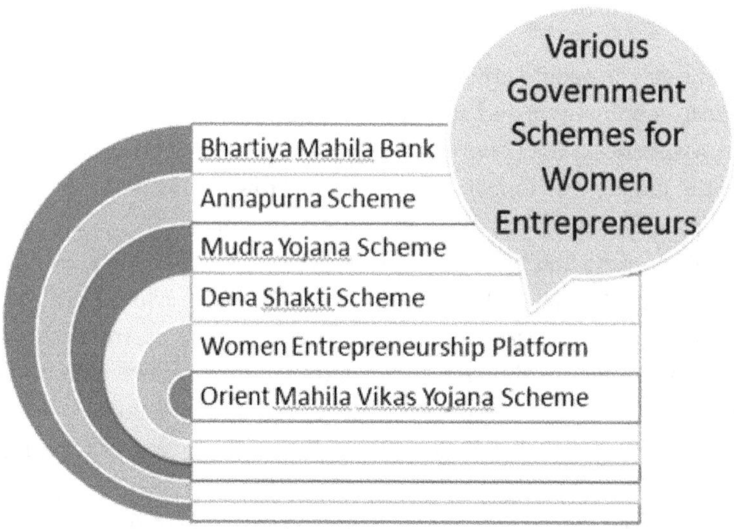

- **Bharatiya Mahila Bank:** The bank was established to support underprivileged women by providing financial support in starting their own businesses. The bank loans the manufacturing sector up to 20 lakhs. In addition, Bharatiya Mahila Bank can grant lending for up to 1 crore without any security requirement.
- **Annapurna Scheme:** Women who need to start a food catering business can get a fifty thousand loan under the scheme. The money from this loan can be used to buy kitchen utensils, appliances, and other equipment. After the loan is approved, the woman is not required to pay the EMI for the first month. Banks, as well as the market rate, decide interest rates. A guarantor is required, and the

loan can be paid back in 36 monthly instalments. The scheme, which was first launched in 2000, is offered by Bharatiya Mahila Bank.

- **Mudra Yojana Scheme:** It is proposed for women who want to start a small company without a large production facility like grocery stores, beauty parlours, or schools. The scheme provides new companies with 50 thousand under this system, enterprises that have long been in operation will receive between 50 thousand and 5 lakhs everywhere.
- **Dena Shakti Scheme:** Dena Bank, as the name implies, is the provider of this government scheme. It is designed for women enterprising businesses in agriculture, retail, microcredit, education, housing, retail and small businesses. This is for women and women enterprises. It provides a 0.25% interest rate reduction on the loan. Loans of up to Rs 20 lakh are available to women entrepreneurs in the housing, retail, and education sectors.
- **Women Entrepreneurship Platform:** The NITI Aayog platform, which has collaborated with SIDBI to support this initiative, was decided to launch to create an ecosystem for young female entrepreneurs throughout the country. The platform is built specifically for women who are considering starting a company. Registration within the ecosystem will bring them in front of an audience and connect them to a group that will assist them.
- **Orient Mahila Vikas Yojana Scheme:** The Oriental Bank of Commerce launched the initiative, which provides grants to women who want to start small businesses. Women who own at least 51% of the company are eligible. A 2% interest rate reduction is being offered by the bank.
- There is a slew of government initiatives aimed at encouraging women to start businesses. All these government programmes have been created with women entrepreneurs in mind. It will be difficult to properly execute these programmes, but if done so, millions of Indian women will benefit.

States with Start - Up Policies for Women

The start - up policies taken by different states in India (MCI, 2019) are illustrated in Table 1.

Eight Stats to Know About Women Entrepreneurs in India

There is a slew of government initiatives aimed at encouraging women to start businesses. All these government programmes have been created with women entrepreneurs in mind. It will be difficult to properly execute these programmes, but if done so, millions of Indian women will benefit.

The increasing role of women as entrepreneurs has resulted in a shift in the demographics of industry and the country's economic growth. Female - owned enterprises are becoming more projecting in society, empowering others and expanding job openings all over the world. Women entrepreneurs must develop sustainably in order to foster balanced progress in the country, and start - up India is committed to strengthening the ecosystem of women's entrepreneurship through policies and initiatives, as well as the establishment of enabling networks.

With a projected GDP of $13.7 billion by 2030, India is expected to become the world's third largest economy. With market reforms that strengthened global competitiveness and stabilized inflation and interest rates, the Indian government has made a concerted effort to foster business - friendly conditions. This has enabled an entrepreneur - friendly culture, but it hasn't necessarily resulted in a surge in female founders.

Table 1. Different States of India Promoting Start - Up Policies

S. No.	States	Initiatives
1	Andaman and Nicobar Islands	Administration provides assistance in the form of monthly allowance of Rs.20000 for One year for start - ups with a woman as the founder / co - founder.
2	Andhra Pradesh	Women entrepreneurs who exhibit at one of the notified national / international exhibitions with a room limit of 9 square meter will be reimbursed in full for the cost of the exhibition stall rental. In the case of student start - up teams with at least one woman as a cofounder 5% grace marks and 20% attendance per semester. Can be given by Universities in Andhra Pradesh
3	Assam	For each employed woman, a bonus of fifty thousand onetime bonus, up to maximum of one lakh per start - up for three years.
4	Bihar	Women entrepreneurs would be eligible for a five % increase in grant / exemption / subsidy above the policy's stipulations.
5	Jammu and Kashmir	Start - ups approved by Start - Up task force are eligible to receive twelve thousand month (for a 1 year) and meet any of the following criteria. The Start - up is initiated by a woman: Minimum percentage of shareholding of woman should be 25% .
6	Odisha	Support at the idea / prototype stage: Rs. 22,000 /- per month can be given if the business is founded by woman. 50% or more ownership in the start - up entity in this situation. Financial help until the idea / concept is commercialised: If the start - up initiator is a woman, the monthly payment would be twenty thousand in this case, women should own at least 50% of the start - up firm.
7	Uttarakhand	The marketing support allowance will be Rs. 7.5 lakhs if the start - up is founded by female entrepreneurs in any of the target areas or belongs to a Category A district under the Uttarakhand MSME Policy 2015, subject to approval from the Start - up Council. The Start - Up will only be able to receive this assistance once.
8	Chhattisgarh	More than Rs. 100 crores will be set aside by the Invention Fund, Leap of Faith Rotating Fund to motivate and inspire female entrepreneurs in the state.
9	Goa	All new and existing units will receive a rent / lease reimbursement on the built - up office space rent / lease for a period of two years, up to 50% of the annual Lease Rentals (60% in cases where 30% or more of the workers are female).
10	Gujarat	• As stated in paragraph 1.2, the Nodal Institute is responsible for reimbursement of 75% of expenses incurred for organising a promotional event for Women Entrepreneurs once a year, up to a maximum of Rs. 5.00 lakh, as long as it is recognised by SLIC in accordance with the procedure outlined. • If the innovator's project is effective, they would be compensated 10 thousand per month as a sustenance allowance for a year.
11	Haryana	Using the Model Shops and Establishment Bill of 2016 as a template: • The state is required to put the bill's provisions into effect in order to increase job opportunities for all people, especially women. This law would apply to any business with ten or more employees that is not a manufacturing facility. • This would include the autonomy to operate 365 days a year and set the establishment's opening and closing hours, as well as the ability for women to work night shifts if lodging, rest rooms, ladies' restrooms, passable protection of their dignity and transportation are available. For start - ups, over - all permission will be decided for three shift operations of women employed at night.
12	Himachal Pradesh	• This includes the ability to operate 365 and set up the business's opening and closing hours, as well as the ability for women to work night shifts if they wish. • HPCED will develop a strategy to send particular start - ups, universities, colleges and school students to leading start - up destinations. • Over - all permission will be given for three shift operations of female working at night for start - ups to talk with and meet industry leaders, thinkers, and innovators for example, women entrepreneurs, students, and teachers will be reflected at least one - third of the time.
13	Jharkhand	• A 50% refund on lease rentals up to INR 5 lakhs per annum for a maximum of three years for plug - and - play type built-up office space leased by a Start - up in IT, STPI / IT parks / Multi - purpose SEZs (an extra five % for ST / SC, Divyang, and Women Enterprises). • On submitting self - certified bills, a refund of thirty % of the amount charged to electricity distribution companies will be given, up to Rs 60000 per year (an extra five % for ST / SC, Divyang, and women Enterprises).
14	Karnataka	• All government - backed incubators will be required to set aside at least 10% of seats for women co - founders. • The initiative, which offers grants to women who want to start small businesses, was initiated by the Oriental Bank of Commerce. Women with a 51% ownership interest in the company are eligible.
15	Kerala	The Women Start - up Summit is a Kerala Start - Up Mission (KSUM) initiative aimed at encouraging young female professionals to start their own businesses and assisting Kerala in developing a more sustainable entrepreneurship ecosystem. On a common platform, the conference brings together experienced female leaders, start - up founders, politicians, and young female entrepreneurs to share their knowledge, experiences and accomplishments. • The Kerala Start - Up Mission (KSUM) provides a soft loan plan of up to fifteen lakhs as working capital for completing projects and works obtained from government and public sector undertakings in Kerala. For women in the age group of 18 to 45 and SC / ST entrepreneurs the assistance is 20% maximum 30 Lakhs.
16	Maharashtra	To qualify for the above incentives, the Maharashtra government will give priority to early stage start - ups (up to 3 years from the date of incorporation) and FinTech start - ups with female founders. It will set aside a certain percentage of the overall fund for such Start - ups: • Top - Rated Start - ups Incentive Fund • Establishment of an investment fund • Internet and energy costs reimbursed • Reimbursement of costs associated with hosting resources • FinTech Corpus Fund is a fund that invests in fintech start - ups.
17	Manipur	Through Facilitation Centres, rural Start - ups and Start - ups by women entrepreneurs receive neighbourhood hand - holding and mentoring support.
18	Nagaland	● In both urban and rural Nagaland, a special effort will be made to recognise female entrepreneurs. ● A special effort will be made to raise awareness of various State and Centrally funded schemes among women entrepreneurs. ● To encourage female entrepreneurs, 25% of funds are set aside for them.
19	Puducherry	A monthly allowance of 10,000 rupees will be provided to each citizen, up to a maximum of five people. If the start - up's founder or co - founder is a woman SC / PH / Transgender then monthly allowance will be Rs. 15000.

continued on following page

Table 1. Continued

S. No.	States	Initiatives
20	Punjab	• IKG Punjab Technical University will establish a Rs. 100 crore Start - up Fund in collaboration with the State Government to help State youth become entrepreneurs. The fund will be used to fund incubation centres, seed capital for scale - up funding, start - ups, and other support to Start - up units. A quarter of the funds will be used to encourage the start - ups of SC and female entrepreneurs. • Women Enterprises receive a yearly award of three lakh per unit for quality in production, export, and efficiency. • Only SC / Women Entrepreneurs are eligible for a five % interest subsidy per year for a period of three years, up to a maximum of Rs. 10 lakh per year.
21	Rajasthan	The Bhamashah Techno Fund for Start - ups has a fund size of INR 500 crore. A total of INR 100 crore has been set aside for women entrepreneurs from this project.
22	Tamil Nadu	• Women - led start - ups should be prioritised. • Women - led start - ups should have training and awareness programmes. • Female - led businesses • Women are given first priority in the allocation of industrial plots in industrial estates. Start - ups and funding will be provided to the founders / co - founders for production, marketing / publicity and participation in trade shows and exhibitions.
23	West Bengal	Rural start - ups and start - ups run by women entrepreneurs receive special neighbourhood handholding and mentoring support through MSME Facilitation Centres (MFC).
24	Dadar and Nagar Haveli & Daman and Dui	• The Administration will assist women entrepreneurs by providing special and additional benefits. There will also be specific training courses added. • To encourage women's participation, extra mechanisms in subsidy systems and preference in industrial plot allocation can be used.

Source: Own

Here are some statistics about women entrepreneurs in India that you should be aware of:

- Nearly 14% of India's 58.5 million entrepreneurs are women.
- 13.45 million People are employed by women - owned companies in India.
- Agriculture employs about a third of Indian women entrepreneurs, followed by manufacturing and retail trade.
- Only 2% of start - up funding went to women founders in 2017.
- A total of $ 8.5 billion was raised in the top ten fund raises of 2017. Just $ 136 million was raised in the top ten fund raises by female - led start - ups.
- According to the McKinsey Global Institute report (2015) India's GDP could increase by 16 - 60% by 2025 if women and men participated equally in the economy. According to projections, this could result in a $2.9 trillion boost to the economy.
- 30% of India's tech workforce is female. Although, 51% of entry - level jobs in India's IT and BPM industries are women, indicating that women are leaving at junior and mid - levels.
- Radhika Aggarwal of e - commerce marketplace Shop Clues made history as India's first female co - founder of a billion - Dollar Company.

None of these stats mean that the future is bleak for women entrepreneurs in India. There are successful founders aplenty, including these inspiring women business owners.

Status of Women Entrepreneurship in India

In India, women's entrepreneurship is still in its beginnings. The participation of women as entrepreneurs is very limited. In this section, data from key government publications is used to examine the representation of women entrepreneurs in India. According to the Global Surveys, India's ranking on the parameter of women's entrepreneurship is also very low. According to the Global Entrepreneurship Development Institute's 2015 "Female Entrepreneurship Index Report," India ranked 70th out of 77 countries surveyed, with a low score of 25.3. India lags behind even African countries in terms of economic growth.

Figure 5. Women Entrepreneurial Activity in India

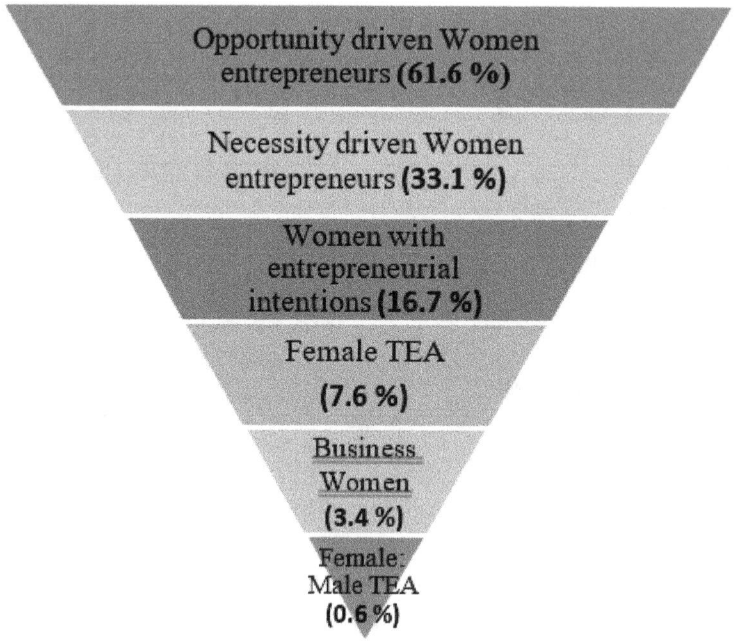

India has a long way to go in terms of women entrepreneurship (GEM, 2018). According to the Global Entrepreneurship Monitor Report on Women's Entrepreneurship 2016 - 17. Figure 5 depicts women's

Figure 6. Women Owned Establishments in India

entrepreneurial activity. The percentage of Indian women engaged in early - stage entrepreneurial activity (TEA) is only 7.6%, while the percentage of women engaged in established business activity is only 3.4%.

As per the Sixth Economic Census, (MOSPI, 2016), the overview of Indian women entrepreneurs is shown in Figure 6, which reported approximately 13.76% establishments are owned by women. Out of which the majority of women owned establishments are non - agricultural (65.7%) and run without hiring workers (83.19%). About 45.36% non - agricultural establishments include manufacturing activities whereas the majority of agricultural establishments i.e., 92.20% involve livestock activities. Agriculture, manufacturing, trading, other services and accommodation and food services are the five topmost economic activities taken by women entrepreneurs and corresponds to 34.3%, 29.8%, 18.23%, 5.38%, and 2.77%, respectively.

Figure 7. % of Women Entrepreneurs in Some States of India

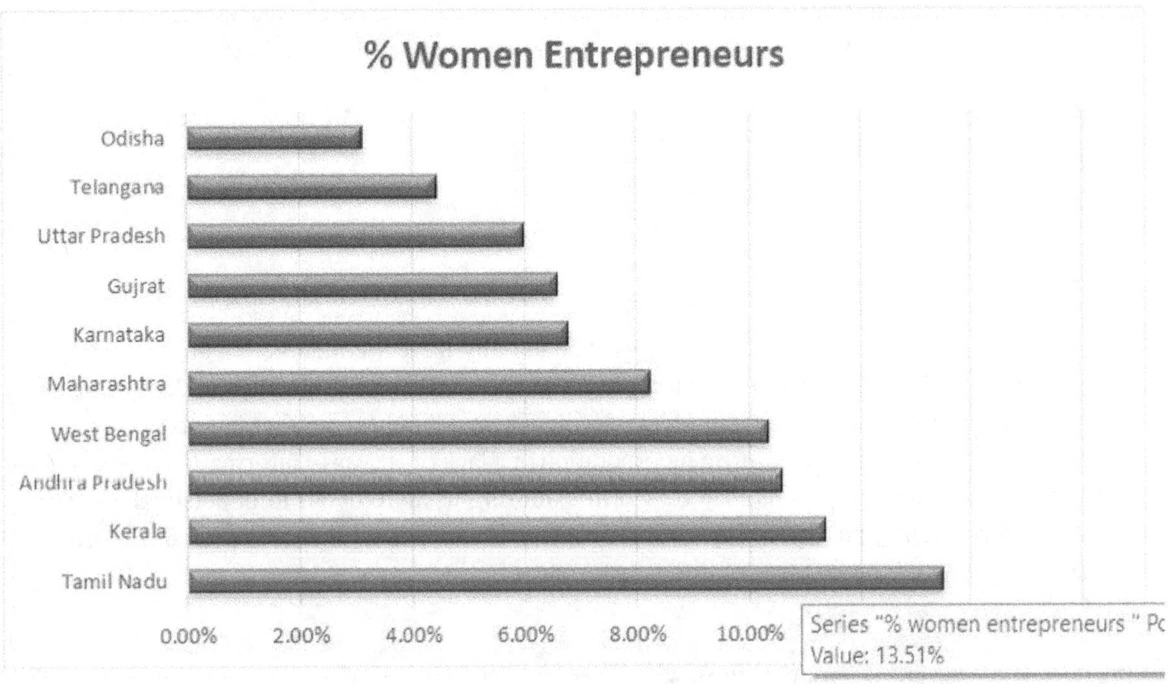

Overall, the largest share in the number of establishments under women entrepreneurship are clustered in the southern states of India, namely: Tamil Nadu (13.51%), Kerala (11.35%), and Andhra Pradesh (10.56%) (Figure 7). This suggests that there is a more favourable environment for women entrepreneurship in the South of India to set up their business. The top four states with the highest distribution of female owned proprietary establishments from both rural and urban areas are Manipur (80%), Arunachal Pradesh (56%), Meghalaya (54%), and Kerala (51%). Six of the top ten States are from the Northeast of India. There is a similar distribution when only the urban proprietary establishments are considered.

The top three states with the highest distribution of female owned urban proprietary establishments are: Manipur, Meghalaya, and Nagaland, and overall, six of the top ten are clustered in Northeast India (Figure 8). This data suggests that Northeast India has a favourable enabling environment for women -

Figure 8. Five Topmost States in India with Women Owned Rural and Urban Establishments

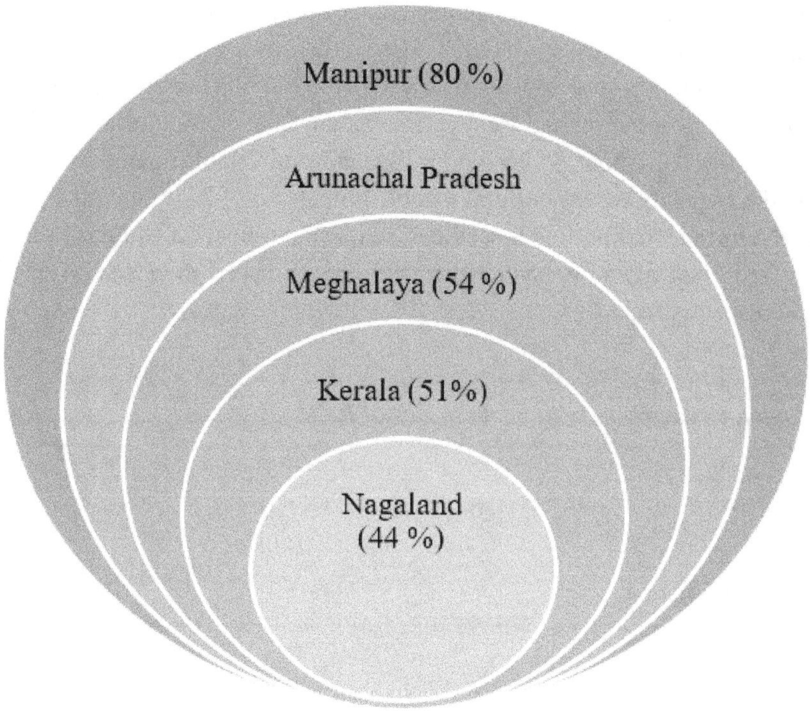

owned enterprises to set up an enterprise, however potentially there are factors that are restricting this entrepreneurship to the micro level and incentivising women to co - own the business with other business partners or adopt other ownership models (Mile, 2019). There could be a number of reasons explaining these, such as tax incentives for enterprise incorporation or a lack of access to information on the diverse models of business ownership. This may be worth exploring in more detail to understand any policy implications. Support may be required to scale proprietary enterprises as well as to promote information on the advantages and disadvantages of different forms of business ownership.

FUTURE RESEARCH DIRECTIONS

The spirit of entrepreneurship among a country's citizens drives and contributes significantly to the country's development process. Gender biases between men and women do not exist in this move. The Indian government has taken several steps to increase the participation of women entrepreneurs and thus make them a partner in the country's growth and development. A great deal of research has been done on this topic over the years. However, in many cases, the investigation is broad and does not focus on gender. Females face different challenges and barriers than males; therefore, gender - specific entrepreneurial research could aid in the development and improvement of female entrepreneurship. Because research findings may be used directly or indirectly to improve or amend management policies in the same cases, having more high - impact data available may be beneficial in some cases.

Figure 9. Five Topmost States in India with Women Owned Urban Establishments

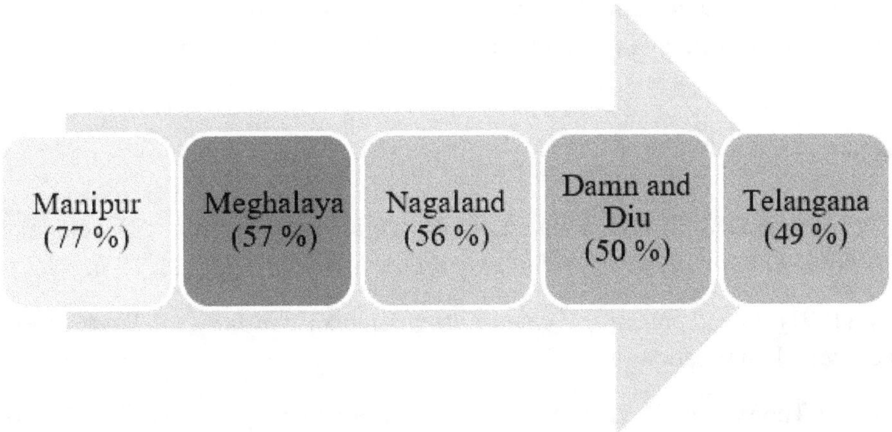

The current researches on women entrepreneurship have revealed the following research gaps. More cross - country research and comparisons of different female groups or samples are required. Further research is needed into the role of human capital, strategic choices, and structural barriers in female entrepreneurship. Aside from that, important questions will need to be addressed in future research like how do various contexts i.e. organisational, family environments, high technology, etc. and cultural environments influence women's business management? In such circumstances, what do female entrepreneurs do? How can theories from fields other than entrepreneurship and small business shed light on women's entrepreneurship and management strategies?

Entrepreneurship is more than just starting a business; it also represents the will and desire to manage an existing business. There appears to be a scarcity of research in this area. A careful examination of female entrepreneurs may aid in better understanding of how to exploit these resources. Because large data sets are becoming more widely available, we can better understand potential disadvantages among various groups of female entrepreneurs. Comparisons between different female groups in social, cultural, and socio - family abstractions continue to be important fields of study and investigation.

CONCLUSION

Women's entrepreneurship is important for economic and societal development. Women's economic participation in India is extremely limited, despite the fact that they make up roughly half of the population. Female entrepreneurs in India are now gaining recognition in non - traditional sectors.

Women entrepreneurs are a diverse group with a range of demographic, economic, and educational characteristics. It is important that policies and programmes address the specific needs of each segment. It is undeniable that women face various obstacles during their entrepreneurial careers. To address these issues, a detailed action plan is needed. Tamil Nadu, Kerala, Andhra Pradesh, West Bengal, and Maharashtra have the highest concentration of women entrepreneurship. These states' policies and interventions should be investigated so that best practices can be replicated in other states.

Despite the government's attempts to enable women to start companies, India has an alarmingly low number of female entrepreneurs. Since the majority of women - owned businesses are unregistered, they are unable to take advantage of government assistance. Analysing the effects of current policies and initiatives will uncover new approaches to encourage women to start businesses. Women's entrepreneurship is a dynamic and nuanced area that requires in - depth research to fully comprehend its dynamics.

REFERENCES

Brush, C. G., & Cooper, S. Y. (2012). Female Entrepreneurship and Economic Development: An International Perspective. *Entrepreneurship and Regional Development, 24*(1 - 2), 1 - 6.

Chandra, K. S. (1991). *Development of Women Entrepreneurship in India: A Study of Public Policies & Programmes*. Mittal Publications.

Coughlin, J. H., & Thomas, A. R. (2002). *The rise of women entrepreneurs: People, processes, and global trends*. Greenwood Publishing Group.

Dhameja, S. K., Bhatia, B. S., & Saini, J. S. (2000). Women Entrepreneurs - Their Perceptions, About Business Opportunities and Attitudes towards Entrepreneurial Support Agencies (A study of Haryana State). *Small Enterprises Development Management Extension Journal, 27*(4), 37–50.

Global Entrepreneurship Monitor (GEM). (2018). *2017 - 2018 Global Report*. https://www.gemconsortium.org/report

Jayashree, G., & Priya, I. C. M. (2016). A Study on Role of Banking Sector in Women Entrepreneurship. *International Journal of Social Relevance & Concern, 4*(11), 1–7.

Mauchi, F. N., Mutengezanwa, M., & Damiyano, D. (2014). Challenges faced by women entrepreneurs: A case study of Mashonaland Central Province. *International Journal of Development and Sustainability, 3*(3), 466–480.

Mile, K. S. (2019). *An Analysis of Women Entrepreneurship in India*. Deutsche Gesellschaft für Internationale Zusammenarbeit GmbH.

Ministry of Commerce and Industry (MCI). (2019). *States with start - up policies for women*. https://www.startupindia.gov.in/content/sih/en/women_entrepreneurs.html

Ministry of Statistics and Programme Implementation (MOSPI). (2016). *All India Report of Sixth Economic Census*. http://mospi.nic.in/all-india-report-sixth-economic-census

Pramanik, A. (2020). *The thing that's holding back Indian women entrepreneurs*. https://m.economictimes.com/news/company/corporate-trends/the-thing-thats-holding-back-indian-women-entrepreneurs/articleshow/77754878.cms

KEY TERMS AND DEFINITIONS

Autonomy: Being empowered to make your own decisions without being influenced by others.

Economic Forces: The nature and direction of the economy in which businesses operate are referred to as economic forces.

Entrepreneurial Aptitude: Ability to think beyond the box, as well as creative service and product concepts to ensure great results.

Gender Gap: The gender gap focuses on the systematic differences in labour-market outcomes between men and women. The numbers of men and women in the labour force, the types of jobs they choose, and their relative salaries or hourly wages all reflect these disparities.

Global Competitiveness: Global competitiveness refers to an ability of nations to supply high - quality goods and services at reasonable costs, resulting in satisfactory returns.

Industrialization: Industrialization is the process by which an economy shifts from being primarily agricultural to one based on the production of goods.

Marketing Cooperative: A marketing cooperative works as a sales outlet for the products that its members supply. It is a cost-effective way for smaller farmers to sell their products at a higher price than they could achieve on their own, especially when selling to large food companies.

Sustainable Growth: Basic concepts of sustainable growth refer to the amount of growth that a business or country can achieve without running into problems.

Unemployment: Unemployment takes place when a person seeking work is unable to find a job. Unemployment is frequently used to evaluate the performance of the market.

Women-Owned Enterprises: A women-owned and managed enterprise with a minimum financial stake of 51% of capital and at least 51% of the enterprise's jobs produced by women.

Chapter 10
The Role of University, Structural, and Social Support Means on the Intention of Entrepreneurship:
An Empirical Study on the Sample of University Youth

Redouan Ainous
https://orcid.org/0000-0001-9646-5774
University of Algiers 3, Algeria

ABSTRACT

This chapter aims at studying the effect of the implicit factors on the intention of establishing an institution for the students of an Algerian university. The structural model of the study was proposed based on the Shapiro and Sokol model and the Ajzen model. The authors tested it on a sample of 163 university students at the University of Algeria 3. The model consists of a set of variables (the intention of establishing an institution as a dependent variable, structural and social educational support as independent variables). The results of the study showed that educational and social support factors affect the entrepreneurial spirit of students more than structural support. Value/authenticity of research enrich knowledge management literature that contributes to the search for how to support investment and support the intention to establish a special institution for young people through various mechanisms and means of support.

INTRODUCTION

Describe the general perspective of the chapter. End by specifically stating the objectives of the concept of establishing an institution has taken a great deal of interest from many researchers and decision - makers during the past decades. And because the main reason for this attention to the growing need for contractors

DOI: 10.4018/978-1-7998-7951-0.ch010

who speed up economic development through the generation of new ideas and turn them into profitable projects. The activities are to create an institution that is not just incubators for creativity; it creates job opportunities and increases competitiveness as well (Reynolds, 1987). Whereas encouraging the establishment of an institution is necessary to stimulate growth in a 'growth conscious world' (Zahra et al., 1999). We can try to figure out how can stimulates one's size and intensity of activity entrepreneurial. In such an educational process, both decision - makers and researchers should focus on the question of why some people choose the profession of establishing an institution, and that others do not.

BACKGROUND

The Chapter looks at the background to the main definitions, incorporate views of others, entrepreneurial intention, Educational Support, Structural Support, and Social Support. Study Titled 'Do entrepreneurship programmes raise entrepreneurial intention of science and engineering students? The effect of learning, inspiration and resources' Do the establishment programs of the Spiritual Intentions Foundation stimulate the creation of an institution for science and engineering students? Impact of learning, inspiration and resources". Based on the theory of planned behaviour, this study examines the effect of foundation programs on the attitudes and intentions of establishing an institution for science and engineering students. This is necessary in order to confirm (or reject) the conventional wisdom that education increases the entrepreneurial spirit of the start of the business establishment of an institution. The results show that the programs raise some overall entrepreneurial positions and intentions. The findings contribute to theories of planned behaviour and education, and have broader implications for the theory of intent to set up an institution and also for the practice of teaching establishment.

Study Titled: Entrepreneurship education and entrepreneurial intention: Do female students benefit? 'Teaching the establishment of an institution and the intention of entrepreneurship: Can female students benefit?' This study aims to link participation in the Education of Establishing an institution (EE) Vigilance, risk - taking skills, and intensity of intent set up a corporation related to joining contractors. Guided by the theories of stereotypes learned socially, this study tried to understand the Wa test new hypotheses with the taking into account the potential impact of gender disparities and participation in the Education Establishment of an institution (EE). Students were compared management business participants in the education standards set up Foundation (EE). With engineering students excluded from these programs. Hierarchical regression analysis revealed that students participating in the Education of Establishing an institution (EE). They have a high density of intent to entrepreneurial; however, participation in the Education of Establishing a foundation was not born (EE) Equal benefits for all students. The women were much less likely to express a high density of intent to entrepreneurial; However, those who cite mindfulness skills were more likely to express a high intensity of non - requests entrepreneurial intent.

Study Academic entrepreneurial intention: the role of gender the intention entrepreneurial for academics: the role of the type of individuals. The purpose of this study is to analyse whether the factors determining the intentions to establish an institution among academics are the same for men and women, to test whether the degree of its importance varies according to gender, and also to test whether there is a spirit (direction) to establish an institution for women. After conducting a survey on a sample of 1178 students, the results of the linear regression model confirmed the hypothesis that female students have less desire to establish an institution. Moreover, it was observed, through lysis Blinder - Oaxaca. That this less entrepreneurial behaviour among women is not due to the absence of factors that are determinants of intentions to establish an institution, but rather it is related to the existence of implicit obstacles for women that affect their intention to establish an institution.

MAIN FOCUS OF THE CHAPTER

Problems

The company And the establishment One Most important Threads Which increase Interest Researchers Out, and this is important Growing Which Generating it On Economic the countries in different Aspects. Where the spirit of establishing an institution that occupies an important part of the concerns of university graduates in Algeria has become, especially after the transformation of the Algerian economy from a controlled economy to a market economy. On the other hand, appears related to the literature shows an institution that most researchers focused their studies on adult contractors. In fact, it has been proven that the people who are most likely to start an entrepreneurial activity are in the age group from 25 to 44 years (Liles, 1974), it is also important to focus on people under the age of 25 who are university graduates in particular, and to understand the factors that affect their intentions to start an entrepreneurial activity in the future, especially since this category is active in Algeria and represents more than two - thirds of society. Saying, 'the work environment in the future will depend on the creativity and individual young people. However, only a relatively little about the views of young people known about the establishment of an institution.' Thus, in order for the percentage of entrepreneurial work to be increased among young university graduates, the entrepreneurial trend (spirit) must be carefully studied through understanding the implicit factors that affect young people's choice of entrepreneurship as a career path and the biggest obstacles they face in this. Through the above, we can formulate the problematic of our research as follows:

What is the impact of the implicit factors on the spirit of the establishment of an institution's Algerians students?

The Importance of This Chapter

This research derives its importance from a mixture of the following scientific and practical considerations:

1. It deals with linking two important variables, the first relates to means of support and the second relates to establishing an institution. The first variable in the first section reflects the university's responsibility to provide the community with individuals who are able to carry ideas for entrepreneurial projects. The second component reflects the structural means of support provided by the political and economic environment. The latter part reflects social support, which mainly refers to emotional and financial support for families and friends. The second variable P reflects the importance of entrepreneurship in the development of the economies of communities. Thus, the value of each variable is determined by the extent of its success in performing the task assigned to it.
2. Through the findings, this research provided an opportunity to reconsider university training programs and curricula, especially the part related to establishing an institution.

The Objective of This Chapter

This study seeks to achieve a number of objectives, which can be summarised in the following points:

1. Theoretical enrichment of the relevant aspects by clarifying the intellectual and conceptual basis of the study variables.
2. Knowing the most important variables and factors affecting students' choice of entrepreneurship and measuring their entrepreneurial orientation.
3. Processing phenomena the company, I have Young As reality a sociologist by trying to understand the impact of the social dimension on the spirit of establishing an institution among Algerian youth.

CONCEPTUAL MODEL AND HYPOTHESES DEVELOPMENT

The Model Research

In our study we will rely on a model theory planned behaviour and model the event Entrepreneurialism, as they are two main references in most of the previous studies in preparing any model related to the entrepreneurial orientation (intention):

1. Entrepreneurial Event Form (Shapero & Sokol, 1982): The authors provided a model to configure the event Entrepreneurial Is based to me Concept of transfers. The basic idea of the model is based on the premise that any individual's decision to change his important directions in life, such as the decision to establish a private institution, will inevitably be preceded by an event that stops and breaks the usual routine. They interpret their model across three groups of factors (the transitions) that characterise the important changes in life. (Negative transfers' refer to divorce, emigration, or dismissal from work; The 'intermediate cases' are the exit from the army, school, or prison; While 'positive moves' could be the influence of the family, the presence of a market or potential investors, etc. And set the authors two groups From Variables Intermediate They: Realisation of desire Comprising Factors Social And cultural which effect On System Value For individuals, realising potential Achievement - perceptions of feasibility - that arise from During Realisation The individual to all Species the support and help available he has to achieve his idea.
2. Planned Behaviour Theory (Ajzen & Fishbein, 1980): Psychology is of great importance in the study of behavioural prediction. It highlights the processes that influence individual and implicit factors on intent to establish an institution. For this purpose, the theory of planned behaviour. It is an undeniable contribution to explaining the spirit of establishing an institution. This theory is based on the logical business model established by Ajzen & Fishbein, 1980. It gives the individual's attitudes the main place in the origin of behaviour, through three sets of variables. Attitudes associated with behaviours include an individual's evaluation of the desired behaviour. It builds on the possible consequences of the latter and is embedded in the actions to make it a reality. While self - standards arise as a result of the social pressure that the individual is exposed to from his close surroundings - family and friends. Whereas, behavioural observation perceptions take into consideration one's own qualifications and the degree of knowledge possessed.

The theoretical model of our study consists of four variables, the dependent variable which is the intention to establish an institution, while the independent variables are educational support; structural support and social support.

The structural model of our study is based on two basic models:

- The first model is for because it provides a general framework for analysing the spirit of establishing an enterprise for the individual, and it is more compatible with the social criteria proposed in our model, which would influence the intention to establish an institution, as the model suggests the direct impact of social factors on the entrepreneurial orientation of individuals.
- The second model is for (Shapero & Sokol, 1982). It takes effect implicit factors on the spirit of the establishment of an institution for individuals, especially educational support factors, social, and structural (Turker & Sonmez, 2009).

The Research Hypotheses

In light of previous studies, we suggested in our study a set of implicit factors that can influence the intention to establish an institution among university students, which we mention as follows:

1. Factor 1 (Educational Support): It is clear that university education is an effective way to obtain the necessary knowledge about setting up an institution. A study Wang & Wong (2004) concluded despite its focus mainly on the students 'personality characteristics, the fact that the intention to establish an institution for many students is hindered by insufficient preparation and training. P knowledge to create an institution is not sufficient, because the students are graduates are not prepared to take risks to achieve their dreams. Therefore, the fact that academic institutions sometimes care for students to be very academic and do not encourage them to choose the profession of establishing an institution sufficiently. (Gibb, 1996). And in order to overcome this shortcoming, most universities offered Algerian courses or programs create an institution at the university level and postgraduate studies. In the literature, the decomposition of some studies how the influence of this educational support for the Entrepreneurship universities on the spirit of the establishment of an institution for students. A study showed the features of establishing an institution can be positively affected by educational programs. As indicated Kolvereid & Moen (1997) in their studies, there is also a link between education in the field of establishments and entrepreneurial behaviour. Likewise, a study (Galloway & Brown, 2002) by analysing the impact of options for establishing an institution, and found that the return on investment in education to establish an institution may be long - term and not immediate. It is clear that effective education about starting a business can be a factor that pushes people towards a career in establishing a corporation.

   Hypothesis 1: The intention to establish an institution for university students is positively related to educational support.
2. Factor 2 (Structural Support): We live in a broader context of social, cultural, economic, political and technological factors. The current entrepreneurial context consists mainly of the economic and political mechanisms governed by actors in the public, private and non - governmental sectors. In such a system, there could be some opportunities or threats to the contractors. For example, if there are some barriers to entering the market, people may appear less entrepreneurial. However, if they find that the particular conditions are sufficient and favourable, they are expected to be more likely

to start the entrepreneurial activity. Where he says in this regard that it is when circumstances exist Economical College stable and growth economy sustainable. It disturbs the possibility Appearance of Form leadership Business the value High for the community.

Hypothesis 2: The intention to establish an institution for university students is positively related to the structural support.

3. Factor 3 (Social Support): From previous studies, we concluded that the family background must also be taken into account as a factor affecting the spirit of establishing an institution. For example, a study showed that family is the second factor influencing respondents' career choice - after their personal experience. Therefore, the support of family and friends is likely to influence a person's choice of entrepreneurship. In the current study, this social support mainly refers to the emotional and financial support of family and friends. For that The Algerian family trying it out to improve Application Living Trying giving more possibilities. For her children they are providing them climate appropriate. To study, and encourage them On Learning and in status Failure is based directing them for centres Configuration Professionals and therefore she works to get. On qualifications and experiences qualify them for the position Work.

Hypothesis 3: The intention to establish an institution for university students is positively related to social support.

SOLUTIONS AND RECOMMENDATIONS

Population and Sampling

The study was conducted on a random sample of community members. The distributed forms reached (200) forms, of which (180) were retrieved. After examining them and ensuring their suitability for statistical analysis (17) questionnaires were excluded. Thus, the number of valid forms for analysis is (163) forms, i.e. a response rate equal to (90%), while the valid response rate is (81.5%).

Instrument and Reliability

It was used as a questionnaire to gather information for this study, which created a for the purposes of this study, after taking necessary for the design of the questionnaire of scientific terms, based on previous studies on the subject. We used a questionnaire consisting of 13 statements, in which respondents

Table 1. Source of Measurement

Variables	No. Items	Scale Source	Total α Cronbach
Educational support	3	Turker & Sonmez, 2009	0.932
Structural support	4	Parnell et al., 1995	
social support	2	Lüthje et al., 2003	
Entrepreneurial Intention	4	Liñán et al., 2009	

Source: Own

were able to provide their opinion on these statements using a 5 - point Likert scale. The questionnaire includes four main axes, summarised in the following table:

The questionnaire's consistency is intended to give it the same results if it is redistributed more than once to the same sample members under the same conditions and circumstances. Where a test was conducted by presenting it to a number of researchers and specialists in business administration, as well as the management of organisations with the aim of arbitrating and correcting them, and finally obtaining approval on the percentage (93%) thus achieving the apparent validity of the questionnaire.

Descriptive Information of the Respondents

This study is based on the descriptive and analytical approach, which aims to describe the studied phenomenon, analyse it, and reveal the relationships between its dimensions. Will we at this point presented the results of the descriptive analysis of personal data and variable Intention of Entrepreneurship, and the results of the test study hypotheses that are as follows. The table below shows a set of demographic characteristics of the study sample:

Table 2. Demographic Information of Respondents

Properties		Repetition	percentage
Type	Male	75	46.01%
	female	88	53.99%
Age	Less than 25 years old	100	61.34%
	From 25 to 30 years old	53	32.52%
	From 30 to 40 years old	10	06.14%
	Are over 40 years old	0	0.00%
Specialisation	accounting and finance	32	19.63%
	Management science	98	60.12%
	Economic sciences	33	20.25%
Education level	License	83	50.92%
	Master	80	49.07%
Place area	Urban	105	64.42%
	Rural	58	35.58%

Source: Own

We note from the above table data that (53.99%) of respondents are only females, and this percentage logical because of the increased number of females than males in the university stands Algerian, and it was a spontaneous representation of this class emerged from the study population in the sample. We also find that (61.34%) of the respondents are less than (25) years old, while those between (25) and (30) years old do not exceed. (32.52%.) This indicates that those who will carry contracting projects in the near future will be young Sunnis. The data also show that (50.92%) of students are in the bachelor's phase, and (49.07%) of those who wanted the sample are in the master's phase. So that the two percentages are close to each other, and that is because most students prefer to continue their studies after they skip the first stage of the progression. The data also shows the urban housing area of the respondents is higher than that of the countryside due to the population density concentrated in the cities.

Evaluation Measurement Model

Table 3. The Results of Each Test KMO and the Bartlett's.

KMO		0.829
Test Bartlett's	Chi - square	2080.054
	Degree of freedom	78
	Statistical significance	0.000

Source: Own

Before starting to test the form of the study hypotheses, it is desirable to evaluate the measurement model:

1. Indicators Quality Model: This is a numbered term.

    a. KMO and Bartlett's Test: To do this, a test was carried KMO, by which to judge the adequacy of the sample size. Ranging value KMO In general, it is between 0 and 1, and the closer its value to 1, the greater the reliability of the factors obtained from the analysis. The minimum acceptable level for KMO it is 0.50 in order to judge the adequacy of the sample size and if its value is lower, the sample size must be increased.

b. General SEM Analysis Result:

Table 4. Model Validity and Quality Indicators (Model Fit and Quality Indices)

Indicators	Value	Sig
Average path parameter (APC)	0.349	P <0.001
Average (ARS) R^2	0.913	P <0.001
AverageR^2 the average (AARS)	0.911	P <0.001
Average massAVIF (VIF))	2.630	AVIF <5
Average VIF For the perfect linear Correlation	3.171	AFVIF <5
Indicator GoF for Tenenhaus	0.801	GoF ^{3} 0.36
Model paradox ratio for (SPR) Sympson	1.000	SPR ^{3} 0.7
Contribution rate to (RSCR) R^2	1.000	RSCR ^{3} 0.9
The proportion of the abolition of statisticalSSR))	1.000	SSR ^{3} 0.7
Causal trend ratio for nonlinearity variables (NLBCDR)	1.000	NLBCDR ^{3} 0.7

Source: Own

Through the table, we note that the ten tests to measure the quality of indicators and the validity of the model are all intangible values. These indicators allow us to analyse the study model and test hypotheses according to the method of structural equations.

c. Latent Variable Coefficients:

Table 5. Coefficients of the Latent Variables

Indications	Educational Support	Structural Support	Social Support	Intention
Reliability Vehicle Reliability	0.897	0.885	0.874	0.872
Alpha Cronbach	0.828	0.827	0.711	0.803
Average Contrast Extracted	0.745	0.658	0.776	0.630
Average VIF	1.147	2.591	3.412	1.095

Source: Own

Note from the above table that Alpha Cronbach's Surpassed (0.7) and that Compound reliability coefficients (Composite Reliability) Superior to (0.7), and we note that the extracted variance coefficients (AVE), all of them are outperforming (0.5), also average VIF or the whole linear relationship is less than or equal to, (5) all of these values are significant, and this indicates the quality of the study model.

2. Evaluation Structural Model

- R Square: We note from the result that the coefficient of determination (R^2) is equal to (0.913), and this means that the independent variables 'educational support, structural support and social support' explain (91.3%) of the changes that are challenged in the dependent variable 'spirit of establishing an institution', and the rest is due to factors other.
- Path Coefficient:

Table 6. Path Coefficient

Hypothesis	Independent Variable	Dependent Variable	Value	Sig	Decision
H1	Educational Support	Intention of Entrepreneurship	0.52	P <0.01	Acceptable
H2	Structural Support	Intention of Entrepreneurship	0.21	P <0.01	Acceptable
H3	Social Support	Intention of Entrepreneurship	0.31	P <0.01	Acceptable

Source: Own

We conclude from the above table the following:

There is a direct correlation with statistical significance between the factors of educational support and the intention to establish an institution Where the strength of the relationship (β= 0.52) the first hypothesis is accepted.

There is a direct correlation with statistical significance between the factors of structural support and the intention to establish an institution Where the strength of the relationship ($\beta = 0.21$) the second hypothesis is accepted.

There is a direct correlation with statistical significance between the factors of social support and the intention to establish an institution, where the strength of the relationship reached ($\beta = 0.31$) the third hypothesis is accepted.

FUTURE RESEARCH DIRECTIONS

Concerning future research on entrepreneurship education using intention as an impact factor, scholars should seek to conduct studies with a high standard of methodological rigor. Of particular importance to such studies is the inclusion of a treatment group (students who receive entrepreneurship education) and a control group (students outside the entrepreneurship education sphere). Considering randomization in assignment to treatment and control groups is also possible to avoid sampling biases.

CONCLUSION

The results of the survey revealed that the three factors of the proposed model are important indicators of intent to establish an institution. The first factor is educational support, which mainly refers to a supportive university environment. And according to the results, provide sufficient knowledge The University and inspiration for the establishment of an institution, and the possibility of choosing a career establishment of an institution may increase among students. It is clear that this result confirms the main role of education in developing the spirit of establishing an institution. Therefore, in light of the current study, it can be said that the establishment of an institution can be strengthened with an education process. This finding is not only interesting in theory, but also a challenge for decision - makers. As the establishment activities become vital for economic development, it may focus on designing more effective educational policies. The results of the study also showed that universities should encourage the development of creative ideas to form entrepreneurs, provide the necessary knowledge about the concept of establishing an institution and develop the skills of establishing an enterprise.

The second factor is structural support. It is clear that strengthening the establishment of an institution requires comprehensive support, including cooperation from all sectors of society. Although the explanatory power is weak, the analysis has also shown that this type of structural support may affect the spirit of establishing an institution among university students. Therefore, the structural support for entrepreneurship is very important to motivate people to be entrepreneurs.

Regarding the third factor, it is social support, which refers to the supportive social environment of family and friends. We concluded a social environment of the m circumspection student provides moral support to choose the establishment of an institution and this is a Kdth study results.

REFERENCES

Ajzen, I., & Fishbein, M. (1980). *Understanding Attitudes and Predicting Social Behaviour*. Prentice - Hall.

Galloway, L., & Brown, W. (2002). Entrepreneurship education at university: A driver in the creation of high growth firms? *Education + Training*, *44*(8 / 9), 398–405. doi:10.1108/00400910210449231

Gibb, A. A. (1996). Entrepreneurship and small business management: Can we afford to neglect them in the twenty- first century business school? *British Journal of Management*, *7*(4), 309–321. doi:10.1111/j.1467-8551.1996.tb00121.x

Kolvereid, L., & Moen, Ø. (1997). Entrepreneurship among business graduates: Does a major in entrepreneurship make a difference? *Journal of European Industrial Training*, *21*(4), 154–160. doi:10.1108/03090599710171404

Liles, P. (1974). Who are the entrepreneurs? *MSU Business Topics*, *22*(1).

Reynolds, P. D. (1987). New firms: Societal contribution versus survival potential. *Journal of Business Venturing*, *2*(3), 231–246. doi:10.1016/0883-9026(87)90011-5

Shapero, A. & Sokol, L. (1982). The social dimensions of entrepreneurship. *Encyclopaedia of entrepreneurship*, 72 - 90.

Turker, D., & Sonmez, S. S. (2009). Which factors affect entrepreneurial intention of university students? *Journal of European Industrial Training*, *33*(2), 142–159. doi:10.1108/03090590910939049

Wang, C. K., & Wong, P. K. (2004). Entrepreneurial interest of university students in Singapore. *Technovation*, *24*(2), 163–172. doi:10.1016/S0166-4972(02)00016-0

Zahra, S. A., Nielsen, A. P., & Bogner, W. C. (1999). Corporate entrepreneurship, knowledge, and competence development. *Entrepreneurship Theory and Practice*, *23*(3), 169–189. doi:10.1177/104225879902300310

Chapter 11
Managerial Pamperdom and Prestige Entrepreneurship

Fahri Özsungur
https://orcid.org/0000-0001-6567-766X
Department of Labor Economics and Industrial Relations, Mersin University, Adana, Turkey

ABSTRACT

Entrepreneurship has started to be used as a tool for individual interests as well as the implementation of innovative ideas. Sustainability in entrepreneurship requires corporate social responsibility and ethical principles in leadership. The fact that individual interests are a hidden aim in entrepreneurship puts justice and ethics in the background. Entrepreneurship is based on sustainable, ethical, corporate innovation, and creative thinking. Entrepreneurship, which is set forth with the individual secret goals of entrepreneurs, causes important problems in leadership and managerial context. Especially, managerial pamperdom and prestige entrepreneurship that emerged in professional organizations are introduced to the literature for the first time. It is thought that this chapter will make significant contributions to the fields of entrepreneurship, business, management, and strategy.

INTRODUCTION

Management is an important tool in strategy and enables control of the behavior of people, organizations, and society (Punt et al., 2016). Management is related to the behavior of individuals, organizational coordination, and the process in the operation of the business (Waugh, 1993; Kumar & Chandrakar, 2012). It makes significant contributions to the creation, execution, and maintenance of the management strategy (Lee & Scott, 2009; Kelly, 1997). Today's business strategies are based on the management approach required by these contributions.

Businesses today develop strategies and adopt management approaches to gain sustainable competitive advantage, create a corporate image, organizational value, and identity (Coyne, 1986). Profitability, access to financial resources provide a diminishing contribution to the sustainability of the business due to constantly changing consumer needs, and technological developments (Shee & Abratt, 1989). A management approach that does not include quality perception, prestige, institutionalism, personal

DOI: 10.4018/978-1-7998-7951-0.ch011

ambitions is important for sustainability and competitive advantage (Steenkamp, 1990). On the other hand, the management style is important for businesses in the context of employee commitment to the workplace, performance, and productivity (Teo, Bentley, & Nguyen, 2020; Nor et al., 2020).

Managers' satisfaction and emotions, excessive self-confidence, personal expectations reveal an important management problem for many organizations and businesses (Boyatzis & Cavanagh, 2018). This problem causes leadership and management weaknesses in today's organizations. This situation can also obstruct entrepreneurship. Widespread admiration, individual satisfaction, reputation, entrepreneurship for success can cause significant management and entrepreneurship problems (Piazza & Abrahamson, 2020).

Entrepreneurship has started to be used as a tool for individual interests as well as the implementation of innovative ideas (Zabashta, 2019). Sustainability in entrepreneurship requires corporate social responsibility and ethical principles in leadership (Haldar, 2019; Iannone, 2018). The fact that individual interests are a hidden aim in entrepreneurship puts justice and ethics in the background. Entrepreneurship is based on sustainable, ethical, corporate innovation, and creative thinking (Markman et al., 2016; Bocken et al., 2014). Entrepreneurship, which is set forth with the individual secret goals of entrepreneurs, causes important problems in leadership and managerial context. Therefore, the aim of the chapter is to introduce managerial pamperdom and prestige entrepreneurship to the literature and to determine the dimensions of these concepts. It is thought that both subjects will contribute to the fields of management and strategy, business, organizational behavior, human resources management, and entrepreneurship. The target audience of this chapter is academics, scientists, researchers, practitioners, governmental institutions, and policymakers.

RESEARCH METHODOLOGY

The systematic review method was applied in this chapter. This method is a qualitative research method that includes identification, review and research, classification and data analysis, summarization, extracting data, discussion, and presentation processes (Papaioannou et al., 2010; DeMarrais & Lapan, 2003). First of all, a social source of inspiration was determined to perform the study (Petticrew & Roberts, 2008; Amenta, 2003). Pamperdom and prestige in management and strategy can cause important problems. Managerial pamperdom is the reason for many problems arising in the context of work commitment, employee-employer relations, performance, and productivity. On the other hand, prestige in entrepreneurship is important in terms of corporate and individual purposes. After determining the points of inspiration, the research question was determined as follows: What are "managerial pamperdom" and "prestige entrepreneurship" and what are their dimensions?

After the research question was determined, classification and data analysis was performed with a wide literature review. The information obtained was organized under the headings of summarization and extracting data (Torgerson, 2003). The text organized under topic titles with discussion and presentation processes was reconsidered as a whole (Somekh & Lewin, 2005). Thus, the final form of the chapter was revealed by checking the harmony between the subject headings and the body text.

THEORETICAL FRAMEWORK

Depending on the purpose of the study, putting forward an approach in which individual interests come to the fore in management and entrepreneurship can be explained on the basis of classical management theory, bureaucratic management theory, and institutional theory of entrepreneurship. This is because, in all three theoretical approaches, factors except social, career, emotional and physical needs of the employee are ignored.

Classical Management Theory

The classical management theory focuses on the physical needs of employees (Baglioni, Campling, & Hanlon, 2020; Sulieman, 2019; Kumar, 2017). This narrow approach ignores the social, emotional and career needs of the employees (Mahmood, Basharat, & Bashir, 2012). The management structure, the definition of the roles of the employees, job description are the important issues revealed by this approach (Carroll, & Gillen, 1987). According to this approach, an ideal workplace emerges through profit maximization, central leadership, expertise in labor, productivity, hierarchical structuring (Cole & Kelly, 1996).

The Bureaucratic Management Theory

The bureaucratic management theory includes task specialization, hierarchical management structure, formal selection rules, efficient and uniform requirements, impersonal environment, achievement-based advancement requirements (Singh, 2013). Managers at the top of the hierarchical structure have the main administration power (Boyne, 1998). For this reason, the authority and management power in bureaucracy do not belong to the employees who are at the bottom of the hierarchy (Wise, 2004).

Institutional Theory of Entrepreneurship

The institutional theory is concerned with preserving the current position and legitimacy in harmony with the environment (Bruton, Ahlstrom, & Li, 2010). The sustainability and competitiveness of the organization depends on the strength and harmony of the state policies, laws, decisions of official authorities, and the relations with the courts (Tolbert, David, & Sine, 2011). Factors except the legitimacy and sustainability requirements of the organization are not considered in the context of entrepreneurship according to this theory (Su, Zhai, & Karlsson, 2017).

MANAGERIAL PAMPERDOM

Pamperdom is an important risk and threat factor in management. Managers and leaders experience a significant level of comfort when they are successful (Tom, 2008). This experience causes them to ignore many important issues. Thus, a manager or leader deviates from her/his goals towards achieving her/his managerial goals (Rutherford & Meier, 2015; Keim, 1978). Manager's ignoring important critical factors such as success, purpose, goal, strategy causes failures. The failure process occurs with the expectation of attention, comfort, and kindness. Managerial pamperdom emerges when the manager's feelings of excessive self-confidence, selfishness, and egoism raise individual expectations.

Managerial pamperdom is a state of attention, comfort, an expectation of kindness, excessive self-confidence, managerial selfishness, and egoism that emerge in management. When the manager reaches the status she/he desires, she/he places emphasis on managerial satisfaction (Daddi et al., 2019). Thus, some values and factors such as social, institutional, humanitarian, personal, and employee rights required by management are ignored by the manager who has managerial pamperdom syndrome.

Purpose Deviation in Management

The purpose of management is to determine the route on the way to the goal. The goal becomes clear as a result of the correct selection of the expectations and values revealed by the purpose (Zarbo, Copeland, & Varney, 2017). The purpose is a reason for existence, the sense of determination or resolve of individuals or an organization. The purpose is the desired outcome and intention in achieving the goal of success. The purpose in management is the set of principles, values, rules, plans, behaviors, and decisions that an individual or organization puts forward to achieve the goal factors. For this reason, goals for the future are determined for the realization of the purpose. The goal is chosen to achieve the purpose.

Achieving the purpose in management provides success, performance, strategic renewal, and sustainability. The method to be followed in determining and achieving the goal is important in achieving the purpose. For this reason, it is necessary to proactively identify the factors that prevent the achievement of the administrative purpose and to take the necessary measures. Purpose deviation in management includes leaving the organization's raison d'etre, the method and path determined to achieve the goal. In organizational management, departing from an accepted standard can eliminate the function of strategic management (Zur Muehlen, 2004; Thompson, 1960; Naoum, 2001). Purpose deviation in management accepted standard involves principles, action plans, values, and departing from the process.

Attention Expectation

Attention expectation is an individual's sense of interest or importance (Summerfield & Egner, 2009). When individuals believe that they have proven themselves in terms of management, they can turn to their personal needs outside of managerial purposes. One of these needs is to see managers respected by their subordinates. However, being respected leaves its place to the anticipation of attention after a while. The desire to be accepted constantly within the organization triggers this expectation.

When routine respect and adoption behaviors directed to managers and leaders by employees become insufficient, excessive, and continuous interest or importance behaviors are expected to be realized. Thus, dissatisfaction with the behaviors of respect and acceptance occurs in the manager and leader. Attention expectation is a result of this dissatisfaction. The relevant and important behaviors of the employees and subordinates increase the attention expectation of the manager. On the other hand, the success achieved, the accepted skills and behaviors demonstrated in achieving the goals affect this expectation (Trmal, Bustamam, & Mohamed, 2015).

Comfort Expectation

Comfort in the organization includes the ergonomy, design, sense of physical ease, and well-being regarding the workplace, good mood expectations of managers and company partners (Luo et al., 2018; Califano et al., 2019). The manifestation of managerial skills often depends on inspiration. Inspiration is affected by environment and individual mood (Kast, 1991). Therefore, managers attach importance to comfort while revealing their management skills. Although this situation is normal in organizational management, some managers exaggerate this situation.

Managers are impressed by the physical location of the organization, the workplace climate, the width and spaciousness of the room/office, and the ergonomics of the chairs and tables (Alzghoul et al., 2018; Dastmalchian, Blyton, & Adamson, 2014). Ergonomic features required for occupational health and safety are often not enough for managers and leaders (Kogi, 2012). Although it is ergonomic, the use of some furniture is abandoned by these managers (Shikdar & Sawaqed, 2003). The width of the working office, the brand of the chair and the table, the design of the chandeliers are not liked by the manager or the leader. The separation of the dining halls of the managers from the workers' and the tools and equipment used by the workers differing from the manager's show that the understanding of comfort tends towards luxury use. This understanding of comfort causes unfair practices and discrimination between worker-leader, subordinate-superior.

Kindness Expectation

Kindness is a quality indicator and tool in communication (Erikson, 2019).. This indicator deals with generousness, friendliness, and considerateness. The kindness expectation requires the affability afforded by a close relationship with respect. This expectation includes the thought that more than expected should be demonstrated by the other party. This thought requires the administrator to be careful to avoid losses or inconvenience.

Managers argue that employees should show empathy in anticipation of kindness. Leaders and employers in particular adopt this notion. Kindness is a necessary factor in the relationship between subordinate and superior in management according to ethical principles (Theodosius, 2006). However, the fact that kindness expectation includes more than expected values causes perceptions of disobedience, leader-employee problems, and injustice.

Significant management problems arise when kindness exceeds managerial communication expectations such as expectation, empathy, excessive interest, and understand the feelings (Panko, 1992). In this case, loyalty to the leader and the workplace decreases and employee performance decreases. Managerial pamperdom may arise due to such expectations except for managerial boundaries.

Extreme Self-Confidence in Leadership

Self-confidence is a feeling of trust in the individual. This feeling of trust is related to personal quality, judgment, and abilities. Trust in leadership traits, expectation, and belief in being overly superior in managerial skills cause excessive self-confidence (Mowday, 1979). Being appreciated by business networks, suppliers, stakeholders, and the social environment causes extreme self-confidence.

Leaders' relationships with their followers, being mediatic, popularity can cause self-confidence (Holenweger, Jager, & Kernic, 2017). Leaders who are accepted and appreciated by society increase their self-belief. Leaders fed by this belief may experience stress, anxiety, and depression when interest is low. This situation causes management weaknesses. Managerial pamperdom caused by extreme self-confidence causes blind spots in management skills. For the sustainable management strategies of the organization, measures to eliminate this situation causing managerial pamperdom should be proactively put forward.

Managerial Selfishness and Egocentrism

In managerial self-perception, managers become insensitive to the events in their environment and display selfish behaviors (Deyreh, 2012). Managerial selfishness is related to lack of consideration, self-interest, and being excessively conceited (Rozuel & Kakabadse, 2010). In managerial egocentrism, the leader or manager prefers to serve her/himself rather than serve the organization. Thus, those that do not benefit the individual in the managerial factors of the organization are excluded from the strategy.

Managerial selfishness is a person's excessive sense of self-importance or self-esteem. The state of being excessively conceited leads to deviation in the organizational goals of the manager and leader and failures in the steps taken to achieve the goals. Selfishness and egocentrism create important managerial blind spots that result in self-interest to be held superior to management goals. These blind spots harm the productivity and profitability of the organization, employee-leader, and leader-stakeholder relationships.

"Managerial egocentrism" causes a sense of social responsibility, team spirit, and organizational commitment to decrease and disappear in conflicts of interest that may arise between the organization and the leader-manager (Hattula et al., 2015; Gelfand et al., 2002). Career development, success factors, profit-loss balance are evaluated according to the individual's interests. This situation causes significant damage to the organization.

Managerial Satisfaction

Managerial satisfaction represents the fulfillment of the manager or leader's needs, expectations, wishes, or pleasure (Decker, 1987). Positive outcomes in favor of the manager arising in the process related to the management reveal a sense of satisfaction (Anderson & O'Reilly, 1981). Success outputs during the implementation of the necessary strategies for the mission and vision of the manager are an important indicator of this satisfaction. On the other hand, situations such as performance, productivity, manager-employee relations, organizational climate, organizational culture and identity, institutionalism are important for managerial satisfaction (Pritchard & Karasick, 1973).

Meeting the managerial needs in managerial satisfaction creates a pleasure. In the context of the management of the organization, fulfillment of the expectations and wishes of stakeholders, employees, customers, consumers, leaders ensure a sustainable cycle (Orpen, 1985). This cycle creates a perception of the successful management of the organization. Thus, managers play an active role in managerial satisfaction due to this positive perception of success.

Excessive managerial satisfaction causes the manager to decrease derived pleasure from existing achievements. As pleasure decreases, even if organizational success increases, satisfaction level decreases (Naseem, Sheikh, & Malik, 2011). Thus, a manager profile that is saturated with success and not satisfied appears. This situation results in a managerial pamperdom. Therefore, control and strategy are necessary for managerial satisfaction. A management approach based on the satisfaction of the manager causes the organization to take unnecessary risks and losses.

Managerial Pamperdom Problems in Professional Organizations

Professional organizations are legal entities representing certain professional groups and supporting the activities of their members (Bucher & Stelling, 1969). These legal entities provide important advantages and benefits in many areas such as gaining sustainable competitive advantage, entering new markets, project consultancy, fair support, financial and network support (Montagna, 1968). Members gain a reliable reference in the international or national market as being members of professional organizations.

Professional organizations, which have three types of structures as public, private, or mixed law, operate for the production or service sector (Özsungur, 2019). These organizations assume an intermediary role in relations with the state in order to find solutions to the legal problems of their members. Problems in the implementation of legal rules, economic developments, regional or international developments are closely followed by professional organizations.

Professional organizations are generally governed by a tripartite structure, consisting of the general assembly, the board of directors, and the administrative unit. The general assembly is the highest body of the professional organization, and the important and legal decisions of the organization are taken by this body (Bleiklie, Enders, & Lepori, 2015). The board of directors is managed by the members elected by the general assembly and is the executive body of the organization. The administrative unit consists of employees and sub-managers.

The triple structure in professional organizations reveals important problems in terms of administration (Özsungur, 2019). The management bodies of professional organizations such as chambers of commerce and chambers of the industry have an active function since they are executive bodies. Since the members of the board of directors and council members are elected persons, their expectations are high in terms of management (Özsungur, 2019). Managerial pamperdom occurs most often in these organizations. The reason for this is that the members of the organization are the managers and leaders of the commercial enterprises and companies.

General assembly and board members often do not have sufficient technical knowledge about the basic functions of the professional organization. As the members of the board of directors, which are the executive bodies, meet at certain times of the year and make decisions and their decisions are executed, the expectations of the members increase. Since members have the authority in the management of a professional organization that has a completely different structure from their profession and in the decisions taken, their expectations for attention, comfort, and kindness are very high (Wallace, 1995). They perceive the employees of the organization as the business' or company' employees they own. This perception causes a transformation towards the boss-employee relationship that should not exist in professional organizations. Thus, the function of the administrative body, which is essentially superior to the employees, is harmed.

The habits of the members of the board of directors to executive and decision duties cause conflict between the duties of the current business-professional organization (Özsungur, 2019). This conflict leads to conflict between the employee and the board member, and to enforce obedience behavior. The nature of the execution of the decisions taken increases the self-confidence of the board members and causes the emergence of managerial selfishness and egocentrism. This condition causes managerial pamperdom syndrome. This syndrome emerges after a business/company manager expects service in return by paying a membership fee is elected to the top management of the organization.

PRESTIGE ENTREPRENEURSHIP

Prestige is a set of behaviors, symbols, gestures, words, writing, and perception aimed at showing respect (Wegener, 1992). Prestige is the respect shown and perceived by people, organizations, and institutions. Therefore, having prestige is tantamount to being respectable. However, prestige and respect are different concepts. The reason for this is related to respect widespread admiration and respect felt that is tried to be achieved in prestige. Prestige is a personal or corporate situation that is gained and felt through active activities.

Prestige is a message about the corporate or personal image transferred to the environment (Frandsen, 2012). Although it is not an objective indicator, the perception of achievements or quality revealed by prestige is important in the context of the network in enterprises and organizations. Entry to new markets, sustainability in competitive advantage, access to financial resources, trust, relations with the public can be improved with indicators that represent success and quality. Prestige is a tool that contributes to these indicators. Through innovation and creativity, new methods, products, services, and ideas can be put forward to gain prestige. This shows that entrepreneurship can be revealed for prestige purposes.

Entrepreneurship is the orientation of knowledge, experience, and skills to the setting up of a new business or businesses (Dollinger, 2008; Eckhardt & Shane, 2003; Zahra, 2020). Setting up new business or businesses with individual creativity and innovation requires financial, social, and spiritual risks (Dwivedi & Weerawardena, 2018). Individuals or businesses seize opportunities for future sustainable competitive advantage by risking their resources for entrepreneurship (Peredo & McLean, 2006). Entrepreneurs with proactive personality traits identify opportunities in advance and take the necessary initiatives to transform the risk factor into the benefit (Crant, 1996; Becherer & Maurer, 1999).

Conceptual Framework

Entrepreneurship can be revealed to create financial resources, gain competitive advantage, enter new markets, develop new products and services, gain new customers, and develop new processes (Chen et al., 2007). These purposes contribute to the purposes of the individual or organization. On the other hand, creating brand value, gaining a corporate image, creating a perception of quality and success in third parties are among these purposes (Chaniago, 2020; Teng, 2007). Creating these perceptions in the network of the organization or enterprise, its stakeholders, suppliers, and competitors is for prestige. Entrepreneurship actions to be put forward to gain prestige reveal a new type of entrepreneurship, prestige entrepreneurship.

Prestige entrepreneurship is the set of efforts, ideas, and activities in order to gain prestige put forward to turn opportunities into benefits and make a profit by taking financial, network, legal, and value-based risks to set up new resources, processes, products. The main purpose of this type of entrepreneurship is to gain prestige, to provide brand value, to create a corporate image, to create a perception of quality and success related to the outputs of entrepreneurship action (figure 1). The prestige to be achieved improves the perception of widespread admiration and respect for the entrepreneur. This achieved image becomes a driving force for the resource by providing the necessary motivation for the entrepreneur's future initiatives.

Prestige entrepreneurship includes six basic factors. These factors are entrepreneurial satisfaction, corporate image, widespread admiration, widespread respect, achievement perception, and quality perception.

Figure 1. Prestige entrepreneurship factors

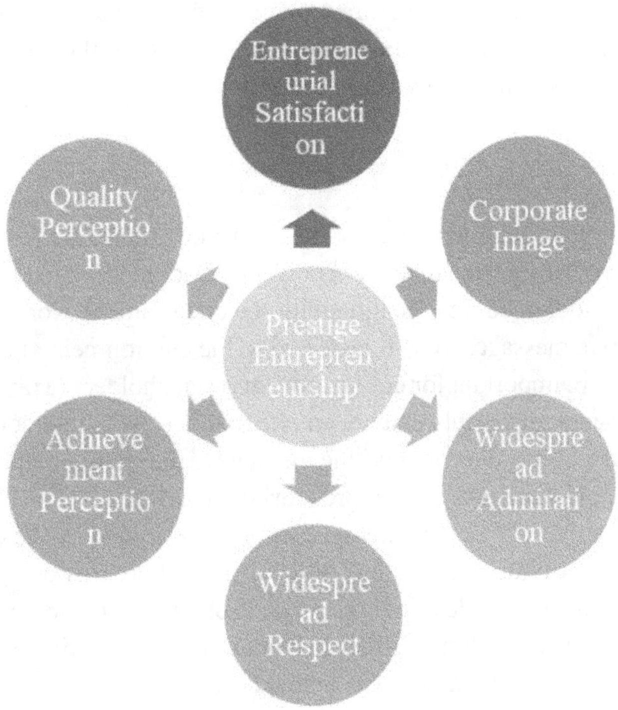

Entrepreneurial Satisfaction

Satisfaction is an important element in prestige entrepreneurship. The entrepreneur provides positive outputs of entrepreneurship fulfillment of the entrepreneur's needs, expectations, wishes, or pleasure (Schjoedt, 2009). The sense of creativity that new products or services will reveal provides a significant level of satisfaction (Kautonen & Palmroos, 2010). Entrepreneurs take risks to generate financial resources and profits (Dawson, 2017). However generally, Profit or financial resources may not be sufficient in terms of expectations from entrepreneurship outputs (Cooper & Artz, 1995).

Entrepreneurs take actions to provide profitability and financial resources, such as entering new markets, acquiring future customers, expanding the business area, operating in new business areas, creating new processes in the business (Lee & Kim, 2019). These initiative actions may not be sufficient to ensure entrepreneurial satisfaction. The entrepreneur's participation in the management bodies of professional organizations, entrepreneurship activities aimed at cooperation with professional organizations and universities are activities aimed at entrepreneurial satisfaction. The entrepreneur is entrepreneurially satisfied with the organizational status she/he has achieved to have an authority in the management body of the entrepreneurial organization and to support other entrepreneurs (Akehurst, Comeche, & Galindo, 2009). Angel investors also support young and women entrepreneurs for achieving this satisfaction (DeGennaro, 2012; Cumming & Zhang, 2019; Ramadani, 2012).

Supporting other entrepreneurs enables the prestige entrepreneur's network and supplier network to expand (Sohl & Hill, 2007). Angel investors or prestige entrepreneurs achieve entrepreneurial satisfaction through resource allocation, enterprise model development, entrepreneurship training, and sharing entrepreneurial ideas on new products and services (Collewaert, 2012). Thus, they make a significant contribution to the encouragement of new entrepreneurs and the emergence of entrepreneurial ideas (Bammens & Collewaert, 2014). This situation causes an increase in the recognition of entrepreneurs who support and respect and admiration by commercial actors.

Corporate Image

Institutional image is the representational image of the legal entity transferred to the environment, related to the organization's identity, institutionalism, and power of resources (Lowrey, 2011). This representative image is an important tool in communicating with the environment. Corporate image is the mirror of the entrepreneur. Positive messages to be transferred to the environment after the implementation of the entrepreneurship idea are important for competitors and stakeholders (Tran et al., 2015). The entrepreneur should use representational tools that are an effective means of interacting and communicating with the environment. Outsourcing dependence, the message to the environment is important in relations with suppliers, and the implementation of entrepreneurial ideas.

In prestige entrepreneurship, the organizational identity determined by the entrepreneur as the goal plays a mediating role in determining the strategy of the organization. However, image is not everything in entrepreneurship. Some factors should be held superior to others in the implementation of the organization's ideas about entrepreneurship. Competition, sustainability, profitability, innovation are prominent factors in entrepreneurship. The corporate image helps these factors.

Gaining Widespread Respect/Reputation Aim

Reputation and respect are important in terms of outsourcing in entrepreneurship. The implementation of the entrepreneurship idea depends on financial, network, supplier, and human resources. The provision and mobilization of these resources are facilitated by the entrepreneur's message of respect for the environment. Reputation is an important pulling factor in the access of business and entrepreneurs to financial, human, spiritual, and moral resources.

The purpose of making a profit in entrepreneurship is not enough for sustainability. The profit obtained adds value to the resources. It is an important indicator for investors. Profitability provides a positive perception of the profile of the business or entrepreneur in a financial context. This perception creates similar results for company shareholders, stakeholders of the company, suppliers, and network.

When the entrepreneur takes financial risks to turn opportunities into benefits by revealing her/his innovative and creative ideas, she/he can adopt the goal of respect/reputation (Kozubíková et al., 2017). The reason for this is the creation of a perception that will ensure that individual success is accepted by competitors, stakeholders, shareholders, and consumers. The perception of dignity created here is the acceptance of the positive outcomes generated by the implementation of entrepreneurial ideas. Acceptance behavior is important for the entrepreneur to promote in the market, to benefit from commercial incentives, to access financial resources, to implement new entrepreneurial ideas.

Gaining Widespread Admiration Aim

Since entrepreneurship action is a set of innovative and creative actions, the implementation of ideas can provide a sense of admiration in individuals. The risk is taken in entrepreneurship, proactive behavior, creativity, implementation of innovative ideas, innovations in products and services, setting up new businesses, and businesses give an impressive impact on followers. Admiration enables the entrepreneur to develop respect for his followers. When this admiration state becomes widespread, a goal that the entrepreneur desires to achieve is realized.

When entrepreneurship is realized at a level that appeals to the admiration of large masses, entrepreneurial outputs provide important elements such as brand, image, corporate identity. Admiration is important for the personal and organizational image. In prestige entrepreneurship, the entrepreneur's personal expectation of admiration is necessary (Örtqvist, Drnovsek, & Wincent, 2007). Beyond the adoption and acceptance of the entrepreneurship idea by competitors, consumers, and stakeholders, creating a commendable perception is among the basic elements of prestige entrepreneurship. The main purpose here is to take the entrepreneur and her/his ideas as an example by the followers and to be a role model. On the other hand, the entrepreneur desires to demonstrate a leader characteristic via prestige entrepreneurship.

Admiration is an important sustainable tool in the relationship between leaders and their followers (Michel, Wallace, & Rawlings, 2013; Chong & Wolf, 2010). Admiration is a necessary factor for the relationship to be permanent (Helfrich & Dietl, 2019). Maintenance of communication is important in relations with stakeholders and the environment that emerge in the implementation of ideas in entrepreneurship. Admiration is an important opportunity in entrepreneurship in the context of outsourcing and incentives (Drakopoulou Dodd, Jack, & Anderson, 2013).

Achievement/Success and Quality Perception

Entrepreneurship is realized to achieve personal and organizational success (Baron, 2000). Entrepreneurs who have goals except for financial factors such as social and academic entrepreneurship focus on quality and success factors for future customers, sustainable competition, new markets and strategies, new processes (Wright, 2007; Siegel & Wright, 2015; Kickul & Lyons, 2020). The perception of success increases the belief that the entrepreneur will put forward new and creative ideas, products, services, processes, businesses. This belief is an important reason for satisfaction for the entrepreneur. On the other hand, the perception of quality is also an important satisfaction tool.

Quality is an indicator of the value, level, status, and standard of the output in entrepreneurship (Sunyigono, Hayati, & Qomariyah, 2020). The perception of quality is a specific standard and degree of excellence regarding new products, services, businesses that are introduced by entrepreneurship (Prasetyo & Kistanti, 2020). High social or network status is a quality indicator revealed by entrepreneurship. It is also a distinguishing and determining tool regarding the characteristics of the quality entrepreneur and the entrepreneurial idea. Therefore, entrepreneurs desire to create a perception of quality to access financial resources, to make a profit, and to set up new businesses. This perception is created to reveal a corporate image by attracting the attention of consumers and suppliers. On the other hand, the entrepreneur creates a perception of quality for entrepreneurial satisfaction and ensures such an entrepreneurship idea to be approved by individuals and organizations.

Entrepreneurial Actions Based on Pleasure

Pleasure deriving is related to enjoyment and happiness (Young & Ferguson, 2020). Individuals enter the business life for success in their lives, self-realization, career development, financial and personal satisfaction. Entrepreneurship is realized to be satisfied and happy from the success and acceptance state of creative and innovative ideas. An entrepreneurship idea and implementation that being inspired by others causes pleasure. Besides, the entrepreneurship idea of someone who is a leader in an existing business is a source of inspiration for employees and followers, causing a significant sense of satisfaction and pleasure.

Entrepreneurship is an enjoyable combination of activities and behaviors that strengthen the individual's behavior. This activity, which is integrated with mental ability and personal skill, allows the feeling of happiness to spread. Enjoyable entrepreneurial action positively affects the entrepreneur stakeholders. As the outcomes resulting from the implementation of the idea of entrepreneurship provide pleasure to the entrepreneur, a driving force and courage emerge for future entrepreneurship. Thus, the entrepreneur tries to get more inspiration to reveal entrepreneurial ideas that they enjoy and are happy with.

SOLUTIONS AND RECOMMENDATIONS

Managerial pamperdom is a state of attention, comfort, an expectation of kindness, excessive self-confidence, managerial selfishness, and egoism that emerge in management. Managerial pamperdom is a state that damages the leader-follower, subordinate-superior, employer-employee relationship. This situation leads to management weaknesses in professional organizations that are public institutions. In order to eliminate this negative situation, the active role of managers in human resources management should be limited and corporate governance principles should be encouraged in organizations.

Prestige entrepreneurship is the set of efforts, ideas, and activities in order to gain prestige put forward to turn opportunities into benefits and make a profit by taking financial, network, legal, and value-based risks to set up new resources, processes, products. Prestige entrepreneurship can cause managerial pamperdom in the case of managerial selfishness and egoism.

Excessive expectation about entrepreneurial satisfaction, reputation, respect, admiration, success, quality, and pleasure causes managerial weakness and pamperdom. Therefore, in prestige entrepreneurship, the expectations of the entrepreneur should be kept under control and personal ambitions and passions should be limited. The desire and ambition exhibited to achieve success should be limited to the purpose of entrepreneurship and its outputs. Behaviors and activities that are put forward due to personal ambitions except for entrepreneurship may cause outcomes except for t the purpose. Managerial selfishness can emerge when the expectation of success is combined with personal ambitions. Managerial selfishness, egoism, and excessive self-confidence in entrepreneurship can reduce the contribution of stakeholders to support the implementation of the idea.

Prestige entrepreneurs should take institutionalism and social responsibility into consideration in revealing innovative and creative ideas about products, services, and processes. Because gaining reputation requires an institutional approach. It is important to demonstrate success and be a role model for widespread admiration. In order to gain prestige in entrepreneurship, the perception of quality must be gained from the followers and stakeholders. Also, the prestige entrepreneur must have ethical leader qualities. Prestige, admiration, and reputation can be gained through the entrepreneurial actions of an ethical leader. Therefore, it is necessary and important not to exaggerate entrepreneurial actions based on pleasure.

FUTURE RESEARCH DIRECTIONS

Empirical research of the relationships between managerial pamperdom and entrepreneurship types is recommended for future research. Managerial pamperdom needs to be investigated qualitatively in the public and private sectors. A scale can be developed in this regard. Besides, it is recommended to develop a scale for prestige entrepreneurship and to determine its dimensions with qualitative studies. The associations of prestige entrepreneurship with ethical leadership, psychological capital, and organizational behavior types should be investigated empirically.

CONCLUSION

In this chapter, it was determined that the dimensions of managerial pamperdom are purpose deviation in management, attention, comfort expectation, kindness expectation, extreme self-confidence in leadership, managerial selfishness and egocentrism, managerial satisfaction. Besides, managerial pamperdom problems in professional organizations were explained in the chapter. Managerial pamperdom is an important problem in management, strategy, and entrepreneurship. For this reason, introducing the subject to literature with its concepts and dimensions will make important contributions to business literature.

Another subject discussed in the study is prestige entrepreneurship. The dimensions of this type of entrepreneurship were determined as entrepreneurial satisfaction, corporate image, gaining widespread respect/reputation aim, gaining widespread admiration aim, achievement/success and quality perception, entrepreneurial actions based on pleasure.

Prestige entrepreneurship reveals the existence of a corporate and personal purpose except for entrepreneurship to access financial resources and to make a profit. Entrepreneurship models such as corporate, social, academic entrepreneurship, and intrapreneurship help to determine the method and path followed in the realization of entrepreneurship. However, prestige entrepreneurship focuses on the purpose and reason for the idea rather than a form of strategic management. Creating an entrepreneurship-based strategy limits entrepreneurship practices with determined methods. On the other hand, the creation of entrepreneurship types based on purposes and reasons is useful for understanding the reasons for the emergence of entrepreneurial ideas.

ACKNOWLEDGMENT

This research received no specific grant from any funding agency in the public, commercial, or not-for-profit sectors.

REFERENCES

Akehurst, G., Comeche, J. M., & Galindo, M. A. (2009). Job satisfaction and commitment in the entrepreneurial SME. *Small Business Economics*, *32*(3), 277–289. doi:10.100711187-008-9116-z

Alzghoul, A., Elrehail, H., Emeagwali, O. L., & AlShboul, M. K. (2018). Knowledge management, workplace climate, creativity and performance. *Journal of Workplace Learning*, *30*(8), 592–612. doi:10.1108/JWL-12-2017-0111

Amenta, E. (2003). *Comparative historical analysis in the social sciences*. Cambridge University Press.

Anderson, J. C., & O'Reilly, C. A. III. (1981). Effects of an organizational control system on managerial satisfaction and performance. *Human Relations*, *34*(6), 491–501. doi:10.1177/001872678103400605

Baglioni, E., Campling, L., & Hanlon, G. (2020). Global value chains as entrepreneurial capture: Insights from management theory. *Review of International Political Economy*, *27*(4), 903–925. doi:10.1080/09692290.2019.1657479

Bammens, Y., & Collewaert, V. (2014). Trust between entrepreneurs and angel investors: Exploring positive and negative implications for venture performance assessments. *Journal of Management*, *40*(7), 1980–2008. doi:10.1177/0149206312463937

Baron, R. A. (2000). Psychological perspectives on entrepreneurship: Cognitive and social factors in entrepreneurs' success. *Current Directions in Psychological Science*, *9*(1), 15–18. doi:10.1111/1467-8721.00050

Becherer, R. C., & Maurer, J. G. (1999). The proactive personality disposition and entrepreneurial behavior among small company presidents. *Journal of Small Business Management*, *37*(1), 28.

Bleiklie, I., Enders, J., & Lepori, B. (2015). Organizations as penetrated hierarchies: Environmental pressures and control in professional organizations. *Organization Studies*, *36*(7), 873–896. doi:10.1177/0170840615571960

Bocken, N. M., Short, S. W., Rana, P., & Evans, S. (2014). A literature and practice review to develop sustainable business model archetypes. *Journal of Cleaner Production*, *65*, 42–56. doi:10.1016/j.jclepro.2013.11.039

Boyatzis, R. E., & Cavanagh, K. V. (2018). Leading change: Developing emotional, social, and cognitive competencies in managers during an MBA program. In *Emotional intelligence in education* (pp. 403–426). Springer. doi:10.1007/978-3-319-90633-1_15

Boyne, G. A. (1998). Bureaucratic theory meets reality: Public choice and service contracting in US local government. *Public Administration Review*, *58*(6), 474–484. doi:10.2307/977575

Bruton, G. D., Ahlstrom, D., & Li, H. L. (2010). Institutional theory and entrepreneurship: Where are we now and where do we need to move in the future? *Entrepreneurship Theory and Practice*, *34*(3), 421–440. doi:10.1111/j.1540-6520.2010.00390.x

Bucher, R., & Stelling, J. (1969). Characteristics of professional organizations. *Journal of Health and Social Behavior*, *10*(1), 3–15. doi:10.2307/2948501 PMID:5776946

Califano, R., Naddeo, A., Gatto, A., Leo, S., Milosa, P., Nazzaro, M., & Straccia, L. (2019). Virtual prototyping for workplace analysis: The effect of expectation on perceived comfort while using office devices. *International Journal on Interactive Design and Manufacturing*, *13*(1), 235–242. doi:10.100712008-018-0521-5

Carroll, S. J., & Gillen, D. I. (1987). Are the classical management functions useful in describing managerial work? *Academy of Management Review*, *12*(1), 38–51. doi:10.5465/amr.1987.4306460

Chaniago, H. (2020). The Effects of Entrepreneurial Personality to Competitiveness and Corporate Image: A Study on Chocolate Agent Entrepreneurs. *International Review of Management and Marketing*, *10*(2), 21–29. doi:10.32479/irmm.9262

Chen, C. N., Tzeng, L. C., Ou, W. M., & Chang, K. T. (2007). The relationship among social capital, entrepreneurial orientation, organizational resources and entrepreneurial performance for new ventures. *Contemporary Management Research*, *3*(3), 213–232. doi:10.7903/cmr.90

Chong, E., & Wolf, H. (2010). Factors influencing followers' perception of organisational leaders. *Leadership and Organization Development Journal*, *31*(5), 402–419. doi:10.1108/01437731011056434

Cole, G. A., & Kelly, P. (1996). *Management: Theory and practice*. Continuum.

Collewaert, V. (2012). Angel investors' and entrepreneurs' intentions to exit their ventures: A conflict perspective. *Entrepreneurship Theory and Practice*, *36*(4), 753–779. doi:10.1111/j.1540-6520.2011.00456.x

Cooper, A. C., & Artz, K. W. (1995). Determinants of satisfaction for entrepreneurs. *Journal of Business Venturing*, *10*(6), 439–457. doi:10.1016/0883-9026(95)00083-K

Coyne, K. P. (1986). Sustainable competitive advantage—What it is, what it isn't. *Business Horizons*, *29*(1), 54–61. doi:10.1016/0007-6813(86)90087-X

Crant, J. M. (1996). The proactive personality scale as a predictor of entrepreneurial intentions. *Journal of Small Business Management*, *34*, 42–49.

Cumming, D., & Zhang, M. (2019). Angel investors around the world. *Journal of International Business Studies*, *50*(5), 692–719. doi:10.105741267-018-0178-0

Daddi, T., Iraldo, F., Testa, F., & De Giacomo, M. R. (2019). The influence of managerial satisfaction on corporate environmental performance and reputation. *Business Strategy and the Environment*, *28*(1), 15–24. doi:10.1002/bse.2177

Dastmalchian, A., Blyton, P., & Adamson, R. (2014). *The Climate of Workplace Relations (Routledge Revivals)*. Routledge. doi:10.4324/9781315772417

Dawson, C. (2017). Financial optimism and entrepreneurial satisfaction. *Strategic Entrepreneurship Journal*, *11*(2), 171–194. doi:10.1002ej.1244

Decker, W. H. (1987). Managerial humor and subordinate satisfaction. *Social Behavior and Personality*, *15*(2), 225–232. doi:10.2224bp.1987.15.2.225

DeGennaro, R. P. (2012). Angel investors and their investments. The Oxford Handbook of Entrepreneurial Finance, 392-423.

DeMarrais, K. B., & Lapan, S. D. (2003). *Foundations for research: Methods of inquiry in education and the social sciences*. Routledge. doi:10.4324/9781410609373

Deyreh, E. (2012). Effects of perceived selfishness among managers on organizational justice. *Procedia: Social and Behavioral Sciences*, *46*, 390–393. doi:10.1016/j.sbspro.2012.05.128

Dollinger, M. (2008). *Entrepreneurship*. Marsh Publications.

Drakopoulou Dodd, S., Jack, S., & Anderson, A. (2013). From admiration to abhorrence: the contentious appeal of entrepreneurship across Europe. *Entrepreneurship and Regional Development, 25*(1-2), 69-89. doi:10.1080/08985626.2012.746878

Dwivedi, A., & Weerawardena, J. (2018). Conceptualizing and operationalizing the social entrepreneurship construct. *Journal of Business Research*, *86*, 32–40. doi:10.1016/j.jbusres.2018.01.053

Eckhardt, J. T., & Shane, S. A. (2003). Opportunities and entrepreneurship. *Journal of Management*, *29*(3), 333–349. doi:10.1177/014920630302900304

Erikson, M. G. (2019). Kindness, Communication and Academic Responsibility in Higher Education. In *Values of the University in a Time of Uncertainty* (pp. 171–184). Springer. doi:10.1007/978-3-030-15970-2_12

Frandsen, S. (2012). Organizational image, identification, and cynical distance: Prestigious professionals in a low-prestige organization. *Management Communication Quarterly*, *26*(3), 351–376. doi:10.1177/0893318912438692

Gelfand, M. J., Higgins, M., Nishii, L. H., Raver, J. L., Dominguez, A., Murakami, F., Yamaguchi, S., & Toyama, M. (2002). Culture and egocentric perceptions of fairness in conflict and negotiation. *The Journal of Applied Psychology*, *87*(5), 833–845. doi:10.1037/0021-9010.87.5.833 PMID:12395808

Haldar, S. (2019). Towards a conceptual understanding of sustainability-driven entrepreneurship. *Corporate Social Responsibility and Environmental Management*, *26*(6), 1157–1170. doi:10.1002/csr.1763

Hattula, J. D., Herzog, W., Dahl, D. W., & Reinecke, S. (2015). Managerial empathy facilitates egocentric predictions of consumer preferences. *JMR, Journal of Marketing Research*, *52*(2), 235–252. doi:10.1509/jmr.13.0296

Helfrich, H., & Dietl, E. (2019). Is employee narcissism always toxic?–The role of narcissistic admiration, rivalry and leaders' implicit followership theories for employee voice. *European Journal of Work and Organizational Psychology*, *28*(2), 259–271. doi:10.1080/1359432X.2019.1575365

Holenweger, M., Jager, M. K., & Kernic, F. (2017). *Leadership in Extreme Situations*. Springer. doi:10.1007/978-3-319-55059-6

Iannone, B. (2018). Sustainability, corporate social responsibility, and corporate reputation in the wine sector: A key performance indicator framework model. *International Journal of Applied Behavioral Economics*, *7*(2), 47–68. doi:10.4018/IJABE.2018040104

Kast, V. (1991). *Joy, inspiration and hope*. Texas A&M University Press.

Kautonen, T., & Palmroos, J. (2010). The impact of a necessity-based start-up on subsequent entrepreneurial satisfaction. *The International Entrepreneurship and Management Journal, 6*(3), 285–300. doi:10.100711365-008-0104-1

Keim, G. D. (1978). Managerial behavior and the social responsibility debate: Goals versus constraints. *Academy of Management Journal, 21*(1), 57–68.

Kelly, A. (1997). *Maintenance strategy*. Elsevier.

Kickul, J., & Lyons, T. S. (2020). *Understanding social entrepreneurship: The relentless pursuit of mission in an ever changing world*. Routledge. doi:10.4324/9780429270406

Kogi, K. (2012). Practical ways to facilitate ergonomics improvements in occupational health practice. *Human Factors, 54*(6), 890–900. doi:10.1177/0018720812456204 PMID:23397801

Kozubíková, L., Dvorský, J., Cepel, M., & Balcerzak, A. P. (2017). Important characteristics of an entrepreneur in relation to risk taking: Czech Republic case study. *Journal of International Students, 10*(3), 220–233. doi:10.14254/2071-8330.2017/10-3/16

Kumar, P. (2017). Analysis the impact of classical management approaches on the management practices. *Asian Journal of Management, 8*(3), 841–853. doi:10.5958/2321-5763.2017.00132.9

Kumar, R., & Chandrakar, R. (2012). Overview of green supply chain management: Operation and environmental impact at different stages of the supply chain. *International Journal of Engineering and Advanced Technology, 1*(3), 1–6.

Lee, H. H. Y., & Scott, D. (2009). Overview of maintenance strategy, acceptable maintenance standard and resources from a building maintenance operation perspective. *Journal of Building Appraisal, 4*(4), 269-278.

Lee, W. S., & Kim, B. Y. (2019). The effects of career orientations on entrepreneurial satisfaction and business sustainability. *The Journal of Asian Finance, Economics, and Business, 6*(4), 235–248. doi:10.13106/jafeb.2019.vol6.no4.235

Lowrey, W. (2011). Institutionalism, news organizations and innovation. *Journalism Studies, 12*(1), 64–79. doi:10.1080/1461670X.2010.511954

Luo, M., Wang, Z., Brager, G., Cao, B., & Zhu, Y. (2018). Indoor climate experience, migration, and thermal comfort expectation in buildings. *Building and Environment, 141*, 262–272. doi:10.1016/j.buildenv.2018.05.047

Mahmood, Z., Basharat, M., & Bashir, Z. (2012). Review of classical management theories. *International Journal of Social Sciences and Education, 2*(1), 512–522.

Markman, G. D., Russo, M., Lumpkin, G. T., Jennings, P. D., & Mair, J. (2016). Entrepreneurship as a platform for pursuing multiple goals: A special issue on sustainability, ethics, and entrepreneurship. *Journal of Management Studies, 53*(5), 673–694. doi:10.1111/joms.12214

Michel, J. W., Wallace, D. L., & Rawlings, R. A. (2013). Charismatic leaders: The role of admiration and system justification. *Leadership and Organization Development Journal, 34*(5), 469–487. doi:10.1108/LODJ-11-0099

Montagna, P. D. (1968). Professionalization and bureaucratization in large professional organizations. *American Journal of Sociology, 74*(2), 138–145. doi:10.1086/224616

Mowday, R. T. (1979). Leader characteristics, self-confidence, and methods of upward influence in organizational decision situations. *Academy of Management Journal, 22*(4), 709–725.

Naoum, S. (2001). *People and organizational management in construction*. Thomas Telford. doi:10.1680/paomic.28746

Naseem, A., Sheikh, S. E., & Malik, K. P. (2011). Impact of employee satisfaction on success of organization: Relation between customer experience and employee satisfaction. *International Journal of Multidisciplinary Sciences and Engineering, 2*(5), 41-46.

Nor, C. S. M., Mohamed, R. K. H., Mohamed, B., & Hassan, N. A. C. (2020). Human Resources Management Practices and its Impact on Employee Commitment Mong Staffs of Road Transport Department, Perak, Malaysia. *Journal of Environmental Treatment Techniques, 8*(1), 28–34.

Orpen, C. (1985). The effects of need for achievement and need for independence on the relationship between perceived job attributes and managerial satisfaction and performance. *International Journal of Psychology, 20*(2), 207–219. doi:10.1080/00207598508247733 PMID:25820002

Örtqvist, D., Drnovsek, M., & Wincent, J. (2007). Entrepreneurs' coping with challenging role expectations. *Baltic Journal of Management, 2*(3), 288–304. doi:10.1108/17465260710817492

Özsungur, F. (2019). Ethical leadership, intrapreneurship, service innovation performance and work engagement in chambers of commerce and industry. *Journal of Human Behavior in the Social Environment, 29*(8), 1059–1081. doi:10.1080/10911359.2019.1664359

Panko, R. R. (1992). Managerial communication patterns. *Journal of Organizational Computing and Electronic Commerce, 2*(1), 95–122. doi:10.1080/10919399209540176

Papaioannou, D., Sutton, A., Carroll, C., Booth, A., & Wong, R. (2010). Literature searching for social science systematic reviews: Consideration of a range of search techniques. *Health Information and Libraries Journal, 27*(2), 114–122. doi:10.1111/j.1471-1842.2009.00863.x PMID:20565552

Peredo, A. M., & McLean, M. (2006). Social entrepreneurship: A critical review of the concept. *Journal of World Business, 41*(1), 56–65. doi:10.1016/j.jwb.2005.10.007

Petticrew, M., & Roberts, H. (2008). *Systematic reviews in the social sciences: A practical guide*. John Wiley & Sons.

Piazza, A., & Abrahamson, E. (2020). Fads and Fashions in Management Practices: Taking Stock and Looking Forward. *International Journal of Management Reviews, 22*(3), 1–23. doi:10.1111/ijmr.12225

Prasetyo, P. E., & Kistanti, N. R. (2020). Human capital, institutional economics and entrepreneurship as a driver for quality & sustainable economic growth. *Entrepreneurship and Sustainability Issues*, *7*(4), 2575–2589. doi:10.9770/jesi.2020.7.4(1)

Pritchard, R. D., & Karasick, B. W. (1973). The effects of organizational climate on managerial job performance and job satisfaction. *Organizational Behavior and Human Performance*, *9*(1), 126–146. doi:10.1016/0030-5073(73)90042-1

Punt, A. E., Butterworth, D. S., de Moor, C. L., De Oliveira, J. A., & Haddon, M. (2016). Management strategy evaluation: Best practices. *Fish and Fisheries*, *17*(2), 303–334. doi:10.1111/faf.12104

Ramadani, V. (2012). The importance of angel investors in financing the growth of small and medium sized enterprises. *International Journal of Academic Research in Business & Social Sciences*, *2*(7), 306–322.

Rozuel, C., & Kakabadse, N. (2010). Ethics, spirituality and self: Managerial perspective and leadership implications. *Business Ethics (Oxford, England)*, *19*(4), 423–436. doi:10.1111/j.1467-8608.2010.01603.x

Rutherford, A., & Meier, K. J. (2015). Managerial goals in a performance-driven system: Theory and empirical tests in higher education. *Public Administration*, *93*(1), 17–33. doi:10.1111/padm.12124

Schjoedt, L. (2009). Entrepreneurial job characteristics: An examination of their effect on entrepreneurial satisfaction. *Entrepreneurship Theory and Practice*, *33*(3), 619–644. doi:10.1111/j.1540-6520.2009.00319.x

Shee, P. S. B., & Abratt, R. (1989). A new approach to the corporate image management process. *Journal of Marketing Management*, *5*(1), 63–76. doi:10.1080/0267257X.1989.9964088

Shikdar, A. A., & Sawaqed, N. M. (2003). Worker productivity, and occupational health and safety issues in selected industries. *Computers & Industrial Engineering*, *45*(4), 563–572. doi:10.1016/S0360-8352(03)00074-3

Siegel, D. S., & Wright, M. (2015). Academic entrepreneurship: Time for a rethink? *British Journal of Management*, *26*(4), 582–595. doi:10.1111/1467-8551.12116

Singh, P. (2013). Transforming traditional bureaucratic management practices by employing the Collegial Leadership Model of Emancipation. *International Business & Economics Research Journal*, *12*(8), 953–968. doi:10.19030/iber.v12i8.7991

Sohl, J. E., & Hill, L. (2007). Women business angels: Insights from angel groups. *Venture Capital*, *9*(3), 207–222. doi:10.1080/13691060701324536

Somekh, B., & Lewin, C. (2005). Research methods in the social sciences. *Sage (Atlanta, Ga.)*.

Steenkamp, J. B. E. (1990). Conceptual model of the quality perception process. *Journal of Business Research*, *21*(4), 309–333. doi:10.1016/0148-2963(90)90019-A

Su, J., Zhai, Q., & Karlsson, T. (2017). Beyond red tape and fools: Institutional theory in entrepreneurship research, 1992–2014. *Entrepreneurship Theory and Practice*, *41*(4), 505–531.

Sulieman, M. S. (2019). Roots of Organizational Knowledge in Classical Management Theories: A Literature Review. *International Journal of Business and Social Science, 10*(10), 8–15. doi:10.30845/ijbss.v10n10a2

Summerfield, C., & Egner, T. (2009). Expectation (and attention) in visual cognition. *Trends in Cognitive Sciences, 13*(9), 403–409. doi:10.1016/j.tics.2009.06.003 PMID:19716752

Sunyigono, A. K., Hayati, M., & Qomariyah, N. (2020). Analysis of Personal Entrepreneurship Quality of The Society in Mandangin Island. *IOP Conference Series. Earth and Environmental Science, 518*(1), 012063. doi:10.1088/1755-1315/518/1/012063

Teng, B. S. (2007). Corporate entrepreneurship activities through strategic alliances: A resource-based approach toward competitive advantage. *Journal of Management Studies, 44*(1), 119–142. doi:10.1111/j.1467-6486.2006.00645.x

Teo, S. T., Bentley, T., & Nguyen, D. (2020). Psychosocial work environment, work engagement, and employee commitment: A moderated, mediation model. *International Journal of Hospitality Management, 88*, 102415. doi:10.1016/j.ijhm.2019.102415

Theodosius, C. (2006). Recovering emotion from emotion management. *Sociology, 40*(5), 893–910. doi:10.1177/0038038506067512

Thompson, J. D. (1960). Organizational management of conflict. *Administrative Science Quarterly, 4*(4), 389–409. doi:10.2307/2390765

Tolbert, P. S., David, R. J., & Sine, W. D. (2011). Studying choice and change: The intersection of institutional theory and entrepreneurship research. *Organization Science, 22*(5), 1332–1344. doi:10.1287/orsc.1100.0601

Tom, S. (2008). Managing energy and comfort. *ASHRAE Journal, 50*(6), 18–27.

Torgerson, C. (2003). *Systematic reviews*. Bloomsbury Publishing.

Tran, M. A., Nguyen, B., Melewar, T. C., & Bodoh, J. (2015). Exploring the corporate image formation process. *Qualitative Market Research, 18*(1), 86–114. doi:10.1108/QMR-05-2014-0046

Trmal, S. A., Bustamam, U. S. A., & Mohamed, Z. A. (2015). The Effect of Transformational Leadership in Achieving High Performance Workforce That Exceeds Organisational Expectation: A Study from a Global and Islamic Perspective. *Global Business and Management Research, 7*(2), 88–94.

Wallace, J. E. (1995). Organizational and professional commitment in professional and nonprofessional organizations. *Administrative Science Quarterly, 40*(2), 228–255. doi:10.2307/2393637

Waugh, W. L. (1993). Coordination or control: Organizational design and the emergency management function. *International Journal of Disaster Prevention and Management, 2*(4), 17–31.

Wegener, B. (1992). Concepts and measurement of prestige. *Annual Review of Sociology, 18*(1), 253–280. doi:10.1146/annurev.so.18.080192.001345

Wise, L. R. (2004). Bureaucratic posture: On the need for a composite theory of bureaucratic behavior. *Public Administration Review, 64*(6), 669–680. doi:10.1111/j.1540-6210.2004.00414.x

Wright, M. (2007). *Academic entrepreneurship in Europe*. Edward Elgar Publishing. doi:10.4337/9781847205575

Young, R., & Ferguson, F. (2020). *Writing For Pleasure: theory, research and practice*. Routledge. doi:10.4324/9780429268984

Zabashta, E. (2019). Theoretical fundamentals of formation of innovative development of entrepreneurship. *Baltic Journal of Economic Studies*, *5*(4), 97–104. doi:10.30525/2256-0742/2019-5-4-97-104

Zahra, S. A. (2020). International entrepreneurship in the post Covid world. *Journal of World Business*, *56*(1), 101143. doi:10.1016/j.jwb.2020.101143

Zarbo, R. J., Copeland, J. R., & Varney, R. C. (2017). Deviation ManagementKey Management Subsystem Driver of Knowledge-Based Continuous Improvement in the Henry Ford Production System. *American Journal of Clinical Pathology*, *148*(4), 354–367. doi:10.1093/ajcp/aqx084 PMID:28967954

Zur Muehlen, M. (2004). Organizational management in workflow applications–issues and perspectives. *Information Technology and Management*, *5*(3-4), 271–291. doi:10.1023/B:ITEM.0000031582.55219.2b

KEY TERMS AND DEFINITIONS

Attention Expectation: An individual's sense of interest or importance.

Comfort in the Organization: The ergonomy, design, sense of physical ease, and well-being regarding the workplace, good mood expectations of managers and company partners.

Kindness: A quality indicator and tool in communication.

Managerial Egocentrism: A sense of social responsibility, team spirit, and organizational commitment to decrease and disappear in conflicts of interest that may arise between the organization and the leader-manager.

Managerial Pamperdom: A state of attention, comfort, an expectation of kindness, excessive self-confidence, managerial selfishness, and egoism that emerge in management.

Managerial Satisfaction: The fulfillment of the manager or leader's needs, expectations, wishes, or pleasure.

Managerial Selfishness: Lack of consideration, self-interest, and being excessively conceited.

Prestige Entrepreneurship: The set of efforts, ideas, and activities in order to gain prestige put forward to turn opportunities into benefits and make a profit by taking financial, network, legal, and value-based risks to set up new resources, processes, products.

Chapter 12
Moderated Mediation Effect of Institutional Environment and Entrepreneurship Orientation:
The Enterprising Self-Efficacy and SME Advancement

Anthony Eniola
Landmark University, UK

Ademola Sajuyigbe
Department of Business Studies, Landmark University, UK

Wasiu Sanyaolu
Department of Accounting, Dominican University, USA

Nwoye Obi
Department of Business Studies, Landmark University, UK

ABSTRACT

Business enterprise is a significant driver of feasible financial development, autonomous of social, economic, and international conditions. Nonetheless, the creation and support of effective small and medium-sized enterprises (SMEs) zeroed in on business is a significant test. This exploration took a gander at the job of enterprising self-efficacy and the institutional environment in the innovative direction and improvement of an effective SME dependent on the business. The objective is to coordinate the institutional environment, self-efficacy, and resolve the previously mentioned difficulties for the development of business enterprise-based SMEs in Nigeria. The investigation utilized an adapted scale; information was gathered from owners of small and medium enterprises in Nigeria. The exploration utilized PLS-SEM to assess the proposed moderate intervention model. The discoveries of the examination empowered the job of innovative self-viability and the institutional atmosphere in the advancement of an effective SME dependent on the business enterprise.

DOI: 10.4018/978-1-7998-7951-0.ch012

INTRODUCTION

This chapter contribution provides an outline of the research. The study looks at how enterprising self-efficacy influences SME advancement and how formal and informal institutional environments impact SME advancement in Nigeria. This chapter contribution thus provides a path map for the study by offering insights into the study's context, research issues and goals, and the study's importance and contributions to the body of knowledge.

Both becoming an autonomous company founder or an small and medium (SMEs) business owners and participating in intrapreneurship in existing companies are critical in today's work environment, as individuals progressively face uncertain career paths. Entrepreneurship is commonly described in market analysis as the process of dig up or co-creating, assessing, and utilizing opportunities to create products and services. Individuals' entrepreneurial thought and action has been an important tool for scholars, students, and politicians wanting to promote entrepreneurial practises conducted individually by individuals or inside organisations (Eniola, 2021; Newman et al., 2019).

Individual qualities of entrepreneurs are thought to play imperative purposes in the institutional environment and personal accomplishment (Wei et al., 2020), such as self-efficacy, which relates to a person's confidence that they will accomplish specific objectives. Entrepreneurial Self-Efficacy (ESE) is the use of self-efficacy in entrepreneurship knowledge, relating to how optimistic entrepreneurs are in their own entrepreneurial abilities to achieve different tasks and programmes (Wei et al., 2020). The entrepreneur's journey is fraught with failures, necessitating the presence of strong psychological traits. ESE, a common trait of entrepreneurs, reflects the entrepreneurs' confidence and mentality toward overcoming different challenges and achieving entrepreneurial achievement. Accordingly, ESE plays a significant role in predicting entrepreneurship advancement. In this manner, the core of entrepreneurship is seizing possibilities, incorporating resources, and then innovating and acting rapidly.

However, scholars have criticised entrepreneurship studies in developing nations for focusing on portrayals instead of clarifications, and despite the fact that there is substantial research in entrepreneurship, the majority of it is centred on North America and Europe, with little thought given to Africa (Dana & Ratten, 2017; Eniola, 2020a, 2020b, 2020c). The explanation is not mindboggling; Africa was neglected in standard entrepreneurship study owing to a lack of reported studies. Africa is a significant participant in the global economy, representing 20 percent of total global land space, addressing a high extent of land for business intentions, with an approximate population of over 1 billion people and the continent being the second largest after Asia in terms of ethnic heterogeneity (Dana & Ratten, 2017; Eniola, 2020a). Current entrepreneurship research study focuses on industrialised countries rather than addressing the diverse forms in which entrepreneurship is conducted in developing, evolving, and transformation economies. As a result of its economic turnaround and development curve, Africa's entrepreneurship study has gained traction.

Business enterprise in the place of small and medium (SME) means the broad prospects for hypothetical examination and reasonable ramifications in Nigeria (Eniola, 2020b, 2020c). Researchers recognize the monstrous portion of SMEs in the economic improvement of countries and embraced that the development of an economy is vitally connected with an expansion in the SMEs (Eniola, 2020a). However, in Nigeria, economic growth has remained sluggish since 2015, and uncertainty in oil prices continues to affect growth output (World Bank, 2019).

This might be as a result of a non-entrepreneurial mind-set in the Nigerian youth be induced by the government's generous public support policies seeking to win goodwill. This is why the new generation that includes the half of populace, (NBS, 2018), prefers to enter public sector organizations instead of moving toward the private sector. Furthermore, the modern generation be short of the necessary combination of qualities and skills. The 'rentier' economy suffers from the often-cited condition of 'Dutch Disease' (Alarjani et al., 2020; Eniola, 2020b, 2020c). Subsequently, different difficulties have emerged, including; ineffectively created private sector, absence of talented work power, and confound between the training and market need notwithstanding many (Hendrix & Noland, 2014; Pitan & Adedeji, 2012).

The nation, however, is lagging behind the two fundamental prerequisites for designing an integrated enterprise sector. These two variables are about the nation's enterprising conduct and business framework or potentially institutional environment. Initially, the enterprise as a cycle requires certain powerful abilities that empower people to distinguish and exploit as well as make innovative opportunities within an institutional framework to build up viable SMEs (Ben-Letaifa & Goglio-Primard, 2016). Also, both academic and expert examination habitually support that individual and organizational efficiency, SMEs for this situation, is a result of certain conduct attributes (Eniola, 2018a, 2020b, 2020c; Eniola et al., 2019; Fishbein & Ajzen, 1975; Herron & Robinson, 1993) and that impact of enterprises activities and practices is intervened by people's motivation got from his / her apparent competence or efficacy. Third, the previously mentioned source additionally recognized a moderating impact of the person's capacities as financial and other aptitudes and assets which are an essential capacity of the market framework and other encouraging establishments.

Similarly, delayed and substantial dependence on natural assets, oil-based commodities, have prompted the absence of appropriate market advancement policies that have delayed the development of a legitimate market and institutional framework that encourages SME advancement. The oil segment's establishing a huge 94.1 percent exports from the nation (Workman, 2019). As indicated by the previously mentioned government measurements about 80 percent of the obstacles to SMEs are made by either absence of legitimate institutions or ill-advised policies of the established institutions.

SMEs without question have an immense commitment towards the feasible improvement of an economy. This is the explanation, at both the industrial and economic levels, that there is an overall accentuation of SMEs for feasible economic advancement (Eniola, 2020b, 2020c; Kelley et al., 2011). Nonetheless, the economic development-related ramifications of business and SMEs are faulty in Nigeria setting due to the two in advance of referenced elements; absence of entrepreneurial propensity and befuddle between education attaining and market-based aptitudes prerequisite; absence of appropriate institutional substructure that encourages in creation, identification, and abuse of chances and securing of assets (Alarjani et al., 2020; Eniola, 2020b; Pitan & Adedeji, 2012).

Several analyses have looked into the connection between enterprising self-efficacy and entrepreneurial intentions (Alarjani et al., 2020; Eniola, 2020b, 2020c; Naktiyok et al., 2010). In any case, investigations have for the most part been led in different countries, but society's cultural environment could have an impact on the venturesome of enterprising self-efficacy. The above association deserves examination, as institutional infrastructure and culture may assume a remarkable function in the assurance motivational infrastructure. Likewise, there is a necessity to expand previous examinations in this field. For example, the self-efficacy that initiates a company in the developed and developing environment, where individualism is high and uncertainty avoidance is low, can encourage people. On the contrary, national culture could reduce self-efficiency in Nigeria, where collectivism and avoidance of uncertainty are high.

Considering Nigeria's unique social, political, and economic context, this study establishes its methodology concerning the exact examination of the accompanying suppositions; as cited in Alarjani et al. (2020); Eniola (2020b, 2020c) that individuals evaluate their capacity to question activities more regarding their insight of the knowledge; Consistently, the research suggests that the business is at any rate to a limited extent a consequence of the entrepreneurs. The formal and informal institution has a task to carry out in economic growth by way of SME creation underpinning entrepreneurship. Therefore, the institutional environment should positively modify the relationship between Enterprising self-efficacy, Business enterprising orientation, and SME advancement (Eniola, 2020b, 2020c; Schmutzler et al., 2018), and that the previously mentioned assumptions might be valid in a traditional industrialist market framework, yet are as yet unsure, requiring further investigation. Having said that, a nitty-gritty outline of the Nigerian setting and related examination holes concerning enterprise, organizations, and their job (assuming any) in the development of SMEs is important.

Considering the above-mentioned context and the previously mentioned suppositions related to business enterprise-based SME, the more extensive reason for this examination is to experimentally research the part of how moderated mediation effect of the institutional environment and entrepreneurship orientation on enterprising self-efficacy and SME advancement. The examination is noteworthy as it would energize the part of the enterprising intentions, self-viability, and institutional environment in the advancement of an effective enterprise-based SME.

BACKGROUND

ESE, EO, and SME Advancement

Contemporary academic literature consistently encourages the willingness of effective entrepreneurs to endorse ambidexterity as a basic trait. According to Alarjani et al. (2020), Eniola (2020b, 2020c), and Volery et al. (2013) entrepreneurs can properly identify market opportunities and profit from them. The researchers recommend further investigation of this creative individual behaviour. Alarjani et al., (2020); Eniola, (2020b); Fang, Lee, and Schilling (2010) position that the attributes allow business people to understand and maximize the possibilities of proven and natural methods while at the same time seeking to identify new opportunities and approaches that add productivity. That is the reason the character drives the production and makes the enterprise maintainable.

Self-efficacy is one's confidence in its ability to coordinate its intellectual qualities, inspiration, and succession of acts in a way that gives it power over occasions in life (Alarjani et al., 2020; Eniola, 2020b, 2020c). Individuals with low self-efficacy will in general abstain from building abilities or facing challenges whereas high self-efficacy can, on the opposite, According to the principle of ambidexterity academic exploration, as a result, habitually supports ESE as the main catalyst for a new SME to start. ESE to them is the self-concept of entrepreneurs of being able to play out an undertaking that helps them to establish a necessary motivation to act (Eniola, 2020b, 2020c; McGee et al., 2009).

While empirical evidence exists about the correlation of ESE with results related to entrepreneurial success, for instance (Alarjani et al., 2020; Eniola, 2020b; Naktiyok et al., 2010) recognized that the capacities of entrepreneurs' to settle for far-reaching strategic decisions was essentially influenced by their ESEs. Likewise, in the sense of transition economies (Alarjani et al., 2020; Eniola, 2020b); McGee et al. (2009) found evidence regarding ESE's direct and mediating impact on results. But the effect of ESE on venture efficiency is not plain enough (Alarjani et al., 2020; Eniola, 2020b; Hmieleski & Baron, 2008) and needs more context-specific empirical studies (Eniola, 2020b; Markman et al., 2016). This examination is especially significant in the Nigerian setting because as summed up before, the contradiction between obtaining education and having market-based skills has led to a lack of entrepreneurial propensity and/or orientation (Eniola, 2020b; Pitan & Adedeji, 2012).

Scholars argue that entrepreneurial intent / orientation is crucial for deciphering enterprising qualities, in this case, self-efficacy, into firm-level results (Ahlin et al., 2014; Fillis & Rentschler, 2010). This paper does not distinguish between entrepreneurship and entrepreneurial orientation, as compared to Richard, Barnett, Dwyer, and Chadwick (2004) who consider entrepreneurial orientation to be a firm-level construct. Nonetheless, at the same time, it concurs simultaneously with the contention that enterprising is a process construct and is related to the managers' strategic approach and activities (decision making, processes, practices) (Eniola, 2018a, 2018b; Eniola & Entebang, 2014; Richard et al., 2004). Consequently, established on Hambrick and Mason (1984), upper echelon perspective, this paper deciphers entrepreneurial orientation as the goals of entrepreneurs rather than the company. That an individual tends to develop and or recognize market-based opportunities and react proactively through creativity and risk-taking while creating a new small and medium-sized enterprise. Centred on the above-mentioned scholarly dialog this study, therefore posits its first hypothesis as follows:

H1: The relationship between enterprising self-efficacy and SME advancement in Nigeria is mediated by Entrepreneurial orientation

Institutional Environment

Multiple empiric sources acknowledge that external environmental dimensions, such as market substructures and other formal and informal institutions, need to be discussed causally between entrepreneurial orientation and performance-related strictures (Eniola, 2020b, 2020c; Naman & Slevin, 1993; Zahra & Covin, 1995). As cited in Eniola (2020b) based on institutional economic observations (North, 1991) the study reads between the institutional lines: formally, informally, explicitly, and implicitly, rules and regulations regulating decision making, describing and developing choices, determining risks, recognizing alliances and networking and speeding up entrepreneurship. Institutions are the human constraints that set the law of the game of business practices and thus their result in the form of competitive SMEs. Various scholars in business literature (Alarjani et al., 2020; Eniola, 2020b, 2020c; Guerrero et al., 2016; Thornton et al., 2013; Urbano et al., 2018; Urbano & Guerrero, 2013; Welter & Smallbone, 2011) support North concept of competitive new projects in an institutional context. Nevertheless, recent research in the transitional economies indicates that countries have seen tremendous growth in business-based institutions and industry activity both weak formal and informal institutions (Eniola, 2020b; Zhou, 2013). China is a common event. Scholars consider that in transition economies, despite the conventional presumption of science, institutional environments are improving; this is not true (Banalieva et al., 2015).

Researchers have always been paradoxical about entrepreneurial and business development (Alarjani et al., 2020; Eniola, 2020b, 2020c; Huang, Liu, & Li, 2019; Naktiyok et al., 2010). While market stability, the rule of law, and the business climate are considered unfavourable to enterprises, the country has seen one of the most rising entrepreneurship classes in the world. The paradox has drawn considerable attention from scholars and practitioners towards the way their institutional environment is influenced by the success of SMEs in China (Pistrui et al., 2001; Yang & Li, 2008) performance (Banalieva et al., 2015; Kshetri, 2007; Peng & Jiang, 2010). Nigeria is more complicated than China, since abundant natural resources and religious tourism in the country, together with the political structure of democracy and the unique social-cultural climate, will exacerbate further the need for investigations into business phenomena. The neglect of social drives which lead to organizational activities (Barley & Tolbert, 1997) by theories of efficiency is the fundamental reason why the promoters of institutional perspectives are dissatisfied with entrepreneurship. Empirically, the research of Ngek (2015) showed a significant relationship between ESE and firm performance. While the empirical result of Chao.et.al (2016) indicates a moderate relationship between ESE and firm performance. The viewpoint that projects the role of the organizational behaviour norms, values, and rules and that these factors differ widely across borders and cultures (Fang et al., 2010; Scott, 2008). In a market background like Nigeria, where religious, political, social, cultural, and economic perspectives challenge the potential of the traditional capitalist approaches to entrepreneurship (Jepperson, 1991).

H2: Institutional Environment positively enhances the mediation impact between enterprising self-efficacy and SME Advancement.

Three sub-hypotheses about the above-mentioned impact of moderation follow.

H2a: An institutional environment moderates the relationship between enterprising self-efficacy and entrepreneurial orientation.
H2b: The relationship between the orientation of entrepreneurship and the progress of SMEs is moderated by the institutional environment.
H2c: The relationship between enterprising self-efficacy and SME advancement is moderated by the institutional environment.

MAIN FOCUS OF THE CHAPTER

Methodology

As a result of the up to referenced reasons in the literature identified with the disposition and propensities of the Nigeria youth, more premium in the middle-class occupations, and the confound between their learning and market-based abilities as far as an entrepreneurial necessity, this exploration did not put into consideration business/financial aspects or potentially business graduates, but entrepreneurs with high school education as the least form of education and in the framework of 10-49 workers (Eniola, 2020b; MSME Survey 2013). In this way, to gather substantial reactions, via questionnaire review approach, we chose our respondents among entrepreneurs and SME owners in the south-western region of the country, (26,744), which form the population, as defined by SMEDAN (MSME Survey, 2013). The exploration was conveyed in the south-west because it has the most noteworthy absolute SMEs in the country (MSME Survey, 2013). Through stratified random sampling, respondents were chosen from companies across different organizations going from transportation, agriculture, construction, agriculture, ICT, taken into cognizance are the respondent capacities to fathom the ideas of business advancement and innovation, business venture, and viable expansion. In deciding the sample size from the entire population, the study utilizes Krejcie and Morgan (1970) that resulted in 379 and was distributed with 343 surveys returned and 17 disposed of because of incomplete replies. Subsequently, 326 substantial returns were analysed using Partial Least Square-Structural Equation Method (PLS-SEM).

The vital variable in this examination was simply the development of Entrepreneurial Self-Efficacy (ESE), Entrepreneurial Orientation (EO), Institutional Environment (IE), and SMEs Advancement. To guarantee its validity and reliability, several scales from previous studies of a similar nature were used. The researchers measure ESE with 20-item (Ebrahimi & Mirbargkar, 2017) and EO with 13-item (Alarjani et al., 2020; Eniola, 2020b), IE with 13-item (Covin & Slevin, 1989), and SME advancement with 9-item (Alarjani et al., 2020; Eniola, 2020b).

Analysing Reliability

Table1 demonstrated that every one of the four scales was dependent upon singular reliability analysis and all show an alpha value of Cronbach of at least .86, surpassing the suggested and generally acknowledged lower limit of 0.7, as shown below following a small modification, by removing unreliable items (Eniola, 2020a, 2020b; Hair et al., 2019).

Table 1. Factor Loading

Constructs	Item	Loading	CA	CR	AVE
ESE	CR1 CR2 CR4 CR5	0.630 0.575 0.611 0.654	**0.727**	**0.778**	**0.643**
	PL1 PL2 PL3	0.857 0.868 0.707	**0.750**	**0.854**	**0.663**
	M1 M2	0.904 0.684	**0.846**	**0.779**	**0.642**
	MA2 MA3 MA4 MA5	0.785 0.813 0.810 0.729	**0.792**	**0.865**	**0.616**
	FL1 FL2 FL3 FL4	0.694 0.711 0.799 0.727	**0.713**	**0.823**	**0.538**
EO	RT1 RT2 RT3	0.858 0.852 0.593	**0.865**	**0.795**	**0.509**
	PR1 PR2	0.858 0.619	**0.722**	**0.712**	**0.559**
	AU1 AU2 AU3	0.505 0.688 0.672	**0.732**	**0.835**	**0.636**
SMEs-A	IE1 IE2 IE3	0.572 0.897 0.883	**0.711**	**0.836**	**0.637**
	FP1 FP2 FP3	0.815 0.886 0.869	**0.713**	**0.892**	**0.735**
	NCE1 NCE2 NCE3	0.817 0.861 0.848	**0.795**	**0.880**	**0.709**
	LE2 LE3	0.865 0.512	**0.954**	**0.941**	**0.721**
	CE1 CE3 CE4	0.654 0.565 0.587	**0.895**	**0.925**	**0.669**
	NE3	0.982	**0.915**	**0.935**	**0.689**

Source: Own

Validity of Discrimination

Discriminant validity was achieved when the AVE square root was higher than the association of the model variables (Eniola, 2020; Eniola & Entebang, 2017; Fornell & Larcker, 1981), The discriminant measures utilized normalized factor loadings, AVE, CR esteems and an examination of the AVE with the elements' connection (between measurements for this situation) squared for every one of the models. The rundown of the fit indices and the different measurements got during reliability and validity analysis are shown in Table 1 above and 2 underneath.

Table 2. Correlations

Con.	AVE	Au	Ce	Cr	Ei	Fl	Fp	Le	Ma	M	Nce	Ne	Pl	Pr	Rt
Au	**0.636**	**0.79**													
Ce	**0.669**	0.54	**0.82**												
Cr	**0.643**	0.42	0.43	**0.80**											
Ei	**0.637**	0.50	0.47	0.53	**0.79**										
Fi	**0.538**	0.44	0.44	0.64	0.52	**0.73**									
Fp	**0.735**	0.47	0.43	0.67	0.48	0.59	**0.86**								
Le	**0.721**	0.49	0.41	0.56	0.49	0.61	0.60	**0.85**							
Ma	**0.616**	0.49	0.49	0.66	0.53	0.64	0.59	0.58	**0.79**						
M	**0.642**	0.54	0.46	0.54	0.64	0.56	0.57	0.49	0.55	**0.80**					
Nce	**0.709**	0.54	0.54	0.54	0.54	0.54	0.67	0.50	0.60	0.59	**0.84**				
Ne	**0.689**	0.42	0.42	0.42	0.42	0.42	0.43	0.58	0.39	0.40	0.43	**0.83**			
Pl	**0.663**	0.50	0.50	0.50	0.50	0.50	0.56	0.50	0.54	0.61	0.56	0.49	**0.81**		
Pr	**0.559**	0.53	0.53	0.53	0.53	0.53	0.66	0.50	0.67	0.64	0.66	0.53	0.50	**0.75**	
Rt	**0.509**	0.45	0.45	0.45	0.45	0.45	0.54	0.58	0.54	0.56	0.54	0.64	0.58	0.54	**0.71**

Source: Own

The underlying theory of this investigation was that entrepreneurial orientation plays a part by intercedes in the relationship between enterprising self-efficiency and SME advancement. The results show that there is no correlation between enterprising self-efficiency and SME advancement. This results from the failure of self-employed people, especially green enterprises, to grow or recognize opportunities to a full degree of self-efficiency in SMEs, which can be attributed to the social-cultural and religious contexts of Nigeria. The results indicate that the entrepreneur is innovative and that the strategy is appropriate, but the entrepreneur needs the capacity to resolve the weak business momentum and structural barriers to deliver feasible opportunities and strive for global competitiveness.

The performance in Table 3 above further confirms Nigeria's full intercession effect on entrepreneurship between self-efficacy and the success of SMEs. The results show that young entrepreneurs can achieve maximum self-efficiency by employing proper schooling, social-cultural, and market-oriented standards to improve entrepreneurship, build or recognize certain opportunities (Alarjani et al., 2020;

Table 3. Hypotheses Testing

	Original Sample (O)	Sample Mean (M)	Standard Deviation (STDEV)	T Statistics (|O/STDEV|)	P Values	Significant value
Entrepreneurial Orientation-> Employment Increase	0.498	0.508	0.034	14.450	**0.000**	**Positive**
Entrepreneurial Orientation-> Financial Performance	0.528	0.530	0.032	16.682	**0.000**	**Positive**
Entrepreneurial Orientation-> New Commercial Enterprise	0.525	0.525	0.032	16.528	**0.000**	**Positive.**
Enterprising Self-Efficacy-> Autonomy	0.256	0.263	0.032	7.918	**0.000**	**Positive.**
Enterprising Self-Efficacy-> Employment Increase	0.458	0.480	0.032	14.332	**0.000**	**Positive.**
Enterprising Self-Efficacy-> Financial Performance	0.486	0.501	0.028	17.596	**0.000**	**Positive.**
Enterprising Self-Efficacy-> New Commercial Enterprise	0.483	0.496	0.028	17.265	**0.000**	**Positive.**
Enterprising Self-Efficacy-> Proactiveness	0.131	0.137	0.038	3.471	**0.001**	**Positive.**
Enterprising Self-Efficacy-> Risk-Taking	0.468	0.481	0.035	13.317	**0.000**	**Positive.**
Enterprising Self-Efficacy-> SME Advancement	-0.252	0.045	0.273	0.925	**0.356**	**Negatlve**
Enterprising Self-Efficacy-> Entrepreneurial Orientation-> SME Advancement (H1)	0.299	0.308	0.028	10.720	**0.000**	**Positive.**

Source: Own

Eniola, 2020). The above results demonstrated the full mediating impact of enterprising self-efficiency and SME advancement, which led to the acceptance of the first hypothesis in Nigeria.

The second hypothesis is the positive moderating effect of the institutional environment on the direct relationship between ESE and SME advancement and their indirect relationship via enterprise guidance. Three versions of the complete structural equation model have therefore been executed and the bootstrapping is calculated to determine the moderating effect in three different phases / paths as suggested in hypotheses 2a, 2b, and 2c. The statistics obtained during the analysis are summarized in Table 4 below.

Table 4 above presents the findings obtained from our three sub-hypotheses of hypothesis 2 discussing the moderating impact of institutional environments. The results show that the institutional environment moderates the correlation between enterprising self-efficacy and the advancement of SMEs that could enhance the impact of entrepreneurial self-efficacy on small and medium-sized Nigerian companies. The same relates to changes in a positive attitude towards entrepreneurial business development, i.e. entrepreneurial orientation and effect of growth and proliferation on SME-based economic progress. This study, consequently, acknowledged all three under-hypotheses which assume that the improved institutional environment can favour the advancement of SMEs in Nigeria directly and indirectly through entrepreneurship.

Table 4. Hypothesis Analysis with moderating variables

	Original Sample (O)	Sample Mean (M)	Standard Deviation (STDEV)	T Statistics (|O/STDEV|)	P Values	Significant value
Entrepreneurial Orientation-> Employment Increase	0.498	0.508	0.034	14.450	**0.000**	**Positive**
Entrepreneurial Orientation-> Financial Performance	0.528	0.530	0.032	16.682	**0.000**	**Positive**
Entrepreneurial Orientation-> New Commercial Enterprise	0.525	0.525	0.032	16.528	**0.000**	**Positive.**
Enterprising Self-Efficacy-> Autonomy	0.256	0.263	0.032	7.918	**0.000**	**Positive.**
Enterprising Self-Efficacy-> Employment Increase	0.458	0.480	0.032	14.332	**0.000**	**Positive.**
Enterprising Self-Efficacy-> Financial Performance	0.486	0.501	0.028	17.596	**0.000**	**Positive.**
Enterprising Self-Efficacy-> New Commercial Enterprise	0.483	0.496	0.028	17.265	**0.000**	**Positive.**
Enterprising Self-Efficacy-> Proactiveness	0.131	0.137	0.038	3.471	**0.001**	**Positive.**
Enterprising Self-Efficacy-> Risk-Taking	0.468	0.481	0.035	13.317	**0.000**	**Positive.**
Enterprising Self-Efficacy-> SME Advancement	-0.252	0.045	0.273	0.925	**0.356**	**Negative**
Enterprising Self-Efficacy-> Entrepreneurial Orientation-> SME Advancement (H1)	0.299	0.308	0.028	10.720	**0.000**	**Positive.**

Source: Own [***: p<0.001; **: p<0.01; *: p<0.05]

SOLUTIONS AND RECOMMENDATIONS

Policy Implications: In this way, this exploration proposes a strategic plan that successfully coordinates the aforementioned educational and market institutions that can assist in building, preparing, and promoting youth in Nigeria into capable business ventures. By searching for and helping the best business enterprise to start a new business, this model can be applied by policymakers. Also, this model could be set up to create a lot of innovative orientations and behaviours among young people in Nigeria. This could be achieved by offering the right values to young people through intensive training that could very well help improve their self-viability. Likewise, their levels of self-ampleness could be extended with real planning modules and the right philosophy. The association between self-viability and entrepreneurial orientations could, from a comparable point of view, be used as a strategy for recognizing ambitious vocations for youth. The creation, progression, and enhancement of understudy self-efficacy should be highlighted in colleges and schools as self-viability is essential for creating enterprising directions.

Managerial Implications: One of Nigeria's Vision 2030's critical topics is a sharp focus on improving the limits and the ability to expand the industrial area's quality and reliability. The focus is therefore on the use and modification of the legitimate, fiscal, and other non-commercial institutional frameworks for streamlining the commercial environment, specifically for the advancement of SME ventures (UNDP, 2015). The main concern is to create and upgrade the economic system of Nigeria from a renewed nation to an independent economy dependent on the internal market. Business enterprises can utilize the entrepreneurial orientation concept in the same way as a tool to break down entrepreneurship and management designs that can promote quantifiable human resource profits. For example, the positive association between business orientation and achievement has been shown by past findings of the examination, and the archetypal set up in this investigation could therefore shape the establishment of qualities that business owners can support among themselves so that high self-viability can be easily acquired, regardless of whether inventive, helpful or both.

Theoretical Implication: Following Ajzen's planned behavioural theory (2011), the investigation likewise underpins the requirement for establishments to empower youngsters and business people to create and depict a positive, market-based way to deal with the improvement of the private sector dependent on SME. In Nigeria, where the market and social norms block the innovative mentality of young graduates, this is especially important (Alarjani et al., 2020; Eniola, 2020b). Most investigators utilized traditional analytical techniques, principally SPSS. By applying further psychometric measures, the SEM-PLS Model set up more knowledge on the current appraisal, which gave increasingly more broad solutions. Thus, the endeavour to apply the SEM-PLS model with a more definite examination could be emulated by other researchers. Another important methodological implication is the utilization of SMEs as tests in various businesses. Past exploration overview results were gathered principally for understudies, executives, and non-business visionaries (Ebrahimi and Mirbargkar, 2017; Pitan and Adedeji, 2012). The findings were consequently conceivable, considering a veritable example of the current populace of entrepreneurs, to extend the actual scenario of small and medium-sized enterprises with reliable and meaningful conclusions.

FUTURE RESEARCH DIRECTIONS

This investigation experiences a couple of limitations, among others. The examination didn't distinguish and separate entrepreneurs by necessity and opportunity as the data gathered dependent on deliberate testing from a pool of SMEs. Explicitly distinguishing the opportunities-entrepreneurs, uniquely, incipient business visionaries and getting their reactions may give better logical comprehension. Also, the examination has received scales created in an altogether different financial, social, lawful, and strict setting that may scrutinize the legitimacy of the reactions assembled identified with the factors of intrigue. Future analysts ought to in such a manner centre around the correct example choice and structure of appropriate setting explicit instruments for variable estimation.

CONCLUSION

The examination reasons that the development of SMEs and increasing entrepreneurial self-efficacy within a society, especially among young entrepreneurs, is a critical issue that requires the attention of all stakeholders. Despite the fact that there is no single best approach to encourage entrepreneurship, it does necessitate a detailed comprehension of the context in terms of the social-cultural and market-oriented standards. As a result, governments, intergovernmental organisations, and non-governmental organisations must collaborate to offer entrepreneurship proper exposure and funding.

According to the analysis, successful entrepreneurship literacy, learning, and training, as well as the presence of mentoring and support centres for the youth community across the states, would have a substantial and positive impact on the potential and perceived desirability of entrepreneurial involvement and company start-up.

Finally, institutional environment must legitimise company start-up as a feasible career choice. Similarly, the establishment of market development centres where ideas and tools for business development can be exchanged would undoubtedly aid in harnessing the potentials of our green entrepreneurs for greater socioeconomic advancement. Along with the limitations listed above, the results of this study open up a range of avenues for potential studies in the areas of individual self-efficacy, entrepreneurial focus, and institutional climate. In light of this, it will be intriguing to use a focus group approach to explore how cultural considerations hinder the progress of SMEs. Furthermore, future studies should empirically investigate the degree to which the dimensions of institutional environments mediate or influence individual entrepreneurial orientation and SMEs development among green entrepreneurs utilising a broader sample that covers all geographical regions of Nigeria.

REFERENCES

Ahlin, B., Drnovšek, M., & Hisrich, R. D. (2014). Entrepreneurs' creativity and firm innovation: The moderating role of entrepreneurial self-efficacy. *Small Business Economics*, *43*(1), 101–117. doi:10.100711187-013-9531-7

Alarjani, F. N. F., Anwar, B., Danial Aslam, H., Iqbal, S., & Ayub, A. (2020). A Moderated Mediation Model of Entrepreneurial Self-Efficacy, Institutional Environment, and Entrepreneurial Orientation for SME Development. *SAGE Open*, *10*(3), 1–18. doi:10.1177/2158244020941000

Banalieva, E. R., Eddleston, K. A., & Zellweger, T. M. (2015). When do family firms have an advantage in transitioning economies? Toward a dynamic institution-based view. *Strategic Management Journal*, *36*(9), 1358–1377. doi:10.1002mj.2288

Barley, S. R., & Tolbert, P. S. (1997). Institutionalization and Structuration: Studying the Links between Action and Institution. *Organization Studies*, *18*(1), 93–117. doi:10.1177/017084069701800106

Ben Letaifa, S., & Goglio-Primard, K. (2016). How does institutional context shape entrepreneurship conceptualizations? *Journal of Business Research*, *69*(11), 5128–5134. doi:10.1016/j.jbusres.2016.04.092

Dana, L.-P., & Ratten, V. (2017). International entrepreneurship in resource-rich landlocked African countries. *Journal of International Entrepreneurship*, *15*(4), 416–435. doi:10.100710843-017-0211-6

Eniola, A. A. (2018a). Entrepreneur-SME Manager Traits and Sources of Financing. In African Entrepreneurship (pp. 223-259). Springer.

Eniola, A. A. (2018b). SME firm characteristics impact the choice of sources of financing in South-West, Nigeria. *International Journal of Business and Globalisation*, *21*(3), 344–366. doi:10.1504/IJBG.2018.095482

Eniola, A. A. (2020a). Entrepreneurial self-efficacy and orientation for SME development. *Small Enterprise Research*, *27*(2), 125–145. doi:10.1080/13215906.2020.1752295

Eniola, A. A. (2020a). Cultural Identity and Entrepreneurial Performance. In R. Vanessa (Ed.), *Entrepreneurship as Empowerment: Knowledge Spill-overs and Entrepreneurial Ecosystems* (pp. 23–44). Emerald Publishing Limited. doi:10.1108/978-1-83982-550-720201004

Eniola, A. A. (2020b). Entrepreneurial Self-efficacy, Entrepreneurial Orientation, and Institutional Environment: SME in Nigeria. *SCMS Journal of Indian Management, 17*(1), 16–27.

Eniola, A. A. (2020b). Entrepreneurial self-efficacy and orientation for SME development. *Small Enterprise Research*, 1-21. doi:10.1080/13215906.2020.1752295

Eniola, A. A. (2020c). Institutional Environment, Entrepreneurial Self-efficacy and Orientation for SME in Nigeria. *International Journal of Engineering, 4*, 17.

Eniola, A. A. (2020c). Entrepreneurial Self-efficacy, Entrepreneurial Orientation, and Institutional Environment: SME in Nigeria. *SCMS Journal of Indian Management, 17*(1), 16–27.

Eniola, A.A. (2021). The Entrepreneur Motivation and Financing Sources. *Journal of Open Innovation, Technology, Marketing, and Complex, 7*, 25. doi:10.3390/joitmc7010025

Eniola, A. A., & Entebang, H. (2014). SME firms performance in Nigeria: Competitive advantage and its impact. *International Journal of Research Studies in Management, 3*(2), 75–86. doi:10.5861/ijrsm.2014.854

Eniola, A. A., & Entebang, H. (2017). SME managers and financial literacy. *Global Business Review, 18*(3), 559–576. doi:10.1177/0972150917692063

Eniola, A. A., Olorunleke, G. K., Akintimehin, O. O., Ojeka, J. D., & Oyetunji, B. (2019). The impact of organizational culture on total quality management in SMEs in Nigeria. *Heliyon, 5*(8), e02293. doi:10.1016/j.heliyon.2019.e02293 PMID:31508519

Fang, C., Lee, J., & Schilling, M. A. (2010). Balancing Exploration and Exploitation through Structural Design: The Isolation of Subgroups and Organizational Learning. *Organization Science, 21*(3), 625–642. doi:10.1287/orsc.1090.0468

Fillis, I., & Rentschler, R. (2010). The role of creativity in entrepreneurship. *Journal of Enterprising Culture, 18*(01), 49–81. doi:10.1142/S0218495810000501

Fishbein, M., & Ajzen, I. (1975). *Belief, attitude, intention, and behaviour: an introduction to theory and research.* Addison-Wesley.

Fornell, C., & Larcker, D. F. (1981). Evaluating structural equation models with unobservable variables and measurement error. *JMR, Journal of Marketing Research, 18*(1), 39–50. doi:10.1177/002224378101800104

Guerrero, M., Urbano, D., & Fayolle, A. (2016). Entrepreneurial activity and regional competitiveness: Evidence from European entrepreneurial universities. *The Journal of Technology Transfer, 41*(1), 105–131. doi:10.100710961-014-9377-4

Hair, J. F., Black, W. C., Babin, B. J., & Anderson, R. E. (2019). *Multivariate data analysis* (8th ed.). Cengage Learning.

Hambrick, D. C., & Mason, P. A. (1984). Upper echelons: The organization as a reflection of its top managers. *Academy of Management Review*, *9*(2), 193–206. doi:10.5465/amr.1984.4277628

Hendrix, C., & Noland, M. (2014). *Confronting the curse: The economics and geopolitics of natural resource governance*. Peterson Institute for International Economics: Columbia University Press.

Herron, L., & Robinson, R. B. (1993). A structural model of the effects of entrepreneurial characteristics on venture performance. *Journal of Business Venturing, 8*(3), 281-294. doi: (93)90032-z doi:10.1016/0883-9026

Hmieleski, K. M., & Baron, R. A. (2008). When does entrepreneurial self-efficacy enhance versus reduce firm performance? *Strategic Entrepreneurship Journal*, *2*(1), 57–72. doi:10.1002ej.42

Huang, Q., Liu, X., & Li, J. (2019). Contextualization of Chinese entrepreneurship research: an overview and some future research directions. *Entrepreneurship & Regional Development,* 1-17. doi:10.1080/08985626.2019.1640437

Jepperson, R. (1991). Institutions, institutional effects, and institutionalism. In W. W. Powell & P. J. DiMaggio (Eds.), *The new institutionalism in organizational analysis* (pp. 143–163). University of Chicago Press.

Kelley, D., Singer, S., & Herrington, M. (2011). *Global Entrepreneurship Monitor (GEM): Global Report*. Babson College.

Kline, R. B. (2016). *Principles and practice of structural equation modelling*. The Guilford Press.

Krejcie, R. V., & Morgan, D. W. (1970). Determining sample size for research activities. *Educational and Psychological Measurement*, *30*(3), 607–610. doi:10.1177/001316447003000308

Kshetri, N. (2007). Institutional factors affecting the offshore business process and information technology outsourcing. *Journal of International Management*, *13*(1), 38–56. doi:10.1016/j.intman.2006.05.003

Markman, G. D., Russo, M., Lumpkin, G. T., Jennings, P. D. D., & Mair, J. (2016). Entrepreneurship as a Platform for Pursuing Multiple Goals: A Special Issue on Sustainability, Ethics, and Entrepreneurship. *Journal of Management Studies*, *53*(5), 673–694. doi:10.1111/joms.12214

McGee, J. E., Peterson, M., Mueller, S. L., & Sequeira, J. M. (2009). Entrepreneurial Self-Efficacy: Refining the Measure. *Entrepreneurship Theory and Practice*, *33*(4), 965–988. doi:10.1111/j.1540-6520.2009.00304.x

MSME Survey. (2013). *Smedan and National Bureau of Statistics Collaborative Survey: Selected Findings*. Retrieved from Abuja, Nigeria: https://www.google.com/url?sa=t&rct=j&q=&esrc=s&source=web&cd=4&cad=rja&uact=8&ved=2ahUKEwiPgrSJtrflAhWBiVwKHT-iA3cQFjADegQIBhAC&url=https%3A%2F%2Fwww.smedan.gov.ng%2Fimages%2FPDF%2F2013-MSME-Survey-Summary-Report.pdf&usg=AOvVaw18wZux7m5XYOaHaR_uI9Z2

Naktiyok, A., Nur Karabey, C., & Caglar Gulluce, A. (2010). Entrepreneurial self-efficacy and entrepreneurial intention: The Turkish case. *The International Entrepreneurship and Management Journal*, *6*(4), 419–435. doi:10.100711365-009-0123-6

Naman, J. L., & Slevin, D. P. (1993). Entrepreneurship and the concept of fit: A model and empirical tests. *Strategic Management Journal*, *14*(2), 137–153. doi:10.1002mj.4250140205

NBS. (2018). *Demographic statistics bulletin*. Retrieved from Abuja, Nigeria: https://www.google.com/url?sa=t&rct=j&q=&esrc=s&source=web&cd=18&ved=2ahUKEwi36Jn1lrflAhVChlwKHTKbBmEQFjARegQICRAC&url=https%3A%2F%2Fnigerianstat.gov.ng%2Fdownload%2F775&usg=AOvVaw1HuYamjCJoZk8geCvTnFYr

Newman, A., Obschonka, M., Schwarz, S., Cohen, M., & Nielsen, I. (2019). Entrepreneurial self-efficacy: A systematic review of the literature on its theoretical foundations, measurement, antecedents, and outcomes, and an agenda for future research. *Journal of Vocational Behavior*, *110*, 403–419. doi:10.1016/j.jvb.2018.05.012

North, D. C. (1991). Institutions. *The Journal of Economic Perspectives*, *5*(1), 97–112. doi:10.1257/jep.5.1.97

Peng, M. W., & Jiang, Y. (2010). Institutions behind family ownership and control in large firms. *Journal of Management Studies*, *47*(2), 253–273. doi:10.1111/j.1467-6486.2009.00890.x

Pistrui, D., Huang, W., Oksoy, D., Jing, Z., & Welsch, H. (2001). Entrepreneurship in China: Characteristics, attributes, and family forces shaping the emerging private sector. *Family Business Review*, *14*(2), 141–152. doi:10.1111/j.1741-6248.2001.00141.x

Pitan, O. S., & Adedeji, S. (2012). Skills Mismatch among University Graduates in the Nigeria Labour Market. *US-China Education Review*, *A*(1), 90-98.

Richard, O. C., Barnett, T., Dwyer, S., & Chadwick, K. (2004). Cultural diversity in management, firm performance, and the moderating role of entrepreneurial orientation dimensions. *Academy of Management Journal*, *47*(2), 255–266.

Schmutzler, J., Andonova, V., & Diaz-Serrano, L. (2018). How Context Shapes Entrepreneurial Self-Efficacy as a Driver of Entrepreneurial Intentions: A Multilevel Approach. *Entrepreneurship Theory and Practice*, *43*(5), 880–920. doi:10.1177/1042258717753142

Scott, W. R. (2008). Approaching adulthood: The maturing of institutional theory. *Theory and Society*, *37*(5), 427–442. doi:10.100711186-008-9067-z

Thornton, P. H., Lounsbury, M., & Ocasio, W. (2013). *The institutional logics perspective: a new approach to culture, structure, and process*. Oxford Univ. Press.

UNDP. (2015). Nigeria's road to SDGs: Country transition strategy. Abuja, Nigeria: MDGs Nigeria.

Urbano, D., Aparicio, S., & Audretsch, D. (2018). Twenty-five years of research on institutions, entrepreneurship, and economic growth: What has been learned? *Small Business Economics*, *53*(1), 21–49. doi:10.100711187-018-0038-0

Urbano, D., & Guerrero, M. (2013). Entrepreneurial universities: Socioeconomic impacts of academic entrepreneurship in a European region. *Economic Development Quarterly*, *27*(1), 40–55. doi:10.1177/0891242412471973

Volery, T., Mueller, S., & von Siemens, B. (2013). Entrepreneur ambidexterity: A study of entrepreneur behaviours and competencies in growth-oriented small and medium-sized enterprises. *International Small Business Journal: Researching Entrepreneurship, 33*(2), 109–129. doi:10.1177/0266242613484777

Wei, J., Chen, Y., Zhang, Y., & Zhang, J. (2020). How Does Entrepreneurial Self-Efficacy Influence Innovation Behaviour? Exploring the Mechanism of Job Satisfaction and Zhongyong Thinking. *Frontiers in Psychology, 11*(708), 708. Advance online publication. doi:10.3389/fpsyg.2020.00708 PMID:32457676

Welter, F., & Smallbone, D. (2011). Institutional perspectives on entrepreneurial behaviour in challenging environments. *Journal of Small Business Management, 49*(1), 107–125. doi:10.1111/j.1540-627X.2010.00317.x

Workman, D. (2019). *Nigeria's Top 10 Exports*. http://www.worldstopexports.com/nigerias-top-10-exports/

World Bank. (2019). *The World Bank In Nigeria-The World Bank is helping to fight poverty and improve living standards for the people of Nigeria with more than 130 IBRD loans and IDA credits since 1958.* The World Bank in Nigeria. https://www.worldbank.org/en/country/nigeria/overview#1

Yang, J. Y., & Li, J. (2008). The development of entrepreneurship in China. *Asia Pacific Journal of Management, 25*(2), 335–359. doi:10.100710490-007-9078-8

Zahra, S. A., & Covin, J. G. (1995). Contextual influences on the corporate entrepreneurship-performance relationship: A longitudinal analysis. *Journal of Business Venturing, 10*(1), 43–58. doi:10.1016/0883-9026(94)00004-E

Zhou, W. (2013). Political connections and entrepreneurial investment: Evidence from China's transition economy. *Journal of Business Venturing, 28*(2), 299–315. doi:10.1016/j.jbusvent.2012.05.004

KEY TERMS AND DEFINITIONS

Enterprising: Enterprising is the desire to consider opportunities whenever they through present themselves, as well as the courage to accept the risk so that the chance is not lost but completely used. It is the capacity to understand the value of preparing, establishing realistic targets (objectives), and having in place the means to accomplish the specified goals of the company.

Enterprising Self-Efficacy: Enterprising self-efficacy is a business start-up or development by an individual with expectations that are based on mission or result objectives, and the valence of the beliefs, whether optimistic or negative, influence beliefs to achieve particular market success attainments. Entrepreneurial self-efficacy is described as the entrepreneurs' understanding of their own trust in themselves and their own entrepreneurial capacities to achieve particular market success outcomes.

Entrepreneur: An entrepreneur is described as a person who starts a new company, bears the majority of the costs, and reaps the majority of the rewards. An entrepreneur is widely regarded as an innovator, a source of innovative technologies, products, facilities, and business/or practises, who employs the expertise and effort required to anticipate requirements and introduce successful new concepts to market.

Entrepreneurship: Entrepreneurship is described as the process of planning, launching, and operating a new company, as well as the skill and desire to create, coordinate, and handle a business venture and all of its risks in order to make a profit. Similarly, entrepreneurship is a risky endeavour that involves starting a venture, often a start-up company, and selling distinct goods and services to target clients, which may or may not be successful.

Entrepreneurship Orientation: Entrepreneurial orientation (EO) can be defined as an organisation strategic orientation that encompasses an organization's entrepreneurial strategy-making activities, management ideologies, and firm behaviours. The structures, procedures, and decision-making styles of organisations that function entrepreneurially are referred to as EO. Entrepreneurial orientation (EO) is a central principle when companies are designing plans in the hopes of doing something better and capitalising on prospects that most businesses cannot.

Institutional Environment: The institutional environment is characterised as the series of social, economic, political, and legal agreements that serve as the basis for trade and development. Institutional environments have both casual and structured elements that apply to a broad variety of unrelated transactions that influence the activities of organisations and individuals.

SMEs Advancement: Small and medium-sized enterprises (SMEs) Advancement is described as companies that keep sales, properties, or the number of employees below a certain threshold when going forward in place or progressing through the provision of market advice and networking help to the creation of financial and non-financial rewards and expenditure in supporting services and/or facilities.

Chapter 13
Enhanced Innovation Process as a Key Driver of Bakery Performance

Kafigi Jeje
Institute of Accountancy, Arusha, Tanzania

Vannie Naidoo
https://orcid.org/0000-0001-8435-4348
University of KwaZulu-Natal, South Africa

Rahul Verma
Delhi University, India

ABSTRACT

Small and medium-sized enterprises (SME) in the food sector play a pivotal role in contributing to the developing county's economy. In order to improve a small and medium-sized enterprises (SME), one key driver is innovation, and for innovation initiatives to grow and succeed, they depend largely on the leadership and the innovation capabilities of the firm. This chapter will shed more light on the impact of the enhanced innovation process on the performance of small and medium-sized enterprise (SME) bakeries. A qualitative study was conducted on 186 registered bakery owners/managers of bakeries. The results indicated that the relationship between enhanced innovation process and output level in small and medium-sized enterprises (SME) bakeries are significant. It has been revealed that the workforce's professional behaviour, the acquired competency through training, and the rewarding systems moderate the relationship between enhanced innovation process and output level in small and medium-sized enterprise (SME) bakeries.

DOI: 10.4018/978-1-7998-7951-0.ch013

INTRODUCTION

Small and Medium-sized Enterprises (SME) are the key role-players in stimulating growth and economic activities within African countries. In Tanzania's food sector there are many Small and Medium-sized Enterprises (SME) bakeries. Many factors contribute to promoting the performance of bakeries. In this paper the researchers' highlight the importance of innovation. Innovation takes place within product development, marketing and communication areas of the small business. The success of the innovation process depends on the ability of the Small and Medium-sized Enterprises (SME) to enhance the customer offerings.

To determine the contribution of innovation strategies on the performance of Small and Medium-sized Enterprises (SME) bakeries in Tanzania. Understanding the effective entrepreneurial strategies that enable Small and Medium-sized Enterprises (SME) to compete fosters core competences needed to address various challenges facing Tanzanian Small and Medium-sized Enterprises (SME) particularly those in the food sector such as bakeries. Although the sector is one of the major job creators in Tanzania, there is no research that links entrepreneurial strategies with specific relation to innovation and how it impacts on Small and Medium-sized Enterprises (SME) performance in Tanzania. The study will assist in knowledge creation in the area of Small and Medium-sized Enterprises (SME) innovation and its impact on performance. The study will also inform business practitioners, Small and Medium-sized Enterprises (SME) owners / managers, and entrepreneurs about the approaches needed to compete and drive their growth and sustainability.

BACKGROUND

Small and Medium-sized Enterprises (SME) play a vital role in driving socio-economic development in many countries including developing nations. It is estimated that 99% of all of the operating businesses around the globe are Small and Medium-sized Enterprises (SME) (Robu, 2013; Savlovschi & Robu, 2011). They also account for 99% of all of the enterprises in developing countries, and 95% in Sub-Saharan Africa (Fjose et al., 2010). Small and Medium-sized Enterprises (SME) contribute significantly in poverty reduction and are the sources of employment opportunities (Katua, 2014; Savlovschi & Robu, 2011). They employ 60-70% of all employees (Robu, 2013; Savlovschi & Robu, 2011). In Tanzania, Small and Medium-sized Enterprises (SME) are also an engine in poverty reduction (URT, 2012), job creation (Maliti & Mnenwa, 2008), and GDP growth. For example, in 2010, about 27% of the GDP was contributed to by small enterprises (URT, 2012). The benefits of Small and Medium-sized Enterprises (SME) are numerous in various economies. For example, they can prevent large enterprises from controlling the market, and are drivers of innovation (Savlovschi & Robu, 2011), and competitiveness (Robu, 2013). Their competitive advantages can be translated in terms of their efficient utilization of resources and high capital productivity (Huang, 2003; Savlovschi & Robu, 2011), low production cost, management cost (Keskìn et al., 2010; Robu, 2013), high flexibility and fast decision making process, and their lower cost of creating employment opportunities than is in large firms (Savlovschi & Robu, 2011). Also, Small and Medium-sized Enterprises (SME) need small capital (Keskìn et al., 2010). However, in order to continue realizing their contribution to the socio-economic development of various economies such as Tanzania, Small and Medium-sized Enterprises (SME) need to realize growth. This can be realized when a positive performance is achieved. This performance can be influenced by Small and Medium-sized Enterprises (SME) entrepreneurial initiatives.

Entrepreneurship is at the heart of Small and Medium-sized Enterprises (SME) performance and sustainability. Entrepreneurship is a process of identifying and pursuing opportunities beyond the limits of the resources under control. Entrepreneurial opportunities are situations in which products can satisfy a need. Entrepreneurs can be independent persons or individuals within a firm who pursue an entrepreneurial opportunity and encompass an entrepreneurial mind-set that can be regarded as a driver of competitive advantages in business entities. A competitive advantage is achieved when entrepreneurs develop capabilities that will help the firm to compete (Hitt et al., 2007). Small and Medium-sized Enterprises (SME) owners develop products, and through these products, managers achieve the firm's competitive advantage. The firm's positive performance is attained when strategic actions are integrated with entrepreneurial actions (Hitt et al., 2002). An entrepreneurial action is the one that discovers opportunities that are used to create business (Johnson & Van-de-Ven, 2002). This is because; an entrepreneurship's center of attention is creation while the strategic management's focal point is firm performance. The creation-performance link is referred to as strategic entrepreneurship (Meyer et al., 2002). Strategic entrepreneurship is an entrepreneurial conduct under a strategic perspective. It can be translated as introducing a product in the market and making efforts that intend to sustain its survival (Hitt et al., 2007). Entrepreneurship and strategic management are joined by various factors such as innovation, networking, learning, governance, and flexibility to mention a few. On the other hand, Hitt et al. (2001) claim that the two perspectives: entrepreneurial and strategic, can be joined to study entrepreneurial strategies that generate wealth.

An entrepreneurial strategy involves identifying and selecting a value creating option for a firm among a set of various choices (Gans et al., 2016). It is made up of both internal and external factors that impact a business (Wang et al., 2015) and allows a firm to develop capabilities, and position itself in the market (Gans et al., 2016). Research has for quite long focused on establishing the contribution of entrepreneurial orientation on firm performance. According to Lumpkin & Dess (1996), a combination of all activities that propel a decision in making a new entry is referred to as an entrepreneurial orientation. Miller (1983) characterized an entrepreneurial orientation as innovation, risk-taking, and pro-activeness. Lumpkin & Dess (1996) adopted Miller's (1983) facets and added two more dimensions: autonomy, and competitive aggressiveness. In meeting their research objectives, various studies characterize an entrepreneurial orientation based on Miller's (1983) or Lumpkin & Dess' (1996) dimensions. This means that a three dimension model (Kurtulmuş & Warner, 2015; Dai et al., 2014; Wang et al., 2015) or a five dimension model (Brownhilder, 2016; Mason et al., 2015; Singh, 2015) can contribute to Small and Medium-sized Enterprises (SME) performance. Apart from the five dimension model, Mason et al. (2015), and Singh (2015) have added competitive energy, and knowledge respectively. However, entrepreneurial orientation is sometimes likened to entrepreneurial strategies. For example, dimensions such as innovativeness, risk-taking, and pro-activeness have been referred to by Duarte (2011) as innovation, risk, and proactivity strategies. Based on this concept, entrepreneurial strategies can be defined in terms of innovation, risk-taking, marketing, knowledge management, and networking. In this regard, an understanding of the entrepreneurial practices in Small and Medium-sized Enterprises (SME) is of paramount importance. These are the innovation, risk-taking, marketing, knowledge management, and networking practices in Small and Medium-sized Enterprises (SME). For the purpose of this chapter the researchers will concentrate on Small and Medium-sized Enterprises (SME) 's that are bakeries and the innovation aspect in Small and Medium-sized Enterprises (SME) bakeries will be discussed further.

MAIN FOCUS OF THE CHAPTER

Entrepreneurial Practices in Bakeries

There is a significant growth in the bakery business in Tanzania (Bennett et al., 2012). Women are the major producers and suppliers of bakery products in Tanzania (Maro & Barreiro-Hurlé, 2012). Most of these bakeries are micro, and small enterprises. The production and selling of bakery products is a famous and old business around the world. The process (baking) can take place in various baking appliances, using flour, and baking technology to produce breads, pastries, cakes, and biscuits / cookies (Lai & Lin, 2006). Other types of bakery products include pizzas, samosas, pies, scones, and doughnuts (Fellows & Axtell, 2004). However, the most famous bakery product is bread (Souki et al., 2016). The bakery products produced and supplied in Tanzania include breads, scones, cakes, cookies, buns, doughnuts, chapatti, and biscuits (Bennett et al., 2012; Chongela et al., 2014). The most consumed are breads, buns, chapatti, and biscuits (Chongela et al., 2014).

Like any other business, producers and suppliers of bakery products take into consideration various internal and external environmental factors. For example, Fellows & Axtell (2004) suggest that the products produced should match the requirements, needs, and preferences of customers in terms of packaging, taste, ingredients, price, and size to mention a few. They also argue that bakeries need to carry out a competitor diagnosis, treat all stakeholders fairly, institute effective customer relationship management strategies, and possess a technical know-how, and necessary machinery in the production of bakery products. They also suggest that segmentation of bakery market is essential. Therefore, the bakery may decide to produce and sell bakery products based on gender, age, income, working environment, nutritional preferences, ceremonies, and geographical location such as rural, urban, or semi-urban. That is why Fellows & Axtell (2004) further argue that bakeries need to enhance their customers to access the bakery products conveniently including timely product delivery. This will capture customers who like bakery products that are produced and sold at the respective bakeries (Souki et al., 2016). That is why convenience, pleasure, and health determine the innovation in bakery products (Martínez-Monzó et al., 2013). The health factor for example, can be in terms of whole grain bread vis-à-vis white bread (Souki et al., 2016). On the other hand, the marketing practices that are honest are expected to capture the attention of potential bakery customers. For example, promotion of bakery products can be enhanced by the use of media such as radio and newspapers as well as signboards, leaflets, and cards. Another important method is personal contacts (Fellows & Axtell, 2004).

Innovation Practices in Small and Medium-sized Enterprises (SME)

The internal business environment plays a vital role in enhancing innovation capabilities in Small and Medium-sized Enterprises (SME) and eventually performance (Bayarçelik et al., 2014). Nevertheless, diversity and dynamics in market influence innovation initiatives that ultimately foster Small and Medium-sized Enterprises (SME) competitiveness (Seo & Chae, 2016). However, these initiatives vary. To a great extent, Small and Medium-sized Enterprises (SME) tend to make frequent innovations in product development (Nicolescu & Nicolescu, 2012), and in process innovation. They also execute marketing innovations by designing and implementing enhanced promotion, product, and pricing techniques (Bozkurt & Kalkan, 2014). This is why successful innovation requires the integration of customer's requirements and ideas in the innovation processes (Bayarçelik et al., 2014). These innovative initiatives include exploration and creativity (Seo & Chae, 2016) and can be enhanced by the use of Information and Communications Technology (ICT) (Nicolescu & Nicolescu, 2012) especially when the Small and Medium-sized Enterprises (SME) owners / managers are willing to adopt such usage. That is why the adoption of innovation is always predicted by management styles within business organizations (Bayarçelik et al., 2014). Small and Medium-sized Enterprises (SME) are flexible in adopting innovative ideas (Garbelli, 2016). Small and Medium-sized Enterprises (SME) are ready to engage in innovative practices that improve their technology. They also strive to engage in developing open and effective innovation plans, and establish control mechanisms in a participatory manner (Yanes-Estévez et al., 2018). It should however be noted that the strategic innovation depends on the awareness of Small and Medium-sized Enterprises (SME) owners / managers on effective risk management practices (Le-Roy & Yami, 2007). This is why, Small and Medium-sized Enterprises (SME) that strive to manage uncertainties in the business environment are likely to influence enhanced innovation operations and Small and Medium-sized Enterprises (SME) performance (Seo & Chae, 2016). The contribution of innovation on Small and Medium-sized Enterprises (SME) performance is evident (Rosli & Sidek, 2013; Nicolescu & Nicolescu, 2012). This contribution is mainly driven by both product and process innovations (Rosli & Sidek, 2013). These include the innovation in product development, and development in information and communication technology. They also include improvement in management, marketing, human resource management, and other business practices (Nicolescu & Nicolescu, 2012). However, the success of innovation initiatives depends on innovation capabilities of the firm. These capabilities include the problem-solving processes, structures, and firm resources (Bayarçelik et al., 2014).

It has been noted that there are several challenges affecting the innovation practices in Small and Medium-sized Enterprises (SME). These include lack of high skilled and experienced staff in innovation, and failure to integrate Small and Medium-sized Enterprises (SME) sections through effective communications. Others include volatility in the market, and failure of the Small and Medium-sized Enterprises (SME) to get support from government, research and academic institutions (Bozkurt & Kalkan, 2014). However, in order to influence growth and sustainability, Small and Medium-sized Enterprises (SME) have the responsibility of investing in enhanced innovation practices that will bring about economic changes (Nicolescu & Nicolescu, 2012). Small and Medium-sized Enterprises (SME) need to commit themselves in monitoring changes in markets. They can also invest their resources to carry out a competitor diagnosis in order to understand innovation initiatives and practices of their rivals (Bozkurt & Kalkan, 2014). Nevertheless, innovation can be enhanced through cooperation among Small and Medium-sized Enterprises (SME) from various industries. Through cooperation, Small and Medium-sized Enterprises (SME) access knowledge on innovation opportunities, and matters pertaining to industrial property protection. In most cases, collaborations among Small and Medium-sized Enterprises (SME) take place in Small and Medium-sized Enterprises (SME) that share similar characteristics and diversities. These diversities are translated by the Small and Medium-sized Enterprises (SME) knowledge, capabilities, and product portfolio and characteristics (Seo & Chae, 2016). Apart from collaborating with other Small and Medium-sized Enterprises (SME), they can also collaborate with other entities particularly in research and development. In this regard, Small and Medium-sized Enterprises (SME) need to improve their communication processes and structures, and enhance their relations with key innovation stakeholders in order to facilitate innovation activities (Bozkurt & Kalkan, 2014). The cooperation that should exist among Small and Medium-sized Enterprises (SME) may be in the form of joint innovation projects. The cooperation between Small and Medium-sized Enterprises (SME) and the research and development community should seek to enhance innovation practices and address innovation challenges within the innovation system. Generally, all of the innovation initiatives and practices in Small and Medium-sized Enterprises (SME) require the commitment of Small and Medium-sized Enterprises (SME) owners / managers in devising strategies that will address the shortage of competent staff, and financial resources. These strategies should intend to increase Small and Medium-sized Enterprises (SME) capabilities in managing innovation processes, and confronting bureaucracy in the process of accessing support from government institutions, and academic and research centers (Bozkurt & Kalkan, 2014).

Diffusion of Innovation Theory

The theory provides details about the mechanisms and rate at which new ideas, practices and technology spread into a social system (Rogers, 2003; Al-Jabri & Sohail, 2012). The rate of adoption is defined as "the relative speed with which an innovation is adopted by members of a social system" (Rogers, 2003). Therefore, diffusion comprises of the communication, acceptance, adoption, implementation, and institutionalization of innovation within a social system (Rogers, 2003; Koçak et al., 2013; Murray, 2009). An innovation is "an idea, practice, or object that is perceived as new by an individual or other unit of adoption" (Rogers, 2003). Accordingly, diffusion is made possible when there is an accumulation of technology and knowledge transfer within an organization. The theory confirms that adoption of new technologies is associated with "five attributes of innovations: relative advantage, compatibility, complexity, trial-ability, and observe-ability" (Rogers, 1995). The relative advantage "is the degree to which an innovation is perceived as being better than the idea it supersedes" (Rogers, 1995; Rogers, 2003). The social prestige and economic prosperity mainly define the degree of relative advantage. In this regard, increased relative advantage is likely to influence users in adopting a particular innovation (Rogers, 1995; Perkins, 2007; Lee et al., 2011). Compatibility "is the degree to which an innovation is perceived as consistent with the existing values, past experiences, and needs of potential adopters" (Rogers, 1995; Rogers, 2003). According to Rogers (1995), a more compatible idea is "less uncertain to the potential adopter, and fits more closely with the individual's life situation". Another attribute in the theory is complexity. This is defined as "the degree to which an innovation is perceived as relatively difficult to understand and use" (Rogers, 1995; Rogers, 2003). In this regard, adopters are likely to adopt innovations that can easily be interpreted and applied (Rogers, 1995). The theory regards trial-ability as an important attribute of innovation. This is defined as "the degree to which an innovation may be experimented with on a limited basis" (Rogers, 1995; Rogers, 2003). The intention of trial-ability is to dismiss uncertainty about a new innovation. In this regard, information regarding an innovation should be clearly understood by the managers in order to address confusions, and avoid any severe consequences (Perkins, 2007). Also, the theory tells about Observe-ability. This is defined as the "degree to which the results of an innovation are visible to others" (Rogers, 1995; Rogers, 2003). Observe-ability suggests that ideas should give out results that can easily be observed and well explained. The rate of adoption is likely to increase when other players see and understand the results brought by an innovation (Rogers, 1995; Rogers, 2003). Through the diffusion of innovation theory, the study finds how Small and Medium-sized Enterprises (SME) can interpret the attributes of their innovations and adopt various innovation strategies to foster their positive performance.

Diffusion of Innovation in Small and Medium-Sized Enterprises (SME)

SME performance is heavily supported by innovation practices. The level of innovation in Small and Medium-sized Enterprises (SME) depends on both formal and informal processes and practices (Robbins & O'Gorman, 2016). That is why the use of social media networks is regarded as an innovation in Small and Medium-sized Enterprises (SME) (Sarosa, 2012). Both formal and informal processes in innovation are supported by idea generation. Ideas come from both internal and external Small and Medium-sized Enterprises (SME) boundaries. Investing in novel ideas is enhanced by the culture of an SME. For example, risk-taking attitude is higher in Small and Medium-sized Enterprises (SME) that have formal innovation process than those with informal innovation process (Robbins & O'Gorman, 2016). Processes are affected by several characteristics such as relative advantages, Observe-ability, complexity and compatibility (Gazem & Rahman, 2013). In turn, these processes are the ones compelling a Small and Medium-sized Enterprises (SME) to adopt a particular innovation or not (Ramdani & Kawalek, 2007). In this regard, Small and Medium-sized Enterprises (SME) need capabilities to test an innovation before they adopt it (Gazem & Rahman, 2013).

Innovation in Small and Medium-sized Enterprises (SME) is challenged by several factors. They include lack of business know-how and limited financial resources (Vega et al., 2008). However, in developed countries such as Australia, lack of knowledge is no more a challenge to innovation adoption. Their main challenge is the difficulty experienced in ascertaining the benefits of innovation especially for small-sized projects. In turn, this makes innovation adoption a risky decision due to the limited resources Small and Medium-sized Enterprises (SME) own (Hosseini, et al., 2016; Al-Mamun, 2018; Boonsiritomachai et al., 2016). Risky actions may endanger Small and Medium-sized Enterprises (SME) performance (Peltier et al., 2012). Small and Medium-sized Enterprises (SME) do face difficulty in overcoming the costs involved in the innovation process or adoption (Sawang & Unsworth, 2011). That is why only Small and Medium-sized Enterprises (SME) with tight financial muscles are able to adopt innovation (Boonsiritomachai et al., 2016).

Innovation adoption is contributed to by several factors. Generally, the availability of organizational resources is crucial for innovation adoption in Small and Medium-sized Enterprises (SME) (Boonsiritomachai et al., 2016). Technical know-how plays a vital role in the adoption (Vega et al., 2008). Small and Medium-sized Enterprises (SME) need to invest in training their workforce including the owners / managers. In this regard, top management support is required (Chiu et al., 2017). Before adopting any innovation, Small and Medium-sized Enterprises (SME) need to ensure that owners / managers have the relevant information and are able to foresee benefits associated with such innovation (Boonsiritomachai et al., 2016). This is because; the adoption is partly influenced by the perception of Small and Medium-sized Enterprises (SME) owners / managers (Peltier et al., 2012). They greatly control the innovation processes within their enterprises. The skills and knowledge of the workforce play a key role in the innovation adoption (Peltier et al. 2012; Sawang & Unsworth, 2011; Al-Mamun, 2018). Without the required training, the Small and Medium-sized Enterprises (SME) workforce will not be able to cope with changes in business environment (Ben-Youssef et al., 2011). Given this context, Small and Medium-sized Enterprises (SME) owners / managers need to depend upon human capital and be ready to accept and adopt innovations from their employees in order to withstand pressures from the environment. Other factors include attitude towards change. Their readiness to accept new innovation determines their readiness to adopt innovation (Al-Mamun, 2018; Peltier et al., 2012). There are also; relative advantage (Peltier et al., 2012; Chiu et al., 2017), Observe-ability (Gazem & Rahman, 2013; Chiu et al., 2017), trial-ability, and compatibility (Chiu et al., 2017). Small and Medium-sized Enterprises (SME) need to see evidence of benefits associated with innovative products before they adopt such innovations (Gazem & Rahman, 2013; Chiu et al., 2017; Boonsiritomachai et al., 2016).

The innovation adoption among Small and Medium-sized Enterprises (SME) is also dependent on Small and Medium-sized Enterprises (SME) capabilities in new product development, and ability to adapt and manage new business processes that create value (Al-Mamun, 2018). For example, new business practices could be managing the supply chain (Hosseini, et al., 2016; Boonsiritomachai et al., 2016) or managing market uncertainty and environmental hostility (Peltier et al., 2012). This is part of the external or competitive pressure that influences innovation adoption in Small and Medium-sized Enterprises (SME) (Sawang & Unsworth, 2011; Chiu et al., 2017; Boonsiritomachai et al., 2016). For example, in order to adapt to the competitive pressure and increase knowledge capital and address financial constraints, some Small and Medium-sized Enterprises (SME) have realized the need to take part in the innovation processes of key industry players especially the large scale enterprises. This is because; to a great extent, most of the large enterprises adopt innovations existing in the market, and their adoptions are not barricaded by financial inadequacy (Sawang & Unsworth, 2011). In order to respond to various changes and competitive pressures from the business environment, Small and Medium-sized Enterprises (SME) need capabilities to adopt and manage innovations, and foresee their economic benefits and rewards. They also need to manage risk, cost and time (Al-Mamun, 2018). Time is one of the main factors of innovation diffusion (Ben-Youssef et al., 2011).

Enhanced Innovation Process in Bakeries

SME owners / managers need to critically assess the link between their innovation practices with business strategy and operating environment (Palmer et al., 2001). For about quarter a century, the advice given to bakeries has dwelt on their need to develop capabilities in order to manage operations through development of cross-functional teams. This advice has consistently urged bakeries to improve process-improvement skills. The skills involve capabilities in capturing of data regarding consumer behaviors and trends, as well as information on rivals. The advice given has also concentrated on the need to develop effective and efficient costing systems (Darling & Davis, 1994). Small and Medium-sized Enterprises (SME) strive to develop and manage production processes that enhance cost reduction in order to attain price competitiveness. Cost reduction strategies facilitate the relationship between process innovations and Small and Medium-sized Enterprises (SME) performance. Cost reduction strategies translated by process innovations should focus on enabling the bakery to attain price competitiveness and reputation (Palmer et al., 2001). Food enterprises dwell more on product and process innovations (Matopoulos & Vlachopoulou, 2008). Bakeries need to understand that the diffusion of innovation depends on imitation process (Garzia, 2017). Literature confirms that bakery products can easily be imitated (Kim, 2015). That is why most of the food companies link innovation with product development initiatives, and research activities (Matopoulos & Vlachopoulou, 2008). Given this scenario, Small and Medium-sized Enterprises (SME) need to concentrate on product improvement in order to attain competitive advantage (Palmer, Wright, & Powers, 2001). Bakeries need to attain greater performance and competitiveness by introducing new product attributes (Sulistiyani, 2017). Bakeries need to concentrate on improving their products so that they can attain longer shelf life (Martínez-Monzó et al., 2013). One way of guaranteeing longer shelf life is through innovative packaging. An effective packaging such as custom-made packaging in bakeries also facilitates smooth distribution of bakery products (White & Hall, 2013). Bakery products need packaging variation in order to compete (Martínez-Monzó et al., 2013). By focusing on packaging variation, and creativity and utilization of creative ideas on other innovation matters, bakeries are likely to influence their growth (Sulistiyani, 2017).

There is evidence showing bakeries adopting quality management practices. The quality management practices in bakeries include control of strategy, resource management and planning, production management, and supply chain management (Van-Der-Spiegel et al., 2006). Quality management practices are the main sources of survival in bakeries (Kim, 2015). Commitment to quality management practices results into innovative bakery products (White & Hall, 2013). Effective quality management practices are reflected in significant production quality, and they reduce the rate of rejected bakery products, and complaints about quality and availability of bakery products (Van-Der-Spiegel et al., 2006). Quality management practices and innovation should be highly emphasized in order to compete (Stowe & Grider, 2014). Bakeries that adopt a differentiation strategy intertwined with quality management initiatives realize great competitiveness (Palmer, Wright, & Powers, 2001). Generally, in order to attain competitiveness, bakeries need more information related to production quality (Van-Der-Spiegel et al., 2006). Production quality is linked with production processes. Production processes in bakeries entail flexibility in effecting changes and entail the use of advanced technological tools such as modern baking ovens, and electronic mixers (Nwewi et al., 2017). A bakery should understand that when other bakeries adopt a new technology and continue using it, there is evidence that the technology is of paramount significance and it should be adopted (Garzia, 2017). For example, consumer preferences have shifted to healthy products. This preference has forced bakeries to develop production processes and techniques that satisfy these needs (Martínez-Monzó et al., 2013). That is why bakeries may need to adopt innovation strategies that seek to institute differentiation such as modifying the main ingredients of bakery products (Zulkarnain et al., 2018). For example, the production of bakery products involves the use of fats and oils as one of their key materials and ingredients. In this regard, firms that strive to adopt effective cost reduction strategies may prefer using fat substitutes when developing their products (Rios et al., 2014). Product improvement is a key innovation strategy that influences Small and Medium-sized Enterprises (SME) performance (Palmer et al., 2001). Apart from the enhanced innovation process, the customer-focused innovation is also part of the innovation strategies in bakeries.

Customer-Focused Innovation in Bakeries

Food companies should first seek to understand information on customer preferences before adopting a new technology (Nguyen & Nguyen, 2013). The motive behind any innovative practices adopted by bakeries should be value creation (Nwewi et al., 2017). Food enterprises should seek to adopt innovation strategies that drive value (Matopoulos & Vlachopoulou, 2008). In order to confront stiff competition, and absorb changing customer preferences, bakeries need to concentrate in developing products with peculiar features that are able to withstand the pressures in the market (Jabłońska-Porzuczek & Smoluk-Sikorska, 2016). Understanding customer preferences and changing needs, as well as strengths and weaknesses of rivals should be the prime objective of bakeries that seek to increase their sales performance (Sulistiyani, 2017). The objective of effective innovation practices facilitated by technology in bakeries should allow the consumer to comprehend the concept of innovative products (Martínez-Monzó et al., 2013). Effective innovative practices in bakeries should be able to institute product differentiation (Nwewi et al., 2017). Bakeries can attain competitiveness through taste variation (Sulistiyani, 2017). Food enterprises that seek to attain competitiveness need to develop products whose characteristics such as taste, milky and creamy appearance, and smoothness are on the preference list of consumers (Rios et al., 2014). For example, customers have now shifted their interest on quality bakery products particularly those considering health issues and trends (Garzia, 2017). One of the innovative strategies is to develop products that seek to satisfy the growing needs of customers to consume products rich in nutrition value (Martínez-Monzó et al., 2013). For example, enterprises can develop capabilities in order to develop low fat products that reduce overweight or obesity (Rios et al., 2014) and take greater consideration of customers with special health concerns such as allergies or celiac disease (Martínez-Monzó et al., 2013). Apart from the customer-focused innovation, the enhanced innovation environment is also part of the innovation strategies in bakeries.

Enhanced Innovation Environment in Bakeries

Firms need to promote practices that influence organizational development (Stowe & Grider, 2014). Through function coordination, bakeries are likely to realize competitiveness (Sulistiyani, 2017). In that regard, employees should be given opportunities to assess their performances in order to develop more knowledgeable teams (White & Hall, 2013). Firms need to encourage their workforce to generate creative ideas in order to improve innovation and performance (Stowe & Grider, 2014). For decades, bakeries have been advised to train their workforce to understand the preferences of their customers, to be able to analyses the performance trend, and develop capabilities in coordinating operations (Darling & Davis, 1994). Today, effective innovation practices in bakeries cannot be achieved unless the workforce is empowered through the provision of necessary training, attractive compensation scheme, as well as employing skilled workforce (Nwewi et al., 2017). Firms need to foster motivation among leaders through enhanced working environment that is translated by positive compensation schemes and reduced employee turnover. Effective innovative practices foster innovative working environment (Stowe & Grider, 2014). For decades, bakery capabilities have been seen in exploitation of various opportunities from the business environment (Darling & Davis, 1994). Bakery competitiveness is also influenced by efforts in exploring new inspiration (Sulistiyani, 2017). In order to realize effective product development and innovation strategies, there should be a process that integrates ideas from all employees in order to combat frustration among the workforce. Firms can also facilitate the interaction of their workforce with external practitioners in order to stimulate fresh ideas (Stowe & Grider, 2014). The integration of ideas from the entire workforce should also include the front line workers. Front line employees are critical in influencing the performance of bakeries. Bakeries need to trust and have confidence in decisions made by front line employees. These bakery front line employees need to be given responsibilities that ultimately increase their motivation (Darling & Davis, 1994). Apart from the innovation strategies, the risk-taking strategies are also part of the entrepreneurial strategies in bakeries.

Entrepreneurial Strategies in Bakeries: Risk-Taking

Bakeries also face risks associated with planning and growth (Sum & Mahussin, 2017). Bakeries and all related enterprises need to establish their target markets before embarking on business operations in order to guarantee success and growth (Louw et al., 2013). Food enterprises need capabilities to forecast market needs as a crucial way of satisfying their customer needs (Cantaleano et al., 2018). In order to mitigate risks, contingency plan is essential (Ariyanti & Andika, 2016). However, bakery owners / managers are highly involved in the development process of strategic plans than other employees (Mithwani, 2015). On the other hand, large bakeries employ production plan, and act as the basis for improving their long-term plan. On the contrary, small bakeries' plans are based on experience (Van-Der-Spiegel et al., 2005). In this regard, bakeries need to train their staff on matters pertaining to food chain in order to increase their competitive advantages and performance (Marques et al., 2012). However, training on risk awareness and mitigation is done at a lesser extent in bakeries (Alexopoulos et al., 2009). Also, bakeries and other related enterprises lack the necessary knowledge and capabilities in managing key business operations such as cash flow management, executing effective pricing strategies, and mitigating risks (Louw et al., 2013). These could be risks associated with demand, raw materials, and recession (Ariyanti & Andika, 2016). Bakeries do as well meet a variety of risks related to ergonomics, hygiene, machinery, and logistics (Alexopoulos et al., 2009). Bakeries also face financial, operational, and strategic risks. They also face risks associated with planning, sustainability and the workforce (Sum & Mahussin, 2017). There are also work-related risks in bakeries which are mainly influenced by managing big load, temperatures, noise, stress, and highly demanding and time consuming tasks (Alexopoulos et al., 2009). These risks negatively affect cost management especially the rising costs of raw materials, logistics, and costs related to machinery. Also, risks in bakeries negatively affect production output level, and revenues (Sum & Mahussin, 2017). However, a lot of challenges facing bakeries such as poor sales revenues, profitability, and productivity are to a great extent happening in bakeries with a single owner and family-owned bakeries as well (Náglová & Horáková, 2017). In most cases, this type of ownership is likely to happen in small bakeries with a small workforce size. That is why planning in bakeries with many employees is much effective and efficient than bakeries with small size of workforce (Van-Der-Spiegel et al., 2005). Therefore, governance and its effective structures are crucial in the management and performance of Small and Medium-sized Enterprises (SME).

Innovation and Small and Medium-Sized Enterprises (SME) Performance

The relationship between innovation and business performance of Small and Medium-sized Enterprises (SME) has been an area of great concern in Small and Medium-sized Enterprises (SME) research. Most of these studies such as Olughor (2015); Zwingina & Opusunju (2017); van-Auken et al. (2008); Rosli & Sidek (2013); and Mbizi et al., (2013) find how innovation influences Small and Medium-sized Enterprises (SME) performance. Innovation has been classified in terms of product, process, organizational, administrative, managerial and system, marketing innovation (van-Auken et al., 2008; Rosli & Sidek, 2013; Zwingina & Opusunju, 2017) while Small and Medium-sized Enterprises (SME) performance measures have been defined in terms of sales level (Zwingina & Opusunju, 2017), financial, production, and market indicators. Control variables such as size and age have been a preference in innovation-Small and Medium-sized Enterprises (SME) performance studies in which both size of the firm and its age are measured as the logarithm of number of employees and years of operation respectively (van-Auken et al., 2008). It is also believed that the findings of the studies may also be affected by the environment in which they were carried out such as Nigeria (Zwingina & Opusunju, 2017), Zimbabwe (Mbizi et al., 2013), Spain (van-Auken et al., 2008), and Malaysia to mention a few (Rosli & Sidek, 2013). Differences can also emerge due to the type of industry or sector such as manufacturing (van-Auken et al., 2008), textiles, clothing, wood, and beverage (Rosli & Sidek, 2013) in which Small and Medium-sized Enterprises (SME) under study operate in.

Most of the innovation-Small and Medium-sized Enterprises (SME) performance studies use a survey design methodology (Mbizi et al., 2013; Zwingina & Opusunju, 2017; Rosli & Sidek, 2013; van-Auken et al., 2008). However, sampling strategies differ. For example, random selection and stratification have been adopted by Mbizi et al., (2013), and van-Auken et al., (2008). The sample size of 30 Small and Medium-sized Enterprises (SME) (Mbizi et al., 2013), 9,337 firms (but only 1,091 responded) (van-Auken et al., 2008), 348 Small and Medium-sized Enterprises (SME) owners (Zwingina & Opusunju, 2017), and 284 Small and Medium-sized Enterprises (SME) (Rosli & Sidek, 2013). The Yamane's (1967) formula to determine the sample size when the population is known has been used by Zwingina & Opusunju (2017) who also use a 5 year period to measure the relationship between innovation and Small and Medium-sized Enterprises (SME) performance. Although both interviews and questionnaires can be used to collect information from Small and Medium-sized Enterprises (SME) (Mbizi et al., 2013), most studies collect data using questionnaires (Zwingina & Opusunju, 2017; van-Auken et al., 2008; Rosli & Sidek, 2013) particularly from the top officials (Zwingina & Opusunju, 2017; van-Auken et al., 2008). The relationship between innovation and Small and Medium-sized Enterprises (SME) performance can be developed by the aid of hierarchical regression analysis (Rosli & Sidek, 2013); although a multiple regression analysis has also become a top priority (Olughor, 2015; Zwingina & Opusunju, 2017; van-Auken et al., 2008). A factor analysis has also been used to show how the indicators can be summarized by a single factor (van-Auken et al., 2008) whereby Cronbach's Alpha has become a preferred tool in testing reliability (Olughor, 2015; van-Auken et al., 2008; Rosli & Sidek, 2013).

Research shows that innovation influences Small and Medium-sized Enterprises (SME) performance (Zwingina & Opusunju, 2017; van-Auken et al., 2008), competitiveness and sustainability (Mbizi et al., 2013; van-Auken et al., 2008). This is mainly contributed to by technological innovation, market innovation, product innovation, process innovation (Zwingina & Opusunju, 2017; van-Auken et al., 2008; Rosli & Sidek, 2013), and managerial and systems innovation (van-Auken et al., 2008). However, both organizational innovation and administrative innovation do not influence Small and Medium-sized Enterprises (SME) performance (Zwingina & Opusunju, 2017). This study seeks to link innovation strategies: enhanced innovation process, customer-focused innovation, and enhanced innovation environment, with Small and Medium-sized Enterprises (SME) performance: production / output level, and sales level. These links are moderated by human resource competency, and Small and Medium-sized Enterprises (SME) size respectively.

Methodology

This study adopted a quantitative approach. The study took place in the United Republic of Tanzania. The United Republic of Tanzania is made up of Mainland Tanzania, and Zanzibar. However, the study was based in Mainland Tanzania. This is the largest part of Tanzania with 26 geographical regions while Zanzibar comprises of only 5 regions. The study population was 359 bakeries. These bakeries are registered within the Tanzania Food and Drugs Authority (TFDA) in Mainland Tanzania. The sample size is estimated based on Krejcie & Morgan's (1970) Table for sample size determination. With a population of 359 bakeries, the sample size becomes 186 registered bakeries. The study employed probability sampling. A multi-stage sampling technique was applied. This technique "entails two or more stages of random sampling based on the hierarchical structure of natural clusters within the population" (Sedgwick, 2015). It is useful when the population is geographically diverse (Sedgwick, 2015). The intention of applying a multi-stage sampling technique was to accommodate all zones of the study area in sampling and make sure each zone was fairly represented. Firstly, all the 26 regions of Mainland Tanzania were stratified into 7 geographical zones based on Tanzania Food and Drugs Authority (TFDA)'s zone classification.

Secondly, the study applied the Probability Proportional to Size (PPS) to decide on the number of bakeries incorporated in the sample from each zone. Lastly, respondents (bakeries from each zone) were identified by adopting a simple random sampling technique. Data were collected using questionnaires that were distributed in person to Small and Medium-sized Enterprises (SME) bakery owners / managers. The questionnaire was designed using a 7-Point LIKERT scale. Each bakery filled in one questionnaire. A total of 161 completed questionnaires were returned. The Principal Component Analysis (PCA) and the Moderator Analysis were used in the analysis. Principal Component Analysis (PCA) was adopted for variable reduction (Karamizadeh et al., 2013). The Cronbach Alpha was used to test Reliability. The Cronbach Alpha score were excellent and were as follows: for Enhanced Innovation Process was 88.6%, Customer-Focused Innovation 86.5% and Enhanced Innovation Environment was 80.9%.

SOLUTIONS AND RECOMMENDATIONS

It has been revealed that the workforce's professional behavior, the acquired competency through training, and the rewarding systems moderate the relationship between enhanced innovation process and output level in Small and Medium-sized Enterprises (SME) bakeries. The positive linear relationship between enhanced innovation process and output level in bakeries with advanced human resource competency suggests that Small and Medium-sized Enterprises (SME) need to frequently train their employees and develop relevant and attractive packages that will eventually motivate their employees to effectively facilitate the innovation processes and increase their production. This is because; employee training and reward have a significant influence on innovation. On the other hand, it has been revealed that the size of the bakery moderates the relationship between enhanced innovation process and sales level. The positive linear relationship between enhanced innovation process and sales level in bakeries with an advanced size suggests that Small and Medium-sized Enterprises (SME) with a considerable number of employees should develop mechanisms that will involve all their employees in the innovation processes so that to blend their vast innovation knowledge and experience and apply them in fuelling sales performance. Similar mechanisms should also be applied in Small and Medium-sized Enterprises (SME) with basic size. This is due to the fact that in competitive business environment, collective knowledge needs to be applied in business operations in order to create economic benefits (Akram et al., 2011).

Since enhanced innovation process is linked to idea generation particularly from employees, bakery owners / managers need to embrace working environment that stimulate idea generation. They should avoid being the sole idea generators in their bakeries in order to pave way for an innovation process that is internalized by their employees. They need as well to incorporate the ideas generated by employees in enhancing an innovation process so that they can continue enjoying repetitive idea generation from their employees. These employees are the ones who manage all the business operations in their bakeries. In this regard, their useful ideas need to be incorporated in respective innovation processes in order to guarantee long lasting competitive advantages in Small and Medium-sized Enterprises (SME) bakeries. Small and Medium-sized Enterprises (SME) owners / managers may also develop a rewarding policy for all useful ideas that contribute significantly to the bakery performance. There is evidence in which firms that fail to integrate their human resource policies with innovation practices barricade idea generation and implementation (Searle & Ball, 2003).

In order to enhance their innovation processes through analyzing reasons for any improvement made to their products, Small and Medium-sized Enterprises (SME) need both competent staff and capabilities in managing marketing intelligence. Bakeries need to employ their efforts in offering necessary and frequent training to their staff, and manage the recruitment and selection process in order to acquire employees who are able to gather, and analyses relevant reasons for product improvement. The government needs to provide marketing assistance to Small and Medium-sized Enterprises (SME) (Osei et al., 2016) and design and implement mechanisms that allow Small and Medium-sized Enterprises (SME) too easily and freely access important marketing information in order to spend less in marketing intelligence. This is because; the success of such analysis depends on the quality of the information gathered and utilized. Due to their size, and financial constraints, Small and Medium-sized Enterprises (SME) bakeries in Tanzania need to adopt affordable and effective training programs that will enable their employees to foster enhanced innovation processes that improve bakery products. The owners / managers need to priorities training and other techniques geared towards influencing the competency of bakery workforce during the development of Small and Medium-sized Enterprises (SME) budget. They should not perceive training as wastage of financial resources. Instead, training should be considered as a strategic driver of results and bakery performance in terms of both increased output, and sales levels. It is argued that the success of innovation execution is linked to the competency of the manager (Szczepańska-Woszczyna & Dacko-Pikiewicz, 2014). Institutions that promote entrepreneurship should employ their efforts in designing and sponsoring training programs to Small and Medium-sized Enterprises (SME) in order to enable them enhance innovation process in improving their products. Similar support should also come from study policy development entities including the government since the increase in production of bakery products, and sales benefits her in terms of tax revenue and eventually improves the living standard of her own people.

It has been concluded that testing the performance of any improvement made to bakery products before they are delivered in the market is an essential component in an enhanced innovation process. This study urges bakery owners / managers to design and implement an effective testing mechanism that is able to foresee the performance of improved bakery products in the markets. An effective testing mechanism needs to be linked with bakery marketing intelligence so that improvements made are the ones reflecting the needs and preferences of the market. This will help the bakery to control risks associated with product failure. Risk is an essential factor in the examination of an innovation (Townsend, 2010). Small and Medium-sized Enterprises (SME) bakeries need not to be discouraged with costs related with testing the performance of improved products. They can outweigh such costs by implementing simple testing initiatives such as offering free bakery products with their respective prices to friends, family members, bakery employees, and a few selected customers so that they can receive feedback that is useful in making informed decisions.

The study tells that an enhanced innovation process is enriched by the frequent evaluation of the performance of improved bakery products. In order to outweigh costs related to evaluation process for improved bakery products, both performance indicators and evaluation criteria need to be well defined. The process should also be simple. In this regard, owners / managers need to train their employees so that they can efficiently manage the evaluation process. The training will also provide them with capabilities to integrate marketing intelligence with an evaluation process. They are also likely to design a simple evaluation process that is cost effective. That is why; research tells that Small and Medium-sized Enterprises (SME) owners / managers have the responsibility of assessing their innovation capability before measuring their innovation performance (Saunila, 2017). Nevertheless, this study urges research and academic institutions that are involved in entrepreneurship, and the food sector to design evaluation processes that are simple and can be managed by Small and Medium-sized Enterprises (SME) particularly

Small and Medium-sized Enterprises (SME) bakeries in a developing economy such as Tanzania. They can also offer necessary training to bakery employees on how to manage their marketing intelligence and link them with their respective evaluation processes. Apart from the recommendations based on the managerial, and policy implications regarding the contribution of enhanced innovation process on bakery performance, the recommendations are also made regarding the contribution of customer-focused innovation.

The results of the study were very interesting. The relationship between enhanced innovation process and output level in Small and Medium-sized Enterprises (SME) has been realized. The workforce's professional behavior, the acquired competency through training and the rewarding systems moderate the relationship between enhanced innovation process and output level in Small and Medium-sized Enterprises (SME) bakeries. There is a positive linear relationship between enhanced innovation process and output level in bakeries with advanced human resource competency but a negative linear relationship in bakeries with low human resource competency. It can be concluded that the professional training and great reward given to employees is a major driver of enhanced innovation processes that ultimately influences greater output. On the other hand, the size of the bakery moderates the relationship between enhanced innovation process and sales level. There is a positive linear relationship between enhanced innovation process and sales level in bakeries with an advanced size but a negative linear relationship in bakeries with a basic size. It can be concluded that inasmuch as the number of employee increases in Small and Medium-sized Enterprises (SME), the higher chances of acquiring innovation knowledge and experiences increases. However, it should be noted that depending on the firm's size, there are different knowledge management techniques that can be adopted. For example, Kruger & Johnson (2013) suggest that small entities mainly adopt a personal approach in knowledge sharing, whilst large entities heavily rely on technology.

Idea generation is an important ingredient in innovation process (Dorow et al., 2015). The study confirms that employees who are frequently encouraged to generate ideas play a vital role in enhancing innovation process and ultimately enable their Small and Medium-sized Enterprises (SME) bakeries to increase their competitiveness. Nevertheless, the favorable working environment in bakeries greatly stimulates idea generation. This is because; such an environment persuades employees by making them feel that they 'own' both the innovation processes and their respective bakeries and are also responsible for any business outcome.

Also, this study confirms that an innovation process is enhanced by the bakery's commitment to analyzing the reasons for any improvement of its products. This commitment will have a greater impact to its competitive advantage. Research tells that such competitive advantage is driven by innovation practices and ultimately the firm's economic success is achieved (Urbancová, 2013). In that regard, bakeries are responsible for enhancing their innovation processes through gathering key marketing information that in turn, when analyzed by competent staff, can increase bakery performance in terms of sales and output levels. In this regard, costs related to marketing intelligence, and those related to acquiring well trained and experienced staff are inevitable and can be easily outweighed in the long run.

The enhanced innovation process in bakeries is characterized by the need for employees to have knowledge and technical know-how in improving bakery products. These capabilities affect the output and sales levels in bakeries. In order to behave professionally, employees need training. The costs associated with training should not discourage bakeries from conducting one. Instead, low cost training models need to be adopted in order to influence employee competency. Additionally, such costs are in the long run offset by the benefits of training in improving business performance. This is because; employee training drives employee satisfaction in Small and Medium-sized Enterprises (SME) (Lyons & Mattare, 2011). Satisfied employees are likely to influence Small and Medium-sized Enterprises (SME) performance.

The study has also confirmed that testing the performance of any improvement made to bakery products is one of the key components defining an enhanced innovation process in Small and Medium-sized Enterprises (SME) bakeries. The testing process needs to be linked with other factors that contribute significantly to bakery performance. These include marketing factors from both internal and external environment so that improved product characteristics such as color, texture, ingredients, packaging, taste, appearance, and perishability reflect the level of competition, delivery systems, technology, marketing strategies, and characteristics of key business stakeholders such as customers.

Also, as it has been seen earlier, evaluating the performance of product is one of the components defining an enhanced innovation process that can contribute significantly to the Small and Medium-sized Enterprises (SME) performance in terms of increased output and sales levels. However, an evaluation process needs to be simple, and that which is able to define both performance indicators and evaluation criteria for improved bakery products. Given this scenario, effective evaluation should be integrated with marketing intelligence of bakeries. Nevertheless, it needs the commitment and involvement of the firm's top leadership (Boer & During, 2001).

FUTURE RESEARCH DIRECTIONS

The focus of the study was on the organizational practices, operations, and initiatives. In this regard, the study got information from the bakery owners / managers since they are the heads, and chief spokespersons of their organizations. However, employees participate fully in designing and implementing their bakeries' business strategies. Therefore, they have a lot of information that would provide a broad picture in regard to practices, operations, and initiatives within the bakeries and in the market. Although, there were a few cases in which the owners / managers involved employees to discuss and uniformly provide answers to the questionnaire, and the survey; to a great extent, everything was left in the hands of the owners / managers who might not be able to provide specific and detailed information at all times.

The study recommends that entrepreneurial-Small and Medium-sized Enterprises (SME) performance studies can be conducted in other sectors other than bakeries and in other developing economies other than Tanzania in order to widen up the understanding of the framework. These studies can involve the participation of other stakeholders such as customers, employees, suppliers, competitors, and the regulatory bodies. The studies can also seek to provide insights on the challenges facing the development and implementation of entrepreneurial strategies in Small and Medium-sized Enterprises (SME) across sectors and in different economies. Nevertheless, a study can be done to compare the frameworks between developing and developed economies.

CONCLUSION

SME's are major drivers of economic growth and will remain so in years to come. Bakeries in the food sector are crucial in stimulating economic growth through job creation and elevation of a country's' poverty. In order to improve bakeries performance, innovation is crucial. Since innovation can have a positive effect on driving performance, Small and Medium-sized Enterprises (SME) owners have a duty and responsibility to incorporate innovation in all aspects of their business operations where possible.

REFERENCES

Akram, K., Siddiqui, S. H., Nawaz, M. A., Ghauri, T. A., & Cheema, A. K. (2011). Role of Knowledge Management to Bring Innovation: An Integrated Approach. *International Bulletin of Business Administration, 11*(1), 121–134.

Al-Jabri, I. M., & Sohail, M. S. (2012). Mobile Banking Adoption: Application of Diffusion of Innovation Theory. *Journal of Electronic Commerce Research, 13*(4), 379–391.

Al-Mamun, A. (2018). Diffusion of Innovation among Malaysian Manufacturing Small and Medium-sized Enterprises (SME). *European Journal of Innovation Management, 21*(1), 113–141. doi:10.1108/EJIM-02-2017-0017

Alexopoulos, E. C., Kavadi, Z., Bakoyannis, G., & Papantonopoulos, S. (2009). Subjective Risk Assessment and Perception in the Greek and English Bakery Industries. *Journal of Environmental and Public Health, 1*(1), 1–8. doi:10.1155/2009/891754 PMID:20041018

Ariyanti, F. D., & Andika, A. (2016). Supply Chain Risk Management in the Indonesian Flavor Industry: Case Study from a Multinational Flavor Company in Indonesia. *Proceedings of the 2016 International Conference on Industrial Engineering and Operations Management*, 1448-1455.

Bayarçelik, E. B., Taşel, F., & Apak, S. (2014). A Research on Determining Innovation Factors for Small and Medium-sized Enterprises (SME). *Procedia: Social and Behavioral Sciences, 150*(1), 202–211. doi:10.1016/j.sbspro.2014.09.032

Ben-Youssef, A., Hadhri, W., & M'Henni, H. (2011). Intra-Firm Diffusion of Innovation: Evidence from Tunisian Small and Medium-sized Enterprises (SME) Regarding Information and Communication Technologies. *Middle East Development Journal, 3*(1), 75–97.

Bennett, B., Naziri, D., Mahende, G., & Towo, E. (2012). *Driving Demand for Cassava in Tanzania: The Next Steps.* Natural Recourse Institute, University of Greenwich.

Boer, H., & During, W. E. (2001). Innovation, What Innovation? A Comparison between Product, Process and Organizational Innovation. *International Journal of Technology Management, 22*(1/2/3), 83-107.

Boonsiritomachai, W., McGrath, G. M., & Burgess, S. (2016). Exploring Business Intelligence and Its Depth of Maturity in Thai Small and Medium-sized Enterprises (SME). *Cogent Business & Management, 3*(1), 1–17. doi:10.1080/23311975.2016.1220663

Bozkurt, Ö. Ç., & Kalkan, A. (2014). Business Strategies of SME's, Innovation Types and Factors Influencing Their Innovation: Burdur Model. *Ege Academic Review, 14*(2), 189–19.

Brownhilder, N. (2016). Examining the Moderating Effect of Environmental Hostility on the Entrepreneurial Orientation Performance Relationship. *Journal of Economics and Behavioral Studies, 8*(6), 6–18.

Cantaleano, K. R., Rodrigues, G. P., & Martins, T. S. (2018). The Mediating Effect of Proactive Market Orientation Capability in Entrepreneurial Orientation and Service Innovation. *Revista de Administração Mackenzie*, *19*(1), 1–27. doi:10.1590/1678-6971/eramr180038

Chiu, C.-Y., Chen, S., & Chen, C.-L. (2017). An Integrated Perspective of TOE Framework and Innovation Diffusion in Broadband Mobile Applications Adoption by Enterprises. International Journal of Management. *Economics and Social Sciences*, *6*(1), 14–39.

Chongela, J., Nandala, V., & Korabandi, S. (2014). Consumer Demand System of Agri-food in Tanzania. *Journal of Development and Agricultural Economics*, *6*(1), 42–48. doi:10.5897/JDAE2013.0475

Dai, L., Maksimov, V., Gilbert, B. A., & Fernhaber, S. A. (2014). Entrepreneurial Orientation and International scope: The Differential Roles of Innovativeness, Pro-activeness, and Risk-taking. *Journal of Business Venturing*, *29*(4), 511–524. doi:10.1016/j.jbusvent.2013.07.004

Darling, B. L., & Davis, T. R. (1994). Super Bakery Inc.: Innovating in a Mature Market Is Not Just a Piece of Cake. *Planning Review*, *22*(1), 8–17.

Darling, B. L., & Davis, T. R. (1994). Super Bakery Inc.: Innovating in a Mature Market Is Not Just a Piece of Cake. *Planning Review*, *22*(1), 8–17. doi:10.1108/eb054450

Dorow, P. F., Dávila, G., Varvakis, G., & Vallejos, R. V. (2015). Generation of Ideas, Ideation and Idea Management. Navus. *Revista de Gestão e Tecnologia*, *5*(2), 51–59. doi:10.22279/navus.2015.v5n2.p51-59.248

Duarte, N. (2011). Innovation, Risk and Proactivity: Are Firms Following these Strategies? *WSEAS Transactions on Business and Economics*, *8*(3), 110–120.

Fellows, P., & Axtell, B. (2004). Setting up and Running a Small Flour Mill or Bakery. In Opportunities in Food Processing Series. Wageningen: ACP-EU Technical Centre for Agricultural and Rural Cooperation (CTA).

Fjose, S., Grünfeld, L. A., & Green, C. (2010). *Small and Medium-sized Enterprises (SME) and Growth in Sub-Saharan Africa: Identifying Small and Medium-sized Enterprises (SME) Roles and Obstacles to Small and Medium-sized Enterprises (SME) Growth*. MENON Business Economics.

Gans, J., Stern, S., & Wu, J. (2016). *The Foundations of Entrepreneurial Strategy*. SSRN Working Paper #2844843.

Garbelli, M. E. (2016). Competitive Networking for SME: A Case Study of its Success in Italy. *European Scientific Journal*, *12*(7), 1–19. doi:10.19044/esj.2016.v12n7p1

Garzia, C. (2017). Innovation Diffusion and Bandwagon Effect: The Palm Oil in the Italian Bakery Industry. In *Proceedings of the 35th International Conference of the System Dynamics Society*. Cambridge, MA: System Dynamics Society.

Gazem, N. A., & Rahman, A. A. (2013). Promoting the Systematic Innovation Process in Small and Medium Enterprises. *Journal of Convergence Information Technology*, *8*(11), 528–535. doi:10.4156/jcit.vol8.issue11.59

Hitt, M. A., Ireland, R. D., Camp, S. M., & Sexton, D. L. (2001). Strategic Entrepreneurship: Entrepreneurial Strategies for Wealth Creation. *Strategic Management Journal, 22*(6-7), 479-491.

Hitt, M. A., Ireland, R. D., Camp, S. M., & Sexton, D. L. (2002). Strategic Entrepreneurship: Integrating Entrepreneurial and Strategic Management Perspectives. In M. A. Hitt, R. D. Ireland, S. M. Camp, & D. L. Sexton (Eds.), *Strategic Entrepreneurship: Creating a New Mindset* (pp. 1–16). Blackwell Publishers. doi:10.1111/b.9780631234104.2002.00001.x

Hitt, M. A., Ireland, R. D., & Hoskisson, R. E. (2007). *Strategic Management: Competitiveness and Globalization (Concepts and Cases)* (7th ed.). Thomson South-Western.

Hosseini, M. R., Banihashemi, S., Chileshe, N., Namzadi, M. O., Udaeja, C., Rameezdeen, R., & McCuen, T. (2016). BIM Adoption within Australian Small and Medium-sized Enterprises (SME)): An Innovation Diffusion Model. *Construction Economics and Building, 16*(3), 71–86. doi:10.5130/AJCEB.v16i3.5159

Huang, I. W. (2003). Importance of Small and Medium-sized Enterprises (SME) Development in Thailand. *Forum of International Development Studies, 23*(1), 159–176.

Jabłońska-Porzuczek, L., & Smoluk-Sikorska, J. (2016). Factors of Competitiveness of Enterprises Operating in the Confectionary-Bakery Industry in Wielkopolska Voivodship. Optimum. *Studia Ekonomiczne, 84*(6), 99–110.

Johnson, S., & Van-de-Ven, A. H. (2002). A Framework for Entrepreneurial Strategy. In M. A. Hitt, R. D. Ireland, S. M. Camp, & D. L. Sexton (Eds.), *Strategic Entrepreneurship: Creating a New Mindset* (pp. 66-85). Oxford: Blackwell Publishers.

Karamizadeh, S., Abdullah, S. M., Manaf, A. A., Zamani, M., & Hooman, A. (2013). An Overview of Principal Component Analysis. *Journal of Signal and Information Processing, 4*(03, 3b), 173–175. doi:10.4236/jsip.2013.43B031

Katua, N. T. (2014). The Role of Small and Medium-sized Enterprises (SME) in Employment Creation and Economic Growth in Selected Countries. *International Journal of Education and Research, 2*(12), 461–472.

Keskìn, H., Şentürk, C., Sungur, O., & Kìrìş, H. M. (2010). The Importance of Small and Medium-sized Enterprises (SME) in Developing Economies. *2nd International Symposium on Sustainable Development*, 183-192.

Kim, K. (2015). What Made a Bakery Franchise No. 1 in Korea? The Story of Paris Baguette and Its Success Factors. *Journal of Marketing Thought, 2*(1), 14–26.

Koçak, N. G., Kaya, S., & Erol, E. (2013). Social Media from the Perspective of Diffusion of Innovation Approach. *The Macrotheme Review, 2*(3), 22–29.

Krejcie, R. V., & Morgan, D. W. (1970). Determining Sample Size for Research Activities. *Educational and Psychological Measurement, 30*(1), 607–610. doi:10.1177/001316447003000308

Kruger, C. J., & Johnson, R. D. (2013). Knowledge Management according to Organizational Size: A South African Perspective. *South African Journal of Information Management, 15*(1), 1–11. doi:10.4102ajim.v15i1.526

Kurtulmuş, B. E., & Warner, B. (2015). Entrepreneurial Orientation and Perceived Financial Performance. Does Environment Always Moderate EO Performance Relation. *Procedia: Social and Behavioral Sciences, 207*(1), 739–748. doi:10.1016/j.sbspro.2015.10.151

Lai, H. M., & Lin, T. C. (2006). Bakery Products: Science and Technology. In Y. H. Hui (Ed.), *Bakery Products: Science and Technology* (pp. 3–65). Blackwell Publishing. doi:10.1002/9780470277553.ch1

Le-Roy, F., & Yami, S. (2007). The Development of an Innovation Strategy in the Small and Medium-sized Enterprises (SME) Context. *International Journal of Entrepreneurship and Small Business, 4*(4), 431–449. doi:10.1504/IJESB.2007.013690

Lee, Y. H., Hsieh, Y. C., & Hsu, C.-N. (2011). Adding Innovation Diffusion Theory to the Technology Acceptance Model: Supporting Employees' Intentions to use E-Learning Systems. *Journal of Educational Technology & Society, 14*(4), 124–137.

Louw, A., Troskie, G., & Geyser, M. (2013). Small Millers' and Bakers' Perceptions of the Limitations of Agro-processing Development in the Wheat-milling and Baking Industries in Rural Areas in South Africa. *Agrekon, 52*(3), 101–122. doi:10.1080/03031853.2013.821746

Lumpkin, G. T., & Dess, G. G. (1996). Clarifying the Entrepreneurial Orientation Construct and Linking It to Performance. *Academy of Management Review, 21*(1), 135–172. doi:10.5465/amr.1996.9602161568

Lyons, P., & Mattare, M. (2011). How can Very Small and Medium-sized Enterprises (SME) Make the Time for Training and Development: Skill charting as an Example of Taking a Scenistic Approach. *Development and Learning in Organizations, 25*(4), 15–19. doi:10.1108/14777281111147053

Maliti, E., & Mnenwa, R. (2008). The Role of Small Businesses in Poverty Alleviation: The Case of Dar es Salaam, Tanzania. Dar es Salaam: Research on Poverty Alleviation (REPOA).

Maro, F., & Barreiro-Hurlé, J. (2012). *Analysis of Incentives and Disincentives for Wheat in the United Republic of Tanzania.* Rome: Monitoring African Food and Agricultural Policies (MAFAP), Food and Agriculture Organization of the United Nations (FAO).

Marques, N. R., Matias, J. C., Teixeira, R. R., & Brojo, F. M. (2012). Implementation of Hazard Analysis Critical Control Points (HACCP) in a SME: Case Study of a Bakery. *Polish Journal of Food and Nutrition Sciences, 62*(4), 215–227. doi:10.2478/v10222-012-0057-5

Martínez-Monzó, J., García-Segovia, P., & Albors-Garrigos, J. (2013). Trends and Innovations in Bread, Bakery and Pastry. *Journal of Culinary Science & Technology, 11*(1), 56–65. doi:10.1080/15428052.2012.728980

Mason, M. C., Floreani, J., Miani, S., Beltrame, F., & Cappelletto, R. (2015). Understanding the Impact of Entrepreneurial Orientation on Small and Medium-sized Enterprises (SME) Performance. The Role of the Financing Structure. *Procedia Economics and Finance, 23*(1), 1649–1661. doi:10.1016/S2212-5671(15)00470-0

Matopoulos, A., & Vlachopoulou, M. (2008). Identifying Innovation Strategies: Insights from the Greek Food Industry. In *110th EAAE Seminar 'System Dynamics and Innovation in Food Networks*. Innsbruck-Igls: European Association of Agricultural Economists (EAAE).

Mbizi, R., Hove, L., Thondhlana, A., & Kakava, N. (2013). Innovation in Small and Medium-sized Enterprises (SME): A Review of Its Role to Organizational Performance and Small and Medium-sized Enterprises (SME) Operations Sustainability. *Interdisciplinary Journal of Contemporary Research in Business*, *4*(11), 370–389.

Meyer, G. D., Neck, H. M., & Meeks, M. D. (2002). The Entrepreneurship-Strategic Management Interface. In M. A. Hitt, R. D. Ireland, S. M. Camp, & D. L. Sexton (Eds.), *Strategic Entrepreneurship: Creating a New Mindset* (pp. 19–44). Blackwell Publishers.

Miller, D. (1983). The Correlates of Entrepreneurship in Three Types of Firms. *Management Science*, *29*(7), 770–791. doi:10.1287/mnsc.29.7.770

Mithwani, A. M. (2015). Factors Influencing Strategy Implementation in the Bakery Industry in Mombasa County. *International Journal of Business and Management*, *3*(8), 185–200.

Murray, C. E. (2009). Diffusion of Innovation Theory: A Bridge for the Research-Practice Gap in Counseling. *Journal of Counseling and Development*, *87*(1), 108–116. doi:10.1002/j.1556-6678.2009.tb00556.x

Náglová, Z., & Horáková, T. (2017). Position of the Bakery Enterprises in the Czech Republic According to Detailed Specification of the Businesses. *Acta Universitatis Agriculturae et Silviculturae Mendelianae Brunensis*, *65*(5), 1719–1727. doi:10.11118/actaun201765051719

Nguyen, M. Q., & Nguyen, P. V. (2013). The Impact of External Environment, Technology and Innovation Capacities, and Leadership Development on Organizational Performance in Food Industry. A Qualitative Study of Food Enterprises in Ho Chi Minh City, Vietnam. *International Journal of Business. Human Technology*, *3*(4), 49–60.

Nicolescu, L., & Nicolescu, C. (2012). Innovation in Small and Medium-sized Enterprises (SME)-Findings from Romania. *Economia e Sociologia*, *5*(2a), 71–85.

Nwewi, H. N., Onwuka, E. M., & Ogbotubo, E. (2017). Entrepreneurial Thinking and Competitiveness in Bakery Industry in Delta State of Nigeria. International Journal of Business. *Management and Social Research*, *4*(1), 192–197.

Olughor, R. J. (2015). Effect of Innovation on the Performance of Small and Medium-sized Enterprises (SME) Organizations in Nigeria. *Management*, *5*(3), 90–95.

Osei, A., Forkuoh, K. S., Shao, Y., & Osei, M. A. (2016). The Impact of Institutional Support in Small and Medium-sized Enterprises (SME) marketing, and Growth-A Case Study of Retail Small and Medium-sized Enterprises (SME) in Ghana. *Open Journal of Business and Management*, *4*(3), 408–426. doi:10.4236/ojbm.2016.43043

Palmer, J. C., Wright, R. E., & Powers, J. B. (2001). Innovation and Competitive Advantage in Small Businesses: Effects of Environments and Business Strategy. *Journal of Small Business Strategy*, *12*(1), 30–41.

Peltier, J. W., Zhao, Y., & Schibrowsky, J. A. (2012). Technology Adoption by Small Businesses: An Exploratory Study of the Interrelationships of Owner and Environmental Factors. *International Small Business Journal*, *30*(4), 406–431. doi:10.1177/0266242610365512

Perkins, R. A. (2007). Using Rogers' Theory of Perceived Attributes as a Framework for Understanding the Challenges of Adoption of Open Educational Resources. *International Journal of Humanities and Social Science, 1*(18), 59–66.

Ramdani, B., & Kawalek, P. (2007). Small and Medium-sized Enterprises (SME) & IS Innovations Adoption: A Review & Assessment of Previous Research. Academia. *Revista Latino Americana de Administration, 39*(1), 47–70.

Rios, R. V., Pessanha, M. D., Almeida, P. F., Viana, C. L., & Lannes, S. C. (2014). Application of Fats in Some Food Products. *Food Science and Technology (Campinas), 34*(1), 3–15. doi:10.1590/S0101-20612014000100001

Robbins, P., & O'Gorman, C. (2016). Innovation Processes: Do They Help or Hinder New Product Development Outcomes in Irish Small and Medium-sized Enterprises (SME)? *Irish Journal of Management, 35*(1), 88–103. doi:10.1515/ijm-2016-0006

Robu, M. (2013). The Dynamic and Importance of Small and Medium-sized Enterprises (SME) in Economy. *The USV Annals of Economics and Public Administration, 13*(17), 84-89.

Rogers, E. M. (2003). Diffusion of Innovations (5th ed.). New York: Free Press.

Rosli, M. M., & Sidek, S. (2013). The Impact of Innovation on the Performance of Small and Medium Manufacturing Enterprises: Evidence from Malaysia. *Journal of Innovation Management in Small & Medium Enterprise, 1*(1), 123–128. doi:10.5171/2013.885666

Sarosa, S. (2012). Adoption of Social Media Networks by Indonesian SME: A Case Study. *Procedia Economics and Finance, 4*(1), 244–254. doi:10.1016/S2212-5671(12)00339-5

Saunila, M. (2017). Understanding innovation performance measurement in Small and Medium-sized Enterprises (SME). *Measuring Business Excellence, 21*(1), 1–16. doi:10.1108/MBE-01-2016-0005

Savlovschi, L. I., & Robu, N. R. (2011). The Role of Small and Medium-sized Enterprises (SME) in Modern Economy. Economia. *Seria Management, 14*(1), 277–281.

Sawang, S., & Unsworth, K. L. (2011). Why Adopt Now? Multiple Case Studies and Survey Studies Comparing Small, Medium and Large Firms. *Technovation, 31*(10-11), 554-559.

Searle, R. H., & Ball, K. S. (2003). Supporting Innovation through HR Policy: Evidence from the UK. *Creativity and Innovation Management, 12*(1), 50–62. doi:10.1111/1467-8691.00268

Sedgwick, P. (2015). Multistage Sampling. *BMJ (Clinical Research Ed.), 351*, h4155. doi:10.1136/bmj.h4155 PMID:26231184

Seo, Y. W., & Chae, S. W. (2016). Market Dynamics and Innovation Management on Performance in Small and Medium-sized Enterprises (SME): Multi-agent Simulation Approach. *Procedia Computer Science, 91*(1), 707–714. doi:10.1016/j.procs.2016.07.060

Singh, R. (2015). The Genesis of the Entrepreneurial Orientation and the Proposed Model. *International Journal of Business and Management, 3*(7), 17–21.

Souki, G. Q., Reis, V. C., & Moura, L. R. (2016). The Behavior of Bakery Consumers. *Organizações Rurais & Agroindustriais, 18*(1), 1–12.

Stowe, C. R., & Grider, D. (2014). Strategies for Advancing Organizational Innovation. *Journal of Management and Marketing Research, 15*(1), 1–17.

Sulistiyani, S. (2017). Performance Marketing Model through Acculturation Innovation and Market Orientation in the Bakery Industry. *Expert Journal of Marketing, 5*(1), 1–9.

Sum, R. M., & Mahussin, N. (2017). Risk Management Practices of a Small Enterprise: A Case Study on a Bakery Shop. In *Proceedings of 4th International Muamalat and Entrepreneurship Conference (IMEC4)*. Nilai: Islamic Finance and Wealth Management Institute (IFWMI).

Szczepańska-Woszczyna, K., & Dacko-Pikiewicz, Z. (2014). Managerial Competencies and Innovations in the Company-The Case of Enterprises in Poland. Business. *Management in Education, 12*(2), 266–282.

Townsend, W. (2010). Innovation and the Value of Failure. *International Journal of Management and Marketing Research, 3*(1), 75–84.

Urbancová, H. (2013). Competitive Advantage Achievement through Innovation and Knowledge. *Journal of Competitiveness, 5*(1), 82–96. doi:10.7441/joc.2013.01.06

URT. (2012). *National Baseline Survey Report for Micro, Small, and Medium Enterprises in Tanzania. United Republic of Tanzania: Ministry of Industry and Trade (MIT) and Financial Sector Deepening Trust*. FSDT.

Van-Auken, H., Madrid-Guijarro, A., & García-Pérez-de-Lema, D. (2008). Innovation and Performance in Spanish Manufacturing Small and Medium-sized Enterprises (SME). *International Journal of Entrepreneurship and Innovation Management, 8*(1), 36–56. doi:10.1504/IJEIM.2008.018611

Van Der Spiegel, M., Luning, P. A., De Boer, W. J., Ziggers, G. W., & Jongen, W. M. F.Van-Der-Spiegel. (2005). How to Improve Food Quality Management in the Bakery Sector. *NJAS Wageningen Journal of Life Sciences, 53*(2), 131–150. doi:10.1016/S1573-5214(05)80002-8

Vega, A., Chiasson, M., & Brown, D. (2008). Extending the Research Agenda on Diffusion: The Case of Public Program Interventions for the Adoption of E-Business Systems in Small and Medium-sized Enterprises (SME). *Journal of Information Technology, 23*(2), 109–117. doi:10.1057/palgrave.jit.2000135

Wang, K. Y., Hermens, A., Huang, K. P., & Chelliah, J. (2015). Entrepreneurial Orientation and Organizational Learning on Small and Medium-sized Enterprises (SME) Innovation. *International Journal of Organizational Innovation, 7*(3), 65–75.

White, K., & Hall, H. (2013). *Chatman's Bakery: Diversification and Innovation in the Family Business*. Retrieved August 29, 2018, from Canadian Regional Development: A Critical Review of Theory, Practice and Potentials: http://ruralresilience.ca/wp-content/uploads/2013/10/Chatmans.pdf

Yanes-Estévez, V., García-Pérez, A. M., & Oreja-Rodríguez, J. R. (2018). The Strategic Behavior of Small and Medium-sized Enterprises (SME). *Administrative Sciences, 8*(4), 1–21.

Zulkarnain, A., Wahyuningtias, D., & Putranto, T. S. (2018). Analysis of IFE, EFE and QSPM Matrix on Business Development Strategy. *IOP Conference Series. Earth and Environmental Science*, *126*, 126. doi:10.1088/1755-1315/126/1/012062

Zwingina, C. T., & Opusunju, M. I. (2017). Impact of Innovation on the Performance of Small and Medium Scale Enterprise in Gwagwalada, Abuja. International Journal of Entrepreneurial Development. *Education and Science Research*, *4*(1), 31–45.

KEY TERMS AND DEFINITIONS

Bakery: A confectionery/bake shop/pastry shop/patisserie.

Innovation: A new product/idea/method.

Key Driver: It is somewhat that has a great effect on whether the business does well or not.

Performance: The process or action of performing a function or task.

Small and Medium-Sized Enterprises (SME): These are operational Small and Medium Enterprises.

Chapter 14
Business Environment as Key Driver of SME Performance

Olalekan Asikhia
University of KwaZulu-Natal, South Africa

Vannie Naidoo
https://orcid.org/0000-0001-8435-4348
University of KwaZulu-Natal, South Africa

ABSTRACT

The chapter established the effects of Nigerian market environment on SMEs performance. An empirical study was conducted with survey research design of 21,444 firms and a sample size of 1,102 was arrived at scientifically. Probability sampling methods were employed. An adapted validated questionnaire, and a 0.82-0.96 reliability coefficients range was used. Inferential statistics were used to analyse the data using SPSS software version 22.0. The findings reveal that Nigerian market environment had significant negative effects on the SME performance. The different components of the Nigerian market environment have different effects on the SME performance. The results imply that the environmental turbulence could be responsible for the high failure rate of SMEs in Nigeria. The study contributes to the body of knowledge on environmental and performance management by noting the criticality of the industry market environment in facilitating organizational performance.

1. INTRODUCTION

Small and Medium-sized Enterprises (SMEs) are a crucial driver that drives a country's GDP and GNP. They create jobs and reduce poverty within a country. Governments are now seeing the value in supporting SMEs. However, SMEs' main goal is to maintain its' sustainability within a volatile business environment. This research study evaluated business values and other factors that are instrumental in facilitating Nigerian SMEs performance. SMEs in the South West, Nigeria which is the region that has the highest number of functional SMEs in Nigeria (Smedan, 2016). To be sustainable, SMEs performance needs to be consistently maintained. Key drivers of performance amongst SMEs vary. Some important

DOI: 10.4018/978-1-7998-7951-0.ch014

drivers of performance are quality of goods/services sold, the competitive performance of the business against other firms in the same industry, firms resource capabilities and constraints and the ability of SMEs to adopt innovation into their business operations.

2. BACKGROUND

The study of the drivers of performance is important in facilitating the growth of firms. Different researchers have researched different aspects of the Nigerian environment and its impact on SMEs performance. For example, Eze & Ogiji (2013) assessed the impact of fiscal policy on the manufacturing output of Nigerian firms. Adelegan (2011) examined the effects of infrastructural development on the performance of Nigerian firms. Gado & Nmadu (2011) evaluated the infrastructural resource impact on textile companies' performance. Few researchers have specifically studied the totality of the Nigerian market environment impacts on SMEs' performance.

Recent events revealed that the World Bank's ease of 'doing business report' of 2016 ranked Nigeria 169 out of 189 countries, though this position is the same as the previous year, yet it was regarded as a positive development because the nation's ranking has been on the decrease in the last 8 years. The major indicators of ease of doing business are; starting a business, dealing with construction permits, registering property, getting credit, protecting investors, paying taxes, trading across borders, enforcing contracts, resolving insolvency, and getting electricity. Specifically, the nation ranked 138th on starting a business, 174th on getting a construction permit, 182nd on registering property, 44th on getting credit, 32nd on protecting minority investors, 182nd on paying taxes, 181ston trading across borders, 138th on enforcing contracts, 140th on resoling insolvency and 180th on getting electricity. However, the 2019 ranking revealed a position of 146 in the country's ranking of ease of doing business, the rank deteriorated to 146 in 2018 from 145 in 2017, though business confidence increased from 22.10 INDEX points to 28.20 points (World Bank Report, 2019).

3. MAIN FOCUS OF THE CHAPTER

3.1 Issues, Controversies, and Problem

There is no consensus on how the different aspects of the business environment impinge on the performance of firms (Enu & Havi, 2014; Muogbo & Enemuo-Uzoezie, 2019). Hence, it is important to establish how the Nigerian market environment drives SMEs performance. A report of eighty-five per cent failure rate of SMEs before their 5th anniversary, adduced to lack of knowledge of the market environment has been corroborated with the recent closure of 216 manufacturing companies identified by the Manufacturing Association of Nigerian (SMEDAN, 2012; Manufacturing Association of Nigerian, 2016). It is therefore important to establish the components of the Nigerian market environment that affect the performance of SMEs.

Different researchers have researched different aspects of the Nigerian environment and its' impact on SMEs performance. For example, Eze & Ogiji (2013) in assessing part of the macro-environment; evaluated the impact of fiscal policy on the manufacturing output of Nigerian firms. Igwe et al. (2018) assessed the factors affecting the investment climate, SMEs productivity and entrepreneurship in Nigeria and noted the criticality of the macro and industry environment on the business. Their result was corroborated by Asikhia et al. (2020) that collateral requirement and loan administration have a positive and significant effect on revenue growth of small and medium enterprises in Southwest, Nigeria. Jayeola et al. (2018) also showed that the macro environment of business affected the performance of micro and small enterprises in Ondo state, Nigeria. Del-Pilar et al. (2019) noted that inadequate government programs' information is deemed the most crucial for stakeholders to tackle as it impacts the premature closure of businesses significantly. Similarly, Boso et al.(2019) established that the internationalization of African firms is first affected by the environment of businesses in Africa. Few researchers have specifically studied the Nigerian market environment that impacts SMEs performance.

3.2 Theoretical Foundation

The study is anchored on the Dynamic Capabilities Theory. The theory tried to address one of the major shortcomings of RBV which is the assumptions that the firm resources are static. Dynamic Capability Theory advanced that the firm's ability to integrate, build and reconfigure internal and external capabilities to address rapidly changing environments. It thus advanced that firm's resource mix can be adjusted to maintain the sustainability of the firm's competitive advantage, which can easily be eroded.

The major assumptions are; firstly, that ability of firms to successfully respond to environmental changes is premised on timely response and market positioning to market dynamics. Secondly, the theory views competition in the light of Schumpeterian context when firms strive to create new resource combinations to march up with competitors, and competitors are also striving to improve on their competences. Thirdly, Teece & Pisano (1994) and Teece, et al. (1997) advanced that dynamic capabilities consist of certain factors that determine a firm's distinctive competences. Such factors include processes (how things are done) positions (organizations' current portfolio assets) and paths (strategic alternatives available to firms and attractiveness of the opportunities that lie ahead). These are the core model of dynamic capabilities.

However, the critics of the theory deduced that the theory lacks a clear theoretical foundation and clarity of basic definitional approach (Arend & Bromiley, 2009; Di-Stefano et al., 2010). Zahra et al. (2006) opined that the confusion of Dynamic Capability theory stemmed from whether dynamic capabilities refer to substantive capabilities in volatile environments or the organization's ability to alter existing substantive capabilities, regardless of the volatility. Davis (2004) criticized it for its lack of explicit measures and lack of evidence of contribution to differences in performance at the firm level because most papers focused on conceptual clarifications rather than evidential empirical data. Collins (1994) agrees that dynamic capabilities could be valuable but doubts its ability to sustain a competitive advantage. He argued that capabilities are vulnerable to being superseded by higher-order capabilities. The capability to innovate would thus be superseded by the capability that develops the capability to innovate, and so on, which leads to an infinite regress.

One of the indisputable facts is the focus of the theory on market dynamism; the Resource-Based View addresses the internal resource efficiency and effectiveness. The Dynamic Capability Theory supplied the reason why enterprises can achieve competitive advantage in dynamic markets (Ferdinand et al., 2004; Poulis et al., 2013). It is evident from the above that Dynamic Capability Theory provides an integrated framework revealing conceptual and empirical knowledge on competitive advantage. It results in the creation of resources that allows the firm to achieve a competitive advantage. Noteworthy is the fact that ordinary capabilities make organizations operate effectively and efficiently in their chosen lines of business while dynamic capabilities upgrade the ordinary capabilities to create new ones (Winter, 2003).

3.3 Literature Review and Hypothesis Development

3.3.1 Market Environment

The market environment is an aggregate of all conditions, events, circumstances, and influences that surround and affect the business organization from delivering on its promises to the customers. Business organizations like SMEs must interact with these conditions or forces which may be opportunistic or a threat to achieving a competitive advantage and hence make a profit (Fernando, 2011).

Researchers are divided on the classification of the factors that make up the environment. These factors are divided into internal, industry and external environments. The internal environment is the immediate environment of the business comprising; the vision, mission, resources, customers, suppliers, competitors and employees of the business. Muogbo & Enemuo-Uzoezie (2019) called the environment comprising the customers, suppliers, competitors and employees the task or microenvironment. However, Porter (1985) separated the set of factors that directly influence a firm and its' competitive actions and responses as the industry environment, that is, the interactions with the competitors, customers and suppliers. While the vision, mission, objectives, resources; capabilities and core competencies are seen as firm level-specific factors or environment. The last category is the external environment; researchers agreed that it comprised the factors that are beyond the control of the firm, like; economic, political, legal, socio-cultural and technological (Asikhia, 2016; Ekakitie-Emonena 2019; Tahir &Inuwa 2019). Other factors, on which the researchers differ, are demographic and physical environment.

Atsegbua (2002) sees the business environment from the point of view of symbiosis. He describes it as the system of abiotic and biotic which the firm interacts with as it adapts and transforms it to satisfy the needs of the customers. Ibidunni & Ogundele (2013) see the market environment as being dynamic, with a tendency to be stable or unstable depending on the degree of changes that are occurring per time. Schoemaker et al. (2018) described the environment in which businesses operate as VUCA that is, Volatile, Uncertain, Complex, and Ambiguous. They further said that it will be difficult for businesses that got attached to a traditional way of doing things to succeed.

Adeola (2016), Chidermbaran & Alagappon (2017) identified the features of business/market environment as the total of all factors external to the firm which affects its functions, it is dynamic and unpredictable. However, it is important to the business because it determines the degree of opportunity and threats, hence an impetus for growth and continuous learning by alerting the firm on its weaknesses and strengths. So, how well the internal environment is manipulated to contain the variations in the external environment determines the level of performance (Oginni &Adesanya 2013). In sustaining this view, Thanos et al. (2017) found that the hostility of the international environment reduces the effects of international entrepreneurial orientation on performance.

Some researchers have noted that the market environments of the developing countries are much different from the developed countries where the environmental variables are less unpredictable (Planing, 2017; Wang & Rafig, 2014). As earlier enunciated, the emerging market environments are very dynamic with a high level of uncertainty characterized by information deficit necessary to identify and evaluate the causes of the factors and the interaction between these factors. The concomitant changes necessitated that this dynamism is often non-linear and discontinuous which often translated to opportunities or threat to the organization (Schilke 2014). Planing (2017) though affirmed that the business environment provided the incentive for growth of firms, they however established that the business environment is characterized with low appropriability, high cost of capital with scarce human capital. Aligning with this position, Dinh (2011) and Lee (2014) agreed that the market environment of the developing countries is harsh and that it has had negative effects on SMEs' performance which include contraction of opportunities (Planing, 2017) as well as general entrepreneurial development (Ayegba & Omale, 2016). Wang & Rafig (2014) pointed out that emerging markets like Turkey, Nigeria, Ghana, and so on are often characterized with turbulence due to inconsistent policies, weak macroeconomic framework, deficient infrastructural support, and these gave room to rapid and discontinuous changes and hence the need for organizations in such environments to have resources and capabilities fitted to arrest these changes.

Aside, the macro-environmental factors, there are the Industry and environmental firms specific factors, that relate directly to the industry and the firm; Zhu, et al. (2018) insist that there is a firm-specific environment, in that some environment may be created for creativity and innovation while others may be created for some other purposes. They assert that a collaborative team environment or climate relate well with creativity and operate through intrinsic motivation while a competitive team climate relates positively with extrinsic motivation but did not directly relate to creativity. And that extrinsic motivation has a strong relationship with creativity when intrinsic motivation is low. All environment created is tailored towards driving performance.

3.3.2 SMEs' Performance

Al-Asheq & MdUzzal (2019) believe that firm performance is how an organization reacts, understands, and influences the environment. It reflects the health status of the SMEs over a dedicated period and in the light of the degree of uncertainty and dynamism of the environment in which the SMEs operate, continuous improvement of their performance is critical.

Firm performance is often measured by several indices (Aladejebi & Oladimeji, 2019). Performance often ensures organizational survival and growth (Laosebikan et al., 2013). How well an organization is performing tells of its seriousness to remain a going concern. Cicea, et al. (2019) assessed enterprise performance using both hard quantitative financial measures and soft qualitative measures. The former concerns cost elements and try to quantify performance solely in financial terms. However, many improvements particularly processes may be hard to measure directly in monetary value (Mafundu & Mafini, 2019). The three most common financial measures include profit margin or return on sales and this determines the enterprise's ability to withstand competition, adverse rising costs, falling prices and future declining sales; return on assets that determine the ability to utilize assets and return on equity which is the payment of dividends or shares bonus to the shareholders. Non-financial issues such as customer and employee satisfaction are by hard measurement practice. For large enterprises, profitability is a favorite financial tool for measuring enterprise performance.

Some researchers noted that a high percentage of SMEs adopts non-financial internal standards, ranging in descending order of importance from a quality, competitive performance, resource utilization, flexibility, and innovation (Sadiku-Dushia et al., 2019; Tahir &Inuwa, 2019; Al-Asheq & MdUzzal, 2019) And in assessing factors that can affect performance apart from environmental factors, Thibault et al. (2002) identified organizational experience, business strategies and entrepreneurial goals. The relevance of performance was highlighted by Baumann et al. (2018); they advised that managers need to make high performing contribution of independent choices, that is; identifying the peak in a performance landscape brought about by different components of environments and management factors in a different context. Asikhia & Naidoo (2020a) identified a significant difference in the evaluations of management success determinants to performance, thus noting the importance of performance in assessing the workability of the management success determinants or factors.

3.3.3 Market Environment and SMEs' Performance

The relationship between SMEs and the environment is seen as being mutual, the market environment exerts pressure on the SMEs and the SMEs in turn influence the environment through its output and operations (Adeola, 2016). Akinbogun (2008) asserts that the Nigerian SMEs in the manufacturing sector has been performing below expectations because of the unfavorable external environment dominant by the economic factors. Also, Awino (2011) affirmed that environmental factors of business affect both the strategy formulation and implementation while Machuki & Aosa (2011) established that only some parts of the business that are contingent on the operations of the business affects the performance. Khoury & Prasad (2015) posited that forces in the market environment of business-like geopolitical systems constitute hindrance that could affect the ability of the firms to mobilize resources and access relevant market opportunities that could create competitive advantage. Asikhia & Naidoo (2020b) affirmed that Nigerian SMEs' decisions under intense environmental turbulence are mostly ineffective, and the effects of management success determinants in facilitating performance were also drastically reduced as well as firms' system flexibility.

Menguc et al. (2010) investigated the interactive effects between internal and external factors of the environment on strategy and discovered that these factors moderated the intensity of entrepreneurial orientation on proactive environmental strategy. Hence, Ibidunni & Ogundele (2013) explained that the understanding and effective comprehension of the market environment would help in the positioning of the firm. Juma & Sequeria (2017) confirmed this when they established that the way entrepreneurs experience their contextual environment affect the environment's effects on SMEs' performance, that is, the knowledge of the entrepreneurs concerning the interactions of the factors of their environment moderate the kind of effects the environment will have on their performance.

However, Leick (2016) suggested that institutional entrepreneurship could help to introduce new patterns of behavior that would arrest the uncertainties associated with market changes prevalent in the environment of SMEs' operations.

Hence from the foregoing; the major gap identified from the studies reviewed is the scarcity of studies on the Nigerian market environment bearing in mind the peculiarity of the environment and particularly the market variables in terms of industry specifics and environmentally firm-level skills required. We thus hypothesize that:

H1: Macro environmental factors will have a significant effect on SMEs Performance
H2: Industry Market-specific factors will have a significant effect on SMEs Performance
H3: Environmental firm-specific factors will have a significant effect on SMEs Performance
H4: Nigerian Market Environment will have a significant effect on SMEs Performance

3.3.4 Conceptual Model

The conceptual model was developed based on the review of the literature to reflect the effects of the Nigerian market environment and its sub-variables on SMEs performance.

Figure 1. Conceptual Framework

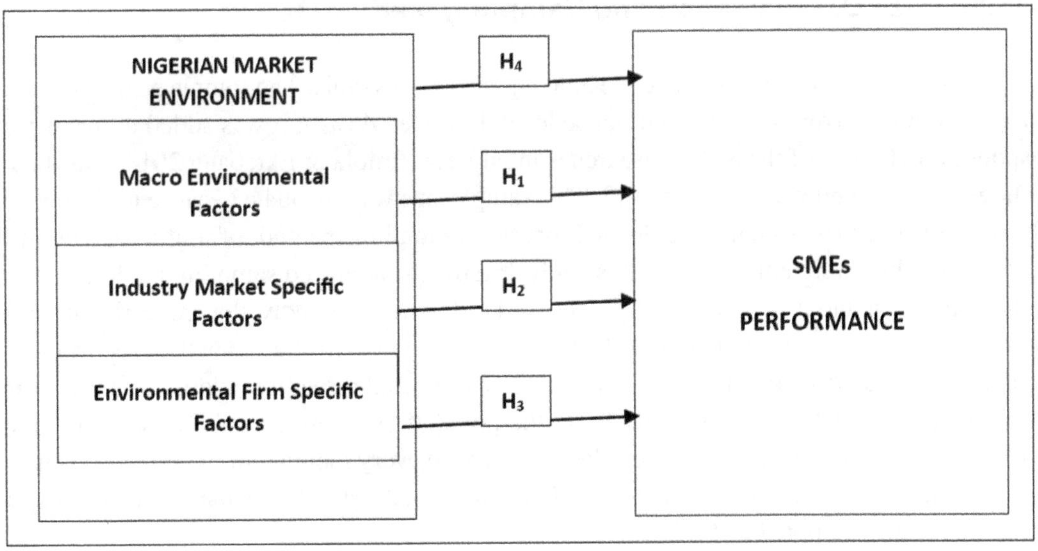

The model shows how the Nigerian market environment sub-variables relate to SMEs performance. The first hypothesis H1 measures the effect of Macro-environmental factors on the performance of SMEs in Nigeria; H2 measures the effect of the Industry market-specific factors on the SMEs performance while H3 measures the Environmental firm-specific market factors on the performance of the SMEs. The last Hypothesis; H4 depicts the combined effects of the Nigerian market environment on SMEs performance.

4. METHODOLOGY

The methodology expands on the research design, method of data collection, and description of the research instrument used in the study and data analysis.

4.1 Research Design

A survey research design was adopted to elicit reliable information and generate numeric data on the variables of the study as used by Asikhia (2016), Aragon-Sanchez & Sanchez-Marin (2005) and Gadenne (1998). This method was adopted because it is capable of producing data based on real-world observations apart from its breadth of coverage and ability to produce a representative sample whose responses can be generalized to the whole population. The population of the study comprised the Chief executive officers (CEOs) of the registered small and medium scale businesses with a maximum asset base of

N200million, excluding land and working capital, and 10 to 300 employees in the selected Nigerian market of Lagos, Ogun, and Oyo states; these were states with the highest number of functional SMEs in Nigeria whose number stood at 21,444 as at February 2017 (CAC, 2017). The sampling frame was drawn from the Small and Medium Enterprises Development Agency of Nigeria (SMEDAN) that has a comprehensive list of the registered SMEs with the Corporate Affairs Commission in Nigeria (CAC, 2017; SMEDAN, 2017).

4.2 Sample Size Determination and Sampling Method

The sample size was calculated using Krejcie & Morgan (1970)'s table. The sample size of 760 was gotten at a 3.5 margin of error and 95% confidence level, however, 45% of it was added to make room for non-response rate typical of the SMEs researches in Nigeria (Eniola & Ektebang 2014; Muritala et al., 2012; Olughor, 2015) and we arrived at 1102. This sample size was adequate because it was determined at 3.5% margin error and 95% confidence level. Probability sampling methods of stratified, proportionate, and random sampling were employed for this study. Firstly, the stratified sampling method was used to divide the population into different strata by states and Industries. Secondly, the proportionate sampling method was used to know the number of SMEs to be contained in each stratum in the proportion of what is present in the population. Finally, the sample size was selected through random sampling from each stratum in the proportion of what was present in the population, These probability sampling methods have the advantage of reducing bias due to selection because every member of the population had equal chances of being selected (Cooper & Schinder, 2006; Kothari, 2004), all population and corresponding sample size by states are noted in Table 1.

Table 1. Proportionate Sample size distribution by States

S/N	STATES	SMEs' POPULATION	PROPORTION	SAMPLE SIZE
1.	Lagos	11, 663	0.544	600
2.	Ogun	1794	0.084	92
3.	Oyo	7987	0.372	410
	TOTAL	21, 444	1.00	1102

Source: CAC, 2017; SMEDAN, 2017.

4.3 Data Collection Methods

Responses were collected through a questionnaire with a predetermined set of questions. The questionnaire was self-administered. The method reduced costs, increased timeliness and improved data quality (Bhattacherjee, 2012; Greener, 2008; Cooper & Schinder, 2006). The researcher was assisted by research fieldworkers familiar with the sample frame, and adequate training was provided to enable them to cope with other technical demands of the work. The average time for filling the questionnaire was between 20 to 25minutes. The research instrument was a questionnaire consisting of 3 major sections and 18 subsections. The 3 major sections are; Firstly, biographic details of the companies; secondly, Nigerian Market

Environment (NME) (which comprised; Macro Environmental factors (MEF), Industry Market Specific Factors (IMSF), and Environmental Firm-Specific Skills (EFSS)), and finally, SMEs' Performance.

4.4 Measurement of the Variables and Sources

All the variables were measured on a five-point scale of Likert type; this made it possible for us to quantify the responses, and compute for statistical analysis, as respondents easily understood them and it was easy to draw conclusions, reports and results from the responses. The Management success determinants and other variables were majorly sourced from Arasa & K'Obonyo (2012), Frank et al. (2017), and Tutar et al. (2015).

4.5 Pilot Study

Recent discourse on pilot study sample size showed that opinions were diverse on the appropriate sample size for the pilot study. Herzog (2008) cautioned that the determination of the sample size for the pilot study was not a simple direct issue because it should depend on the research context. Isaac & Michael (1995) and Hill (1998) advised that 10-30 respondents were sufficient for an average study. However, Julious (2005) and Van-Belle (2002) suggested 12 for medical research, while Connelly (2008) and Treece & Treece (1982) suggested 10% of the sample size.

However, the pilot study for this study was conducted using 20 chief executive officers of the SMEs who were not part of the study but are had similar characteristics as the intended participants of the study, as suggested by Isaac & Michael (1995) and Hill (1998). The validity and reliability of the research instrument were also determined.

4.6 Validity

The validity of the instrument was done through content and construct validity. To achieve content validity, the researcher made sure that the concepts and theories from which the items in the instrument were developed related well with the items. For construct validity, Blumberg et al. (2014) recommended that factor analysis could be used to determine the construct adequacy of a measuring device. Construct validity of the instrument was determined using exploratory factor analysis which included; principal component analysis, the Kaiser-Meyer-Olkin (KMO) measure of sampling adequacy and Bartlett's Test of Sphericity. The Kaiser-Meyer-Olkin (KMO) values indicated the proportion of variance in the variables that might be caused by underlying factors, Kaiser-Meyer-Olkin (KMO) value of greater than 0.5 is acceptable. The Kaiser-Meyer-Olkin (KMO) values of the variables are all acceptable as seen in table 2. Bartlett's test of Sphericity ensures that the correlation matrix is an identity matrix, which indicated if the variables are unrelated and therefore unsuitable for structure detection. Table 2 also showed that the variables are suitable for structure detection.

4.7 Reliability

The reliability of the instrument was determined using the test-retest method in the pilot study. This was to test whether the developed factors measure consistently what they ought to measure. The internal consistency of the variables was measured, that is; the interrelatedness of one variable to the other by use of the Cronbach's alpha, which consists of the alpha coefficient that ranges from 0 to 1, the value of 0.7 or above indicated that the items rightly measured the variable as reflected in Table 2.

Table 2. Reliability and Principal Components Factor Analysis for Validity of Variables

Variables	No. of Items	Cronbach Alpha	KMO	Bartlett's Test of Sphericity	Average Variance Explained	Sig.
Macro Environmental Factors	5	0.873	0.637	1053.903	0.531	0.000
Industry Market Specific Factors	11	0.721	0.666	2409.021	0.563	0.000
Environmental Specific Factors	7	0.741	0.530	1840.382	0.513	0.000
Small and Medium-sized Enterprises (SMEs) Performance	58	0.878	0.637	29970.798	0.546	0.000
Nigerian Market Environment	27	0.737	0.661	8582.084	0.585	0.000

Source: Field Survey Report

4.8 Methods of Data Analysis

The quantitative method of data analysis was used. It has the advantage of providing accurate results about a phenomenon or a set of activities and facilitates easy hypotheses testing by ensuring easy development of models and theories from empirical data (Bali et al., 2007). Responses were collated, coded and summed up for each of the variables and each of the participant. Descriptive statistical analysis of mean, median, and mode, degree of skewness, standard deviation, and variation was measured using the SPSS 22.0. The result was used to answer the research questions.

The convergent validity of the measurement model was evaluated using construct reliability and standardized factor loading of the observed variables as recommended by Kothari (2004). The fit indices for the final measurement model and the structural model were estimated in line with the recommended cut off values advised by Byme (2016): Chi-square/Degree of freedom < 3.0, Goodness of Fit Index (GFI) > 0.9, Root Mean Residual (RMR) > 0.08, Comparative Fit Index (CFI) > 0.9, Tucker-Lewis Index (TLI) > 0.90, Root Mean Square Error of Approximation(RMSEA) > 0.08.The standardized regression weights of the structural model were used to evaluate hypotheses 1 to 4. The significance tested at 0.01 and 0.05 levels of significances for all other hypotheses. The path analysis of each variable was also done.

5. RESULTS OF THE STUDY

5.1 Response Rate

1102 questionnaires were administered to the owners/managers of selected small and medium scale enterprises in Lagos, Ogun, and Oyo states of South Western, Nigeria to ensure that the sample size would be achieved. 988 copies of questionnaires were correctly completed and returned and this represents a response rate of 89.66% while 114 representing 10.34% of the questionnaire were either not returned or not correctly completed. Table 3 shows the analysis of the questionnaire distribution. This response rate is adequate and sufficient for this kind of research (Isaac & Michael, 1997; Hill, 1998).

Table 3. Analysis of The Questionnaire Distribution

Description	Copies of the Questionnaire			Percentage %
Number of respondents	1,102			
Number of questionnaires distributed		1,102		
Number retrieved			988	89.66%
Number not returned			114	10.34%
Total			1,102	100%

Source: Field Survey Report

5.1 Descriptive Statistics of Nigerian Market Environments and SMEs' Performance

Table 4 shows that SMEs performance has the highest mean of 60.84 and deviation of 6.84 which means there is much disparity between the SMEs in terms of performance. The mean of each of the variables: the SME performance mean is the highest with 60.84 having had the highest number of items followed by the industry market-specific 11.76, environmental specific factors, 10.60 and finally, macro-environmental factors, 10.38. The standard deviation reveals 6.844 for the SMEs performance meaning there is a high deviation from the mean, showing that the performance of the SMEs under study differ greatly from one another. And the industry market-specific factors have the lowest of 1.199 showing that not much variations exist in the industry environment of the SMEs.

Table 4. Descriptive statistics of Nigerian market environments and SMEs performance

Descriptive Statistics			
	Mean	Std. Deviation	N
SMEs' Performance	60.84	6.844	988
Macro Environmental Factors	10.38	2.026	988
Industry Market Specific Factors	11.79	1.199	988
Environmental Firm-Specific Factors	10.60	2.023	988

Source: Field Survey Results

5.3 Demographic Profile of Respondents

Table 5. Demographic Characteristics of Respondents

Variables	Category	Frequency	Percentage
Age	20-30 years	140	14.2%
	31-40 years	696	70.4%
	41-above	152	15.4%
Gender	Male	531	53.7%
	Female	457	46.3%
Education	Primary	7	0.7%
	Secondary	59	6.0%
	University	922	93.3%
Marital Status	Single	209	21.2%
	Married	750	75.9%
	Divorced	29	2.9%
Business Experience	1-5 years	151	15.3%
	6 10 years	621	62.9%
	11-20 years	182	18.4%
	20 and above	34	3.4%
Industry of operation	Retailing	103	10.4%
	Insurance	105	10.6%
	Health Sector	85	8.6%
	Advertising	69	7.0%
	Manufacturing	65	6.6%
	Marketing	81	8.2%
	ICT	71	7.2%
	Fashion	45	4.6%
	Banking	74	7.5%
	Food and Beverages	75	7.6%
	Agriculture	66	6.7%
	Wholesale	59	6.0%
	Entertainment	45	4.6%
	Sport	45	4.6%
State of operation	Oyo	303	30.7%
	Lagos	427	43.2%
	Ogun	258	26.1%
Types of enterprise	Small (10-49 employees)	563	57.0%
	Medium (50-199 employees)	425	43.0%

Source: Field Survey Results

The demographic profile of respondents and its interpretation are presented in Table 5. It showed the frequency distribution and percentages of the respondents as contained in section A of the questionnaire.

Table 5 revealed the demographic characteristics of the respondents; this becomes necessary as Diehl et al. (2018) affirmed that poor socioeconomic conditions raise the strength of the relationship between task performance and citizenship behavior. And also evaluating the age, gender, and educational qualification, Heyden et al. (2018) affirmed that there is a professional similarity between the top and middle management of most enterprises and there is cross-echelon similarity in age and gender characteristics (Bio-demographics). For this study, the majority of the CEOs are young with the age bracket of 31-40years (70.4%) as against 14.2% for 20-30 years and 15.4% for 41 years and above. The majority is male (53.7%). Better performance of the firms is expected, emphasizing the advantage of having young people in an organization. Bonsdorff et al. (2018) affirmed that the company average age (employee ages) was negatively related to company workability and the workability of the company is positively related to company performance. While high involvements work practice was positively related to the company workability. The older a company average age of the employees is less effective and efficient.

The educational qualification revealed that most CEOs are quite educated with 93.3% being university certificated and are married (75.9%). It is expected that the average performance of the firms will be high given the high percentage of university education amongst the CEOs, and as noted by Swift (2018) who emphasized the need for educational and professional proficiency in workplace performance by stating that PhD board members with different professional knowledge are more valuable as board members through their level and the depth of contribution to the decision making. Similarly, the quality of decision of the CEOs understudy is expected to be high.

The business experience of the CEOs varies; it spanned 6-10 years (62.9%),1-5years (15.3%) and 11-20years (18.4%), 20years and above (3.4%). This shows that a greater percentage of the CEOs have surpassed the 5thyear anniversary mark for failure as noted by SMEDAN (2012)'s study. The Insurance and Retail industries had the highest respondents (105, 10.6%; 103, 10.4%) while Fashion, Entertainment and Sport had the lowest (45, 4.6%) each.

The general spread of the industries from which the respondents were drawn is expected to enhance the generalization of the findings. Lagos State had the highest number of respondents of 427 which is 43.2% against 303 (30.7%) of Oyo state and 258 (26.1%) of Ogun state because of the higher industrial presence in the state. And finally, the businesses were defined by the number of employees' small businesses (10-49) and the medium businesses (50-199).

Table 6. Regression model of selected Nigerian Market Environments and SMEs' Performance

Model Summary[b]					
Model	**R**	**R Square**	**Adjusted R Square**	**Std. Error of the Estimate**	**Durbin-Watson**
1	.-556[a]	.309	.307	5.696	1.522
a. Predictors: (Constant), Environmental Specific Factors, Industry Market Specific, Factors					
b. Dependent Variable: SMEs' Performance					

Source: Field Survey Results

5.4 Inferential Statistics

5.4.1 Regression Analysis of Effects of Nigerian Market Environment on SMEs' Performance

Table 6 shows the regression model of selected Nigerian market environments and SMEs performance. The Adjusted R square is 0.307 meaning 30.7% of the variation observed in SMEs' performance is accounted for by the Nigerian market environment. This is statistically significant as shown in table 7 with F (3,985) =146.915, ρ=0.00.

Table 8 shows the Regression model (b) of the selected Nigerian Market Environments and SMEs' performance. The different effects that each component of the Nigerian Market Environment have on the SMEs' performance are; Macro-environmental factors ($\beta = -.60$, $\rho < 0.05$) showing that the macro-environment has a negative and significant effect on the SMEs' performance. It also showed that one

Table 7. Analysis of Variance of selected Nigerian Market Environments and SMEs' Performance

ANOVA[a]						
Model		Sum of Squares	df	Mean Square	F	Sig.
1	Regression	14302.084	3	4767.361	146.915	.000[b]
	Residual	31930.649	984	32.450		
	Total	46232.733	987			
a. Dependent Variable: SMEs' Performance						
b. Predictors: (Constant), Environmental Specific Factors, Industry Market Specific, Factors						

Source: Field Survey Results

Table 8. Regression model (b) of selected Nigerian Market Environments and SMEs' Performance

Coefficients[a]								
Model		Unstandardized Coefficients		Standardized Coefficients	T	Sig.	Co-linearity Statistics	
		B	Std. Error	Beta			Tolerance	VIF
1	Constant	24.356	1.896		12.843	.000		
	Macro Environmental Factors	-.203	.098	-.600	-12.078	.038	.842	1.187
	Industry Market Specific factors	-1.919	.159	-.336	-12.072	.000	.905	1.105
	Environmental Firm Specific Factors	1.108	.099	.328	11.192	.000	.819	1.220
a. Dependent Variable: SMEs' Performance								

Source: Field Survey Results

unit increase in the macro-environmental factors caused 0.60-unit decrease in SMEs' performance. This is a reflection of the degree of turbulence of the Nigerian market environment.

The industry market-specific factors have $\beta = -0.336$, $\rho < 0.05$ indicating an inverse and significant effect of the industry market-specific factors on SMEs' performance. It also showed that a unit increase in industry-specific factors causes a 0.336-unit decrease in SMEs' performance. However, the Environmental Firm-Specific factors have positive and significant effects on the SMEs' performance ($\beta = 0.328$, $\rho < 0.05$). It also shows that a one-unit increase in Environmental Firm-Specific factors leads to a 0.328 unit increase in SMEs' performance. The positivity of this effect is understandable from the point of view that this is the only factor of the environment that is controllable, the other two environmental factors are uncontrollable; macro and industry environments. A similar result was obtained through path dependencies measure results in table 9 and figure 2, additionally figure 2 showed that the macro environment has the highest path effects on the Nigerian market environment (β=.87). Hence the overall effects of the Nigerian Market environment on the SMEs' performance was negative (R= -.56).

Given that:
Macro-Environmental Factors = MEF
Industry Market Specific Factors = IMSF
Environmental Firm-Specific Factors = EFSF
SMEs' Performance = SMEP
The regression model is:
SMEP = 24.356-.600 MEF-.336 IMSF + .328 EFSF

Table 9. Results of Path Analysis

Proposed Hypothesis Relationship	Hypothesis	Path coefficient estimates	Decision
Macro-environment factors→ SMEs' Performance	H_1	-0.60	Accepted
Industry market-specific factors → SMEs' Performance	H_2	-0.34	Accepted
Environmental Firm-Specific Market → SMEs' Performance	H_3	0.33	Accepted
Nigerian Market Environment → SMEs' Performance	H_4	-0.56	Accepted

Source: Field Survey Results

6. SOLUTIONS AND RECOMMENDATIONS

Both the macro environment and the industry environment show a negative relationship with SMEs' performance, this indicates that the lower the intensity of this environment in terms of volatility, uncertainty, complexity and ambiguity the better the performance of SMEs. This is so because the factors in these two environments are uncontrollable (Schoemaker et al., 2018). However, the firm-specific factors have positive effects on the SMEs performance, apart from being controllable, it relates directly with the availability of resources in the firm.

Figure 2. Path Analysis

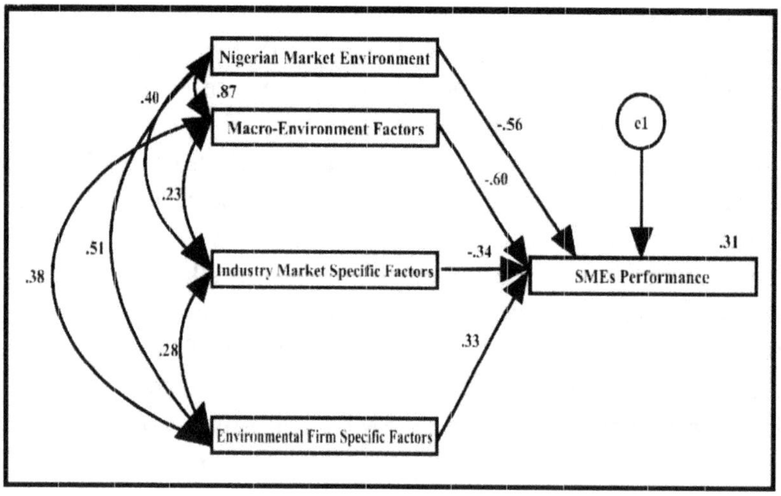

The Dynamic Capability Theory argues that the SMEs possess intangible resources like knowledge and skills that could be configured and reconfigured continuously and adapted to changes in the environment to achieve competitive advantage which dovetails into better performance (Poulis et al., 2013) which means there would be congruence between the changing environment and the SMEs' portfolio of activities. But, before this congruence is formed there is bound to be negative effects of the environment on the SMEs' performance as seen in this study. For the organization for the environment fit to be formed, the firm needs to upgrade ordinary capabilities in line with the changes in the environment. This upgrade may not be too easy with the SMEs' because of the resource poverty, lack of current knowledge, skills and experience (Juma & Sequeria, 2017).

The findings of this study concur with the works of Akinbogun (2008), Awino (2011), and Khoury & Prasad (2015) that assert that the Nigerian SMEs has been performing below expectations because of the unfavorable external environment. The environmental factors have also affected the business strategy formulation and implementation and abilities of the firms to mobilize resources.

The positive effects of the firm-specific factors can be explained from dynamic capability which believed that firms could use their configured resources in such a way as to arrest the changes in the environment. So, the SMEs will be able to arrest the volatility, uncertainty, complexity and ambiguity in the environment as they deploy their resources profitably thus facilitating better performance.

These findings align with Tutar et al. (2015) that affirm that profitable business strategies can arrest the dynamism of the business environment; other researchers like Agwu & Emeti (2014) and Eruemegbe (2015) establish a positive relationship between business environment and performance which are contrary to the findings of this study. Soriano (2010) and Okpara & Wynn (2007) also believe that SMEs will perform better when they could change management styles as the environment changes no matter the degree of negativity.

The following recommendations are made based on the findings and conclusion of this study:

- The macro-environment is revealed to have a negative effect on the performance of the SMEs, it is therefore imperative that SMEs' operators must put in place an Environmental Assessment

Management Strategy(EAMS) that will facilitate the continuous assessment of the effects of the environment on the business parameters through effective environmental scanning, forecasting, and impact measurements. It is recommended that a department should be set up to manage this function and a weekly report submitted to ensure adequate integration into the decision making framework.

- The industry market-specific factors also had a negative effect on the performance of the SMEs'. This could be reversed through effective Market Re-Positioning Strategy (MREPS) through assessments of the features of the products or services and identifying areas where the firms have a competitive advantage within the industry and the features that engender these advantages, and thus repositioning the service or products in line with these advantages. By this method, there will be a realignment of forces within the industry in favor of the firms.
- The environmental firm-specific factors have positive effects on the SMEs' performance, these factors could be re-engineered to facilitate better performance since all these factors are controllable. A Factor Resource Management (FACReM) strategy will help through resource generation and allocation to factors of immense importance or with higher effects on performance. Such factors are thus enhanced to facilitate better performance.

7. FUTURE RESEARCH DIRECTIONS

The selected Nigerian environment was operationally defined following the prevailing situations in the research context and the existing literature. Other studies could redefine the Nigerian market environment based on industries' characteristics and peculiarities.

Comparative studies on other countries in Africa and what factors impact SMEs' performance should be conducted. It would be good to contrast and see common factors in countries and unique factors affecting SMEs performance.

Innovation as a key driver of SMEs' performance in the 4thindustrial revolution should also be examined. This will add to the knowledge gap on this theme in Africa.

8. CONCLUSION

SMEs' are very important to any economy. However, they operate in an environment that is volatile, uncertain, complex and ambiguous. This necessitates the need to align the organizational resources and capabilities in such a way as to contain these complexities. The study revealed that the environmental firm-specific factors had positive and significant effects on SMEs' performance, while the macro and industry environments had negative and significant effects on SMEs performance. Three different studies in Kenya revealed similar results; Bowen et al.(2009), Suh (2010), and Yusuf & Dansu (2013) reported that Kenyan SMEs performance was grossly affected by the business environment, to the extent that it reduced the contribution to GDP to 18%.

Given the findings of this study, it could be inferred that the failure experienced by these firms in the time past may be partly due to the volatile, uncertain, complex and ambiguous nature of the environment. More so, that the macro and industry environments had negative effects on SMEs' performance, this implies that the higher the intensity of the environment the lower the performance of the SMEs. The implication is that for the SMEs to enhance performance there is a need to reduce the unpredictability of the macro and industry environment, if this is impossible then, they may need to reconfigure their capabilities to align with the variability of the environment.

It is important to note that the three components of the market environment used in this study did not have the same effects on the performance of SMEs. Hence management should note that the styles needed to arrest the impact of these components may differ. The macro-environment due to its' uncontrollability should be constantly assessed and forecasted to reduce its' negative effects on the performance of the SMEs.

The study revealed that the macro environment of business is affected by the performance of the SMEs in a negative manner. This implies that the macro environment of the business was unfavorable which could be traced to instability in government policies, abnormality in the functionality of all relevant regulatory bodies and mechanisms. It is noted that the more the activities of the regulatory bodies become aligned with the performance objectives of SMEs, the more favorable the market environment is likely to be and the less unpredictable the macro environment. The market environment of business could be brought closer to the SMEs operators if stable government policies are enthroned and the effectiveness of various agencies serving the SMEs are investigated. The less effective these agencies are, the more vulnerable the SMEs are.

SMEs need to undertake strategic modifications that would facilitate proper environmental assessments particularly forecasting of the demand and competitive intensity apart from proper monitoring of industry/market trends.

REFERENCES

Adelegan, O. (2011). Infrastructure deficiencies and investment in manufacturing firms in Nigeria. *Journal of Economics & International Finance*, *3*(9), 542–552.

Adeola, A. (2016). Impact of external business environment on organization performance of Small and Medium-sized Enterprises (SMEs) in Osun State, Nigeria. *Scholedge International Journal of Business Policy & Governance*, *3*(10), 155–166.

Agwu, M. O., & Emeti, C. I. (2014). Issues, challenges and prospects of small and medium scale enterprises (Small and Medium-sized Enterprises (SMEs)) in Port-Harcourt City, Nigeria. *European Journal of Sustainable Development*, *3*(1), 101–114. doi:10.14207/ejsd.2014.v3n1p101

Akinbogun, T. L. (2008). The impact of Nigerian business environment on the survival of small scale ceramic industries. Journal of Asia &. *African Studies*, *43*(6), 663–679.

Al-Asheq. A. & MdUzzal H. (2019). SME performance: impact of market, customer and brand orientation. Academy of Marketing Studies Journal, 23(1), 1-9.

Aladejebi, O., & Oladimeji, J. O. (2019). The impact of record keeping on the performance of selected small and medium enterprises in Lagos Metropolis. *Journal of Small Business & Entrepreneurship Development*, *7*(1), 28–40. doi:10.15640/jsbed.v7n1a3

Aragon-Sanchez, A. & Sanchez-Marin, G. (2005). Strategic orientation, management characteristics and performance: A study of Spanish Small and Medium-sized Enterprises (SMEs). *Journal of Small Business Management*, *43*(3), 287–308. doi:10.1111/j.1540-627X.2005.00138.x

Arasa, R. & K'Obonyo, P. (2012). The relationship between strategic planning and firm performance. *International Journal of Humanities and Social Science*, 2(22), 201–213.

Arend, R. J., & Bromiley, P. (2009). Assessing the dynamic capabilities view: Spare change everyone? *Strategic Organization*, *7*(1), 75–90. doi:10.1177/1476127008100132

Asikhia, O., & Naidoo, V. (2020a). Assessment of the moderating effects of Nigerian market environment on the relationship between management success determinants and Small and Medium-sized Enterprises (SMEs)' performance. *Problems and Perspectives in Management*, *18*(4), 1–14. doi:10.21511/ppm.18(4).2020.31

Asikhia, O., & Naidoo, V. (2020b). Small and Medium-sized Enterprises (SMEs) management success determinants and its implications on their performance in South West, Nigeria. *International Journal of Economics & Business Administration*, *8*(4), 1057–1072. doi:10.35808/ijeba/650

Asikhia, O. U. (2016). Small and Medium-sized Enterprises (SMEs) wealth creation and poverty alleviation in Nigeria. *Journal of Economics and Behavioral Studies*, *8*(4), 17–31. doi:10.22610/jebs.v8i4(J).1360

Asikhia, O. U., Fasola, I. O., Makinde, G. O., & Akinlabi, B. H. (2020). Business Credit Affordability and Revenue Growth of Small and Medium Scale Enterprises: Evidence from Southwest, Nigeria. *IOSR Journal of Business and Management*, *22*(3), 24–37.

Atsegbua, K. (2002). *Changing Organization: Essays on the Development and Evaluation of Human Organization*. McGraw-Hill.

Awino, B. Z. (2011). Strategic management: An empirical investigation of selected strategy variables on firms: A study of supply chain management in large private manufacturing firms in Kenya. *Prime Journals*, *1*(1), 9–18.

Ayegha, O., & Omale, S. (2016). A study on factors affecting entrepreneurial development in Nigeria. *European Journal of Business and Management*, *8*(12), 43–51.

Bali, N. P., Gupta, P. N., & Gandhi, C. P. (2007). *A textbook of quantitative techniques*. Firewall Media.

Baumann, O., Schmidt, J., & Stieglitz, N. (2018). Effective search in rugged performance landscapes: A review and outlook. *Journal of Management*, *45*(1), 285–318. doi:10.1177/0149206318808594

Bhattacherjee, A. (2012). Social Science Research: Principles, Methods and Practices (2nd ed.). Global Text Project.

Blumberg, B. F., Cooper, D. R., & Schindler, P. S. (2014). *Business research methods*. McGraw-Hill Education.

Bonsdorff, M. E., Zhou, L., Wang, M., Vanhala, S., von Bonsdorff, M. B., & Rantanen, T. (2018). Employee age and company performance: An integrated model of aging and human resource management practices. *Journal of Management*, *44*(8), 3124–3150. doi:10.1177/0149206316662314

Boso, N., Adeleye, I., Ibeh, K., & Chizema, A. (2019). The internationalization of African firms: Opportunities, challenges and risks. *Thunderbird International Business Review*, *61*(1), 5–12. doi:10.1002/tie.21977

Bowen, M., Morara, M., & Mureithi, M. (2009). Management of business challenges among small and Microenterprises in Nairobi-Kenya. KCA. *Journal of Business and Management*, *2*(1), 16–31.

Byme, B. M. (2016). *Structural equation models with AMOS: Basic concepts, applications, and programming (3rd ed.)*. Routledge.

CAC. (2017). *Corporate Affairs Commission business directory*. Macmillan.

Chidermbaran, K. & Alageppon, V.C. (2017). *Business environment*. Vikas Publishing Houseput Ltd.

Cicea, C., Popa, I., Marinescu, C., & Simona, C. Ş. (2019). Determinants of Small and Medium-sized Enterprises (SMEs)' performance: Evidence from European countries. *Economic Research Journal*, *32*(1), 1602–1620.

Collins, D. J. (1994). Research note: How valuable are organizational capabilities? *Strategic Management Journal*, *15*(S1), 143–152. doi:10.1002mj.4250150910

Connelly, L. M. (2008). Pilot studies. *Medsurg Nursing*, *17*(6), 411–412. PMID:19248407

Cooper, D., & Schindler, P. (2006). *Research Methods*. McGraw-Hill.

Davis, J. G. (2004). Capabilities: A different perspective. *Australian Journal of Management*, *29*(1), 1–44. doi:10.1177/031289620402900108

del Pilar, E. C., Alegado, I., & Bongo, M. F. (2019). Structural relationships among critical failure factors of micro-businesses. *Journal of Small Business and Enterprise Development*, *27*(1), 148–174. doi:10.1108/JSBED-01-2019-0001

Di-Stefano, G., Peteraf, M. & Verona, G. (2010). Dynamic capabilities deconstructed: A bibliographic investigation into the origins, development, and future directions of the research domain. *Industrial and Corporate Change*, *19*(14), 1187–1204.

Diehl, M.-R., Richter, A., & Sarnecki, A. (2018). Variations in employee performance in response to organizational justice: The sensitizing effect of socioeconomic conditions. *Journal of Management*, *44*(6), 2375–2404. doi:10.1177/0149206316671581

Dinh, C. N. (2011). *Performance of small and medium enterprises and the impact of environmental variables: Evidence from Vietnam* [Unpublished Doctoral Thesis]. Aston University, Birmingham, UK.

Ekakitie–Emonena, S. (2019). Managing turbulent business environments in Nigeria: A model approach. Journal of Education, Society &. *Behavioral Science*, *29*(3), 1–11.

Eniola, A. A., & Ektebang, H. (2014). SME firms performance in Nigeria: Competitive Advantage and its impact. *International Journal of Research Studies in Management*, *3*(2), 75–86. doi:10.5861/ijrsm.2014.854

Enu, P., & Havi, E. D. K. (2014). Macroeconomic determinants of inflation in Ghana: A co-integration approach. *International Journal of Academic Research & Social Sciences*, *4*(7), 95–110. doi:10.6007/IJARBSS/v4-i7/993

Eruemegbe, G. O. (2015). Impact of business environment on organizational performance in Nigeria: A study of Union Bank of Nigeria. *European Scientific Journal*, *11*(10), 478–494.

Eze, O., & Ogiji, F. (2013). Impact of fiscal policy on manufacturing sector output in Nigeria: An error correction analysis. *International Journal of Business & Management Review*, *1*(3), 35–55.

Ferdinand, J., Graca, M., Antonacopoulou, E. & Easterby-Smith, M. (2004). *Dynamic capability: tracking the development of a concept.* In 5thEuropean Conference on Organizational Knowledge, Learning, and Capabilities, Innsbruck, UK.

Fernando, A. C. (2011). *Business environment.* Dorling Kindersley.

Frank, H., Güttel, W., & Kessler, A. (2017). Environmental dynamism, hostility, and dynamic capabilities in medium-sized enterprises. *International Journal of Entrepreneurship and Innovation*, *18*(3), 185–194. doi:10.1177/1465750317723219

Gadenne, D. (1998). Critical success factors for small business: An inter-industry comparison. *International Small Business Journal*, *17*(1), 36–57. doi:10.1177/0266242698171002

Gado, N., & Nmadu, T. (2011). The performance of textile companies in the North-West zone of Nigeria: The role of Infrastructure as a resource. *International Journal of Human Resource Studies*, *2*(1), 89–100. doi:10.5296/ijhrs.v2i1.1259

Greener, S. (2008). *Business Research Methods.* Ventus Publishing.

Herzog, M. A. (2008). Considerations in determining sample size for pilot studies. *Research in Nursing & Health*, *30*(2), 180–191. doi:10.1002/nur.20247 PMID:18183564

Heyden, M. L. M., Sidhu, J. S., & Volberda, H. W. (2018). The conjoint influence of top and middle management characteristics on management innovation. *Journal of Management*, *44*(4), 1505–1529. doi:10.1177/0149206315614373

Hill, R. (1998). What sample size is 'enough' in internet survey research? *Interpersonal Computing and Technology. An Electronic Journal for the 21st Century*, *6*(3-4), 1-10.

Ibidunni, O. S., & Ogundele, O. J. K. (2013). Competition in marketing survival yardstick for Small and Medium-sized Enterprises (SMEs) in Nigeria. *Mediterranean Journal of Social Sciences*, *4*(1), 231–240.

Igwe, P. A., Amaugo, A. N., Ogundana, O. M., Egere, O. M., & Anigbo, J. A. (2018). Factors affecting the investment climate, Small and Medium-sized Enterprises (SMEs) productivity and entrepreneurship in Nigeria. *European Journal of Sustainable Development*, *7*(1), 182–200. doi:10.14207/ejsd.2018.v7n1p182

Isaac, S., & Michael, W. B. (1995). *Handbook in research and evaluation.* Educational and Industrial Testing Services.

Jayeola, O., Ihinmoyan, T., & Kazeem, Y. K. (2018). Environmental factors and the performance of micro and small scale enterprises (MSEs) in Nigeria: Lessons from some selected MSEs in Ondo State Nigeria. Journal of Economics. *Management & Trade, 21*(6), 1–14. doi:10.9734/JEMT/2018/42079

Julious, S. A. (2005). Sample size of 12 per group rule of thumb for a pilot study. *Pharmaceutical Statistics, 4*(4), 287–291. doi:10.1002/pst.185

Juma, N., & Sequeria, J. M. (2017). Effects of entrepreneur's individual factors and environmental contingencies on venture performance: A case study of African American women-owned ventures. *Journal of Small Business and Entrepreneurship, 29*(2), 91–119. doi:10.1080/08276331.2016.1248276

Khoury, T. A., & Prasad, A. (2015). Entrepreneurship amid concurrent institutional constraints in less developed countries. *Business & Society, 55*(7), 934–969. doi:10.1177/0007650314567641

Kothari, C. R. (2004). *Research methodology: methods and techniques*. New Age International Limited.

Krejcie, R., & Morgan, D. (1970). Determining sample size for research activities. *Educational and Psychological Measurement, 30*(3), 607–610. doi:10.1177/001316447003000308

Laosebikan, J. S., Ogunni, B. O., & Ogunlusi, C. F. (2013). Evaluation of time management for growth and development in developing economies: Nigerian experience. *International Journal of Innovative Research and Development, 2*(7), 490–496.

Lee, Y. A. (2014). Insight for writing qualitative research paper. *Family and Consumer Sciences Research Journal, 43*(1), 94–97. doi:10.1111/fcsr.12084

Leick, B. (2016). Institutional entrepreneurs and small firms: How firm practices are being shaped in the context of demographic transformations. *Journal of Small Business and Entrepreneurship, 29*(1), 1–24. doi:10.1080/08276331.2016.1248055

Machuki, V. N., & Aosa, E. (2011). *The influence of the external business environment on the performance of publicly quoted companies in Kenya* [Unpublished Doctoral Dissertation]. University of Nairobi Kenya.

Mafundu, R. H., & Mafini, C. (2019). Internal constraints to business performance in black-owned small to medium enterprises in the construction industry. *Southern African Journal of Entrepreneurship & Small Business Management, 11*(1), 1–10. doi:10.4102ajesbm.v11i1.165

Manufacturing Association of Nigeria. (2016). *Report*. Macmillian.

Menguc, B., Auh, S., & Ozanne, L. (2010). The interactive effect of internal and external factors on a proactive environmental strategy and its influence on a firm's performance. *Journal of Business Ethics, 94*(2), 279–298. doi:10.100710551-009-0264-0

Muogbo, U. S., & Chuka, E.-U. (2019). Environmental factors: A panacea for survival and growth of small and medium scale businesses in Nigeria. *International Journal of Business & Management Invention, 8*(3), 30–40. doi:10.2139srn.3432188

Muritala, T. A., Awolaja, A. M., & Bako, Y. A. (2012). Impact of small and medium enterprises on economic growth and development. *American Journal of Business and Management, 1*(1), 18–22.

Oginni, B. O., & Adesanya, A. S. (2013). Business environmental factors: Implications on the survival and growth of business organizations in the manufacturing sector of Lagos metropolis. *Business & Management Research*, *2*(3), 146–155. doi:10.5430/bmr.v2n3p146

Okpara, J., & Wynn, P. (2007). Determinants of small business growth constraints in a sub-Sahara African economy. *S.A.M. Advanced Management Journal*, *72*(2), 24–35.

Olughor, R. J. (2015). Effect of innovation on the performance of Small and Medium-sized Enterprises (SMEs) organizations in Nigeria. *Management*, *5*(3), 90–95.

Planing, P. (2017). On the origin of innovations-the opportunity vacuum as a conceptual model for the explanation of innovation. *Journal of Innovation & Entrepreneurship*, *6*(5), 1–18. doi:10.118613731-017-0063-2

Porter, M. E. (1985). *Competitive Strategy*. Free press.

Poulis, E., Poulis, K., & Christodoulou, I. (2013). *Developing dynamic capabilities to address 'mutating' forces. Track: dynamic capabilities: Theoretical Approaches and Practical Applications'. European Academy of Management*. EURAM.

Sadiku-Dushia, N., Leo-Paul, D., & Veland, R. (2019). Entrepreneurial marketing dimensions and Small and Medium-sized Enterprises (SMEs) performance. *Journal of Business Research*, *100*, 86–99. doi:10.1016/j.jbusres.2019.03.025

Schilke, O. (2014). On the contingent value of dynamic capabilities for competitive advantage: The nonlinear moderating effect of environmental dynamism. *Strategic Management Journal*, *35*(2), 179–203. doi:10.1002mj.2099

Schoemaker, P. J., Heaton, S., & Teece, D. (2018). Innovation, dynamic capabilities, and leadership. *California Management Review*, *61*(1), 15–42. doi:10.1177/0008125618790246

SMEDAN. (2012). *Small and Medium Enterprises Development Agency of Nigeria*. Survey report on MSmall and Medium-sized Enterprises (SMEs) in Nigeria.

SMEDAN. (2016). *Small and Medium Enterprises Development Agency of Nigeria*. Survey report on MSmall and Medium-sized Enterprises (SMEs) in Nigeria.

SMEDAN. (2017). *Small and Medium Enterprises Development Agency of Nigeria*. Survey report on MSmall and Medium-sized Enterprises (SMEs) in Nigeria.

Soriano, D. R. (2010). Management factors affecting the performance of technology firms. *Journal of Business Research*, *63*(5), 463–470. doi:10.1016/j.jbusres.2009.04.003

Suh, F. D. (2010). Risks and opportunities facing Small and Medium-sized Enterprises (SMEs) in the post-crisis Era [Paper Presentation]. The APEC Small and Medium-sized Enterprises (SMEs) training workshop, Taipei, Korea.

Swift, T. (2018). PhD scientists in the boardroom: The innovation impact. *Journal of Strategy & Management*, *11*(2), 184–202. doi:10.1108/JSMA-06-2017-0040

Tahir, F. A., & Inuwa, F. U. (2019). Empirical investigation of the factors affecting micro, small and medium scale enterprises performance in Borno State, Nigeria. *International Business Research*, *12*(4), 30–39. doi:10.5539/ibr.v12n4p30

Teece, D. J., & Pisano, G. (1994). The dynamic capabilities of firms: An introduction. *Industrial and Corporate Change*, *3*(3), 537–556. doi:10.1093/icc/3.3.537-a

Teece, D. J., Pisano, G., & Shuen, A. (1997). Dynamic capabilities and strategic management. *Strategic Management Journal*, *18*(7), 509–533. doi:10.1002/(SICI)1097-0266(199708)18:7<509::AID-SMJ882>3.0.CO;2-Z

Thanos, I. C., Dimitratos, P., & Sapouna, P. (2017). The implications of international entrepreneurial orientation, politicization, and hostility upon SME international performance. *International Small Business Journal*, *35*(4), 495–514. doi:10.1177/0266242616641749

Thibault, M., Wilcock, A., & Kanetker, U. (2002). An exploratory study of factors influencing sales performance of Small and Medium-sized Enterprises (SMEs). *Proceedings of the administrative sciences association of Canada.*

Treece, E. W., & Treece, J. W. (1982). *Elements of Research in Nursing* (3rd ed.). Mosby.

Tutar, H., Nart, S., & Bingöl, D. (2015). The effect of strategic orientations on innovation capabilities and market performance: The case of ASEM. *Procedia: Social and Behavioral Sciences*, *207*, 709–719. doi:10.1016/j.sbspro.2015.10.144

Van-Belle, G. (2002). Statistical rules of thumb. John Wiley.

Wang, C., & Rafiq, M. (2014). Ambidextrous organizational culture, contextual ambidexterity and new product innovation: A comparative study of U.K and Chinese high tech firms. *British Journal of Management*, *25*(1), 58–76. doi:10.1111/j.1467-8551.2012.00832.x

Winter, S. (2003). Understanding dynamic capabilities. *Strategic Management Journal*, *24*(10), 991–995. doi:10.1002mj.318

World Bank Report. (2019). *Data and Report on Nigeria.* World Bank Group.

Yusuf, T. O., & Dansu, F. S. (2013). Small and Medium-sized Enterprises (SMEs), business risk and sustainability in Nigeria. *European Journal of Business & Social Sciences*, *2*(9), 76–94.

Zahra, S. A., Sapienza, H. J., & Davidsson, P. (2006). Entrepreneurship and dynamic capabilities: A review model and research agenda. *Journal of Management Studies*, *43*(2), 917–955. doi:10.1111/j.1467-6486.2006.00616.x

Zhu, Y., Gardner, D. G., & Chen, H. (2018). Relationships between work team climate, individual motivation, and creativity. *Journal of Management*, *44*(5), 2094–2115. doi:10.1177/0149206316638161

KEY TERMS AND DEFINITIONS

Business Environment: It is a combination of all factors both controllable and uncontrollable that affect the performance of a firm.

Business Failure: It defines the inability of firms to meet performance targets and satisfy the stakeholders profitably.

Environmental Turbulence: High degree of uncontrollability of the environment.

Industry Market Specific Factors: These are market uncontrollable factors operational in the immediate environment of the business.

Macro-Environment: Are the uncontrollable factors external to the business unit.

Nigeria: It is a West African country and the venues of the research.

Organizational Performance: It is a measure of the accomplishment of the set objectives of a firm.

Small and Medium Development Agency of Nigeria: This is a government agency that coordinates the activities of the Small and Medium Enterprises in Nigeria.

Small and Medium-Sized Enterprises (SMEs): These are operational Small and Medium Enterprises in Nigeria.

Chapter 15
Key Drivers of Performance and Profitability in a Social Business

Daisy Isabella van Steenbergen
Fernando Pessoa University, Portugal

Paulo Graça Ramos
Fernando Pessoa University, Portugal

Bruno Barbosa Sousa
https://orcid.org/0000-0002-8588-2422
Polytechnic Institute of Cávado and Ave, Portugal & CiTUR, Portugal & UNIAG, Portugal

ABSTRACT

In order to build a successful strategy for any type of business, a strategic analysis needs to be performed. A strategic analysis consists of multiple elements, but it always starts with environmental scanning. This research focuses on that very first step by conducting an environmental analysis. It is a strategic tool that identifies all the external and internal elements, which could possibly affect the organization's performance. The aim of this research was not to provide all the final and conclusive answers. It was merely to explore the research topic with varying levels of depth. Additionally, this research tended to tackle new problems on which little or no previous research has been done by combining and elaborating well-known models, such as PESTEL, Porter´s 5 forces, and SWOT. The research problem of this chapter can be described as to determine the possibilities of starting a successful commercial business within the social welfare sector of Portugal.

INTRODUCTION

Is it possible for a private commercial business to gain a place within the Portuguese social care system? Due to current vulnerabilities within the social sector, as well as the economy, the sustainability of this sector is being questioned and for that reason it is a good time to explore new possibilities and opportunities. The aim of this chapter is to execute an environmental analysis that differentiates four layers, based

DOI: 10.4018/978-1-7998-7951-0.ch015

on the technique from Johnson et al. (2018) in order to create a complete vision on the social sector of Portugal. Based on those layers, the research objectives have been established. The first layer concerns the macro - environment, focusing on the broad environmental factors that impact to a greater or lesser extent on almost all organisations.

- **Objective 1:** To establish a benchmark between Portugal and the Netherlands in order to identify the general factors that play a major part on a macro - level basis when starting a new business in the social sector of Portugal. To achieve this, the PESTEL tool will be applied. Continuously on the next layer, attention is moved to the sector and its competitive forces. Here, objective 2 is applicable.
- **Objective 2:** To scan the Portuguese social sector together with its competitors to classify the financial mechanism that allows the business to be profitable. The model of Porter's 5 forces is implemented to obtain a picture of the main forces that shape this sector within Portugal. Additionally, the power - interest matrix will be applied to identify key stakeholders and their influence on the business. Thirdly, the layer of direct competitors together with market segments, where we define the third objective.
- **Objective 3:** To focus on direct competitors and to look for unexploited opportunities as well as 'black holes' by looking at the market segment and defining the differences in customer's needs. Finally, it is important to apply the information on the organisation itself to understand where strengths and weaknesses lie. This brings us to the fourth and final objective.
- **Objective 4:** To describe the critical factors of success for this organisation and based on those factors, to identify the main constrains and opportunities for the business by means of a dynamic SWOT analysis. Further recommendations and the conclusion of this research will also be implemented in this final chapter.

BACKGROUND

Building a Strategy

The basics for thinking and decision - making are perception and cognition together with the gathering and analysing of information. These factors will form the footing of this research, where an environmental analysis will be performed in order to formulate the strategy for a profitable social business in Portugal. The first two chapters derive from a literature review about the processes of strategic and environmental analysis. An environmental analysis is always performed as a base for the strategic analysis. As it is important to understand where it leads to, there will first follow an indication of the strategic analysis process. Chapter I will contain a description of the steps, the mission, vision, and values and finally the three phases a strategic analysis exists of. Strategic analysis comes from strategy. As it is described by Henderson, the concept of strategy can be traced in ancient times with the central idea being: to gain advantage over someone or something (Henderson, 1989). According to the perspective of Johnson et al. (2008), strategy is the direction and scope of an organisation over the long term. Their definition has other concerns besides the planning process, it also pays special attention to the main players in the internal and external environment of the organisation. Mintzberg (1992) defines strategy as follows: as a ''plan'', strategy is seen as a guideline to deal with a situation. Furthermore, as a ''ploy'', because it is a specific 'manoeuvre' intended to outwit an opponent or competitor. As a ''pattern'', as it is consistent in behaviour, whether or not intended. As a ''position'', because strategy can be seen as a means of locating an organisation in an 'environment' and as a ''perspective'', it is chosen position, and an ingrained way of perceiving the world (Mintzberg, 1992).

Each of these definitions deals with a specific aspect of the organisation and they complement each other. The next step would be to look at these strategies as plans, doing so, two essential characteristics arise: they are made in advance of actions and they are developed consciously and purposefully (Mintzberg, 1992). With other words, strategic analysis refers to the process of conducting research on a company and its environment to formulate a strategy, in this case it concerns a start - up company, which does not exist yet.

The definition of strategic analysis can differ between an academic or business perspective, but every book and paper indicates that the process involves the following common factors: Identifying and evaluating data relevant to the company's strategy; Defining the internal and external environments to be analysed; Applying the usage of several analytic methods and tools, such as SWOT analysis, PESTEL analysis, and Porter's five Forces (CFI, 2019). To specify further, Poole indicates that the strategic planning process can be seen as a continuous cycle in which the activities occur simultaneously or in varying order (Poole, 1990).'' He describes the following elements or activities: Environment scanning; Developing a mission statement; Setting goals and objectives; Developing implementation plans; Implementing plans; Monitoring the progress; and Formal evaluation.

Due to the limitations of this research it is not possible to execute all of these steps. It is, however, important to name the continuous steps and perhaps keep them in mind for a follow - up research. In the continuation of this research, the first step of environment scanning will be deliberated. As it concerns a start - up, the vision, mission and values have not yet been written. These will be based on what is achievable, what is necessary and what is desired, given by the outcome of this research. This will mainly depend on the wishes and desires of the management, but also on the requirements from key stakeholders.

For example, the company can have the mission to offer services for people with money problems, but if those people are not open to receive the services for whatever reason, the mission is not applicable with its stakeholders, in this case its client base, and therefore won't be sustainable for the future of the company. Thus, to prevent mistakes from happening and be well prepared, executing an environment analysis is fundamental. Lastly, each strategy analysis is composed of multiple phases and different authors describe different phases. Wright et al. identifies three phases within strategic management for the development of business strategies, which are: Strategy formulation: formulation of corporate, business, and functional strategies that will match the organisation's strengths, and weaknesses with its environment's opportunities and threats. Strategy implementation: implement strategies. Strategic control: activities to ensure that the organisation's goals are attainted (Wright, Pringle, & Kroll, 1992).

These three phases are more difficult to apply on this research as it concerns a start - up company and thus the implementation and control cannot be executed. For that reason, it has been decided to also evaluate the three phases described by Johnson, Scholes and Wellington (2008): Strategic position; Strategic choices; Strategy in action.

There are many definitions of the concept 'strategy'. In order to come up with a solid strategy, a strategic analysis needs to be conducted. Conclusively, to formulate the mission, vision and values, three phases need to be performed. First of all, the strategic position that indicates four forces in order to come up with a strategy. It indicates an evaluation of the environment, the strategic capability, the strategic purpose and the culture. Secondly, the overarching strategic choices that need to be made by answering the three questions: How does the organisation position itself in relation to its competitors? Should the scope of the company be broader or smaller, when considering the products and markets? And finally, how will the strategies be pursued? The third and final phase, is the phase of implementation, where the formulated strategy will be implemented and also its development will be considered. Looking at strategic analysis, it has become clear that it starts with an environmental analysis. Especially if the aim is to start up a profitable business in the social sector, an extensive environmental analysis can be considered key. The next section will enlighten what an environmental analysis consists of.

Environmental Analysis Process

After evaluating how a company's strategy is built, it is now important to further specify the environmental analysis process. This will be achieved by separating the environment in four different layers and analyse each layer separately by applying the appropriate tool. Numerous theories describe different amounts of layers. A more general approach by Anthony Taylor, only distinctions the external and internal analysis. He explains that there a businesses that can have infinite directions of where it could go and therefore there are far more factors to manage the internal strategy then the external (Taylor, 2019). Other theories usually recognise three layers: macro level (e.g. economical, political, socio - cultural, technological and legislation factor), micro level (e.g. industry, competition, external stakeholders) and internal assessment of the company (e.g. finance, internal processes, productions, human resources).

Furthermore, Johnson, Scholes and Whittington (2008) add an extra layer, after the macro environment and before the internal organisation, they fist describe the industry (or sector) followed by the competitors' market. As the environmental analysis forms the core for this research it was chosen to follow this, more defined, approach. The information will be gathered by using different tools and methods. In order to discover which tools are most applicable for each layer, it is essential to first define the differences between each of the layers that from around the organization.

The first layer, the macro - environment, ranks the highest level, consisting of the general and global (or national) factors which might influence the lower layers in the economic activities. It consists of broad environmental factors that impact to a greater or lesser extent on almost all organisations. This layer can be analysed applying the PESTEL tool, from which key drivers of change can be identified. Alternative scenarios about the future can be constructed according to how the key drives develop. Scenarios consider how strategies might need to change depending on the different ways in which the business environment might change.

The PESTEL framework provides a comprehensive list of influences on the possible success or failure of particular strategies. It can identify the future trends in political, economic, social, technological, environmental and legal environments. In order to apply this tool successfully it is necessary to identify the key drives for change. Key drives for change are the high impact factors likely to affect significantly the success or failure of strategy. In this case possible key drivers could be considered to be the government and municipalities in regard to funding as well as the clients in regards to be open to a different type of care. For example: the implementation of a new act that implements social security for Portuguese citizens. This model helps to indicate what acts already exist and what acts might still appear in the future. Changing social acts can be a crucial factor for either failure or success of the business. Additionally, this tool contains scenario analyses, where analyses are carried out to allow for different possibilities and help prevent managers from closing their minds to alternatives. Note that scenario planning does not attempt to predict the unpredictable: the point is to consider plausible alternative futures.

Despite being a popular and well used model, it also has its limitations. One of them is the wide focus, when covering a broad spectrum of macroeconomic variables, it is easy to get overwhelmed with the gathered information (del Marmol & Feys, 2016). For this research this was prevented by only focus on the national level of Portugal and the Netherlands and by looking within the social sector and no other sectors, such as healthcare or psychiatry. Furthermore, the usage of this tool can make future predictions, but never with certainty. A business can identify the major trends, but not prepare for the unexpected. For example, it can predict that the county´s economy will grow or stabilize, but if an unexpected event occurs, such as a virus like Covid - 19, this could cause an economic crisis. On one side this can lead to failure, because the government might make more cuts in the social sector. On the other side it can lead to success, because there are more people in need of help and thus an increase in demand. Finally, using this model alone is interesting, but insufficient. Porter´s five forces analysis and the SWOT analysis can prove to be a useful aid in the analysis of the business environment (del Marmol & Feys, 2016).

Where the previous section looked at how forces in the macro - environment might influence the success or failure of an organisation's strategies, this section will focus on the more immediate environment through changes in the competitive forces surroundings organizations. Economic theory defines an industry as 'a group of firms producing the same principal product or service (Rutherford, 1995)´or, more broadly, ´´a group of firms producing products that are close substitutes for each other´´ (Porter M. E., 1980). This concept of an industry can be extended into the public services through the idea of a sector. Social services, health care or education also have many producers of the same kinds of services, which are effectively competing for resources. As this research concerns a profitable business in the social sector, the main attention will be focused to the area of sector rather than industry. The five forces framework helps identify the attractiveness of a sector in terms of competitive forces. It includes: barriers to entry; substitutes; buyer power; supplier power and rivalry. Also, it can help set an agenda for action on the various pinch - points that they identify. Porter's essential message is that where these five forces are high, then industries are not attractive to compete in. As this social business shall effectively compete for resources within the same sector, evaluating every force on a scale from 0 to 10 will enable the research to see who has the power in the sector and how profitable the market is. The stronger the forces are, the greater challenge to make profits (Taylor, 2019). Recent studies have elaborated in order to improve this model. Baburaj and Narayanan (2019) state that this framework assumes relative stability in the structural characteristics and for that reason does not explain the distribution of profits among industry/sector players over time. For example, within the social sector, there are multiple businesses striving towards the same goal: provide care for those in need. Through collaboration, innovations appear and opportunities are created. As this also can be considered a factor for success, it should not be forgotten, whilst looking at the competitive environment. Especially within the social sector of Portugal, it can be helpful to know whether other businesses are striving for more governmental support or whether they are innovating the methods they are using with their clients. As it concerns a collective public, more can be achieved whilst working together to improve the care that is being given.

Many industries contain a range of companies, each of which has different capabilities and competes on different bases. For example, Ford and Porsche may be in the same broad industry (automobiles), but they are positioned differently: they face different kinds of buyer power and supplier power at the very least (Johnson, Scholes, & Whittington, 2008). In the case of this business, there is the broad industry of delivering care, this can be done by pharmaceutical medication, social care, psychiatric care, psychological care, private as well as public care and so on. For that reason, it helpful to channel the focus on more specific competitors. The concepts and frameworks discussed earlier should be helpful in understanding the factors in the macro -, industry and competitor/market environments of the business. However, the critical issue is the implications that are drawn from this understanding in guiding strategic decisions and choices. The crucial next stage is to draw from the environmental analysis specific strategic opportunities and threats for the organisation. Identifying these opportunities and threats is extremely valuable when thinking about strategic choices for the future. Opportunities and threats can be formed on behave of the strengths, weaknesses, opportunities and threats (SWOT) analyses that shape many companies' strategy formulation. In responding strategically to the environment, the goal is to reduce identified threats and take advantage of the best opportunities (Johnson, Scholes, & Whittington, 2008). SWOT summarises the key issues from the business environment and the strategic capability of an organisation that are most likely to impact on strategy development. The aim is to identify the extent to which strengths and weaknesses are relevant to the changes taking place in the business environment. It is important to emphasise that this analysis is only useful if it is comparative, so if it examines strengths, weaknesses, opportunities and threats in relation to competitors. This means to compare the services that this company will offer with the services that are already being offered on the market.

MAIN FOCUS OF THE CHAPTER

Methods

In this chapter the literature review will be complemented by describing the appropriate methodology of this dissertation. The research will apply both a desk research and a field research to answer the question 'How to determine the possibilities of starting a successful commercial business within the social welfare sector of Portugal?'. Previously, it was stated that an extensive environmental analysis is critical and can be achieved by applying different tools that are adapted to each of the four environmental layers. To better understand those, it is valuable to first gain broad knowledge on the matter through a desk research. Here, a benchmark between Portugal and The Netherlands is performed. The outcome of the desk research is used as a base for the field research, where in - depth interviews will be conducted from a carefully selected group of professionals and experts. Eventually, the objectives that are stated below will be shaped further during the desk research and reflected upon, deepened and specified during the field research. The aim of the data method is to get a clear view on the Portuguese social sector by conducting a desk research followed by a field research, where experts and professionals are being interviewed in order to execute an environmental analysis.

As described earlier on, two methods are applied to collect data. A desk research to increase reliability by adding secondary data and a field research to gather primary data by conducting in - depth interviews. Interviewing is an extremely flexible research tool (Breakwell, 1995). The philosophy behind qualitative interview is described by H. and I. Rubin (1995) as followed: 'Find out what others think and know and avoid dominating your interviewees by imposing your world on theirs.' Before getting into the interviews, there will now be a closer look at the benchmark structure for the desk research.

The benchmark will be conducted to gain general information on a macro - level by demonstrating the differences and similarities between two countries. It was chosen to compare Portugal with the Netherlands as this country build an extensive social care system after World War II (Bijlsma, 2012). Consequently, that extensive system has been creating many business opportunities for innovative commercial businesses in the social sector. Through a benchmark, the differences and similarities between both countries will be demonstrated, which will lead to the knowledge whether a similar set up for business could be applied in Portugal.

Many qualitative interviews have both more structured and less structured parts, but vary in the balance between them. In the less structured parts, the interviewee does most of the talking, perhaps explaining what an idea, event, or a bit of background means. In this case that will take place after the first general questions. There will be an explanation of the set - up and aim of this company. Later on, there is a direct referral to the 5 cultural issues of Hofstede and in order for the interviewee to answer the questions correctly, this model will be further explained. In the more structured part of the interview, the interviewer poses specific questions to get detail, example and context. Such as the questions where the direct professional opinion of the interviewee is asked, here it is expected to hear the details of the specific area of that professional/expert. As Saunders, Lewis and Thornhill (2000) describe it: 'In semi - structured interviews, the researcher will have a list of themes and questions to be covered. During the interview there will be a balance between structured and unstructured as the researchers are ought to listen to each answer and determine the next question based on what was said. Because of that it is important for the qualitative interviewer to listen intently to pick up on key words and ideas and to mark important omissions. In qualitative interviews you listen to as to hear the meaning of what is being said.' Furthermore P. Brewerton and L. Millward (2001) state that semi - structured interviews incorporate elements of both quantifiable, fixed choice responding and the facility to explore, and probe in more depth, certain areas of interest. The advantage is that they are generally easy to analyse, quantify and compare, but also allow interviewees to explain their responses and to provide more in - depth information where necessary. There is the disadvantage of spending too long on peripheral subjects, or to lose control to the interviewee and finally the disadvantage of the reduction in reliability when using a non - standardized approach. Whilst analysing the environment it is key to apply this type of primary data collection. Environment is a dynamic mechanism, based many segments, such as culture, history, finance, etc. Thus, the interviews and data collection should also be flexible and able to move along instead of set in stone. The research design should help in choosing what will be asked from whom and why. It is important to have a design from the beginning to keep the research on target, but also bear in mind that the design has to be flexible, iterative, continuous and cannot be fully planned in advance as it will change based on the gathered data from interviewing (Rubin & Rubin, 1995).

First of all, the design needs to be flexible in order to process the gathered data and continue accordingly. This flexibility makes it impossible to create a static design at the beginning and that remains the same throughout the entire process. However, the set - up of this flexible design can be initiated by talking and discussing initial ideas with people of interest.

Secondly, there is the iterative design, that enhances the approach to have in the early stages of interviewing, a design that will emphasize more the gathering of many themes and ideas; towards the middle of the research, the concentration will lie within winnowing it and here a limited number of themes are being explored. Finally, in the final stages, there is a higher emphasize on analysing and testing the understandings. This design complements the Delphi - method, where the data is also analysed by winnowing the results to eventually end up with a specific and concrete outcome. Eventually, the iterative design stops when the information that is put together supports a small number of integrated themes and each additional interview adds no more ideas or issues to the themes that are now being questioned. Glaser and Strauss (1967) call this point the theoretical saturation. To finalize, the continuous nature of qualitative interviewing means that the questioning is redesigned throughout the project. It allows exploration of new topics while keeping the research organized and focused. It points the research in a direction to ensure that it pursues core topics in sufficient depth to end up with adequate evidence for the conclusions and results.

As for the interviewees, these will be carefully selected as only a limited number of interviews will take place. Whom is chosen to interview should match the definition of the research subject and should satisfy three requirements: interviewees should be knowledgeable about the specific area that is valuable to the study; they should be willing to talk; and when people in the area have different perspectives, the interviewees should represent the range of points of view (Rubin & Rubin, 1995). So, with other words, they should be willing to share their knowledge that is applicable to the study and they should be able to share different perspectives in common areas to give a wide range of ideas and themes.

Furthermore, during the interview it is important to limit the number of main topics, as it could be overwhelming for an interviewee and the result would be a jumble with inadequate depth on any one subject. It was decided to choose 5 main topics that were also formed out of the 4 environmental layers:

A: The benchmark between Portugal and the Netherlands (macro layer)
B: The financial mechanism (macro layer)
C: The social care system (sector layer)
D: The target group (competition/market layer)
E: The critical success factors (organisational layer)

Most sampling in qualitative research entails purposive sampling. It is a non - probability form of sampling, which has essentially to do with the selection of units (which may be people, organizations, documents, departments, etc.). The researcher does not seek to sample research participants on a random basis. The goal of purposive sampling is to sample participants in a strategic way, so that those sampled are relevant to the research questions that are being posed. In purposive sampling the researcher samples with certain research goals in mind. Therefore, it needs to be clear what the criteria are that will be relevant to inclusion or exclusion of participants (Bryman, 2008). In the case of this research, the sample unit will be people and the relevant criteria can be described in three segments: the Portuguese welfare system segment, the Legal and financing segment and finally, the segment of culture and migration. Theoretical sampling is one form of purposive sampling. As Glaser and Strauss (1967) put it: ''Theoretical sampling is done in order to discover categories and their properties and to suggest the interrelationships into a theory. Statistical sampling is done to obtain accurate evidence on distributions of people among categories to be used in descriptions and verifications.' You carry on collecting data until you have achieved theoretical saturation.

Thus, for this research there will be one level of sampling, namely the sampling of interviewees. As the theoretical sampling entails, a sampling of interviewees will take place until the 5 categories (earlier described as topics) achieve theoretical saturation, when the information that is being put together supports a small number of integrated themes and each additional interview adds no more ideas or issues to the themes that are now being questioned. As it is impossible to know how many people should be interviewed before theoretical saturation has been achieved, it was chosen to execute 5 interviews and based on the gathered data, it will be decided whether theoretical saturation has been achieved or not.

Desk Research: Benchmark Portugal - Nederland

During the desk research, also known as the literate review, a comparison will be made between the start of social business in Portugal with the start of a social business in the Netherlands. As these countries have different cultures as well as healthcare systems and financial mechanisms, making a comparison holds crucial value in order to understand how this factor impacts a company.

Legal and Financing

The Portuguese healthcare system is based on the Beveridge Model, whilst the Dutch System is based on the Bismarck Model. As there is no separate financing system for social care, it was decided to analyse the general healthcare systems as this also covers the costs for (public) social care. Later on, closer attention is paid to the historical context, the cultural differences, indicated by Geert Hofsteede and to statistics that indicate where these countries differ. The European healthcare systems can be divided into two broad categories: National Health Services, short NHS, and Social Security (based) Health care systems, in short SSH. Both systems are named after their founding fathers Beveridge (NHS) and Bismarck (SSH). Existing literature is inconclusive about which system performs best. Therefore, the pros and cons of both systems will now be further analysed.

The inclusion of a country's system into one of the two categories is mainly based on the way the systems are funded, but these funding differences also correlate with the differences in the way the systems are organised. An NHS is funded by means of general taxation. Responsibility for the budget is in hands of the Ministry of Health and as such the NHS is associated with a strong influence of the state. An SSH is funded by means of earmarked premiums, mainly from salaried employees. The system is more loosely organised, with less state influence and more pluralistic, with a strong influence of health care providers and (social) insurers (van der Zee & Kroneman, 2007).

Table 1. The division of countries with SSH and NHS systems.

Countries with SSH system	Countries with NHS system
• Austria • Belgium • France • Germany • Luxembourg • Netherlands • Switzerland • Portugal (until 1978)	• Denmark • Finland • Greece • Ireland • Italy • Norway • Portugal (from 1979) • Spain • Sweden • United Kingdom

Source: Own

Striking differences between both systems are firstly that the health spending per capita of SSH has become increasingly higher compared to the NHS systems. Also, the satisfaction with the healthcare system of the population in SSH - countries is much higher compared to NHS countries, this is indicated in the graphic below. In 1998, Portugal was just below 20%, where the Netherlands was 70%. After, however, Portugal made a bigger growth as visible until 1999.

In SSH countries about two - third of the population is very or fairly satisfied with the system, whereas in NHS countries this is the case for only half of the population. Regardless of the system there is a strong improvement of life expectancy and a reduction in infant mortality. According to the study of van der Zee and Kroneman, there were no differences in health outcomes between NHS and SSH systems (van der Zee & Kroneman, 2007).

It is important to keep in mind that international comparison of health data is severely hampered by differences in national definitions and differences in national methods of data collection. Dissatisfaction with a health care system seemed to be related to problematic organisational items like waiting lists and limitations in accessibility. To elaborate more, a closer look will be taken at Portugal as well as the Netherlands and explain this theory in a more practical terms by using examples.

The hierarchal structure of the Beveridge (NHS) model, was used in Portugal. This model is also being used in the United Kingdom, it was designed by William Beveridge and established in 1948. Nowadays, it is still funded from general taxation and national insurance contributions paid by employees, employers and the self - employed. Almost all healthcare is provided free of charge to everyone, according to clinical need. As for the Netherlands, they use the Bismarck model (SSH) instead. This system is funded by employers and employees who pay into "sickness funds" that subsequently cover medical care. A key feature to this system, much like the Beveridge Model, is that it is strictly non - profit and government - run. No one is denied coverage in the Bismarck Model. Most hospitals are privately run (Health Care Systems: Differences Around the Globe, 2014).

Both models might be non - profit and government - run, however, their different structure has a huge impact on the legal & financing fragment. First of all, in the Netherlands each citizen is obligated to have a health insurance, whereas in Portugal, citizens can go to public hospitals or pay more for the received care in private hospitals. As a result, it is more difficult to receive paying customers in Portugal, because the citizens expect the government to provide them with the services they need. This is important to keep in mind, when starting this profitable social business. It could be considered to open a public service, however, instead of it being a commercial business, it would be an association. And as that was not the aim for this research, that idea has been ruled out. Keeping this in mind, it is important to deliver a service that is required and asked for by the appropriate consumers. Only then will they be willing to buy your services. Moreover, if the focus of the business is on a group that is need of help and which is recognised by the government, it can increase the change of receiving funding from the municipalities. Which brings us back to the importance of analysing the environment thoroughly.

Historical Context

To analyse the historical context of both countries, a timeline was designed to indicate the most significant factors for the welfare sector together with implemented acts. On the bottom the Netherlands is demonstrated and on the top Portugal. The timeline starts just before the Second World War that ended in 1945 and it ends with a general idea where both countries are nowadays. Before the war, the conditions in which people lived and worked in the Netherlands were often appalling. Workers soon combined to form unions to campaign for change. It was a Liberal member of parliament, Samuel van Houten, who in 1874, initiated legislation to stop children under twelve of being employed in factories. This can be considered to be the first step on the road to reform. In 1889 the Labour Law was implemented and its updated version in 1911 regulated the hours that women and children could work, as well as men. In the years following the Second World War a miracle occurred in the Netherlands: despite the high birth rate, unemployment fell, and the economy grew at an astonishing pace. For those unable to provide for themselves, the welfare state set up under Willem Drees offered support. In 1947, as minister of social affairs, Willem Drees had already begun to extend the welfare state: the system in which the government took responsibility for the basic needs of its citizens. Seniors without resources now received a regular pension. Ten years later, in 1957, a general pension law was passed (Algemene Ouderdoms Wet – AOW) and successive governments after Drees introduced more benefits: child support in 1963 (Algemene Kinderbijslagwet) and social security in 1965 (Algemene bijstandswet), making financial assistance to families and those without means a right. People in need were no longer dependent on charity from religious or private organization. The cost of this extensive system of benefits, public health services and affordable education would be henceforth be borne by the state (Timeline of Dutch History, 2020).

Since the late 1980s a changing government attitude towards social welfare provision and the role of civil society organisations therein can be observed. It has been argued that a fundamental shift from a collective solidarity model towards one of personal responsibility is highly visible, through the introduction of neoliberal elements and cutbacks in the degree of social spending by the state (van Oorschot, 2006). From a global comparative perspective, the Dutch welfare state has traditionally been characterised by its comprehensiveness and can still be regarded as generous. As in other Western European welfare states, government interventions affect various domains of economic and social life, including health, work, income and housing.

The consensus in the Netherlands about devolving sickness absence issues to local actors led to the allocation of both financial and return - to - work responsibilities to employers (and employees. The degree of responsibility for Dutch employers has become unique in Europe and it has been labelled 'going Dutch' in sickness absence policies. The shift from a disability scheme to an ability scheme reflects the normative shift in the Netherlands toward a 'participation society' characterised by a strong emphasis on individual responsibility.

Moving on to Portugal that is demonstrated in the upper part of the timeline it is clear to see that the country was under a dictatorship, whilst the Netherlands was evolving the social sector. During the Salazar dictatorship the social welfare was primitive.

As a result, many of the citizens experienced poverty, lengthy military service and stagnation. 900,000 emigrated, mainly to France, West - Germany and Brazil. At the same time, the 1960s are marked by the 1962 Social Welfare Reform, which led to the development of a unified social welfare scheme. Several institutions merged into one body and the resultant structure underpins the social security scheme that operates today. This rationalization is considered a milestone in the process of the development of the welfare state in Portugal, as argued by and it led to a significant increase in social expenditure, which reached 4 per cent of GDP in 1969. The increase in social expenditure was even greater from 1969 to the end of the New State in 1974, during the Estado Social (social state) phase under the leadership of the Prime Minister, Marcelo Caetano. During this period several important gaps in the social protection network were filled, namely those corresponding to certain groups that had not been considered to be participating in the labour market (e.g. family allowance and old age pensions were extended to rural workers), as well as to professions that had previously been excluded from the social insurance scheme (such as hairdressers, newspaper sellers and maids).

Further important developments of the welfare state in Portugal took place in the period of transition to democracy, between 1974 and the early 1980s. These changes resulted from the recognition of rights subsequent to the political institutionalization of social benefits. Social policies at this time were also directed towards expanding the scope of benefits, with the establishment of an unemployment benefit (1975) and social pensions that were based not on contributions but on citizenship (1977). In 1979, the provisional government of Maria de Lourdes Pintassilgo legislated a minimal social protection scheme in Portugal, including a social pension, a pension supplement for severe incapacity, an orphan pension, family allowance, a monthly cash benefit for handicapped minors and social services (da Soledade Carolo & Pereirinha, 2017). On the other, some resources state that this reestablishment of the democratic system, also resulted in some difficulties. The long period of dictatorship made it impossible for Portugal to take advantage of the thirty years of post - World War II economic growth that help to create the basis for a mature welfare state in several European countries (Brito, 2019). Only in the 1980s Portugal had the stability and resources to begin their implementation. Portugal's admission to the EU in the 1980s was a turning point for the country; it meant admittance into (Western) Europe policymaking, in political terms. It also meant access to substantive financial, cognitive and strategic resources.

Between 1995 - 2001 public spending grew by eight per cent per year, and thousands of new jobs were created. Nonetheless, there was still a weaker economic growth, when compared with other European countries and associated with the high unemployment rates continued to shape Portuguese economy throughout the 2000s. The socialist governments of 2005 - 2012 implemented several cuts and reforms in order to control the deficit and to stimulate growth. However, these reforms did not have the expected results and, in April 2011, Portugal requested a bail - out, with devastating social, economic and legal impacts (Araújo, S., Ferreira, S., & Safradin, B., 2018). Simultaneously, Portugal has also benefited considerably from the EU's structural funds, vital to financing public services and to developing several social policies, in order to adapt to the European Union 'way of thought'. One major example was the creation of a minimum income scheme, later renamed 'Social Insertion Income' (SII – see Meneses et al., 2018; Brito, 2018). The effort made by the Portuguese government to match high European standards and the strong welfare state, unfortunately, was not complemented by a growing economy. Nowadays, the Portuguese social protection system has left unprotected a growing number of persons and the increase in long - term unemployment suggests that the system is inefficient in reducing unemployment time (Valadas, 2013). Currently, for a vast sector of the Portuguese population (63%), unemployment remains the main concern, a reality that is a consequence the low protection created by a weak welfare state (Brito, 2019).

SOLUTIONS AND RECOMMENDATIONS

To finalize this benchmark, a final comparison is made between Portugal and the Netherlands. There are some crucial differences between both countries and those are demonstrated in the table below. Part of the information is also conducted from the interviews. These will be enlightened in the next chapter, but to make the comparison complete, it has already been applied. The desk research has shown that in the Netherlands, the government provides care for every citizen. It also shown that in Portugal, the effort made by the Portuguese government to match high European standards and the strong welfare state, unfortunately, was not complemented by a growing economy. There is a high unemployment rate together with an insufficient social sector and a system, where one is sustaining the other.

Culturally, the Netherlands has a high score with individualism and Portugal a high score with uncertainty avoidance. Having a higher social responsibility could explain this high number in individualism.

Looking at the high number of uncertainty avoidance, could indicate the level of dependency the citizens have on its government. They rather not take a risk and expect the government to find a solution. As it concerns a collective problem, it could be agreed that it is upon the government to find a collective solution in order to increase the sustainability of the social sector. Thus, where in the Netherlands professional help is provided to those that don't fit in society, which is a big group of a lot of different people, in Portugal, those people will mainly depend on family, friends and/or associations. In both countries there is a big group of elderly that often require extra help, when households exist of two cost winners, it often leaves them with not enough time to also deliver care. In Portugal it is often friends, family or charity that take responsibility and, in the Netherlands, it is more often institutions or professional home care. As a result, the professionalism within the care sector of Portugal is lower and problems have a higher risk of escalation. A comparison was made between Portugal and The Netherlands in order to understand the impact of different legal and financing systems. Portugal is using the Beveridge model (NHS), with no prohibited insurances and The Netherlands has always used the Bismarck model (SSH), where every citizen is ought to have a private health insurance. Striking differences between both systems are firstly that the health spending per capita of SSH has become increasingly higher compared to the NHS systems. Also, the satisfaction with the healthcare system of the population in SSH - countries is much higher compared to NHS countries. The historical timeline indicates the differences between both countries. Where the Netherlands was implementing social act´s and profiting from the post - war economic growth, Portugal was under a conservative dictatorship, which led to economic instability and a smaller amount social act´s. As stated by Nunn (2012) cultural change and persistence are important channels through which history continues to matter today. For that reason, the important aspect of culture was also discussed. If you were to compare a large number of cultures around the world, you would see that although each culture is different, they all contain 5 basic problems: power distance, individualism, masculinity, uncertainty avoidance and long - term orientation. What stands out in the model of Geert Hofsteede is that Portugal scores high on uncertainty avoidance and the Netherlands scores high on individualism and long - term orientation.

The Delphi method was applied by indicating the three levels of the pyramid with its categories. This led to the main results that are shown in the final evaluation, demonstrated in table 3. Each category has its own outcome, in general, there is little financial support, which causes the sector to stagnate. Also, there is an ongoing social stigma on looking for professional help, which could also contribute to stagnation. Furthermore, elderly is a group that is recognised as in need of help and there is a lot of ongoing research towards this target group, which could be a possible strength for the business. In conclusion, it became clear that there is need for a change within the social sector of Portugal. However, there are many ideas on how this could be achieved and on what this change should be focused. Based on the gathered data, the best - case scenario would be to have financial support from the government to set up this business. Whilst performing this strategic analysis, having governmental support will be assumed. In the first chapter, it was stated that strategic analysis refers to the process of conducting research on a company and its environment to formulate a strategy. To formulate a strategy, three steps, described by Johnson, Scholes and Wellington (2008), need to be evaluated. For this company, the aim will be to pay close attention to the differentiation strategy, the company will seek to provide a service that offers benefits that are different from those of competitors and that are widely valued by buyers. The best way to achieve this would be to make the following strategic choices:

- Make a switch and cooperate with health insurances to make the businesses partly public and partly private. It would create a system to work alongside its competitors.
- Make the scope smaller to reach the clients by indicating the essence of the services you are selling. First of all, by reinsuring the importance of professionalism within care and make your business easily accessible by going to client's houses.
- Focus on the elderly, because not only is Portugal an aging country, the elderly are recognised as a target group in need and there is a high demand for more care due to the high number of emigrants the and growing number 2 of workers within a household.
- Pursue the strategies by maintaining communication with other professionals of the field and the government in order to share the results and outcomes from this new service. It is a manner to also reinsure them of the quality and the effect that innovative methods can bring and how it can eventually lead to return of investment.

The final step would be to make the strategy happen. As was stated earlier on in the research, this would not necessarily need to be a big obstacle. Anybody can start a business online with a start capital of €1, - . Before starting though, it is of the essence to first clarify all the doubts in regard to this innovative company. Also, it would be interesting to reach out to the government and share the findings and ideas regarding this business plan.

FUTURE RESEARCH DIRECTIONS

Further research could consider also conducting interviews in the Netherlands as this dissertation is mainly focused on the Portuguese care system and culture. It is compared with the general Dutch WMO (The Dutch Social Act) approach, but it could be further refined by also comparing it with other social care approaches from the Netherlands and focus more on the element of the Dutch culture.

Additional research could also mean conducting a survey amongst Portuguese citizens to either confirm or deny ideas about the Portuguese culture that have been discussed during the gathering of data. Outside of interviews with experts of the field, it could be interesting to interview business analytics that focus their main attention on innovation to also hear their perspective and ideas on this organisation. Furthermore, an interesting follow - up research could be about the drug use of Portuguese citizens and, in particular, the anti - depressants. Where this high number comes from, the effectiveness, the entire process, etc. By creating a clearer picture on the drug use, it could be monitored better and based on the results, improvements could be set in place. This could be the set up to improve the methods by implementing preventive methods instead of using medication as a solution.

CONCLUSION

Based on multiple studies, a common understanding to what should be considered a strategic analysis was described in order to better understand what an environmental analysis to should lead to. Performing an environmental analysis on the social sector of Portugal begun by gaining a deeper understanding on this process and its appropriate tools. Chapter II, first, demonstrates the four layers of the environmental analysis: the macro environment, the industry or sector, the competitors and the organisation, based on the theory of Johnson, Scholes and Whittington (2008) and after it indicates the appropriate tools for each layer. These tools are: PESTEL, Porter´s 5 forces, Power - interest matrix and the SWOT, Throughout the research it became clear that certain concerns, that seemed to be important at the beginning, such as determining the target group, appeared to be les vital in a later stage. On the other hand, points that seemed to be unimportant, such as the governmental role, turned out to be rather significant. After explaining the tools that would be applied, in chapter II and presenting the methods in chapter III, the data gathering begun. The desk research indicated that there are several noteworthy differences between Portugal and the Netherlands. The Netherlands has been working on its social acts for a longer period of time and Portugal has fewer financial resources to support its social sector. Factors that were taken into consideration here, were: the financial mechanism, history, culture and current graphics. During the gathering of secondary data, rather than being locked into one set of questions for all the interviewees, it was chosen to adjust the questioning to each individual. They were asked about the particularities of a subject that they knew best. Eventually, this led to a dynamic research where multiple levels were explored and many ideas and opinions where shared. When combining these outcomes with secondary data, the credibility increased and it allowed the tools and models to be processed, based upon a complete and extensive amount of data. Eventually, this led to a clear conclusion in order to answer the research problem: to determine the possibilities of starting a successful commercial business within the social welfare sector of Portugal.

The research shows that there is a need and urgency to strengthen the social care in Portugal. The current generation of elderly can still rely on the historical Portuguese model of social support from family, neighbours and denominations. However, due to the economic, cultural political and social developments, this social care system, does not appear to be sustainable. This creates a business opportunity for a new type of business that responds to the high demand within the social sector, especially focussing on the elderly in this aging country. The main threat, however, would be the financial mechanism. As there is a collective problem due to limited financial resources, the government can be held responsible. It is called a collective problem, because not only do the public systems appear to be overloaded, the satisfaction levels of Portuguese citizens are low and the medication usage is high.

For that reason, it could be considered to be the right time for a shift in the sector. A commercial business that provides a high level of professionalism can be a great opportunity for both the organisation and the government. It does, however, require financial support from the government as citizens have little financial possibilities. As the critical success factor for this business is highly depending on an external factor, the government´s financial support, it can be considered that it is still too early to start a commercial business in the social care sector of Portugal today. There are too few financial recourses available and there is still too little recognition of value to start within the private sector. The option right now would be to start this business as an association in order to build reputation and test how it is received by the people. After a couple of years and an increase in stability, it can be decided to make it commercial. By that time, perhaps there also has been a drastic change of the care system, which could create new opportunities to commercialize this business.

REFERENCES

Ackermann, F., & Eden, C. (2011). *Strategic management of stakeholders: theory and practice*. Elsevier.

Araújo, S., Ferreira, S., & Safradin, B. (2018). Comparative report on the types of distributive claims, interests and capabilities of various groups of the population evoked in the political and economic debates at the EU and at the nation state level. *Ethos (Berkeley, Calif.), D6*, 2.

Baburaj, Y., & Narayanan, V. (2016). *Five Forces Framework*. Drexel University. doi:10.1057/978-1-349-94848-2_632-1

Bijlsma, J. (2012). *Sociaal werk in Nederland*. Coutinho.

Breakwell, G. (1995). *Research methods in Psychology*. Sage Publications.

Brewerton, P., & Millward, L. (2001). *Organizational Research Methods*. Sage Publications Ltd. doi:10.4135/9781849209533

Brito, L. (2019). *Social justice and the Portuguese Welfare State – National Report*. Coimbra: ETHOS consortium.

Bryman, A. (2008). *Social Research Methods*. New York: Oxford Universtiy Press.

Carrilho, P., & Perista, H. (2016, February 15). *Portugal: High and rising emigration in a context of high, but decerasing, unemployment*. Retrieved from Eurofound: https://www.eurofound.europa.eu/publications/article/2016/portugal - high - and - rising - emigration - in - a - context - of - high - but - decreasing - unemployment

CFI. (2019, November 19). *Strategic Analyis*. Retrieved from CFI: https://corporatefinanceinstitute.com/resources/knowledge/strategy/strategic - analysis/

Chen, J. (2019, June 30). *Stakeholders*. Retrieved from Investopedia: https://www.investopedia.com/terms/s/stakeholder.asp

Child, J. (1984). *Organization: A Guide to Problems and Practice*. Harper and Row. doi:10.4135/9781446280348

da Soledade Carolo, D., & Pereirinha, J. (2017). *The development of the Welfare State in Portugal: trends in social expenditure between 1938 and 2003*. Lisbon University.

del Marmol, T., & Feys, B. (2016). *Pestle Analysis*. 50minutes.

Freeman, E. (1984). *Strategic Management - A Stakeholder Approach*. Pitman Publishing Inc.

Gerard, H., & Bruijl, T. (2018). The Relevance Of Porter's Five Forces In Today's Innovative And Changing Business Environment. SSRN *Electronic Journal*.

Gibson, K. (2000). The Moral Basis of Stakholder Theory. *Journal of Business Ethics*, 26.

Glaser, B., & Strauss, A. (1967). *The discovery of grounded theory*. Aldine.

Health at a glance 2019: OECD indicators. (2019). Retrieved from OECD iLibrary: https://www.oecd - ilibrary.org/sites/4dd50c09 - en/1/2/10/3/index.html?itemId=/content/publication/4dd50c09 - en&_csp _=82587932df7c06a6a3f9dab95304095d&itemIGO=oecd&itemContentType=book

Health Care Systems: Differences Around the Globe. (2014, February 22). Retrieved from Global, Pre - Meds: https://www.globalpremeds.com/blog/2014/02/22/health - care - systems - differences - around - the - globe/

Henderson, B. D. (1989). The Origin of Strategy. *Harvard Business Review*. PMID:10303992

Hofer, C. W., & Schendel, D. (1978). *Strategy formulation: analytical concepts*. West Publising Co.

Hofstede, G. (2019, December 12). *Insights*. Retrieved from Hofstede insights: https://www.hofstede - insights.com/country - comparison/the - netherlands,portugal/

Hofstede, G., Pedersen, P. B., & Hofstede, G. (2002). *Exploring Culture*. Nicholas Brealey Publishing.

Johnson, G., Scholes, K., & Whittington, R. (2008). *Exploring corporate strategy*. Harlow: Financial Times Prentice Hall.

Kangas, J., Pesonen, M., Kurttila, M., & Kajanus, M. (2001). *A'WOT: Integrating the AHO with SWOT analysis*. ISAHP.

Kisi, N. (2019). *A Strategic Approach to Sustainable Tourism Development Using the A+WOT Hybrid Method: A Case Study of Zonguldak, Turkey*. MDPI.

Malheiros, J. (2002). Portugal Seeks Balance of Emigration, Immigration. Brussels: Migration Policy Institute (MPI).

Mintzberg, H. (1992). *Five Ps for Strategy*. Prentice - Hall.

NA. (2015, September 24). *Strategic analysis: Layers of business environment*. Retrieved from PyramiDNA: https://pyramidna.wordpress.com/2015/09/24/strategic - analysis - layers - of - business - environment/

Nazarko, J., Ejdys, J., Halicka, K., Magruk, A., Nazarko, L., & Skorek, A. (2017). *Application of Ehanced SWOT Analysis in the Future - oriented Public Management of Technology*. Elsevier.

Nunn, N. (2012). *Culture and the historical process*. Harvard University. doi:10.3386/w17869

OECD. (2019). *OECD Economic Surveyes*. OECD.

Papulova, Z., & Gazova, A. (2015). *Role of Strategic Analysis in Strategic Decision - Making*. Elsevier.

Poole, M. L. (1990). *Recommended Data for the First Step in External Environment Scanning for Public Schools*. University of Maryland.

Porter, M. E. (1980). *Competitive Strategy: Techniques for analysing industries and competitors*. Free Press.

Porter, M. E. (1987). *From Competitive Advantage to Corporate Strategy*. Harvard Business Review.

Prahalad, C. K., & Hamel, G. (1994). Competing for the Future. *Harvard Business Review*, 9.

Rubin, H. J., & Rubin, I. S. (1995). *Qualitative interviewing; The art of hearing data.* SAGE Publications.

Rutherford, D. (1995). *Routledge Dictionary of Economics* (2nd ed.). Routledge.

Saunders, M., Lewis, P., & Thornhill, A. (2000). *Research methods for business students.* Pearson Education Limited.

Schein, E. H. (1997). *Organizational Culture and Leadership.* Jossey - Bass.

Taylor, A. (2019, April 20). *Strategic Planning and Management Insights.* Retrieved from SME - Strategy Management Consultant: smestrategy.net/blog/business - strategy - frameworks - for - strategic - planning

Timeline of Dutch History. (2020, July 13). Retrieved from Rijksmuseum: https://www.rijksmuseum.nl/en/rijksstudio/timeline - dutch - history/reconstruction - welfare - state

Valadas, C. (2013). *Mudanças nas políticas: do (des)emprego à empregabilidade.* Revista Críticas de Ciências Sociais.

van der Zee, J., & Kroneman, M. W. (2007). Bismarck or Beveridge: A beauty contest between dinosaurs. *BMC Health Services Research, 7*(1), 94. doi:10.1186/1472-6963-7-94 PMID:17594476

van Oorschot, W. (2006). The Dutch Welfare State: Recent Trends and Challenges in Historical Perspective. Leuven. *European Journal of Social Security, 8*(1), 57–76. doi:10.1177/138826270600800104

Wanhoni, J. M. (2014, June 17). *Research Objectives.* Nairobi, Kenya: Academic Press.

Wright, P., Pringle, C. D., & Kroll, M. J. (1992). *Strategic management: Text and Cases.* Allyn and Bacon.

KEY TERMS AND DEFINITIONS

Non-Profit Organization: They are organizations of a legal nature with no purpose of accumulating capital for the profit of their directors.

PESTEL: A PESTEL analysis or PESTLE analysis (formerly known as PEST analysis) is a framework or tool used to analyse and monitor the macro - environmental factors that may have a profound impact on an organisation's performance. This tool is especially useful when starting a new business or entering a foreign market.

Porter's Five Forces Framework: Is a method for analysing competition of a business. It draws from industrial organization (IO) economics to derive five forces that determine the competitive intensity and, therefore, the attractiveness (or lack thereof) of an industry in terms of its profitability. An "unattractive" industry is one in which the effect of these five forces reduces overall profitability.

Strategic Management: In the field of management, strategic management involves the formulation and implementation of the major goals and initiatives taken by an organization's managers on behalf of stakeholders, based on consideration of resources and an assessment of the internal and external environments in which the organization operates.

Third Sector: The third sector is made up of non - profit and non - governmental organizations, whose objective is to generate public services.

Compilation of References

Abdelnaeim, S. M., & El-Bassiouny, N. (2020). The relationship between entrepreneurial cognitions and sustainability orientation: The case of an emerging market. *Journal of Entrepreneurship in Emerging Economies, 20*(12), 12–29.

Abosede, A. J., Obasan, K. A., & Alese, O. J. (2016). Strategic Management and Small and Medium Enterprises (SMEs) Development: A Review of Literature. *International Review of Management and Business Research, 5*(1), 315–335.

AboutKOSGEB. (n.d.). Retrieved from https://en.kosgeb.gov.tr/site/tr/genel/detay/347/about-kosgeb

Abrahamsson, A. (2006). Sustainopreneurship - Business with a Cause. in Science Sustainable Development - Starting Points and Critical Reflections. Uppsala: VHU - Föreningen Vetenskap för Hållbar Utveckling.

Abrahamsson, A. (2007a). *Sustainopreneurship - Business with a Cause: Conceptualizing Entrepreneurship for Sustainability* [Master Thesis in Business Administration]. Växjö: Reports from Växjö University: Business Administration and Economics. http://www.diva-portal.org/vxu/abstract.xsql?dbid=1254

Abrahamsson, A. (2007b). *Researching Sustainopreneurship - conditions, concepts, approaches, arenas and questions. An invitation to authentic sustainability business forces*. Paper presented at the 13th International Sustainable Development Research Conference, Mälardalens Högskola, Västerås.

Abrahamsson, A. (2008). Sustainopreneurship - Business with a Cause. The Promise of Creative Organizing for Sustainability. In Bridging the Functional and Territorial Views on Regional Entrepreneurship and Development. Örebro: FSF (Swedish Foundation for Small Business Research).

Ackermann, F., & Eden, C. (2011). *Strategic management of stakeholders: theory and practice*. Elsevier.

Adams, M. J. D., & Umbach, P. D. (2012). Nonresponse and Online Student Evaluations of Teaching: Understanding the Influence of Salience, Fatigue, and Academic Environments. *Research in Higher Education, 53*(5), 576–591. doi:10.100711162-011-9240-5

Adelegan, O. (2011). Infrastructure deficiencies and investment in manufacturing firms in Nigeria. *Journal of Economics & International Finance, 3*(9), 542–552.

Adeola, A. (2016). Impact of external business environment on organization performance of Small and Medium-sized Enterprises (SMEs) in Osun State, Nigeria. *Scholedge International Journal of Business Policy & Governance, 3*(10), 155–166.

Afonina, A., & Chalupský, V. (2013). Investigation of strategic management tools and techniques. *Acta Universitatis Agriculturae et Silviculturae Mendelianae Brunensis, 61*(4), 833–840. doi:10.11118/actaun201361040833

Aghayeva, K., & Ślusarczyk, B. (2019). Analytic Hierarchy of Motivating and Demotivating Factors Affecting Labour Productivity in the Construction Industry: The Case of Azerbaijan. *Sustainability, 11*(21), 5975. doi:10.3390u11215975

Agwu, M. O., & Emeti, C. I. (2014). Issues, challenges and prospects of small and medium scale enterprises (Small and Medium-sized Enterprises (SMEs)) in Port-Harcourt City, Nigeria. *European Journal of Sustainable Development, 3*(1), 101–114. doi:10.14207/ejsd.2014.v3n1p101

Ahlin, B., Drnovšek, M., & Hisrich, R. D. (2014). Entrepreneurs' creativity and firm innovation: The moderating role of entrepreneurial self-efficacy. *Small Business Economics, 43*(1), 101–117. doi:10.100711187-013-9531-7

Ajzen, I., & Fishbein, M. (1980). *Understanding Attitudes and Predicting Social Behaviour.* Prentice - Hall.

Akehurst, G., Comeche, J. M., & Galindo, M. A. (2009). Job satisfaction and commitment in the entrepreneurial SME. *Small Business Economics, 32*(3), 277–289. doi:10.100711187-008-9116-z

Akinbogun, T. L. (2008). The impact of Nigerian business environment on the survival of small scale ceramic industries. Journal of Asia &. *African Studies, 43*(6), 663–679.

Akram, K., Siddiqui, S. H., Nawaz, M. A., Ghauri, T. A., & Cheema, A. K. (2011). Role of Knowledge Management to Bring Innovation: An Integrated Approach. *International Bulletin of Business Administration, 11*(1), 121–134.

Aladejebi, O., & Oladimeji, J. O. (2019). The impact of record keeping on the performance of selected small and medium enterprises in Lagos Metropolis. *Journal of Small Business & Entrepreneurship Development, 7*(1), 28–40. doi:10.15640/jsbed.v7n1a3

Alarjani, F. N. F., Anwar, B., Danial Aslam, H., Iqbal, S., & Ayub, A. (2020). A Moderated Mediation Model of Entrepreneurial Self-Efficacy, Institutional Environment, and Entrepreneurial Orientation for SME Development. *SAGE Open, 10*(3), 1–18. doi:10.1177/2158244020941000

Al-Asheq. A. & MdUzzal H. (2019). SME performance: impact of market, customer and brand orientation. Academy of Marketing Studies Journal, 23(1), 1-9.

Alaslani, M., & Collins, J. (2017). The Blocked Mobility Hypothesis and Muslim Immigrant Entrepreneurship in Sydney, Australia. *Review of Integrative Business and Economics Research, 6*(3), 333–357.

Alexopoulos, E. C., Kavadi, Z., Bakoyannis, G., & Papantonopoulos, S. (2009). Subjective Risk Assessment and Perception in the Greek and English Bakery Industries. *Journal of Environmental and Public Health, 1*(1), 1–8. doi:10.1155/2009/891754 PMID:20041018

Al-Jabri, I. M., & Sohail, M. S. (2012). Mobile Banking Adoption: Application of Diffusion of Innovation Theory. *Journal of Electronic Commerce Research, 13*(4), 379–391.

Alkan, A., & Bozkurt, Ö. Ç. (2013). The Choice and Use of Strategic Planning Tools and Techniques in Turkish SMEs According to Attitudes of Executives. *Procedia: Social and Behavioral Sciences, 99*, 1016–1025. doi:10.1016/j.sbspro.2013.10.575

Alkaraan, F., & Northcott, D. (2006). Capital investment decision - making: A role for strategic management accounting. *The British Accounting Review, 38*(2), 49–73. doi:10.1016/j.bar.2005.10.003

Al-Mamun, A. (2018). Diffusion of Innovation among Malaysian Manufacturing Small and Medium-sized Enterprises (SME). *European Journal of Innovation Management, 21*(1), 113–141. doi:10.1108/EJIM-02-2017-0017

Almeida, C. M. V. B., Bonilla, S. H., Giannetti, B. F., & Huisingh, D. (2013). Cleaner Production initiatives and challenges for a sustainable world: An introduction to this special volume. *Journal of Cleaner Production, 47*, 1–10.

Alvarado-Lagunas, E., Ramirez, D. M., & Tellez, E. A. (2016). Perception of educational quality: Case applied to students of the Autonomous University of Nuevo León and the Technological Institute of Higher Studies of Monterrey. *Revista de la Educación Superior, 45*(180), 55–74.

Álvarez-Rojo, V., Garcia-Jimenez, E., & Gil Flores, J. (1999). The quality of university education from the perspective of the professors who are best valued by students. *Review of Education, 319*, 273–290.

Alzghoul, A., Elrehail, H., Emeagwali, O. L., & AlShboul, M. K. (2018). Knowledge management, workplace climate, creativity and performance. *Journal of Workplace Learning, 30*(8), 592–612. doi:10.1108/JWL-12-2017-0111

Amenta, E. (2003). *Comparative historical analysis in the social sciences*. Cambridge University Press.

Andersen, L. L., Jensen, P. H., Meng, A., & Sundstrup, E. (2019). Strong Labour Market Inequality of Opportunities at the Workplace for Supporting a Long and Healthy Work - Life: The Senior Working Life Study. *International Journal of Environmental Research and Public Health, 16*(18), 3264. doi:10.3390/ijerph16183264

Anderson, J. C., & O'Reilly, C. A. III. (1981). Effects of an organizational control system on managerial satisfaction and performance. *Human Relations, 34*(6), 491–501. doi:10.1177/001872678103400605

Androniceanu, A., & Drăgulănescu, I. V. (2012). Sustainability of the Organizational Changes in the Context of Global Economic Crisis. *Amfiteatru Economic, 14*(32), 366–379.

Ansoff, H. I. (1965). *Corporate strategy*. Prentice Hall.

Apaydın, Ş. (2018). The Relations Between Unemployment and Entrepreneurship in Turkey: Schumpeter or Refugee Effect? *Fiscaoeconomia, 2*(2).

Aquino, R. S., Luck, M., & Schanzel, H. A. (2018). A conceptual framework of tourism social entrepreneurship for sustainable community development. *Journal of Hospitality and Tourism Management, 37*, 23–32. doi:10.1016/j.jhtm.2018.09.001

Aragón-Correa, J. A., & Sharma, S. (2003). A Contingent Resource - Based View of Proactive Corporate Environmental Strategy. The Academy of Management Review, 28(1), 71 - 88.

Aragon-Sanchez, A. & Sanchez-Marin, G. (2005). Strategic orientation, management characteristics and performance: A study of Spanish Small and Medium-sized Enterprises (SMEs). *Journal of Small Business Management, 43*(3), 287–308. doi:10.1111/j.1540-627X.2005.00138.x

Arasa, R. & K'Obonyo, P. (2012). The relationship between strategic planning and firm performance. *International Journal of Humanities and Social Science, 2*(22), 201–213.

Araújo, S., Ferreira, S., & Safradin, B. (2018). Comparative report on the types of distributive claims, interests and capabilities of various groups of the population evoked in the political and economic debates at the EU and at the nation state level. *Ethos (Berkeley, Calif.), D6*, 2.

Aravossis, K. G., Kapsalis, V. C., Kyriakopoulos, G. L., & Xouleis, T. G. (2019). Development of a holistic assessment framework for industrial organizations. *Sustainability, 11*(14), 3946.

Arend, R. J., & Bromiley, P. (2009). Assessing the dynamic capabilities view: Spare change everyone? *Strategic Organization, 7*(1), 75–90. doi:10.1177/1476127008100132

Argyris, C. (1960). *Understanding Organizational Behaviour*. Dorsey Press.

Ariyanti, F. D., & Andika, A. (2016). Supply Chain Risk Management in the Indonesian Flavor Industry: Case Study from a Multinational Flavor Company in Indonesia. *Proceedings of the 2016 International Conference on Industrial Engineering and Operations Management*, 1448-1455.

Armstrong, M. (2006). *A Handbook of Human Resource Management Practice* (8th ed.). Kogan Page.

Asikhia, O. U. (2016). Small and Medium-sized Enterprises (SMEs) wealth creation and poverty alleviation in Nigeria. *Journal of Economics and Behavioral Studies*, *8*(4), 17–31. doi:10.22610/jebs.v8i4(J).1360

Asikhia, O. U., Fasola, I. O., Makinde, G. O., & Akinlabi, B. H. (2020). Business Credit Affordability and Revenue Growth of Small and Medium Scale Enterprises: Evidence from Southwest, Nigeria. *IOSR Journal of Business and Management*, *22*(3), 24–37.

Asikhia, O., & Naidoo, V. (2020a). Assessment of the moderating effects of Nigerian market environment on the relationship between management success determinants and Small and Medium-sized Enterprises (SMEs)' performance. *Problems and Perspectives in Management*, *18*(4), 1–14. doi:10.21511/ppm.18(4).2020.31

Asikhia, O., & Naidoo, V. (2020b). Small and Medium-sized Enterprises (SMEs) management success determinants and its implications on their performance in South West, Nigeria. *International Journal of Economics & Business Administration*, *8*(4), 1057–1072. doi:10.35808/ijeba/650

Astanaqulov, O., & Asatullayev, K. (2020). Improving Investment Decisions in the Context of the Coronavirus Pandemy. *International Finance and Accounting*, *3*(28), 1–12.

Atsegbua, K. (2002). *Changing Organization: Essays on the Development and Evaluation of Human Organization*. McGraw-Hill.

Awino, B. Z. (2011). Strategic management: An empirical investigation of selected strategy variables on firms: A study of supply chain management in large private manufacturing firms in Kenya. *Prime Journals*, *1*(1), 9–18.

Ayegha, O., & Omale, S. (2016). A study on factors affecting entrepreneurial development in Nigeria. *European Journal of Business and Management*, *8*(12), 43–51.

Aykan, E., Karakuş, G., & Karakoç, H. (2019). The Effect of University Students' Individual Innovation and Lifelong Learning Trends on Entrepreneurship Orientation. *Sustainability*, *11*(22), 6201. doi:10.3390u11226201

Baburaj, Y., & Narayanan, V. (2016). *Five Forces Framework*. Drexel University. doi:10.1057/978-1-349-94848-2_632-1

Baglioni, E., Campling, L., & Hanlon, G. (2020). Global value chains as entrepreneurial capture: Insights from management theory. *Review of International Political Economy*, *27*(4), 903–925. doi:10.1080/09692290.2019.1657479

Bakker, A. B., Demerouti, E., & Verbeke, W. (2004). Using the job demands: Resources model to predict burnout and performance. *Human Resource Management*, *43*(1), 83–104. doi:10.1002/hrm.20004

Bakker, A. B., Gierveld, J. H., & Van Rijswijk, K. (2006). *Success factors among female school principals in primary teaching: A Study on Burnout, Work Engagement, and Performance, Right Management Consultants*. Diemen.

Bakker, A. B., & Schaufeli, W. B. (2008). Positive organizational behavior: Engaged employees in flourishing organizations. *Journal of Organizational Behavior*, *29*(2), 147–154. doi:10.1002/job.515

Balaguru, P., Raj, B. V., & Vignesh, B. E. (2013). Low Cost Energy Production Using Wind Belt Technology. *International Journal of Engineering and Innovative Technology*, *2*(9).

Bali, N. P., Gupta, P. N., & Gandhi, C. P. (2007). *A textbook of quantitative techniques*. Firewall Media.

Bammens, Y., & Collewaert, V. (2014). Trust between entrepreneurs and angel investors: Exploring positive and negative implications for venture performance assessments. *Journal of Management*, *40*(7), 1980–2008. doi:10.1177/0149206312463937

Banalieva, E. R., Eddleston, K. A., & Zellweger, T. M. (2015). When do family firms have an advantage in transitioning economies? Toward a dynamic institution-based view. *Strategic Management Journal*, *36*(9), 1358–1377. doi:10.1002mj.2288

Bangert, A. W. (2006). The development of an instrument for assessing online teaching effectiveness. *Journal of Educational Computing Research*, *35*(3), 227–244. doi:10.2190/B3XP-5K61-7Q07-U443

Barley, S. R., & Tolbert, P. S. (1997). Institutionalization and Structuration: Studying the Links between Action and Institution. *Organization Studies*, *18*(1), 93–117. doi:10.1177/017084069701800106

Barney, J. B. (1991). Firm Resources and Sustained Competitive Advantage. *Journal of Management*, *17*(1), 99–120. doi:10.1177/014920639101700108

Baron, R. A. (2000). Psychological perspectives on entrepreneurship: Cognitive and social factors in entrepreneurs' success. *Current Directions in Psychological Science*, *9*(1), 15–18. doi:10.1111/1467-8721.00050

Bartosova, V., & Kral, P. (2017). Methodological framework of financial analysis results objectification in Slovak Republic. *J. Mod. Account. Audit.*, *13*, 394–400.

Baumann, O., Schmidt, J., & Stieglitz, N. (2018). Effective search in rugged performance landscapes: A review and outlook. *Journal of Management*, *45*(1), 285–318. doi:10.1177/0149206318808594

Bayarçelik, E. B., Taşel, F., & Apak, S. (2014). A Research on Determining Innovation Factors for Small and Medium-sized Enterprises (SME). *Procedia: Social and Behavioral Sciences*, *150*(1), 202–211. doi:10.1016/j.sbspro.2014.09.032

Becherer, R. C., & Maurer, J. G. (1999). The proactive personality disposition and entrepreneurial behavior among small company presidents. *Journal of Small Business Management*, *37*(1), 28.

Becker, G. S. (1964). *Human Capital: A Theoretical and Empirical Analysis, with Special Reference to Education*. National Bureau of Economic Research.

Beck, T., & Demirguc-Kunt, A. (2006). Small and medium - size enterprises: Access to finance as a growth constraint. *Journal of Banking & Finance*, *30*(11), 2931–2943.

Beier, M. E., Kell, H. J., & Lang, J. W. B. (2019). Commenting on the "Great Debate": General Abilities, Specific Abilities, and the Tools of the Trade. *Journal of Intelligence*, *7*(1), 5. doi:10.3390/jintelligence7010005 PMID:31162384

Bell, M., & Pavitt, K. (1993). Technological Accumulation and Industrial Growth: Contrasts between Developed and Developing Countries. *Industrial and Corporate Change*, *2*, 157–210.

Ben Letaifa, S., & Goglio-Primard, K. (2016). How does institutional context shape entrepreneurship conceptualizations? *Journal of Business Research*, *69*(11), 5128–5134. doi:10.1016/j.jbusres.2016.04.092

Bennett, B., Naziri, D., Mahende, G., & Towo, E. (2012). *Driving Demand for Cassava in Tanzania: The Next Steps*. Natural Recourse Institute, University of Greenwich.

Ben-Youssef, A., Hadhri, W., & M'Henni, H. (2011). Intra-Firm Diffusion of Innovation: Evidence from Tunisian Small and Medium-sized Enterprises (SME) Regarding Information and Communication Technologies. *Middle East Development Journal*, *3*(1), 75–97.

Berisha, Q. A., Kutllovci, E., & Shiroka, P. J. (2017). Strategic Management Tools and Techniques: A Comparative Analysis of Empirical Studies. *Croatian Economic Survey*, *19*(1), 67–99. doi:10.15179/ces.19.1.3

Bernardin, H. J. (1977). Behavioral expectation scales versus summated scales. *The Journal of Applied Psychology, 62*(4), 422–427. doi:10.1037/0021-9010.62.4.422

Bhattacherjee, A. (2012). Social Science Research: Principles, Methods and Practices (2nd ed.). Global Text Project.

Bijlsma, J. (2012). *Sociaal werk in Nederland*. Coutinho.

Bisht, R. (2019). The children are cursing us: Can we rescue humanity from the Suicide Pact of the 7 Billion? *Times of India*.

Blažková, I., & Dvouletý, O. (2020). Zombies: Who are they and how do firms become zombies? *Journal of Small Business Management*, 1–27. Advance online publication. doi:10.1080/00472778.2019.1696100

Blechová, B. (2011). The influence of tax policy on the emergence of financial crisis. In *13th International Conference on Finance and Banking*. Karvina: SU OPF.

Bleiklie, I., Enders, J., & Lepori, B. (2015). Organizations as penetrated hierarchies: Environmental pressures and control in professional organizations. *Organization Studies, 36*(7), 873–896. doi:10.1177/0170840615571960

Bloom, P. N., & Dees, J. G. (2008). Cultivate Your Ecosystem. *Stanford Social Innovation Review, 6*(1), 47–53.

Blumberg, B. F., Cooper, D. R., & Schindler, P. S. (2014). *Business research methods*. McGraw-Hill Education.

Bocken, N. M., Short, S. W., Rana, P., & Evans, S. (2014). A literature and practice review to develop sustainable business model archetypes. *Journal of Cleaner Production, 65*, 42–56. doi:10.1016/j.jclepro.2013.11.039

Boer, H., & During, W. E. (2001). Innovation, What Innovation? A Comparison between Product, Process and Organizational Innovation. *International Journal of Technology Management, 22*(1/2/3), 83-107.

Boie, I., Fernandes, C., Frías, P., & Klobasa, M. (2014). Efficient strategies for the integration of renewable energy into future energy infrastructures in Europe - An analysis based on transnational modelling and case studies for none European regions. *Energy Policy, 67*, 170–185.

Bonsdorff, M. E., Zhou, L., Wang, M., Vanhala, S., von Bonsdorff, M. B., & Rantanen, T. (2018). Employee age and company performance: An integrated model of aging and human resource management practices. *Journal of Management, 44*(8), 3124–3150. doi:10.1177/0149206316662314

Boonsiritomachai, W., McGrath, G. M., & Burgess, S. (2016). Exploring Business Intelligence and Its Depth of Maturity in Thai Small and Medium-sized Enterprises (SME). *Cogent Business & Management, 3*(1), 1–17. doi:10.1080/23311975.2016.1220663

Boso, N., Adeleye, I., Ibeh, K., & Chizema, A. (2019). The internationalization of African firms: Opportunities, challenges and risks. *Thunderbird International Business Review, 61*(1), 5–12. doi:10.1002/tie.21977

Bourdeau, P. (2004). The man - nature relationship and environmental ethics. *Journal of Environmental Radioactivity, 72*(1 - 2), 9 - 15.

Bowen, H. R. (1953). *Social responsibilities of the businessman*. Harper and Row.

Bowen, M., Morara, M., & Mureithi, M. (2009). Management of business challenges among small and Microenterprises in Nairobi-Kenya. KCA. *Journal of Business and Management, 2*(1), 16–31.

Boyatzis, R. E., & Cavanagh, K. V. (2018). Leading change: Developing emotional, social, and cognitive competencies in managers during an MBA program. In *Emotional intelligence in education* (pp. 403–426). Springer. doi:10.1007/978-3-319-90633-1_15

Boyatzis, R., & McKee, A. (2011). Neuroscience and leadership: The promise of insights. *Ivey Business Journal, 75*(1), 1–3.

Boyne, G. A. (1998). Bureaucratic theory meets reality: Public choice and service contracting in US local government. *Public Administration Review, 58*(6), 474–484. doi:10.2307/977575

Bozkurt, Ö. Ç., & Kalkan, A. (2014). Business Strategies of SME's, Innovation Types and Factors Influencing Their Innovation: Burdur Model. *Ege Academic Review, 14*(2), 189–19.

Breakwell, G. (1995). *Research methods in Psychology*. Sage Publications.

Brewerton, P., & Millward, L. (2001). *Organizational Research Methods*. Sage Publications Ltd. doi:10.4135/9781849209533

Brinckmann, J., Grichnik, D., & Kapsa, D. (2010). Should entrepreneurs plan or just storm the castle? A Meta - analysis on contextual factors impacting the business planning - performance relationship in small firms. *Journal of Business Venturing, 25*(1), 24–40. doi:10.1016/j.jbusvent.2008.10.007

Brito, L. (2019). *Social justice and the Portuguese Welfare State – National Report*. Coimbra: ETHOS consortium.

Bronzini, R., & Piselli, P. (2016). The impact of R&D subsidies on firm innovation. *Research Policy, 45*(2), 442–457.

Brooking, A. (1996). *Intellectual Capital, Core Assets for the Third Millennium Enterprise*. International Thomson Business Press.

Browne, O., Poletti, S., & Young, D. (2015). How does market power affect the impact of large scale wind investment in 'energy only' wholesale electricity markets? *Energy Policy, 87*, 17–27. doi:10.1016/j.enpol.2015.08.030

Brownhilder, N. (2016). Examining the Moderating Effect of Environmental Hostility on the Entrepreneurial Orientation Performance Relationship. *Journal of Economics and Behavioral Studies, 8*(6), 6–18.

Brown, P. G., & Garver, G. (2009). *Right relationship: Building a whole earth economy*. Berrett - Koehler Publishers.

Brown, S. L., & Eisenhardt, K. M. (1998). *Competing on the edge: strategy as structured chaos*. Harvard Business School Press.

Brush, C. G., & Cooper, S. Y. (2012). Female Entrepreneurship and Economic Development: An International Perspective. *Entrepreneurship and Regional Development, 24*(1 - 2), 1 - 6.

Bruton, G. D., Ahlstrom, D., & Li, H. L. (2010). Institutional theory and entrepreneurship: Where are we now and where do we need to move in the future? *Entrepreneurship Theory and Practice, 34*(3), 421–440. doi:10.1111/j.1540-6520.2010.00390.x

Bryman, A. (2008). *Social Research Methods*. New York: Oxford Universtiy Press.

Bucher, R., & Stelling, J. (1969). Characteristics of professional organizations. *Journal of Health and Social Behavior, 10*(1), 3–15. doi:10.2307/2948501 PMID:5776946

Bülbül, Y. (2010). *Osmanlı'dan Cumhuriyet'e Özel Girişimciliğe Yönelik Devlet Politikaları*. İTO Yayınları.

Burke, W. W., & Litwin, G. H. (1992). A causal model of organizational performance and change. *Journal of Management, 18*(3), 523–545. doi:10.1177/014920639201800306

Byme, B. M. (2016). *Structural equation models with AMOS: Basic concepts, applications, and programming (3rd ed.)*. Routledge.

Byrnes, L., Brown, C., Foster, J., & Wagner, L. D. (2013). Australian renewable energy policy: Barriers and challenges. *Renewable Energy, 60*(1), 711–721. doi:10.1016/j.renene.2013.06.024

CAC. (2017). *Corporate Affairs Commission business directory*. Macmillan.

Cadoret, I., & Padovano, F. (2016). The political drivers of renewable energies policies. *Energy Economics*, *56*, 261–269. doi:10.1016/j.eneco.2016.03.003

Califano, R., Naddeo, A., Gatto, A., Leo, S., Milosa, P., Nazzaro, M., & Straccia, L. (2019). Virtual prototyping for workplace analysis: The effect of expectation on perceived comfort while using office devices. *International Journal on Interactive Design and Manufacturing*, *13*(1), 235–242. doi:10.100712008-018-0521-5

Cantaleano, K. R., Rodrigues, G. P., & Martins, T. S. (2018). The Mediating Effect of Proactive Market Orientation Capability in Entrepreneurial Orientation and Service Innovation. *Revista de Administração Mackenzie*, *19*(1), 1–27. doi:10.1590/1678-6971/eramr180038

Carr, C., Kolehmainen, K., & Mitchell, F. (2010). Strategic investment decision making practices: A contextual approach. *Management Accounting Research*, *21*(3), 167–184. doi:10.1016/j.mar.2010.03.004

Carrilho, P., & Perista, H. (2016, February 15). *Portugal: High and rising emigration in a context of high, but decerasing, unemployment*. Retrieved from Eurofound: https://www.eurofound.europa.eu/publications/article/2016/portugal - high - and - rising - emigration - in - a - context - of - high - but - decreasing - unemployment

Carroll, S. J., & Gillen, D. I. (1987). Are the classical management functions useful in describing managerial work? *Academy of Management Review*, *12*(1), 38–51. doi:10.5465/amr.1987.4306460

Cave, M., Hanney, S., Henkel, M., & Kogan, M. (1997). The use of performance indicators in higher education. In *Higher Education Policy Series*. Jessica Kingsley Publishers.

Cervelló-Royo, R., Moya-Clemente, I., Perelló-Marín, M. R., & Ribes-Giner, G. (2020). Sustainable development, economic and financial factors that influence the opportunity-driven entrepreneurship. An fsQCA approach. *Journal of Business Research*, *115*, 393–402. doi:10.1016/j.jbusres.2019.10.031

CFI. (2019, November 19). *Strategic Analyis*. Retrieved from CFI: https://corporatefinanceinstitute.com/resources/knowledge/strategy/strategic - analysis/

Chakravarty, S., & Meifang, X. (2011). Determinants of Profit Reinvestment by Small Businesses in Emerging Economies. *Financial Management*, *40*(3), 553–590. doi:10.1111/j.1755-053X.2011.01153.x

Chalikias, M., Kyriakopoulos, G., Skordoulis, M., & Koniordos, M. (2014). Knowledge Management for Business Processes: Employees' Recruitment and Human Resources' Selection: A Combined Literature Review and a Case Study. *Communications in Computer and Information Science, 466*, 505 - 520.

Chandler, A. D. (1962). *Strategy and structure: Chapters in the history of American enterprise*. M.I.T. Press.

Chandra, K. S. (1991). *Development of Women Entrepreneurship in India: A Study of Public Policies & Programmes*. Mittal Publications.

Chaniago, H. (2020). The Effects of Entrepreneurial Personality to Competitiveness and Corporate Image: A Study on Chocolate Agent Entrepreneurs. *International Review of Management and Marketing*, *10*(2), 21–29. doi:10.32479/irmm.9262

Chaudhuri, S. K., & Lovley, D. R. (2003). Electricity generation by direct oxidation of glucose in mediator less microbial fuel cells. *Nature Biotechnology*, *21*(10), 1229–1232. PMID:12960964

Chen, J. (2019, June 30). *Stakeholders*. Retrieved from Investopedia: https://www.investopedia.com/terms/s/stakeholder.asp

Chen, C. N., Tzeng, L. C., Ou, W. M., & Chang, K. T. (2007). The relationship among social capital, entrepreneurial orientation, organizational resources and entrepreneurial performance for new ventures. *Contemporary Management Research, 3*(3), 213–232. doi:10.7903/cmr.90

Chen, J., Cheng, S., Vinko, N., & Song, M. (2018). Quo Vadis? Major players in global coal consumption and emissions reduction. *Transformations in Business & Economics, 17*(1), 112–132.

Chen, S. (1995). An empirical examination of capital budgeting techniques: Impact of investment types and firm characteristics. *The Engineering Economist, 40*(2), 145–170. doi:10.1080/00137919508903142

Chidermbaran, K. & Alageppon, V.C. (2017). *Business environment.* Vikas Publishing Houseput Ltd.

Child, J. (1984). *Organization: A Guide to Problems and Practice.* Harper and Row. doi:10.4135/9781446280348

Chiu, C.-Y., Chen, S., & Chen, C.-L. (2017). An Integrated Perspective of TOE Framework and Innovation Diffusion in Broadband Mobile Applications Adoption by Enterprises. International Journal of Management. *Economics and Social Sciences, 6*(1), 14–39.

Cho, C., Yang, L., Chu, Y., & Yang, H. (2013). Renewable energy and renewable R&D in EU countries: A cointegration analysis. *Asian Journal of Natural and Applied Sciences, 2*(1), 10–16.

Cho, H. J., & Ahn, J. Y. (2018). The Dark Side of Wars for Talent and Layoffs: Evidence from Korean Firms. *Sustainability, 10*(5), 1365. doi:10.3390u10051365

Choi, D. Y., & Gray, E. R. (2008). Socially responsible entrepreneurs: What do they do to create and build their companies? *Business Horizons, 51*, 341–352.

Chong, E., & Wolf, H. (2010). Factors influencing followers' perception of organisational leaders. *Leadership and Organization Development Journal, 31*(5), 402–419. doi:10.1108/01437731011056434

Chongela, J., Nandala, V., & Korabandi, S. (2014). Consumer Demand System of Agri-food in Tanzania. *Journal of Development and Agricultural Economics, 6*(1), 42–48. doi:10.5897/JDAE2013.0475

Cicea, C., Popa, I., Marinescu, C., & Simona, C. Ş. (2019). Determinants of Small and Medium-sized Enterprises (SMEs)' performance: Evidence from European countries. *Economic Research Journal, 32*(1), 1602–1620.

Clausen, T. H. (2009). Do subsidies have positive impacts on R&D and innovation activities at the firm level? *Structural Change and Economic Dynamics, 20*(4), 239–253.

Cohen, B., & Winn, M. I. (2007). Market imperfections, opportunity and sustainable entrepreneurship. *Journal of Business Venturing, 22*, 29–49.

Cohen, M. D. (2006). What's Different is Routine. *Industrial and Corporate Change, 15*(2), 387–390. doi:10.1093/icc/dtl001

Cohen, M. D., & Bacdayan, P. (1994). Organizational Routines Are Stored As Procedural Memory: Evidence from a Laboratory Study. *Organization Science, 5*(4), 554–568. doi:10.1287/orsc.5.4.554

Cole, G. A. (2011). *Management Theory and Practice* (8th ed.). South - Western Cengage Learning.

Cole, G. A., & Kelly, P. (1996). *Management: Theory and practice.* Continuum.

Collewaert, V. (2012). Angel investors' and entrepreneurs' intentions to exit their ventures: A conflict perspective. *Entrepreneurship Theory and Practice, 36*(4), 753–779. doi:10.1111/j.1540-6520.2011.00456.x

Collins, D. J. (1994). Research note: How valuable are organizational capabilities? *Strategic Management Journal*, *15*(S1), 143–152. doi:10.1002mj.4250150910

Connelly, L. M. (2008). Pilot studies. *Medsurg Nursing*, *17*(6), 411–412. PMID:19248407

Cooper, A. C., & Artz, K. W. (1995). Determinants of satisfaction for entrepreneurs. *Journal of Business Venturing*, *10*(6), 439–457. doi:10.1016/0883-9026(95)00083-K

Cooper, D., & Schindler, P. (2006). *Research Methods*. McGraw-Hill.

Cooremans, C. (2011). Make it strategic! Financial investment logic is not enough. *Energy Efficiency*, *4*(4), 473–492. doi:10.100712053-011-9125-7

Coughlin, J. H., & Thomas, A. R. (2002). *The rise of women entrepreneurs: People, processes, and global trends*. Greenwood Publishing Group.

Coyne, K. P. (1986). Sustainable competitive advantage—What it is, what it isn't. *Business Horizons*, *29*(1), 54–61. doi:10.1016/0007-6813(86)90087-X

Crabtree. (2013). *Worldwide, 13% of employees are engaged at work*. Available at https://www.gallup.com/poll/165269/worldwide-employees-engaged-work.aspx

Crant, J. M. (1996). The proactive personality scale as a predictor of entrepreneurial intentions. *Journal of Small Business Management*, *34*, 42–49.

Cumming, D., & Zhang, M. (2019). Angel investors around the world. *Journal of International Business Studies*, *50*(5), 692–719. doi:10.105741267-018-0178-0

D'Amico, G., Lika, A., & Petroni, F. (2019). Risk Management of Pension Fund: A Model for Salary Evolution. *Int. J. Financial Stud.*, *7*(3), 44. doi:10.3390/ijfs7030044

D'Monte, L. (2019). *Five technologies that may alter India in 2020*. Retrieved from mint: https://www.livemint.com/technology/tech-news/five-technologies-that-may-alter-india-in-2020-11575819146057.html

da Soledade Carolo, D., & Pereirinha, J. (2017). *The development of the Welfare State in Portugal: trends in social expenditure between 1938 and 2003*. Lisbon University.

Daddi, T., Iraldo, F., Testa, F., & De Giacomo, M. R. (2019). The influence of managerial satisfaction on corporate environmental performance and reputation. *Business Strategy and the Environment*, *28*(1), 15–24. doi:10.1002/bse.2177

Dahlsrud, A. (2006). How Corporate Social Responsibility is defined: An Analysis of 37 Definitions. *Corporate Social Responsibility and Environmental Management*, *15*, 1–13.

Dai, L., Maksimov, V., Gilbert, B. A., & Fernhaber, S. A. (2014). Entrepreneurial Orientation and International scope: The Differential Roles of Innovativeness, Pro-activeness, and Risk-taking. *Journal of Business Venturing*, *29*(4), 511–524. doi:10.1016/j.jbusvent.2013.07.004

Dai, W. (2019). V - Shaped Responsibility of China's Social Welfare for the Elderly: Based on Analysing Historical Evolution and Future Sustainability. *Sustainability*, *11*(8), 2385. doi:10.3390u11082385

Damanpour, F. (1991). Organizational innovation: A Meta - analysis of effects of determinants and moderators. *Academy of Management Journal*, *34*(3), 555–590.

Dana, L.-P., & Ratten, V. (2017). International entrepreneurship in resource-rich landlocked African countries. *Journal of International Entrepreneurship*, *15*(4), 416–435. doi:10.100710843-017-0211-6

Darling, B. L., & Davis, T. R. (1994). Super Bakery Inc.: Innovating in a Mature Market Is Not Just a Piece of Cake. *Planning Review*, *22*(1), 8–17.

Darooneh, A. H. (2005). Physical Premium Principle: A New Way for Insurance Pricing. *Entropy (Basel, Switzerland)*, *7*(1), 97–107. doi:10.3390/e7010097

Dastmalchian, A., Blyton, P., & Adamson, R. (2014). *The Climate of Workplace Relations (Routledge Revivals)*. Routledge. doi:10.4324/9781315772417

Davis, J. G. (2004). Capabilities: A different perspective. *Australian Journal of Management*, *29*(1), 1–44. doi:10.1177/031289620402900108

Dawson, C. (2017). Financial optimism and entrepreneurial satisfaction. *Strategic Entrepreneurship Journal*, *11*(2), 171–194. doi:10.1002ej.1244

De Bodt, E., & Bouquin, H. (2001). Le contrôle de l'investissement. In *Images de l'investissement, Ouvrage collectif coordonné par G. Charreaux* (pp. 115–166). Vuibert.

De-Bruin, A., & Teasdale, S. (2019). A Research Agenda for Social Entrepreneurship. Edward Elgar Publishing.

Decker, W. H. (1987). Managerial humor and subordinate satisfaction. *Social Behavior and Personality*, *15*(2), 225–232. doi:10.2224bp.1987.15.2.225

Dees, J. G. (2001). *The Meaning of Social Entrepreneurship*. Caseatduke.org.

DeGennaro, R. P. (2012). Angel investors and their investments. The Oxford Handbook of Entrepreneurial Finance, 392-423.

del Marmol, T., & Feys, B. (2016). *Pestle Analysis*. 50minutes.

del Pilar, E. C., Alegado, I., & Bongo, M. F. (2019). Structural relationships among critical failure factors of micro-businesses. *Journal of Small Business and Enterprise Development*, *27*(1), 148–174. doi:10.1108/JSBED-01-2019-0001

De-La-Orden, A. (2009). Quality and evaluation: Analysis of a model. *Estudios Sobre Educación*, *16*, 17–36.

Delmar, F., & Shane, S. (2003). Does Business Planning Facilitate the Development of New Ventures? *Strategic Management Journal*, *24*(12), 1165–1185. doi:10.1002mj.349

DeMarrais, K. B., & Lapan, S. D. (2003). *Foundations for research: Methods of inquiry in education and the social sciences*. Routledge. doi:10.4324/9781410609373

Demirci, A. E. (2013). Cross-Cultural Differencies in Entrepreneurial Tendencies: An Exploratory View in Turkey and Canada. *International Journal of Entrepreneurship*, 17.

Deyreh, E. (2012). Effects of perceived selfishness among managers on organizational justice. *Procedia: Social and Behavioral Sciences*, *46*, 390–393. doi:10.1016/j.sbspro.2012.05.128

Dhameja, S. K., Bhatia, B. S., & Saini, J. S. (2000). Women Entrepreneurs - Their Perceptions, About Business Opportunities and Attitudes towards Entrepreneurial Support Agencies (A study of Haryana State). *Small Enterprises Development Management Extension Journal*, *27*(4), 37–50.

Dickinson, T. L., & Zellinger, P. M. (1980). A comparison of the behaviorally anchored rating and mixed standard scale formats. *The Journal of Applied Psychology*, *65*(2), 147–154. doi:10.1037/0021-9010.65.2.147

Diehl, M.-R., Richter, A., & Sarnecki, A. (2018). Variations in employee performance in response to organizational justice: The sensitizing effect of socioeconomic conditions. *Journal of Management*, *44*(6), 2375–2404. doi:10.1177/0149206316671581

Dinh, C. N. (2011). *Performance of small and medium enterprises and the impact of environmental variables: Evidence from Vietnam* [Unpublished Doctoral Thesis]. Aston University, Birmingham, UK.

Di-Stefano, G., Peteraf, M. & Verona, G. (2010). Dynamic capabilities deconstructed: A bibliographic investigation into the origins, development, and future directions of the research domain. *Industrial and Corporate Change, 19*(14), 1187–1204.

Dobrin, C. O., Popescu, G. N., Popescu, V. A., & Popescu, C. R. G. (2012). The concept of performance in business organizations - Case study on the employee performance in Romanian business organizations, In *Proceedings of the 6th International Management Conference: Approaches in Organisational Management* (pp. 310 - 316). Editura ASE.

Dollinger, M. (2008). *Entrepreneurship.* Marsh Publications.

Donnelley, S. (2009). *Minding Nature, Minding Ourselves.* Centre for Humans & Nature.

Dorow, P. F., Dávila, G., Varvakis, G., & Vallejos, R. V. (2015). Generation of Ideas, Ideation and Idea Management. Navus. *Revista de Gestão e Tecnologia, 5*(2), 51–59. doi:10.22279/navus.2015.v5n2.p51-59.248

Drakopoulou Dodd, S., Jack, S., & Anderson, A. (2013). From admiration to abhorrence: the contentious appeal of entrepreneurship across Europe. *Entrepreneurship and Regional Development, 25*(1-2), 69-89. doi:10.1080/08985626.2012.746878

Drucker, P. F. (1985). *Innovation and Entrepreneurship: Practice and Principles.* Harper Business.

Duarte, N. (2011). Innovation, Risk and Proactivity: Are Firms Following these Strategies? *WSEAS Transactions on Business and Economics, 8*(3), 110–120.

Dwivedi, A., & Weerawardena, J. (2018). Conceptualizing and operationalizing the social entrepreneurship construct. *Journal of Business Research, 86*, 32–40. doi:10.1016/j.jbusres.2018.01.053

Eckhardt, J. T., & Shane, S. A. (2003). Opportunities and entrepreneurship. *Journal of Management, 29*(3), 333–349. doi:10.1177/014920630302900304

Edomah, N., Foulds, C., & Jones, A. (2017). Influences on energy supply infrastructure: A comparison of different theoretical perspectives. *Renewable & Sustainable Energy Reviews, 79*, 765–778. doi:10.1016/j.rser.2017.05.072

Ekakitie–Emonena, S. (2019). Managing turbulent business environments in Nigeria: A model approach. Journal of Education, Society &. *Behavioral Science, 29*(3), 1–11.

Eniola, A. A. (2018a). Entrepreneur-SME Manager Traits and Sources of Financing. In African Entrepreneurship (pp. 223-259). Springer.

Eniola, A.A. (2021). The Entrepreneur Motivation and Financing Sources. *Journal of Open Innovation, Technology, Marketing, and Complex, 7*, 25. doi:10.3390/joitmc7010025

Eniola, A. A. (2018b). SME firm characteristics impact the choice of sources of financing in South-West, Nigeria. *International Journal of Business and Globalisation, 21*(3), 344–366. doi:10.1504/IJBG.2018.095482

Eniola, A. A. (2020a). Cultural Identity and Entrepreneurial Performance. In R. Vanessa (Ed.), *Entrepreneurship as Empowerment: Knowledge Spill-overs and Entrepreneurial Ecosystems* (pp. 23–44). Emerald Publishing Limited. doi:10.1108/978-1-83982-550-720201004

Eniola, A. A. (2020a). Entrepreneurial self-efficacy and orientation for SME development. *Small Enterprise Research, 27*(2), 125–145. doi:10.1080/13215906.2020.1752295

Eniola, A. A. (2020b). Entrepreneurial Self-efficacy, Entrepreneurial Orientation, and Institutional Environment: SME in Nigeria. *SCMS Journal of Indian Management*, *17*(1), 16–27.

Eniola, A. A. (2020c). Institutional Environment, Entrepreneurial Self-efficacy and Orientation for SME in Nigeria. *International Journal of Engineering*, *4*, 17.

Eniola, A. A., & Entebang, H. (2014). SME firms performance in Nigeria: Competitive advantage and its impact. *International Journal of Research Studies in Management*, *3*(2), 75–86. doi:10.5861/ijrsm.2014.854

Eniola, A. A., & Entebang, H. (2017). SME managers and financial literacy. *Global Business Review*, *18*(3), 559–576. doi:10.1177/0972150917692063

Eniola, A. A., Olorunleke, G. K., Akintimehin, O. O., Ojeka, J. D., & Oyetunji, B. (2019). The impact of organizational culture on total quality management in SMEs in Nigeria. *Heliyon*, *5*(8), e02293. doi:10.1016/j.heliyon.2019.e02293 PMID:31508519

Enu, P., & Havi, E. D. K. (2014). Macroeconomic determinants of inflation in Ghana: A co-integration approach. *International Journal of Academic Research & Social Sciences*, *4*(7), 95–110. doi:10.6007/IJARBSS/v4-i7/993

Erikson, M. G. (2019). Kindness, Communication and Academic Responsibility in Higher Education. In *Values of the University in a Time of Uncertainty* (pp. 171–184). Springer. doi:10.1007/978-3-030-15970-2_12

Ernst, E. (2019). Finance and Jobs: How Financial Markets and Prudential Regulation Shape Unemployment Dynamics. *J. Risk Financial Manag.*, *12*(1), 20. doi:10.3390/jrfm12010020

Eruemegbe, G. O. (2015). Impact of business environment on organizational performance in Nigeria: A study of Union Bank of Nigeria. *European Scientific Journal*, *11*(10), 478–494.

European Commission. (2017). *Directorate General Human Resources and Security: Performance through People, Management Plan 2017*. Retrieved from https://ec.europa.eu/info/sites/info/files/management-plan-hr-2017_en_0.pdf

European Commission. (2018a). *Directorate General Human Resources and Security: Performance through People, Management Plan 2018*. Retrieved from https://ec.europa.eu/info/sites/info/files/management-plan-hr-2018_en.pdf

European Commission. (2018b). Thematic Paper: Human Resource Management: How to Attract, Retain and Develop Talent. doi:10.2767/89866

European Commission. (2018c). Human Resources: Performance through People, Human Resources in 2018. Luxembourg: Publications Office of the European Union. doi:10.2774/259615

European Commission. (2019). *Directorate General Human Resources and Security: Performance through People, Management Plan 2018*. Retrieved from https://ec.europa.eu/info/sites/info/files/management-plan-hr-2019_en.pdf

Eze, O., & Ogiji, F. (2013). Impact of fiscal policy on manufacturing sector output in Nigeria: An error correction analysis. *International Journal of Business & Management Review*, *1*(3), 35–55.

Fang, C., Lee, J., & Schilling, M. A. (2010). Balancing Exploration and Exploitation through Structural Design: The Isolation of Subgroups and Organizational Learning. *Organization Science*, *21*(3), 625–642. doi:10.1287/orsc.1090.0468

FAPI. (2020). *Průzkum COVID - 19: Víme, jak koronavirus zasáhl podnikatele a firmy*. Retrieved from https://fapi.cz/pruzkum-covid-19-vime-jak-koronavirus-zasahl-podnikatele-a-firmy/

Fazzari, S. M., Hubbard, R. G., & Peterson, B. C. (1998). Financing Constraints and Corporate Investment. *Brookings Papers on Economic Activity*, *1*, 141–195.

Fellows, P., & Axtell, B. (2004). Setting up and Running a Small Flour Mill or Bakery. In Opportunities in Food Processing Series. Wageningen: ACP-EU Technical Centre for Agricultural and Rural Cooperation (CTA).

Ferdinand, J., Graca, M., Antonacopoulou, E. & Easterby-Smith, M. (2004). *Dynamic capability: tracking the development of a concept.* In 5[th]European Conference on Organizational Knowledge, Learning, and Capabilities, Innsbruck, UK.

Fernando, A. C. (2011). *Business environment.* Dorling Kindersley.

Fichter, K., & Tiemann, I. (2020). Impacts of promoting sustainable entrepreneurship in generic business plan competitions. *Journal of Cleaner Production, 267*, 122076. Advance online publication. doi:10.1016/j.jclepro.2020.122076

Fiet, J. O. (2001). The pedagogical side of entrepreneurship theory. *Journal of Business Venturing, 16*(2), 101–117. doi:10.1016/S0883-9026(99)00042-7

Fillis, I., & Rentschler, R. (2010). The role of creativity in entrepreneurship. *Journal of Enterprising Culture, 18*(01), 49–81. doi:10.1142/S0218495810000501

Fishbein, M., & Ajzen, I. (1975). *Belief, attitude, intention, and behaviour: an introduction to theory and research.* Addison-Wesley.

Fjose, S., Grünfeld, L. A., & Green, C. (2010). *Small and Medium-sized Enterprises (SME) and Growth in Sub-Saharan Africa: Identifying Small and Medium-sized Enterprises (SME) Roles and Obstacles to Small and Medium-sized Enterprises (SME) Growth.* MENON Business Economics.

Fornell, C., & Larcker, D. F. (1981). Evaluating structural equation models with unobservable variables and measurement error. *JMR, Journal of Marketing Research, 18*(1), 39–50. doi:10.1177/002224378101800104

Fournier, G., Zimmermann, H., Masdonati, J., & Gauthier, C. (2018). Job Loss in a Group of Older Canadian Workers: Challenges in the Sustainable Labour Market Reintegration Process. *Sustainability, 10*(7), 2245. doi:10.3390u10072245

Fourth Sector Network. (2009). *The Emerging Fourth Sector About Fourth Sector Network.* Fourth Sector Network.

Frandsen, S. (2012). Organizational image, identification, and cynical distance: Prestigious professionals in a low-prestige organization. *Management Communication Quarterly, 26*(3), 351–376. doi:10.1177/0893318912438692

Frank, H., Güttel, W., & Kessler, A. (2017). Environmental dynamism, hostility, and dynamic capabilities in medium-sized enterprises. *International Journal of Entrepreneurship and Innovation, 18*(3), 185–194. doi:10.1177/1465750317723219

Freeman, E. (1984). *Strategic Management - A Stakeholder Approach.* Pitman Publishing Inc.

Frenken, K., & Hekkert, M. P. (2017). *Innovatiebeleid in tijden van maatschappelijke uitdagingen.* Retrieved on https://www.mejudice.nl/artikelen/detail/innovatiebeleid-in-tijden-van-maatschappelijke-uitdagingen

Gadenne, D. (1998). Critical success factors for small business: An inter-industry comparison. *International Small Business Journal, 17*(1), 36–57. doi:10.1177/0266242698171002

Gado, N., & Nmadu, T. (2011). The performance of textile companies in the North-West zone of Nigeria: The role of Infrastructure as a resource. *International Journal of Human Resource Studies, 2*(1), 89–100. doi:10.5296/ijhrs.v2i1.1259

Gallagher, H., Yang, L., & Liang, J. (2019). 'I Respect You but I Am Not Willing to Be You': Critical Reflections of Western Teaching of Social Work to Students in China - What Can be Learned Both Ways? *Soc. Sci., 8*(10), 272. doi:10.3390ocsci8100272

Galloway, L., & Brown, W. (2002). Entrepreneurship education at university: A driver in the creation of high growth firms? *Education + Training, 44*(8 / 9), 398–405. doi:10.1108/00400910210449231

Gans, J., Stern, S., & Wu, J. (2016). *The Foundations of Entrepreneurial Strategy*. SSRN Working Paper #2844843.

Garbelli, M. E. (2016). Competitive Networking for SME: A Case Study of its Success in Italy. *European Scientific Journal, 12*(7), 1–19. doi:10.19044/esj.2016.v12n7p1

García Mestanza, J., Cerezo Medina, A., & Cruz Morato, M. A. (2019). A Model for Measuring Fair Labour Justice in Hotels: Design for the Spanish Case. *Sustainability, 11*(17), 4639. doi:10.3390u11174639

García-Alcaraz, J. L., Alor-Hernández, G., Sánchez-Ramírez, C., Jiménez-Macías, E., Blanco-Fernández, J., & Latorre-Biel, J. I. (2018). Mediating Role of the Six Sigma Implementation Strategy and Investment in Human Resources in Economic Success and Sustainability. *Sustainability,* 10.

García-Alcaraz, J. L., Flor-Montalvo, F. J., Avelar-Sosa, L., Sánchez-Ramírez, C., & Jiménez-Macías, E. (2019). Human Resource Abilities and Skills in TQM for Sustainable Enterprises. *Sustainability, 11*(22), 6488. doi:10.3390u11226488

García-Sánchez, E., García-Morales, V., & Martín-Rojas, R. (2018). Influence of Technological Assets on Organizational Performance through Absorptive Capacity, Organizational Innovation and Internal Labour Flexibility. *Sustainability, 10*(3), 770. doi:10.3390u10030770

Garzia, C. (2017). Innovation Diffusion and Bandwagon Effect: The Palm Oil in the Italian Bakery Industry. In *Proceedings of the 35th International Conference of the System Dynamics Society*. Cambridge, MA: System Dynamics Society.

Gazem, N. A., & Rahman, A. A. (2013). Promoting the Systematic Innovation Process in Small and Medium Enterprises. *Journal of Convergence Information Technology, 8*(11), 528–535. doi:10.4156/jcit.vol8.issue11.59

Gelfand, M. J., Higgins, M., Nishii, L. H., Raver, J. L., Dominguez, A., Murakami, F., Yamaguchi, S., & Toyama, M. (2002). Culture and egocentric perceptions of fairness in conflict and negotiation. *The Journal of Applied Psychology, 87*(5), 833–845. doi:10.1037/0021-9010.87.5.833 PMID:12395808

GEM. (2010). *Report, Entrepreneurship in Turkey*. Author.

Gerard, H., & Bruijl, T. (2018). The Relevance Of Porter's Five Forces In Today's Innovative And Changing Business Environment. SSRN *Electronic Journal.*

Gerlach, A. (2003a). *Sustainable entrepreneurship and innovation.* Centre for Sustainability Management. University of Lueneburg.

Gerlach, A. (2003b). *Innovativität und Sustainability Intrapreneurship.* Paper presented at Sustainable Management in Action '03, University of St. Gallen, Schweiz.

Gibb, A. A. (1996). Entrepreneurship and small business management: Can we afford to neglect them in the twenty-first century business school? *British Journal of Management, 7*(4), 309–321. doi:10.1111/j.1467-8551.1996.tb00121.x

Gibson, K. (2000). The Moral Basis of Stakholder Theory. *Journal of Business Ethics,* 26.

Gil-Edo, M. T., Roca Puig, V., & Camisón Zornoza, C. (1999). Towards customer - oriented service quality models in public universities: The case of Universitat Jaume I. *Investigaciones Europeas de Dirección y Economía de la Empresa, 5*(2), 69–92.

Gill, A. S., Sharma, S. P., & Mathur, N. (2012). The Impact of Debt Policy on the Investment Decision of Small Business Owners in India. *International Research Journal of Finance and Economics*, (97), 6–13.

Gismera, E., Fernández, J. L., Labrador, J., & Gismera, L. (2019). Suffering at Work: A Challenge for Corporate Sustainability in the Spanish Context. *Sustainability, 11*(15), 4152. doi:10.3390u11154152

Glaser, B., & Strauss, A. (1967). *The discovery of grounded theory*. Aldine.

Global Entrepreneurship Monitor (GEM). (2018). *2017 - 2018 Global Report*. https://www.gemconsortium.org/report

Golsorkhi, D., Rouleau, L., Seidl, D., & Vaara, E. (2010). *Cambridge handbook of strategy as practice*. Cambridge University Press. doi:10.1017/CBO9780511777882

Gómez-Bezares, F., Przychodzen, W., & Przychodzen, J. (2019). Corporate Sustainability and CEO - Employee Pay Gap—Buster or Booster? *Sustainability*, *11*(21), 6023. doi:10.3390u11216023

Greener, S. (2008). *Business Research Methods*. Ventus Publishing.

Guerrero, M., Urbano, D., & Fayolle, A. (2016). Entrepreneurial activity and regional competitiveness: Evidence from European entrepreneurial universities. *The Journal of Technology Transfer*, *41*(1), 105–131. doi:10.100710961-014-9377-4

Guiyang, Z. (2007). Energy subsidy policies and their reform: Providing economic incentives for climate change mitigation. *Advances in Climate Change Research*, *3*, 92–96.

Gullberg, A. T., Ohlhorst, D., & Schreurs, M. (2014). Towards a low carbon energy Future - Renewable energy cooperation between Germany and Norway. *Renewable Energy*, *68*, 216–222. doi:10.1016/j.renene.2014.02.001

Gupta, J., Gregoriou, A., & Healey, J. (2015). Forecasting bankruptcy for SMEs using hazard function: To what extent does size matter? *Review of Quantitative Finance and Accounting*, *45*(4), 845–869. doi:10.100711156-014-0458-0

Gupta, V. (2020). A Case Study on Economic Development of Tanzania. *Journal of the International Academy for Case Studies*, *26*(1), 1–16.

Gürol, Y., & Atsan, N. (2006). Entrepreneurial characteristics amongst university students. *Education + Training*, *48*(1), 25–38. doi:10.1108/00400910610645716

Guthrie, J., & Neumann, R. (2007). Economic and non - financial performance indicators in universities. *Public Management Review*, *9*(2), 231–252. doi:10.1080/14719030701340390

Hadjimanolis, A. (1999). Barriers to innovation for SMEs in a small less developed country (Cyprus). *Technovation*, *19*(9), 561–570.

Hair, J. F., Black, W. C., Babin, B. J., & Anderson, R. E. (2019). *Multivariate data analysis* (8th ed.). Cengage Learning.

Haldar, S. (2019). Towards a conceptual understanding of sustainability-driven entrepreneurship. *Corporate Social Responsibility and Environmental Management*, *26*(6), 1157–1170. doi:10.1002/csr.1763

Hall, J. K., Daneke, G. A., & Lenox, M. J. (2010). Sustainable Development and Entrepreneurship: Past Contributions and Future Directions. *Journal of Business Venturing*, *25*, 439–448.

Hamadamin, H. H., & Atan, T. (2019). The Impact of Strategic Human Resource Management Practices on Competitive Advantage Sustainability: The Mediation of Human Capital Development and Employee Commitment. *Sustainability*, *11*(20), 5782. doi:10.3390u11205782

Hambrick, D. C., & Mason, P. A. (1984). Upper echelons: The organization as a reflection of its top managers. *Academy of Management Review*, *9*(2), 193–206. doi:10.5465/amr.1984.4277628

Hargreaves, A., & Fink, D. (2004). The seven principles of sustainable leadership. Educational Leadership. *Journal of the Department of Supervision and Curriculum Development, NEA*, *61*(7), 8–13.

Harrison, B. (2015). Expanding the renewable energy industry through tax subsidies using the structure and rationale of traditional energy tax subsidies. *University of Michigan Journal of Law Reform. University of Michigan. Law School, 48*(3), 845–877.

Hart, S. L. (2005). *Capitalism at the Crossroads: the Unlimited Business Opportunities in Solving the World's Most Difficult Problems*. Wharton School Publishing.

Harwood, R. (2016). What Has Limited the Impact of UK Disability Equality Law on Social Justice? *Laws, 5*(4), 42. doi:10.3390/laws5040042

Hasuch, H., & Pyka, A. (2007). *Elgar companion to Neo - Schumpeterian Economics*. Edward Elgar Publishing.

Hattula, J. D., Herzog, W., Dahl, D. W., & Reinecke, S. (2015). Managerial empathy facilitates egocentric predictions of consumer preferences. *JMR, Journal of Marketing Research, 52*(2), 235–252. doi:10.1509/jmr.13.0296

Häuser, S. (2007). *Krizové řízení v turbulentním prostředí.Studijní opora*. Slezská univerzita v Opavě. Matematický ústav v Opavě.

Havlíček, K. (2011). Strategické řízení podniku. *Moderní řízení*, 32 - 34.

Hawken, P. (1992). The ecology of commerce. *Inc., 14*(4), 93–97.

Health at a glance 2019: OECD indicators. (2019). Retrieved from OECD iLibrary: https://www.oecd - ilibrary.org/sites/4dd50c09 - en/1/2/10/3/index.html?itemId=/content/publication/4dd50c09 - en&_csp_=82587932df7c06a6a3f9dab95304095d&itemIGO=oecd&itemContentType=book

Health Care Systems: Differences Around the Globe. (2014, February 22). Retrieved from Global, Pre - Meds: https://www.globalpremeds.com/blog/2014/02/22/health - care - systems - differences - around - the - globe/

Helfrich, H., & Dietl, E. (2019). Is employee narcissism always toxic?–The role of narcissistic admiration, rivalry and leaders' implicit followership theories for employee voice. *European Journal of Work and Organizational Psychology, 28*(2), 259–271. doi:10.1080/1359432X.2019.1575365

Henderson, B. D. (1989). The Origin of Strategy. *Harvard Business Review*. PMID:10303992

Hendrix, C., & Noland, M. (2014). *Confronting the curse: The economics and geopolitics of natural resource governance*. Peterson Institute for International Economics: Columbia University Press.

Hernandez-Pina, F., & Maquilón-Sánchez, J. J. (2010). Conceptions of teaching. Contributions to teacher training. *Revista Electrónica Interuniversitaria de Formación Del Profesorado, 13*(3), 17–25.

Herron, L., & Robinson, R. B. (1993). A structural model of the effects of entrepreneurial characteristics on venture performance. *Journal of Business Venturing, 8*(3), 281-294. doi: (93)90032-z doi:10.1016/0883-9026

Herzog, M. A. (2008). Considerations in determining sample size for pilot studies. *Research in Nursing & Health, 30*(2), 180–191. doi:10.1002/nur.20247 PMID:18183564

Heyden, M. L. M., Sidhu, J. S., & Volberda, H. W. (2018). The conjoint influence of top and middle management characteristics on management innovation. *Journal of Management, 44*(4), 1505–1529. doi:10.1177/0149206315614373

Hill, R. (1998). What sample size is 'enough' in internet survey research? *Interpersonal Computing and Technology. An Electronic Journal for the 21st Century, 6*(3-4), 1-10.

Hitt, M. A., Ireland, R. D., Camp, S. M., & Sexton, D. L. (2001). Strategic Entrepreneurship: Entrepreneurial Strategies for Wealth Creation. *Strategic Management Journal, 22*(6-7), 479-491.

Hitt, M. A., Ireland, R. D., Camp, S. M., & Sexton, D. L. (2002). Strategic Entrepreneurship: Integrating Entrepreneurial and Strategic Management Perspectives. In M. A. Hitt, R. D. Ireland, S. M. Camp, & D. L. Sexton (Eds.), *Strategic Entrepreneurship: Creating a New Mindset* (pp. 1–16). Blackwell Publishers. doi:10.1111/b.9780631234104.2002.00001.x

Hitt, M. A., Ireland, R. D., & Hoskisson, R. E. (2007). *Strategic Management: Competitiveness and Globalization (Concepts and Cases)* (7th ed.). Thomson South-Western.

Hmieleski, K. M., & Baron, R. A. (2008). When does entrepreneurial self-efficacy enhance versus reduce firm performance? *Strategic Entrepreneurship Journal*, *2*(1), 57–72. doi:10.1002ej.42

Hoang, D. (2019). Labour Standards in the Global Supply Chain: Workers' Agency and Reciprocal Exchange Perspective. *Societies (Basel, Switzerland)*, *9*(2), 38. doi:10.3390oc9020038

Hockerts, K. (2003). *Sustainability Innovation: Ecological and Social Entrepreneurship and the Managing of Antagonistic Assets* (PhD Dissertation). University of St. Gallen, Schweiz.

Hofer, C. W., & Schendel, D. (1978). *Strategy formulation: analytical concepts*. West Publising Co.

Hofstede, G. (2019, December 12). *Insights*. Retrieved from Hofstede insights: https://www.hofstede - insights.com/country - comparison/the - netherlands,portugal/

Hofstede, G., Pedersen, P. B., & Hofstede, G. (2002). *Exploring Culture*. Nicholas Brealey Publishing.

Holban, E., Diacu, E., Matei, M., Ghita, G., Raischi, M., Fronescu, S., Daescu, A., Gheorghe, I. P., Ilie, M., Szep, R., Daescu, V., Dumitru, D., Marinescu, F., Tociu, C., Popescu, I., & Gh. Popescu, C. R. (2017). Assessment of atmospheric pollution in a cement factory area situated in the eastern part of Romania. *Journal of Environmental Protection and Ecology*, *18*(3), 819–830.

Holenweger, M., Jager, M. K., & Kernic, F. (2017). *Leadership in Extreme Situations*. Springer. doi:10.1007/978-3-319-55059-6

Holmes, H., & Ferriill, M. (2005). The application of operation and technology road - mapping to aid Singaporean SMEs identify and select emerging technologies. *Technological Forecasting and Social Change*, *72*(3), 349–357. doi:10.1016/j.techfore.2004.08.010

Homero-Orozco, G., Sola-Olalla, M. R., & Martinez-Abad, F. (2018). Didactic Models at the High Education: A reality that can change. Profesorado. *Revista de Curriculum y Formación Del Profesorado*, *22*(2), 447–469.

Hoogendoorn, B., Van der Zwan, P., & Thurik, R. (2019). Sustainable Entrepreneurship: The Role of Perceived Barriers and Risk. *Journal of Business Ethics*, *157*(3). Advance online publication. doi:10.100710551 - 017 - 3646 - 8

Hosseini, M. R., Banihashemi, S., Chileshe, N., Namzadi, M. O., Udaeja, C., Rameezdeen, R., & McCuen, T. (2016). BIM Adoption within Australian Small and Medium-sized Enterprises (SME)): An Innovation Diffusion Model. *Construction Economics and Building*, *16*(3), 71–86. doi:10.5130/AJCEB.v16i3.5159

Hosseininia, G., & Ramezani, A. (2016). Factors Influencing Sustainable Entrepreneurship in Small and Medium - Sized Enterprises in Iran: A Case Study of Food Industry. *Sustainability*, *8*(10), 1010. doi:10.3390u8101010

Huang, Q., Liu, X., & Li, J. (2019). Contextualization of Chinese entrepreneurship research: an overview and some future research directions. *Entrepreneurship & Regional Development,* 1-17. doi:10.1080/08985626.2019.1640437

Huang, I. W. (2003). Importance of Small and Medium-sized Enterprises (SME) Development in Thailand. *Forum of International Development Studies*, *23*(1), 159–176.

Huang, K.-W., Huang, J.-H., & Tzeng, G.-H. (2016). New Hybrid Multiple Attribute Decision - Making Model for Improving Competence Sets: Enhancing a Company's Core Competitiveness. *Sustainability*, *8*(2), 175. doi:10.3390u8020175

Huang, S., Lo, S., & Lin, Y. (2013). To re - explore the causality between barriers to renewable energy development: A case study of wind energy. *Energies*, *6*(9), 4465–4488. doi:10.3390/en6094465

Hurst, D. K. (2002). *Crisis: meeting the challenge of organizational change*. Harvard Business School Press.

Iannone, B. (2018). Sustainability, corporate social responsibility, and corporate reputation in the wine sector: A key performance indicator framework model. *International Journal of Applied Behavioral Economics*, *7*(2), 47–68. doi:10.4018/IJABE.2018040104

Ibidunni, O. S., & Ogundele, O. J. K. (2013). Competition in marketing survival yardstick for Small and Medium-sized Enterprises (SMEs) in Nigeria. *Mediterranean Journal of Social Sciences*, *4*(1), 231–240.

IEA, IRENA, UNSD, WB, & WHO. (2019). Tracking SDG 7: The Energy Progress Report 2019. Washington, DC: Author.

Igwe, P. A., Amaugo, A. N., Ogundana, O. M., Egere, O. M., & Anigbo, J. A. (2018). Factors affecting the investment climate, Small and Medium-sized Enterprises (SMEs) productivity and entrepreneurship in Nigeria. *European Journal of Sustainable Development*, *7*(1), 182–200. doi:10.14207/ejsd.2018.v7n1p182

Ijadi Maghsoodi, A., Azizi-ari, I., Barzegar-Kasani, Z., Azad, M., Zavadskas, E., & Antucheviciene, J. (2019). Evaluation of the Influencing Factors on Job Satisfaction Based on Combination of PLS - SEM and F - MULTIMOORA Approach. *Symmetry*, *11*(1), 24. doi:10.3390ym11010024

Illés, M. (2016). The Real Reinvestment Rate Assumption as a Hidden Pitfall. Theory, Methodology. *Practice*, *12*(1), 47–60.

IPCC. (2012). *Intergovernmental panel on climate change. Renewable energy sources and climate change mitigation. Summary for policymakers and technical summary*. https://archive.ipcc.ch/

Isaac, S., & Michael, W. B. (1995). *Handbook in research and evaluation*. Educational and Industrial Testing Services.

Jabłońska-Porzuczek, L., & Smoluk-Sikorska, J. (2016). Factors of Competitiveness of Enterprises Operating in the Confectionary-Bakery Industry in Wielkopolska Voivodship. Optimum. *Studia Ekonomiczne*, *84*(6), 99–110.

Jayashree, G., & Priya, I. C. M. (2016). A Study on Role of Banking Sector in Women Entrepreneurship. *International Journal of Social Relevance & Concern*, *4*(11), 1–7.

Jayeola, O., Ihinmoyan, T., & Kazeem, Y. K. (2018). Environmental factors and the performance of micro and small scale enterprises (MSEs) in Nigeria: Lessons from some selected MSEs in Ondo State Nigeria. Journal of Economics. *Management & Trade*, *21*(6), 1–14. doi:10.9734/JEMT/2018/42079

Jensen, M. C. (1986). Agency costs of free cash flow, corporate finance, and takeovers. *The American Economic Review*, *76*, 323–329.

Jepperson, R. (1991). Institutions, institutional effects, and institutionalism. In W. W. Powell & P. J. DiMaggio (Eds.), *The new institutionalism in organizational analysis* (pp. 143–163). University of Chicago Press.

Johannisson, B. (2002). *Enacting Entrepreneurship - Using Auto - Ethnography to Study Organization Creation*. Paper presented the conference Ethnographic Organizational Studies, University of St. Gallen, Switzerland.

Johannisson, B. (2005). *Entreprenörskapets väsen*. Studentlitteratur.

Johnson, G., Scholes, K., & Whittington, R. (2008). *Exploring corporate strategy*. Harlow: Financial Times Prentice Hall.

Johnson, S., & Van-de-Ven, A. H. (2002). A Framework for Entrepreneurial Strategy. In M. A. Hitt, R. D. Ireland, S. M. Camp, & D. L. Sexton (Eds.), *Strategic Entrepreneurship: Creating a New Mindset* (pp. 66-85). Oxford: Blackwell Publishers.

Joshi, P. R., & Islam, S. (2018). E - Government Maturity Model for Sustainable E - Government Services from the Perspective of Developing Countries. *Sustainability, 10*(6), 1882. doi:10.3390u10061882

Jovovic, R., Simanaviciene, Z., & Dirma, V. (2017). Assessment of Heat Production Savings Resulting from Replacement of Gas with Biofuels. *Transformations in Business & Economics, 16*(1), 34–51.

Julious, S. A. (2005). Sample size of 12 per group rule of thumb for a pilot study. *Pharmaceutical Statistics, 4*(4), 287–291. doi:10.1002/pst.185

Juma, N., & Sequeria, J. M. (2017). Effects of entrepreneur's individual factors and environmental contingencies on venture performance: A case study of African American women-owned ventures. *Journal of Small Business and Entrepreneurship, 29*(2), 91–119. doi:10.1080/08276331.2016.1248276

Jun, S. P., Seo, J. H., & Son, J. K. (2013). A study of the SME technology road - mapping program to strengthen R&D planning capability of Korean SMEs. *Technological Forecasting and Social Change, 80*(5), 1002–1014. doi:10.1016/j.techfore.2012.10.022

Kaczmarek, J. (2014). Czynnik czasu a modyfikacja dynamicznych miar oceny efektywności inwestycji. Zeszyty Naukowe Uniwersytetu Szczecińskiego. Finanse, Rynki Finansowe. *Ubezpieczenia, 66*, 111–121.

Kahn, W. A. (1990). Psychological conditions of personal engagement and disengagement at work. *Academy of Management Journal, 33*, 692–724.

Kangas, J., Pesonen, M., Kurttila, M., & Kajanus, M. (2001). *A'WOT: Integrating the AHO with SWOT analysis*. ISAHP.

Kaplan, S. N., & Zingales, L. (1997). Do financing constraints explain why investment is correlated with cash flow? *The Quarterly Journal of Economics, 112*, 169–215. doi:10.1162/003355397555163

Kapsalis, V. C., Kyriakopoulos, G. L., & Aravossis, K. G. I. (2019). Investigation of ecosystem services and circular economy interactions under an inter - organizational framework. *Energies, 12*(9), 1734.

Karakaya, E., & Sriwannawit, P. (2015). Barriers to the adoption of photovoltaic systems: The state of the art. *Renewable & Sustainable Energy Reviews, 49*, 60–66. doi:10.1016/j.rser.2015.04.058

Karamizadeh, S., Abdullah, S. M., Manaf, A. A., Zamani, M., & Hooman, A. (2013). An Overview of Principal Component Analysis. *Journal of Signal and Information Processing, 4*(03, 3b), 173–175. doi:10.4236/jsip.2013.43B031

Kast, V. (1991). *Joy, inspiration and hope*. Texas A&M University Press.

Katua, N. T. (2014). The Role of Small and Medium-sized Enterprises (SME) in Employment Creation and Economic Growth in Selected Countries. *International Journal of Education and Research, 2*(12), 461–472.

Kaufmann, A., & Tödtling, F. (2002). How effective is innovation support for SMEs? An analysis of the region of Upper Austria. *Technovation, 22*(3), 147–159.

Kautonen, T., & Palmroos, J. (2010). The impact of a necessity-based start-up on subsequent entrepreneurial satisfaction. *The International Entrepreneurship and Management Journal, 6*(3), 285–300. doi:10.100711365-008-0104-1

Kędzierski, L. (2017). Determinanty oddziaływania inwestycji finansowych na maksymalizację wartości rynkowej przedsiębiorstwa. *Studia Gdańskie. Wizje i rzeczywistość, 14*, 179 - 196.

Keeley, R. H., & Roure, J. B. (1990). Management, Strategy, and Industry Structure As Influences on the Success of New Firms: A Structural Model. *Management Science*, *36*(10), 1256–1267. doi:10.1287/mnsc.36.10.1256

Keenan, T. (2015). *Human Resource Management*. Edinburgh Business School Heriot - Watt University. Retrieved from https://www.ebsglobal.net/EBS/media/EBS/PDFs/Human-Resource-Management-Course-Taster.pdf

Keim, G. D. (1978). Managerial behavior and the social responsibility debate: Goals versus constraints. *Academy of Management Journal*, *21*(1), 57–68.

Kelley, D., Singer, S., & Herrington, M. (2011). *Global Entrepreneurship Monitor (GEM): Global Report*. Babson College.

Kell, H. J., & Lang, J. W. (2017). Specific Abilities in the Workplace: More Important Than g? *Journal of Intelligence*, *5*(2), 13. doi:10.3390/jintelligence5020013 PMID:31162404

Kelly, A. (1997). *Maintenance strategy*. Elsevier.

Kember, D. (1997). A reconceptualization of the research into university academics' conceptions of teaching. *Learning and Instruction*, *7*(3), 255–275. doi:10.1016/S0959-4752(96)00028-X

Kember, D., & Wong, A. (2000). Implications for evaluation from a study of students' perceptions. *Higher Education*, *40*(1), 69–97. doi:10.1023/A:1004068500314

Keskìn, H., Şentürk, C., Sungur, O., & Kìrìş, H. M. (2010). The Importance of Small and Medium-sized Enterprises (SME) in Developing Economies. *2nd International Symposium on Sustainable Development*, 183-192.

Khoury, T. A., & Prasad, A. (2015). Entrepreneurship amid concurrent institutional constraints in less developed countries. *Business & Society*, *55*(7), 934–969. doi:10.1177/0007650314567641

Kickul, J., & Lyons, T. S. (2020). *Understanding social entrepreneurship: The relentless pursuit of mission in an ever changing world*. Routledge. doi:10.4324/9780429270406

Kilinc - Ata, N. (2016). The evaluation of renewable energy policies across EU countries and US states: An econometric approach. *Energy for Sustainable Development*, *31*, 83–90. doi:10.1016/j.esd.2015.12.006

Kimberly, J., & Cook, J. M. (2008). Organizational Measurement and the Implementation of Innovations in Mental Health Services. *Administration and Policy in Mental Health*, *35*(1-2), 11–20. doi:10.100710488-007-0143-x PMID:17990096

Kim, J. Y., Lee, K., Coates, N. E., Moses, D., Nguyen, T. Q., Dante, M., & Heeger, A. J. (2007). Efficient tandem polymer solar cells fabricated by all - solution processing. *Science*, *317*(5835), 222–225. PMID:17626879

Kim, K. (2015). What Made a Bakery Franchise No. 1 in Korea? The Story of Paris Baguette and Its Success Factors. *Journal of Marketing Thought*, *2*(1), 14–26.

Kiseľáková, D., Šofranková, B., Gombár, M., Čabinová, V., & Onuferová, E. (2019). Competitiveness and Its Impact on Sustainability, Business Environment, and Human Development of EU (28) Countries in terms of Global Multi - Criteria Indices. *Sustainability*, *11*(12), 3365. doi:10.3390u11123365

Kisi, N. (2019). *A Strategic Approach to Sustainable Tourism Development Using the A+WOT Hybrid Method: A Case Study of Zonguldak, Turkey*. MDPI.

Kivarina, M., Kulikov, S., Zagorodnikov, K., Zhiltsov, V., & Khan, N. (2020). Economic Growth Humanization: Responsibility of Business and Social Entrepreneurship. *Quality - Access to Success*, *21*(176), 16–21.

Kline, R. B. (2016). *Principles and practice of structural equation modelling*. The Guilford Press.

Kobayashi, S. (2000). *Renewal of logistics: how to define global physical distribution strategies. Traduzido por Valéria Custódio dos Santos*. Atlas.

Koçak, N. G., Kaya, S., & Erol, E. (2013). Social Media from the Perspective of Diffusion of Innovation Approach. *The Macrotheme Review*, *2*(3), 22–29.

Kogi, K. (2012). Practical ways to facilitate ergonomics improvements in occupational health practice. *Human Factors*, *54*(6), 890–900. doi:10.1177/0018720812456204 PMID:23397801

Kolk, A., & van de Buuse, D. (2012). In search of viable business models for development: Sustainable energy in developing countries. *Corporate Governance*, *12*(4), 551–567. doi:10.1108/14720701211267865

Kolumber, Š., Tkačíková, L., & Menšík, M. (2020). Increasing the Competitiveness of Businesses By Using The Balance Scorecard Methodology. *Economics Management Innovation*, *12*(3), 49–68.

Kolvereid, L., & Moen, Ø. (1997). Entrepreneurship among business graduates: Does a major in entrepreneurship make a difference? *Journal of European Industrial Training*, *21*(4), 154–160. doi:10.1108/03090599710171404

KOSGEB. (n.d.). *Türkiye Girişimcilik Stratejisi ve Eylem Planı (GISEP) (2015-2018)*. https://www.ko sgeb.gov.tr/Content/Upload/Dosya/Mali%20Tablolar/Gisep_2015-2018_TR.pdf

Kothari, C. R. (2004). *Research methodology: methods and techniques*. New Age International Limited.

Kozubíková, L., Dvorský, J., Cepel, M., & Balcerzak, A. P. (2017). Important characteristics of an entrepreneur in relation to risk taking: Czech Republic case study. *Journal of International Students*, *10*(3), 220–233. doi:10.14254/2071-8330.2017/10-3/16

Krasniqi, E., & Kume, A. (2013). Entrepreneurship and Strategic Management In Emerging Economies: Kosovo's Perspective. *Annales Universitatis Apulensis Series Oeconomica*, *15*(1), 267–279. doi:10.29302/oeconomica.2013.15.1.22

Krejcie, R. V., & Morgan, D. W. (1970). Determining sample size for research activities. *Educational and Psychological Measurement*, *30*(3), 607–610. doi:10.1177/001316447003000308

Kruger, C. J., & Johnson, R. D. (2013). Knowledge Management according to Organizational Size: A South African Perspective. *South African Journal of Information Management*, *15*(1), 1–11. doi:10.4102ajim.v15i1.526

Krupski, R. (2005). *Zarządzanie przedsiębiorstwem w turbulentnym otoczeniu. Ku superelastycznej organizacji*. PWE.

Kshetri, N. (2007). Institutional factors affecting the offshore business process and information technology outsourcing. *Journal of International Management*, *13*(1), 38–56. doi:10.1016/j.intman.2006.05.003

Kucharcikova, A., Miciak, M., Malichova, E., Durisova, M., & Tokarcikova, E. (2019). The Motivation of Students at Universities as a Prerequisite of the Education's Sustainability within the Business Value Generation Context. *Sustainability*, *11*(20), 5577. doi:10.3390u11205577

Kuitto, K., Salonen, J., & Helmdag, J. (2019). Gender Inequalities in Early Career Trajectories and Parental Leaves: Evidence from a Nordic Welfare State. *Soc. Sci.*, *8*(9), 253. doi:10.3390ocsci8090253

Kumar, P. (2017). Analysis the impact of classical management approaches on the management practices. *Asian Journal of Management*, *8*(3), 841–853. doi:10.5958/2321-5763.2017.00132.9

Kumar, R., & Chandrakar, R. (2012). Overview of green supply chain management: Operation and environmental impact at different stages of the supply chain. *International Journal of Engineering and Advanced Technology*, *1*(3), 1–6.

Kuravi, S., Trahan, J., Goswami, D. Y., Rahman, M. M., & Stefanakos, E. K. (2013). Thermal energy storage technologies and systems for concentrating solar power plants. *Progress in Energy and Combustion Science*, *39*(4), 285–319.

Kurtulmuş, B. E., & Warner, B. (2015). Entrepreneurial Orientation and Perceived Financial Performance. Does Environment Always Moderate EO Performance Relation. *Procedia: Social and Behavioral Sciences*, *207*(1), 739–748. doi:10.1016/j.sbspro.2015.10.151

Kurtuluş, K. (1987). Entrepreneurship in Turkey. *Journal of Small Business Management.*

Kyriakopoulos, G. L., Kapsalis, V. C., Aravossis, K. G., Zamparas, M., & Mitsikas, A. (2019). Evaluating circular economy under a multi - parametric approach: A technological review. *Sustainability*, *11*(21), 6139.

Kyriakopoulos, G. L., Kolovos, K. G., & Chalikias, M. S. (2010). Woodfuels prosperity towards a more sustainable energy production. *Communications in Computer and Information Science*, *112*, 19–25.

Lai, H. M., & Lin, T. C. (2006). Bakery Products: Science and Technology. In Y. H. Hui (Ed.), *Bakery Products: Science and Technology* (pp. 3–65). Blackwell Publishing. doi:10.1002/9780470277553.ch1

Lai, S. L., Pham, H.-H., Nguyen, H.-K. T., Nguyen, T.-C., & Le, A.-V. (2019). Toward Sustainable Overseas Mobility of Vietnamese Students: Understanding Determinants of Attitudinal and Behavioural Loyalty in Students of Higher Education. *Sustainability*, *11*(2), 383. doi:10.3390u11020383

Laosebikan, J. S., Ogunni, B. O., & Ogunlusi, C. F. (2013). Evaluation of time management for growth and development in developing economies: Nigerian experience. *International Journal of Innovative Research and Development*, *2*(7), 490–496.

Latifi, K. A. N., & Lim, S. (2019). Strategic Human Resource Management in the Afghanistan Ministry of Mines and Petroleum: A Network Perspective. *Sustainability*, *11*(14), 3830. doi:10.3390u11143830

Lazonick, W. (2014). Profits without prosperity. *Harvard Business Review*, *92*(9), 46–55.

Lee, H. H. Y., & Scott, D. (2009). Overview of maintenance strategy, acceptable maintenance standard and resources from a building maintenance operation perspective. *Journal of Building Appraisal*, *4*(4), 269-278.

Lee, W. S., & Kim, B. Y. (2019). The effects of career orientations on entrepreneurial satisfaction and business sustainability. *The Journal of Asian Finance, Economics, and Business*, *6*(4), 235–248. doi:10.13106/jafeb.2019.vol6.no4.235

Lee, Y. A. (2014). Insight for writing qualitative research paper. *Family and Consumer Sciences Research Journal*, *43*(1), 94–97. doi:10.1111/fcsr.12084

Lee, Y. H., Hsieh, Y. C., & Hsu, C.-N. (2011). Adding Innovation Diffusion Theory to the Technology Acceptance Model: Supporting Employees' Intentions to use E-Learning Systems. *Journal of Educational Technology & Society*, *14*(4), 124–137.

Leick, B. (2016). Institutional entrepreneurs and small firms: How firm practices are being shaped in the context of demographic transformations. *Journal of Small Business and Entrepreneurship*, *29*(1), 1–24. doi:10.1080/08276331.2016.1248055

Leksono, E. B., Suparno, S., & Vanany, I. (2019). Integration of a Balanced Scorecard, DEMATEL, and ANP for Measuring the Performance of a Sustainable Healthcare Supply Chain. *Sustainability*, *11*(13), 3626. doi:10.3390u11133626

Lemos, M. S., Queirós, C., Teixeira, P. M., & Menezes, I. (2011). Development and validation of a theoretically based, multidimensional questionnaire of student evaluation of university teaching. *Assessment & Evaluation in Higher Education*, *36*(7), 843–864. doi:10.1080/02602938.2010.493969

Le-Roy, F., & Yami, S. (2007). The Development of an Innovation Strategy in the Small and Medium-sized Enterprises (SME) Context. *International Journal of Entrepreneurship and Small Business, 4*(4), 431–449. doi:10.1504/IJESB.2007.013690

Liles, P. (1974). Who are the entrepreneurs? *MSU Business Topics, 22*(1).

Liu, J., & Pang, D. (2009). Financial Factors and Company Investment Decisions in Transitional China. *Managerial and Decision Economics, 30*(2), 91–108. doi:10.1002/mde.1440

Liu, Y., Wang, G. G., & Chen, Y. (2019). Why Are Corporations Willing to Take on Public CSR? An Organizational Traits Approach. *Sustainability, 11*(2), 524. doi:10.3390u11020524

Lo, C.-H. (2019). A Study of the Influence of Career Counselling Perception on the Employment Competencies of Design Students in Central Taiwan. *Applied Sciences (Basel, Switzerland), 9*(23), 5072. doi:10.3390/app9235072

Lo, F. Y. (2013). The dynamic adjustment of environment, strategy, structure, and resources on firm performance. *The International Entrepreneurship and Management Journal, 9*(2), 217–227. doi:10.100711365-012-0222-7

Louw, A., Troskie, G., & Geyser, M. (2013). Small Millers' and Bakers' Perceptions of the Limitations of Agro-processing Development in the Wheat-milling and Baking Industries in Rural Areas in South Africa. *Agrekon, 52*(3), 101–122. doi:10.1080/03031853.2013.821746

Lowrey, W. (2011). Institutionalism, news organizations and innovation. *Journalism Studies, 12*(1), 64–79. doi:10.1080/1461670X.2010.511954

Lüdeke-Freund, F. (2020). Sustainable Entrepreneurship, Innovation, and Business Models: Integrative Framework and Propositions for Future Research. *Business Strategy and the Environment, 29*(2), 665–681.

Lumpkin, G. T., & Dess, G. G. (1996). Clarifying the Entrepreneurial Orientation Construct and Linking It to Performance. *Academy of Management Review, 21*(1), 135–172. doi:10.5465/amr.1996.9602161568

Luo, M., Wang, Z., Brager, G., Cao, B., & Zhu, Y. (2018). Indoor climate experience, migration, and thermal comfort expectation in buildings. *Building and Environment, 141*, 262–272. doi:10.1016/j.buildenv.2018.05.047

Lyons, P., & Mattare, M. (2011). How can Very Small and Medium-sized Enterprises (SME) Make the Time for Training and Development: Skill charting as an Example of Taking a Scenistic Approach. *Development and Learning in Organizations, 25*(4), 15–19. doi:10.1108/14777281111147053

Lyu, X., & Shi, A. (2018). Research on the Renewable Energy Industry Financing Efficiency Assessment and Mode Selection. *Sustainability, 10*(1), 222. doi:10.3390u10010222

Macey, W. H., & Schneider, B. (2008). The meaning of employee engagement. *Industrial and Organizational Psychology: Perspectives on Science and Practice, 1*(1), 3–30. doi:10.1111/j.1754-9434.2007.0002.x

MacGregor Pelikánová, R. (2019). Corporate Social Responsibility Information in Annual Reports in the EU - A Czech Case Study. *Sustainability, 11*(1), 237. doi:10.3390u11010237

Machuki, V. N., & Aosa, E. (2011). *The influence of the external business environment on the performance of publicly quoted companies in Kenya* [Unpublished Doctoral Dissertation]. University of Nairobi Kenya.

Madhavan, M. R. (2007). *You are here.* Penguin Books India.

Mafundu, R. H., & Mafini, C. (2019). Internal constraints to business performance in black-owned small to medium enterprises in the construction industry. *Southern African Journal of Entrepreneurship & Small Business Management, 11*(1), 1–10. doi:10.4102ajesbm.v11i1.165

Mahmood, Z., Basharat, M., & Bashir, Z. (2012). Review of classical management theories. *International Journal of Social Sciences and Education*, *2*(1), 512–522.

Malara, J., Plebankiewicz, E., & Juszczyk, M. (2019). Formula for Determining the Construction Workers Productivity Including Environmental Factors. *Buildings*, *9*(12), 240. doi:10.3390/buildings9120240

Malheiros, J. (2002). Portugal Seeks Balance of Emigration, Immigration. Brussels: Migration Policy Institute (MPI).

Malik, K., Rahman, S. M., Khondaker, A. N., Abubakar, I. R., Aina, Y. A., & Hasan, M. A. (2019). Renewable energy utilization to promote sustainability in GCC countries: Policies, drivers, and barriers. *Environmental Science and Pollution Research International*, *26*(20), 20798–20814. doi:10.100711356 - 019 - 06138 - 2 PMID:31104248

Maliti, E., & Mnenwa, R. (2008). The Role of Small Businesses in Poverty Alleviation: The Case of Dar es Salaam, Tanzania. Dar es Salaam: Research on Poverty Alleviation (REPOA).

Manufacturing Association of Nigeria. (2016). *Report*. Macmillian.

March, J. G. (1991). Exploration and Exploitation in Organizational Learning. *Organization Science*, *2*(1), 71–87. doi:10.1287/orsc.2.1.71

Maree, J. G., & Di Fabio, A. (2018). Integrating Personal and Career Counselling to Promote Sustainable Development and Change. *Sustainability*, *10*(11), 4176. doi:10.3390u10114176

Markman, G. D., Russo, M., Lumpkin, G. T., Jennings, P. D., & Mair, J. (2016). Entrepreneurship as a platform for pursuing multiple goals: A special issue on sustainability, ethics, and entrepreneurship. *Journal of Management Studies*, *53*(5), 673–694. doi:10.1111/joms.12214

Maro, F., & Barreiro-Hurlé, J. (2012). *Analysis of Incentives and Disincentives for Wheat in the United Republic of Tanzania.* Rome: Monitoring African Food and Agricultural Policies (MAFAP), Food and Agriculture Organization of the United Nations (FAO).

Marques, N. R., Matias, J. C., Teixeira, R. R., & Brojo, F. M. (2012). Implementation of Hazard Analysis Critical Control Points (HACCP) in a SME: Case Study of a Bakery. *Polish Journal of Food and Nutrition Sciences*, *62*(4), 215–227. doi:10.2478/v10222-012-0057-5

Marsh, H. W. (1982). SEEQ: A reliable, valid, and useful instrument for collecting students' evaluations of university teaching. *The British Journal of Educational Psychology*, *52*(2), 77–95. doi:10.1111/j.2044-8279.1982.tb02505.x

Martínez-Geijo, P. (2008). Learning styles: Methodological guidelines for working in the classroom. *Revista Complutense de Educación*, *19*(1), 77–94.

Martínez-Monzó, J., García-Segovia, P., & Albors-Garrigos, J. (2013). Trends and Innovations in Bread, Bakery and Pastry. *Journal of Culinary Science & Technology*, *11*(1), 56–65. doi:10.1080/15428052.2012.728980

Maslach, C., Schaufeli, W. B., & Leiter, M. P. (2001). Job burnout. *Annual Review of Psychology*, *52*(1), 397–422. doi:10.1146/annurev.psych.52.1.397 PMID:11148311

Mason, M. C., Floreani, J., Miani, S., Beltrame, F., & Cappelletto, R. (2015). Understanding the Impact of Entrepreneurial Orientation on Small and Medium-sized Enterprises (SME) Performance. The Role of the Financing Structure. *Procedia Economics and Finance*, *23*(1), 1649–1661. doi:10.1016/S2212-5671(15)00470-0

Matei, A. (2017). *Technology is changing our relationship with nature as we know it*. Retrieved from Quartz: https://qz.com/1048433/technology-is-changing-our-relationship-with-nature-as-we-know-it/

Matopoulos, A., & Vlachopoulou, M. (2008). Identifying Innovation Strategies: Insights from the Greek Food Industry. In *110th EAAE Seminar 'System Dynamics and Innovation in Food Networks*. Innsbruck-Igls: European Association of Agricultural Economists (EAAE).

Matosas, L. (2018). Core behavioral aspects of university professors in Student Evaluation of Teaching (SET) for blended learning models. *Espacios, 39*(10), 10–24.

Matosas-Lopez, L., Leguey-Galan, S., & Doncel-Pedrera, L. M. (2019). Converting Likert scales into Behavioral Anchored Rating Scales (Bars) for the evaluation of teaching effectiveness for formative purposes. *Journal of University Teaching & Learning Practice, 16*(3), 1–24.

Matos, S., & Hall, J. (2007). Integrating sustainable development in the extended value chain: The case of life cycle assessment in the oil and gas and agricultural biotechnology industries. *Journal of Operations Management, 25*, 1083–1102.

Mauchi, F. N., Mutengezanwa, M., & Damiyano, D. (2014). Challenges faced by women entrepreneurs: A case study of Mashonaland Central Province. *International Journal of Development and Sustainability, 3*(3), 466–480.

Mbizi, R., Hove, L., Thondhlana, A., & Kakava, N. (2013). Innovation in Small and Medium-sized Enterprises (SME): A Review of Its Role to Organizational Performance and Small and Medium-sized Enterprises (SME) Operations Sustainability. *Interdisciplinary Journal of Contemporary Research in Business, 4*(11), 370–389.

McGee, J. E., Peterson, M., Mueller, S. L., & Sequeira, J. M. (2009). Entrepreneurial Self-Efficacy: Refining the Measure. *Entrepreneurship Theory and Practice, 33*(4), 965–988. doi:10.1111/j.1540-6520.2009.00304.x

McGuire, J. W. (1963). *Business and society*. McGrawHill.

McKenzie, D. J. (2006). Disentangling age, cohort, and time effects in the additive model. *Oxford Bulletin of Economics and Statistics, 68*(4), 473–495. doi:10.1111/j.1468-0084.2006.00173.x

Meade, A. W., & Craig, S. B. (2012). Identifying careless responses in survey data. *Psychological Methods, 17*(3), 437–455. doi:10.1037/a0028085 PMID:22506584

Menguc, B., Auh, S., & Ozanne, L. (2010). The interactive effect of internal and external factors on a proactive environmental strategy and its influence on a firm's performance. *Journal of Business Ethics, 94*(2), 279–298. doi:10.100710551-009-0264-0

Meyer, G. D., Neck, H. M., & Meeks, M. D. (2002). The Entrepreneurship-Strategic Management Interface. In M. A. Hitt, R. D. Ireland, S. M. Camp, & D. L. Sexton (Eds.), *Strategic Entrepreneurship: Creating a New Mindset* (pp. 19–44). Blackwell Publishers.

Meyer, R. L. (1979). A Note on Capital Budgeting Techniques and the Reinvestment Rate. *The Journal of Finance, 34*(5), 1251–1254. doi:10.1111/j.1540-6261.1979.tb00070.x

Michel, J. W., Wallace, D. L., & Rawlings, R. A. (2013). Charismatic leaders: The role of admiration and system justification. *Leadership and Organization Development Journal, 34*(5), 469–487. doi:10.1108/LODJ-11-0099

Midttun, A., Næss, K. M., & Piccini, P. B. (2019). Biofuel Policy and Industrial Transition - A Nordic Perspective. *Energies, 12*(14), 2740. doi:10.3390/en12142740

Mile, K. S. (2019). *An Analysis of Women Entrepreneurship in India*. Deutsche Gesellschaft für Internationale Zusammenarbeit GmbH.

Miller, D. (1983). The Correlates of Entrepreneurship in Three Types of Firms. *Management Science, 29*(7), 770–791. doi:10.1287/mnsc.29.7.770

Miller, M., Bustamante, C., Roesch, R., Boshell, F., & Ayuso, M. (2015). *Renewable Energy Technology Innovation Policy. A Process Development Guide*. IRENA Innovation and Technology Centre.

Ministry of Commerce and Industry (MCI). (2019). *States with start - up policies for women*. https://www.startupindia.gov.in/content/sih/en/women_entrepreneurs.html

Ministry of Statistics and Programme Implementation (MOSPI). (2016). *All India Report of Sixth Economic Census*. http://mospi.nic.in/all-india-report-sixth-economic-census

Mintzberg, H. (1992). *Five Ps for Strategy*. Prentice - Hall.

Mithwani, A. M. (2015). Factors Influencing Strategy Implementation in the Bakery Industry in Mombasa County. *International Journal of Business and Management*, *3*(8), 185–200.

Montagna, P. D. (1968). Professionalization and bureaucratization in large professional organizations. *American Journal of Sociology*, *74*(2), 138–145. doi:10.1086/224616

Moore, T. (2006). Teacher Evaluations and Grades: Additional Evidence. *The Journal of American Academy of Business, Cambridge*, *9*(2).

Mowday, R. T. (1979). Leader characteristics, self-confidence, and methods of upward influence in organizational decision situations. *Academy of Management Journal*, *22*(4), 709–725.

MSME Survey. (2013). *Smedan and National Bureau of Statistics Collaborative Survey: Selected Findings*. Retrieved from Abuja, Nigeria: https://www.google.com/url?sa=t&rct=j&q=&esrc=s&source=web&cd=4&cad=rja&uact=8&ved=2ahUKEwiPgrSJtrflAhWBiVwKHT-iA3cQFjADegQIBhAC&url=https%3A%2F%2Fwww.smedan.gov.ng%2Fimages%2FPDF%2F2013-MSME-Survey-Summary-Report.pdf&usg=AOvVaw18wZux7m5XYOaHaR_uI9Z2

Muogbo, U. S., & Chuka, E.-U. (2019). Environmental factors: A panacea for survival and growth of small and medium scale businesses in Nigeria. *International Journal of Business & Management Invention*, *8*(3), 30–40. doi:10.2139srn.3432188

Muritala, T. A., Awolaja, A. M., & Bako, Y. A. (2012). Impact of small and medium enterprises on economic growth and development. *American Journal of Business and Management*, *1*(1), 18–22.

Murray, C. E. (2009). Diffusion of Innovation Theory: A Bridge for the Research-Practice Gap in Counseling. *Journal of Counseling and Development*, *87*(1), 108–116. doi:10.1002/j.1556-6678.2009.tb00556.x

Musiolik, J., & Markard, J. (2011). Creating and Shaping Innovation Systems: Formal Networks in the Innovation System for Stationary Fuel Cells in Germany. *Energy Policy*, *39*(4), 1909–1922.

Myers, L., & Bahaj, A. S. (2007). Wake studies of a 1/30th scale horizontal axis marine current turbine. *Ocean Engineering*, *34*(5), 758–762.

NA. (2015, September 24). *Strategic analysis: Layers of business environment*. Retrieved from PyramiDNA: https://pyramidna.wordpress.com/2015/09/24/strategic - analysis - layers - of - business - environment/

Náglová, Z., & Horáková, T. (2017). Position of the Bakery Enterprises in the Czech Republic According to Detailed Specification of the Businesses. *Acta Universitatis Agriculturae et Silviculturae Mendelianae Brunensis*, *65*(5), 1719–1727. doi:10.11118/actaun201765051719

Naktiyok, A., Nur Karabey, C., & Caglar Gulluce, A. (2010). Entrepreneurial self-efficacy and entrepreneurial intention: The Turkish case. *The International Entrepreneurship and Management Journal*, *6*(4), 419–435. doi:10.100711365-009-0123-6

Naman, J. L., & Slevin, D. P. (1993). Entrepreneurship and the concept of fit: A model and empirical tests. *Strategic Management Journal, 14*(2), 137–153. doi:10.1002mj.4250140205

Naoum, S. (2001). *People and organizational management in construction.* Thomas Telford. doi:10.1680/paomic.28746

Naseem, A., Sheikh, S. E., & Malik, K. P. (2011). Impact of employee satisfaction on success of organization: Relation between customer experience and employee satisfaction. *International Journal of Multidisciplinary Sciences and Engineering, 2*(5), 41-46.

Nasirov, S., Silva, C., & Agostini, C. A. (2015). Investors' perspectives on barriers to the deployment of renewable energy sources in Chile. *Energies, 8*(5), 3794–3814. doi:10.3390/en8053794

Naveed, A., Ahmad, N., Esmaeilzadeh, R., & Naz, A. (2019). Self - Employment Dynamics of Immigrants and Natives: Individual - level Analysis for the Canadian Labour Market. *Sustainability, 11*(23), 6671. doi:10.3390u11236671

Nazarko, J., Ejdys, J., Halicka, K., Magruk, A., Nazarko, L., & Skorek, A. (2017). *Application of Ehanced SWOT Analysis in the Future - oriented Public Management of Technology.* Elsevier.

NBS. (2018). *Demographic statistics bulletin.* Retrieved from Abuja, Nigeria: https://www.google.com/url?sa=t&rct=j&q=&esrc=s&source=web&cd=18&ved=2ahUKEwi36Jn1lrflAhVChlwKHTKbBmEQFjARegQICRAC&url=https%3A%2F%2Fnigerianstat.gov.ng%2Fdownload%2F775&usg=AOvVaw1HuYamjCJoZk8geCvTnFYr

Nelson, R. R. (1991). Why do firms differ, and how does it matter? *Strategic Management Journal, 12*(2), 61–74. doi:10.1002mj.4250121006

Newman, A., Obschonka, M., Schwarz, S., Cohen, M., & Nielsen, I. (2019). Entrepreneurial self-efficacy: A systematic review of the literature on its theoretical foundations, measurement, antecedents, and outcomes, and an agenda for future research. *Journal of Vocational Behavior, 110*, 403–419. doi:10.1016/j.jvb.2018.05.012

Nguyen, H. V., Nguyen, N., Nguyen, B. K., Lobo, A., & Vu, P. A. (2019). Organic Food Purchases in an Emerging Market: The Influence of Consumers'. *Personal Factors and Green Marketing Practices of Food Stores. Int. J. Environ. Res. Public Health, 16*, 1037. PMID:30909390

Nguyen, M. Q., & Nguyen, P. V. (2013). The Impact of External Environment, Technology and Innovation Capacities, and Leadership Development on Organizational Performance in Food Industry. A Qualitative Study of Food Enterprises in Ho Chi Minh City, Vietnam. *International Journal of Business. Human Technology, 3*(4), 49–60.

Nicolescu, L., & Nicolescu, C. (2012). Innovation in Small and Medium-sized Enterprises (SME)-Findings from Romania. *Economia e Sociologia, 5*(2a), 71–85.

Nor-Aishah, H., Ahmad, N. H., & Thurasamy, R. (2020). Entrepreneurial Leadership and Sustainable Performance of Manufacturing SMEs in Malaysia: The Contingent Role of Entrepreneurial Bricolage. *Sustainability, 12*(8), 3100. doi:10.3390u12083100

Nor, C. S. M., Mohamed, R. K. H., Mohamed, B., & Hassan, N. A. C. (2020). Human Resources Management Practices and its Impact on Employee Commitment Mong Staffs of Road Transport Department, Perak, Malaysia. *Journal of Environmental Treatment Techniques, 8*(1), 28–34.

North, D. C. (1991). Institutions. *The Journal of Economic Perspectives, 5*(1), 97–112. doi:10.1257/jep.5.1.97

Nunn, N. (2012). *Culture and the historical process.* Harvard University. doi:10.3386/w17869

Nwewi, H. N., Onwuka, E. M., & Ogbotubo, E. (2017). Entrepreneurial Thinking and Competitiveness in Bakery Industry in Delta State of Nigeria. International Journal of Business. *Management and Social Research, 4*(1), 192–197.

OECD. (2019). *OECD Economic Surveyes*. OECD.

Ogbadu, E., Aduku, D., & Nafiu, A. (2017). Small Firms' Strategy Adoption and Business Outcomes in Business Games: An Empirical Investigation from Nigeria. Asian Journal of Economics. *Business and Accounting*, *4*(1), 1–13.

Oginni, B. O., & Adesanya, A. S. (2013). Business environmental factors: Implications on the survival and growth of business organizations in the manufacturing sector of Lagos metropolis. *Business & Management Research*, *2*(3), 146–155. doi:10.5430/bmr.v2n3p146

Ohunakin, O. S., Adaramola, M. S., Oyewola, O. M., & Fagbenle, R. O. (2014). Solar energy applications and development in Nigeria: Drivers and barriers. *Renewable & Sustainable Energy Reviews*, *32*, 294–301. doi:10.1016/j.rser.2014.01.014

Okpara, J., & Wynn, P. (2007). Determinants of small business growth constraints in a sub-Sahara African economy. *S.A.M. Advanced Management Journal*, *72*(2), 24–35.

Olughor, R. J. (2015). Effect of Innovation on the Performance of Small and Medium-sized Enterprises (SME) Organizations in Nigeria. *Management*, *5*(3), 90–95.

Olughor, R. J. (2015). Effect of innovation on the performance of Small and Medium-sized Enterprises (SMEs) organizations in Nigeria. *Management*, *5*(3), 90–95.

Öner, M. A., & Kunday, Ö. (2016). A study on Schumpeterian and Kirznerian entrepreneurship in Turkey: 2006–2013. *Technological Forecasting and Social Change*, 102.

Orpen, C. (1985). The effects of need for achievement and need for independence on the relationship between perceived job attributes and managerial satisfaction and performance. *International Journal of Psychology*, *20*(2), 207–219. doi:10.1080/00207598508247733 PMID:25820002

Örtqvist, D., Drnovsek, M., & Wincent, J. (2007). Entrepreneurs' coping with challenging role expectations. *Baltic Journal of Management*, *2*(3), 288–304. doi:10.1108/17465260710817492

Osei, A., Forkuoh, K. S., Shao, Y., & Osei, M. A. (2016). The Impact of Institutional Support in Small and Medium-sized Enterprises (SME) marketing, and Growth-A Case Study of Retail Small and Medium-sized Enterprises (SME) in Ghana. *Open Journal of Business and Management*, *4*(3), 408–426. doi:10.4236/ojbm.2016.43043

Osterwalder, A., Pigneur, Y., & Clark, T. (2010). *Business model generation: a handbook for visionaries, game changers, and challengers*. Wiley.

Özsungur, F. (2019). Ethical leadership, intrapreneurship, service innovation performance and work engagement in chambers of commerce and industry. *Journal of Human Behavior in the Social Environment*, *29*(8), 1059–1081. doi:10.1080/10911359.2019.1664359

Painuly, J. P. (2001). Barriers to renewable energy penetration; a framework for analysis. *Renewable Energy*, *24*(1), 73 - 89. https://doi: (00)00186-5 doi:10.1016/S0960 - 1481

Pakšiová, R. (2017). The Critical Analysis of Profit for its Allocation Decision - Making. *Scientific Annals of Economics and Business*, *64*(s1), 41–56. doi:10.1515aeb-2017-0039

Palmer, J. C., Wright, R. E., & Powers, J. B. (2001). Innovation and Competitive Advantage in Small Businesses: Effects of Environments and Business Strategy. *Journal of Small Business Strategy*, *12*(1), 30–41.

Palová, Z., & Šebestová, J. (2020). Competencies, Skills, and Goals Needed for Social Enterprises: Case of the Czech Republic. In Developing Entrepreneurial Competencies for Start - Ups and Small Business (pp. 109 - 128). IGI Global. .ch008 doi:10.4018/978-1-7998-2714-6

Panko, R. R. (1992). Managerial communication patterns. *Journal of Organizational Computing and Electronic Commerce, 2*(1), 95–122. doi:10.1080/10919399209540176

Papaioannou, D., Sutton, A., Carroll, C., Booth, A., & Wong, R. (2010). Literature searching for social science systematic reviews: Consideration of a range of search techniques. *Health Information and Libraries Journal, 27*(2), 114–122. doi:10.1111/j.1471-1842.2009.00863.x PMID:20565552

Paprocka, I. (2019). Evaluation of the Effects of a Machine Failure on the Robustness of a Job Shop System - Proactive Approaches. *Sustainability, 11*(1), 65. doi:10.3390u11010065

Papulova, Z., & Gazova, A. (2015). *Role of Strategic Analysis in Strategic Decision - Making*. Elsevier.

Parastuty, Z., & Bögenhold, D. (2019). Paving the Way for Self - Employment: Does Society Matter? *Sustainability, 11*(3), 747. doi:10.3390u11030747

Paravantis, J. A., Stigka, E. K., & Mihalakakou, G. K. (2014). An analysis of public attitudes towards renewable energy in Western Greece. *Renewable & Sustainable Energy Reviews, 32*, 100–106. doi:10.1109/IISA.2014.6878776

PBS Foundation. (2021). *What is a Social Entrepreneur. Enterprising Ideas. A social entrepreneur, in our view, is a person or entity that takes a business approach to effectively solving a social problem*. Author.

Pegalajar-Palomino, M. D. C. (2016). Percepciones del alumnado de posgrado acerca de la metodología docente y evaluativa. Profesorado. *Revista de Curriculum y Formación Del Profesorado, 20*(2), 98–119.

Pelkmans, J., & Renda, A. (2014). *Does EU regulation hinder or stimulate innovation?* https://www.ceps.eu/ceps-publications/does-eu-regulation-hinder-or-stimulate-innovation/

Peltier, J. W., Zhao, Y., & Schibrowsky, J. A. (2012). Technology Adoption by Small Businesses: An Exploratory Study of the Interrelationships of Owner and Environmental Factors. *International Small Business Journal, 30*(4), 406–431. doi:10.1177/0266242610365512

Peng, M. W., & Jiang, Y. (2010). Institutions behind family ownership and control in large firms. *Journal of Management Studies, 47*(2), 253–273. doi:10.1111/j.1467-6486.2009.00890.x

Peredo, A. M., & McLean, M. (2006). Social entrepreneurship: A critical review of the concept. *Journal of World Business, 41*(1), 56–65. doi:10.1016/j.jwb.2005.10.007

Perera, S., Harrison, G., & Poole, M. (1997). Customer - focused manufacturing strategy and the use of operations - based non - financial performance measures: A research note. *Accounting, Organizations and Society, 22*(6), 557–572. doi:10.1016/S0361-3682(96)00048-7

Pérez-Ordás, R., Aznar Cebamanos, M., Nuviala, R., & Nuviala, A. (2019). Evaluation of Extracurricular Sports Activities as an Educational Element for Sustainable Development in Educational Institutions. *Sustainability, 11*(12), 3474. doi:10.3390u11123474

Perkins, R. A. (2007). Using Rogers' Theory of Perceived Attributes as a Framework for Understanding the Challenges of Adoption of Open Educational Resources. *International Journal of Humanities and Social Science, 1*(18), 59–66.

Petticrew, M., & Roberts, H. (2008). *Systematic reviews in the social sciences: A practical guide*. John Wiley & Sons.

Pfeffer, J., & Salanick, G. R. (1978). *The External Control of Organization*. Harper and Row.

Phillips, J. (2013). *Technology foresight for small - to medium - sized enterprises*. LAP Lambert Academic Publishing.

Piaget, J. (1981). Piaget's theory. *Journal for the Study of Education and Development, 4*(sup 2), 13 - 54.

Piazza, A., & Abrahamson, E. (2020). Fads and Fashions in Management Practices: Taking Stock and Looking Forward. *International Journal of Management Reviews*, *22*(3), 1–23. doi:10.1111/ijmr.12225

Pino, L., Vita, A., Cordaro, M., Recupero, V., & Hegde, M. S. (2003). A comparative study of Pt/CeO 2 catalysts for catalytic partial oxidation of methane to syngas for application in fuel cell electric vehicles. *Applied Catalysis A, General*, *243*(1), 135–146.

Pirmana, V., Alisjahbana, A. S., Hoekstra, R., & Tukker, A. (2019). Implementation Barriers for a System of Environmental - Economic Accounting in Developing Countries and Its Implications for Monitoring Sustainable Development Goals. *Sustainability*, *11*(22), 6417. doi:10.3390u11226417

Pistrui, D., Huang, W., Oksoy, D., Jing, Z., & Welsch, H. (2001). Entrepreneurship in China: Characteristics, attributes, and family forces shaping the emerging private sector. *Family Business Review*, *14*(2), 141–152. doi:10.1111/j.1741-6248.2001.00141.x

Pitan, O. S., & Adedeji, S. (2012). Skills Mismatch among University Graduates in the Nigeria Labour Market. *US-China Education Review*, *A*(1), 90-98.

Pittaway, L., & Cope, J. (2016). Entrepreneurship Education. *International Small Business Journal: Researching Entrepreneurship*, *25*(5), 479–510. doi:10.1177/0266242607080656

Pizzi, S., Caputo, A., Corvino, A., & Venturelli, A. (2020). Management research and the UN sustainable development goals (SDGs): A bibliometric investigation and systematic review. *Journal of Cleaner Production*, *276*, 1–15. doi:10.1016/j.jclepro.2020.124033

Planing, P. (2017). On the origin of innovations-the opportunity vacuum as a conceptual model for the explanation of innovation. *Journal of Innovation & Entrepreneurship*, *6*(5), 1–18. doi:10.118613731-017-0063-2

Ploum, L., Blok, V., Lans, T., & Omta, O. (2018). Toward a validated competence framework for sustainable entrepreneurship. *Organization & Environment*, *31*, 113–132. PMID:30886514

Pokorná, P. (2020). Financial Sources for Company Scale - Up. In J. Šebestová (Ed.), *Developing Entrepreneurial Competencies for Start - Ups and Small Business* (pp. 97–108). Advances in Business Strategy and Competitive Advantage. IGI Global. doi:10.4018/978-1-7998-2714-6.ch007

Pokorná, P., Šebestová, J., & Čemerková, Š. (2019). Dilemma of Directions for Reinvestment. *Forum Scientiae Oeconomia*, *7*(4), 83–99. doi:10.23762/FSO_VOL7_NO4_6

Pokrovskaia, N. N., Ababkova, M. Y., & Fedorov, D. A. (2019). Educational Services for Intellectual Capital Growth or Transmission of Culture for Transfer of Knowledge - Consumer Satisfaction at St. Petersburg Universities. *Education in Science*, *9*(3), 183. doi:10.3390/educsci9030183

Poole, M. L. (1990). *Recommended Data for the First Step in External Environment Scanning for Public Schools*. University of Maryland.

Popescu, C. R. G. & Popescu, G. N. (2018a). Risks of cyber - attacks on financial audit activity. *Audit Financiar, 16*(1), 140 – 147. Doi:10.20869/AUDITF/2018/149/006

Popescu, C. R. G. (2017). The Role of Total Quality Management in Developing the Concept of Social Responsibility to Protect Public Interest in Associations of Liberal Professions. *Amfiteatru Economic, 19*(11), 1091 – 1106. Retrieved from https://www.amfiteatrueconomic.ro/temp/Article_2685.pdf

Popescu, C. R. G. (2018). "Intellectual Capital" - Role, Importance, Components and Influences on the Performance of Organizations - A Theoretical Approach. *Proceedings of the 32nd International Business Information Management Association Conference.*

Popescu, C. R. G. (2019a). Evaluating intellectual capital and its influence on companies' performance - a Case Study on Romania's Experience. *INTED2019 Proceedings*. doi: 10.21125/inted.2019

Popescu, C. R. G., & Popescu, V. A. (2015). The Assessment Methodology PDCA/PDSA - A Methodology for Coordinating the Efforts to Improve the Organizational Processes to Achieve Excellence. In Proceedings "CKS - Challenges of the Knowledge Society" (pp. 693 - 696). "Nicolae Titulescu" University Publishing House.

Popescu, G. N., Popescu, V. A., & Popescu, C. R. G. (2008) Interdisciplinary Research regarding the Role of Virtual Components in Knowing and Modelling Complex Economical - Social Phenomena and Processes. In *Proceedings of The International Scientific Session "Challenges of the Knowledge Society"*. University of Bucharest Publishing House.

Popescu, V. A., & Popescu, G. N. (2002). Manualul inspectorului de salarii. Bucharest: Editura Gestiunea.

Popescu, V. A., Popescu, G. N., & Popescu, C. R. G. (2015). Competitiveness and sustainability - a modern economic approach to the industrial policy. *Metalurgija, 54*(2), 426 - 428.

Popescu, C. R. G. (2019). Addressing Intellectual Capital in the Context of Integrated Strategy and Performance: Emphasizing the Role of Companies' Unique Value Creation Mechanism, While Targeting Better Organizational Reporting In Romania: The Case of Green Marketing and Green Marketing Strategies. *Journal of Marketing Research & Case Studies, 672821*. Advance online publication. doi:10.5171/2019.672821

Popescu, C. R. G. (2019c). "Intellectual Capital": Major Role, Key Importance and Decisive Influences on Organizations' Performance. *Journal of Human Resources Management Research.* doi:10. 5171/2019

Popescu, C. R. G. (2019e). Business development opportunities: Demonstrating present and future performance, auditing intellectual capital - a case study on Romanian organizations. *Proceedings of the 33nd International Business Information Management Association Conference.*

Popescu, C. R. G. (2019f). Intellectual capital, integrated strategy and performance: focusing on companies' unique value creation mechanism and promoting better organizational reporting in Romania - a framework dominated by the impact of green marketing and green marketing strategies. *Proceedings of the 33nd International Business Information Management Association Conference.*

Popescu, C. R. G. (2019g). Corporate Social Responsibility, Corporate Governance and Business Performance: Limits and Challenges Imposed by the Implementation of Directive 2013/34/EU in Romania. *Sustainability, 11*(19), 5146. doi:10.3390u11195146

Popescu, C. R. G. (2020). Sustainability Assessment: Does the OECD/G20 Inclusive Framework for BEPS (Base Erosion and Profit Shifting Project) Put an End to Disputes Over The Recognition and Measurement of Intellectual Capital? *Sustainability, 12*(23), 10004. doi:10.3390u122310004

Popescu, C. R. G., & Banța, V. C. (2019). Performance Evaluation of the Implementation of the 2013/34/EU Directive in Romania on the Basis of Corporate Social Responsibility Reports. *Sustainability, 11*(9), 2531. doi:10.3390u11092531

Popescu, C. R. G., & Dumitrescu, M. (2016a). The Importance of Change Typology - a Key Element in the Enterprise's Organizational Dynamics. *Manager Journal, Issue,* (23), 116–123.

Popescu, C. R. G., & Dumitrescu, M. (2016b). A New Configuration: Management's Paradigms - Acting in the Context of Social Economy. *Manager Journal, Issue,* (23), 124–137.

Popescu, C. R. G., & Popescu, G. N. (2018b). Methods of Evaluating "Intellectual capital" of an Organization and Ways of Enhancing Performance in the Knowledge - based Economy - A Synthetically Approach. *Proceedings of the 32nd International Business Information Management Association Conference.*

Popescu, C. R. G., & Popescu, G. N. (2019b). An Exploratory Study Based on a Questionnaire Concerning Green and Sustainable Finance, Corporate Social Responsibility, and Performance: Evidence from the Romanian Business Environment. *J. Risk Financial Manag., 2019*(12), 162. doi:10.3390/jrfm12040162

Popescu, C. R. G., Popescu, G. N., & Popescu, V. A. (2017a). Assessment of the State of Implementation of Excellence Model Common Assessment Framework (CAF) 2013 by the National Institutes of Research - Development - Innovation in Romania. *Amfiteatru Economic, 19*(44), 41–60. https://www.amfiteatrueconomic.ro/temp/Articol_2593.pdf

Popescu, C. R. G., Popescu, G. N., & Popescu, V. A. (2017b). Sustainability Leadership, the Key to a Better World - A Case Study on Romania's Situation. *Proceedings of the 29th International Business Information Management Association Conference.*

Popescu, C. R. G., Popescu, G. N., & Popescu, V. A. (2017c). Creating Comprehensive Human Resources Management Policies and Instruments by Using Strategic Personnel Planning - A Case Study on Romania's Situation: A Quantitative and Qualitative Analysis. *Manager Journal, Issue*, (25), 133–146.

Popescu, C. R. G., Popescu, V. A., & Popescu, G. N. (2015). The Entrepreneur's Role in the Performance Growth of the Financial Audit Activity in Romania. *Amfiteatru Economic, 17*(38), 228–246.

Popescu, C. R. G., Popescu, V. A., & Popescu, G. N. (2017d). Forecasting of Financial Markets and Monetary, Fiscal, Financial, Economic and Political Freedom Features in Nowadays Society - A Case Study on Romania's Situation. *Manager Journal, Issue*, (25), 116–132.

Popescu, C. R., & Popescu, G. N. (2019). The Social, Economic, and Environmental Impact of Ecological Beekeeping in Romania. In G. Popescu (Ed.), *Agrifood Economics and Sustainable Development in Contemporary Society* (pp. 75–96). IGI Global. doi:10.4018/978 - 1 - 5225 - 5739 - 5.ch004

Popescu, G. N. (1997). *Procedurile controlului intern şi auditul financiar.* Editura Gestiunea.

Popescu, G. N., Popescu, C. R. G., & Popescu, V. A. (2016). The Macro Environment and the Companies' Economic, Social and Research - Development - Innovation Potential - Nowadays Key Elements. *Perspectives and Challenges, Manager Journal, Issue*, (24), 214–230.

Popescu, G. N., & Popescu, V. A. (2000). *Impozitul pe venit şi contabilitatea în partidă simplă.* Editura Gestiunea.

Popper, R. (2008). *Foresight methodology. The Handbook of Technology Foresight. Northhampton.* Edward Elgar.

Porter, M. E. (1996). Competitive Advantage, Agglomeration Economies, and Regional Policy. *International Regional Science Review, 19*(1 - 2), 85 - 90.

Porter, M. E. (1980). *Competitive Strategy: Techniques for analysing industries and competitors.* Free Press.

Porter, M. E. (1985). *Competitive Strategy.* Free press.

Porter, M. E. (1987). *From Competitive Advantage to Corporate Strategy.* Harvard Business Review.

Poulis, E., Poulis, K., & Christodoulou, I. (2013). *Developing dynamic capabilities to address 'mutating' forces. Track: dynamic capabilities: Theoretical Approaches and Practical Applications'. European Academy of Management.* EURAM.

Prahalad, C. K. (2004). *The Fortune at the Bottom of the Pyramid - Eradicating Poverty Through Profits.* Wharton School Publishing.

Prahalad, C. K., & Hamel, G. (1994). Competing for the Future. *Harvard Business Review*, 9.

Pramanik, A. (2020). *The thing that's holding back Indian women entrepreneurs.* https://m.economictimes.com/news/company/corporate-trends/the-thing-thats-holding-back-indian-women-entrepreneurs/articleshow/77754878.cms

Prasetyo, P. E., & Kistanti, N. R. (2020). Human capital, institutional economics and entrepreneurship as a driver for quality & sustainable economic growth. *Entrepreneurship and Sustainability Issues*, *7*(4), 2575–2589. doi:10.9770/jesi.2020.7.4(1)

Preuss, U. (2016). Sustainable Digitalization of Cultural Heritage - Report on Initiatives and Projects in Brandenburg, Germany. *Sustainability*, *8*(9), 891. doi:10.3390u8090891

Pritchard, R. D., & Karasick, B. W. (1973). The effects of organizational climate on managerial job performance and job satisfaction. *Organizational Behavior and Human Performance*, *9*(1), 126–146. doi:10.1016/0030-5073(73)90042-1

Punt, A. E., Butterworth, D. S., de Moor, C. L., De Oliveira, J. A., & Haddon, M. (2016). Management strategy evaluation: Best practices. *Fish and Fisheries*, *17*(2), 303–334. doi:10.1111/faf.12104

Purkayastha, D., Tripathy, T., & Das, B. (2020). Understanding the ecosystem of microfinance institutions in India. *Social Enterprise Journal,* 243 - 261.

Qiblawey, H. M., & Banat, F. (2008). Solar thermal desalination technologies. *Desalination*, *220*(1), 633–644.

Rahdari, A., Sepasi, S., & Moradi, M. (2016). Achieving sustainability through Schumpeterian social entrepreneurship: The role of social enterprises. *Journal of Cleaner Production*, *137*, 347–360.

Ramadani, V. (2012). The importance of angel investors in financing the growth of small and medium sized enterprises. *International Journal of Academic Research in Business & Social Sciences*, *2*(7), 306–322.

Ramdani, B., & Kawalek, P. (2007). Small and Medium-sized Enterprises (SME) & IS Innovations Adoption: A Review & Assessment of Previous Research. Academia. *Revista Latino Americana de Administration*, *39*(1), 47–70.

Rampal, N. (2019). *India Today.* Retrieved from https://www.indiatoday.in/diu/story/delhi-air-quality-toxic-smoke-smog-cigarettes-1621410-2019-11-21

Rao, R., Zhang, X., Shi, Z., Luo, K., Tan, Z., & Feng, Y. (2014). A Systematical Framework of Schedule Risk Management for Power Grid Engineering Projects' Sustainable Development. *Sustainability*, *6*(10), 6872–6901. doi:10.3390u6106872

Razak, J. A., Sopian, K., Ali, Y., Alghoul, M. A., Zaharim, A., & Ahmad, I. (2009). Optimization of PV - wind - hydro - diesel hybrid system by minimizing excess capacity. *European Journal of Scientific Research*, *25*(4), 663–671.

Raza, W., Saula, H., Islam, S. U., Ayub, M., Saleem, M., & Raza, N. (2015). Renewable energy resources: Current status and barriers in their adaptation for Pakistan. *Journal of Bioprocessing and Chemical Engineerin*, *3*(3), 1–9.

Remmers, H. H. (1928). The relationship between students' marks and student attitude toward instructors. *School & Society*, *28*, 759–760.

Rennings, K. (2000). Redefining Innovation— Ecoinnovation Research and the Contribution from Ecological Economics. *Ecological Economics*, *32*(2), 319–332.

Resino-Blázquez, J. J., Chamizo Gonzalez, J., Cano Montero, E. I., & Gutierrez Broncano, S. (2013). Quality of college life: Identifying the key indicators of student satisfaction. *Review of Education*, *362*, 458–484.

Restrepo-Abondano, J. M. (2008). Managerial consequences of credit system introduction: A Colombian case. *Cuadernos Americanos*, *21*(37), 11–36.

Reynolds, P. D. (1987). New firms: Societal contribution versus survival potential. *Journal of Business Venturing*, *2*(3), 231–246. doi:10.1016/0883-9026(87)90011-5

Richard, O. C., Barnett, T., Dwyer, S., & Chadwick, K. (2004). Cultural diversity in management, firm performance, and the moderating role of entrepreneurial orientation dimensions. *Academy of Management Journal*, *47*(2), 255–266.

Rigby, D., & Bilodeau, B. (2018). *Management tools and trends 2017.* Bain & Company. Retrieved from http://www.bain.com/publications/articles/management-tools-and-trends-2017.aspx

Rios, R. V., Pessanha, M. D., Almeida, P. F., Viana, C. L., & Lannes, S. C. (2014). Application of Fats in Some Food Products. *Food Science and Technology (Campinas)*, *34*(1), 3–15. doi:10.1590/S0101-20612014000100001

Robbins, P., & O'Gorman, C. (2016). Innovation Processes: Do They Help or Hinder New Product Development Outcomes in Irish Small and Medium-sized Enterprises (SME)? *Irish Journal of Management*, *35*(1), 88–103. doi:10.1515/ijm-2016-0006

Robinson, D., Perryman, S., & Hayday, S. (2004). *The Drivers of Employee Engagement, Institute for Employment Studies*. IES Report 408.

Robinson, J. (2004). Squaring the Circle? Some thoughts on the idea of Sustainable Development. *Ecological Economics*, *48*(4), 369–384. doi:10.1016/j.ecolecon.2003.10.017

Robu, M. (2013). The Dynamic and Importance of Small and Medium-sized Enterprises (SME) in Economy. *The USV Annals of Economics and Public Administration*, *13*(17), 84-89.

Rodríguez-Sánchez, J.-L., Montero-Navarro, A., & Gallego-Losada, R. (2019). The Opportunity Presented by Technological Innovation to Attract Valuable Human Resources. *Sustainability*, *11*(20), 5785. doi:10.3390u11205785

Rogers, E. M. (2003). Diffusion of Innovations (5th ed.). New York: Free Press.

Rosli, M. M., & Sidek, S. (2013). The Impact of Innovation on the Performance of Small and Medium Manufacturing Enterprises: Evidence from Malaysia. *Journal of Innovation Management in Small & Medium Enterprise*, *1*(1), 123–128. doi:10.5171/2013.885666

Rothmann, S., & Storm, K. (2003). *Work engagement in the South African Police Service*. Paper presented at the 11th European Congress of Work and Organizational Psychology, Lisbon.

Rozuel, C., & Kakabadse, N. (2010). Ethics, spirituality and self: Managerial perspective and leadership implications. *Business Ethics (Oxford, England)*, *19*(4), 423–436. doi:10.1111/j.1467-8608.2010.01603.x

Ruan, Z., Liu, W., Na, S., Tan, X., & Xue, T. (2019). Regional Marketization, OFDI, and Sustainable Employment: Empirical Analysis in China. *Sustainability*, *11*(15), 4101. doi:10.3390u11154101

Rubin, H. J., & Rubin, I. S. (1995). *Qualitative interviewing; The art of hearing data*. SAGE Publications.

Ruiz-Carrascosa, J. (2000). The evaluation of teaching by students in the national plan for evaluating the quality of universities. Construction of an assessment instrument. *Revista de Investigación Educacional*, *18*(2), 433–445.

Ruiz-Carrascosa, J. (2005). The evaluation of the teaching process in universities quality improvement plans. *Educación XX1*, *8*(5), 87 - 102.

Rutherford, A., & Meier, K. J. (2015). Managerial goals in a performance-driven system: Theory and empirical tests in higher education. *Public Administration*, *93*(1), 17–33. doi:10.1111/padm.12124

Rutherford, D. (1995). *Routledge Dictionary of Economics* (2nd ed.). Routledge.

Rylková, Ž. & Chobotová, M. (2011). Přizpůsobování organizací na změny v konkurenčním prostředí. *Periodica Academica, 6*, 65 - 82.

Sadiku-Dushia, N., Leo-Paul, D., & Veland, R. (2019). Entrepreneurial marketing dimensions and Small and Medium-sized Enterprises (SMEs) performance. *Journal of Business Research, 100*, 86–99. doi:10.1016/j.jbusres.2019.03.025

Sakaki, S. (2019). Equality in Income and Sustainability in Economic Growth: Agent - Based Simulations on OECD Data. *Sustainability, 11*(20), 5803. doi:10.3390u11205803

Samuelowicz, K., & Bain, J. D. (1992). Conceptions of teaching held by academic teachers. *Higher Education, 24*(1), 93–111. doi:10.1007/BF00138620

Samuelowicz, K., & Bain, J. D. (2001). Revisiting academics' beliefs about teaching and learning. *Higher Education, 41*(3), 299–325. doi:10.1023/A:1004130031247

Sandberg, P., & Söderström, M. (2003). Industrial energy efficiency: The need for investment decision support from a manager perspective. *Energy Policy, 31*(15), 1623–1634. doi:10.1016/S0301-4215(02)00228-8

Sarosa, S. (2012). Adoption of Social Media Networks by Indonesian SME: A Case Study. *Procedia Economics and Finance, 4*(1), 244–254. doi:10.1016/S2212-5671(12)00339-5

Saunders, M., Lewis, P., & Thornhill, A. (2000). *Research methods for business students*. Pearson Education Limited.

Saunila, M. (2017). Understanding innovation performance measurement in Small and Medium-sized Enterprises (SME). *Measuring Business Excellence, 21*(1), 1–16. doi:10.1108/MBE-01-2016-0005

Savlovschi, L. I., & Robu, N. R. (2011). The Role of Small and Medium-sized Enterprises (SME) in Modern Economy. Economia. *Seria Management, 14*(1), 277–281.

Sawang, S., & Unsworth, K. L. (2011). Why Adopt Now? Multiple Case Studies and Survey Studies Comparing Small, Medium and Large Firms. *Technovation, 31*(10-11), 554-559.

Schaltegger, S. (2000). *Vom Bionier zum Sustainopreneur*. Presentation at Rio Impuls Management Forum 2000.

Schaufeli, W. B., & Bakker, A. B. (2003). *UWES – utrecht work engagement scale: test manual*. Department of Psychology, Utrecht University. Available at www.schaufeli.com

Schein, E. H. (1997). *Organizational Culture and Leadership*. Jossey - Bass.

Schilke, O. (2014). On the contingent value of dynamic capabilities for competitive advantage: The non-linear moderating effect of environmental dynamism. *Strategic Management Journal, 35*(2), 179–203. doi:10.1002mj.2099

Schjoedt, L. (2009). Entrepreneurial job characteristics: An examination of their effect on entrepreneurial satisfaction. *Entrepreneurship Theory and Practice, 33*(3), 619–644. doi:10.1111/j.1540-6520.2009.00319.x

Schmutzler, J., Andonova, V., & Diaz-Serrano, L. (2018). How Context Shapes Entrepreneurial Self-Efficacy as a Driver of Entrepreneurial Intentions: A Multilevel Approach. *Entrepreneurship Theory and Practice, 43*(5), 880–920. doi:10.1177/1042258717753142

Schoemaker, P. J., Heaton, S., & Teece, D. (2018). Innovation, dynamic capabilities, and leadership. *California Management Review, 61*(1), 15–42. doi:10.1177/0008125618790246

Schumpeter, J. (1934). *The Theory of Economic Development*. Harvard University Press.

Schumpeter, J. (1942). *Capitalism, Socialism, and Democracy*. Harper.

Scott, W. R. (2008). Approaching adulthood: The maturing of institutional theory. *Theory and Society*, *37*(5), 427–442. doi:10.100711186-008-9067-z

Searle, R. H., & Ball, K. S. (2003). Supporting Innovation through HR Policy: Evidence from the UK. *Creativity and Innovation Management*, *12*(1), 50–62. doi:10.1111/1467-8691.00268

Šebestová, J. (2018). Strategic Management Tools in the Small and Medium Sized Enterprises: A Long - Term View. In International Day of Science 2018 - Economics, Management, Innovation. In *Proceedings of the International Scientific Conference*. Olomouc: Moravian University College Olomouc.

Šebestová, J., & Antonová, B. (2011). Adaptabilita podnikání v reakci na turbulentní politicko - ekonomické prostředí v kontextu strategického řízení. *Periodica Academica*, *6*(1), 218–230.

Šebestová, J., & Nowáková, K. (2013). Dynamic strategy and sustainable business development: Lessons learned from the crisis. *Acta Universitatis Agriculturae et Silviculturae Mendelianae Brunensis*, *61*(7), 2827–2833. doi:10.11118/actaun201361072827

Šebestová, J., & Sroka, W. (2020). Sustainable development goals and SMEs decisions: Czech Republic vs. Poland. *Journal of Eastern European and Central Asian Research*, *7*(1), 39–50. doi:10.15549/jeecar.v7i1.418

Sedgwick, P. (2015). Multistage Sampling. *BMJ (Clinical Research Ed.)*, *351*, h4155. doi:10.1136/bmj.h4155 PMID:26231184

Seetharaman, M. K., Patwa, N., Saravan, & Gupta, Y. (2019). Breaking barriers in deployment of renewable energy. *Heliyon*, *5*(1), 1–23. doi:10.1016/j.heliyon.2019.e01166 PMID:30723834

Seijts, G. H., & Crim, D. (2006). What engages employees the most or The Ten C's of employee engagement. Ivey Business Journal, 70(4), 1-5.

Seisebaeva, N. G. (2015). Analysis of theoretical approaches to the definition of the essence of the concept of crisis financial management in the enterprise. *Bulletin of the Zaporizhzhya National University*, *4*, 116–123.

Senge, P., Lichtenstein, B., Kaeufer, K., Bradbury, H., & Carroll, J. (2007). Collaborating for systemic change. *MIT Sloan Management Review*, *48*, 44–53.

Seo, Y. W., & Chae, S. W. (2016). Market Dynamics and Innovation Management on Performance in Small and Medium-sized Enterprises (SME): Multi-agent Simulation Approach. *Procedia Computer Science*, *91*(1), 707–714. doi:10.1016/j.procs.2016.07.060

Shapero, A. & Sokol, L. (1982). The social dimensions of entrepreneurship. *Encyclopaedia of entrepreneurship*, 72 - 90.

Shaw, K. (2005). An engagement strategy process for communicators. *Strategic Communication Management*, *9*(3), 26–29.

Shee, P. S. B., & Abratt, R. (1989). A new approach to the corporate image management process. *Journal of Marketing Management*, *5*(1), 63–76. doi:10.1080/0267257X.1989.9964088

She, Q., Jin, X., & Tang, C. Y. (2012). Osmotic power production from salinity gradient resource by pressure retarded osmosis: Effects of operating conditions and reverse solute diffusion. *Journal of Membrane Science*, *401*, 262–273.

Shikdar, A. A., & Sawaqed, N. M. (2003). Worker productivity, and occupational health and safety issues in selected industries. *Computers & Industrial Engineering*, *45*(4), 563–572. doi:10.1016/S0360-8352(03)00074-3

Siegel, D. S., & Wright, M. (2015). Academic entrepreneurship: Time for a rethink? *British Journal of Management*, *26*(4), 582–595. doi:10.1111/1467-8551.12116

Sierra-Sánchez, J. (2012). Factors influencing a student's decision to pursue a communications degree in Spain. *Intangible Capital, 8*(1), 43–60.

Silvestre, B. S. (2015). A hard nut to crack! Implementing supply chain sustainability in an emerging economy. *Journal of Cleaner Production, 96*, 171–181.

Simon, H. (1979). Rational Decision Making in Business Organizations. *The American Economic Review, 69*(4), 493–513.

Sinclair, M., & Phillips, C. J. C. (2018). International Animal Protection Society Leadership: The Right People for the Right Issues. *Animals (Basel), 8*(6), 89. doi:10.3390/ani8060089 PMID:29880748

Singh, P. (2013). Transforming traditional bureaucratic management practices by employing the Collegial Leadership Model of Emancipation. *International Business & Economics Research Journal, 12*(8), 953–968. doi:10.19030/iber.v12i8.7991

Singh, R. (2015). The Genesis of the Entrepreneurial Orientation and the Proposed Model. *International Journal of Business and Management, 3*(7), 17–21.

SMEDAN. (2012). *Small and Medium Enterprises Development Agency of Nigeria.* Survey report on MSmall and Medium-sized Enterprises (SMEs) in Nigeria.

SMEDAN. (2016). *Small and Medium Enterprises Development Agency of Nigeria.* Survey report on MSmall and Medium-sized Enterprises (SMEs) in Nigeria.

SMEDAN. (2017). *Small and Medium Enterprises Development Agency of Nigeria.* Survey report on MSmall and Medium-sized Enterprises (SMEs) in Nigeria.

Sobrino-Morrás, Á. (2011). Teaching-learning process and web 2.0: Valuation of connectivism as a post - constructivist learning theory. *Estudios Sobre Educación, 20*, 117–140.

Sohl, J. E., & Hill, L. (2007). Women business angels: Insights from angel groups. *Venture Capital, 9*(3), 207–222. doi:10.1080/13691060701324536

Sokas, R. K., Dong, X. S., & Cain, C. T. (2019). Building a Sustainable Construction Workforce. *International Journal of Environmental Research and Public Health, 16*(21), 4202. doi:10.3390/ijerph16214202 PMID:31671567

Somekh, B., & Lewin, C. (2005). Research methods in the social sciences. *Sage (Atlanta, Ga.).*

Sönmez, A., & Toksoy, A. (2014). Türkiye'de Girişimcilik ve Türk Girişimci Profili Üzerine Bir Analiz. *Yönetim ve Ekonomi, 21*(2).

Soriano, D. R. (2010). Management factors affecting the performance of technology firms. *Journal of Business Research, 63*(5), 463–470. doi:10.1016/j.jbusres.2009.04.003

Sorrell, S. (2000). *Reducing barriers to energy efficiency in public and private organisations.* Final Report, SPRU, JOS3CT970022, Research funded in part by the European Commission in the framework of the Non-Nuclear Energy Programme JOULE III.

Souki, G. Q., Reis, V. C., & Moura, L. R. (2016). The Behavior of Bakery Consumers. *Organizações Rurais & Agroindustriais, 18*(1), 1–12.

Sovacool, B. K. (2009). Rejecting renewables: The socio - technical impediments to renewable electricity in the United States. *Energy Policy, 37*(11), 4500–4513. doi:10.1016/j.enpol.2009.05.073

Stankevičiūtė, Ž., & Savanevičienė, A. (2018). Raising the Curtain in People Management by Exploring How Sustainable HRM Translates to Practice: The Case of Lithuanian Organizations. *Sustainability, 10*(12), 4356. doi:10.3390u10124356

Stanny, C. J., & Arruda, J. E. (2017). A comparison of student evaluations of teaching with online and paper - based administration. *Scholarship of Teaching and Learning in Psychology, 3*(3), 198–207. doi:10.1037tl0000087

Steenkamp, J. B. E. (1990). Conceptual model of the quality perception process. *Journal of Business Research, 21*(4), 309–333. doi:10.1016/0148-2963(90)90019-A

Stenfors, S., Tanner, L., Syrjänen, M., Seppälä, T., & Haapalinna, I. (2007). Executive views concerning decision support tools. *European Journal of Operational Research, 181*(2), 929–938. doi:10.1016/j.ejor.2006.06.024

Steyaert, C., & Katz, J. (2004). Reclaiming the space of entrepreneurship in society: Geographical, discursive and social dimensions. *Entrepreneurship and Business Development, 2004*(3), 179–196.

Stiglitz, J. (2016). An agenda for sustainable and Inclusive growth for emerging Markets. *Journal of Policy Modeling, 38*(4), 693–710.

Stjepcevic, J., Siksnelyte, I. (2017). Corporate Social Responsibility in Energy Sector. *Transformations in Business & Economics, 16*(1), 21 - 33.

Stonehouse, G., & Pemberton, J. (2002). Strategic planning in SMEs - some empirical findings. *Management Decision, 40*(9), 853–861. doi:10.1108/00251740210441072

Stowe, C. R., & Grider, D. (2014). Strategies for Advancing Organizational Innovation. *Journal of Management and Marketing Research, 15*(1), 1–17.

Streimikiene, D., & Balezentis, T. (2019). Innovative Policy Schemes to Promote Renovation of Multi - Flat Residential Buildings and Address the Problems of Energy Poverty of Aging Societies in Former Socialist Countries. *Sustainability, 11*(7). . doi:10.3390u11072015

Štreimikienė, D., Mikalauskienė, A., Atkočiūnienė, Z., & Mikalauskas, I. (2019). Renewable energy strategies of the Baltic States. *Energy & Environment, 30*(2), 363–381. doi:10.1177/0958305X18790961

Suh, F. D. (2010). Risks and opportunities facing Small and Medium-sized Enterprises (SMEs) in the post-crisis Era [Paper Presentation]. The APEC Small and Medium-sized Enterprises (SMEs) training workshop, Taipei, Korea.

Su, J., Zhai, Q., & Karlsson, T. (2017). Beyond red tape and fools: Institutional theory in entrepreneurship research, 1992–2014. *Entrepreneurship Theory and Practice, 41*(4), 505–531.

Sulieman, M. S. (2019). Roots of Organizational Knowledge in Classical Management Theories: A Literature Review. *International Journal of Business and Social Science, 10*(10), 8–15. doi:10.30845/ijbss.v10n10a2

Sulistiyani, S. (2017). Performance Marketing Model through Acculturation Innovation and Market Orientation in the Bakery Industry. *Expert Journal of Marketing, 5*(1), 1–9.

Sum, R. M., & Mahussin, N. (2017). Risk Management Practices of a Small Enterprise: A Case Study on a Bakery Shop. In *Proceedings of 4th International Muamalat and Entrepreneurship Conference (IMEC4).* Nilai: Islamic Finance and Wealth Management Institute (IFWMI).

Summerfield, C., & Egner, T. (2009). Expectation (and attention) in visual cognition. *Trends in Cognitive Sciences, 13*(9), 403–409. doi:10.1016/j.tics.2009.06.003 PMID:19716752

Sun, P., & Nie, P. (2015). A comparative study of feed - in tariff and renewable portfolio standard policy in renewable energy industry. *Renewable Energy, 74*, 255–262. doi:10.1016/j.renene.2014.08.027

Sunyigono, A. K., Hayati, M., & Qomariyah, N. (2020). Analysis of Personal Entrepreneurship Quality of The Society in Mandangin Island. *IOP Conference Series. Earth and Environmental Science, 518*(1), 012063. doi:10.1088/1755-1315/518/1/012063

Swayne, L. E., Duncan, W., & Ginter, P. M. (2006). *Strategic management of health care organizations* (5th ed.). Blackwell Pub.

Swift, T. (2018). PhD scientists in the boardroom: The innovation impact. *Journal of Strategy & Management, 11*(2), 184–202. doi:10.1108/JSMA-06-2017-0040

Szczepańska-Woszczyna, K., & Dacko-Pikiewicz, Z. (2014). Managerial Competencies and Innovations in the Company-The Case of Enterprises in Poland. Business. *Management in Education, 12*(2), 266–282.

Taft, K. (2017). *Oil's Deep State: How the petroleum industry undermines democracy and stops action on global warming - in Alberta, and in Ottawa.* James Lorimer & Company.

Tahir, F. A., & Inuwa, F. U. (2019). Empirical investigation of the factors affecting micro, small and medium scale enterprises performance in Borno State, Nigeria. *International Business Research, 12*(4), 30–39. doi:10.5539/ibr.v12n4p30

Tak, J., Seo, J., & Roh, T. (2019). The Influence of Authentic Leadership on Authentic Followership, Positive Psychological Capital, and Project Performance: Testing for the Mediation Effects. *Sustainability, 11*(21), 6028. doi:10.3390u11216028

Tang, C., Liu, C., Fang, P., Xiang, Y., & Min, R. (2019). Work - Related Accumulated Fatigue among Doctors in Tertiary Hospitals: A Cross - Sectional Survey in Six Provinces of China. *International Journal of Environmental Research and Public Health, 16*(17), 3049. doi:10.3390/ijerph16173049 PMID:31443480

Tan, H. P., Plowman, D., & Hancock, P. (2008). The evolving research on intellectual capital. *Journal of Intellectual Capital, 9*(4), 585–608. doi:10.1108/14691930810913177

Tassigny, M. (2013). *Sustainable Entrepreneurship in the Energy Sector.* https://www.researchgate.net/publication/292604425_Sustainable_Entrepreneurship_in_the_Energy_Sector

Tauraitė-Janušauskienė, G. (2019). The role of organizational social entrepreneurship in the context of sustainable development. *Regional Formation and Development Studies, 3*(29).

Taylor, A. (2019, April 20). *Strategic Planning and Management Insights.* Retrieved from SME - Strategy Management Consultant: smestrategy.net/blog/business - strategy - frameworks - for - strategic - planning

Taylor, M. B., & van der Velden. (2019). Resistance to Regulation: Failing Sustainability in Product Lifecycles. *Sustainability, 11*(22), 6526. doi:10.3390u11226526

Teece, D. J., & Pisano, G. (1994). The dynamic capabilities of firms: An introduction. *Industrial and Corporate Change, 3*(3), 537–556. doi:10.1093/icc/3.3.537-a

Teece, D. J., Pisano, G., & Shuen, A. (1997). Dynamic capabilities and strategic management. *Strategic Management Journal, 18*(7), 509–533. doi:10.1002/(SICI)1097-0266(199708)18:7<509::AID-SMJ882>3.0.CO;2-Z

Teng, B. S. (2007). Corporate entrepreneurship activities through strategic alliances: A resource-based approach toward competitive advantage. *Journal of Management Studies, 44*(1), 119–142. doi:10.1111/j.1467-6486.2006.00645.x

Teo, S. T., Bentley, T., & Nguyen, D. (2020). Psychosocial work environment, work engagement, and employee commitment: A moderated, mediation model. *International Journal of Hospitality Management, 88*, 102415. doi:10.1016/j.ijhm.2019.102415

Thanos, I. C., Dimitratos, P., & Sapouna, P. (2017). The implications of international entrepreneurial orientation, politicization, and hostility upon SME international performance. *International Small Business Journal, 35*(4), 495–514. doi:10.1177/0266242616641749

Theodosius, C. (2006). Recovering emotion from emotion management. *Sociology, 40*(5), 893–910. doi:10.1177/0038038506067512

Thibault, M., Wilcock, A., & Kanetker, U. (2002). An exploratory study of factors influencing sales performance of Small and Medium-sized Enterprises (SMEs). *Proceedings of the administrative sciences association of Canada.*

Thompson, J. L. (2002). The World of the Social Entrepreneur. *The International Journal of Public Sector Management, 15*(4/5), 413. Doi: 10.1108 / 09513550210435746

Thompson, J. D. (1960). Organizational management of conflict. *Administrative Science Quarterly, 4*(4), 389–409. doi:10.2307/2390765

Thornton, P. H., Lounsbury, M., & Ocasio, W. (2013). *The institutional logics perspective: a new approach to culture, structure, and process.* Oxford Univ. Press.

Tidd, J., Bessant, J., & Pavitt, K. (2007). *Řízení inovací.* Computer Press.

Timeline of Dutch History. (2020, July 13). Retrieved from Rijksmuseum: https://www.rijksmuseum.nl/en/rijksstudio/timeline - dutch - history/reconstruction - welfare - state

Tociu, C., Szep, R., Anghel, A. M., Marinescu, F., Ilie, M., Holban, E., Ghita, G., Matei, M., Dumitru, F. D., Popescu, I., Moncea, A., Laslo, L., Daescu, A. I., & Gh. Popescu, C. R. (2017). Possibilities For Efficient Use Of Valuable Materials From Aluminium Slag To Remove Specific Pollutants In Wastewater. *Journal of Environmental Protection and Ecology, 18*(3), 842–852.

Tolbert, P. S., David, R. J., & Sine, W. D. (2011). Studying choice and change: The intersection of institutional theory and entrepreneurship research. *Organization Science, 22*(5), 1332–1344. doi:10.1287/orsc.1100.0601

Tom, S. (2008). Managing energy and comfort. *ASHRAE Journal, 50*(6), 18–27.

Torgerson, C. (2003). *Systematic reviews.* Bloomsbury Publishing.

Townsend, W. (2010). Innovation and the Value of Failure. *International Journal of Management and Marketing Research, 3*(1), 75–84.

Tran, M. A., Nguyen, B., Melewar, T. C., & Bodoh, J. (2015). Exploring the corporate image formation process. *Qualitative Market Research, 18*(1), 86–114. doi:10.1108/QMR-05-2014-0046

Treece, E. W., & Treece, J. W. (1982). *Elements of Research in Nursing* (3rd ed.). Mosby.

Trmal, S. A., Bustamam, U. S. A., & Mohamed, Z. A. (2015). The Effect of Transformational Leadership in Achieving High Performance Workforce That Exceeds Organisational Expectation: A Study from a Global and Islamic Perspective. *Global Business and Management Research, 7*(2), 88–94.

Turker, D., & Sonmez, S. S. (2009). Which factors affect entrepreneurial intention of university students? *Journal of European Industrial Training, 33*(2), 142–159. doi:10.1108/03090590910939049

Tutar, H., Nart, S., & Bingöl, D. (2015). The effect of strategic orientations on innovation capabilities and market performance: The case of ASEM. *Procedia: Social and Behavioral Sciences, 207*, 709–719. doi:10.1016/j.sbspro.2015.10.144

Tytell, E. D. (2006). Median fin function in bluegill sunfish Lepomis macrochirus: Stream wise vortex structure during steady swimming. *The Journal of Experimental Biology*, *209*(8), 1516–1534. PMID:16574809

Ullrich, D., Koleňák, J., Ambrozová, E., Pokorný, V., & Milichovský, F. (2019). Global X - tream Index and its Partial Parameters for Identifying the Level of Potential Individual Characteristics in the Challenging Conditions of a Modern Corporate and Security Environment. *Sustainability*, *11*(12), 3325. doi:10.3390u11123325

Ulrich, E., Hurdelbrink, J., Perepelkin, J., & Welter, K. (2019). Financial Incentive Required for Pharmacy Students to Accept a Post - Graduation Position in Rural and Undesirable Pharmacy Settings. *Pharmacy (Basel, Switzerland)*, *7*(3), 109. doi:10.3390/pharmacy7030109 PMID:31390805

UN. (1987). *World Commission on Environment and Development. Our Common Future*. Oxford University Press.

UN. (1992a). *Conference on Environment and Development Main Documents*. https://www.un.org/esa/sustdev/documents/docs_unced.htm

UN. (2000). *Millennium Development Goals*. https://www.un.org/millenniumgoals

UN. (2002b). *World Summit on Sustainable Development*. http://www.johannesburgsummit.org

UNDP. (2015). Nigeria's road to SDGs: Country transition strategy. Abuja, Nigeria: MDGs Nigeria.

United Nations & United Nations Economic Commission for Europe. (2013). *Human Resources Management and Training: Compilation of good practices in statistical offices*. Retrieved from https://www.unece.org/fileadmin/DAM/stats/publications/HRMT_w_cover_resized.pdf

United Nations Conference on Trade and Development (UNCTAD). (2020). *Intellectual Property*. https://unctad.org/Topic/Science-Technology-and-Innovation/Intellectual-Property

United Nations. (2015). Post - 2015 Development Agenda. In Integrated and coordinated implementation and monitoring of the results of major United Nations conferences and summits in the economic and social and related fields: Vol. A 69/L.85. Author.

United Nations. (2019). *Responsible and Sustainable Business Practices and Corporate Social Responsibility and Enterprise Development*. United Nations Conference on Trade and Development, Trade and Development Board Investment, Enterprise and Development Commission Multi - year Expert Meeting on Investment, Innovation and Entrepreneurship for Productive Capacity - building and Sustainable Development, Seventh session Geneva, 17 - 19 June 2019, Item 3 of the provisional agenda. Retrieved from https://unctad.org/system/files/official-document/ciimem4d20_en.pdf

Urbancová, H. (2013). Competitive Advantage Achievement through Innovation and Knowledge. *Journal of Competitiveness*, *5*(1), 82–96. doi:10.7441/joc.2013.01.06

Urbano, D., Aparicio, S., & Audretsch, D. (2018). Twenty-five years of research on institutions, entrepreneurship, and economic growth: What has been learned? *Small Business Economics*, *53*(1), 21–49. doi:10.100711187-018-0038-0

Urbano, D., & Guerrero, M. (2013). Entrepreneurial universities: Socioeconomic impacts of academic entrepreneurship in a European region. *Economic Development Quarterly*, *27*(1), 40–55. doi:10.1177/0891242412471973

Urquijo, I., Extremera, N., & Azanza, G. (2019). The Contribution of Emotional Intelligence to Career Success: Beyond Personality Traits. *International Journal of Environmental Research and Public Health*, *16*(23), 4809. doi:10.3390/ijerph16234809 PMID:31795505

URT. (2012). *National Baseline Survey Report for Micro, Small, and Medium Enterprises in Tanzania. United Republic of Tanzania: Ministry of Industry and Trade (MIT) and Financial Sector Deepening Trust*. FSDT.

Vaara, E., & Whittington, R. (2012). Strategy as practice: Taking social practices seriously. *The Academy of Management Annals*, *6*(1), 285–336. doi:10.5465/19416520.2012.672039

Valadas, C. (2013). *Mudanças nas políticas: do (des)emprego à empregabilidade.* Revista Críticas de Ciências Sociàis.

Valaskova, K., Kliestik, T., Svabova, L., & Adamko, P. (2018). Financial Risk Measurement and Prediction Modelling for Sustainable Development of Business Entities Using Regression Analysis. *Sustainability*, *10*(7), 2144. doi:10.3390u10072144

Van Der Spiegel, M., Luning, P. A., De Boer, W. J., Ziggers, G. W., & Jongen, W. M. F.Van-Der-Spiegel. (2005). How to Improve Food Quality Management in the Bakery Sector. *NJAS Wageningen Journal of Life Sciences*, *53*(2), 131–150. doi:10.1016/S1573-5214(05)80002-8

van der Zee, J., & Kroneman, M. W. (2007). Bismarck or Beveridge: A beauty contest between dinosaurs. *BMC Health Services Research*, *7*(1), 94. doi:10.1186/1472-6963-7-94 PMID:17594476

Van Dierendonck, D., Lankester, A., Zmyslona, M., & Rothweiler, H. (2016). Linking HRM Practices and Institutional Setting to Collective Turnover: An Empirical Exploration. *Administrative Sciences*, *6*(4), 18. doi:10.3390/admsci6040018

van Oorschot, W. (2006). The Dutch Welfare State: Recent Trends and Challenges in Historical Perspective. Leuven. *European Journal of Social Security*, *8*(1), 57–76. doi:10.1177/138826270600800104

Van-Auken, H., Madrid-Guijarro, A., & García-Pérez-de-Lema, D. (2008). Innovation and Performance in Spanish Manufacturing Small and Medium-sized Enterprises (SME). *International Journal of Entrepreneurship and Innovation Management*, *8*(1), 36–56. doi:10.1504/IJEIM.2008.018611

Van-Belle, G. (2002). Statistical rules of thumb. John Wiley.

Veciana-Vergés, J. M., & Capelleras-I-Segura, J. L. (2004). Quality of service in university teaching development and validation of a measurement scale. *Revista Europea de Dirección y Economía de La Empresa*, *13*(4), 55–72.

Vega, A., Chiasson, M., & Brown, D. (2008). Extending the Research Agenda on Diffusion: The Case of Public Program Interventions for the Adoption of E-Business Systems in Small and Medium-sized Enterprises (SME). *Journal of Information Technology*, *23*(2), 109–117. doi:10.1057/palgrave.jit.2000135

Velenturf, A. P., Jensen, P. D., Purnell, P., Jopson, J., & Ebner, N. (2019). A Call to Integrate Economic, Social and Environmental Motives into Guidance for Business Support for the Transition to a Circular Economy. *Administrative Sciences*, *9*(4), 92. doi:10.3390/admsci9040092

Venkatasubramanian, V. (2009). What is Fair Pay for Executives? An Information Theoretic Analysis of Wage Distributions. *Entropy (Basel, Switzerland)*, *11*(4), 766–781. doi:10.3390/e11040766

Vishnevskiy, K., & Egorova, O. (2015). *Strategic Foresight for SMEs: Choice of the Most Relevant Methods.* XXVI ISPIM Conference - Shaping the Frontiers of Innovation Management, Budapest, Hungary.

Volery, T., Mueller, S., & von Siemens, B. (2013). Entrepreneur ambidexterity: A study of entrepreneur behaviours and competencies in growth-oriented small and medium-sized enterprises. *International Small Business Journal: Researching Entrepreneurship*, *33*(2), 109–129. doi:10.1177/0266242613484777

Vygotskiĭ, L. S. (1978). *Mind in society: The development of higher psychological processes.* Harvard University Press.

Wade, N. S., Taylor, P. C., Lang, P. D., & Jones, P. R. (2010). Evaluating the benefits of an electrical energy storage system in a future smart grid. *Energy Policy*, *38*(11), 7180–7188.

Walker, J. S., Check, H. F. Jr, & Randall, K. L. (2011). Does the Internal Rate of Return Calculation Require a Reinvestment Rate Assumption? There Is Still No Consensus. *West Chester University: Pennsylvania Economic Association Proceedings Annual Conference*, 118 - 130.

Wallace, J. E. (1995). Organizational and professional commitment in professional and nonprofessional organizations. *Administrative Science Quarterly*, *40*(2), 228–255. doi:10.2307/2393637

Wang, C. K., & Wong, P. K. (2004). Entrepreneurial interest of university students in Singapore. *Technovation*, *24*(2), 163–172. doi:10.1016/S0166-4972(02)00016-0

Wang, C., & Rafiq, M. (2014). Ambidextrous organizational culture, contextual ambidexterity and new product innovation: A comparative study of U.K and Chinese high tech firms. *British Journal of Management*, *25*(1), 58–76. doi:10.1111/j.1467-8551.2012.00832.x

Wang, K. Y., Hermens, A., Huang, K. P., & Chelliah, J. (2015). Entrepreneurial Orientation and Organizational Learning on Small and Medium-sized Enterprises (SME) Innovation. *International Journal of Organizational Innovation*, *7*(3), 65–75.

Wanhoni, J. M. (2014, June 17). *Research Objectives*. Nairobi, Kenya: Academic Press.

Watkin, L. J., Ruangpan, L., Vojinovic, Z., Weesakul, S., & Torres, A. S. (2019). A Framework for Assessing Benefits of Implemented Nature - Based Solutions. *Sustainability*, *11*(23), 6788. doi:10.3390u11236788

Watson, J. B. (1970). *Behaviorism*. The Norton Library.

Waugh, W. L. (1993). Coordination or control: Organizational design and the emergency management function. *International Journal of Disaster Prevention and Management*, 2(4), 17–31.

Wegener, B. (1992). Concepts and measurement of prestige. *Annual Review of Sociology*, *18*(1), 253–280. doi:10.1146/annurev.so.18.080192.001345

Wei, J., Chen, Y., Zhang, Y., & Zhang, J. (2020). How Does Entrepreneurial Self-Efficacy Influence Innovation Behaviour? Exploring the Mechanism of Job Satisfaction and Zhongyong Thinking. *Frontiers in Psychology*, *11*(708), 708. Advance online publication. doi:10.3389/fpsyg.2020.00708 PMID:32457676

Wellalage, N. H., & Reddy, K. (2020). Determinants of profit reinvestment undertaken by SMEs in the small island countries. *Global Finance Journal*, *43*, 1–13. doi:10.1016/j.gfj.2017.11.001

Wellins, R., & Concelman, J. (2005). *Creating a culture for engagement*. Workforce Performance Solutions. Retrieved from www.WPSmag.com

Welter, F., & Smallbone, D. (2011). Institutional perspectives on entrepreneurial behaviour in challenging environments. *Journal of Small Business Management*, *49*(1), 107–125. doi:10.1111/j.1540-627X.2010.00317.x

Wheeler, D., McKague, K., Thomson, J., Davies, R., Medalye, M., & Prada, M. (2005). Creating sustainable local enterprise networks. *MIT Sloan Management Review*, *47*, 33–40.

White, K., & Hall, H. (2013). *Chatman's Bakery: Diversification and Innovation in the Family Business*. Retrieved August 29, 2018, from Canadian Regional Development: A Critical Review of Theory, Practice and Potentials: http://ruralresilience.ca/wp-content/uploads/2013/10/Chatmans.pdf

Winter, S. (2003). Understanding dynamic capabilities. *Strategic Management Journal*, *24*(10), 991–995. doi:10.1002mj.318

Winter, S. G. (2000). The Satisficing Principle in Capability Learning. *Strategic Management Journal*, *21*(10-11), 981–996. doi:10.1002/1097-0266(200010/11)21:10/11<981::AID-SMJ125>3.0.CO;2-4

Wise, L. R. (2004). Bureaucratic posture: On the need for a composite theory of bureaucratic behavior. *Public Administration Review, 64*(6), 669–680. doi:10.1111/j.1540-6210.2004.00414.x

Witek-Crabb, A. (2019). CSR Maturity in Polish Listed Companies: A Qualitative Diagnosis Based on a Progression Model. *Sustainability,* 11.

Workman, D. (2019). *Nigeria's Top 10 Exports.* http://www.worldstopexports.com/nigerias-top-10-exports/

World Bank Report. (2019). *Data and Report on Nigeria.* World Bank Group.

World Bank. (2019). *The World Bank In Nigeria-The World Bank is helping to fight poverty and improve living standards for the people of Nigeria with more than 130 IBRD loans and IDA credits since 1958.* The World Bank in Nigeria. https://www.worldbank.org/en/country/nigeria/overview#1

Wright, M. (2007). *Academic entrepreneurship in Europe.* Edward Elgar Publishing. doi:10.4337/9781847205575

Wright, P., Pringle, C. D., & Kroll, M. J. (1992). *Strategic management: Text and Cases.* Allyn and Bacon.

Wu, K. J., Chen, Q., Qi, Y., Jiang, X., Gao, S., & Tseng, M. L. (2019). Sustainable Development Performance for Small and Medium Enterprises Using a Fuzzy Synthetic Method - DEMATEL. *Sustainability, 11*(15), 4119. doi:10.3390u11154119

Xanthopoulou, D., Bakker, A. B., Demerouti, E., & Schaufeli, W. B. (2007). *How job and personal resources influence work engagement and financial turnover: A diary study in a Greek fast - Food Company.* Academic Press.

Xu, S., Cavusgil, S. T., & White, J. C. (2006). The impact of strategic fit among strategy, structure, and processes on multinational corporation performance: A multi - method assessment. *Journal of International Marketing, 14*(2), 1–31. doi:10.1509/jimk.14.2.1

Yanes-Estévez, V., García-Pérez, A. M., & Oreja-Rodríguez, J. R. (2018). The Strategic Behavior of Small and Medium-sized Enterprises (SME). *Administrative Sciences, 8*(4), 1–21.

Yang, J. Y., & Li, J. (2008). The development of entrepreneurship in China. *Asia Pacific Journal of Management, 25*(2), 335–359. doi:10.100710490-007-9078-8

Yavuzaslan, A., & Barıscıl, A. (2017). Career in Entrepreneurship: Perceptions of Hungarian and Turkish Students. *Revista Romaneasca pentru Educatie Multidimensionala, 9*(3).

Yi, L., Uddin, M. A., Das, A. K., Mahmood, M., & Sohel, S. M. (2019). Do Transformational Leaders Engage Employees in Sustainable Innovative Work Behaviour? Perspective from a Developing Country. *Sustainability, 11*(9), 2485. doi:10.3390u11092485

Yin, J., Yan, Q., Lei, K., Baležentis, T., & Streimikiene, D. (2019). Economic and Efficiency Analysis of China Electricity Market Reform Using Computable General Equilibrium Model. *Sustainability, 11*(2), 350. . doi:10.3390u11020350

Ying Lee, C., Lotsu, S., Islam, M., Yoshida, Y., & Kaneko, S. (2019). The Impact of an Energy Efficiency Improvement Policy on the Economic Performance of Electricity - Intensive Firms in Ghana. *Energies, 12*(19), 3684. doi:10.3390/en12193684

Yoo, S., Domercq, B., & Kippelen, B. (2004). Efficient thin - film organic solar cells based on pentacene/C - 60 heterojunctions. *Applied Physics Letters, 85*(22), 5427–5429.

York, J. G., & Venkataraman, S. (2010). The entrepreneur - environment nexus: Uncertainty, innovation, and allocation. *Journal of Business Venturing, 25*, 449–463.

Young, R., & Ferguson, F. (2020). *Writing For Pleasure: theory, research and practice*. Routledge. doi:10.4324/9780429268984

Yusuf, T. O., & Dansu, F. S. (2013). Small and Medium-sized Enterprises (SMEs), business risk and sustainability in Nigeria. *European Journal of Business & Social Sciences*, *2*(9), 76–94.

Zabashta, E. (2019). Theoretical fundamentals of formation of innovative development of entrepreneurship. *Baltic Journal of Economic Studies*, *5*(4), 97–104. doi:10.30525/2256-0742/2019-5-4-97-104

Zagonari, F. (2016). Four Sustainability Paradigms for Environmental Management: A Methodological Analysis and an Empirical Study Based on 30 Italian Industries. *Sustainability*, *8*(6), 504. doi:10.3390u8060504

Zahra, S. A. (2020). International entrepreneurship in the post Covid world. *Journal of World Business*, *56*(1), 101143. doi:10.1016/j.jwb.2020.101143

Zahra, S. A., & Covin, J. G. (1995). Contextual influences on the corporate entrepreneurship-performance relationship: A longitudinal analysis. *Journal of Business Venturing*, *10*(1), 43–58. doi:10.1016/0883-9026(94)00004-E

Zahra, S. A., Nielsen, A. P., & Bogner, W. C. (1999). Corporate entrepreneurship, knowledge, and competence development. *Entrepreneurship Theory and Practice*, *23*(3), 169–189. doi:10.1177/104225879902300310

Zahra, S. A., Sapienza, H. J., & Davidsson, P. (2006). Entrepreneurship and dynamic capabilities: A review model and research agenda. *Journal of Management Studies*, *43*(2), 917–955. doi:10.1111/j.1467-6486.2006.00616.x

Zappalà, S., Toscano, F., & Licciardello, S. A. (2019). Towards Sustainable Organizations: Supervisor Support, Commitment to Change and the Mediating Role of Organizational Identification. *Sustainability*, *11*(3), 805. doi:10.3390u11030805

Zarbo, R. J., Copeland, J. R., & Varney, R. C. (2017). Deviation ManagementKey Management Subsystem Driver of Knowledge-Based Continuous Improvement in the Henry Ford Production System. *American Journal of Clinical Pathology*, *148*(4), 354–367. doi:10.1093/ajcp/aqx084 PMID:28967954

Zbierowski, P. (2015). New impulse for European economy? Comparison of entrepreneurship in Turkey and Poland. *Journal of Economics and Management*, *20*(A).

Zeng, S., Jiang, C., Ma, C., & Su, B. (2018). Investment efficiency of the new energy industry in China. *Energy Economics*, *70*, 536–544. doi:10.1016/j.eneco.2017.12.023

Zhang, H., Li, L., Zhou, D., & Zhou, P. (2014). Political connections, government subsidies and firm financial performance: Evidence from renewable energy manufacturing in China. *Renewable Energy*, *63*, 330–336. doi:10.1016/j.renene.2013.09.029

Zhang, L., Guo, X., Lei, Z., & Lim, M. K. (2019). Social Network Analysis of Sustainable Human Resource Management from the Employee Training's Perspective. *Sustainability*, *11*(2), 380. doi:10.3390u11020380

Zhao, H., Zhao, Q. H., & Ślusarczyk, B. (2019). Sustainability and Digitalization of Corporate Management Based on Augmented / Virtual Reality Tools Usage: China and Other World IT Companies' Experience. *Sustainability*, *11*(17), 4717. doi:10.3390u11174717

Zhao, Z., Chang, R., & Chen, Y. (2016). What hinder the further development of wind power in China? A socio - technical barrier study. *Energy Policy*, *88*, 465–476. doi:0.1016/j.enpol.2015.11.004

Zhou, W. (2013). Political connections and entrepreneurial investment: Evidence from China's transition economy. *Journal of Business Venturing*, *28*(2), 299–315. doi:10.1016/j.jbusvent.2012.05.004

Zhou, W. (2017). Institutional environment, public - private hybrid forms, and entrepreneurial reinvestment in a transition economy. *Journal of Business Venturing*, *32*(2), 197–214. doi:10.1016/j.jbusvent.2016.11.002

Zhu, K., Neale, N. R., Miedaner, A., & Frank, A. J. (2006). Enhanced charge - collection efficiencies and light scattering in dye - sensitized solar cells using oriented TiO2 nanotubes arrays. *Nano Letters*, *7*(1), 69–74. PMID:17212442

Zhu, Y., Gardner, D. G., & Chen, H. (2018). Relationships between work team climate, individual motivation, and creativity. *Journal of Management*, *44*(5), 2094–2115. doi:10.1177/0149206316638161

Zott, C., Amit, R., & Massa, L. (2011). The Business Model: Recent Developments and Future Research. *Journal of Management*, *37*(4), 1019–1042. doi:10.1177/0149206311406265

Zulkarnain, A., Wahyuningtias, D., & Putranto, T. S. (2018). Analysis of IFE, EFE and QSPM Matrix on Business Development Strategy. *IOP Conference Series. Earth and Environmental Science*, *126*, 126. doi:10.1088/1755-1315/126/1/012062

Zuo, Z., Li, Y., Fu, J., & Wu, J. (2019). Human Resource Scheduling Model and Algorithm with Time Windows and Multi - Skill Constraints. *Mathematics*, *7*(7), 598. doi:10.3390/math7070598

Zur Muehlen, M. (2004). Organizational management in workflow applications–issues and perspectives. *Information Technology and Management*, *5*(3-4), 271–291. doi:10.1023/B:ITEM.0000031582.55219.2b

Zwingina, C. T., & Opusunju, M. I. (2017). Impact of Innovation on the Performance of Small and Medium Scale Enterprise in Gwagwalada, Abuja. International Journal of Entrepreneurial Development. *Education and Science Research*, *4*(1), 31–45.

Zyadin, A., Halder, P., Kähkönen, T., & Puhakka, A. (2014). Challenges to renewable energy: A bulletin of perceptions from international academic arena. *Renewable Energy*, *69*, 82–88. doi:10.1016/j.renene.2014.03.029

About the Contributors

Cristina Raluca Gh. Popescu is Full-Professor Habil. at University of Bucharest and PhD. Supervisor and Doctoral School Member at The Bucharest University of Economic Studies, Romania. She collaborates with University of Craiova and is scientific researcher at The National Institute of Research and Development for Environmental Protection and the National Institute for Research and Development Comoti Turbomotors, Romania. She is Public Policy Expert at the Ministry of Research, Innovation and Digitization, Romania. She is Member of Chamber of Financial Auditors of Romania (CAFR), Romania as Financial Auditor, and Member of Authority for the Public Oversight of the Statutory Audit Activity (ASPAAS), Ministry of Public Finance, Romania as Financial auditor. She is review board member: IBIMA Conferences and Journal of E-Government Studies and Best Practices, IBIMA Publishing, USA; IGI Global – Publishing House; International Journal of Health Economics (IJHE), University of Bucharest; Multidisciplinary Digital Publishing Institute (MDPI) (Basel, Switzerland) for Journal of Risk and Financial Management, Mathematics, Sustainability, Journal of Open Innovation: Technology, Market, and Complexity, Symmetry, Administrative Sciences, World, and Informatics.

Rahul Verma, MCom (International Business) & PGDBA (Finance & Marketing), is a Lecturer in Commerce with the Delhi University, India, for the last 10 years. His research interests include Marketing, International Business, and Finance. He has attended / presented / published more than 30 research papers / chapters in several national / international conferences / seminars and has edited 7 books with prestigious publishers like IGI Global, Apple Academic Press, etc. till date. He is also on editorial boards of several peer - reviewed journals.

* * *

Redouan Ainous is an Assistant Professor at the University of Algiers3, Algeria. He obtained a doctorate degree in marketing. He has a group of academic research published on the local and international. He participated in a number of international Conference. He worked as an associate professor at the University of Tlemcen, University of Bel-abbes and the High School of Management.

Olalekan Asikhia is a Professor of Business Administration and Entrepreneurship at the Babcock Business School of Babcock University, Ilishan Remo, Ogun State. He attended Government College, Ikorodu and University of Benin, Edo State for his Secondary and University Education before undertaking Postgraduate studies at the University of Lagos, Nigerian Institute of Journalism, Olabisi Onabanjo University, Ago-Iwoye, Ogun State, University of South Africa for Master and Doctoral degrees respectively. He also undertakes another doctoral degree programme at the University of Kwa-Zulu Natal, South Africa. He is an erudite scholar and a Research Professor at Graduate School of Business Leadership, University of South Africa (2014-2016). He had earlier lectured at Covenant University, Ota, Ogun State as well as Olabisi Onabanjo University, Ago-Iwoye, Ogun State. He has published over hundred articles and books in Entrepreneurship, Marketing and Management areas. He has supervised and graduated 80 doctoral students. He had a brief stint in Marketing/Management Training and Consultancy before joining the academics. He trained and consulted for Nemeith Pharmaceutical, Lagos, NCAA Shell Development Corporation, Nigeria, Nigeria Liquefied Natural Gas Company (NLNG), National Communication Commission (NCC), Nigerian National Assembly members Personal Assistants, CITA Petroleum Ltd, Electronic Marketing- Connect, Ikeja, Lagos. Professor Olalekan Asikhia is happily married to Dr (Mrs) Busayo Asikhia and blessed with two children.

Amit Bhattacharya has 30 years of banking experience now engaged in social research for the benefits of society. Worked as professor in economics and management in two universities for 6 years post retirement, also to credit are around 70 research papers and 05 edited books.

Moussa Boumadan has a PhD in Education from the Autonomous University of Madrid. He is currently an Associate Lecturer of the Department of Education at the Faculty of Languages and Education of Nebrija University. He is an expert in active learning methodologies with an emphasis on "learning by doing". He is an expert in research methodologies based on design, that is, those that seek to determine the value of an innovative pedagogical approach (mediated by hardware or software) from teaching practice. Finally, he is a founding member of TalentPlant, a non-profit organization oriented to the integral development of people. He works with people at risk of exclusion, the acquisition of social skills for social and labour integration from an innovative methodology centred on the metaphor of Campbell's Hero Way.

Jarmila Duháček Šebestová is Associate Professor at Silesian University in Opava, SBA Karviná, an experienced researcher focusing on Small Businesses. She has participated in a number of international projects, including IPREG (Innovative Policy Research for Economic Growth) and the E-WORLD project (International Entrepreneurs Network). She is Vice President of the European Council of Small Businesses for the Czech Republic. Research interests: Small business performance, small business dynamics.

Melchor Gómez is a Lecturer in Educational Technology at the Faculty of Teacher Training and Education of the Autonomous University of Madrid. Director and coordinator of the Digital Education and Innovation research group at the Autonomous University of Madrid. He has published different books and research articles in scientific journals focusing on the use of ICT in the classroom and the key elements for educational change and improvement through technologies. He teaches at the Master's Degree in Information and Communication Technologies in Education and Training at the UAM. He is the director of the master's degree in Management of Educational Centres in the new digital environment, which is part of the UAM, and a participant in master's degrees from the Universidad Nacional a Distancia and the Universidad de Comillas. He has held different positions in innovation management, from Vice-Dean of Studies and Educational Innovation (5 years) in the Faculty of Teacher Training, Delegate of the Rector for Teaching Network and Teaching Innovation (5 years), and Director of DISEI Design Innovation Educational Software and Internet (3 years).

Pallavi Jain has a very luminous academic and professional career. She is currently serving as Head-Incharge in Department of Chemistry, SRM Institute of Science and Technology Delhi-NCR Campus, Modinagar, Ghaziabad, India. Dr. Jain received her Ph.D. degrees in Chemistry from the Department of Chemistry, Banasthali Vidyapith, Jaipur, Rajasthan, India. She has extensive teaching experience of about 15 years. She has authored and co-authored over 20 publications in journals of international repute, and contributed more than a dozen book chapters.

(Kafigi Jeje - Contributing Author) Dr. Kafigi Jeje is a Lecturer in the Department of Business Management at the Institute of Accountancy Arusha, Tanzania. He received his PhD (Management) from the University of KwaZulu-Natal, South Africa.

Luis Matosas-López is a professor at Rey Juan Carlos University. PhD in Economics, Master in Marketing, Degree in Marketing and Market Research and Bachelor's Degree in Business from Rey Juan Carlos University. He has also studied at Francisco de Vitoria University or at the IMC University of Applied Sciences in Austria. His research focuses on the applicability of ICTs in the social sciences and quality management in higher education. On both topics, he has published different book chapters with international publishers such as McGraw-Hill, Dykinson, Tecnos, Pirámide, or Ramon Areces, as well as more tan fifteen articles in international impact journals indexed in first quartiles of WOS (JCR) and SCOPUS (SJR). He has also developed an extensive professional activity as a marketing consultant, working in companies such as France Telecom - Orange or Vodafone Spain within the areas of loyalty and CRM. Currently, in addition to being a member of the CIBERIMAGINARIO research group from Rey Juan Carlos University, he is an external collaborator of Digital Education and Innovation (EID) research group at the Autonomous University of Madrid.

Asta Mikalauskiene has a PhD in Economics, Professor of Vilnius University. Her main areas of research are sustainable development, sustainability assessment, climate change and evaluation of economic processes. She has conducted interdisciplinary research on issues related to sustainable development and climate change, analysis and evaluation of economic processes, and she has published 12 scientific articles in publications included in the list of the Institute of Scientific Information (ISI), more than 20 scientific articles in peer-reviewed international, foreign periodicals. She is the co-author of 3 collective monographs and 3 monographs. The scientist is an active participant in international scientific conferences, seminars and trainings.

Vannie Naidoo is a full-time staff member at the University of KwaZulu-Natal, South Africa, in the Faculty of Management and Law. Her field of teaching is in management, corporate strategy, project management, marketing, project management research methodology and entrepreneurship. The research areas pursued by Prof. Naidoo are in the areas of management, management, marketing, service marketing, entrepreneurship and social media and e-learning or learning with new technologies. She has presented papers at international conferences throughout the world and has written on various issues in management and marketing in journal articles and books.

Fahri Özsungur was graduated from Ataturk University Faculty of Law, Hacettepe University Department of Family and Consumer Sciences PhD. and Aksaray University Department of Business PhD. He serves as a Higher Degrees by Research (HDR) Examiner /PhD Examiner for the University of New England. He is a Eurostars Technical Expert (EUREKA Secretariat). He is affiliated to Mersin University Faculty of Economics and Administrative Sciences Department of Labor Economics and Industrial Relations, Adana Science and Technology University, Rotary International, Osmaniye Korkut Ata University, Çağ University, WEGATE- European Gateway for Women's Entrepreneurship and Canadian Institute for International Law Expertise (CIFILE). He has 4 books, 9 book chapters, and more than 78 (4 SSCI/SCI/SCI-Expanded,10 ESCI) published articles and 18 international conference papers. He is the editor of 14 Journals (1 SSCI/SCI/SCI-Expanded), and the reviewer of 109 Journals (9 SSCI/SCI/SCI-Expanded,26 ESCI).

Paulo Ramos has a PhD in Management Sciences, Marketing and Strategy, Faculty of Economics, University of Porto MSc in Marketing and Product Management, Cranfield University, UK, BA in International Relations, University of Minho. Assistant Professor in University Lusíada Norte. Coordinator of the Marketing Degree. Assistant Professor at the Lusiada and Fernando Pessoa University (member of the Scientific Board of UFP) Former Management Departmental Coordinator, Marketing Degree and Erasmus coordinator. Guest lecturer in the Catholic University School of Biotechnology, Faculty of Sciences of University of Porto,and in the past in the Católica Business School, University of Lisbon and in the IPVC. He has lectured in several international universities: International School of Management, Dortmund, Germany. Lutheran University - Brazil ULBRA, Rio Grande do Sul, Brazil, Kufstein Universitat, Áustria. Member of the Editorial Board of the "Journal of Organisational Studies and Innovation" UK Reviewer in EMAC International Journal of Wine Business Research, Marketing Trends conference (Paris, Venice) Partner and board member of several companies in the areas of Agro food (Wine), Education, Real Estate and Consultancy. External expert and adviser of the Coordinating Commission for Northern Regional Development of the Portuguese Government. (External evaluator of the Norte 2015 program). He has several research papers in journals and proceedings of national and international conferences in the fields of Wine, Tourism, Brands and Services. Keynote speaker, guest speaker, Member of the Scientific Committee, Session Chair in international conferences. Awarded in 2012: "best short communication" in Economy and Law in OIV XXIV World Congress of Vine and Wine. Specialties: Market research, data analysis (quantitative & qualitative), focus group and personal in-depth interviews, questionnaire design, lecturer, marketing audits, marketing plans, label designer.

Rinkal Sharma has an extensive experience of teaching for over 17 years. She has been associated with various renowned educational organizations as teacher educator. She has obtained her Master Degree in Arts (M.A. English & Hindi), Mater Degree in Education (M.Ed. & M.Phil.) and Ph.D.in Education. Academically obtained top position at Secondary, senior Secondary & graduation level, she had always secured position at college and university level. She has presented various papers in National and International Seminars & Conferences and also has several publications to her credit. Her area of specialization includes English Methodology, Hindi Methodology, Comparative Education, & Educational Psychology. She worked as Assistant Superintendent (AS) in B.Ed. and Professional course examination of Ch.Charan Singh University, Meerut. She is an active participant for live T.V. Telecast for Swayam Prabha Channel of NIOS and Radio Counselling programme of NIOS.

Roberto Soto-Varela has a PhD in Education from the Autonomous University of Madrid. He is currently an Associate Lecturer of the Department of Education at the Faculty of Languages and Education of Nebrija University. He develops research in the area of education and training mediated by technology, especially in the area of communication and mathematics. He has been a research fellow at the Universidad Autónoma de Madrid. He has also worked as a teacher for different autonomous administrations. As far as research is concerned, he has presented several papers in International Congresses, has a publication in a journal indexed in Web of Sciences and Scopus; and has collaborated in some financed projects.

Bruno Sousa is a Professor in Polytechnic Institute of Cavado and Ave (IPCA, Portugal) Head of Master Program - Tourism Management - PhD Marketing and Strategy. He was Market Analist at Sonae Distribuição – Modelo e Continente, S.A. (2006 to 2009) and he was Marketing Assistant - Jornal O Jogo at Controlinveste (2005) - Best Paper Award in Strategic Marketing & Value Creation (International Conference on Innovation and Entrepreneurship in Marketing and Consumer Behaviour 2020) Teaching Award of the School of Economics and Management of the University of Minho 2015/2016 - Best Thesis in Tourism Award - ICIEMC 2015 - Management Graduation, University of Minho Award - Best performance (2006) - Merit Scholarship for Students in Public Higher Education Awards of Merit Scholarship by University of Minho in 2001/02 - 2002/03 - 2003/04 Rresearch centre: CiTUR and Applied Management Research Unit (UNIAG). He is author or co-author of several papers and her research interests include tourism management, marketing and strategy. Editorial board member of several peer reviewed scientific journals and ad-hoc reviewer of several peer-reviewed scientific journals. Member of the scientific committee of several national and international congresses and conferences.

Dalia Streimikiene, PhD in Economics; Professor of Vilnius University. She is working in the area of sustainable development since 1998 and is an internationally recognized expert in this field. She works on behalf of UNFCCC, European Commission, the United Nations Economic Commission for Europe, the United Nations Development Programme, World Energy Council, the IAEA etc. on sustainable energy, environmental and climate change mitigation policies. D. Streimikiene consults Lithuanian Ministry of Environment on Climate Change and participates in preparation of national reports to the UNFCCC Secretariat and the national greenhouse gas inventories. She is a member of State Commission for allocation of National Scientific Grants of Republic of Lithuania which is the most prestigious award by Lithuanian State for scientists. She represents expertise in Economics in this Commission. She has published over 200 articles in Web of Science (WoS) referred journals with high IF. She is a co-author of 15 monographs and presented many papers at many international conferences and forums around the world. She is Editor-in-Chief of Transformations in Business and Management journal indexed in WoS and SCOPUS databases.

Nishi Tyagi has a diverse academic and professional career. She obtained her Ph.D. degree (Education & Sanskrit Literature) from CCS University, Meerut, UP, India. Her research interests include Educational Management, Language Education, Teacher Education, and Psychological aspects of Education. She has contributed to the Development of Handbook for Teachers working in Special Training Centres Department of Elementary Education, NCERT, New Delhi. She has immense experience designing curriculum and conducting professional development programs on Teacher Education at National and International level. She has edited and authored several books and contributed chapters in various books. She has published numerous research papers in reputed journals on multidimensional issues of education. She is an active member of the editorial board of several journals and professional bodies. She has extensive experience teaching in leading institutions / universities in India for about 15 years. She is currently working as an Assistant Professor at the School of Education, Sharda University.

Index

P

R

S

T

U

V

W

www.ingramcontent.com/pod-product-compliance
Lightning Source LLC
LaVergne TN
LVHW062137300926
849161LV00010B/2558